all the time she seems doomed to trouble. I did not com
home as she did — Will came down and we stayed 'till dark
almost and brought up some things [...] [...] so
sweet among the trees at home [...] [...] [...]uld
make a new fence. Wendle [...] [...]s in
the paper this morning — the one "thi [...] [...]
wanted there I suppose.

Fourth day 2 ond

This morning we spent some
hours working in the yard I wonder if I ever will
forget how like a fright I fix up when I work in the garden
this morning I wore an old skirt pinned around my
shoulders — and old bonnet and veil — and old pair of gloves
I must have looked like a fright — but then there is
no need of getting so black and having our hands
rough when we can help it. The wind is blowing
very hard a perfect hurricane almost I cannot step out
but my dress flows half over my head. I have had a
long "nap" this evening overslept myself entirely.

Poland Number Ten is not taken yet and report
says there is a great battle yet to come off at that point.

I think the war will last longer than many persons
think of. The paper today has the "Exposition of the
Knights of the Golden Circle" a band of traitors scattered
all over the north and south for the overthrow of
the government — there is no hope of quelling the
rebellion when we have so many traitors among us
I hope the Kn. G. C. will be exposed and brought to
punishment.

Fifth day 3 d 1862

Such a beautiful morning — we are going to Carma[n's]
to dinner —— Will is working on our fence I think it is go[ing]
to be so pretty I am anxious to see it done. —— I am so
discouraged about the war I think the clouds grow darker
all the time I have not as much hope of peace as I
had months ago but I never believed we would have a
short war. It is even asserted that McClelland is a Kn[ight]

To
Cindy
with warmest wishes
Christie

The Civil War Period Journals

of

Paulena Stevens Janney

1859–1866

The Civil War Period Journals

of

Paulena Stevens Janney

1859–1866

Edited and Annotated

by

Christie Hill Russell

Transcribed by

Betty Hill Kochan and Christie Hill Russell

GATEWAY PRESS, INC.
Baltimore, MD   2007

Copyright © 2007 by
Christie Hill Russell
All rights reserved.

Permission to reproduce in any form
must be secured from the author.

Please direct all correspondence to:
Christie Hill Russell
Paris, Illinois
For additions and corrections see
www.cartar.com

ISBN.0-9792886-090000

Library of Congress Control Number
2007920468
Subject: PCN for The Civil War Period Journals
of Paulena Stevens Janney 1859-1866

Published for the author by
Gateway Press, Inc.
3600 Clipper Mill Road, Suite 260
Baltimore, Maryland 21211-1953

www.gatewaypress.com

Printed in the United States of America

Dedication

In memory of my great-grandmother, Paulena Stevens Janney,
author of these journals,
my mother, Georgia Janney Hill, and
my uncle, Andrew Palmer "Jack" Janney

To my husband, T. Alan Russell,
our children, Scott A. Russell and Sheryl Russell Clark, and
our grandsons, Kendrick P. Russell, Grant M. Clark, and Evan A. Clark

In memory of our son Brian K. Russell

꿍 ✿ 꿍

Fourthday, December 31st, 1862

Where will we be in one year or two or three?
What a helping it is, we cannot know.

Paulena Stevens Janney
Martinsville, Ohio

꿍 ✿ 꿍

Table *of* Contents

Newberry Friends
Meeting House,
Martinsville, Ohio, 1843

Acknowledgments

I am deeply grateful to a number of people whose assistance has made it possible for this book to be brought to publication.

I am thankful that my great-grandmother, Paulena Stevens Janney, was interested in keeping an almost daily account of her life for us to share today. Her desire to have her children, grandchildren, and great-grandchildren read her journals many years after she had penned them was a major motivation for proceeding with this book. My mother, Georgia Janney Hill, and her brother, Jack Janney, made early attempts to read, copy, and collect bits of family history from the journals' pages. Those notes stirred in me an early interest and curiosity about an ancestor I had never known.

As my sister, Betty Hill Kochan, and I began reading portions of the journals to each other, we soon realized the unique experience we shared in reading and hearing our great-grandmother's words. As the ink faded further and the pages became more worn with human contact, it was apparent that the time had come to capture Paulena's thoughts before they were gone forever. The tedious task of reading the faded iron-gall ink was accomplished with the help of a magnifying glass, a black light, and photocopies from which handwritten transcriptions were transferred to a word processor.

Betty Hill Kochan worked on the transcription of Journals Two and Three. Her interest in and commitment to the tasks she undertakes have always been hallmarks of her work ethic. I greatly appreciate her contributions toward turning this material into a workable manuscript. I'm sure that our great-grandmother, mother, and uncle would be pleased to see this project culminate in published form.

While transcribing Journal One, I realized that I needed to do further research to have a better understanding of the time period, society, and events Paulena described. Among the subjects that required study were the Quaker community she lived in, Civil War battles, social issues of the day such as abolition of slavery and temperance, and the general lifestyle of the period. Soon I was annotating and making minor editorial changes. I was gaining a more intimate view of my great-grandmother and learning a valuable lesson about life in the United States in the nineteenth century.

To that point, I had been researching and compiling the genealogy of the family based on the early work of my mother and uncle; however, little was known beyond the third generation, and for that reason not much was known about individuals Paulena referred to on an everyday basis. Therefore, I began a more in-depth search of the Quaker Meeting records, census and tax records, deeds, wills, newspaper articles, county histories, and obituaries. Tom Hamm, archivist for the Quaker Collection at Earlham College, was most helpful in providing insight into the practices of the Society of Friends of the nineteenth century, especially regarding the Indiana Yearly Meeting. The Earlham Boarding School records and college photographs were made available to me as well as much information on the early years of the Boarding School and College. My thanks go to the Philadelphia-based staff of the Haverford College Quaker Collection and Swarthmore College Friends Historical Library where Mary Ellen Chijioke was of great help in directing me through the unpublished Quaker Meeting records. She is now at the Friends Historical Collection at Guilford College Library in Greensboro, North Carolina. My appreciation to Ina Kelly of the Quaker Special Collections, Wilmington College, Wilmington, Ohio, who assisted me with the transcribed Newberry Monthly Meeting minutes. My thanks go to Joyce Pinkerton, Gladys Williams, and the late Adrian Roberts at the Genealogical Library of Clinton County Ohio Historical and Genealogical Society for assistance with tax, land, and probate records, collections of family histories, and the history of Clinton County.

I extend special thanks to Ruth Connolly whose keen eye for editorial accuracy and knowledge of the surrounding geographical area improved this manuscript. My sincere thanks to Dan Kirklin and Shawn Woodyard, editors, and Cherie Wood, graphic artist and typographer, for their skillful transformation of the printed pages into the handsome book you are now holding.

My appreciation and love to my husband, Alan Russell, who has not only been a source of encouragement and support but has also provided a great deal of technical expertise in the formatting of the text, scanning, and restoring photographs from the family collections.

Introduction

Paulena (Stevens) Janney was an eighteen-year-old bride of ten days when she began writing the first of three journals spanning the years 1859 to late 1866. She could not have known as she penned her routine life experiences that she would be recording events of one of the most tragic periods in our nation's history. Just two years after she began her journals, our country was embroiled in civil war. As she wrote:

> Everything seems so beautiful were it not for the cloud resting over our country which casts so many shadows on our hearts. . . . [W]hat good will come of this bloody war sufficient to compensate for the desolated homes, the murdered sons and fathers, the destroyed cities, the demoralizing effect upon the people that the evil war is scattering abroad over our once beautiful and happy country. (See December 17, 1862, entry.)

With her journal on her lap and the light of her east window, a candle, or an oil lamp as illumination,[1] Paulena dipped her pen in iron-gall ink[2] to record daily life in the rural Ohio community of Martinsville, Clinton County, in the mid-nineteenth century. Today, the ink has faded and her words have almost disappeared from the pages. Paulena's journals would have been lost forever if not for this transcription. Her record provides us with a personal view of life in that time: weather conditions, family and community life, and social issues. She seems to express joy, anger, sorrow, grief, melancholy, depression, and

---

1. Coal oil lamps, now known as kerosene lamps, appeared on the market in 1857, and by 1860 there were at least thirty kerosene plants in the United States. Coal oil was first distilled from petroleum by Abraham Gesner, a Canadian, in 1849, and it rapidly replaced whale oil as a fuel for illumination. In 1846, there were 735 ships in the U.S. whaling fleet. By 1876, the fleet was down to 39 ships. The price of sperm oil reached its apex, $1.77 per gallon, in 1856; by 1896 it was 40 cents per gallon. Several of Paulena's relatives were captains or owners of whale ships out of Nantucket. The Coffin branch of the family removed from Nantucket to Guilford County, North Carolina, in 1772. Source: http://www.littletechshoppe.com/ns1625/gesner.html.

2. "Iron-gall ink was the most important ink in Western history. Leonardo da Vinci wrote his notes using iron-gall ink. Bach composed with it. Rembrandt and Van Gogh drew with it. The Constitution of the United States was drafted with it. . . . And, when the black ink on the Dead Sea Scrolls was analyzed using a cyclotron at the Davis campus of the University of California, it was found to be iron-gall ink. The gallic acid was mixed with water and vitriol (iron (II) sulfate). Gum arabic from acacia trees was added as the suspension agent. The result was iron-gall ink." Source: http://www.realscience.breckschool.org/upper/fruen/files/Enrichmentarticle/files/IronGallInk/IronGallInk.html.

loneliness easily, commenting on subjects such as Civil War battles, the call for volunteers, the draft, reports of casualties, Lee's surrender, and Lincoln's assassination.

The grammar, spelling, and punctuation of Paulena's writing have been retained for the most part. However, for clarification and ease of reading, punctuation and capitalization have been added in some places. Repetition of words and phrases, rambling thoughts, and writing too faint to read have been omitted. Bracketed words, dates, and comments are editorial additions intended to help the reader place the journal in historic context.

Dates have been moved from their original positions on the right side of the page to the left side. The name of the month is included in each day's entry, whereas Paulena wrote the name of the month only at the beginning of that month. However, the original style of using Sabbath, Firstday, Secondday, etc. instead of Sunday, Monday, Tuesday, etc. has been retained.

Editorial footnotes contain information that was not included in the original journal entries. Genealogical notations have been made, and a directory of individuals mentioned in the journals has been added. A prologue and an epilogue have been included to provide the reader with information leading up to Journal One and events that occurred after the last entry in Journal Three. An appendix contains biographical sketches of Paulena's notable relatives who would be well known to most readers.

$\mathcal{P}$rologue

$\mathcal{T}$he eldest of the four children of Evan and Priscilla (Betts) Stephens (Stevens),[3] Paulena, nicknamed "Lena," was born on July 1, 1840, close to the village of Martinsville in Clark Township, Clinton County, Ohio, fifty miles northeast of Cincinnati on the Marietta and Cincinnati Rail Road[4] (now the B&O). The 1860 census recorded the village's population as 338. Martinsville was the largest community in the township. Both village and township were close-knit and composed of numerous related families, most of which were members of the Newberry Friends (Quaker) Meeting.

Paulena was a "birthright Quaker," which meant that both of her parents were members in good standing of the Society of Friends. By virtue of her birthright, she was a member of the Quaker meeting without any further confession or confirmation of her own. The Religious Society of Friends dated back to the mid-1600s in England where George Fox[5] sought "The Devine Presence" in the

3. Later, the spelling of the name was changed to Stevens.

4. Source: http://www.lib.umich.edu/spec-coll/ohio-mich/marietta.html.

5. "George Fox was born in Fenny Drayton, Leicestershire, in 1624. Apprenticed to a Nottingham shoemaker, Fox developed strong opinions about religion. Fox rebelled against the state control of the Church of England and in 1643 began touring the country giving sermons where he argued that consecrated buildings and ordained ministers were irrelevant to the individual seeking God. George Fox was arrested many times for his religious views. On one occasion the judge told Fox 'to quake in the presence of the Lord' and afterwards members of his movement became known as Quakers." Source: "George Fox," http://www.raptureme.com/resource/gfox/george_fox.html.

Twenty-year old Thomas Janney was living in Pownall Fee, Cheshire, England, in 1654, when he and his first cousin, Mary Janney, and her husband, John Bancroft, are reported to have been converted to the doctrines of the Society of Friends by George Fox, in his first sermon preached in Cheshire at the Market Cross in Stockport. Thomas Janney became a ministering Friend about two years later. His parents were also early Quaker converts. In 1660, Thomas Janney married Margery Heath at the home in Pownall Fee of his brother-in-law, James Harrison. James Harrison had married Anne Heath, sister of Margery, and another sister, Jane Heath, married William Yardley. These three couples eventually removed to Bucks County, Pennsylvania, in 1682 and 1683. Thomas Janney and William Yardley were ministers in the Society of Friends and served in the Provincial Council. James Harrison was William Penn's friend as well as property commissioner and steward of Penn's home, Pennsbury, on the Delaware River outside Philadelphia.

"Thomas Janney was imprisoned for two months in 1665 for attending a Quaker meeting near his home, he also had goods restrained for refusing to pay tithes on at least nine occasions between 1663 and 1681. He visited Quaker meetings in Ireland in 1669, and scattered evidence indicates he undertook tours to spread the Quaker message in England." Source: *Law Making and Legislators in Pennsylvania,* vol. 1. Non-quoted

"Inner Light" that spoke directly to each person. Friends believed in baptism by the Holy Spirit and did not observe the sacraments of baptism by water or Holy Communion found in other Christian churches. Friends believed that both baptism and communion were spiritual; therefore, they did not observe either outwardly or physically. The best systematic statement of Quaker theology is Robert Barclay's "Apology for the True Christian Divinity," which can be found at http://www.qhpress.org/texts/barclay/apology. It was written in the late 1600s and remained the formal theological statement on baptism and communion. Baptism by the Holy Spirit was and still is recognized as an authentic spiritual experience by Friends (Barclay, Proposition 12). Communion was viewed as "inward and spiritual," and the outward forms were viewed as rituals that might lose their meaning (Barclay, Proposition 13). Friends believe in both sacraments, but not in the rituals, which take many forms in the Christian church (A. Crosman, Quaker Roots Web List, April 11, 2005).

Who are the Friends (Quakers)?

According to *Quakers of Richmond and Wayne County, Indiana:*

> Quakers believe that God speaks to the heart and mind of every person. Equality is centrally important to Friends, who strive to address "that of God" in each person. Quaker worship and decision-making are both shaped by a common search for the Truth as revealed by the prompting of the Spirit. In practical terms, one result is that Quaker organizations make many of their decisions by a process of gradually discerning, as a community, what is the best decision for the entire group—in other words, by building consensus. Another result of the Quaker belief in equality is that many Friends are active in social justice concerns, sharing the conviction that each of us is called to work for peace and understanding, treat all persons with respect regardless of differences, and discern the active presence of the Spirit at work in the world among us. Some Quaker meetings worship in silence, with attenders providing "vocal ministry" as they are led by the Spirit.[6] Others have pastors, and follow a programmed tradition similar to many Protestant Christian denominations. In either case, Friends believe that each person is called to be a minister to others. . . .

---

material paraphrased from *Law Making and Legislators; Colonial Families of the United States,* vol. 5, p. 40; and *History of Bucks County,* William W. H. Davis, New York–Chicago, Lewis Publishing, 1905, vol. 3. Note: Thomas Janney was William Janney's great-great-great-grandfather.

6. "Quaker worship meetings were silent and contemplative, with each participant 'centering down' to find the 'Inner Light' that would allow them to communicate on an individual level with God. Only then might a Quaker rise in meeting to share this experience with the assembled worshipers. Adornments like pulpits, statuary, steeples, and

Prior to and during the Civil War, Quakers expressed their opposition to slavery in various ways, with many becoming actively involved in the Underground Railroad that helped escaped slaves travel to freedom. Differences over how to express opposition to slavery, over theology, and over how to respond to revival movements sweeping the Midwest in the 1800's challenged the unity of Friends and led to some organizational divisions still reflected in the diversity of Quaker worship practices today. Source: *Quakers of Richmond and Wayne County, Indiana,* www.earlham.edu/Q/brochure1.

Paulena's early education consisted of attending a subscription school overseen by the Newberry Friends Meeting. She fondly recalls her school days and childhood play in her journals. At the age of sixteen, Paulena began attending Friends' Boarding School, Earlham,[7] in Richmond, Wayne County, Indiana, and she was there from 1856 to 1857. The school, founded by the Indiana Yearly Meeting of the Society of Friends for high school age students, would later become a nationally ranked liberal arts institution, Earlham College. Paulena's future husband, William Janney, attended the school during the same years; however, he and Paulena had known each other prior to attending Earlham, as both were members of Newberry Meeting and William lived in Clark Township near Martinsville.

William Janney was the tenth of twelve children of Joseph and Elizabeth (Russell) Janney. The Janneys came to Clinton County, Ohio, from Loudoun County, Virginia, in 1817, one year after their marriage. William Janney was twenty-four years old when he and Paulena were married on April 7, 1859. His mother had died on December 15, 1851, when he was fifteen years old, and his father died on March 13, 1852, only three months later. Because Will had only reached his sixteenth birthday in January 1852, Reuben Hunt was appointed guardian of the three minor children of Joseph and Elizabeth Janney: Stephen, William, and Caroline.[8] Reuben Hunt was a first cousin once removed of Paulena Stevens and a

---

stained glass were unnecessary distractions in achieving these goals." Source: http://www.newporthistorical.org/the great.htm.

"A story related of a person who told a Quaker that the silent meeting of Friends was enough to kill the Devil; to which the Quaker replied, that it was the very thing the silent assembly was trying to do." Source: *The Clinton Republican,* April 29, 1859.

7. Friends' Boarding School was founded in 1847 and named Earlham after an English Quaker's estate. No diplomas were issued until 1859 when the school became Earlham College. Source: *The Indiana Genealogist* 12, June 2002.

8. No will has been found for Joseph Janney. Jesse Coffin was the administrator of the estate, and Joseph Moon and Reuben Hunt were bondsmen, dated March 17, 1852. The inventory valued the property at $1,126.71, with cash in the amount of $350.93, for a total of $1,477.64. There were outstanding notes due the estate and $3,000

member of the Newberry Meeting. William Janney was also a birthright Quaker. For the first five months of their marriage, William and Paulena lived with her parents, the Evan Stevenses, on the family farm just west of Martinsville, off State Road 28. Besides Evan, Priscilla, William, and Paulena, the household included Paulena's siblings: Alma, thirteen; Elva, seven; and Willie, four.

William Janney, or "Will," as Paulena referred to him, was a carpenter and house builder by trade, but he was also an inventor who applied for patents for a fruit pan and butter churn, as is reported in these journals. He and his brother, George, were contracted to build the new schoolhouse in Martinsville in 1857.[9] Their father, Joseph Janney, was also a builder and farmer. In 1844 he had been appointed by the Newberry Meeting to construct a new Meeting House to replace the original log structure built in 1816, which had burned. The new house of worship was a simple brick building in traditional Quaker style. That structure was replaced in 1883 with the current building, which stands in the original location of the first log building.[10] Paulena reported in her journals that Will also worked on rebuilding bridges destroyed by Rebels when Morgan's Raiders swept into southern Ohio during the Civil War.

---

paid into the Cincinnati & Marietta Rail Road Co. on January 8, 1852. The bill of sale shows that the property brought $1,349.10, with $350.93 in cash still in the account and $739.32 in notes, for a total of $2,439.35 less $75. The sale took place on September 6, 1852, as shown in book 1, p. 96. The first account was given in 1853, p. 233, and the second account was given in December 1857, book 2, p. 268.

Distributions were made to Lot Janney, Jane [Janney] Haworth, George Janney, Mary [Janney] Bailey, J. M. Moon [John Milton Moon, husband of Rebecca Janney], and Daniel Coffin [husband of Patience Janney] in the amount of $170 each.

Reuben Hunt was appointed guardian of the minor children Stephen Janney, William Janney, and Caroline Janney. Cash from the sale of land was $510 with additional sums totaling $1,037.92. It is believed that Reuben Hunt had purchased the land for $510. No deed of transfer has been located. From Probate Administration of Joseph Janney, Clinton County Court House, collected by Christie Russell, 1999.

9. "When a special school district was formed in Martinsville, Ohio, authorization to build a schoolhouse and establish a graded school were granted. Christopher Columbus Betts [uncle to Paulena], Robert Fulton [who had performed Will and Paulena's marriage], and Dr. John Carman, as directors and prime movers in the enterprise, called the patrons of the school together and submitted a proposition to build a house costing not less than $2,500 or $3,000. The proposition was carried, there being only two dissenting voices. The contract was given to George and William Janney, who built the house, which cost, when completed about $2,800." Miss Josie (Josephine, or Jo in the journal) White (sister to Lydia White who married Steven Janney) was in charge of the second department of the school. Source: *History of Clinton County, Ohio,* Clark Township, 1882, p. 702.

10. "Newberry Meeting House Dates Back to 1816," *Clinton County Shopper's Guide,* June 17, 1987, front page.

Will worked on the construction of Dr. John Carman's house in Martinsville, located on lot 47. On June 1, 1859, William Janney purchased two lots in Martinsville, numbers 55 and 56, from Paulena's uncle, Christopher Betts, for $200. Shortly afterward, he began construction of a new house on lot 55 that Paulena later named Grapevine Cottage. They moved into their new home in August 1859.

Life in the Mid-Nineteenth Century

In 1859, it had been only eighty-three years since the signing of the Declaration of Independence and seventy-two years since the ratification of the U.S. Constitution.

James Buchanan was president of the United States from 1857 to 1861, when Paulena began her journals. Abraham Lincoln was president from 1861 to 1865, and Andrew Johnson became president after Lincoln's assassination, serving from 1865 to 1869, the later years of Paulena's journals. Queen Victoria reigned in Britain from 1836 to 1901. The United States consisted of thirty-three states and had a population of thirty-one million, four million of whom were slaves. Just one month before the first journal entry, Oregon gained statehood on March 17, 1859. During the years from 1859 to 1866, when the last journal entry was made, three more states would be added to the Union: Kansas in 1861, West Virginia in 1863, and Nevada in 1864. Shortly thereafter, in 1867, Nebraska would join the Union, but it would be nine more years before the next state, Colorado, would gain statehood, the thirty-eighth of the fifty states we have today.

As one can imagine, life in the nineteenth century was quite different from life in the twenty-first century. Many conveniences we take for granted today did not exist then. Labor-saving devices and technology have made our lives more comfortable and healthful. In the mid-nineteenth century, there was no electricity for lights and appliances, no central heat or air-conditioning, no indoor plumbing or running water, no refrigeration, no gas or electric stoves or microwaves, no automobiles, bicycles, airplanes, telephones, cell phones, answering machines, voice mail, PDAs, radios, CD or DVD players, televisions, or computers. Cooking and baking were accomplished by using a wood-burning stove, which also served as the heat source for the kitchen. Wood or coal burning fireplaces or stoves were sources of heat in other rooms of the house. Wood was chopped, stacked, and stored in a woodhouse. Water was drawn from a well and brought to the house for drinking, cooking, and cleaning. The laundry was done by heating water on the stove, pouring it into a tub, and scrubbing the clothes by hand on a washboard with homemade soap.[11] Clothes were hung out

---

11. At the end of Journal Three, Paulena lists among her recipes one for making soap: "Dissolve one pound of soda and a half a pound of hot lime in one gallon of boiling

to dry on a line in the yard or indoors on whatever was available to hang them on. Heavy irons had to be heated on the stove before ironing could be done.

The toilet was an outbuilding called a privy or an outhouse, which was designed with a board seat positioned over a pit. The chamber pot that held waste from indoor use was emptied into the pit, and lime was added to facilitate decomposition. Leaves, sticks, and corncobs served as toilet paper at that time in Ohio. Toilet paper was not invented until 1880, and the Sears Roebuck Catalog, whose pages were often used for toilet paper, was not printed until 1894.

Vegetables and fruit were stored in the cool, dark root cellar, which in the Janneys' case was under the house and was entered from outside. It is still visible today at the home on lot 55. Canning was a seasonal chore. Wildflower roots were brought in from the fields, transplanted, and lovingly tended to add a touch of beauty to the yard. Some apparel was purchased, but most clothing was sewn by hand until Paulena's mother bought a sewing machine that the women of the family shared. Traveling was done on foot; on horseback; by horse and buggy, wagon, or carriage; or by train or steamboat.

Martinsville's location on the Marietta and Cincinnati Rail Road provided relatively convenient long-distance travel and linked its residents to steamboat transportation on the Ohio River at Cincinnati or Marietta. The trains carried passengers and troops in the war, freight, mail, and news, providing an important link to the outside world. The telegraph came into use in Martinsville in 1864 with an office in the train depot, which was located on a two-block-long hill south of Lena and Will's home in Martinsville.[12] The post office, one block east, had been established several years earlier.

Among the businesses listed on an 1859 map of Martinsville were Moon, Nordyke & Burns Saw and Flouring Mill, Betts & Hunt Merchants, A. Bilderback

---

water. Dissolve one pound of sliced hard soap in two quarts of boiling water. When cool mix them together soak the clothes and boil them half an hour in the suds of this soap. Then rinse." The hard soap she refers to here might be rendered animal fat that had been mixed with wood ash to form lye. Lye soap was good for chigger bites, mosquito bites, poison ivy, chicken pox, and cleaning just about anything.

12. "1844 May 24—(Samuel) Morse . . . gives first official demonstration of his telegraph using over-head wire from the Supreme Court Chamber in the Capitol Building in Washington (his location) to Baltimore (Vail's location). Using his letter code, Annie Ellsworth's selected biblical phrase 'What Hath God Wrought,' from Numbers 23:23, is sent from Washington to Baltimore . . . 1859 Western Union sets up the '92 Code' of numbered phrases. '73' is included and means 'Accept my compliments.' '30' is defined to mean 'The end. No more.' 1860 Apr 3—The Pony Express, officially the Central Overland California and Pike's Peak Express Company, is initiated. A letter from St. Joseph, Missouri to Sacramento, California typically requires ten days transit time." Source: http://members.tripod.com/morse_telegraph_club/images/newpage1.htm.

Wagon Shop, J. B. Puckett Chair Factory, L. Townsend Grocery & Provisions Store, R. Fulton Merchant, West & Lyttles Store, J. W. Vance Smith Shop, Mairs Shoe Shop, White & Ford Saddle & Harness Shop, John Hunt Maker and Dealer in Furniture, T. E. & D. Carey Drugs & Jewelry, and John Carey Blacksmith. Down at the railroad depot were F. Moon's Store, R. Fulton's Warehouse, and C. C. Betts's Warehouse. Also listed are physicians John Carman, F. M. Sanderson, A. Guttery, and D. Carey, as well as the M. E. Church [Methodist Episcopal] and the Friends Meetinghouse Ground. By 1863, a bank had been established in the village.

Paulena was an avid reader. She recorded the titles of books, magazines, and newspapers she read. A library had been established by members of the Newberry Meeting in 1843. A committee was appointed to oversee the selection, purchase, distribution, and repair of the books, which were at first located in Paulena's uncle William S. Betts's home and later were placed in Aaron Betts's (Paulena's grandfather's) home. The library was organized in honor of Professor Milton Hollingsworth, educated at Earlham, who was a noted instructor at the Newberry Subscription School. It was this library that provided most of the books that Lena read, many of which are now considered classics. Several of those books were still in the libraries of descendants of former library members living in Martinsville as late as 1953. Lot Janney, Paulena's brother-in-law, also sent books that Paulena happily devoured. She enjoyed writing prose and poetry and was often called on by friends and family to write a piece for a paper or some correspondence. It was her dream to be a writer, and she realized that dream by becoming a diarist. The exchange of letters was an important aspect of daily life in the mid-nineteenth century and a significant means of communication.

Women did not have the right to vote. Paulena wrote a short piece expressing her opinion concerning equal rights for women. She mentioned attending at least one debate on the subject. It would be sixty years before women won the right to vote with the ratification of the Nineteenth Amendment on August 20, 1920.

The Janneys, Bettses, Hiatts, Hunts, Stevenses, and Coffins had moved west from Virginia and North Carolina to escape the slave-owning culture of the South and live in the Old Northwest Territory where slavery was prohibited by the Northwest Ordinance of 1787. They were also drawn by the prospect of inexpensive, fertile farmland. The soil in Virginia and North Carolina had become depleted from overuse, and land became scarce when property was divided among several sons in one family. Younger sons tended to be the ones who moved on, however, because of the right of primogeniture, the exclusive right of the first-born male to succeed to the family property to the exclusion of all other siblings, the widow, and all other relatives, regardless of need. In 1784 and 1785, North Carolina and Virginia, respectively, abolished primogeniture.

Paulena's grandfather, Aaron Betts, and her great-uncle, Christopher Hiatt, as well as her cousins Levi and Vestal Coffin were deeply involved in the

Underground Railroad.[13] Betts and Hiatt lived in Clinton County, Ohio. Vestal Coffin lived in Guilford County, North Carolina, and Levi Coffin lived first in Fountain City, Indiana, and later in Cincinnati, Ohio. Paulena's cousins Lucretia Coffin Mott of Philadelphia and John Woolman,[14] deceased, of New Jersey, were early noted Quakers in the abolitionist movement.

There was no better way for members of the Quaker community to express their concern for the welfare of slaves and the abolition of slavery than to set their own slaves free. As early as 1783, a number of Janney men signed

---

13. "The Underground Railroad was the name given to the system by which escaped slaves from the South were helped in their flight to the North. . . . Opponents of slavery allowed their homes, called stations, to be used as places where escaped slaves were provided with food, shelter and money. The various routes went through 14 Northern states and Canada. It is estimated that by 1850 around 3,000 people worked on the underground railroad. Some of the best known of the people who provided help on the route included Frederick Douglass, Henry David Thoreau, Lucretia Mott, Susan B. Anthony. . . .

"Stations were usually about twenty miles apart. Conductors used covered wagons or carts with false bottoms to carry slaves from one station to another. Runaway slaves usually hid during the day and traveled at night. Some of those involved notified runaways of their stations by brightly lit candles in a window or by lanterns positioned in the front yard. . . .

"Plantation owners became concerned at the large number of slaves escaping to the North and in 1850 managed to persuade Congress to pass the Fugitive Slave Act. In future, any federal marshal who did not arrest an alleged runaway slave could be fined $1,000. Any person aiding a runaway slave by providing shelter, food or any other form of assistance was liable to six months' imprisonment and a $1,000 fine." Source: "Freedom's Trail: The Underground Railroad," http://www.nyjournalnews.com/blackhistory/main.html.

"Polaris [the North Star] became a symbol of freedom to slaves as well as a guide star. As soon as they were old enough to understand, slave children were taught to locate Polaris by using the stars of the Big Dipper.

"Slaves passed the travel instructions from plantation to plantation by song. Slaves brought from the tribal cultures of Africa the custom of creating songs to transmit factual information. In America slaves turned song into codes that secretly transmitted information they wished to keep from whites.

"'Follow the Drinking Gourd' is a coded song that gives the route for an escape from Alabama and Mississippi. Of all the routes out of the Deep South, this is the only one for which the details survive. The route instructions were given to slaves by an old man named Peg Leg Joe. Working as an itinerant carpenter, he spent winters in the South, moving from plantation to plantation, teaching slaves this escape route. Unfortunately, we know nothing more about Peg Leg Joe." Source: "Follow the Drinking Gourd," http://quest.arc.nasa.gov/ltc/special/mlk/gourd1.html.

14. "[John] Woolman, whose simple, unpretentious journal—the record of a pure and beautiful life—has become an American classic, spoke for the Negro, the Indian, the cruelly exploited everywhere. 'To labor hard,' he wrote in his homely way, 'or

the Anti-Slavery Petition to the United States Congress from the [Philadelphia] Yearly Meeting of the People called Quakers, dated 4th Day of the Tenth Month 1783.[15] No record has been found that any of these Janneys ever owned slaves. The family of Elizabeth Russell Janney, whose members were not Quakers, did own slaves.

As a member of the "contraband society," as Paulena referred to it, organized by the Newberry Meeting, Paulena made clothing and was appointed to serve on the procurement committee. That clothing was conveyed to Cincinnati to newly freed slaves or those escaping from the South to freedom in Canada along the Underground Railroad. For many African Americans who lived in the slave states prior to and during the Civil War, the Underground Railroad provided the opportunity and assistance to escape slavery and find freedom. Several Underground Railroad stations were known to exist in Clinton County, and one was at the home of Paulena's great-uncle, Christopher Hiatt.[16]

Among the social issues found in Paulena's journals are many that are still debated. Capital punishment and the effects of alcohol abuse were two such issues. Paulena expressed her opinion of capital punishment at the time of John Brown's execution. Alcohol abuse led to the founding of the temperance movement. Paulena attended temperance meetings and contributed written material for the Martinsville Division 67, as her journal demonstrates.

Journal entries that deal with Civil War battles, the call for volunteers, the draft, and military leadership provide insight into the impact the war had on family life. William Janney's two older brothers, Stephen and George Janney,

---

cause others to do so, that we may live comfortably to customs which our redeemer discountenanced by his example, and which are contrary to divine order, is to manure a soil for propagating an evil seed on earth.' Woolman never resorted to harsh abuse, but his journal (as the Quaker poet, John Greenleaf Whittier, later wrote) was a life-long testimony against wrong, and one of the finest expressions of eighteenth-century benevolence." Source: Richard Hofstadter, William Miller, and Daniel Aaron, *The American Republic* to 1865, 1960, vol. 1, p. 108.

15. The anti-slavery petition reads, "Being through the favour of Divine Providence met as usual at this season in our annual Assembly to promote the cause of Piety and Virtue. We find with great satisfaction our well meant endeavours for the relief of an oppressed part of our fellow Men have been so far blessed, that those of them who have been held in bondage by Members of our Religious Society are generally restored to freedom, their natural and just right." Among those signing were Joseph Janney, grandfather of William Janney, Mahlon Janney, a nephew to Joseph Janney Sr., and Blackstone Janney, a son of Joseph Janney Sr. Source: *Papers of the Continental Congress*, National Archives, microfilm.

16. "Christopher Hiatt was one of the first advocates of the abolition of slavery. Some traveling speakers for the cause stopped at his home over night and violence was feared by the community. Nothing happened except that the manes and tails of

and Henry "Clay" Cowgill, Alma Stevens's future husband, had volunteered to serve in the Union Army. The strain in their own household because they were unsure whether Will would go if drafted, pay to have a substitute, or declare himself "conscientious" became obvious. If he went as a draftee or volunteer or paid for a substitute, he would violate the Quaker "peace testimony," which opposed violence as a means of reconciling differences. Four years of civil war not only took a toll in human life but also powerfully affected the economy. Construction came to a halt and Will found little work. The months and years dragged on until, at last, in the spring of 1865, Paulena was able to record the closing days of the war, Lee's surrender, Lincoln's assassination, and the capture of John Wilkes Booth and Jefferson Davis. Life did go on.

Most married women of the nineteenth century could expect to have a child within the first year or two of marriage. Paulena longed for a child in the household to fulfill her maternal instincts, give her greater purpose in life, and bring the happiness and companionship she so desired. However, seven long, childless years passed before Will and Lena were blessed with the birth of their first surviving child, a daughter, Alma, named for Paulena's sister. Although she never mentioned the nature of her illness, Paulena often recorded that she was not feeling well, and it is quite clear that on at least one occasion the birth of an anticipated child for whom a cradle was prepared never took place. There was a six-month lapse when nothing was recorded in her journal. When she did resume writing, there was no mention of the reason for the long absence in writing or what had transpired in those months. The childless years provided her with time to keep these journals and leave a treasured legacy for her descendants and other interested readers.

An epilogue follows the last journal entry of 1867. It gives the rest of the story, providing the reader with the family's history in the years following the Civil War, including the migration to Carthage, in Jasper County, Missouri.

---

the traveler's horses were trimmed in the barn. Christopher Hiatt was a shelterer of runaway slaves. Once he was in the field with one of these refugees when they saw his nephew Evan Stephens approaching. Christopher knew that they must name the black man quickly. So they called him Martin Davis. That name stuck to the negro for the rest of his life and was passed on to his children and descendants." Source: *History of Clinton County, Ohio,* Clark Township, 1882.

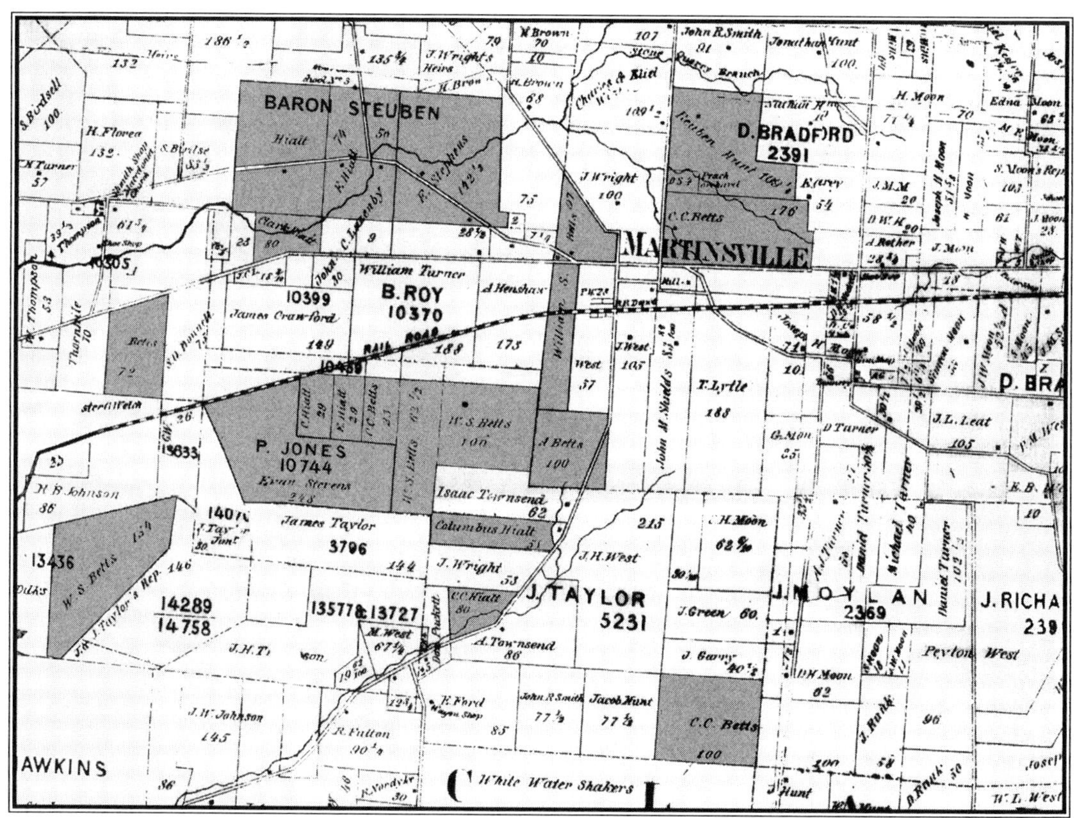

1865 Martinsville area map.
Shaded areas are parcels of family land.

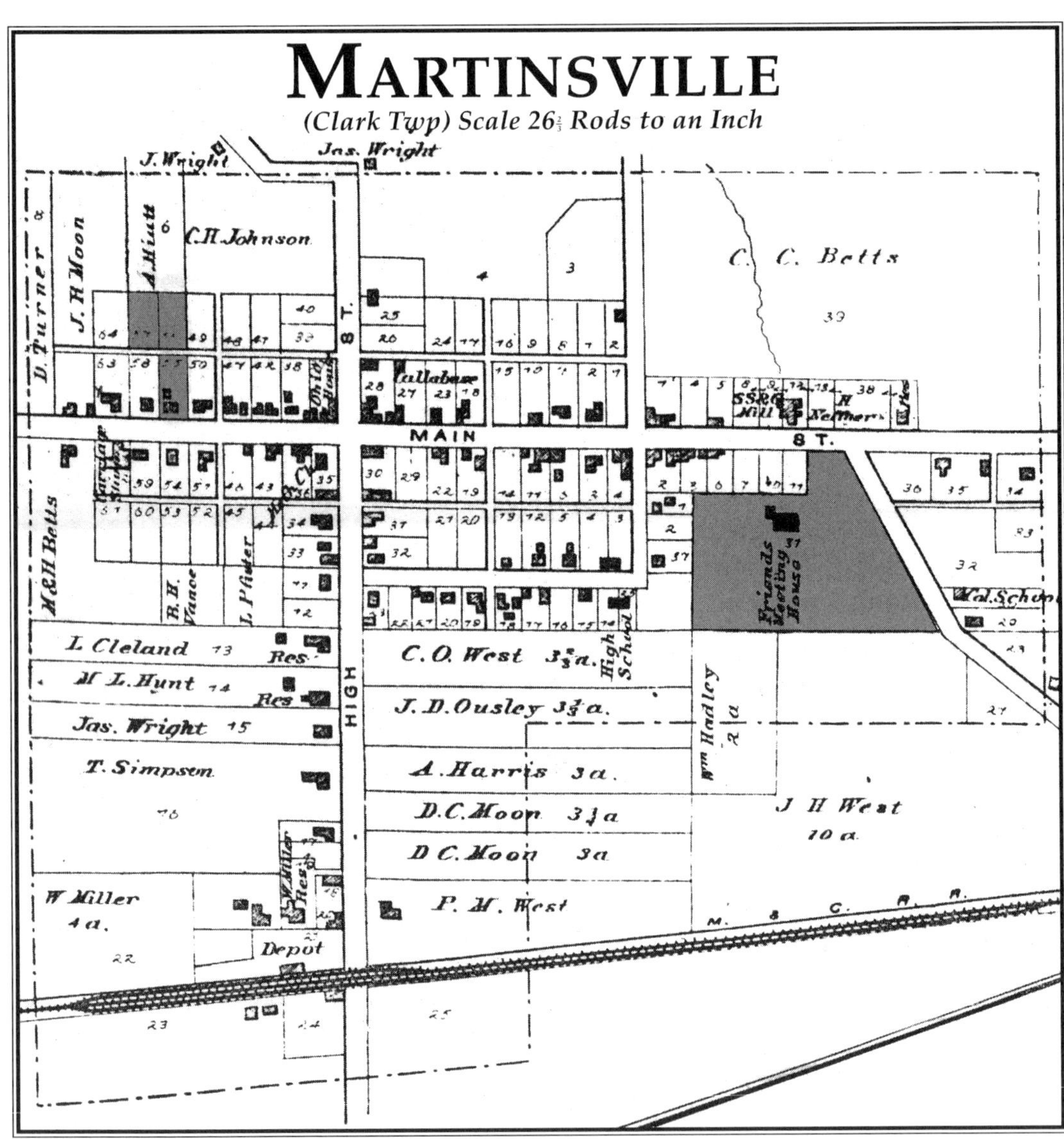

Martinsville Village map
showing lot 55 and Friends Meeting House

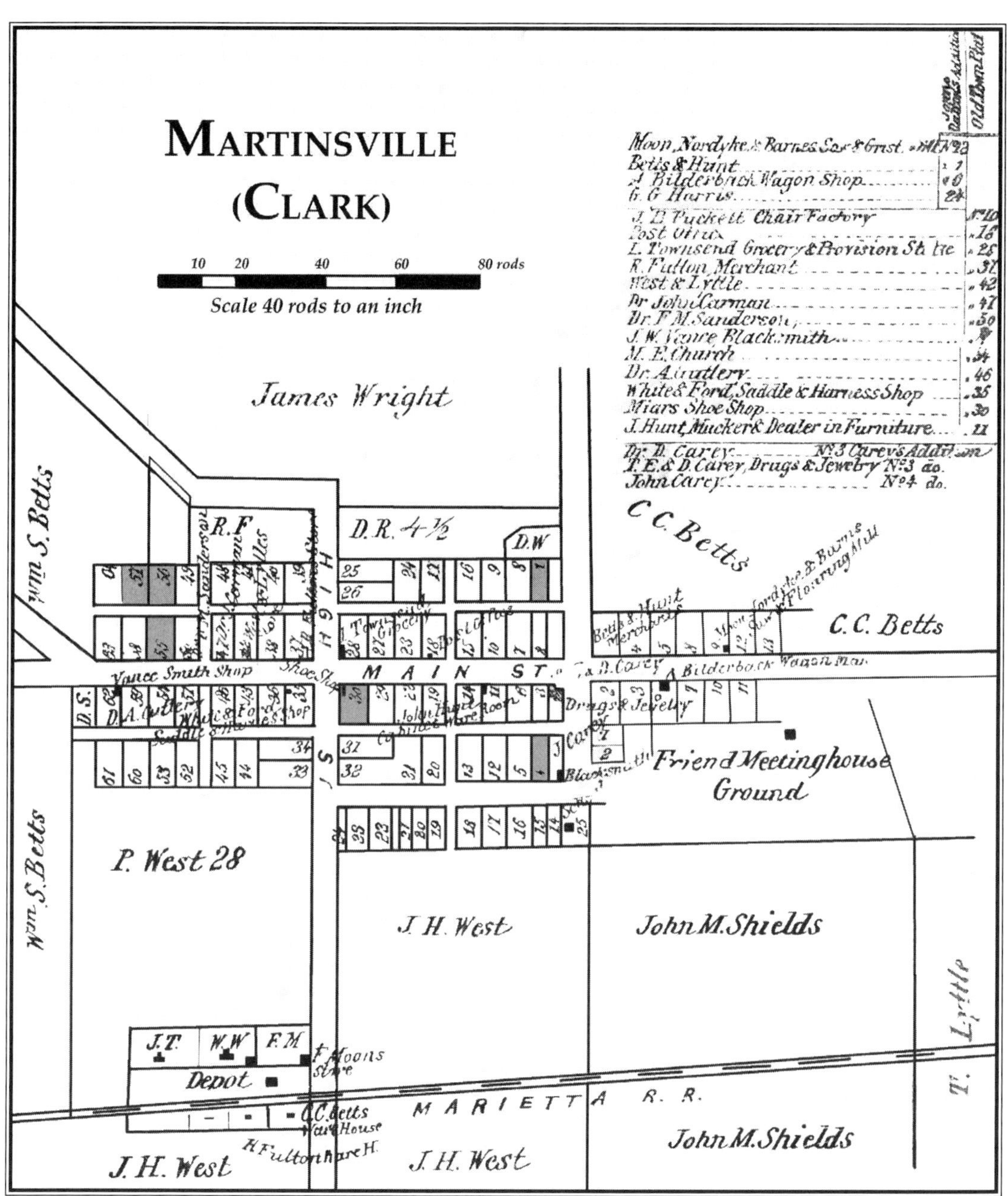

1859 Martinsville atlas with
directory of businesses.
Shaded areas are parcels of family land.

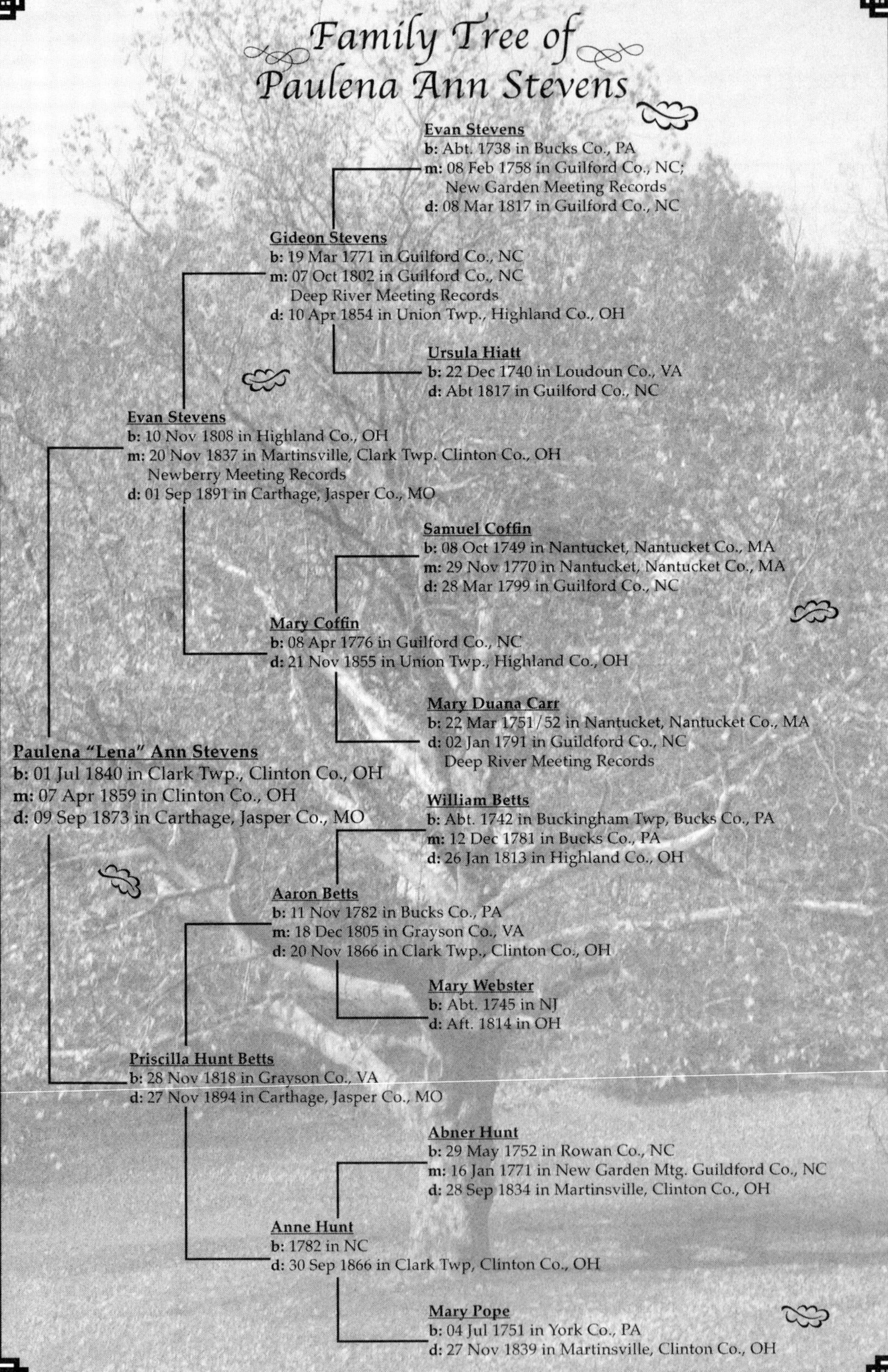

Family Tree of
Paulena Ann Stevens

Evan Stevens
b: Abt. 1738 in Bucks Co., PA
m: 08 Feb 1758 in Guilford Co., NC;
New Garden Meeting Records
d: 08 Mar 1817 in Guilford Co., NC

Gideon Stevens
b: 19 Mar 1771 in Guilford Co., NC
m: 07 Oct 1802 in Guilford Co., NC
Deep River Meeting Records
d: 10 Apr 1854 in Union Twp., Highland Co., OH

Ursula Hiatt
b: 22 Dec 1740 in Loudoun Co., VA
d: Abt 1817 in Guilford Co., NC

Evan Stevens
b: 10 Nov 1808 in Highland Co., OH
m: 20 Nov 1837 in Martinsville, Clark Twp. Clinton Co., OH
Newberry Meeting Records
d: 01 Sep 1891 in Carthage, Jasper Co., MO

Samuel Coffin
b: 08 Oct 1749 in Nantucket, Nantucket Co., MA
m: 29 Nov 1770 in Nantucket, Nantucket Co., MA
d: 28 Mar 1799 in Guilford Co., NC

Mary Coffin
b: 08 Apr 1776 in Guilford Co., NC
d: 21 Nov 1855 in Union Twp., Highland Co., OH

Mary Duana Carr
b: 22 Mar 1751/52 in Nantucket, Nantucket Co., MA
d: 02 Jan 1791 in Guildford Co., NC
Deep River Meeting Records

Paulena "Lena" Ann Stevens
b: 01 Jul 1840 in Clark Twp., Clinton Co., OH
m: 07 Apr 1859 in Clinton Co., OH
d: 09 Sep 1873 in Carthage, Jasper Co., MO

William Betts
b: Abt. 1742 in Buckingham Twp, Bucks Co., PA
m: 12 Dec 1781 in Bucks Co., PA
d: 26 Jan 1813 in Highland Co., OH

Aaron Betts
b: 11 Nov 1782 in Bucks Co., PA
m: 18 Dec 1805 in Grayson Co., VA
d: 20 Nov 1866 in Clark Twp., Clinton Co., OH

Mary Webster
b: Abt. 1745 in NJ
d: Aft. 1814 in OH

Priscilla Hunt Betts
b: 28 Nov 1818 in Grayson Co., VA
d: 27 Nov 1894 in Carthage, Jasper Co., MO

Abner Hunt
b: 29 May 1752 in Rowan Co., NC
m: 16 Jan 1771 in New Garden Mtg. Guildford Co., NC
d: 28 Sep 1834 in Martinsville, Clinton Co., OH

Anne Hunt
b: 1782 in NC
d: 30 Sep 1866 in Clark Twp, Clinton Co., OH

Mary Pope
b: 04 Jul 1751 in York Co., PA
d: 27 Nov 1839 in Martinsville, Clinton Co., OH

$\mathcal{D}$irectory of Individuals in Paulena's Journals

Author   **Paulena "Lena" Ann Stevens,** daughter of Evan Stevens and Priscilla Hunt Betts; married to William Janney; migrated to Carthage, Missouri, 1868; buried in Park Cemetery, Carthage, Missouri

Mother   **Priscilla Hunt Betts,** daughter of Aaron Betts and Anne Hunt married to Evan Stevens; migrated to Carthage, Missouri, 1868; buried in Park Cemetery, Carthage, Missouri

Father   **Evan Stevens (Stephens),** son of Gideon Stephens and Mary Coffin (deceased 1854 and 1855, respectively), grandson of Evan Stevens and Ursula Hiatt, and Samuel Coffin and Mary Duana Carr; buried in Park Cemetery, Carthage, Missouri

Alma   **Mary "Alma" Stevens,** Paulena's sister; married to Henry Clay Cowgill; student at Earlham, 1862; migrated to Carthage, Missouri, 1868; buried in Park Cemetery, Carthage, Missouri

Elva   **Lydia Elva Stevens,** Paulena's sister; married to Curtis Brinton Wood; migrated to Carthage, Missouri, 1868; buried in Park Cemetery, Carthage, Missouri

Willie   **William Land Stevens,** Paulena's younger brother who died at age sixteen in a hunting accident in Carthage; buried in Park Cemetery, Carthage, Missouri

Will   **William Janney,** Paulena's husband, son of Joseph Janney and Elizabeth Russell (deceased 1852 and 1851, respectively) and grandson of Joseph Janney and Mary Holmes, and Robert Russell and Mary Leedom, deceased, of Loudoun County, Virginia; buried in Thresher Cemetery, Neosho, Missouri

Grandmother **Anne (Hunt) Betts,** daughter of Abner Hunt and Mary Pope; buried in Newberry Meeting Cemetery, Martinsville, Ohio

Grandfather **Aaron Betts,** son of William Betts and Mary (Webster) Paxson; buried in Newberry Meeting Cemetery, Martinsville, Ohio

George   **George Janney,** brother-in-law, older brother of William Janney; married to Rebecca Betts, first cousin of Paulena; Union Army, Civil War; buried in Newberry Meeting Cemetery, Martinsville, Ohio

Jane

Jane (Janney) Haworth, sister-in-law, older sister of William Janney; married to Richard M. Haworth, son of Mahlon Haworth and Phoebe Frazier; buried in Sugar Grove Friends Cemetery, Plainfield, Indiana

Rebecca "Beck"

Rebecca (Janney) Moon, sister-in-law, older sister of William Janney; married to John Milton Moon, son of Henry Moon and Sarah Mills; buried in Newberry Meeting Cemetery, Martinsville, Ohio

Steve

Stephen Janney, brother-in-law, older brother of William Janney; married to Lydia White, daughter of Benjamin J. White and Lavinia Coffin; Union Army, Civil War; buried in Cherokee Cemetery, Crawford County, Kansas

Lot

Lot Janney, brother-in-law, older brother of William Janney; married to Fannie Wood, daughter of Caius Martius Wood and Sophia Hall; buried in Olathe, Johnson County, Kansas

Mary

Mary Janney, sister-in-law, older sister of William Janney; married first to David Bailey, son of Daniel Bailey and Mary Haworth, and second to James Fisher

Call

Carolyn (Janney) Betts, sister-in-law, younger sister of William Janney; married to Madison Betts, Paulena's first cousin, son of Christopher Betts and Lydia Huff; buried in Sugar Grove Cemetery, Wilmington, Ohio

Cal

Anna Carolyn Betts, first cousin, daughter of William S. Betts, brother of Paulena's mother, and Anna Hadley; married to Jacob Jackson; migrated to Missouri in 1868

Jake

Jacob Jackson, son of Josiah and Ruth Hiatt Jackson, and third cousin once removed to Paulena; married Carolyn Betts

Jimmy

James P. Betts, first cousin and brother to Anna Carolyn Betts; married to Nancy Perry of Covington, Kentucky; migrated to Jasper County, Missouri

"Jo," Jose

Josephine White, good friend, daughter of Benjamin White and Lavinia Coffin, second cousin to Paulena, married to Milton Morgan

Lyd   **Lydia White,** sister to above, second cousin to Paulena; married to Stephen Janney and therefore Paulena's sister-in-law; buried in Cherokee Cemetery, Crawford County, Kansas

Uncle William   **William S. Betts,** brother to Paulena's mother; married to Anna Hadley; migrated to Carthage, Missouri, in 1868

Uncle Christopher   **Christopher Columbus Betts,** older brother of Paulena's mother; married to Lydia Huff, daughter of Daniel Huff and Sarah Burnside; remained in Clinton County, Ohio; buried in Sugar Grove Cemetery, Wilmington, Ohio

Uncle David   **David James,** son of Isaac James and Sarah; married first to Mary Hunt (first cousin twice removed to Paulena) and next to Deborah Stevens, Paulena's aunt (her father's sister)

Matt and Jonathan   **Martha "Matt" Ann Ladd,** Paulena's dear friend who lived near Leesburg, Highland County, Ohio; married to Addison Pushee. Jonathan Ladd, married to Louisa Lazenby. Matt and Jonathan were the children of Asa Ladd and Mary Chalfant and were Paulena's third cousins. She is buried in Fairfield Friends Cemetery, Highland County, Ohio.

Mary   **Mary Hunt,** Paulena's younger second cousin, the daughter of Jesse Hunt and Anna Moon, born April 21, 1842

Jim Hunt   **James E. Hunt** was the son of Jonathan and Margaret Hadley Hunt. He was a second cousin to Paulena. Margaret Hadley was a sister of Anna Hadley who was married to William S. Betts, Paulena's uncle.

Sallie   **Sallie James,** Paulena's second cousin once removed, the daughter of David James and Mary Hunt

Aunt Lizzie   **Elizabeth Betts** lived in the household of Paulena's grandfather, Aaron Betts, according to the 1860 census. She was two years older than Aaron, but Aaron did not have a sister named Elizabeth that we know of. She may be the widow of Aaron's older half-brother, Hezekiah.

Uncle Tom   **Thomas Stevens,** brother of Paulena's father, Evan, lived in Highland County on land inherited from his father's estate

Lenna	**Paulena Stevens,** daughter of Thomas Stevens and cousin to Paulena. At the death of her mother, Evan and Priscilla Stevens, her aunt and uncle, adopted her. She migrated to Carthage, Missouri, in 1868, and is buried in Park Cemetery, Carthage, Missouri.
Jesse Coffin	**Jesse Coffin,** first cousin, son of David Coffin and Mary Kenworthy; married to Emily Janney, older sister of Will Janney and brother to Daniel
Daniel Coffin	**Daniel Coffin,** first cousin, son of David Coffin and Mary Kenworth, and brother of Jesse; married to Patience Janney, older sister of Will Janney
Lib	**Elizabeth (West) Haynes,** sister of George West, daughter of James Hadley West and Elizabeth Loggett; married to Asa Haynes
Cousin William Paxson	**William Paxson,** son of Arthur Paxson, cousin of Paulena; lived in Loudoun County, Virginia
Aaron	**Aaron Betts,** first cousin, son of William S. Betts and Anna Hadley
Willie	**William C. Betts,** Paulena's first cousin and brother to Aaron; student at Earlham 1863–1865
Ella and Nannie	**Mary Ellen and Nancy Janney** were cousins of William Janney, daughters of Jonas Janney and Ruth Davis, living in Waynesville, Warren County, Ohio
Elma	**Gulielma Hunt,** Paulena's dear friend and second cousin, the daughter of Reuben Hunt and Rebecca Henley
Lizzie	**Elizabeth Vance,** next-door-neighbor of Paulena in Martinsville, Ohio. Benjamin H. Vance and Elizabeth Bates were married on December 19, 1858.
Alf	**Alfred P. James,** son of David James and Mary Hunt, second cousin once removed to Paulena
Lib	**Lib Hockett,** formerly Elizabeth Huff, married Amos Hockett, son of David Hockett and Lydia Hiatt

Carmens   **Dr. John Carmen** and wife, Margaret Moon, daughter of Joseph and Eleanor Moon

Eli Newlin   **Eli Newlin,** son of John Newlin and Esther Stubbs; married to Lydia Osborn. Calvin Newlin, his nephew, married Leonora Haworth, daughter of Jane Janney and Richard M. Haworth. Leonora was a niece of William Janney. Eli was a Quaker minister.

Parents of Paulena Stevens Janney

| **Evan Stevens** | **Priscilla Betts Stevens** |
| November 10, 1808—September 1, 1891 | November 27, 1818—November 28, 1894 |

Parents of Paulena "Lena" Stevens Janney, Alma Stevens Cowgill, Elva Stevens Wood, and William "Willie" Stevens

Grandparents of Paulena Stevens Janney

Aaron Betts
November 11, 1782—November 20 , 1866

Anne Hunt Betts
1782—September 30, 1866

**Parents of William S. Betts, Christopher Columbus Betts
and Priscilla Betts Stevens**

Parents of William Janney

Joseph Janney   **Elizabeth "Betsy" Russell**
March 8, 1781—March 13, 1852   July 31, 1795—December 15, 1851

**Parents of Mary Janney Bailey Fishers, Emily Janney Coffin,
Hannah Janney, Rebecca Janney Moon, Patience Janney Coffin,
Lot Janney, Jane Janney Haworth, George Janney,
Stephen Janney, William "Will" Janney, Amos Janney
and Caroline "Cal" Janney Betts**

Journal One

April 17, 1859—January 9, 1861

Paulena Stevens Janney
About nineteen years old

But, Oh, the hum of the bees
And the sight of the budding trees

They bring something more joyous to me
Than the making of butter and cheese

Paulena Stevens Janney

April 1859

Sabbath, April 17th, 1859

We went to church this morning for the first time since our marriage.[17] Left Call and Matt Ladd at home.[18] After meeting we took dinner at grandfathers, they invited all the relations. I never felt so well acquainted with Cal Janney before, I think I will like her, she suits my disposition so much better than Rebecca or Jane, we had quite a pleasant time. I wonder if we will ever be there altogether again. Lindley James is dead![19] Oh, it seems too sad, but some of my friends are ever dying, we know not who will go next.

Newberry Friends Meeting House, Martinsville, Ohio. In 1844, Joseph Janney built the second meeting house set in a grove of locust trees. In 1883, the meeting house was replaced by a brick building that is still in use.

---

17. Paulena and William's marriage was performed by Robert Fulton, Minister of the Gospel, April 7, 1859. This little rhyme is in reference to one of Will's brothers and speaks of Will's strong affection for Paulena:

> His brother, Will, a sober lad,
> And serious of demeanor,
> Made business of his early love
> And carried off Paulina

Rhyme read at Reunion of Martinsville School. August 23, 1878, by Amos Hockett.

18. Call was Carolyn Betts, first cousin. Matt Ladd was Paulena's best friend and third cousin. Will and Paulena were living with her parents, Evan and Priscilla, until their new house was built.

19. Lindley James was a second cousin once removed to Paulena. He was the son of David James and Mary Hunt. His sister, Sarah, one year younger, is probably the one referred to here. Sarah married Jacob Green Hunt, son of Nathaniel and Rachel Huff Hunt.

Secondday, April 18th, 1859
Matt has gone home. Oh, I love her so dearly. Ed took me to the funeral today, it was a sad sad time for he who had mingled with us, as classmate and student was being lowered in the cold ground. I pity Sarah so for I know she will miss him. Will did not go but he will always be willing for me to go any place I want to. I saw Harry, he said he was coming up to quarterly meeting.[20]

Thirdday, April 19th, 1859
Will and I were at Lizzie Risers for tea[21] this evening, Beck is there, I like her so well. Lizzie, Beck, Jennie Porter and I took a walk to the church yard, it seemed so lonely though I could but feel sad thinking of the many loved friends lying there, on some graves were planted the myrtle and white roses, and the modest white tombstone marked the resting place of many [a] mother, many a sister, and brother and two sweet infants who [were] transplanted in Heaven. I wonder if when I die if I will be buried here where I so often go with loved companions, and wonder too who will plant the rose upon my grave, and shed tears above me when they come there in the evening time!

Fourthday, April 20th, 1859
It has been so gloomy all day till this evening the sun broke forth through the mist and sheds a halo of sunlight on everything. It looks so beautiful far away over the green hills and meadows, where the grass is so soft and green and where the early daisies and violets are blooming in their secluded homes. How I am longing for a ramble wild and free away deep in the dark wood where the spring birds are merry all the long day and the trees are growing green. I wish I could go to some romantic spot where the flowers grow away up among the rocks, and where the water does not glide along so dreamily but where it dashed over the stones with solemn dirge like music that makes one almost fancy themselves away on the sea coast with the waves rolling onward and the shells just waiting to be gathered. Will will be home soon and I will be glad.

---

20. "The Religious Society of Friends is organized into Monthly, Quarterly and Yearly Meetings. The basic unit is the Monthly Meeting, the equivalent to the local congregation in most other churches. It is customary for Friends to worship every Sunday at a designated time. It is also the practice to hold business meetings once a month. Members of a Monthly Meeting are also members of the Quarterly meeting which meets for worship and business every three months. Similarly, all members within a certain geographic region belong to a Yearly Meeting which meets for several days once a year." Source: *Bucks Quarterly Meeting of the Society of Friends (Quakers)*, http://quakersbucks. org/.

21. Paulena often mentions "taking tea" which appears to have been an early evening light meal that today we might call "supper" but did not seem to have been just the serving of tea.

Fifthday, April 21st, 1859
Raining this morning, strange the sun cannot shine five days in succession, but when the right time comes it will be bright and beautiful just as I love for it to be. I will be so glad when we can all go "Maying" ["a-Maying" meant celebrating the first day of May] again just as we used to. I am going up to Ladds after awhile, then I can gather flowers just such wild ones as I love, those which bloom along the creek and cliffs [near Leesburg, Highland Co., Ohio]. I know I feel sad for the water always did make me lonely and this time I will think of happy days long ago when we wandered there when Matt was healthful and joyous and we could laugh such merry heart laughs which did us so much good. I do want Will to go there for I know it is such a romantic spot as he loves. I would love to live where there were cliffs and hills and everything romantic. I would love to live near the ocean if I ever had trouble, and when there were storms coming I would get on some high rock which overlooked the "mighty waters" and I could almost forget my sorrow or if I did not live there, which I know I never can, I would love to live away in some foreign land where the orange and lemon trees shed their fragrance but I suppose I can be happy at home with Will for I will just fix things to my own notion and I know Will will like things beautiful and so I must school my rebellious little heart, and quiet all my longings for some undefined something and learn to be a good true woman.

Sixthday, April 22nd, 1859
One of those cold rainy days when there is no sunshine and when everything without, looks so desolate and gloomy—such a day when warm fires and interesting books are hailed joyfully to pass away the tedious hours. I think I have spent my time in quite a profitable manner this evening, for I was making a cake. I flatter myself that it was real good for a new beginner. This evening I stood looking out from my window watching the snow flakes, as they were rapidly descending. Thinking of those winter school days when I rejoiced at the very thought of a snow storm, then I thought I would go and write while I was in the mood. Then I remembered how nice it would be to wait till Will came home and we could have a cheerful fire. I have been reading a portion of the "Sickles" trial, it seems so awful.[22] There will be vacations of school next week Alma says, and they are going to have a "May Party" on second day following.

---

22. "February 27, 1859, in a fit of jealous rage, Dan Sickles murdered Philip Barton Key (United States Attorney for the District of Columbia, son of Francis Scott Key) in broad daylight near the White House for having an affair with his wife Teresa. April 4, 1859, Dan Sickles went on trial for the murder of Barton Key. His attorney was the flamboyant James Brady. April 26, 1859, Dan Sickles was found not guilty of the murder of Barton Key by reason of "temporary insanity." That was the first use of "temporary insanity" to prove innocence." Sources: *Great American Trials,* ISBN 0-8103-9134-1, 1944; http://users.commkey.net/fussichen/otdsick.htm.

Sabbath, April 24th, 1859
Went to Sabbath school this morning, then went to our meeting. We were all going to gather flowers this evening but when I arrived home I was too much fatigued to go, so I rested awhile, and Will and I took a nice walk down by the creek where everything is so romantic and beautiful, then we came home, and found Call had been enjoying herself upstairs reading. Last evening we were at Whites party, we had a very nice time, nuts and everything good, we played Sociability too. Oh, it is beautiful this evening, but when I listen to the frogs I get sad. I think they sound like graveyard frogs. We were all there this morning in the graveyard. Lide, Jose, Lyd, Will and I, it looks so lonely, but I don't see why they are so careless, for signs of neglect were plainly visible, the graves are sinking in front of them, and there are no trees to make it beautiful, and the grass is ruined by the dumb brutes. Oh, I think it too holy a place for such as they, what can they read of its deep solemnity? On one grave I saw a bouquet of early flowers, it looked so pretty, some young hand had placed it there upon the grave of some loved one.

Secondday, April 25th, 1859
Raining this morning, the sun did come out beautiful and bright, but now the rain is falling gently, and I think after [a] while the sun will come forth. I forget myself and listen for the school bell[23] or imagine I hear it, but this is vacation week. I hope it will be pleasant next second day for the "May Party" (night). I was up at Uncle Williams and began my new bracelet. Will has gone to night, I do wish he could come home. I am getting so uneasy about him, I guess I won't let him go anymore. Will has come.

G. W. Coffin Buckeye Bell Foundry.
Cincinnati, Ohio, 1857

---

23. The school bell was cast by G. W. Coffin Buckeye Bell Foundry, Cincinnati, Ohio, in 1857 when the schoolhouse was built by William and George Janney. "George W. Coffin started his Buckeye Bell Foundry in Cincinnati, Ohio, in 1837. The bells were dated because they were sold with a 10-year warranty against breakage. The foundry was located on Second Street near Broadway on part of the site now covered by the parking lot between Paul Brown Stadium and the Great American Ballpark. Leonard Slye, better known as Roy Rogers, was born in a house which stood on the stadium site in 1911. In one season the foundry had made four hundred and forty-seven bells of all sizes, from a dinner alarm to the largest class of church bells, which weighed four thousand and ninety five pounds. The aggregate weight of theses bells was forty thousand and seventy six pounds. It was the only bell foundry in the United States in which bells were constructed "based on purely scientific principles, and made to conform rigidly to the laws of acoustics." Source: *Sketches and Statistics of Cincinnati in 1859,* by Charles

Thirdday, April 26th, 1859

Have been at home all the day long, wrote some in Matt's diary this evening. I expect she will wish she had not forgot it. Poor little thing, I am afraid it will be literally used up and bear the imprint of pen and pencil of years to come. It is raining real hard. I am so afraid it will rain on second day which would ruin the May party and I hope it will be so nice.

I do want to go to Ladds so bad. It reminds me of there, when I heard it raining for I remember we were doomed to some rainy days and nights but we could enjoy ourselves any place where we could laugh. I wonder if ever will I forget in the years to come how much I used to laugh especially Matt and I and how much fun I have seen. Wonder if I will ever get-to-be just like anyone else? And do just like them. I know I never will become ill and just forget all the joyous impulses of my youthful nature but it makes me grow young again. If I ever get old—to think of my girlhood days and all the high styles and brightness thinking of the dear girls Elma, Matt, Call, Jo[24] and oh, so many of them. I know I love them still though years have rolled away and some of them be lying in their graves. I will ever hold their memories dear and perchance I can scatter the early flowers upon the graves of the dead when spring time cometh. It may be I too will be gone, sleeping in the graveyard where tonight the cold rain is falling, and someone will read this and if they never knew me will perhaps carelessly pass by it, and if it is a dear one who has loved me it will cause them to feel very sad, if I indeed am gone. I expect little Eva will die for she was so bad this morning and this rain and thunder always reminds of some person dead. It sounds so lonesome. I think she is so sweet, but she will be better off.

Fourthday, April 27th, 1859

It has been so gloomy looking, I do wish it would be nice weather. I began a piece for the paper this evening. I don't know whether I will get it finished or not. Have got no letter from Matt yet I don't look for her a bit to quarterly meeting and wish she would come. Will is so weary tonight, he don't feel like writing or anything. I don't feel in the mood for writing either.

Cist. G. W. Coffin died sometime after the 1870 census and before the 1880 census. The company came under new ownership (E. W. Vanduzen) but kept the Buckeye name. Under that ownership, many bells were made for churches, schools, and battleships in World War I. One was cast as a commemorative bell for the Lewis and Clark Centennial Exposition in Portland, Oregon, in 1905. George W. Coffin was a cousin of Paulena through her grandmother Mary Coffin Stephens. The school bell is currently displayed presently in a small structure built of bricks from the former school building on the original school site in Martinsville, Ohio.

24. These four girls were Elma [Gulielma Hunt, a cousin and a loving friend as well, died less than a year later in February 1860; see memorials written for her by Paulena in this journal], Matt [Martha Ladd], a cousin, Call [Carolyn Betts, a cousin] and Jo [Josephine White], sister of Lydia White who married Stephen Janney, brother of Will.

Fifthday, April 28th, 1859
I am going to division (a temperance meeting) tonight. Beck Irwin and I met. There are a great many going but they don't belong to us.

Sixthday, April 29th, 1859
I was up to take Will's dinner today and after I came home I heard such a sea of storys about me that I felt like crying. I don't see why people cant just let me alone. Sarah Ellen Hunt[25] —I thought she was some of a different girl from what she is but I know now how to trust her here after. I find no friends so true among all the girls, as Jo, Call and Matt—others I can trust them not for to my face they profess friendship yet they pause not, to injure me when away. Such friends I can not call friends.

Seventhday, April 30th, 1859
 I went to meeting. Mary, John, Matt Hussey were here again. We went to the depot after supper as usual. We got acquainted with a girl I have seen so often but never spoke to. I met her at Richmond [Indiana] several times at Fairfield [Highland County, Ohio] and Wilmington [Clinton County Seat, Ohio]. I like her so well.

May 1859

Sabbath, May 1st, 1859
Bright and beautiful dawn. Went to meeting today it was so crowded when I got there but my new friend had saved me a seat by her. Mary and John came down this evening.

Secondday, May 2nd, 1859
Joyous "May party" today.[26] We have had a sweet time. Went to the school house to listen to the exercises or a portion of them—we marched to the grove—I as much a school girl as any. We had dinner and then at the ringing of the school bell we went to the school house. Danny was there he enjoyed it so much then we were all at Uncle Williams to spend the evening—we were so tired.

---

25. Sarah Ellen Hunt was the daughter of Amos Hunt and Hannah Moon. She married James Hadley. She was a second cousin to Paulena.

26. "[S]ome were well aware of May Day and its allure. Many took strolls through the fields in early May to enjoy wild flowers and the splendor of nature's rebirth. Some even read about how their stern Puritan fathers reacted in 1637 to the May Day revels of Thomas Morton and his followers in 'The Maypole of Merry Mount,' penned by a young Massachusetts author named Nathaniel Hawthorne. [Nathaniel Hawthorne was a distant cousin to Paulena Stevens Janney.] And there was an emerging practice of observation by the young Aaron Greenwood of Gardner, Massachusetts, noted on May 1, 1860, that, 'A party of young folks occupied the Town Hall this forenoon in having a

Thirdday, May 3rd, 1859
Jo began her school today. I wonder how she will do. It is such a pretty day—but I think it has been a very long one for Will stayed unusually late for something.

Fourthday, May 4th, 1859
I came over with Jo this morning—I think she will have a hard time to get them started. It shows very plain that they have never had a good teacher for they don't know anything about reading. They are all little barefooted things. I would hate to raise children this way. There is no ambition or life about them—some intelligent faces yet not scholarly ones. It looked so beautiful out in the green woods. I don't see why there is not more poetry about the children but they are all "plain matter of fact ones."

Fifthday, May 5th, 1859
Went to the "Lodge."[27] I am so tired, but I know Will is tired too every night.

Sixthday, May 6th, 1859
Had such a nice time this evening. Beck Erwin and after Jo came home, we went to gather flowers. We gave each other a tiny bouquet for remembrance. I thought to myself that perhaps in future years when parted the sight of those might recall olden feelings, but before enjoying myself so well, I was destined to pass through some of the preliminaries of cooking. I made a cake and thought all would be so nice. But behold! when putting it in to bake I found I had left the most important ingredient out—sugar. I quickly stirred in some and was just putting in the pan again when I heard a knock . . .

---

good time, it being May Day. They occupied some of the time in marching and dancing to the music of a fiddle and bass viola.'" Source: *A-Maying We Will Go*, Thomas Kelleher, Old Sturbridge Village, 2003.

Others described May Day celebrations as follows: "At daybreak on the first day of the fifth month we youngsters went 'a-maying.' We brought back freshly picked wild flowers and put them in little baskets which we hung on the front door knobs of our favorite people. If you were secretly sweet on some winsome lass she got a special basket, maybe with a bow of ribbons on the handle." Source: *Nature Bulletin* 715, April 27, 1963, http://www.newton.dep.anl.gov/natbltn/700 799/nb715.htm.

27. The Lodge is thought to be the Rebekah Lodge of the Independent Order of Odd Fellows. Odd Fellows added the degree of Rebekah in 1851. It was founded upon the principles of faithfulness, hospitality, purity, and dedication to the principles of the order as portrayed by women characters of the Bible. Emblems were used to teach lessons to a prospective Rebekah. The beehive represented associated industry and the result of united effort. The moon and seven stars taught the value of regularity in all work. The dove was the emblem of peace. The white lily was a symbol of purity. Source: *The Sovereign Grand Lodge, Independent Order of Odd Fellows,* http://www.ioof.org/rebekahs.htm.

Seventhday, May 7th, 1859
This evening, I went to grandfather's and went to gather flowers down by the creek. I took my Bible along to read my Sabbath lesson over in the grove. Oh! It is such a beautiful place there. The grass is as green and it is so cool and shady. I gathered a bouquet and when I went up they had tea waiting. Had sweet potatoes and I like them so well.

A Long Time Ago
[By Paulena Stevens Janney][28]

I remember a long time ago when I took my little dinner basket and trundled off to school[29] in the hot summer days. My ideas were not so exalted then for my ambition was not much higher than to read in the first-reader and have a ramble in the green woods—or a playhouse up under the old oak tree where the roots came out making beautiful recesses which we appropriated as our rooms. Then we gathered flowers to deck our parlors and acorn shells our teacups. Here we spent many hours of the every days blessed noon—till the school bell called us away to spend a few more hours in the hot school room. Oh! how inviting the cool shade looked—far more desirable than to pour over the spelling book.

After a while as I grew older, new impulses and wishes twined their selves around my heart and made things wear a new appearance. I formed associations that will never be forgotten though many of them who shared my best feelings passed away softly as evenings last light. I used to almost dread to see night come for we had so much fun. Perhaps that was an absorbing item that caused the sorrow for night fall. But, Oh, can anyone who went thru them forget the joyous hours spent around the old school room at those gleeful play times. Teacher was exchanged for teacher—yet we scholars kept journeying along in the same old paths that first received our childish footsteps. Ever joyous, ever gay, past the summer came on winter with her punching cold, who made us draw close around the stove and we had to play all the more at recess to keep ourselves warm.

---

28. Paulena began school in about 1846.

29. *Review of Education in the Martinsville Community* by Clara E. Smith, former principal and superintendent, at the sesquicentennial program, Monday night, September 14, 1953. This material was received at the Alumni Banquet, Martinsville, 1994, by Francis R. Brown from Harry C. Ertel [Martinsville High School class of 1935] who was associate professor emeritus at Wright State University. Francis Brown sent the material to Christie Russell in 1997 shortly before his death. Francis Brown was a descendant of Aaron Betts through his son, Christopher Betts.

"The first school in the community was a subscription school taught by Jonah Wright in about 1812. The school was under the control of the Society of Friends (Quakers) and classes were held in their meeting house. Pupils came from four or five districts surrounding Martinsville as well as from distant areas. The school was overseen by Daniel Moon, John Beales, and Christopher Hiatt. Mr. John Rowe was listed as a

It was then, Jo[30] first came among us. We were attracted by her dark eyes and then at last I ventured so far as to ask her what her name was. Thus things past long till we found ourselves in the fifth reader and spelling in the dictionary—wonder how we ever had achieved so much was a mystery to me—but for all we never deserted our playhouses and they accordingly began to expand—as the owners wanted things to correspond. So we gathered moss for our carpets enlarged our rooms by placing rails which were mysteriously constructed from high fences—to separate our kitchens from our parlors. I am sorry I can't say everything past along in harmony but now and then some moments of disagreement would jar our pleasure produced by feelings of envy because one playhouse excelled another.

---

teacher and taught night classes which were free to adults. In the early years no women teachers were found in the classrooms. The salary allowed the teacher was $1.50 to $2.00 per scholar for a class of 25 for a term of 13 weeks, consisting of 65 working days. Teachers often took produce for their salaries. Reading, writing, arithmetic and spelling were the subjects taught in the early schools. . . . In Albert J. Brown's Book, *History of Clinton County, Ohio*, we learn that 'until 1852 only reading, writing, arithmetic, and spelling were required to be taught in Ohio Schools. Male Teachers were required to be examined in each of these subjects except spelling and female teachers were allowed to substitute spelling for arithmetic.

"After the adoption of the Constitution in 1852, grammar and geography were added to the curriculum. . . . There is no complete list of teachers, however, records indicate that James Hadley, Elizabeth Wasson, Milton Hollingsworth, Sarah Gibson, William Houghton, and Hiram Moore made up a partial list. Milton Hollingsworth, was a very popular and effective teacher. He was educated at Earlham College, Richmond, Indiana. Elementary subjects listed were reading, geography, English grammar. Advanced studies included composition, natural philosophy, chemistry, physiology, algebra, geometry, and astronomy. The School had daily Bible readings and Scriptures were used as a class book. The subscription school was discontinued about 1855 as the public schools were being developed. The Aaron Betts home was one of the homes open to student boarders. A large library was established in honor of Milton Hollingsworth. When Madison Betts took over the Betts home, these books were distributed among the library members and as late as 1953 many of these books could be found. About 1858 the Martinsville Special School District was formed with Robert Fulton, Christopher Betts, and Reuben Hunt as members of the Board of Education and leaders of this new movement. The bond issue of $2500 or $3000 was submitted to the voters to build a substantial four room building. During the next few years numerous excellent 'administrators' and teachers helped to build a strong curriculum. Among those named were: Amos Hockett, Mr. and Mrs. Adams, Charles and Sattie Oren. The Orens studied under Horace Mann at Antioch College. Others named were Milton L. Hunt, Mary Hunt, Armanice Hixon, Thomas J. Moore, Edward Ellis, and C.L. Foster."

30. Josephine "Jo" B. White, Paulena Stevens, Will Janney, and Madison Betts all attended Earlham, the twentieth session, 1856–1857. Source: Enrollment Records for *Friends Boarding School Found in the Quaker Collection,* Earlham College Library, by Christie Russell in 1999.

Sabbath, May 8th, 1859
Went to Sabbath school this morning—did not go to meeting—stopped at Lizzies a while. John is no better. I am so sorry for Lizzie. Will and I took such a pleasant walk this evening in the grove. Call and Cj came down a while and this evening I put on my bridal dress and we went to Uncle Williams—the girls all went out walking, but I did not feel like going up there for it is so much nicer down here. Everything looks so beautiful and there is such nice dark shade in the woods.

Night—have just returned from church—have seen much of the manifestations or pretensions of religions. Matt did not get to go to church—so I did not laugh, when Anna James was lying to comfort mourners. [Anna James was Paulena's cousin and the younger sister of Lindley James, whose death was reported on April 17th.]

Secondday, May 9th, 1859
Raining—I wonder how Jo and them will get home and Will. I believe I will go after them.

Thirdday, May 10th, 1859
Jo and I went up town [Martinsville was literally up the road from the Evan Steven's house where Paulena was living at that time] this evening. Did not stay long. Got some ribbon for our regalia [costume]. Beck and all the girls came down and stayed a while. Matt came to talk. Jo and I felt sorry for her but I think it is all the better. Call stayed the night.

Fourthday, May 11th, 1859
I finished our regalia. All but binding. Jo has gone home tonight. We received a letter from Elma this evening. I must answer it soon. Mary and Hannah Jane just pained me so much—she said in a year from today I would be packing a little baby round, she said I would have to wash him. Will is so tired tonight. I wish he didn't have to work so hard.

Fifthday, May 12th, 1859
Went to the Lodge. Got there late—felt a little excited going in [with] my regalia on. Will did not feel like going but wanted me to. Lin and Jimmy came home with us. All the band boys are going in next night.

Sixthday, May 13th, 1859
Read some in Mrs. Stowe's new story—*The Minister's Wooing*. I think it is good and such fine language. I like her sentiments in regard to romance. She says all but this dead grind and doldrums that come through the mill is by them thrown into one waste "catch all" and labeled romance. Perhaps there was a time in Mr. Smith's youth he remembers now when he read poetry when his cheek was wet with strange tears when a little song ground out by some organ-grinder in the

street had power to set his heart beating and bring a mist before his eyes[31]—
Ah! in those days . . .

> She was alone in her chamber from below came the sound of music and
> the dance but it brought no light in her eye or blush to her cheek as once
> it did—why was Ada all alone? was there naught in the gay throng to
> make the blood bound through her veins and bring all the girlish glad-
> ness back?

I wrote a letter to Matt Ladd and sent a bouquet to Beck Irwin. She is going
home in the morning. I do like her so well. I took a nice nap this evening.

They Are Not All Here!
[By Paulena Stevens Janney]

I look around the old school room and repeat to myself, they are not all
here. Oh! sad indeed has been the changes within a few short months.
Once we all mingled here as students and as friends but there are some
away, some gone from the class bench, gone from the playground, gone
from all associations which make the school house dear and gone from
the home the childhood's home never never to return. Yes, some are
sleeping today in the quiet graveyard where the long grass is waving,
the trees looking down in gloomy solem dignaty over the white grave-
stones and green mounds. They will come not again to the old schoolroom, be welcomed never more by eager schollars, but winter and summer will roll away bringing new faces and associations and the absent
will be almost forgotten—Not forgotten either for if early associations
are formed through and cherished properly they will not so soon pass
away—yet time wafts along with her changing periods and the dead
the absent to many become merely as the things that were.

Seventhday, May 14th, 1859
Jo came down this evening and I went up town—then Will came back with me
and we went fishing. I caught six and a crawfish and Will caught 4 and Call not
any. I don't know how many Jo and Miss Porter caught. Will did not like the
idea of being beaten in such a business and by a woman.

Sabbath, May 15th, 1859
Will and I went out to Moons. Henry looked so bad and Aunt Sarah (Mills)[32]

---

31. Harriett Beecher Stowe's *The Minister's Wooing* (1859) is a historical novel
and a domestic comedy. Set in eighteenth-century Newport, Rhode Island, it was considered a powerful examination of slavery, Protestant theology, and gender differences
in early America.

32. Sarah Mills was an older cousin to Paulena. She married Henry Moon.

too. Call is going down to the city with us this week. I went to Sabbath school this morning after we came back and then went to Uncle Christophers and took dinner. We had such a pleasant time—took a nice walk in the grove and this evening Call, Jo, Elwood and Elma were there and they came for us to go again. I am very happy Will is so good to me and I know he always will be—sometimes I think that if I was to die, he would never love anyone else as well as me. I know he would never forget me.

Secondday, May 16th, 1859
Just have been at home all day. I wonder if Matt has got my letter yet. I want to see her so bad. I have been so sick today.

Thirdday, May 17th, 1859
Oh May, sweet May, will soon be gone. I prize May highly for remembrance of long ago but other Mays will come and times roll along unmindful of our little sorrows, caring not for farewells bespoken again for tears shed in hallowed spots. Out we are born along on the tossing ocean of life just as the winds of fate see fit to lift our floating barge through quiet, dreary moments when the treasured gems of the past come back to us—thus ours—even though storms be around us we can still think calmly of the past.

Fourthday, May 18th, 1859
Been at home—I expect Will will be back at home pretty soon; I will be glad.

Fifthday, May 19th, 1859
At the Lodge—wore my pink dress. Got there late but soon had a very nice time. The band was in town; it played so nice. It almost charmed some 23 invitations to come away before it was over.

Sixthday, May 20th, 1859 [Cincinnati]
Went to the city—got there in time to go out shopping. I purchased Alma a bonnet and myself a headdress—did not go out much only we went to the theater. Next day I felt so bad, so tired.

Seventhday, May 21st, 1859 [Returned from Cincinnati]
Came home this evening stopped at Lizzies a while—John is worse. Will got strawberries at the city and we had them for supper.

Sabbath, May 22nd, 1859
Again—balmy Sabbath has come. I feel too lazy to go to church or Sabbath school, so I'll stay home but I think I will do better in the future. We went to

---

"Aunt" may have been a term of endearment used by all who knew her in deference to her age.

Rizers this evening. Lizzie and I took a walk to the graveyard. I expect little Eva will die for she was so bad this morning and this rain and thunder—it always reminds of some person dead—it sounds so lonesome. I think she is so sweet but she will be better off.

Secondday, May 23rd, 1859
How swiftly time passes. It seems but a few days ago that we were talking about going to Cincinnati and now it is all over before it is fully realized.

Thirdday, May 24th, 1859
I received a letter from Matt this evening. It breathed of sadness and loneliness. I know she must be very lonely. I am going there this week. Oh, I do hate to leave Will so bad—Dear Will—I am afraid I cannot do right by him for he is so good to me. I wonder why they were all so opposed to Will marrying me. They know they have talked about me and I know it just as much as I know there is a heaven. I feel myself above stooping to such a thing as telling things to injure others as I know they have done, and I would not have the nerve of fussing anymore for Will loved me anyhow and I don't care for the rest. Oh! I do hate to leave Will's bed. He will be so lonesome.

Fourthday, May 25th, 1859
Supper late—all alone—Will sweetly sleeping. I have got the last button sewed on his shirt and the buttons on his vest. I am going to Ladds tomorrow—am going to stop at Vienna in the morning. I know Will will be lonesome. I did not go to the lecture—Jo did—Heard the bands. I am glad I don't have to walk home now though.

Fifthday, May 26th, 1859 [New Vienna on to Leesburg, Highland County, Ohio]
Went as far as Vienna—Stopped at Franks a while then went to Husseys. Matt and I went to school in the evening. Went to Ladds this evening

Sixthday, May 27th, 1859 [Leesburg, Ohio]
I wanted to see Will so bad this evening. Wondered if he was lonesome. Matt and I went to the bridge where cars [railroad] came along and it swayed like it used to. We were at Johns house too and I built a playhouse. Quite exalted business for a "married lady," good as any I think. Matt was sick when we got back. I do wish she was well—Just thinking—tomorrow night Will will be here.

Seventhday, May 28th, 1859 [Leesburg, Ohio]
Went to the cliffs, it seemed so sad and beautiful reminding me of lonely things and bringing lonely thoughts. I sat down upon a shaded rock near the water and while the water was gliding along thinking of bright days even when I was not alone, thinking of a dear one who when with me dearly loved to ramble there

but whose brow could feel not now the cool breeze that was wafted through the dark trees which stood looking down on us on those days gone by. Thinking if I would go far, far away and return to be alone again. Thinking how sad I would feel if Matt was gone forever. It would indeed be lonely there. I would sit in the same old spot perhaps thinking calmly and sadly of the absent whose ears the murmur of the water was sweetly born. Will came I was so glad to see him.

Sabbath, May 29th, 1859 [Leesburg, Ohio]
Will and I went to the cliffs—gathered so many shells. Will wove a basket for them. Matt gave me a pet too. I am going to keep it, we can carry it home in our basket of shells. There were several boys here this morning—some came a horse back and I took a ride. I got a hat and climbed up one side with a rose—Matt and I. Louisa[33] came home this evening. I never did see as curious [a] thing. I don't believe she enjoyed herself any place for she is so backward and she would hardly speak to me. I don't see any use of her being this way. I do wish Matt would get well and come down. I just love her so well.

Secondday, May 30th, 1859 [Martinsville, Ohio]
Arrived home safe—brought our shells and bird. Sarah Porter came down this morning. Lid Fulton and Emma Hunt were down this evening Will will be so tired tonight for they are going to plaster our house this week.

Thirdday, May 31st, 1859
Raining this morning—company came—got dinner. Call and baby came down—gathered strawberries for tea got only a few to eat—for little sweet Willie kept begging for a "little" of them after supper so I had to give him some. I wonder when Willie is grown if he will be good and smart and I wonder if he will like me as well as I like him. I know if he lives, I will do every thing for him if he has no one else to. Just be as good to him and I hope he will be a noble man—not just merely a bubble—to float-along doing no good to others or himself—not merely a "poke easy" man or so called man.[34] Will is weary.

June 1859

Fourthday, June 1st, 1859
Joyous first of June, I welcome here again. Perhaps we think—how we sat in the old schoolroom and watched the blue clouds float along and listened to the birds melody longing all the while to be free from the old grammar lessons.

---

33. Louisa Lazenby, a cousin, the daughter of John C. Lazenby and Mary Hiatt, lived near Paulena's grandparents, the Bettses, near Martinsville. She married Jonathan Ladd, the brother of Matt.

34. Willie was not to grow to manhood. In 1872, he died at the age of sixteen of a gunshot wound in a hunting accident in Jasper County, Missouri.

Fifthday, June 2nd, 1859
Liz Porter and Lizzie came down this morning.

Sixthday, June 3rd, 1859
Bright and pleasant—dawned this morning. I was up to our house this morning. I think it will look nice and I know I will feel odd when we first move. It seems now like it would be a pleasure first to arrange things to my own way. I recon some people wonder what I got married for when I don't know how to do anything.

Seventhday, June 4th, 1859
I was down at grandfathers this evening and grandmother washed some potatoes for me.

Sabbath, June 5th, 1859
Went to church this morning—came home read a while—took a nap then went to grandfathers this evening. George, Jane and Beck were there.

Secondday, June 6th, 1859
Call came down—went up town saw Dave. I just know he will take Jo to the picnic—well I don't care if he does. I hope they will marry indeed I do. I just imagine her living across from me and Lizzie. Trimmed my shaker [article of clothing] today.

Thirdday, June 7th, 1859 [Wilmington, Clinton County, Ohio]
Went to Wilmington and stayed at Wests all night. I and Emma Shoody took a pony ride. Em Hughs,[35] the girl I knew I would like, I saw her too she said she was glad she got acquainted. I am too. I like her real well. I felt sorry for Will I just won't leave him any more—but indeed I did have to stay all night for he will be so lonely.

Fourthday, June 8th, 1859
Came home this morning. I did some shopping—got Alma a new dress. I was so glad to see Will. It seemed almost a week since I left him. Our blinds came today. I think they look real nice.

Fifthday, June 9th, 1859
Went to the Lodge—had a nice time.

Sixthday, June 10th, 1859
Rained today. I thought some of going to the "Picnic" but I don't care about

---

35. In 1860, Emma Hughs married Elias M. Wright. Source: Clinton County, Ohio, marriage records.

going myself. Will could go but I am such a baby that I have to cry a little. Call and Alma I expect will go. I wish they would.

Seventhday, June 11th, 1859
This evening I had a nice nap and when the band came in I listened to the delicious music without one pang of regret for not getting to go and Will brought down some nice books—*Charlotte Bronte*,[36] [and] *The Hidden Path*.[37] Jimmys horse ran away this evening—caused by the band—no serious injuries done. Alma and Call went or started but I guess they went the wrong way.

Sabbath, June 12th, 1859
Bright beautiful Sabbath has come again. I did not go to church today—Wills eye is sore and he did not feel like it. Will is quite the same to me all the time—so good.

Thirdday, June 14th, 1859
Matilda washed today and is coming tomorrow to clean up everything.

Fourthday, June 15th, 1859
Matilda came and scoured everything and things look as clean, can't bear dirty things. I don't see how some people live who pay no regard for cleanliness.

Fifthday, June 16th, 1859
Went to Lodge. Jo stayed home to come down then in the morning. Dave went home. I wish they would get married it would be so funny to have Jo for a neighbor. We would have such good times. I was up at Lizzies this evening.

Sixthday, June 17th, 1859
Been home today making Will some clothes. Hannah Jane was here this evening and Grandmother brought up some peas. I do like them so well. I wish I could put up some. Milton Hunt was here this evening. Guilelma [Hunt] sent for us to go out there but Will does not feel like going. I have not seen her for so long.

Seventhday, June 18th, 1859
[Went to] Uncle Williams this evening. Call and I called at Cys—they are fixed

---

36. *The Life of Charlotte Brontë,* by Elizabeth Gaskell, was published in 1857.

37. *The Hidden Path* by Mary Virginia Hawes Terhune [1830–1922], published by Derby, 1855. "Mary Virginia Terhune was a celebrated writer on domestic economy. Her pen name Marian Harland was a household word during her lifetime. She was known for her charming combination of home making with literary work. She possessed a masterful way of making duties fit each other without fuss." Source: Passaic County Historical Society, Passaic, New Jersey.

very nice. I wish we were moved too. Call and I went to our house. It is all cleaned out nice except washing. Jim and Will took a buggy ride.

Sabbath, June 19th, 1859
Raining—how glad I am it is raining now. I can get to read all day without being molested. Will opened "Lots Books"[38] this morning oh I wish I had as many.

Secondday, June 20th, 1859
Aaron Betts came down this morning. We went to grandfathers and stayed a long time had such a good dinner—peas and potatoes. It rained very hard this evening. I received a letter from Jennie Henley it was so good—perhaps she will come this fall. Will brought a note for Jo from Dave.

Thirdday, June 21st, 1859
Call and Jane were here. I have been to a concert tonight. The "Glee Club" sang so sweet and also nice music by the band.

Fourthday, June 22nd, 1859
Company today. I will be so glad when we get moved. Lydia came, Rebecca, George, Aaron Hunt, Jimmy were here for tea.

Fifthday, June 23rd, 1859
Did not go to the Lodge tonight. Jo and I went to grandfathers this evening. We had such a good supper—Lizzie and Miss Porter are here this evening. Will is tired. I will be so glad when we get independent enough so Will can rest whenever he chooses.

Sixthday, June 24th, 1859
Guttery is dead. Mrs. Guttery almost grieves herself to death. I was in fanning her this evening. She said if she could only die she did not want to stay any longer in this wide wicked world. Mary Ellen cries so much I don't see how they can bear it but we all have to bear things which before we think impossible.

Seventhday, June 25th, 1859
Such a sad day has this been. Guttery was buried this afternoon—a little before 3 o'clock. So many there—the "Odd Fellows" marched. Fulton preached the funeral in the grove at the meeting house.

Sabbath, June 26th, 1859
Another funeral this evening—Henry Moon [married to Sarah Mills] was buried.

---

38. Lot Janney, older brother of Will, was a portrait photographer living in Portsmouth, Ohio. He often sent books for Will and Paulena to read.

There was a great many out—we stopped at Amos Hocketts. Call came home with us. I have to write for the paper and don't know what to write.

Fifthday, June 30th, 1859
The wedding [marriage of Madison Betts to Caroline Janney] is over. Had quite a nice time. Charley Lewis was there. I think he is interesting to be with. We all went to the grove.

July 1859

Seventhday, July 1st, 1859
Went to school this morning. Will came at noon with my dinner and the examination was mostly in the morning. Charley and Aaron took tea with us. This evening we went to school and got home just before the rains. Call had on her wreath.[39] [I am] 19 years old today—in three years where be I?

Sabbath, July 2nd, 1859 [Date confusion; Paulena might have thought there were thirty-one days in June]

Firstday, July 3rd, 1859
Will and I went to church this morning. Matt Chaffin [Chalfant?] and Lib Pope were here this evening—we had such a good time. Ed was here too. Will has been reading all day long and now has gone to sleep.

4th of July 1859
Went to the celebration—had quite a nice time—a very eloquent speaker—saw so many familiar faces but had forgotten their names—saw Ann Nut—Em Templin—Julia Steward—and so many others. Had lemonade and sodas. Went to the depot. Will had toothache and headache so came home. Jo and I marched a little piece.

Thirdday, July 5th, 1859
Jo came down today—went to school but no scholars came so she stayed with me—after a nap we went up town saw Miss Porter. Lizzie and [illegible] was at our house too. I wonder how I will feel when we get moved—it will be so funny—so strange.

Fourthday, July 6th, 1859
Jo came down stayed all day we had a fine sleep in our accustomed places.

---

39. Call Janney Betts apparently wore a bridal wreath for her wedding on June 30. The wreath was a circular garland of flowers and greens worn on the head of the bride. It is still used today for brides as well as for bridesmaids to wear or carry.

Fifthday, July 7th, 1859
Will has to be so busy now. I will be glad when they get Carmens house raised.

Sixthday, July 8th 1859
They are going to raise Carmens house tomorrow. [The raising of a house was a construction process, similar to a barn raising, in which a crew of men assembled the frame of a house and raised each side into position.] I will be so glad when it is over for Will can have a little more rest then and work at our house too. I will be so glad when we are moved. It will be so funny to just do everything myself.

Seventhday, July 9th, 1859
Carmens house is raised. Jim Hunt[40] got hurt a little. I will be so glad when we get moved for Will will not have so far to walk then.

Sabbath, July 10th, 1859
Will and I and Willie went over in the grove this morning it is so pretty there. Will and I were at John Bisers [Bisher's] a while. John is not better. Emma Hunt and Call and Jimmy were there.

Secondday, July 11th, 1859
Went up with Will this morning and I think we will get moved anyhow. Lid Weeks came home at noon. Jane was here—she combed my hair as usual. Mother and Father are away this evening and A [Alma] and I are at home. I have taken my seat under my favorite place—it is so sweet here.

Thirdday, July 12th, 1859
I am reading "Bay of Burgundy."

Fourthday, July 13th, 1859
Went up with Will this morning. He will get only half done this week. I think it looks nice. I will be glad when it is all done. Lizzie came in while I was there. It just seemed like we lived there.

Fifthday, July 14th, 1859
Just as warm as ever. I do wish it would rain. Mother has gone this afternoon. Susan Turner sent for us.

Sixthday, July 15th, 1859
At Uncle Williams today—came home with a toothache—had company.

---

40. The Carmen house was two stories high. Jim Hunt was James E. Hunt, son of Jonathan and Margaret Hadley Hunt. He was a second cousin to Paulena.

Seventhday, July 16th, 1859
Clara Chaffin came down this evening but did not stop.

Sabbath, July 17th, 1859
Sabbath again—with the warm sunshine beating down almost destroys the grass and flowers with its heat. I can not walk to meeting this morning so Will went and I stayed at home. Lot and Steve came down. I was very glad they came. Steve and I had quite a chat under the trees in the grove. Will and I went up town in the evening met with Doctor Wilson at Whites introduced me to him—thought very well of him.

Secondday, July 18th, 1859
Mother went to meeting today left Willie and us at home as a matter of course. Clara and Sophena [Chaffin] called a while. Will and I were at an Ice Cream Supper tonight—I just almost know Jo and Dave will get married—I would be so glad for them—Lizzie and us would be neighbors and it would just seem like we were—pretending we were married just like we used to a long time ago and go to see each other.

Thirdday, July 19th, 1859
Jo and I went to see Call this evening. Will came over at tea—Will and I, Matt and Call took a walk to the graveyard—it seemed so lonesome there at night—the stones resting in the moonlight—the frogs keeping up their music—as it is every night—it makes me feel so sad to go there where so many I loved have been laid—yet even a strangers grave brings the tears to my eyes.

Fourthday, July 20th, 1859
Grandfathers—Willie and I went up to see "Will's house"—Willie said he liked it very well.

Fifthday, July 21st, 1859
Mother, Willie and I went to Reuben Hunts this evening. Elma looks so bad. I can't bear to think of her dying. We had such nice times together a long time ago and yet but then we were children—once little happy girls playing in playhouses up under the oak trees—but it is all over now we will never go to sleep again on the cushions in the meeting house—nor never study our lessons under the trees in the graveyard.

[Paulena's Childhood Memory]

How time whirls us along as it moves—every day opening some new phase in our lives—either something to make us happy or unhappy—it seems almost dream like to glide away so swiftly—it seems but a little while ago—and yet a long time as I take some views of the past since I took my little basket and trundled off to school in the bright—summer mornings—my ambition took not a very lofty flight—for I imagine I would know something when I was advanced to the second class in spelling—and that I would know almost anything when in the syllables—and I felt very proud indeed as I dreamed of a future period when I would get a new first-reader with a green back my favorite color—and stand up by my teacher to read I thought I would know almost everything then—But I had a great love for playhouses, and am inclined to believe I would know more if I had possessed less talent—for ornamenting little tiny rooms and working in little gardens—and I remember I always thought it looked so nice to see a stove pipe extending out— some place about the premises—so I always left a place for one which frequently happened to lie [illegible] handle of some old dilapidated board—but anything would answer just so the smoke came out—but that was when I had more exhalted ideas about house keeping.

Sixthday, July 22nd, 1859
No letter from Matt—today past in the usual way. I have the toothache—been reading *David Copperfield*[41] —it is so interesting. Matt Hussey is not expected to live. I am so sorry. I wish I could go to see her—perhaps Will will take me up. I always hate to ask to go any place now—for I know Will is so busy and he would want me to go if I know he was not willing for me to go places, why I would be sorry to go or leave or have a cry—anyway I want change in the air. I think it would be much benefit to me. I want to see Matt Ladd too. I wonder if she ever thinks of me now?

Seventhday, July 23rd, 1859
Just as usual nothing new only got some paper and envelopes. I am in hopes of something will happen to make me glad. I want some change so much for I am so tired of everyday life. I want something to stir up new thoughts.

Sabbath, July 24th, 1859
Dreary morning—Will wished it would rain all day—but it didn't. We took a ride this evening after we came back we went to grandfathers—George and Rebecca were there.

Secondday, July 25th, 1859
Matilda washing—I wish I could get something—a letter perhaps.

---

41. *David Copperfield*, by Charles Dickens, was first published in 1850 in London. In 1842, Dickens took a tour of Canada and the United States, visiting Boston, New York, Baltimore, Philadelphia, Pittsburgh, Cincinnati, and St. Louis, among other places. He is reported to have stopped in Leesburg, Highland County, Ohio, to exchange horses. His tour is recorded in his *American Notes* (1842).

Thirdday, July 26th, 1859
I have been wishing we would get moved so soon now and had things arranged in my mind when this morning Will received a letter from the painters stating they could not come this week. I almost cried but I know it wasn't Will's fault so I will have to wait for a good time to come. We have had company this evening—Elizabeth Alexander and Mary Hiatt—no letter yet.

Fourthday, July 27th, 1859
Out under the pine tree where everything seems so still and quiet except an occasional stirring of the boughs above my head as the wind sweeps through them—which seems first like music as I close my eyes and hear the leaves rustling in the grove—Oh! everything seem so still—too still—for I want some excitement. I began some shell work today. I do not think it will be very nice though.

Fifthday, July 28th, 1859
Went to meeting today—saw Gulielma (Hunt). I went to Mary's this morning to get Jane to begin my quilt for me. I don't see how I will ever get it done—they had such good fried chicken and biscuits for tea. Willie and Elva were there. Will came for me and we were at the creek getting shells—I have finished my frame—all but putting a picture in it—at the lodge tonight.

Sixthday, July 29th, 1859
Nothing new just the same every day affair. I went up stairs had a long chat with Lizzie—she says John is going South this winter. I will be so sorry for Lizzie to go away.

Seventhday, July 30th, 1859
 Have had the toothache—been in bed. Mother made a poultice[42] for my jaw and some tea for me to drink—got better—took a nap—read some in *Irving's Sketch Book*[43] —knit some on my [illegible]. Will never home till dark—was wearied and had got the house done. I don't think I will ever say anything about us moving for I think Will gets tired of it.

---

42. A poultice is made by mixing ground herbs with hot water, putting the mixture in a muslin bag, and applying it to the affected area. Source: www.uky.edu/~lhjeng00/herbweb/00000092.

43. *Irving's Sketch Book,* by Washington Irving, was first published in 1819. "Most of the pieces in it were descriptions of England, where Irving had been living. But in two of the stories, he rewrote German folk tales and transplanted them to American

Sabbath, 31st July, 1859

Did not go to church for fear of my tooth getting bad again. The painters are coming tomorrow—but I do not intend to ask how they get along nor anything about them at all—nor about us moving either for Will I *know* is tired of me asking so I won't bother him any more. He used to say anything I done was no bother—I wonder if he thinks so now?

Washington Irving
From a portrait by James Jarvis

Irvings Sketch Book, Paulena's granddaughter, Georgia Janney, used *Irving's Sketch Book* in an English class ca. 1920

soil. The first of these was 'Rip Van Winkle,' about a man who falls asleep during the British rule of the American Colonies, only to wake up years later to find that he lives in the independent United States. The other American story in his *Sketch Book* was the most famous story Irving would ever write. It was set in an area of the Hudson River Valley which he described as 'one of the quietest places in the whole world . . . [where] a drowsy, dreamy influence seems to hang over the land, and to pervade the very atmosphere . . . this sequestered glen . . . known by the name of Sleepy Hollow.'

"In 'The Legend of Sleepy Hollow,' Irving invented one of the first memorable characters of American literature, the visiting schoolteacher, Ichabod Crane, whom Irving described as 'tall, but exceedingly lank, with narrow shoulders, long arms and legs, hands that dangled a mile out of his sleeves, feet that might have served for shovels, and his whole frame most loosely hung together. . . . 'Rip Van Winkle' and 'The Legend of Sleepy Hollow' were revolutionary American short stories because they suggested that the fledgling nation actually had a history. At the time 'Sleepy Hollow' was published, there were no internationally known American fiction writers, leading one English wag to write in 1818, 'The Americans have no national literature and no learned men.' Another said, 'In the four quarters of the globe, who reads an American book?' *Irving's Sketch Book* was the first international bestseller by an American author, and it was greatly admired by British writers, including Sir Walter Scott and Charles Dickens." Source: "It Happened in History," Washington Irving, http://amsaw.org/amsaw ithappenedinhistory 040304 irving.html. Sixty years later, in about 1920, Paulena's granddaughter, Georgia Janney, studied Washington Irving's *Sketch Book* in school.

August 1859

Secondday, August 1st, 1859
Great Cellebration, I wonder if the darkies will have a glorious time today?[44]
Two years ago Matt and I were at Chilicothe. I wonder where Matt is today or if
she thinks of our old times?

Thirdday, August 2nd, 1859
Will says Nan Taylor is in town—she sent for me to come up—I will be so glad
to see her.

Fourthday, August 3rd, 1859
I was at Mary Rogers [David Rogers married Mary Jennings in 1832] this eve-
ning for tea. Mrs. Harris and Miss Johnson were there. I was so glad to see
Nan—she looks just like she used to. We were at Whites a while. Lib [Lin?] and
Jimmy called there—it rained and Will came home and got the carriage for me.

Sixthday, August 5th, 1859
Cloudy this morning—my heart cloudy yet—I wonder what does it mean? for
I feel so lonely. Will comes home so late every night too but then I must not
murmur for I expect Will thinks I am too particular anyhow about things but I
cannot help it—for its my nature to be proud and I can't be any other way—and
I am so impulsive too for I am always too high or to low—in the "valley" or on
the "mountain." I went down in the grove this evening for when I feel sad, I
love to go away off in some lonely spot.

Seventhday, August 6th, 1859
Nan and Jo came down this evening and took tea with me. We walked down
in the grove and had a nice seat to sit on. Nan was telling her experiences. I
think there is some romance connected within her history. Tonight they all came
down—we played Sociability and had a real good time.

August 7th, 1859
Will did not work at Carmens today his hand was too sore. I was up at Lizzies
this evening. Miss Porter is there.

---

44. This may refer to an inflammatory speech delivered by Frederick Douglass
in the Chambersburg Public Hall the previous Saturday, reported by *The Franklin Repository,* August 24, 1859. "John M. Cooper, sat in the front row — evidently as the 'right
supporter' of the sable speaker." This compels *The Franklin Repository* editor to ask,
"What expedients will not that party resort to in order to rescue their sinking political
ship? . . . Are they now about to don the garb of abolitionism?" Source: www.iath.vir-
ginia.edu / vshadow2 / Browser1 / frbrowser / fr.topic.african.

Sabbath, August 8th, 1859
Went to church saw Jane and Call—we had company—Craft [Milton Craft, carpenter—age twenty-nine in the 1860 census] came down and drew our house this evening.

Secondday, August 9th, 1859
Just like it always is on second day—Matilda washing—I have been up stairs this evening fixing away some of my things which "by the way" are very miss-nervious—for I find a ribbon—a piece of lace, or fringe one place, and a letter or book or pattern another—and so I just gather them up and stow them away in some of my numberless boxes. I wonder how I ever will get things all put away nice! This morning Jo sent down to get a piece to put in her paper and I had to sit down and write as quick as I could and I did not feel at all poetical so I just wrote a few common extracts from "Aunt Mary's Diary"—or someone else. Will and I took a walk in the grove it seemed just like old times. Just think this time next week and some of our things will be gone from our good old room and good old home. I wonder if it wont seem odd! I want to get moved and just see how everything will look and how I will feel keeping house all to myself and can arrange things just as I please but still I will feel bad to leave home—yet it will not be like going away off—among strangers.

Thirdday, August 10th, 1859
I ironed today and Matilda is here working—I am free for a while now so I have come up stairs. I wonder if I will get a letter or something this week? I wish some person would send me a book beautifully bound with gold clasps—and I would not know who sent it—or I wish I would get a letter from Jennie that she was coming soon. I feel so sorry for Will I know his face hurts so bad. I want to go to the concert—I wonder if I can go?

Fourthday, August 11th, 1859
Matilda has cleaned up things real clean and I washed all the dishes in the cupboard I was up at Whites this evening and Lizzies. Lizzie had received a letter from Beck—she had been crying—I do wish I could see her before she marrys—it seems so strange just last spring we were gathering violets in the woods talking merrily of the future. I am so sorry Johns are going away. I am afraid they will never come back again

Fifthday, August 12th, 1859
Hannah Jane came over today to help me. It seems so strange to talk of moving—I wonder if it is a tour to Europe—or only to some bright cottage home embowered among trees and flowers where the balmy air of home makes everything cheerful? I wonder if I will ever see the bright skies and fair gardens of Italy—or feel the balmy breeze of the mountains of Switzerland fan my brow? But I must keep down my dreaming for I am poetical.

Sixthday, August 13, 1859
This time two weeks we will be moved. I want "Matt Ladd" to come—remembering when [we were] so light and free we rambled over the hills—the wild pleasure of climbing hills and gathering flowers.

Seventhday, August 14th, 1859
Alma and I had a nice ride this evening—we went down the State Road [State Road 28] a long piece and then turned off in the woods—and it was so nice—so cool and dark. I am glad Will will be home all day tomorrow.

Sabbath, August 15th, 1859
Went to church—Will and I came home went down to grandfathers for dinner they had such good fried chicken—after dinner we went over in the grove. I selected a nice place and Will and Homer and Willie got some good apples. Pretty soon I wanted a drink so they brought a bucket of good cold water—it was such a delightful place. Will, Willie and I took a buggy ride this evening went down to a new place—to Granols [or Crants] we got such good water melons[45] to eat—then we went to Harts—for Willie kept saying "I'd rather go to Tilda's house"—I had to punch him to keep him from it—at last we got there—and Matilda [The 1860 census, Union Township, Clinton County, Ohio, listed Levi Hart, age 50, born in Kentucky; Matilda, age 43, born in Virginia; and presumably their children, John H., Peter M., James, Robley D., Alfred M., and Anna L. This was a free black family among several listed in the census for Clinton County. Matilda is mentioned in Paulena's journals as doing washing and house cleaning for her mother.] gave Willie a duck and us two melons so we came home very much pleased with our visit to the "quarters." [The quarters must have been the neighborhood where black families lived.]

Secondday, August 16th, 1859
Matilda washed up all our clothes so I think we can move next week. I think I will leave them at home next week too for we have no *wash* board—and I know Will would never think of one in the world and I would not go for one—Will is reading *Never Too Late* and I am writing—I recon I won't forget that thought.

Thirdday, August 17th, 1859
Been "fixing up" my books and papers and Wills clothes. I have so many things I hardly know what to do with all of them. Matilda brought me some potatoes this evening—they look so nice I think I will have them for dinner tomorrow.

---

45. "Watermelon, a vine native to Africa, first appears in English in 1605. Cultivated for thousands of years in the Middle East and Russia, the watermelon was brought to America by African slaves." Source: *The Encyclopedia of American Food and Drink,* John F. Mariani, New York, Lebhar-Friedman Books, 1999, p. 344.

Will says when he gets his money he will give me "lots" and I can go where I please. I wonder where I please to go! I wish Will could go where he pleases. Letter from Jennie.

Fourthday, August 18th, 1859
Something so bad happened this evening. Lazenbys house was burned down—they saved most of the furniture—I feel so sorry for them—I wrote a note for them to inform Louisa.[46]

Fifthday, August 19th, 1859
Matilda and Jane went to clean our house today. I have been there all day too. I made a terrible noise—letting fall, stove pipes, kettles etc.

Sixthday, August 20th, 1859
At home—Louisa came down this morning. I felt sorry for her for it looks so lonely there with nothing but the stones and scorched grass where her house was.

Seventhday, August 21st, 1859
We actually moved today partly—"fixed our carpets down" and I am real tired. I wonder if I will get tired of house keeping. I hope not for I would be in a terrible predicament. We had Lot's pictures brought up yesterday. I saw Miss Porter's miniature.[47]

Sabbath, August 22nd, 1859
Will and I stayed at home today and we went away this evening. We went up to see the pictures—they are so nice—We told Miss Porter she was upstairs in our room—she did not know what we meant. Tonight my last night at home—as I have been.

Secondday, August 23rd, 1859 [Moved to lot 55 in Martinsville, Ohio]
Moved today have been so busy putting things up or Will has—for I did not do much this forenoon—my old tooth hurt so bad but this evening with the promise of five dollars, I concluded to have it extracted which almost distracted me,

---

46. The 1850 and 1860 censuses show John C. Lazenby one house away from Evan Stevens's residence, where Paulena and Will were living at the time of the house burning. Louisa Lazenby, daughter of John Lazenby, married Jonathan Ladd, on September 10, 1858. Jonathan was a brother to Matt and a third cousin to Paulena. John Lazenby was married to Mary Hiatt, a cousin of Paulena.

47. Lot Janney was a portrait photographer in Portsmouth, Scioto County, Ohio. His studio was located on the east side of Market Street, one door above Front St. Front or Water Street was next to the Ohio River.

though I said never a word but bore it like a "martyr"—it rained hard this evening—Jimmy and Steve came in and stayed a long time—it will seem so strange to sleep here tonight. We had water melon.

Thirdday, August 24th, 1859
Stayed in the new house last night. Breakfasted at 7—dinner at 1 o'clock pm—tea at 7. Lizzie and Miss Porter were over. Call was up today. I went home this evening—brought a load of my clothes up and some apples—concluded not to go to the cellebration tomorrow. Lizzie has too. Jimmy was here tonight. We opened Lot's pictures tonight—there are some such nice ones—some of them are badly broken[48] —I am sorry—letter from Jennie.

Fourthday, August 25th, 1859
Lizzie and I went to the railroad this morning. I was real glad I was not going—came back home and Will put the pictures up they look real nice—Matt called a while—just as sure as I am real dirty some person comes in but every person knows I am a new housekeeper. Alma and Jane came and brought me a chicken to fry and some apples.

Fifthday, August 26th, 1859
Finished my morning's work—read an hour—May West called—got dinner—Call came this evening. Had a cry. Oh, how lonely how desolate all the world seemed then. I felt like all were against me. I wonder if Matt will ever be as true as now! For Jo I can no longer call a true friend—alas, is it so that those we love and trust can be even worse than our enemies? I know it makes Will feel bad to see me sad but I can't help it sometimes for when tears cannot come my heart almost bursts. Went to the Lodge tonight. Mary was initiated tonight.

Sixthday, August 27th, 1859
Got up feeling very badly—had breakfast about 8 o'clock did my work—read an hour—went to Lizzies a while—we talked over our little troubles—for by the by—my eyes have not recovered last nights flood. Miss Porter and Lizzie said if I had as much trouble as them I would cry all the time. Perhaps Mother will come up this evening. I don't feel like I have any energy about me this morning at all. I wish something would happen to cheer me. Went to the exhibition—it was so good.

Seventhday, August 28th, 1859
Mother and Eva came up this evening and brought me pies—and bread. I am so glad of it. It is such a wet evening but it will be pleasant sitting by a bright fire

---

48. Some photographs were printed on glass plates. If they were broken, the photograph was destroyed.

with some good book—as *Reveres of a Bachelor*[49] before me to read. I will be so sorry when Lizzie goes away it will be so lonely—for I will not have any neighbors at all next door.

Sabbath, August 29th, 1859
This morning at 9 o'clock—heard a rap at the front door and I got up from the breakfast table to see who was there—it was Jo and [Lanny?], Mary Ellen Cowgill. I was very glad to see them—we had a nice fire in the parlor it was quite pleasant in doors—but out—the rain was falling and dark dismal clouds were visible almost everywhere—except when a few rays of light found their way through darkness—just like our lives are when we feel so lonely so destitute for a time—and the cloud begins to clear away and the dim unseen future grows light. Steve and Jim was here today. This evening I went to Whites a while. Jim and Steve, Mary and Call, and Jimmy were there—Jo gave me a muskmelon to bring home. Alma stayed all evening. Will is sick this evening or not very well.

Secondday, August 30th, 1859
Call came up—this evening we took a walk. Miss Porter came to Lizzies this evening. I wish Matt Ladd would come. Lide Hunt[50] and Lide Hiatt were here this evening. Mother has been up all day. I had my washing done too. Lib Hockett [Elizabeth Hiatt married Amos Hockett] called this evening.

Thirdday, August 31st, 1859
Cellebration at Clarksville several went—the band went—I called on Mrs Porter this afternoon. Frank is the greatest fellow. I wonder what kind of a man he will make? I went home today and brought home a water melon and so much— Alma came home with me.

Fourthday, August 31st, 1859 [Paulena has given this entry the same date as the previous one]
Felt gloomy this morning. The wind sighed such a lonely gloomy dirge and it seemed so still every place and I all alone too. But then it was not because I was lonely for such moods come over me let me be where I will, it is just natural for me to have fits of melancholy and I do wish I could be like some person else—but let me be as cheerful as I will and as happy in a little while afterwards if a cloud happens to obscure my sunshine. I feel like another person just so powerless, and lost to all energy. Mrs. Guttery [listed in the 1860 census] and

---

49. *Reveries of a Bachelor, or a Book of the Heart*, Donald G. Mitchell (pen name Ik Marvel), 11th ed., Charles Scribner, New York, 1851, www.alibris.com/search.cfm?qwork=5729708&ptit=Reveries.

50. Lide Hunt is probably the daughter of Nathan Hunt and Rachel Huff. She was a second cousin to Paulena.

Jo brought me a bouquet—I wrote in my diary this morning—read a while and sewed on my dress a while.

September 1859

Fifthday, September 1st, 1859
Feel better this morning and everything looks bright again. I wonder how I can get so down hearted when I have nothing to trouble me—for Will is so good to me and I do not have much to do but read and sew and go. I rose early this morning—got breakfast washed the dishes—washed the potatoes for dinner and pared the apples. I finished *Drama Life* and *Reveries of a Bachelor* and began *Moss Side*[51] —is interesting. Mother and grandmother have been up.

Sixthday, September 2nd, 1859
I went home this morning stayed all day and night. I slept all afternoon and Mother warmed my foots up good. It seemed so good to be at home.

Seventhday, September 3rd, 1859
I came home this morning. Eva came with me. I had such good "luck" with my pies this evening no person would have thought but what I had always been raised to *baking.* Jo came here this evening and Call was here. I called at Carmens this evening. Mr. Mofit lectures here tonight.

Sabbath, September 4th, 1859
Went to church this morning. Mary and Call came home with us for dinner. We got along nicely at dinner. Went to the lecture again this evening—after that went home. Uncle William and Aunt Anna were there. Mother gave us a melon to bring home. I finished *Moss Side.*

Thirdday, September 6th, 1859
Will is at home not very well.

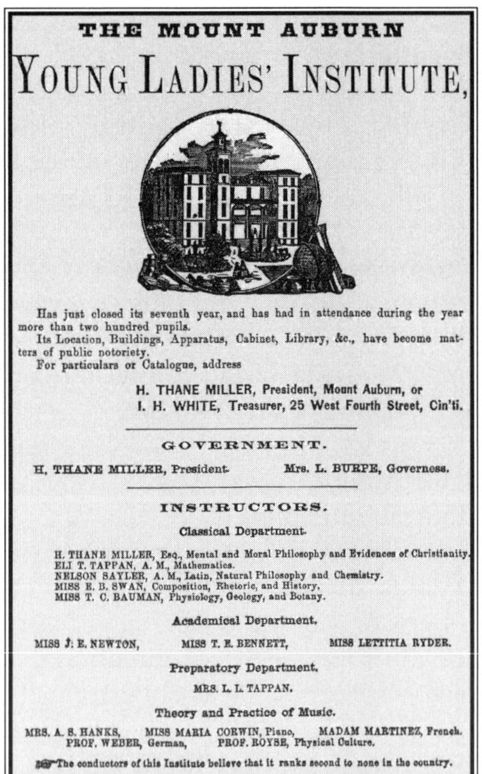

THE MOUNT AUBURN
YOUNG LADIES' INSTITUTE,

Has just closed its seventh year, and has had in attendance during the year more than two hundred pupils.

Its Location, Buildings, Apparatus, Cabinet, Library, &c., have become matters of public notoriety.

For particulars or Catalogue, address

H. THANE MILLER, President, Mount Auburn, or
I. H. WHITE, Treasurer, 25 West Fourth Street, Cin'ti.

GOVERNMENT.

H. THANE MILLER, President.   Mrs. L. BURPE, Governess.

INSTRUCTORS.

Classical Department.

H. THANE MILLER, Esq., Mental and Moral Philosophy and Evidences of Christianity.
ELI T. TAPPAN, A. M., Mathematics.
NELSON SAYLER, A. M., Latin, Natural Philosophy and Chemistry.
MISS E. B. SWAN, Composition, Rhetoric, and History.
MISS T. C. BAUMAN, Physiology, Geology, and Botany.

Academical Department.

MISS J. E. NEWTON,   MISS T. E. BENNETT,   MISS LETTITIA RYDER.

Preparatory Department.

MRS. L. L. TAPPAN.

Theory and Practice of Music.

MRS. A. S. HANKS,   MISS MARIA CORWIN, Piano,   MADAM MARTINEZ, French.
PROF. WEBER, German,   PROF. ROYSE, Physical Culture.

The conductors of this Institute believe that it ranks second to none in the country.

Advertisement for The Mount
Auburn Young Ladies' Institute

---

51. *Moss-Side* was written by Mary Virginia Hawes Terhune (the pen name of Marion Harland). It was published by Derby and Jackson in 1857.

Fourthday, September 7th, 1859 [Cincinnati, Ohio]
Went to the city—Birdsalls[52] and father went. We had a nice time. Went to the fair —and Institute—and Longworth's gardens.[53] I saw such splendid paintings at the Institute and everything fine. I met Charley today in the street. It seemed so funny—I was glad to see him he seems like a brother. This evening there was a girl sit by me to Loveland we had quite a chat. I learned she is attending school in the city. She showed me where she lives and just as she started to go up home from the railroad—she lost her footing and fell. She says there are a great many fall there. Will was real sick while I was away. I ought to have been at home.

The Garden of Nicholas Longworth

---

52. The Birdsalls were in Loudoun County, Virginia, at the same time as the Janneys. On Long Island there were Birdsalls in the records with the Betts family. It is not known whether these families were connected if at all.

53. The Institute may refer to The Mount Auburn Young Ladies' Institute, which was established in 1856 with Rev. J. J. Rowland as the head of the institute. Longworth's Gardens were at the home of Nicholas Longworth, located in a two-block area between Pike and Butler Streets and between East Fifth and East Third Streets. Nicholas Longworth is called the "Father of American Winemaking" and was known for propagation and experiments in his Ohio vineyards. Nicholas Longworth's daughter, Maria Longworth, married Bellamy Storer, a cousin of William Janney. Bellamy Storer was U.S. Ambassador to Belgium, and to Austria under the Hapsburg Empire in the Teddy Roosevelt administration. The grandson of Nicholas Longworth, also Nicholas Longworth, was to become Speaker of the House from 1925 to 1931. He was married to Alice Roosevelt, the daughter of President Teddy Roosevelt. The Longworth Congressional Office Building in Washington, D.C., is named for him. Teddy Roosevelt's first wife, Edith Kermit

Fifthday, September 8th, 1859
Will and I went home this morning and Mother and Willie came up and stayed till evening. I went to the Lodge a while.

Sixthday, September 9th, 1859
I went home this evening. When I came back Jo came down and stayed till after tea. Alma stayed to go to literary—I hope it will be interesting—I do wish Matt would come down and perhaps we would have a laugh for I do not have any good happy laughs like I used to. Jo is getting so old or seems like she is. She is always quilting—and Lizzie has so much to do—and gets the blues sometimes and I have them myself and Call is the best of any to laugh.

Carow, was a distant cousin to Paulena. The William Betts family, which lived near the Longworths, was distantly related to Paulena's grandfather, Aaron Betts, but it is not known whether Aaron Betts ever visited there. The Betts House is the oldest original house in the city of Cincinnati.

"Longworth's . . . conservatories, for the first time in America, saw the Victoria Regia or century plant bloom during a month. They were open nightly for the benefit of botanists who came from far and wide to view this novel spectacle."

"In 1820, Nicholas Longworth, a Cincinnati lawyer, planted Catawba vines near his home on the Ohio River. Early German immigrants called the area their new 'Rhineland' because the terrain reminded them of home. They had tried, with little success, to plant their traditional grapes, But, the hearty Catawba withstood cold Ohio winters and the wine gained consumer acceptance in this country and the salons of Europe. Well known poet of the time Henry Wadsworth Longfellow wrote a tribute to the Catawba. The sparkling, delicate, semi-sweet wine was different from other stronger wines of the time. By 1845, the annual production was over 300,000 gallons. Vines stretched along the river's edge from the foot of Mount Adams, in what is now downtown Cincinnati, toward Ripley. By 1860, the Ohio River Valley led the nation in the production of wine. But, crop diseases, such as black rot and mildew, began to destroy the vineyards as the Civil War left the grape growers with little manpower. Winemaking in southern Ohio succumbed to nature and nurture before California had even begun to be a commercial force." Source: "The Father of American Winemaking and The Longworth Heritage Wine Trail," Ohio Wine Producers Association, http://www2.eos.net/beerwine/longworth.html.

The following verse is from Longfellow's "Ode to Catawba Wine":

"'For richest and best
Is the wine of the West,
That grows by the Beautiful River;
Whose sweet perfume
Fills all the room
With a benison on the giver . . .'"

Source: *Cincinnati, Story of The Queen City,* Clara Longworth De Chambrun, Charles Scribner's Sons, New York, 1939, p. 115.

Seventhday, September 10th, 1859
Will and I went to Moons. Had a very nice visit—melons and apples to eat—Aunt Sarah [Sarah Mills was Henry Moon's widow]—seems so kind and good—if all quakers were like her there would not be so many hypocrites among them. It seems so very lonely there—I could not live there happy—it seems so desolate at evening with the katydids and crickets music—it makes me feel so lonely.

Martinsville, September 10th, 1859
[By William Janney]

Association met persuant to adjournment. But few of the officers were present. President called the house to order. Minutes were read and approved. Vigilence Committee haveing nothing to report. There was next a motion put before the house to levy a tax of 5 cts on each male member of the institution to procure a book suitable to record the minutes each meeting of this society. Carried. Robert Fulton was appointed to take the list of names and collect from each one what the above motion called for. The Speakers were then called on to address the meeting. Elwood Ladd[54] not being present was continued to address us on the next evening. Dr. Carmen was next called for but not being prepared he was excused on the grounds that he should address us on the next evening or be under a heavy penalty. He was reappointed as one of our next speakers. Then on motion adjourned to meet Thursday Evening September 17, 1859.

Will Janney
Sec.

Sabbath, September 11th, 1859
We came by Hunts this morning—had melons to eat—Elwood and Milton[55] were there—we did not go to meeting but this evening we went home. It seemed so nice and cool there—"Emma Hiatt is dead." Oh can it be that thou too art gone when just a year ago I saw? Surely those whom we least think of going, die first. Well I do remember when first I met Ema and thought her cold and proud and her the same of me—but some where I have a little note which read—"When I first saw thee I did not like thee a bit but I love thee now" oh how we remember little words or acts of kindness long after the author is gone forever.

---

54. Thomas "Elwood" Ladd was a brother of Jonathan and Matt Ladd. All were third cousins of Paulena.

55. Elwood, mentioned earlier, and Isaac "Milton" Ladd are thought to have been twins as their birth dates are just one day apart. Perhaps one was born before midnight and the other after. Their maternal grandmother was Ruth Hunt; thus they were cousins of Paulena.

Secondday, September 12th, 1859
Jim Hunt and Call took tea here this evening—we had fried chicken etc.

Thirdday, September 13th, 1859
Cool this morning—I have finished *The Hidden Path*[56] it is good—I am going to have chicken and corn and potatoes for dinner. Afternoon up stairs—I wish I could get a letter from some dear girl friend this evening. Jo and Call have been to stay all night.

[No entries for a week]

Fifthday, September 22nd, 1859
Went to division—Lizzie and I and Will and John stayed at home—we called at Gutterys [Dr. Guttery's medical office] after it closed. Lizzie will not be at any more soon.

Sixthday, September 23rd, 1859
Will has received part of the money. I am so glad—perhaps he will be in better heart now—I hope I won't be extravigant. Alma stayed here and went to the lyceum. I think I will go next night.

Seventhday, September 24th, 1859
Will, Alma and I went Hazel nutting this afternoon—down in the dark dismal swamp. I love to go away off in the forest and gather red leaves and berries etc. Will took a water melon along and we ate it—it tasted real nice there—we got lots of nuts and came home late and had supper about 8 o'clock. John Rizer came in tonight. Will and I are going to George's tomorrow.

Sabbath, September 25th, 1859
We went to Georges had a very nice time—had a good dinner fried chicken etc.—Steve, Jimmy, Dave came home with George for dinner. We all made nice bouquets and brought home. Rebecca and George went to grandfathers and I rode home—all the girls now gone out riding and I did not know what to do with myself—til Marg Carmen came over and we went to get Dr. to take us riding so we had a good ride out to Lutes [Lufts?]—Will brought a melon from home.

Secondday, September 26th, 1859
Mother came up today and brought a chicken and some apples—Margaret washed here this morning—I am glad it is done—Marg Carmen and I took a ride this evening went to Cuba—and her old home—got as many melons as we

---

56. *The Hidden Path* (Derby, 1855) was written by Mary Virginia Hawes Terhune.

could eat and some to bring home. Fall days will soon be here for the leaves are beginning to fall and turn pale.

Thirdday, September 27th, 1859

The sun is all darkened and the rain beginning to fall—pattering among the dead leaves and against the window panes. This evening I have been thinking of the past—all those days—at Boarding [Earlham] of the kind words spoken— and the little acts of kindness done—thinking of those who have gone over the Ocean to "Merry Old England" and some who have crossed that deep ocean of—death.

Fourthday, September 28th, 1859

I went home this evening came back loaded [food items] as usual. Lizzie and I went to Cluxtons—Frank is no better [Frank Cluxton was listed as age eleven in 1860 census] we are going to Greenfield.

Fifthday, September 29th, 1859

Bright this morning—yet not cloudless. I was at church saw the great marriage solimized—quite an imposing affair—the bridegroom wore cotton gloves or worsted—we could not tell which—they took a ride this evening. I expect they enjoy themselves fine—I am sick this morning. Will is house keeper. Mrs. Lindsy brought my bonnet home to night. I like it very well. Johns ate their last dinner to day— it makes me lonely to [see] them packing everything up. I won't have any place to run to now when ever I feel lonesome.

Sixthday, September 30th, 1859

Been over at Lizzies—helping stow away her things which will be there no longer. Miss Porter, Lizzie, John and Jo to tea here this evening.

October 1859

Seventhday, October 1st, 1859

I was at Lib Hocketts this afternoon.

Sabbath, October 2nd, 1859

Went to church this morning—this afternoon Mag and Dr. Will and I went to gather nuts. I am happy all the time only when those

Home Sweet Home. Drawings made by Paulena depicting her parents' home.

dreamy sad spells creep over me which I have no power to keep away but they come over me like shadows that they are and make those around me unhappy when I feel no power to make it otherwise.

Secondday, October 3rd, 1859
"Home Sweet Home." I was there today all day—came home laden with many good things. I made a beginning on those horrable shirts of Wills which surely have to be finished—sometime—I wish some good angel would come along to take the burden from my shoulders.

Thirdday, October 4th, 1859
Just the usual style—new neighbors—I can't be with anyone like I was with Lizzie.

Love Only the Beautiful
[By Paulena Stevens Janney]

Oh, the old spring and the willows dropping their branches near its crystal waters how the breeze sang and the grass waved on those sunny days where I have sat near by it and the old brown house among the trees how I can recall everything connected with it with more sympathy and more love toward all God's creatures. Such homes would more truly be estimated as to be the greatest and best of God's blessings. And when the homestead is exchanged for the cares and vexations of the world perchance for the wind and sea and foreign land, home sweet home will be the brightest, dearest spot on earth.

Look at the homes where there is nothing beautiful, where everything speaks of toil and wherein the atmosphere of the home breaths no spirit of beauty. Is there anything to refine and make the heart sympathetic? If there were forever homes like this, man would be more the likeness of God or women be a bright accent to society.

The Old Brown House
[By Paulena Stevens Janney]

The old house is very grim now. Dimly at evening do the shadows steal over and around making it more desolate. The old brown structure which lies half hidden in large old trees among whose leaves whispers are heard as the wind stirs among them. Near by are large old willow trees which bend low to the ground hung swinging with their branches. As I musingly sat thinking of the by gone, I imagined that I heard the sound of carriage wheels in the distance and saw bright young faces from the windows and open doors and heard gentle whispers of "they're coming" and then young footsteps bounded eagerly to the hall door to catch the sight of a very young bride gliding along quite happily. Dreams only of gladness are pictured from the fair brow of the bride and upon the broad masculine forehead of the bridegroom. [It] speaketh all of goodness and gentleness for the loved one by his side.

Next I saw the windows and heard the prattle of baby voices and heard the little feet tripping along the stairway. And I said, "Oh such happiness dwellith there." But alas, I see why are there tear-drops gushing from that pale, care-warn mother. Is it because one of her treasures has been taken away? Even as seeing yonder in darkened chamber there is a little coffin and flaxen curls are pillowed to never waken again. Oh, one shadow has fallen in the household, only one. God has taken the gentle sister for His own, never again will the world be filled with the same tone, the same smile and kindly spoken words—all, all gone. Then I see at evening a large old bible brought down and a chapter read, but there is one vacant seat, one absent voice that joins in the family no more and a silent tear stealith down the mother's cheek and a sadness hovers over all as they think of the dead.

Again death falls on another and another they are all gone all the fair young forms that so cheered and brightened with their presence. All are gone but the father and mother. Sadly they linger waiting for the blessed time to meet their children in the brighter world. Again the peace is broken and a trembling old woman follows daughter to the last of her early possessions and goes gravely back to her lonely home but the sound of youthful voices greet her ears no more and with every silent footstep, brings tender memories of the dead but she liveth alone in her sadness until the hour cometh when she lay calmly down and slept the last sleep.

I look around me, where is the fair gentle bride—how full of purity and where is the bridegroom? Where are all those young faces that timidly whispered "they've come, they've come"? I slowly wandered through the silent rooms and in the yard where every thing seemed to answer as the night winds sliced among the leaves—all, all gone.

Fourthday, October 5th, 1859
Mary Ann came I was glad to see her—she left on the last train—Alma is here—Lib Hockett called this evening too.

Fifthday, October 6th, 1859
Did not go to Division tonight—Call stayed here while Will went.

Sixthday, October 7th, 1859
Went home [her parents' home down the road] today again. Stayed till after tea—grandmother came up and brought me a chicken to bring home.

Seventhday, October 8th, 1859
Going home tonight—get something good to eat. Birdsalls coming to our house to dinner tomorrow.

Sabbath, October 9th, 1859
Had a good time at home. Birdsalls there—came home this evening—Lide and Sallie, Jamie [Jane?] E. Riser—Call—Jimmy have been here. We had the best melon.

Secondday, October 10th, 1859
Margaret washed here.

Thirdday, October 11th, 1859
Went home this evening. Mother got supper and sent enough home for Wills supper.

Fourthday, October 12th, 1859
Mother, grandmother and I went to Aunt Eliza's [wife of Uncle Thomas Stevens living in Highland County on farm inherited from his father, Gideon Stevens] today—"got along" very well—only Bet kept swishing her tail over the lines [the horse Bet was pulling a buggy] keeping me in continual dread for fear of accident.

Fifthday, October 13th, 1859
Had late supper—Miss Porter, Lide and several of the girls called—Mag Carman came in the back way—they left for home and Mag stayed—did not go to division going to Greenfield tomorrow. Alma and I were sitting in the boudoir—sewing when I, though not certain, thought I hear a knock so I began to say—"if any one knocked just come in"—when it was repeated I started for the door when my "unmentionables" came down and I just caught the glimpse of some person and got out of sight. It was only Dr. Noble[57] though.

Sixthday, October 14th, 1859 [Greenfield, Ohio]
Cloudy—dark—after while began to pour—but I kept on my determination to go [to Greenfield-Highland County] and so did. Will—Alma and Call came so Cary took us down—it cleared off nicely—glad we went—fair very good.

Seventhday, October 15th, 1859
Went to White's for tea this evening staid till bed time. Jo and I took a walk to the graveyard. I have my mind on going home for breakfast in the morning.

---

57. Dr. David Noble was graduated from Starling Medical College, Columbus, Ohio, and had his office on South High Street in Hillsboro, Ohio. Source: *Highland Pioneer Sketches and Family Genealogies*, H. K. Skinner & Son, 1971.

Sabbath, October 16th, 1859
Got up very early walked very fast. Got home just as mother and Alma were dressing. stayed till 8 o'clock—George and Lib were here for dinner—Elma [Hunt] was at Whites today. I only saw her for a few minutes—she looks badly.

> [October 16, 1859—"Abolitionist, John Brown, led a small group of armed men into Harper's Ferry, Virginia (later West Virginia) to seize the federal arsenal and encourage a slave rebellion. Confidently he waited for the slave uprising—but it never came. Ten of his seventeen raiders, including two of his own sons, were killed or fatally wounded. Historians cite this event as a prelude to the Civil War." Source: *John Brown's Raid*, Records and Resources at the Library of Virginia, December, 1999]

Secondday, October 17th, 1859
Mary Rizer came this morning to go to grandmothers. Willie came home with me but didn't stay all night.

Fourthday, October 19th, 1859
Mother was here today and Willie. Treny [Triphena] Lazenby[58] was here a while. I was at Vances—Lib was first like usual. I wonder if she will be sociable now? Will is not at Carmens this week. It seems so much better for him to be at home.

Sixthday, October 21st, 1859
Alma is Editress—we are going to the Society tonight, there is going to be a debate on women's rights[59] —Charles [Oren] and Dr. Carmen are in the affirmative. Warren Johnson the negative.

Seventhday, October 21st, 1859 [Date repeated]
It is such a dreary afternoon so cold and chilly.

---

58. Triphena Lazenby was the daughter of John C. Lazenby and Mary Hiatt, and a sister of Louisa Lazenby. She was a cousin to Paulena. She died on May 31, 1861, and is buried in Newberry Friends Cemetery, Martinsville, Ohio.

59. "The 19th Amendment to the Constitution of the United States (ratified August 1920) provides men and women with equal voting rights. The amendment states that the right of citizens to vote 'shall not be denied or abridged by the United States or by any State on account of sex.' Although this equality was implied in the 14th Amendment (1868), most of the states continued to restrict or prohibit Women's Suffrage. The women's rights movement, which started as early as the 1830s and became intertwined

Sabbath, October 22nd, 1859
Went to church—came home ate dinner—read a while—then Call and Sarah James came and we went to see Lide—from there walking—Will and us went up on the observatory—we had a splendid view of the city in full—but indeed I did enjoy it—exceedingly—it was such a calm quiet afternoon.

Secondday, October 23rd, 1859
This morning I rose so much earlier than usual gathered the dirty clothes all up and Bogy came and took them to be washed. Gulielma was here this morning a while. I will have to work this week—quarterly meeting.

Thirdday, October 24th, 1859
 The terrible task of ironing is over. My hand looked like a boiled lobster and the skin came off in one place. I had a tremendous time soaking it in buttermilk. It don't look quite so bad. I got stung twice today with a wasp. I felt sorry for them and did not like to kill them—but after I was stung I made them fly—that is a pretty good example of my disposition—just when I am angry I can do "lots." Mother was here this evening she wants me to get Jane to help me but I will wait till I go to iron next week.

Fourthday, October 25th, 1859
Afternoon—down in the woods with the dead leaves rustling and falling around me—and the wind sighing over my head like some pent up thunder.

Fifthday, October 26th, 1859
Call came up tonight went down the street just in time. Lide Hunt[60] was married this evening. It seems so funny to think that the girls are getting married. Beck Pidgeon came over to day.

Sixthday, October 27th, 1859
Bright this morning but the clouds gathered before noon and the air grew chilly. I have had a terrible time today baking—in the midst of my working I heard a knock—at leaving all—ran to the door—Miss Pidgeon, Miss Huff, and Lib Hocket called.

---

with the struggle to abolish slavery, resulted in the proposal for the 19th Amendment, introduced in Congress in 1878. This proposed amendment remained a controversial issue for over 40 years, during which the women's rights movement became strongly militant, conducting campaigns and demonstrations for congressional passage of the amendment and then for ratification by the states. This political action, reinforced by the service of women in industry during World War I, resulted in the adoption of the amendment." Source: http://gi.grolier.com/presidents/aae/side/19amend.html.

    60. Eliza Hunt married Eliel West on October 27, 1859, according to the Clinton County Marriage Records.

Seventhday, October 29th, 1859

Matt came this morning and her mother [Mary (Chalfant) Ladd]—glad to see them—went to meeting—Mollie Brown was there. She came home with me for dinner. We had a fine talk about old times. The Governes is dead[61] —it seems so sad and strange. I am very sorry for I wanted to see her so bad and now never will. There were not so many young people this time. Mag and Dr. [Carmen] came over and we had a game of chequers. The *wildcats* marched tonight.

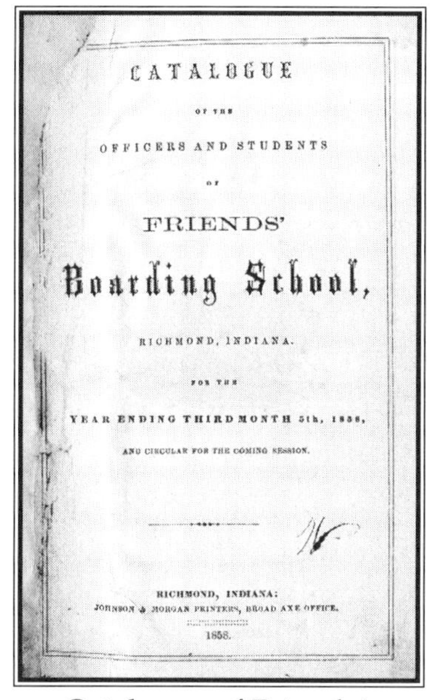

Catalogue of Friends'
Boarding School

Friends' Boarding School, Earlham,
showing separate walks for men and women.

Earlham Hall, 1857.
This was the only building on the campus in 1857. It housed administrative offices, a parlor, classrooms, a dining hall, and separate residences for men and women students.

---

61. Sarah P. Hopkins is listed as Governess at Friends Boarding School, Earlham, Richmond, Indiana, in the 1858 Catalogue. She was also listed as governess in the enrollment records, which listed Paulena Stevens and William Janney as students in the school year 1856–1857. Source: *Quaker Collection*, Earlham College Library, copied by Christie Russell, 1999.

Sabbath, October 30th, 1859
We rose bright and late—had breakfast at 8 o'clock. Harry Miller and his mother called here—Steve also and Matt. I did not go to meeting today—Matt Hussey—Call and Jim Hunter and Jimmy here till bedtime.

Secondday, October 31, 1859
Went home today to see Lizzie Turner. She will not live long. Finished Jennie's letter tonight wrote some poetry.

November 1859

Thirdday, November 1st, 1859
Lizzie is dead. It seems sad that one so young should die—but she is far better off than in this world where life would never have been for her as it should have been. It seems almost like a dream to think quarterly meeting is past. I wish I could go someplace—Will says when we get to be wealthy—we will travel. Nothing would please me better than crossing the Ocean to fair "Ole England" of which I have heard so much of—bright skies and romantic scenery—but perhaps when there I would sigh for the homeland again and think the skies more clear and everything more beautiful.

Fourthday, November 2nd, 1859
Will and I spent the evening at Uncle Williams. Governess is dead and I did not see her—I am so sorry—I did think so much of her. The Boarding School is the first place for forming attachments—just the place for learning to have confidents—and to tell secrets.

Fifthday, November 3rd, 1859
Jo was here this evening and Call—we went to 'Division.' I have read *Fifty Years in Exile*[62] this week and am now reading Lord-Fronlang's Page—Historical Romance. I am very happy for I can read and do anything I please after certain dishes are washed—and certain rooms swept and dusted. I wish Will would get to read as much as I.

Sixthday, November 4th, 1859
I sewed a while on form shirts—it is strange we women—have to make such articles. Call has been up here the usual number of times today—twice or three times.

---

62. *Israel Potter: His Fifty Years in Exile,* by Herman Melville, published in book form in 1855. The book, Melville's eighth, appeared first in serial form in *Putnam's Monthly* by G. P. Putnam & Co. from July 19, 1854, to March 18, 1855. *Moby Dick* had been published in 1851. Paulena was a sixth cousin to Herman Melville through her paternal grandmother, Mary Coffin.

Seventhday, November 5th, 1859
Finished that book this morning—got dinner—and came here to the graveyard
to read and write—it is such a calm, quiet afternoon.

Memories of Childhood Play
[By Paulena Stevens Janney]

Just like a long time ago when I came to school in that old house which
used to be in my eyes a great place—but it looks lonely enough now
with its sloping roof and narrow windows and closed doors. We used to
have *great* and grand times in the meeting house—playing meeting or as
Willie says "just tending on like we had meeting"—we did some things
very wrong too but we were innocent then as we could be. Some of us
used to don plain handkerchiefs and with very solemn expressions get
the highest seat—and preach and pray etc and some others—had great
trouble with imagining babies who seemed to make a terrible noise, but
oh it is all gone now and I will never go to school again—it makes me
feel sad—for I have been very happy at school and very sad too with a
child's sadness.

I am sitting now just where I have sat many and many times
getting my lessons or talking with some friend—I remember one hot
summer afternoon I came out here in the pleasant shade to study—but
I grew very sleepy—and slumbered long and sweetly—my head resting on the grave stone there—but it is all changed now—and many are
sleeping here that last sleep—that were school mates then and very still
now—and very desolate too for the leaves are all falling—and the grass
is green no longer. I wonder if I will be buried here too—or if in some
distant graveyard where the trees will wave over graves that I have
never beheld.[63]

Oh childhood, thou art truly a season of lilies for thy griefs are
transient and joys lingering—the future with its many daring plots is to
thee all brightness—the past—an oblivion—even now I hear the childish voice—and see a little girl of flannel petticoats and shawls—trundled along by a little lump of a girl and followed by two little chubby
boys—one of which the little girl calls Eddy—and they have a playhouse just like *we* made almost in the same very spot—I wonder if there
is anything poetical in that little girl? Just a while ago I heard her say
"Oh good man, good man, Eddy is telling the biggest story"—I wonder
if she will be *anything*.

---

63. Paulena was prophetic in her statement here as her final resting place was
in a "distant graveyard" where the trees waved over graves that she had never beheld.
It was in Carthage, Jasper County, Missouri, that she was first buried, in East/Cedar
Cemetery, but when the Park Cemetery was created, her grave was moved in 1891 to
the Stevens Plot, where her parents were buried. Her husband, Will Janney, would be
buried with his second wife, Sarah, in Thresher Cemetery, outside Neosho, Newton
County, Missouri.

I would like to visit all the orphan asylums and see and study—the children's characters—there would be such a confusion of blue eyes and black eyes and grey eyes, auburn hair, white hair, red, and almost every color except blue—when I travel I will just go every such place—this little girl has started now saying "the baby" and leading Eddy who is carrying the baby's cap—and the other one is holding her bonnet—she speaks so kindly to them too.

Sabbath, November 6th, 1859
Will and I went down home last night this morning we went to Whites—had a very nice time—Steve and Call were there.

Secondday, November 7th, 1859
Just like all second days. Margaret did my washing soon this morning and I wish my ironing was done—it is very smoky [foggy]—can scarcely see before us—I wish the sun would shine it would be such a beautiful day—Lyd, Call and I were to see Danny [Danny Hunt, son of Nathan and Rachel (Huff) Hunt—age twenty-seven] this evening he will not linger much—sad for one so beloved to die.

Thirdday, November 8th, 1859
Will went to see Danny—still living—Elma is failing they say—oh how can I ever bear her death? for we have been schoolmates—and friends—and it will be very sad—but we do not know—perhaps she will live longer than I. Jo and [I] want to get our miniatures taken together. I want hers any how and Jo's so if I live to be old I can look at them in after years and recall our school days and our happy girlhood.

Fourthday, November 9th, 1859
Went home this morning. Mother and grandmother came to Uncle Williams this afternoon, and I went down. Danny is just living—do not suppose he will last through the night. I wish I could [get] a letter from some person. Matt promised to write soon I am afraid such promises are easily forgotten—but it has not been very long yet.

Fifthday, November 10th, 1859
Danny is dead—his suffering is at last ended[64] —this is a sad gloomy looking day—been raining some. Call and I were at Whites this evening a while. Will and I are going home. The committee are out visiting families—now—they will

---

64. Danny was Daniel Hunt, Paulena's second cousin. His death notice, dated December 16, 1859, *Clinton Republican*, Wilmington, Ohio: "Died, on November 10, 1859, Daniel Hunt, age 28 years. At the residence of his father, near Martinsville, Ohio. Son of Nathaniel and Rachel [Huff] Hunt. Rachel Hunt deceased."

give us a call soon.[65] Poor old Brown [John Brown] is going to be hung. I am
very sorry. I wish Governor Wise [Governor of West Virginia where John Brown
was tried] would get ashamed and pardon him. He has a wife too—I pity her.
Phillip Wendel made such a good speech on the subject. I think he must be a
good man. His [Danny's] funeral is to take place on seventh day at 10 o'clock
am.

Sixthday, November 11th, 1859
Came home this morning found a fire in the stove for Will had preceded me—I
have been reading this afternoon—it is such a dreary evening the rain drops are
beginning to patter on the roof reminding us of chilly bleak winter—coming
very near—when we will draw around the pleasant fireside—and listen to the
howling winds ever breath melancholy to my ear.

Seventhday, November 12th, 1859
It rained very hard this morning so much that I did not attend the funeral. Will
went—it is a very bad evening—the rain continually coming down in torrents.

Sabbath, November 13th, 1859
Oh! the snow has come once more—since last it enshrouded the earth—many
changes have come—and it now covers newly made graves that the summer
winds never breathed upon—how it reminds me of other winters when I stood
at the window on Sabbath morning or looked out upon the leafless trees and
white ground—all so cheerless and every vestige of summer disappeared. Mag
and her mother were here while Will and I have been indoors reading by a
cheerful fire.

Secondday, November 14th, 1859
Alma stayed here tonight—I wrote a note to Elma it seemed just like old times
to do that—those old glad school days how quickly they glide away leaving us
only the memory to dwell upon.

Thirdday, November 15th, 1859
Milder today not so cheerless—Call and I visited Joe's school this evening it was
so funny to see the little—red, white and almost every color of little heads—that
kept peeping up in every direction—little dirty things some with stringy hair

---

65. Because Will and Paulena did not follow the Quaker discipline of announc-
ing their intention to marry for two or three meetings prior to their marriage to determine their clearness to marry, and because they were married by a Minister of the
Gospel and not in the gathering of the Society of Friends, a committee from the meeting
was appointed to visit them and inform them of the inappropriateness of their action
and to gain from them some form of acknowledgment that they had not followed the
discipline.

and long dresses—but among them there were some bright eyes and fine bones. Jo and Steve were here to night.

Fourthday, November 16th, 1859
Went home to day Mother brought me back for I came heavily laden as usual after being at home stayed at home to night—finished *Bavengro* going to begin *Never Too Late to Mend*—no letters yet just about time. Mary told [me] to write a letter to Hannah Jane for her. She is so afraid she will marry him.

Fifthday, November 17th, 1859
Mary came over today. I wrote the letter—Lib Hockett was here this evening— Call and I went to division—Dr. Davis spoke—hear we are going to have literary exercises and were complained of today. Jim Hunt came home with me.

Sixthday, November 18th, 1859
We had meeting here to day. Committee called—all preached. Aunt Sarah kissed me and sied [sighed]—she seems like she likes me. I wonder if they all think I am so bad. Call came up in the rain this evening.

Seventhday, November 19th, 1859
Been a dark day. I do not feel lonesome though. I made a nice fire in the grate and we have had fine times reading. I finished *Never Too Late to Mend*.

Sabbath, November 20th, 1859
We went to church this morning. Call came home with us for dinner. Steve and Jenny were here this afternoon—went to Orens found Clara writing which she kept on till Charley took her pen away.[66] I could hardly keep from laughing— but did—then started home calling on Whites. Played chequers.

Secondday, November 21st, 1859
Went home today father is sick—raining today cold and drizzly. David and Deborah were there. After I came home I was sick.

Thirdday, November 22nd, 1859
Been sick today. Jo and Call came here to night we had so much fun and played chequers too. I have been reading Byron[67] today.

---

66. Clara Oren was Charles Oren's younger sister, born on December 16, 1844. Clarissa, the youngest daughter of Elihu and Jane Newcomb Oren, died of scrofulous consumption on June 6, 1862, at age seventeen. She is buried in the Friends Cemetery in Martinsville.

67. "Romantic poet, George Gordon, Lord Byron, was born in 1788. Byron is the most famous and controversial of his contemporaries. He was always a study in contrasts,

Fourthday, November 23rd, 1859
I was ironing this morning when Rebecca Moon came. It is the first time she [was] ever here. Mother came up too—she brought me a chicken to fry. Cook is sentenced to be hung on the 16th of next month. I do hope something will occur to prevent the executions. I feel sorry for them.[68] It is such a bright beautiful day almost like Spring but there are many hearts its brightness cannot cheer—and every morning is to them one day near that terrible sorrow. Surely Brown's wife so and Cook is married too. I don't see how they bear up under such awful sorrow—for it would madden me—but we do not know what we can bear till we are afflicted.

Fifthday, November 24th, 1859
Bright again this morning. Call and Steve and Jimmy were here to night we played chequers as usual.

Sixthday, November 25th, 1859
The examination begins today. Mother and I went to Uncle Thomas's [Thomas Stevens, brother to Evan] today. Cyrus[69] is sick—I saw Althea's girls. I like them real well. I wish Maria would come up and stay a week, Alma stayed here to night.

---

a melancholy satirist, an aristocratic champion of the common man, handsome and adored but obsessed with a small personal deformity. He fled England to escape scandal and a failed marriage and died of fever in 1824. His natural gift for poetry was the only consistency in his troubled life. Yet even during his own lifetime, his personal life overshadowed his work." Source: http://www.englishhistory.net/byron.html.

"Lord George Gordon Byron (1788–1824) was as famous in his lifetime for his personality cult as for his poetry. He created the concept of the 'Byronic hero'—a defiant, melancholy young man, brooding on some mysterious, unforgivable event in his past. Byron's influence on European poetry, music, novel, opera, and painting has been immense, although the poet was widely condemned on moral grounds by his contemporaries." Source: http://www.online literature.com/byron/.

68. "John E. Cook, a veteran of the fight to keep Kansas free from slavery, served as John Brown's front man for the raid. At Harpers Ferry, he held various jobs, including schoolteacher, book-agent, and lock tender on the Chesapeake & Ohio Canal which runs parallel to the Potomac River on the Maryland side. He also married a local Catholic girl, Mary V. Kennedy, on April 18, 1859. She bore him a son that summer. Cook escaped from Harpers Ferry during the raid, but was captured eight miles outside Chambersburg, Pennsylvania. He made a lengthy confession to Virginia authorities in Charlestown [became West Virginia in 1896] where John Brown's trial was held, an act which did not endear him to Brown and his surviving men. He was hanged on December 16, 1859." Source: http://johnbrownsbody.net/Raiders.htm.

69. Cyrus Stevens was the oldest son of Thomas and Elizabeth Harris Stevens. He was born circa 1845.

Seventhday, November 26th, 1859
I went to school this evening it was interesting they recited so well. Dosh Fulton and Call took tea here this evening—and they went to the party. Alma went to night for her first party—but then it was made expressly for the scholars including all of them. I have been reading Byron. I like to read it so well. I wish I could be a writer. I don't see why I was not a "genius" perhaps though I might be more of one if I would cultivate my talents for I know I take more interest in literature and such things than half the rest of the girls in town for just the other day I was speaking of Capt. Brown to a certain lady and she knew nothing about him. Poor old man I pity him so for in his heroic act for freedom he has lost himself—but I pity more his family for they will be left alone—just a few more days and the fatal day will be here.

Sabbath, November 27th, 1859
Will and I went to Methodist church this morning. Noble preached today. We went home for dinner and to grandfathers this evening. Willie knows all his letters and can say them as quick—little toad. He won't go any place and leave Frank at home. [Willie was four years old on September 7, 1859]. Martin Clevenger and Galny came here to play chequers.

Secondday, November 28th, 1859
Bright and beautiful as a spring day. I feel like starting out to gather flowers—or doing something pertaining to spring. My new neighbor came over to borrow some coffee today. If we could see to Virginia [now West Virginia]—we would see them erecting a scaffold oh it is so awful. I am opposed to hanging.

Thirdday, November 29th, 1859
Mother was here today. Jo and Call came up this evening and tonight Lyd, Willie, and Call were here.

Fourthday, November 30th, 1859
This afternoon I went down where Will is working on house—I do wish some person would move there I could visit. Aaron came by and I went down home with him.

December 1859

Fifthday, December 1st, 1859
The last day of Brown's life has dawned at last—dark—a fit emblem of the feelings of thousands. I was at Uncle Williams today and to night Call and I were at division. All the ladies present—I acted as Chaplain—some of the gentlemen complimented us on our courage in coming—going out. I wonder if Brown feels happy to night, his last night on earth! but I pity his family.

Sixthday, December 2nd, 1859
Today is a very wet day and I do not wonder—for the sun would be ashamed to shed its rays over so much cruelty—as will occur today—the Farewell day—Governor Wise refuses to let any person be admitted within hearing distance of Brown. I think it is atrocious, he ought to be hung himself—Governor Willard of Indiana[70]—has gone to Wise to try to get Cook pardoned. I wish Brown would be found dead when they go to bring him out to hang him. It would be a great disappointment to the southerners.

Seventhday, December 3rd, 1859
A very disagreeable day—sleeting and blowing. I am thinking how miserable Brown's family are today—he was hung yesterday at 11 o'clock no one was allowed to be near to the scaffold except the militia. Call is here we have been playing chequers.

Sabbath, December 4th, 1859
Remained at home till late this evening. Read the execution of John Brown. Began a letter to Emma Chaffin. Call came up this evening. Marg and Dr. were here tonight till bed time. I am going to stay at home on Sabbath after this.

Secondday, December 5th, 1859
Very cold this morning. Dreaded to get up so bad—had late breakfast—finished my letter to day—Will and I went to Whites tonight but Dave and Steve came as usual so we came home soon. Alma is here tonight.

[Paulena's ink is very faint and no entries were made for four days.]

Sixthday December 9th, 1859
Ironed today—Call and Jo were here this evening. Will got me a new dress yesterday The band serenaded us tonight it is such a beautiful night.

Seventhday, December 10th, 1859
Not so cold today—Will and I are going home tonight—Mother and father came up in the sleigh and I rode home.

---

70. "Ashbel Willard served in the Indiana House of Representatives (1850–1851), and in 1852 was elected lieutenant governor on the Democratic ticket with Joseph Wright. Willard was only thirty-six years old when he defeated Oliver P. Morton in the 1856 election for governor. Willard's administration was plagued with problems with the legislature, and he was forced to borrow money to pay the interest on the state's debt. A heavy drinker with longstanding health problems, in 1860 Willard, in a vain effort to regain his health, went to Minnesota where he died in October. He was the first of Indiana's chief executives to die in office." Source: Indiana Historical Bureau, "Ashbel Parsons Willard," http://www.statelib.lib.in.us/www/ihb/govportraits/willard.html.

Sabbath, December 11th, 1859
Came home went to church Call stayed here—We called at Chatts—they look very nice. I feel sad this evening but I am not going out any place till night any how for I said I would not and I must keep my promise—I have been writing a piece—"A Reverie" for the division—and I am going to send some poetry.

Secondday, December 12th, 1859
Mother and grandmother were here today and Willie. I received a letter from Jennie this morning—I was so glad to get it—she says she is coming in the spring to see me I will be so glad to see her.

Thirdday, December 13th, 1859
Josy and I were to see Elma today, she looks so pale—I am afraid she will not live long [see February 22, 1860, entry]—poor girl—I will never forget what great times we used to see at school—Will and I were at Carmens tonight—perhaps we had sociability—Alma stayed and kept the fire—Dr. Noble and I had some more conversation to night I guess we are as good friends now as we were before.

Fourthday, December 14th, 1859
How swiftly time wafts us along the weeks seem almost as days as they come and go ever bringing some new change—Jo was here this evening. Oh I will be sorry when her and Dave move to Wilmington—I do not see what I will do.

Fifthday, December 15th, 1859
Went to the division to night—heard our pieces read. I think they suspicioned Alforie as I—Miss Porter, Jo and I are appointed to read the contributions next night I am of the opinion that it is very doubtful about there being any without we write them—no letter from Matt yet—I never did see such a promise breaker.

Sixthday, December 16th, 1859
Jo was here this evening—she braided my hair—it seemed quite like old times—boarding school times—but the Matron[71] could not tell me to take it down—Cook, Coppoc, Copeland and Shields are to be hung today. I feel so sad when I think of it. Cook and Coppque are to be hung at 3 o'clock.[72] I pity their

---

71. Elizabeth B. Hopkins was listed as matron on the enrollment records for Friends' Boarding School, Earlham, in 1856–57, when Paulena was a student. An 1862 photograph of young women students at Earlham College clearly shows that hair braiding and curls were fashionable and must have been permitted by that time, about five years later than when Paulena was a student.

72. "John E. Cook, a veteran of the fight to keep Kansas free from slavery, served as John Brown's front man for the raid. At Harpers Ferry, he held various jobs, including

relations—it would be so terrible to see a friend hung; there is not as much excitement about them as Brown, though many sad thoughts are wafted to them.

Seventhday, December 24th, 1859

And tomorrow is Christmas—how time glides along bearing upon it's bosom how much of grief and joy—three years ago we were at boarding school—I remember how they forbade us saying Christmas gift—but we should "say thanksgiving"—poor old Governess her trials are all over and she is in that better land—we are invited to Uncle Williams tomorrow to dinner and Allemong from the city is going to be there.

Sabbath, 25th December 1859

It did not seem one bit like Christmas today. I forgot it was. We had quite a

---

schoolteacher, book-agent, and lock tender on the Chesapeake & Ohio Canal which runs parallel to the Potomac River on the Maryland side . . . Cook escaped from Harper's Ferry during the raid, but was captured eight miles outside Chambersburg, Pennsylvania. He made a lengthy confession to Virginia authorities in Charlestown where John Brown's trial was held, an act which did not endear him to Brown and his surviving men. He was hanged on December 16, 1859."

"Edwin Coppoc, the older brother of Barclay, was born June 30, 1835. He met John Brown in Springdale, Iowa, in the fall of 1858. During the raid, Edwin shot the mayor of Harpers Ferry, Fontaine Beckham. He was tried, found guilty and sentenced to hang on November 2, 1859. He was hanged December 16, 1859."

"Shields Green, also known as the 'Emperor,' was an escaped slave from Charleston, South Carolina. He lived for a time in Canada and later moved to Rochester, New York, where he met Frederick Douglass and John Brown. Green accompanied Douglass to Chambersburg, Pennsylvania, where Brown had organized a conference of his men in a local rock quarry to discuss the raid on the Ferry. Douglass refused to go with Brown, but Green was willing to follow 'the ole man.' According to some of the raiders, Green was more of a liability than an asset during the raid. He proved to be so lacking in courage that, when Brown's men were finally captured in the Engine House, Green tried to pass himself off as one of the slaves Brown had forcibly pressed into service. Osborn Anderson, on the other hand, praised Green's courage at his willingness to remain with Brown to the end when he could have escaped. He was executed on December 16, 1859."

"John Anthony Copeland, Jr., was born August 15, 1834, in Raleigh, North Carolina. Although an African American, he was a free man. In 1842, he and his parents moved to Oberlin, Ohio, where he attended school and was later enrolled as a student at Oberlin College. While living there, Copeland became involved in the rescue of escaped slave John Price, an act for which he was arrested and jailed in Cleveland. His uncle, Lewis Sheridan Leary, recruited him for John Brown's raid on Harper's Ferry. Copeland was one of the few who survived the raid, but he was captured and put on trial for murder and treason. He was hanged December 16, 1859." Source: http://johnbrownsbody.net/Raiders.htm.

nice time at Uncles. I like Mr. Alimong (Allemong) very well but not so well as Charley. Dr. Noble, Tim and Jim were here tonight and we had quite a fine time (Call too) Aaron, and A [Alma] called a while.

New Years Eve
[By William Janney]

Farewell to the old year, two more hours will fill the time allotted to thee. Yes in two more hours the new year of 1860 will be ushered in and who knows what tidings she may bring about or what shall transpire in her term. Whether incidents of joy or sadness non but god can fathom and tis well that it is so arranged for if we knew our destiny it might be one of such dark forbodings that life would cease to be anything else but terror and death sweet death would be welcome with great joy.

This New years Eve brings recollections of the past of such a character that I love to ponder and reflect what the future will bring forth. Will it be less or more bright than what it has been in the past five years, when I first met the one that I was willing to sacrifice all for her sake; the one which I have since been joined to, the link of which I pledged myself never to brake so long as we both shall live. And one of us will be permitted to trace these lines after the other is gone to that loving home in the skies. A sad thought it is indeed to me, for we know not that it will be more than a day or a year for us to pass time so sweetly together as we have in the past. But one bright hope we have, one that will never fade which is to live together in a brighter world than this beyond the skies where parting with Husband and Wife is no more a serious subject to contemplation than a lone adieu to the old year. Let us have the dangers and trials that may fall to our lot before the new year expires.

Will

Seventhday, Night [December 31st], 1859
Yes! tonight is the last of the old year with its smiles and frowns, it is going— and sadly I bid it good by for we know not what the future one may have in store for us—Will, thee did not know that in five years I would be thy wife did thee—am I a good wife? I will try to be a better one for I know I am very thoughtless now.

[This essay by Paulena Stevens Janney opens with a quoted text and then follows with what I believe are her own words.]

"The old clock upon the mantle that ticked off the hours when Charlie died and when Charlie sighed, it drew on toward midnight, the lamp flame grew dimmer and dimmer and thus it is that home, childhood's home passes away forever like the swaying of the pendulum, like the fading of a shadow on the floor."

Dear home, home how I loved thee true, was that within thy atmosphere, no other spot could give, but the sunny days of childhood pass quickly along and buries childish joys and childish griefs in the certain past, and the uncertain future wears a brighter glow and we are to the world children no longer. Yet in our hearts the gushing fonts of childhood well up ever more keeping in hearts kinder and good if we but listen to its teachings, but home, is it ours yet? Many answer, no, but its memory never fades but our hearts let us go where we may. Sweet home, if it has been a home, is ever near. Someone beautifully said, "Woman, thou are the angel of home, go look not in thy gilded glass, but look down into the dear bright fountain which gave back thy smile in childhood, Art thou an angel of light causing the sunshine over the sill, or of darkness brooding like raven wings over the family alter."

Childhood home passes away just as it grows dearest, the other feet tread the olden walks of the garden where we have watched the flowers bloom and the sun sink in the west and dear dear old playhouse, it is hard to give thee up for my happiest days were spent bringing violets from the brook and acorns from the forest decking thee with every toy and broken dish my hands could find. Then I wove my dreams of the future—Oh, why could I not always be a child—be just as June as childhood ever is. Why should I ever be longing for some thing undefined, grow so weary of everyday life? Why could I not always chase the butterfly and pick the buttercup in the meadows? It is because the world, the great wicked world claims every man, woman and child. Oh, life, life!

Oh, life, life? How like mariners we are tossed upon thy tempestuous ocean and yet we cling to thee though every hour be bitterness.

January 1860

[No entries for January]

February 1860

Sabbath, February 12th, 1860 [Entry By William Janney]

> A pretty Sabbath evening is this and Lena and I are all alone a pleasant time we have musing upon the past present and that which is to come, May Heaven always send us those bright rays as thus she has done for they cherish good thoughts and cite us to noble action, such as it takes to constitute pure happiness on earth and ensure us a peaceful reward in the world to come. Oh how many homes yes

how many hearts are dark as midnight with deep felt sorrow caused
by not studying nature sufficiently to accertain what she has in store
for all of those who investigate great natures laws till they are capable of appreciating all the beauties set forth by our all wise creator
whose works on every hand is studied becomes an interesting theme
for mans consideration—one that will elevate him to the dignity of
pure unsullied manhood when he sees no pleasure only in the pursuit
of an object which tends to raise man from the low sphere which he
is placed in and to occupy in which the glory and the splendor of
the Almighty dims his vision with radiant brightness till he exclaims
aloud Oh Lord God thou has made all things good which should cause
every nation on this wide earth to praise thee forever and ever.

Wm Janney

[On February 22, 1860, Gulielma (Elma) Hunt, daughter of Reuben and Rebecca
Henley Hunt, was buried in Newberry Friends Cemetery in Martinsville, Ohio.
She was Paulena's dear friend and her cousin who was one week younger than
Paulena. She was nineteen years old at the time of her death.]

Memorials to Elma by Paulena

We will never meet thee more Elma
In this world of ours.
For the Spirit clothed in brightness
Joins in the Angel choirs.

Glimpses of the Past

It is a cherished friend that we have loved ever since we were children—together at school, yes come the brightest memories of my
school days are that of a darling friend. Oh, what joyous hours we
spent at school on the long summer noons that were such treats to
us—but that friend is dead now just in the graveyard where we used
to ramble they have laid her down. I have a little package of letters I
treasure more than I can tell for they are her words. I could not realize
that she was dead when I stood and looked upon her as she lay in her
coffin so beautiful yet so white and still. I thought, oh, surely this is
not death—but when I sit down on lonely dark days and read those
tenderly written notes traced either in joy or sadness, I know then
that she is dead—yes, Elma—I will ever treasure them as the dearest
mementos I have of thee.

Oh those precious Olden letters
How I love to look them o'er
For they bring the memory to me
Of the one I'll see no more.
Albone

March 1860

March 1st, 1860
Matt went home today. I was sorry to see her go away for she is very dear to me. Jennie and Call and I went to school this evening.

[March 6, 1860]
Marriage of Mary Jane (Janney) Bailey, widow of David Bailey, to James Fisher

April 1860

[No entries for April]

May 1860

In The Happy Maytime
And a spirit whispers—
Of the long ago
When the fairy vespers
Sighed soft and low.

May 8th, 1860
The rain drops come down this morning with a gentle music that "lulls me into a reverie," I am again a laughing girl bounding over the meadows with a light and buoyant footstep which betokens lightness of heart, abundance of health. Oh I had little thought then of all life had for me, of all the little griefs and the sad ones, I remember how friend after friend was taken away by death or what is equally as bad became estranged forever.

Sixthday, 23rd, 1860 [No month given]
This morning on looking over the "Watchman" I saw a "poem" written for me. It was a kind of parody on the letter I wrote—it is very insulting. I think Amos Hockett is the author of it.

Secondday, 27th, 1860 [No month given]
Lizzie and John were here this morning. Oh! I have lived long enough to know we can trust but few—Jo has been Lizzies friend and Lizzie cares no more for Jo's trouble than a straw—and she made several insinuations I did not like. She said Dave told them last fall he was not going to marry—so much the worse for him—it only makes his sin greater—she said Lib Hockett [Elizabeth Huff was married to Amos Hockett] said she was "thinking glad" he quit when he did—oh how deceitful she is—what will ever become of her for she has no vestige—we may almost say—of truth about her—John, I think is very far of being "sick about it" for he talked worse—if anything than Lizzie.

[Childhood Memory]

I remember a long time ago when I trudged off to school with my little basket upon my arm I felt very happy then for I had in anticipation such grand play at noon up under the old oak tree Oh how pleasantly we wiled all the long summer noon away playing there in forgetfulness of the great world in which we had let to fight our battles and thus we lived on till we were children no more.

[May, 1860, Chicago, Illinois]
The Republican Party nominated Abraham Lincoln and Hannibal Hamlin as its candidates for president and vice president of the United States.

June 1860

[June 18, 1860]
In Baltimore, Maryland, the split among the Democrats made the Republicans' prospects look bright. Stephen Douglas was nominated by what remained of the Democratic convention. The seceders met across town and chose John C. Breckenridge of Kentucky as their nominee. In the meantime, an "old gentlemen's party" of ex-Whigs and Know-Nothings named John Bell of Tennessee to head a Constitutional Union ticket.

July 1860

[July 1, 1860]
Paulena's twentieth birthday]

August, September and October 1860

[No entries]

[31 August, 1860] From *The Clinton Republican*

"Died—Obed Hussey, of Baltimore, the inventor of the celebrated Hussey reaper[73] and mower, lost his life at Exeter, New Hampshire [Maine] on Saturday last [August 4, 1860] by falling between the cars, which ran across his abdomen and was killed instantly." Obed Hussey was a fourth cousin twice removed to Paulena through her Nantucket Bunker line. There were several Hussey family relatives of Obed living in the Clinton and Highland County areas of Ohio.

---

73. "Obed Hussey (1792–1860), working in Baltimore, perfected a device to cut grain—a mechanical reaper—one year before a more developed invention for the same task came from Cyrus McCormick." Source: http://www.americanprofile.com/issues/20010708/20010708ne_1050.asp.

"When *Mechanic Magazine* published an article in April 1834 claiming that Obed Hussey had made a reaper and had acquired a patent on it, McCormick was encouraged to seek his own patent. That was possible because Hussey's reaper varied distinctly from McCormick's. In place of the revolving reel, Hussey's reaper required a man to ride the reaper and to pull the stalks toward the knife with a rake. McCormick's patent was issued on June 21, 1834." Source: http://www.lib.niu.edu/ipo/ihy921213.html.

"The invention of two successful reaping machines—independently by Obed Hussey in Ohio, who obtained the first patent in 1834, and by Cyrus Hall McCormick in Virginia—brought about an end to that tedious handiwork. Further, they apparently encouraged the invention and manufacture of other labor-saving farm implements and machinery: the chilled steel moldboards plow, harrows, seeding drills, corn planters and cultivators, threshing machines, and steam 'traction engines' to pull or propel them." Source: http://www.newton.dep.anl.gov/natbltn/700 799/nb759.htm.

The Hussey and McCormick reapers were exhibited at the New York State Fair in 1851. "It is true, however, that machines designed for reaping grain by horse-power were tried in England fifty years ago, and also at several subsequent periods; but their practical use is of comparatively late origin, the credit, which we are proud to say, belongs to American mechanics. . . . It is known to our readers that two noted American reaping machines, have been introduced into England during the present season, and that to one of these, Mr. McCormick's, the great medal has been awarded at the Industrial Exhibition of all Nations. This machine, as well as that of Mr. Hussey's has been subjected to various trials in England, with results highly satisfactory as to their operation, results which seem to have inspired a conviction that they can be extensively adopted in that country, notwithstanding the comparative cheapness of labor, with profit to the farmer—or at least with profit to the class of farmers who produce grain on a large scale." Source: "Implements from the New York State Fair," *Cultivator,* 1851.

November 1860

Thirdday, November 6th, 1860
The cold relenting winds of winter have come again and it seems very good and pleasant to greet the coming night with bright cheerful fires that cast strange shadows upon the wall and makes brilliant pictures for us to build castles of. Today will decide the great contest—between Lincoln or Douglas—or rather Breckinridge—of who will take the seat in the "White House" on the 4th of March. I do hope Lincoln will. I received a letter from George Paxson, Nellie Weaver, Call, last week and this week I have received two—one from Jennie, one from Matt.

[In the November 6 election, Lincoln received more votes than any of the other three candidates, even though he failed to obtain a majority. His electoral count was 180; Breckenridge in the South received 72; Bell received 39 from the border states; and Douglas received only 12, although his popular vote was second only to Lincoln's.]

[Sometime after the date of November 7, 1860, Paulena wrote to her cousin George Paxson, who is thought to have been living in Leesburg, Loudoun County, Virginia.][74]

Cousin George
I received thy letter—it was just as I was starting to visit Lide Hunt West—for the first time, I had such a pleasant time—she was so glad to hear from thee and bade me send her best friendship to thee. She said she would be so glad for thee to come, come as soon as thee can and I will visit with thee.

If Bell had been elected—we would have congratulated you upon your success for I never heard him spoken of except as an honest man just what Lincoln is, so of course you will congratulate us—The Union is still unserved and I think it will remain so for time indefinite—for all there is much judging about it, there is no danger at all. I am inclined to believe since the "Seventh of November" past away with no deleterious effect. I do not think thee quite understood me in regard to free speech. I did not mean to infer that I believe the northerners possess the right or wished the privilege of interfering

---

74. George Washington Paxson was the son of Samuel and Martha Ellen Wright Paxson. He was a grandson of William Paxson, who was a half-brother to William Betts, the grandfather of Paulena's mother, Priscilla (Betts) Stevens. George had seven children. The youngest was Mary Sue who must be the child Paulena mentions at the close of the letter. George's brother, William, also visited the families in Clinton County.

with the slaves when they go south for I think we have no right at all to meddle with them any way whatever and Old Brown was censured by the Republicans and called a misguided old man for the course he took last winter. What I meant by free speech is a right to our own opinion and for how many innocent people have been murdered and abused just for simply adhering to their principles when questioned! No person ought to deny it. "Yancy" speaks any way he pleases over here and is not molested but just imagine a reverse—yet it is almost invariably said that it is just a certain class in the South who participate in those outrages. They speak of most with respects—I think they are generally more impulsive and warmhearted than the Northerners. An Aunt of mine was in Alabama last winter and she spoke of them being kind. There is just a certain [class] there and here too that cause so much disturbance.

The class here that cause so much disturbance, it would be hard for them to tell whether were Democrats or Republicans—it is those low lifed beings who have no regard for themselves. I do not believe in equality nor do the Republicans as it is stated so often. I hope thee will take everything as kindly as I mean it George, for I think thee a gentleman and I know thee used to be. And so you have a little Un? I know she must be pretty—has she got black eyes? [This may refer to George's daughter, Mary Sue Paxson, who was born on October 22, 1858.]

[On December 20, 1860, South Carolina, rapidly followed by six other Southern states, seceded from the Union in reaction to the election of Abraham Lincoln, who opposed the extension of slavery into western territories.]

Woman's Sphere
[By Paulena Stevens Janney]

I will not get up here to speak of the failings and weak minds of the woman, neither do I think them inferior to man in intellect, but I cannot believe that we should have equal rights with man if it was lawful and we could have the privilege. I do not think it would be the best for us—let us be true woman, noble minded and strong minded to a certain extent—and let us fill truly and as a woman should our sphere alotted, let us read, and inform our selves and not be mere idle and indolent creatures which some of the opposite sex are so ungallant as to denominate us—let us make home the happiest—everything goes to prove that we were intended for a different sphere from man—history tells us of woman noble minded and strong able to combat with any who dare terry that woman is as intellectual as man's spot on earth and in the end we will be satisfied with our work and content that we did not participate in the public political excitement.

Martinsville [Temperance][75] Division No. 67
[By Paulena Stevens Janney]

A great many people have heard of Martinsville Division No. 67—in days gone by it had a place among the flourishing ones of the land—Many moons ago on each succeeding week ladies and gentlemen came forth from their homes to assist each other in the good cause. The erring ones who had been reclaimed were there, and the weak and unstable were there. But there was harmony and friendly feeling for each other a vast amount of good was done. After a time the tempter came, came with the sparkling winecup, and its sweetness proved too strong for some and then the more unpoetical whiskey and sweet cider came and drew many astray, they touched their lips to the sparkling beverage and forgetfulness came over them for a time and no doubt there were truly repentant hearts among them after that and they a rose like men and stood with uncovered heads and folded arms and confessed their fall they were forgiven—for God forgives the erring when his repentant children ask him a right.
The tempter has come again we fear and the tempted have been as strangers. There had been dark nights when there were few—there was still fewer for know you not the wages of sin are death? It is a fearful thing to turn back and make our vows before God to "taste not touch not"—and it must be a wicked thing to break those vows—and a sad thing to pass each day and night knowing we have merited the displeasure of God and yet make atonement.

What I Would Love To Be
[By Paulena Stevens Janney]

In the first place I would love to be a lady. I do not mean one to dress and flirt and dance and every time I was told to go in the kitchen, faint or commit some blunder that our little weak sex, as the gentlemen are pleased to term us, take delight in though I had perhaps better be more explicit for I am not so very fond of going in the kitchen myself yet I never fainted but more often grow very red in the face about the time the stove-fire begins to heat up. But as I was saying I would be a lady. I would have a beautiful home with everything attractive to the sight and I would have music to remind me of the

---

75. "[T]he temperance movement emerged during the first half of the nineteenth century. Temperance advocates formed societies in their communities for mutual support and to promote their campaigns against alcohol." Source: *The Hoosier Genealogist* 44, 3, fall 2004.

Angels for does it not say in the scripture, "Praise God with loud stringed instruments." And I think there is nothing more fit to be compaired to the Angels singing around God's throne, than is delicious music. And I would have books large and splendid volumes to remind me daily that there has been great things accomplished and a great many more yet to be done. I would have flowers the purest of all pure things ever breathing into our souls a gentle minstrelly to cheer us in our daily lives. I would have a home near some wild lone spot—a villa among the mountains where each morning I would gather the dewy mountain flower. And I would be a great woman. I would be a beautiful and fair woman—beautiful as the morning yet gentle as the evening winds. I would be as Beatrice beautiful as an Angel and good to perfection. I would have every thing and every person to love me and obey me and I would rule with no rod of ir, but one of love and at a glance from my eye I could make a pause wheresoever I demanded. And I would be a brave woman, one who would to fear to meet danger but with a fearless and high step march through every dark and narrow way of lie. I would be an artist. I would be as "Rose Bonheur"[76] in one respect not spoil my talent and forget to paint by marrying some one who could not define landscapes from cows or ? pictures from a drove of geese.

Poems
[By Paulena Stevens Janney]

All alone in my room at last
I wonder how far they have traveled now?
They'll be very happy when the night is past
And so would I if I knew but how
How lovely she looked in her wreath and dress!
She is queenlier far than the village girls
Those were roses too in the wreath I guess
Where they made the crimson among her curls

---

76. "Rosa Bonheur, 1822–1899, a French artist, with a passion for animals. The artist received special dispensation from the police to wear trousers and a smock to visit butcher shops and slaughterhouses. It was in these locations that she studied animal anatomy. She also wore her hair short, and rode astride." Source: National Museum of Women in the Arts, The Permanent Collection, http://www.nmwa.org/collection/Profile.asp?LinkID=95.

I am sitting alone in the old house now
And no childish voices sing
To disturb my reverie with their joyous laugh
Or their footsteps merry ring
I wait and watch for their coming still
And weep for they do not come
I will wait in vain for coming light
In the old house sad and lone.

There are little toys gathered away
And dresses but slightly worn
For their owners are sleeping the sleep of death
With their shrouds neath the pillow of stone

So I press the toys to my aching heart
And sadly turn away
How childish tunes and happy thoughts.
Are stealing around me today

Their lowly beds in early spring
With daisies are covered o'er
And the long grass waves

The grass in spring on their lovely beds
And the violet is blooming low
And hearts are weeping in anguish deep
For the sunny head and childish bow

[Letters]

Please to send the *Home Magazine* to the undersigned names, I do not know whether I am entitled to an engraving or not as I do not know whether the getter up of Clubs is considered as one.

Lena Janney
Lena Janney Martinsville Clinton co. Ohio
Mary Hunt
Sallie L. James
Lizzie Vance

Enclosed you will find five dollars for which please send the "Home Magazine" to the following names. I do not know if I am entitled to a premium for so small a number.

                                 Lena Janney

Lena Janney   Martinsville Clinton co. Ohio
Mrs. Lizzie Vance   "   "   "   "
Miss Sallie L. James   "   "   "   "
Miss Mary Hunt   "   "   "   "

New Publications for 1860

The Haunted Homestead by Mrs. E.D.E.N. Southworth

Adela The Octoroon by Hezekiah Lord Hosmer [1765–1814, New York, Follett, Foster & Co., 1860]

Ten Thousand Wonderful Things edited by Edmund Fillingham King, M.A., author of "Life of Newton"

Passing Thoughts on Religion by Elizabeth Sewell

Little Graves
[By Paulena Stevens Janney]

Oh how many little green graves we see when we walk through the church yard. I never see a little grave but I think of the household that has lost its treasure, of how the little toys are gathered up and put away and the empty crib covered and the nursery left all alone, but everything is kept as a sacred memorial of the lost. Every little dress or half worn shoe is cherished and tears are shed over them in secret and they are treasured up to remind us in after years of light footsteps and childish tunes hushed forever.

January 1861

January 8th, 1861
Up stairs Mary sewing Alma reading—my thoughts went back last night when some one spoke of "Bill Winners" and his brother being in town. I remember him as he was long ago with his pant rolled up half way to his knee, one gallow hanging in the wind and his mouth spread wide open. I like him real well and we had many and merry times and little "Othlo" has grown to be a big boy and has forgotten all about me I expect—I want to see them so bad and I must see them before they go. I have not much idea how they will look—for I have them looking like they did years ago. Bill with his good natured face and straw hat. I hope I will like him now.

Editor's Note: The preceding entry was placed on the only empty partial page left in the first journal, and it was the only entry made for the year 1861. It is likely that Paulena did not have another journal to record her thoughts in until 1862. The following calendar of events is not part of Paulena's journal. It has been provided to make it easier for the reader to put previous and later journal entries in perspective.

January 9th, 1861
Will's twenty-sixth birthday.
Mississippi followed South Carolina out of the Union.

January 10th, 1861
Florida seceded.

January 11th, 1861
Alabama seceded.

January 19th, 1861
Georgia seceded.

January 26th, 1861
Louisiana seceded.

January 29th, 1861
Kansas admitted to the Union.

February 1st, 1861
Texas seceded.

February 8th, 1861
The Confederacy had a new constitution.

February 9th, 1861
Election of Mississippi's Jefferson Davis as president of the Confederate States of America, with Alexander H. Stephens of Georgia as vice president. Jefferson Davis was a former soldier, congressman, senator, and secretary of war.

February
At Fort Sumter, South Carolina troops repulsed a supply ship trying to reach federal forces based in the fort. The ship was forced to return to New York, its supplies undelivered. Source: "Timeline of Civil War," http://americancivil-war.com/tl/tl1861.html.

March 4th, 1861
Abraham Lincoln was inaugurated as the sixteenth president of the United States. Sharpshooters were posted at the windows of the Capitol and a flying wedge of artillery was just out of sight. His inaugural address was given to a crowd of 25,000.

April 7th, 1861
Will and Paulena's second wedding anniversary.

April 1861
Attack on Fort Sumter. "When President Lincoln planned to send supplies to Fort Sumter, he alerted the state in advance, in an attempt to avoid hostilities. South Carolina, however, feared a trick. On April 10, 1861, Brig. Gen. Beauregard, in command of the provisional Confederate forces at Charleston, South Carolina, demanded the surrender of the Union garrison of Fort Sumter in Charleston Harbor. The Garrison commander Anderson refused. On April 12, Confederate batteries opened fire on the fort, which was unable to reply effectively. At 2:30 p.m., April 13, Major Anderson surrendered Fort Sumter, evacuating the garrison on the following day.

"The bombardment of Fort Sumter was the opening engagement of the American Civil War. Although there were no casualties during the bombardment, one Union artillerist was killed and three wounded (one mortally) when a cannon exploded prematurely when firing a salute during the evacuation. From 1863 to 1865, the Confederates at Fort Sumter withstood a 22 month siege by Union forces. During this time, most of the fort was reduced to brick rubble. Fort Sumter became a national monument in 1948." Source: "Timeline of the Civil War," http://americancivilwar.com/tl/tl1861.html.

April 15th, 1861
Lincoln called for 75,000 men to be enlisted for ninety days. The precedent for this proclamation went back to Washington's administration, giving "the President power to call the state militia into Federal service whenever the laws were resisted by 'combinations too powerful to be suppressed.'"[77] This was viewed by the Southern states as an act of aggression verging on an invasion.

April 17, 1861
Virginia seceded from the Union.

April 23, 1861
"Many will recall that John Janney[78] was president of the 1861 convention that decided Virginia should leave the Union. An opponent of secession, as was the other Loudoun delegate, John Armistead Carter, Mr. Janney handed his sword to Robert E. Lee and renounced his commission with these words: 'When the Father of his Country made his last will and testament, he gave swords to his favorite nephews with an instruction that they should never be drawn from their scabbards, except in self defense or in defense of the rights and liberties of their Country, and that if drawn for the latter purpose, they should fall with them in their hands, rather than relinquish them.'" *Loudoun Discovered*, vol. 1, p. 47.

John Janney (1798–1872), a Loudoun County attorney, was president of the Virginia convention, which offered Robert E. Lee the position of commander in chief of the military and naval forces of the Commonwealth of Virginia on April 23, 1861. John Janney's speech is reprinted in the *Freeman*, R. E. Lee, 1:466 67, and in the United States Congressional Record, 1967.

---

77. *The American Heritage Picture History of the Civil War*, Bruce Catton, American Heritage Publishing Co., New York, 1982.

78. John Janney (1798–1872) was a first cousin once removed to William Janney, husband of Paulena. John Janney was the son of Elisha and Mary Gibson Janney. Elisha (1761–1827) and Joseph (1749–1829) Janney were brothers and sons of Jacob Janney and Hannah Ingledue. The latter Joseph Janney married Mary Holmes and was William Janney's grandfather, the father of Joseph Janney (1791–1852), who married Elizabeth Russell.

April 1861
With Virginia's secession, Richmond was named the Confederate capital.

May 6, 1861
Arkansas seceded from the Union.

May 20, 1861
North Carolina seceded from the Union.

June 20, 1861
West Virginia was formed. Residents of the western counties of Virginia did not wish to secede along with the rest of the state. This section of Virginia was admitted into the Union as the state of West Virginia.

June 1861
"Four slave states stayed in the Union, despite their acceptance of slavery. Delaware, Kentucky, Maryland, and Missouri did not join the Confederacy. Although divided in their loyalties, a combination of political maneuvering and Union military pressure kept these states from seceding." Source: "Timeline of the Civil War," http://americancivilwar.com/tl/tl1861.html.

July 1, 1861
Paulena's twenty-first birthday

July 4, 1861
"Lincoln's War Message, communicated to Congress as formal government document, 'comprised a history of events, a report of stewardship, a constitutional argument, and an exalted commentary on fundamentals.'" Source: Randall, *Lincoln*, vol. 1, p. 381.

"President reviews state of Union: As of March 4, 1861, functions of government, except for post office, have been suspended in six seceded states; public revenue has been seized by, and large proportion of Federal rifles sent to, these states; many officers of Army and Navy have resigned, and active forces have been sent to scattered posts; an illegal organization, the Confederate States of America, with openly avowed purpose to sever Federal Union, is invoking aid, recognition, and intervention from foreign powers. Inaugural Address declared government's policy was to prevent destruction of Union, that government would exhaust all peaceful means before using stronger ones, would retain public property not already wrested from it, would collect revenue, and in other matters rely on time, discussion, and ballot box. Attack on Fort Sumter, S.C., the Message continues, was designed to drive out visible authority of Federal Union, and has forced on country distinct issue of dissolution or war. To preserve Union, Executive had no choice but to call out war power to resist force; 75,000 militia have been called out, blockade proclaimed, and writ of habeas corpus suspended. Recommends that Congress place at control of government $400 million and 400,000 men. Doctrine that a state may consistently with Constitution withdraw from Union without consent of Union is sophistry. States have neither more nor less power than that reserved to them by Constitution while in Union. Principle of relations of national power to states rights is no other than principle of relation of generality to locality; whatever concerns whole should be entrusted to whole, and whatever concerns state alone should be left exclusively to state. Principle of secession is one of disintegration. Nation purchased lands now forming state of Florida; if latter secedes and gets free of contributing to cost of land, all states may behave in like fashion. Who, then, would pay nation's debts? Executive, after rebellion has been suppressed, will be guided by Constitution and laws as understood and expressed in Inaugural Address. Regrets that duty of employing war power in defense of government has been forced upon him." Sources: *Message to Congress in Special Session*, 4 July 1861; *Collected Works of Abraham Lincoln*, eds. Roy P. Basler, Marion Dolores Pratt, and Lloyd A. Dunlap, vol. 4., Abraham Lincoln Association, Springfield; *Abraham Lincoln*, 1809–1865, New Brunswick, N.J, Rutgers University Press, 1953, pp. 421–41.

"Lincoln adds his name to temperance declaration previously signed by ten Presidents from Madison to Buchanan. Edward C. Delavan, noted temperance worker and lecturer, in letter dated July 4, 1861, writes: 'President Lincoln has recently returned me, signed, the Presidential Temperance Declaration.'" Source: "Temperance Declaration" [c. 4 July 1861], *Collected Works of Abraham Lincoln*, ed. Roy P. Basler, Marion Dolores Pratt, and Lloyd A. Dunlap, vol. 4., Abraham Lincoln Association, Springfield; Abraham Lincoln, 1809–1865, New Brunswick, N.J, Rutgers University Press, 1953, p. 420.

July 5th, 1861
The Battle of Carthage, Jasper County, Missouri. "Early on the morning of July 5, 1861, just hours after President Lincoln formally declared war on the Confederate States of America, Union forces commanded by Colonel Franz Sigel (Third Missouri Infantry) confronted the Missouri State Guard army, under the command of Missouri Governor, Claibourn Fox Jackson, eleven miles north of Carthage, Missouri. The battle ended when the federal forces had been forced southward to Carthage and out of the city. It is considered the first major land battle of the War Between the States." Source: "Battle of Carthage," http://www.geocities.com/battleofcarthage/BOChistory.htm.

"Brig. Gen. Nathaniel Lyon had chased Governor Claiborne Jackson and approximately 4,000 State Militia from the State Capital at Jefferson City and from Boonville, and pursued them. Col. Franz Sigel led another force of about 1,000 into southwest Missouri in search of the governor and his loyal troops. Upon learning that Sigel had encamped at Carthage, on the night of July 4,

Jackson took command of the troops with him and formulated a plan to attack the much smaller Union force. The next morning, Jackson closed up to Sigel, established a battle line on a ridge ten miles north of Carthage, and induced Sigel to attack him. Opening with artillery fire, Sigel closed to the attack. Seeing a large Confederate force, actually unarmed recruits—moving into the woods on his left, he feared that they would turn his flank. He withdrew. The Confederates pursued, but Sigel conducted a successful rearguard action. By evening, Sigel was inside Carthage and under cover of darkness; he retreated to Sarcoxie. The battle had little meaning, but the pro-Southern elements in Missouri, anxious for any good news, championed their first victory." Source: "Carthage, Missouri, American Civil War, July 5, 1861," http://www.americancivilwar. com/statepic/mo/mo002.html. William and Paulena's son, Carl Russell Janney, would one day marry Fannie Kendrick and live in the Kendrick House, where troops had camped just before the first Battle of Carthage. Jasper County, Missouri.

July 21st, 1861
First Battle of Bull Run

August 10th, 1861
Battle of Wilson's Creek, near Springfield, Greene County, Missouri. Union troops fled and Missouri remained in Confederate control.

Paulena's Journal resumes at this point

No other entries were made for the year 1861 except for the following recipes and bits of miscellaneous writing.

Josephine White
I am composed of 14 letters,
my 5, 2, 4 is the name of a distinguished poet
my 10, 11, 12, 5, 3 is what ought to be used for certain people

my 1, 2, 8, 9, 3 is one of law term
my 3, 7, 8 is what we all do

my 6, 7, 8, 9 is the name of a public speaker
My whole the most amiable lady of Martinsville

Mary Alma Stephens
I am composed of 16 letters
My 1, 2, 4, is the name of a beautiful month
My 1, 2, 10 is the name of a friend
My 13, 14, 15, 16 is of great benefit

My 9, 2, 11 is a great a neusance
My 9, 8, 7, is a boys name
My 10, 11, 15, is a number
My 6, 8, 10 is what shoe makers use

Recipes

Custard for Pies

In a pint of new milk, put two or three almonds, a stick of cinnamon piece of lemon peel, sugar: let it simmer till the flavor is extracted, then strain and stir till cold. Beat the yolks of six eggs and mix with the milk then stir the whole over a slow fire till about the thickness of cream.

To Make Salt Meat Fresh

Put a half pound of salt peter into two gallons of boiling water and let the salt meat be put in, let it remain for twelve hours: at the end of that time it will be fresh.

Dessert Biscuits

3/4 pound of flour, 1/4 pound of loaf sugar, the peel of a lemon grated, 1/2 tea cup of cream, two eggs leaving out the whites: roll them out thin.

Almond Cheese Cakes

Boil a pint of new milk—beat three eggs and stir in the milk while boiling. When it boils up, take it from the fire, put in a half a glass of wine, separate the curd from the whey and put to the curd, three eggs, six ounces of powdered sugar beat in together. Mix the whole well together, then form it into small pans lined with [illegible] ornament the top—bake them directly.

Flour Pudding

Into a pint and half of sifted flour stir gradually so that it may not be lumpy, quart of milk, beat seven eggs and put in together with a couple of spoonsful of butter.

Custard Pudding

Stir a quart of milk very gradually into a half a pint of flour—mix it free from lumps and put to it—seven eggs beaten with three table spoons of sugar and half a grated nutmeg. Bake 3/4 of an hour.

Apple Fritters

Take four or five tart mellow apples, pare and cut them into slices and soak them in lemon juice. Make a batter of a quart of milk, a quart of flour, eight eggs, gradually drop the batter by spoonfuls in hot lard having a slice of apple for each fritter.

Prunes

Prunes that are too dry to eat, without stewing, can be made into good pies. Turn enough boiling water on the prunes to cover them, let them stew, till they become plump, add sugar and lemon to taste.

English Stew

Cut the meat in slices, pepper and salt and flour them; lay them in a dish, take a few pickles of any kind or small quantity of pickled cabbage and sprinkle over the meat, then take a tea cup half full of water, add to it a small quantity of vinegar belonging to the pickles, a small quantity of catchup if approved of, any kind of [illegible] stir all together and pour it over the meat—set the meat before the fire in the oven as may be convenient for half an hour before dinner time.

Orange Marmalade

One pound of oranges, half pound of lemons, three quarts of water—boil slowly for two hours, cut all taking out the seeds—to each pound of fruit take two pounds of loaf sugar, one pint of water which the fruit is boiled in—while cutting the fruit into thin slices, pour the water upon the sugar and boil all for half an hour.

Pound Cake

One pound of flour, 3/4 of a pound of butter, 3/4 of a pound of lump sugar, one pound and a half of currants, five eggs, a teaspoon full of yeast and a glass of brandy.

Shrewsberry Cakes

Take a quarter of a pound of butter well worked, mix it with a pound of brown sugar, one egg well beaten as much flour as will make it stiff, roll it out, cut it with a tin mold and bake the cakes in a slow oven.

Paulena's Book List, 1860–1861

Lena Rivers	[Mary Jane Holmes]
Ida May	[Mary Langdon (Mary H. Pike), Phillips, Sampson and Company, Boston, 1854]
Fashion and Famine	[Mrs. Ann S. Stephens, Bunce & Brothers, New York, 1854. Stephens was one of the leading editors and best-selling authors of her day; this is one of her most popular novels. Stephens is best remembered as the author of *Malaeska*, the first Beadle dime novel. Source: *The Nineteenth Century Shop.*]
Tempest and Sunshine	[Mary Jane Holmes]
The Lone Dove	
Homestead On the Hillside	[Mary Jane Holmes]
The Stolen Will	
David Copperfield	[Charles Dickens]
Charlotte Brontë	
Life of Queen Elizabeth	
History of England	
Josephine the Empress	
Twice Married	
Three Brides	
Female Life Among the Mormans	[New York, Derby & Jackson, 1847]
The Lamp Lighter	
The Deserted Wife	[E. D. E. N. Southworth. Many of her novels appeared first in serial form in

	magazines, including the *Saturday Evening Post*. She produced about three novels a year during her working life, many of which were translated into foreign languages. Her novels were still in print in the 1930s.]
Three Eras in Woman's Life	[T. S. Arthur, J. W. Bradley, Philadelphia, 1857]
Gabriel Van His Fortune and His Friends	
Fred	
Uncle Tom's Cabin	[Harriet Beecher Stowe]
Hope on Hope Ever	[Mary Howitt., *Hope on Hope Ever!* or, The Boyhood of Felix Law, New York, A. Appleton, 1852. "This classic romance of 19th century dales life was written after a visit to Dent in 1836 and first published in 1840. The title is taken from a poem by Gerald Massey." Source: *The Lake District*, rare and collectable books, R. F. G. Hollet & Son, Titus Wilson and Son, Kendal, Cumbria, [England].
Miss Paddington	
An Liggommny Letters to Young Ladies	
Danger in the Park	
A Good Time Coming	[T. S. Arthur]
Greatness in Little Things	[Stopford James Ram, pseudonym for Ruth Vernon, Cincinnati, H.M. Rulison, 1855]
History of Hannabal	
Upper Ten and Lower Million	[George Lippard, H.M. Rulison, Cincinnati, 1853]
Fifty Years in Chains	[Charles Ball, H. Dayton, New York, 1860]
May of Burgundy	
Silver Cup of Sparkling Drops	
Ten Leaves	
Fanny Lewis' Portfolio	
Lights and Shadows of Red Life	
The Old Parsonage	
Sunshine of Greystone	

*Loving and Reflecting on
        What Comes of It*
Legends of the West
Three Brides or Love in a Cottage
Twelve Years in Slavery

[*Israel Potter's Twelve Years in Slavery*, Herman Melville. It was first published in serial form in *Putnam's Monthly Magazine* from July 1854 to March 1855. The first American edition was published in March 1855 by G. P. Putnam & Co., New York.
The following is a contemporary book review:
"Mr. Melville's works are unequal, but none of them can be charged with dullness. . .
Among the famous, Benjamin Franklin and Capt. Paul Jones, have a part to play in this veritable history, which is a mixture of fun, gravity, romance and reality very taking from beginning to end.
It will take its place among the best of its predecessors, and may certainly be said to belong to American literature."
—*New Bedford Daily Mercury*, March 12 1855]

The Outcast   Isaac L. Hopper
Annie Clavers
Look Out
Reveries of a Bachelor   [Ik Marvel (Donald G. Mitchell), New York, Charles Scribner, 1851

Peg Woffington   [Charles Reade, Collier, New York]
Alone
Moss Side   [Marion Harland]
The Hidden Path   [Charles Reade]
Never Too Late to Mend   [*It is Never Too Late to Mend*, Charles Reade, Boston, Tichnor and Fields, 1856]
Lavengro   George Borrow, England
Minnie Life   Mrs. Riletie
Bio of Good Wives   L.M. Childs

Hawthorne's Stories
Fortune of Nigle
Live and Let Live
Blanchassed
The Vicar of Wakefield

The Bride of Lamamoor

[Nathaniel Hawthorne]

[Oliver Goldsmith, Philadelphia,
H.C. Peck & Theo. Bliss, 1858]
[*"The Bride of Lammermoor* is an
historical novel by Sir Walter Scott,
set in Scotland in the reign of
Queen Anne. It forms, along with
A Legend of Montrose, the 3rd series
of Scott's Tales of *My Landlord;* the
two novels were published
together in 1819. The story recounts
the tragic love of Edgar, Master of
Ravenswood, with Lucy Ashton,
the daughter of Ravenswood's
enemy Sir William Ashton.
Sir William's wife, Lady Ashton, is
the villain of the piece, haughty
and manipulative; Caleb
Balderstone, an eccentric old
Ravenswood family retainer,
provides some comic relief.
The story is fictional, but was based
(Scott tells us) on an actual incident
in the history of the Stair family.
The novel was taken as the basis
for Donizetti's opera
Lucia di Lammermoor."
Source: *Wikipeida,*
http://en.wikipedia.org/wiki/
The_Bride_of_Lammermoor.
Lucia di Lammermoor was first
performed at the Teatro San Carol,
Naples, Sepetember 26, 1835.
Lucia di Lammermoor, adapted
from a translation by Herbert Gross
man, was performed in English by
Opera Theatre of St. Louis in May
and June 2002, at the Loretto-Hilton
Center. Source: Opera Theatre of St.
Louis Program for the Twenty-
seventh Season, 2002.

Tower of London
Loving and Reaping
Regina
The Earl's Daughters
Mysterious Parchment   [Joel Wakeman, Temp.
                                          Publications, 1858]

Pillar of Fire
Lady of the Lake   [Walter Scott, New York,
                                          Clark & Austin, 1848]

Mother's Recompense   [Grace Aguilar, Leipzig,
                                          Bernhard Tauchnitz, 1859]

Cottage Life

Journal Two

January 12, 1862—July 17, 1863

Paulena Stevens Janney
Twenty-four years old

Photograph by Lot Janney

January 1862

January 12th, 1862

Two weeks of the New Year almost gone and I have left no record—the old year died gently—there was no unusual occurrence in Martinsville at least we all seemed to appreciate the solemnity of its death and so we let it pass away with a stillness quite appropriate. To me it seems no time for such an expression of mirth as we sometimes hail the "New year and bid good bye to the "old"—instead it seems entirely out of place. Let us be cheerful kind and do what we can to make others happy and make a resolution to be better in the year that has just opened to us. When I look back the months of the old year and in fact of all the years of my life I can remember so many instances where I acted very unwise, very foolish and many times very wickedly and I try in vain to recall anything to my credit. I wonder if I ever did anything good or anything worldly [worthy] of the admiration of others. It seems not and if I have any friends I wonder how it happened for I have such a poor opinion of myself. It seems every one else has the same concerning me. I just wish I could go away off where I would with my bundle of sins and mistakes be for a season free and then perhaps when I returned I would be different in some respects.

This is Sabbath. Such a wild strange morning—one moment the sun comes forth bright and radiant cheering up all things and again its brightness is dimmed and clouds dark as night are cast over the sky and the wind is loud—and at last after all the changefulness it has settled down to a wet Sabbath. Just pouring for it "never rains, but it pours." I feel quite dull today have not even put a clean dress on. In fact, I have none I want to put on. I wish I had a new one. I am so tired of my old ones. But I step from the sublime to the ridiculous.

Secondday, January 13th, 1862

A cold morning but seated here by the pleasant fire, I heed not the chilly air without—how thankful we should be for a pleasant home and warm fire. Cal and I are going to enjoy ourselves today in some way. I would be at a great loss for someone to converse with sometimes if it were not for Cal. Only 6 weeks till we start to Richmond [Indiana] if we go. I am terribly afraid I will have a stye or something but "Sufficient for the Day is the Evil Thereof."[79] Alma will be

---

79. Matthew 6:34. "Christ reminded us of the importance of the 'now moment' when He said, 'give us this day our daily bread,' reminding us God will give us the help we need for the problems of each day. He constantly spoke about the fact of worrying over tomorrow's trouble. Christ, in effect, said, you have enough problems to contend with, don't drag the problems of the past or the problems of the future into today's living. When He said, 'sufficient for the day is the evil thereof,' He was saying you have enough to contend with today, forget about yesterday and tomorrow." Source: Rev. Mark Connolly, http://www.spirituality.org/issue30/pg01.html.

surprised to see us for we are not going to tell her when—just when we go.[80] Now I do wonder if I will go to Richmond and come back safe and sound without having done anything to disgrace myself for I am of such a temperament and act so much from impulse that I need someone with me continually to step on my toes when I go to say anything impertinent. Am anxious to see the paper today. I wonder if it is "all quiet on the Potomac."[81] I think it is time our army was accepting something. So many of our troops idle.

---

80. Paulena's younger sister, Alma, was a student at Earlham College by that time. Earlham had become a college in 1859.

81. "The Union catastrophe at First Manassas [Bull Run] was the end of Irvin McDowell's tenure in command. Within a week Lincoln had installed George McClellan, the hero of the West Virginia campaign, to command forces based in Washington. McClellan was a strong organizer, and the situation called for precisely those talents. He brought order out of chaos, got a training program underway, improved the distribution of supplies, organized a staff to support the army in everything from bakeries to post offices. He spent a great deal of time explaining the rudiments of military strategy to amateurs—like the President.

"The Confederates were happy to participate in this quiet period. Their armies needed training, their supply system was even more of a shambles. They too had to equip men, and they had even less material than the Federal Government. Joe Johnston entrenched a long line, with the Potomac on both flanks and the center at Centreville. Johnston's right, on the Potomac, closed the river to Union shipping, a sore point in Washington because the railroads could barely supply the swollen population of the city and the army.

"Being the center of events stroked the worst parts of McClellan's character. He was bolder on paper than in the real world. . . . McClellan came under tremendous pressure to do something aggressive, almost anything. He in turn passed some of the pressure on to some of his subordinates. Charles Stone made the wrong choice in picking the inexperienced Edward Baker to actually command the attack. Baker was well-connected politically—he'd been an Illinois Congressman with Lincoln, had ridden in Lincoln's carriage to the inauguration—but completely green militarily. As a result the battle of Ball's Bluff was a catastrophe for the North. Baker was killed, Stone was politically crucified by the Joint Committee on the Conduct of the War. This was probably the most important result of the battle: it was a tool of the Radical Republicans, which they would use for the rest of the war. Seldom was any measure against the Confederates, military or civilian, strong enough; the Lincoln Administration did very little right in the eyes of the Radicals. On the other hand, the Democrats were even worse, and the Radicals had to save some of their vitriol for them.

"Meanwhile, McClellan was doing, if possible, even less. In December there was a skirmish at Dranesville as Union troops intercepted a Confederate foraging party under JEB Stuart, but it was nothing serious. Along the Potomac, in January 1862, there were some minor efforts to destroy Confederate batteries at Cockpit Point, but they failed. Not all the Confederates were as deliberate as Joe Johnston. Out in the Shenandoah Valley, 'Stonewall' Jackson had been calling for reinforcements so that he could attack. There weren't any spare troops in the Confederacy, but once Robert E. Lee had

Thirdday, January 14th, 1862
It is very cold this morning. I received a letter from Alma yesterday—much longer than usual. I wish I knew whether to go to Richmond or not. Will it be right or not? Mother is here. I am glad of it for I am sick. She is very anxious for me to write to Alma and send her some "chips" for her paper as she requested me to do. I suppose she will think our letters neither few or far between as we write every week. I have another new dress. I do hope I will be a little more respectable in my appearance for a time at least.

Fourthday, January 15th, 1862
Cloudy, dark and perfectly dreary looking. I wrote to Alma last night. I have been thinking of Mrs. Adams this morning. How I would love to see her. I hope the time will come when I will meet her again and little Harry. He was only a little laughing baby. I remember how his bright black eyes would sparkle when pleased or when he heard music. Now if he is living here, so much older and larger, I would not know him at all. Only seven weeks from today till school at Earlham is out. I hope I can have the pleasure of being there. I could enjoy it much better if Will could go but he says that is impossible. I was sick last night and dreamed so many curious dreams, but then I dream every night sick or well. I wish Willie or Elva was here to stay with me today. I would be so glad if I could receive a letter from Matt. Her letters do me so much good. Pretty good news this morning. There has been a battle in Kentucky—Garfields and Marshalls forces. Marshall flies in consternation—Garfield is now occupying Prestonburg. Our loss two killed and 25 wounded. Rebel force 2,500[82] —Cassius

---

been beaten in the West Virginia campaign, some of his men were transferred to Jackson. In the middle of winter Jackson moved. Starting on January 1, 1862, and marching hard, despite inadequate protection against the weather, at first Jackson swept through scattered Union forces. Nobody had expected a campaign in the middle of winter, and the Union troops were dispersed to winter camps, so Jackson's men captured a useful amount of supplies and also damaged the B&O. . . . So the winter of 1861–62 passed in the east. So little happened that the newspapers could sum up the events for their readers with the phrase 'All quiet on the Potomac' which became an accusation of inactivity as well as a report of events." Source: "All Quiet on the Potomac," www.ehistory.com/uscw/features/battles/campaigns/east/0004.cfm.

82. "The largest battle in eastern Kentucky, the Battle of Middle Creek, was fought on the high ridges near Prestonsburg on January 10, 1862. Both sides were evenly matched in this engagement, with forces of about 1500 each. The Confederates were commanded by General Humphrey Marshall, and the Union troops by future President James A. Garfield, who was promoted to Brigadier General after his performance in the battle. Although victory was claimed by both sides after light casualties, a late-night retreat by the Confederate forces left the Union army in control of eastern Kentucky." Source: http://www.thinkwestkentucky.com/civilwar/region4/prestons.

M. Clay[83] is coming home from Russia. Cameron will fill his place. Clay will be Brigadier General I presume such is talked of—says the paper.

Fifthday, Morning January 16th, 1862

The sun is shining brightly this morning but the air is bitter cold. How I pity the poor soldiers for many are doomed to suffer. I think we ought to be thankful for a good home and warm fire without meeting trouble halfway or grieving over little things that cannot be helped, but I cannot help it sometimes.

Sixthday, January 17th, 1862

A pretty day—at home, no letter, no special news in the daily. Will is finishing our wood house today. It will be a greatly improved in appearance when done. Only five weeks after this till we start for Richmond. How glad Alma will be to see us and we her. I can imagine how she will come into the central parlor when we call for her. I will be so glad to go. I said I did not get a letter but I had forgotten I got one from Jennie she did not say a word about meeting me at Earlham—her Mother is at Hunt's and perhaps I will get to see her—Cal has not been in for a day or two—I wonder why? I think Matt had better be writing to me soon.

Seventhday, January 18th, 1862

A dark day. I awoke last night and heard the rain pattering against the window pane. I am always glad to think I have a comfortable home. How many poor persons were drenched last night by the cold rain. If Will was a soldier I would not see a happy moment. How can any person stand it? It would be so awful to me. When I first began my journal I resolved I would write something better or at least try and see if I could not keep a respectable journal, but I am afraid this will prove to be as absurd as any. It is much easier to make good resolutions than to keep them. Tomorrow is Sabbath again. The beginning of another week. [Rev. R. L.] Stillwell preaches his war sermon in the morning and his slavery sermon at night. I hope he will come.

Sabbath, January 19th, 1862

Just the darkest day. The rain came down in torrents all night flooding street and highway. Stillwell did not come to deliver the war sermon this morning and

---

83. Cassius M. Clay was a cousin of Henry Clay. He was a veteran of the Mexican War, governor of Kentucky, and was married to Mary Jane Warfield of Lexington in 1832. He helped create the Republican Party in 1856. He sought the vice presidential nomination in 1860, but lost to Hannibal Hamlin of Maine. Cassius Clay was appointed minister to Russia in 1861, but he delayed his departure to organize a troop of irregulars to help protect Washington, D.C. until regular troops arrived. He was Minister to Russia 1863—1869. Sources: http://www.picturehistory.com/find/p/10597/mcms.html and http://history.sandiego.edu/gen/classes/diplo/cassiusclay.html.

if he had it would have done me little good for it was so muddy. It is still raining, but it suits me very well. I do wish the war was ended. If it is ended without
its effecting us any more than it has yet, I think we should never murmur at
anything let happen what would—for there are so many persons suffering so
much from the war that it seems too good for some others to enjoy home and sit
down in comparative relief while "our Soldiers" are enduring innumerable pri-
vations and for our good more than their own for it all remains with Providence
whether their lives are spared or not among the thousands who are battling for
freedom. One is as likely to fall as another. I have been at home so long I really
am afraid I will get to be real lazy and "greener" than I am now but anyhow I
enjoy home and care little about visiting. I would love to be so I could take a
"journey" once in a while when I get tired with the routine of country life or if
we only lived near the Sea how I would enjoy that . . .

Sitting alone in the twilight
Watching the daylight go
Thinking of scenes that vanished
With the years that past long ago
There are gleeful romps in the meadows
And rides on the hard white snow
And there's many a place I could mention
Where we played so long ago
And a thought goes back to the playhouse
Up under the old oak tree
And I half imagine I'm there again
With my schoolmates glad hearted and free

Secondday, January 20th, 1862
Oh it seems so pleasant this morning almost like spring equally as warm, yet
not so bright. I feel very happy and contented this morning. We have the window open this morning and the mild invigorating air comes in so pure and
fresh—notwithstanding the muddy road and high waters. Stillwell came last
night and delivered a very eloquent sermon from the following text "The word
of God grew and multiplied" [Acts 12:24]. His war and slavery sermons were
deferred until his usual preaching day which is four weeks from yesterday. I
like to hear him so well.

Eva is still here, merry as a bird washing dishes. The weeks are passing
away very quickly. I hope if I go to Richmond it will all be right. Yet I wish I had
some good book to read. It has been a long time since I had new book. Heston
brought in some books to read that are good—A letter from Alma and one from

Clay. He is in Kentucky. He wrote of the scenery as very romantic.[84] Of all the events of today the most startling occurred at Monthly meeting. Mother really was appointed to attend the quarterly meeting to be held at Fairfield this coming week.[85] I must tell Alma. Clay says he is sorry he has not been in a battle yet. [That letter must have been written and sent before the Battle of Middle Creek on January 10th.] He is not coming home till the war is over and I am afraid that will be many months yet.

Thirdday, January 21st, 1862
Cold this morning. There was a light fall of snow last night—very light—indeed. The wind is moaning around the house with its solemn music which almost makes me sad. I heard something last night which made me feel very badly—two soldiers deserted from a camp near Cincinnati [on the] Sabbath and yesterday their captain started in pursuit of them. He passed them—he being aboard the cars and came here and waited till they came up he secured them and took them back on the evening train. It is said one of them will be shot for deserting twice. How badly the poor fellows must feel. They are married men and are from Athens [Ohio]. I must finish Clays letter this morning and he may not remain at Prestonburg long—Night— Carre has been up today. We had a very pleasant time talking of our journey to Richmond. There has been another battle at Somerset between Zollicoffer—I forget how to make Z—and General [George] Thomas' forces. The federals were victorious [Brigadier General Felix Kirk] Zollicoffer killed. Rebel loss said to be 275 over 200 anyhow. The number was more equal than in any battle before 10,000 or near that on each side.[86]

---

84. Henry "Clay" Cowgill was a corporal in Company B, Fortieth Ohio Volunteer Infantry, Union side. From Dyers' Compendium: "40th Regiment Infantry. Organized at Camp Chase, Columbus, Ohio, September to November, and mustered in December 7, 1861. Ordered to Eastern Kentucky December 11, 1861. Attached to 18th Brigade, Army of the Ohio, to March, 1862. Unattached, Army of the Ohio to August, 1862. District of Eastern Kentucky, Dept. of the Ohio, to October, 1862. Service; Garfield's Campaign against Humphrey Marshall December 23, 1861, to January 30, 1862. Advance on Paintsville, Ky., December 31, 1861, to January 7, 1862. Occupation of Paintsville January 8 to February 1. Middle Creek, near Prestonsburg, January 10. Expedition to Pound Gap, Cumberland Mountains, March 14 17. Pound Gap March 16. Moved to Piketon, Ky., and duty there till June 13." Source: *History of Clinton County Ohio*, Beers.

85. Newberry Monthly Meeting Minutes, 1816–1826, transcribed by Amelia W. Herman and Eleanor Swigert, 1936–38, in the Quaker Collection, Wilmington College, Wilmington, Ohio. "Newberry Monthly Meeting of Friends Held 1st 20th 1862: . . . Abigail West, Rebecca Hunt, Priscilla Stephens, & Elizabeth Andrew whom we appoint our representatives therein, to Quarterly Meeting who are to give an account of their attendance at next meeting."

86. "The Battle of Mill Springs is considered one of the most important early battles fought in Kentucky. The event took place approximately one mile south of

Fourthday, January 22nd, 1862
 Breakfast at seven. Buckwheat cakes and coffee. The clouds still hang heavy and leaden passing halfway between rain and snow. Sometimes a few stray flakes will find their way from the far off clouds, then pausing just as the few have reached the ground. I must write to Alma this morning. She says they are through arithmetic, only six weeks more from today. I could not sleep very well last night. So I built air castles. I resolved in my mind that if I ever have the opportunity of so doing I will open an infant school. That is, I would collect all the "poor" children I could find ranging from the eight year old and teach them all in my power. I could just see the schoolroom filled with the curly heads, red heads and black ones and all color of eyes to correspond. Nothing would afford me more pleasure, even were I rich as Crassus.[87] I would enjoy myself in that manner.

Fifthday, January 23rd, 1862
I wonder if any person will come I want to see today. It is still cloudy this morning. Neither snowing or raining. Eva and I are going down home this morning.

Sixthday, Morning January 24th, 1862
The sun is shining this morning. Mother and father are going to Leesburg today and we have to go down and stay with the children. I wish I could get a letter or something. Everything seems dull, but I suppose we should be contented with anything such times as we are having now. The most perilous which ever befell our country. It seems hard to bring myself to believe war is right for us. Seems so dreadful to think of the many souls hurried into Eternity without a moments preparation. Souls full of guilt. It is truly horrible, but how we are to avoid it, I know not. Only four weeks after this till we start to Richmond.

Seventhday, January 25th, 1862 [At her parents' home]
Willie, Eva and myself have had a very nice time. Frederic seems ready to take our heads off, but we never mind him. He speaks very cross to the children. I

Nancy on January 19, 1862. The battle (also known as the Battle for Logan's Crossroads, the Battle of Fishing Creek, and the Battle of Somerset [Pulaski County]) was a decisive Union victory. The battle site is located on KY 235 just south of Nancy." Source: http://www.thinkwestkentucky.com/civilwar/region4/nancy.htm.

"Union Brig. Gen. George Thomas received orders to drive the Rebels across the Cumberland River and break up Maj. Gen. George B. Crittenden's army. He left Lebanon and slowly marched through rain-soaked country, arriving at Logan's Crossroads on January 17, where he waited for Brig. Gen. A. Schoepf's troops from Somerset to join him." Source: http://americancivilwar.com/statepic/ky/ky006.html.

87. Publius Licinius Crassus, d. 87 B.C., was Roman consul in 97 B.C. He was the financial backer of the Roman colony of Narbo (modern Narbonne) in Gaul [France].

don't like it. Will went for my net which Alma sent by Emma. It is not finished. He stayed so long I was real uneasy and doubted whether I would ever see him again or not, but after all my foolishness, he came at last. We have made new arrangements in Mother's room, but I expect she will change again when she comes. We received a letter from Alma today. She says she is discouraged. I am afraid she is sick.

Sabbath, January 26th, 1862

Such a bright morning the birds singing merrily and the sun shining like spring. Will went to church. Heston came home with him from meeting. I mean just before we had dinner ready John[88] brought up some chicken and dumplings and we had them for dinner in the evening. Just as Heston was about starting Willie said if I had not told grandfather Heston was here they would not have sent that chicken. I never was plagued much worse. I just cried and cried and two more events—I had written two letters to Alma today. The first one Elva spilt the ink. Over the last Willie upset the ink. Tonight I went in the other room and wept again for I was so disappointed and it was all the paper I could find. Elva and Willie came in and looked on in amazement. At last Willie said "I didn't know 'Pleny' would cry. I thought she was too big." It sounded so funny I could not keep from laughing and I kissed Willie and he cried then and said he was so sorry. I did not feel anger with him, but I felt so 'outed' I could not help it. I never will forget how funny Willie said that.

Secondday, January 27th, 1862

Mother and father did not come in the morning train as we expected, but at three o'clock. The snow flakes came down beautifully awhile today, but it has changed to rain. No new book. I wish I had *Cecil Dreeme*[89] a novel written by

---

88. The John referred to here was probably John Roberts, listed in the 1860 census in the household of Evan Stevens as a laborer, age sixty-one, born in Prussia.

89. "Theodore Winthrop studied law and was admitted to the bar in 1855. His first position as a lawyer took him to St. Louis, but because of ill health, he returned to New York to practice. Winthrop began to write essays, stories, and novels. During this period, Winthrop, along with many artists, writers, and intellectuals, lived in the NYU University Building that provides the backdrop for *Cecil Dreeme,* his gothic novel about sexual ambiguity that is set in and around Washington Square and NYU. A frequent visitor to his friend Frederic Church, the noted Hudson River School painter, Winthrop came to know the intricate details of art history, painting, and bohemian culture, which also play a central role in the novel *Cecil Dreeme* (Boston: Ticknor and Fields, 1862). Two extra-textual features of this novel are important for placing it in context: 1) it was published by Ticknor and Fields, one of the most important literary publishers of the day, a publisher known for high quality American literature; and 2) the text was incredibly popular, running through several editions in the first year. . . . The text, with its combination of New York scenes, gothic tropes, metaphorical use of Greek history

Theodore Winthrop. He was killed in the Battle of By Bethel. His last piece in the *Atlantic Monthly* was so good. I am sorry he was singled out by the deadly bullet of the enemy for he was a good writer and no doubt his name would have become a name familiar in the "literary world" had his life been spared.

Thirdday, January 28th, 1862
We came up home this morning. I rode Cola. It seems a wonder how I managed to stick for I am not an expert or graceful rider and the muddy roads do any-thing but add to the pleasure of "horse back riding." I propose putting a letter in Colas name T for Flora Temple. The rebels chronicle "our" defeat of Humphry Marshall as a "brilliant victory" on their side quite mistaken. *John Brent* is the title of another novel just out by Major Winthrope. I would like to have it.

Fourthday, Morning January 29th, 1862
How quickly the days go by this month. What a dark morning it is. The rain coming down in showers and although dark the air is warm and it seems genial as a rainy morning in spring. Perhaps I will get a letter from Clay soon and one from Mary. I fed Cola T salt from my hand last evening, but I was fearful she would like the salt better than me and so far forget my kindness as to bite my hand and so sprinkled some of it on the sill for her. I am in hopes Cal will be heroine enough to brave the rain and mind to come up. I do hope she will. The day passes so quickly when she is here.

Fifthday, January 30th, 1862
The wind is moaning round the house this morning and makes me sad. I went out to see Will brush Cola T. this morning. She is becoming quite affectionate. I hope she will remain as gentle as she now is. It snowed more last night, but the ground was so soft there is no chance of a sleigh ride this time. I hope we will get to take buggy rides this summer if nothing happens.

Sixthday, January 31st, 1862
The last day of January. How fleeting roll the years away. I remember when a month seemed a long time away, but now the months glide away almost before we have become accustomed to the name. How anxious we are for the time to pass away ever looking to the future for the realization of some pleasure or anticipated wish and yet every day which passes bears us nearer the grave. I fear we do not improve the passing moments as we ought. I made a great many good resolutions, but I lack firmness in keeping them and let little trivial things

---

and mythology, gender confusion, and sexual ambiguity, provides a glimpse into the American vision of same-sex sexuality before the definition of homosexuality." Source: www.nyu.edu/library/bobst/collections/exhibits/bobst/washsq/voices/volumes/cdreeme/html/CD_int.

cause me to become as bad as ever and then how much unhappiness does it cause me.

I feel like I wanted to hear music. How can any person so little appreciate the power of music! I hope the time will soon come when the evening song will be heard in every household. The children with their bird voices and older, all join in singing and then we will have happier homes and better children. Dear children to love home. It is a peculiarity of all our natures to crave a time of amusement. We like to have some incentive to urge us along with our work. How much more eagerly the children stand at school when they have recess. It is an incentive to them and they study hard that they may play hard and as we all need some recreation why not let that be something of beneficial as well as pleasant and amusing. Some person can endure to see the children holler—scream—and do everything but sing. I think it will be along time before some people become civilized.

February 1862

Seventhday February 1st, 1862
The day has passed quickly away. The coming shadows are beginning to gather on the first day of February. Just one year ago and they were gathering thus "year after year the cowslips fill the meadow, year after year the skylark thrill the air, year after year rolls the world round, love, and finds us as we were, year after year the shadows come at evening, year after year the star lights up the sky, year after year through the darkness and the sunlight rolls the world round and finds us as we were."[90] I think L. A. Hine is to lecture here this evening—

---

90. At first glance it appears that Paulena is quoting the poem "Year After Year, A Love Song," by Dinah Mulock Craik (1826–1887) in 1860. The wording is not quite the same. It is possible that Paulena composed her own version after the first few lines. The poem may have appeared anonymously in *Chamber's Journal*, perhaps in the version Paulena quotes. Source: *Victorian Women Writers Project: An Electronic Collection*, Library of Indiana University, Bloomington, 1996. http://www.indiana.edu/~letrs/vwwp/ craik/craik poem1866.html.

> YEAR after year the cowslips fill the meadow, / Year after year the sky-larks thrill the air, / Year after year, in sunshine or in shadow, / Rolls the world round, love, and finds us as we were.
>
> Year after year, as sure as birds' returning, / Or field-flowers' blossoming above the wintry mould, / Year after year, in work, or mirth, or mourning, / Love we with love's own youth, that never can grow old.
>
> Sweetheart and ladye-love, queen of boyish passion, / Strong hope of manhood, content of age began; /Loved in a hundred ways, each in a different fashion, / Yet loved supremely, solely, as we never love but one.

speak rather. This evening he will take up the continuing thread of the subject he introduced in his previous lecture which he delivered on Sixth day night. He calls it a war subject, but it embraces more. He begins at the fundamental rules. I have almost my net. [Paulena is referring to netting for her hat. See photograph of Paulena at the beginning of Journal Three.] I think it is real pretty.

Sabbath, February 2nd, 1862
Went to church this morning. Mother and father took dinner with us. It is very cold but the sun is shining very bright. I will be glad when spring comes though time is flitting away so rapidly and it will be gone forever when it is gone and we know not "what a day will bring forth" So we should learn to appreciate the present. Only three more weeks and then "On to Richmond" if it is right to go. I must answer Alma's letter this evening.

Secondday, February 3rd, 1862
The ground is covered with snow this morning and the wind sounds lonely, but the little snow birds are twilling about and trying with their songs to bring the sunshine back. I am so busy. George Paxton [Paxson] and Cal were here for dinner. He is going to Virginia as soon as he can go—no letter today. Clay has had time to answer my letter, but then he has no chance to write.

Thirdday, February 4th, 1862
The sun has been shining beautifully all day and the birds seemed joyous as spring. Cal was up here this evening. It seems odd to miss her daily visits. Elva is up here and has been all week.

Fourthday, February 5th, 1862
Such a bright morning. Almost like spring only cooler. How glad I will be when spring comes again with the bright flowers and green trees and everything full of beauty. Lib is going to help me.

Fifthday, February 6th, 1862
It is dark this morning, not nearly as bright as yesterday and the birds not so exhuberent.

Dearest and bonniest! though blanched those curling tresses, / Though loose clings the wedding-ring to that thin hand of thine,— / Brightest of all eyes the eye that love expresses! / Sweetest of all lips the lips long since kissed mine!

So let the world go round with all its sighs and sinning, / Its mad shout o'er fancied bliss, its howl o'er pleasures past: / That which it calls love's end to us was love's beginning:—/ I clasp my arms about thy neck and love thee to the last.

Sixthday, February 7th, 1862
Clay came home this morning and he is sick. I did not get to see him. I am very anxious. I hope he will be well soon. I went home this morning and tonight Will took Cola T. down for me to ride. She was very gentle. We have great times with Cola T. tonight. Will forgot to water her and I had the kindness to go myself, after dark too, and give her a "drink of cold water." Alma is appointed to read an essay the last morning. I received a letter from her this evening. Steve called tonight. I never in my "life" felt so well contented with everything and so evenly happy as I have this winter. I think I will never forget myself and get in my old habit of the blues again, but my health is much better than usual this winter and I think any person is happier that is healthy. They can put a brighter look on things already bright and find a bright side to things really dark. If they will, though, of course the temperament has much to do with that.

Seventhday, February 8th, 1862
The victory of yesterday is confirmed today. Fort Henry is in the United States now.[91] Heston took dinner here today. We had some nice music. Mother came up this evening "Saturday Night." I always love it and more especially do I welcome it now for each one brings the time nearer when we shall see Alma—only two weeks from Fourthday till we go if we go. I have not heard from Clay yet. I do hope his is better.

Sabbath, February 9th, 1862
Bright and beautiful this morning the birds jubilant the air was not quite so cool it would be as bright as spring. Cal and I went to church and Will stayed at home and had a good fire. I wrote to Mary. Steve was here for dinner. Cal and I went to see Lide West. I am afraid she will never be any better than she is. I had no idea she was so sick and looking so frail as she does.

Secondday, February 10th, 1862
Cal and I went home today. Mother had a good dinner. Grandmother was there. The paper says there is a battle in progress at "Roanoke" Gen Burnside. I have not seen Clay yet. I am so anxious. It was cold today. How glad I will be when the winds of winter subside into the pleasant breeze of spring and the green grass come again where now nothing but the cold frozen ground we see.

---

91. "On February 6th 1862, Union soldiers under General Grant attacked Fort Henry on the Tennessee River. The Fort quickly surrendered after a bombardment from Union ships. Federal troops soon surrounded the fort and made the Confederate position untenable, forcing their surrender. Thus, both the Tennessee and Cumberland Rivers were now open to the Union, and the North had a new hero General Grant." Source: History Central, "Capture of Ft. Henry and Ft. Donelson," http://www.multied.com/CivilWar/FTHenry.html.

Thirdday, February 11th, 1862
Company today. Mary Birdsall. We had a pleasant time. I knew yesterday she was coming so I could be with her most of the time. I had so much rather know when I am going to have company. Our paper came today for the last time, unless we subscribe again, which we surely will do for one night as we'll be out of the world as out of news such times as the present. The paper has a very complimentary piece concerning Gen. Burnside. I hope he is worthy of all that is said of him. He is very tender of his soldiers, considered too much so by some, to accomplish much, but I think it rather a good trait than bad. It has snowed and blowed a perfect hurricane part of today, but this evening the sun shone out as though all had been calm as summer. We hear Clay is very bad. I do hope he will get better.

Fourthday, February 12th, 1862
Just two weeks from this morning we will be on our way to Richmond if no unseen event comes to disappoint us. I hope there will not but "We know not what a day will bring forth." I wish Mother would come up today or Cal or some person. When I have company one day it spoils it for the next day. I want some one again to talk to. Night, Mother was in for today. Willie and Elva stayed at Uncle Williams. We went out shopping this evening and Oh, such dismal muddy streets. Just gives me the blues almost. When I go out and see what a dirty little place we do live in. I feel very well contented with our little home and think there is none pleasanter. The news came this morning that our forces have come off victorious at Roanoke. Will has gone to hear the evening news. Here he comes. What is the news, Will? "Two thousand prisoners and 300 killed." Well it is awful to think of so many poor fellows being sent into Eternity unprepared. Our loss from rebel accounts to 4000 killed, but doubtful—yet there must have been many, many killed. It has been a terrible battle.[92] How thankful I am that I have no friends there.

Fifthday, February 13th, 1862
This morning the sun shone bright and the air mild and genial as spring, but now it is all changed and the snow is falling fast. I was at Whites this evening. It had been so long since I was there. Lyd was very busy making a pink dress.

---

92. "On February 7, Brig. Gen. Ambrose E. Burnside landed 7,500 men on the southwestern side of Roanoke Island [on the North Carolina coast] in an amphibious operation launched from Fort Monroe. The next morning, supported by gunboats, the Federals assaulted the Confederate forts on the narrow waist of the island, driving back and out-maneuvering Brig. Gen. Henry Wises outnumbered command. After losing less than 100 men, the Confederate commander on the field, Col. H.M. Shaw, surrendered about 2,500 soldiers and 32 guns. Burnside had secured an important outpost on the Atlantic Coast, tightening the blockade." Casualties [dead, injured, or missing] estimated: 2,907. Source: American Heritage Preservation Services, CWSAC Battle Summaries, Roanoke Island, http://www.cr.nps.gov/hps/abpp/battles/nc002.htm.

The sleeves are faced with pink silk and trimmed in buttons. It looks real pretty. Will was to see Clay this evening. He is better some. "George Train" has made another grand speech in England on American Affairs. I think he is such a good speaker. Alma is very anxious for me to go to Richmond sooner than I expected, but it will be impossible for me to go sooner. Stillwell will be here on Sabbath. I hope I can go to hear him. Someplace "Train" says "Even as I speak I think I hear booming over the ocean, the sweet music of the Union cannon playing the requiem of death to treason."

Sixthday, February 14th, 1862
Bitter, bitter cold and the ground covered with snow. How many poor soldiers will suffer tonight far away from their warm fireside braving a thousand miseries for us. Clay was no better they said.

Seventhday, February 15th, 1862
Such a cold morning and I am so lazy. The *Gazette* contains a fuller account of the battle at Roanoke. The Federals came off victorious. We are taking the *Gazette* now. There is some poetry this morning. It begins:

> Oh the murmur, haunting murmur,
> Ever sounding in my ears.
> Down the stream of life eternal,
> Through the boundless sweep of years.

Stillwell came this morning so there is some prospect of hearing a good sermon. Perhaps Will will go out to see Clay this evening. If he does I must get Cal to go to stay with me. In one of the books Jeff brought there is such a good piece of poetry. I have heard it before but the beautiful never grows old. It begins:

> Over the river they beckon me
> Loved ones who crossed to the further side.
> The gleam of their snowy robes I see,
> But their voices are lost in the rushing tide.
>
> Over the river the boatman hale
> Carried another—the household pet
> Her brown curls waved in the gentle gale.
> Darling Minnie. I see her yet.
>
> N. A. W. Priest

Sabbath, February 16th, 1862
Bright Sabbath morning again. It seems just a little time since last Sabbath. Will has not yet come home. Cal and I met with no adventure last night. Stillwell preached a good sermon from the text "God will preserve them that love him, but all the wicked will be destroyed."[93] Oh! this is such a bright morning. Very cold though. I will be so glad when spring comes again. I used to welcome the spring time eagerly for its "Halcyon Days"[94] were past away merrily in playhouses in the green wood or in some pleasant place where undisturbed we could erect our wonderful little stoves that did such good service in the way of baking our cakes. I wish Will would come. I hope Cola T has not done so badly as let him fall. Went to hear Stillwell this morning and tonight. His text tonight was "Proclaim liberty in all the land and to all the inhabitants thereof" [Leviticus 137]. Jeff was here this afternoon and played and sung. I felt so discouraged when I came from church this morning the tears fell thick and fast for a time and then I felt much happier.

Secondday, February 17th, 1862
George [Paxton/Paxson] came to bid us goodbye this morning. I felt real sorry to see him go. He expects to go to Maryland if prudent for him to do so. He is going home to Virginia. A dark looking morning. Cloudy and drizzling. I have been so fortunate as to pick up a little girl but as I have no class I will have to return her. It is Jennie. Her mother is sick and I brought her over. It sounds odd to hear a childish voice in our house. I feel so idle this morning. There is a great battle at Ft. Donelson. Perhaps decided before this time as it has been in progress two or three days. Our armies seem to be aroused from the lethargy which has seemed for so long a time to possess them but perhaps they knew why they were so idle. But there are so many traitors in our army. Gen . . . has been sent to Ft. Lafayette for treason. It is said while in command he held stated interviews with the enemy. Ft. Donelson taken—the evening paper says. There is great loss on both sides. Generals Buckner, Pillow and Johnson are said to be in the Ft. 15,000 prisoners taken.[95]

---

93. Psalms 145:20 reads: "The Lord preserveth all them that love him: but all the wicked will be destroyed."

94. "Alcyone, in Greek mythology, daughter of Aeolus and wife of Ceyx. When her husband drowned, Halcyone threw herself into the sea. Out of pity the gods changed the pair into kingfishers or halcyons, and Zeus forbade the winds to blow seven days before and after the winter solstice, the breeding season of the halcyon. The expression "alcyone days" comes from this myth and figuratively means a time of peace and tranquility." Source: *The Columbia Encyclopedia,* 6th ed., Columbia University Press, 2004.

95. "(Feb. 11–16, 1862) Fort Donelson Union gunboats led by flag Officer Andrew H. Foote captured Fort Henry on the Tennessee River, and 27,000 troops led by Ulysses

Thirdday, February, 18th, 1862
Such a lovely morning like spring. It gladens my heart to think spring is coming so quickly. Sweet spring is ever dear to my heart. Ft. Donelson is surely taken. The loss was heavy on both sides. [Casualties numbered 19,455, the tenth-greatest loss of life in the war.] There were 25,000 men in the Fort. Lloyd and Pillow escaped with four Regiments the night before the capitulation. The rebels denounced Lloyd as a blackhearted coward. I was down to see Lid this evening. There are so many persons in town suffering for clothes and vituals. I think if the poor increase and the rich remain as sparse as now, the whole town will be turned into an asylum.

S. Grant captured Fort Donelson on the Cumberland, opening both rivers for Union offenses deep into Rebel Territory." Source: *Battles of the Civil War,* Supplement to the *National Geographic,* April 2005.

"Begun in the East, the war was spreading to the West, even beyond the Mississippi where the fate of the important border state of Missouri and the chief city of the West, St. Louis, hung in the balance between slaveholding and non-slaveholding elements. This, from the days of the Kansas-Nebraska troubles in the fifties, had been 'dark and bloody ground.' Both sides claimed Missouri and both sides needed her. In August 1861, a Union army was defeated at Wilson's Creek in southwestern Missouri and the casualties amounted to over 23 per cent of all engaged, among them the stalwart Unionist General Nathaniel Lyon. The following March came the Battle of Pea Ridge in northwestern Arkansas. This was the first clear and decisive victory gained by the North in a pitched battle west of the Mississippi River, and until 1864 the last effort of the South to carry the war into Missouri except by abortive raids. More importantly perhaps, its result made it possible for veterans of a long series of minor engagements west of the Mississippi to reinforce the armies in the mid South under Buell, Rosecrans, Sherman, and Grant.

"In this area the object of the Federal armies was, of course, to cut the Confederacy in half by clearing the Mississippi from St. Louis all the way to the Gulf and to stab at the heart of the Confederacy via the Tennessee and Cumberland rivers. If successful, these maneuvers would cut Texas off from the main body of the South, hold Kentucky firmly in the Union, and make it difficult for Tennessee to cooperate with her sister states.

"In February 1862, Fort Henry, commanding the Tennessee River, was captured with support from gunboats on the river by a taciturn, rumpled, cigar smoking (some said whisky-drinking) character named Ulysses Simpson Grant of Illinois. Ten days later, Fort Donelson, eleven miles away on the Cumberland River and a very much stronger position for the Confederates, followed suit. The North was beside itself, reveling in the victory and in Grant's memorable answer to Buckner, the Confederate commander who had asked for terms. 'No terms except unconditional and immediate surrender can be accepted,' said Grant. 'I propose to move immediately upon your works.' Apparently Mr. Lincoln had at last found a fighting general in Unconditional Surrender Grant." Source: *Battle of Fort Donelson* (February 13–16, 1862), http://www.civilwarhome.com/donelson.htm.

Fourthday, February 19th, 1862
Stormy—the rain and sleet coming down with great violence. Cal braved the storm and came up. The poor soldiers. What a dreadful time it is for them especially those who have to march for their orders would not be reversed for rain or sleet. I am so anxious for the war to close. There is so much suffering all over the land and more still to come. How many homes have been desolated and wrecked of all happiness by this cruel cruel war and the poor wretches who have been sent into Eternity unprepared is almost too terrible to think of. How difficult it must be to fix the mind upon death when in the midst of battle, yet I think there are many fall who have thought of dying before the stern realities came upon them and if those persons felt confident they were doing their duty, it is not so dreadful to think of their doom.

Fifthday, February 20th, 1862
The trees are bending beneath their weight of ice and everything seems to have a shadow over it. I never remember to have seen such a sleet as we had yesterday. The news is still favorable from Europe. I do hope it will continue so. Going down home this evening.

Sixthday, February 21st, 1862
I received a letter from Matt. It was good and came first when I was not expecting it. I rode Cola T. up this evening, but it was not very pleasant riding. The road so dreadful bad and I was afraid she would get her feet hurt. Steve came in this evening. Clarksville "Tenn" is said to be occupied by our troops. All things look encouraging now, but how long they will remain so no one can tell.

Seventhday, February 22nd, 1862
The anniversary of Washington's birthday. There will be an interesting time in the city today. Jesse Coffin was here for dinner. He is going home Secondday. [Jesse Coffin was married to Emily Janney, sister of William, and they lived in Richmond, Indiana]. Jeff came tonight. I am going to learn "Unfurl Your Banners"[96] if I can. President Lincoln's son is dead.[97] Oh, if the war would only

---

96. This may refer to a portion of text from Isaiah 10:11: "In that day the Root of Jesse will stand as a banner for the peoples; the nations will rally to Him, and His place of rest will be glorious."

"Unfurl Your banner, mighty King! Blast Your trumpet Lord! Show Yourself, so we may rally to You. For with You alone can we make a stand. Look on us. Have mercy and send out Your call. Then we will dare to leave our hiding places. Stand above Your beloved elected people and gather us to fight with courage." Source: http://ecn.ab.ca/ salttalk/dev_mar.htm++%22Unfurl+Your+Banner%22&hl=en&lr=&strip=1.

97. "William Wallace Lincoln ("Willie") was born on December 21, 1850. He was the third son of Abraham and Mary Todd Lincoln. Willie was named after Dr. William Wallace who had married Frances, one of Mary Todd's sisters. Willie was more like his

end, but if the rebellion is dashed and liberty and peace is abroad once more it will not restore those who have fallen in battle or languished or died in the hospital. It cannot fill the void that has been left in many a household. Yet the

---

dad than older brother Robert; he had the same magnetic personality of Abraham Lincoln. A 16 year old girl, Julia Taft, described Willie as 'the most lovable boy I ever knew, bright, sensible, sweet-tempered and gentle-mannered.' "In Springfield, Willie attended a private school operated by Miss Corcoran. Like his folks, Willie loved learning. Willie developed lots of interests including writing poetry and drawing up railroad timetables. He had excellent natural ability in math. Additionally, Mary Todd said Willie was 'a most peculiarly religious child.' He was more studious than his younger brother, Tad.

"The Lincolns moved into the White House in March of 1861. Willie and Tad had a great time in their new home. Willie was calmer and more conscientious than his younger brother. The boys loved animals, and gifts of dogs, rabbits, goats, and ponies poured into the White House. Because of the times, war-related games were popular with the boys, and they even constructed a fort on the White House roof. Willie and Tad often accompanied their father when he reviewed the troops in their camps. Additionally, they went with their mother when she took fruit, books, papers, etc. to the soldiers.

"Horatio Nelson Taft, Jr. ("Bud") and Halsey Cook Taft ("Holly") were close friends and playmates of the Lincoln boys in 1861 and early 1862. Mrs. Lincoln hired a tutor for the boys. Willie's mind was amazingly mature for his age. Whereas Tad seems to have disliked the lessons, Willie loved learning. Just before Christmas, 1861, Willie turned 11. His future seemed extremely bright. Shortly thereafter Willie became ill. His condition fluctuated from day to day. Most likely the illness was typhoid fever. Gradually Willie weakened. Both parents spent much time at his bedside. Finally, on Thursday, February 20, 1862, at 5:00 P.M. the young boy passed away. Abraham said, 'My poor boy. He was too good for this earth. God has called him home. I know that he is much better off in heaven, but then we loved him so. It is hard, hard to have him die!' Willie lay in state in the Green Room adjoining the East Room. . . . The funeral took place in the East Room on Monday, February 24. The services were conducted by Reverend Phineas D. Gurley of Washington's New York Avenue Presbyterian Church.

"Willie was buried in Oak Hill Cemetery in Georgetown. After the assassination of Lincoln in 1865, Willie's casket was exhumed, and his remains placed on the Lincoln funeral train which traveled back to Springfield. Willie's remains were placed in the public receiving vault at Oak Ridge Cemetery along with his father on May 4, 1865. On December 21, 1865, the remains were moved to a temporary tomb. On September 19, 1871, the remains of Abraham, Eddie, and Willie were moved to the permanent tomb." Source: Mary Todd Lincoln Research Site, http://home.att.net/~rjnorton/Lincoln68.html.

See also: *Mary: A Biography of the Girl Who Married Abraham Lincoln* by Ruth Painter Randall; *Lincoln's Sons* by Ruth Painter Randall; *Mary Todd Lincoln: A Biography* by Jean H. Baker; and *Twenty Days* by Dorothy Meserve Kunhardt and Philip B. Kunhardt Jr. Although the main focus of John D. Weaver's *Tad Lincoln: Mischief Maker in the White House* is Tad, the book also contains lots of information about Willie. The same is true for Julia Taft Bayne's *Tad Lincoln's Father*. Source: http://home.att.net/~rjnorton/Lincoln68.html.

remembrance that their efforts have assisted in restoring the government will be laurels on their memory.

Sabbath, February 23rd, 1862
A beautiful Sabbath morning. The air mild and pure. The birds musical in their joy and a spring feeling seems to pervade everything. I had a pleasant ride over the meadow early. Cola T and myself scoured the meadow. Our meadow with it's little brook and ravine.[98] Oh, it did seem so sweet. Will kept at a little distance in case of emergency. The sun is so bright and as warm as spring. How glad I will be when spring comes.

Secondday, February 24th, 1862
The dawn up wild and stormy, but this evening has been bright and cold. Lydia was here and Cal awhile. President Lincoln's youngest son is dangerously ill and Jessie Fremont.

Thirdday, February 25th, 1862
We received a letter from Alma. She does not know how to get everything home.

Parlor of Earlham College, 1860

Fourthday, February 26, 1862
[Traveled to Richmond, Indiana]
Morning up early I am in such a hurry I fear I will look shabby. I felt much better than I did yesterday. Oh such an awful time as I had with my dress last night. It just seemed like I never would get it done or go to bed either, but at last the wearisome task was completed and my tired eyes were closed for a season. I hope we will meet with no accident. I hate to leave Will so badly. It has been raining, but it has passed away and I hear a sweet little bird singing so beautiful. Arrived safe at Richmond—Coffins [Jesse and Emily (Janney) Coffin] came for me.[99]

---

98. This description seems to fit a piece of property they may have been renting from Paulena's uncle William Betts and which they later bought. At present, the land has a sloping meadow with what appears to be a creek near a row of trees. Deed transaction follows:

Deed Book 9, Page 473
"February 16, 1865 William S. and Anna Betts to William Janney for $255 being a part of David Bradford's survey No. 2391 beginning at Lot #49 in the town of Martinsville and SW corner of Amos Hiatt's lot of land to James Wright's line in all about 2 1/2 acres."

99. "1857 City Directory of Richmond Indiana, Jesse Coffin, merchant residence

Fifthday, February 27th, 1862
[Richmond, Indiana]
After my return Cal and I started for Earlham. Pretty soon the road was smooth and we soon arrived. Ran up the steps, rang the bell and were ushered into the parlor. Alma was called for and soon made her appearance and in great haste exclaiming, "Oh mercy girls." We took dinner at Earlham and then left. I was taken sick that night and did not recover for some days—indeed have not got well yet. We took dinner at the Gibson house as we went.

Sixthday, February 28th, 1862
[Richmond, Indiana]
This evening Ed [Coffin] took Ada [his sister] and I over to the girls exhibition. Alma did not belong to the Society [Literary Society]. It does seem so nice to be in a land of nice roads. I was not well over at school, but just as I expected, there were some very

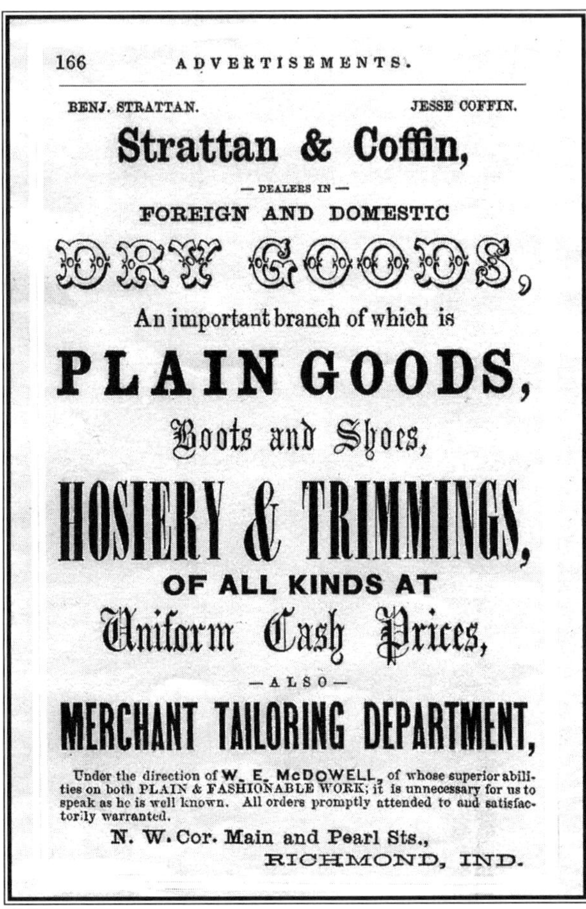

1857 Richmond, Indiana, City Directory

---

at the corner of Main and Green Streets; Advertisements—Strattan & Coffin, Dealers in Foreign and Domestic Dry Goods, An Important branch of which is Plain Goods, Boots and Shoes, Hosiery & Trimmings, of all kinds at Uniform Cash Prices, N.W. Corner Main and Pearl Streets, Richmond, Indiana—Also Merchant Tailoring Department, Under the direction of W.E. McDowell, of whose superior abilities on both Plain and Fashionable Work; it is unnecessary for us to speak as he is well known. All orders promptly attended to and satisfactorily warranted."

"1860 City Directory of Richmond Indiana—B.& J. Coffin, dry goods and merchant tailors, 25 Main, corner of Pearl—Barnabas Coffin residence Economy [Indiana] (B. & J. Coffin) David W. Coffin, clerk B. & J. Coffin—Jesse Coffin, (B. & J. C.) residence N.W. corner Main and Green Streets." Source: *Sutherland & McEvoy's Directory*, 1860.

"1863 City Directory of Richmond Indiana—B. & J. Coffin (Barnabas & Jesse C.) Dry Goods, 46 Main. Jesse Coffin (B. & J. C.) house north west corner Main and Green."

interesting performances all literary. I met Sarah Morgan [Sarah Henley, Mrs. William B. Morgan] and Naomi Harrison[100] this evening. I was thankful I was not under teacher Sarah's control for although I was glad to see her and she looked very smiling and said it was pleasant to see me again, I could see the old haughtiness in her black eyes. We were out shopping this morning. It seems real nice to have good stores to go to.

March 1862

Seventhday, March 1st, 1862 [Richmond, Indiana]
Cal [Carolyn Janney] and I walked over to Earlham again this evening. We were in the central parlor and there were so many visitors, it seemed like old times. The boys were going to have their exhibition and I would have stayed had I listened to the girls, but I felt like I had rather come away.

Sabbath, March 2nd, 1862 [Richmond, Indiana]
A stormy day. I have not been well, but have had a very pleasant time reading. I wished we lived in Richmond. Cal[101] came to Coffins [house was at NW corner of Main and Green Streets] awhile. I have not been anywhere except Hadleys. I called a little while—I like Jennie. It seems so much like a dream to be here when for so long a time it has been our theme of conversation.

Secondday, March 3rd, 1862 [Richmond, Indiana]
How quickly the months are gliding away. Just a little while ago and I commented Feb 1st and now it is another month. This time last week and I was saying soon be time to go to Richmond and now it will soon be time to go home.

---

100. Sarah (Henley) Morgan was a teacher at Earlham Boarding School 1857–1859 and was Governess 1875–1876 at Earlham College. Source: *Earlham, The Story of the College*, 1847–1862, Faculty and Staff Listing, Friends Collection, Lilly Library, Earlham College. Naomi Harrison, 1879–1882 and 1885–1897, members of Governing Ladies of Friends Board School and Earlham College.

101. Carolyn Janney was the youngest of the twelve children of Joseph and Elizabeth Russell Janney and the sister of William Janney. Carolyn was twelve years old when both of her parents died. Reuben Hunt was named her guardian along with Stephen and William, but it is not known where the children lived until they became of age. In October 1853 a certificate of removal was granted by the Newberry meeting in Martinsville to the Whitewater Meeting in Richmond, Indiana. Six years later, in 1859, her certificate of removal from Whitewater to Newberry was granted. She may have lived with her elder sister, Emily, and her husband, Jesse Coffin, while she resided in Richmond.

Thirdday, March 4th, 1862 [Richmond, Indiana]
I am missing all the examination, but want to be well enough to go tomorrow. Father came yesterday. We will have someone to go home with us. I like Ella so well and all of them, AIf and I have great times playing chequers.

Fourthday, March 5th, 1862 [Richmond, Indiana]
School closed this morning. Alma read an essay. There were some very good ones. Just tomorrow and we start home. We were out in town this evening. I wish we lived here or in some nice place. It looks so dull at Martinsville when we go home, but still it will be pleasant to get home again.

Fifthday, March 6th, 1862 [Traveled back to Martinsville, Ohio]
Through the crowd and confusion we came safely without any accident and came home in time to get a good supper. Alma was glad to get home.

Sixthday March 7th, 1862
We came up home this morning. Konner was here for dinner and this evening we have had callers. Steve came tonight and stayed awhile. I wonder when Lyd and him are going to marry.

Women Students of Earlham College, 1862

Seventhday, March 8th, 1862
The sun is shining bright, but the air is cold. I hardly know what to do first. I wish Alma would come up, but mother will keep her at home awhile. I have not seen Clay yet. I wonder if he is mad or anything. It seems to me like something is wrong. I am anxious to see him.

Sabbath, March 9th, 1862
A lonely looking morning, no church bells to ring to fill the air with their sweet music. Alma came up last night. It seemed very natural. Will and her are at church, but I thought it was too muddy for me to go. There was a funeral this morning. Green's little boy. I feel sorry for them. Will put a window harp in the window. It sounds so lonely. So many callers. Jeff came this evening, but only played one time. Alma went home. The last callers were Jim H, Jo White and Jimmy. The bright morning changed into a gloomy evening. I do wonder if Steve and Lyd are going to get married. Wait and see.

Secondday, March 10th, 1862
This morning I wanted to go down home and as Will was going I rode behind, how nice it must have looked. Such dreadful roads. Mud almost knee deep. I guess I will have to content myself at home till the weather is nicer. I will be so glad when we get our buggy done. I hope we will have many pleasant rides this summer. I have always wanted a nice buggy and perhaps my wish will be realized. There has been some more fighting. Leesburg, VA is in our possession again,[102] but there was severe fighting on James River. The rebel gun boat, *Merrimac,* was very near too powerful for our boats as it was shot proof, but at last the Federals came off victorious.[103]

Thirdday, March 11th, 1862
A bright spring morning. Spring indeed. How gladly I hail the bright sunshine and clear sky and soon the grass will be springing up and the violets peering their bright forms from their tiny nestling place. Spring is such a beautiful time. The most gladsome of all the year. My old custom of keeping late hours in the morning is returning. I dream so many golden hours away when I should be out in the fresh morning air. I must not grow so indolent. I am afraid I will build too many air castles. I am sure to meet with some disappointment when for a time I have been very happy. I wonder what my next misfortune will be. Let me hope I will not meet any. I must go down and see Will. He is making our fence. I think we have such a sweet little home. The March wind sounds just as it did a year ago. Can it be that summer autumn and winter have passed away so quickly. It seems a little time ago and I was listening to the wind and sitting here along.

Fourthday, March 12th, 1862
Went home again today. This evening Clay and Ed came down and stayed awhile. I had been thinking how glad I would be to see him and when he came there seemed to be a little reserved on both sides. I laughed afterward to think how cool Alma and I were at the first. Just as though it had been yesterday we had seen him, Alma came up this evening with me. We rode Cola T. I almost

---

102. March 1862, Battle of Leesburg, Loudon Co., Virginia: "In the battle of Leesburg, Welborn's and Campbell's companies (CSA) were first in battle, as part of a detachment, after which the remainder of the regiment marched to the scene of conflict. Colonel Burt, Auditor of the State, fell mortally wounded while gallantly leading the charge upon the Federal battery, and the command fell upon Lieutenant-Colonel Griffin. Reinforced by the Seventeenth (Mississippi) the two regiments, under Colonel W. S. Featherston, drove the enemy into the river, capturing several hundred prisoners." Source: CWSAC Reference No. VA006, http://www.featherstone society.com/sites history/winfield_s_featherstonetimeline.htm.

103. On March 8, 1862, the Confederate gunboat *Merrimac* created havoc with the federal fleet at Hampton Roads, Virginia. It was defeated by the U.S. ironclad *Monitor* on March 9, 1862.

have the blues since I came home. It looks as dull here and black. If it was not for leaving home I would go away gladly.

Fifthday, March 13th, 1862
Mary came today—heard she was at Hunts, so I had been expecting her. Clay came this evening. It seemed like old times. Alma, Mary and Clay all here. Clay seems very sober. I fear he regrets very much that he is a soldier though I do not know. But he seems so down hearted. It has been a beautiful day until this evening. The sky grew cloudy. March is changeable as our lives—sunshine and then shadow.

Sixthday, March 14th, 1862
A gloomy day again. I went to the close of school. Some very interesting essays and addresses, especially Robinson's. I think he is so talented. They had no music. Clay came up and stayed all night for it rained so. Such a muddy time it seems like the streets would never get dry.

Seventhday, March 15th, 1862
Mary left here this morning and Clay Heston was here awhile, Oh dear me. I feel so bad. I am discouraged about our troubles too. I just think before we know it England will be over here and after that will come a king.[104] I do not know what will become of us. It has just been pouring down rain. I feel dreadful bad this morning. Alma has not gone home yet and I do not know how she will get there without she rides Cola T. Stillwell comes tomorrow. It has been a short month. I argue that there is more pleasure in anticipating our visit to Richmond and when I got there was sick most of the time and now it is all over and gone and here I am at home again, but I did have a nice time. I like Coffins so well. I had company for tea last evening. Sarah and Lydia Ann and Milton Hunt, Alma and May.

Sabbath, March 16th, 1862
A day of gloom. Cloudy and wet. Alma stayed until evening. We went to hear

---

104. "The Confederate Bazaar at Liverpool," by John Bennett, originally appeared in *Crossfire—The Magazine of the American Civil War Round Table* (U.K.) 61, December 1999.

"Liverpool during the American Civil War was probably the most pro-Confederate city in Britain. The birthplace of the commerce raider CSS *Florida*, a major port for blockade running, and the scene of frantic speculation in cotton brought out of the beleaguered Confederacy, the fortunes of its large and wealthy merchant class were closely bound up with those of the Southern States. The prominent Liverpool business-man, James Spence, one of the Confederacy's most active sympathizers, described it as 'the headquarters of Southern sentiment.'" Source: http://www.americancivilwar.org.uk/articles/conf_bazaar.htm.

Stillwell at 3 o'clock. His text was "He who serves me will father honor." I finished the *Withered Heart*[105] this morning. I think it is very good.

Secondday, March 17th, 1862
Such a lonely day. The moon has come forth bright and lovely this evening. Oh, I am so glad summer is coming. Sweet summer. I hope I will show my appreciation of it by loving nature more than ever going abroad over the fields and forest gathering flowers and listening to the murmur of the water that ever carry sweet thoughts to my heart.

Thirdday, March 18th, 1862
A sunny morning. I am going down home. I am so anxious to see our new fence done. I think it will improve the appearance of our home very much and I will not grieve to see the old brown fence torn away. I have been reading an account of the battle at Pea Ridge. It is most horrible. The force under Price and McCullagh was near 30,000, many more than Curtis and Sigel had, and then the miserable renegade Albert Pike had a band of wild savages who tore and scalped the mangled bodies of many a poor soldier.[106] It is too horrible to dwell upon. Surely God can look with no favor upon such cruel barbarity and he will hold guilty those who have brought the war upon us and crimsoned our fields with blood.[107]

---

105. *The Withered Heart,* by T. S. Arthur, Philadelphia, J.W. Bradley, 1857. Source: *Wright American Fiction* 1851–1875, Digital Library Program, Indiana University, http://www.letrs.indiana.edu/cgi/t/text/text idx?c=wright2;idno=wright2 0146.

106. "On the night of March 6, Maj. Gen. Earl Van Dorn set out to outflank the Union position near Pea Ridge [Arkansas], dividing his army into two columns. Learning of Van Dorn's approach, the Federals marched north to meet his advance on March 7. This movement—compounded by the killing of two generals, Brig. Gen. Ben McCulloch and Brig. Gen. James McQueen McIntosh, and the capture of their ranking colonel—halted the Rebel attack. Van Dorn led a second column to meet the Federals in the Elkhorn Tavern and Tanyard area. By nightfall, the Confederates controlled Elkhorn Tavern and Telegraph Road. The next day, Maj. Gen. Samuel R. Curtis, having regrouped and consolidated his army, counterattacked near the tavern and, by successfully employing his artillery, slowly forced the Rebels back. Running short of ammunition, Van Dorn abandoned the battlefield. The Union controlled Missouri for the next two years." Casualties [dead, wounded, missing]: 5,549. Source: "The Battle of Pea Ridge" (Elkhorn Tavern), March 7–8, 1862, http://www.civilwarhome.com/pearidge.htm.

107. "Much to the later chagrin of their commander, Albert Pike's Indian troops engaged in barbaric conduct when they overran a detachment of federal cavalry. Pike did not witness the event, but the Northern newspapers told lurid tales of Pike's troops scalping and mutilating bodies of federal dead. This would haunt Pike for the remainder of his long life. . . . The Battle of Pea Ridge has been described as the 'Gettysburg of the West,' a reference to its role as the turning point in securing Missouri for the Union

It looked so sweet among the trees at home and I was under the pine tree and the wind sounded just as it did in summer a half murmur like the music of far off water. It seemed a little spring all to its self, for the birds were making sweet music. The grass getting green and honeysuckle putting forth it's green leaves. The trees at their old whispering again with the sunlight rippling through their branches, while just a little way off the mind was black and deep. The wind had a chilling and all seemed a perfect January.

Fourthday, March 19th, 1862

I am sitting alone by the fire and almost lonely, but then I think it is no use to be so foolish, so I will brave myself to take the day just as it may happen to be. The morning is dull and cloudy and I can not even see the cloud that has the silver lining. Surely it must be somewhere. I wonder if the flowers are blooming at the cliffs yet? I would like to see them. I would like to see Matt, Oh! have we enjoyed some happy moments together and had some gleeful laughs. I remember when we could laugh for half an hour about nothing.

Evening. Sitting by the east window. It looks very cheerless. Cal came up this evening awhile. There has been another battle. Newburn is taken by the federals. The loss on both sides severe.[108]

Fifthday, March 20th, 1862

How sweet that little bird sings. It always reminds me of the times we used to have when we hunted eggs [hens laid eggs in the hay] or played hide and seek in grandfathers barn. What wonderful feats we use to perform jumping out of the haymow [hayloft]. It is a wonder we were not hurt or killed. It has the appearance just now of being a bright day, but March is so much like me, so changeable, that it is doubtful how long the sun will shine. Steve came home this morning or down here I mean. He came last night from Richmond. I dreamed last night that I had the sweetest little baby and it had such a head of hair and such eyes and when only a day old could sit up and laugh and look as bright. What if it was so. Well, I don't know, of course, it would be sweet and of course we would think it the dearest little angel in the world. There is such a sweet little fir tree in the garden—mine. "Will, thee must always remember it is mine." It was broken down soon after we came here and we had no thought of it growing, but how emblematic it is of some human lives, it is now sprung up green and bids fair to become the most beautiful tree we have. Oh, it is just pouring down rain.

---

while at the same time opening Arkansas for invasion." Source: Tom W. Dillard, *Arkansas Democrat-Gazette,* Special Collections Department at the University of Arkansas Libraries in Fayetteville, posted March 13, 2005.

108. The Confederate victory at Newbern, North Carolina, March 14, 1862, was followed by Federal victories near Winchester, Virginia, March 23, by General James Shields.

All my visions of a bright spring day have vanished. "Sic transit glory munda."
[*Sic transit gloria mundi* is Latin for "Thus passes the glory of the world."] Our
new neighbors across the road have come.

Sixthday, March 21st, 1862
It looks odd to see the sun shining for it has been so dark for a few days past.
It is real cold. The cold wind of March seems none the less severe because it is
spring. Clay called last evening and Cal was here all the afternoon. We had so
much fun. We can take rides whenever we please, but I am afraid Cola T will be
bad and a "runaway" or something.

Seventhday, March 22nd, 1862
A disagreeable morning. The snow falling, the wind blowing and everything
in unison with a winter morning. I hope the weather will be pleasanter before
the exhibition for I want to go. Jeff comes here to practice on one of the tunes
they are going to sing and play. They have changed it so as to make it appropriate. I have been real smart this morning and got my work all done in a hurry.
I am anxious to see the paper this morning. I hope Island No 10[109] is taken as
there has been a battle raging there for several days. It is harder to capture than
Columbus would have been. It is said Ella, Billy Hunt and Heston came up to
practice on their song.

Sabbath, March 23rd, 1862
Mary and Will have gone to church, but it is too muddy for Alma and I to venture, so we are sitting here by the fire very happy. I wish I could write something
good, but it seems I was never intended for much but to stay at home and work.
Afternoon the misty clouds hanging dull and leaden shedding in sunlight upon
us.

Secondday, March 24th, 1862
I feel so badly this morning. Everything so dreary. I wonder if the sunshine is
never going to come again to gladden the earth and dry up the mud. It is almost
impossible to go anyplace for the mud is so plentiful and so deep. Alma and

---

109. "From March 2 to April 8, 1862 was the struggle for control of Island No.
10, former island in the Mississippi River, between NW Tennessee and SE Missouri; site
of an important western campaign of the Civil War. With the advance of Union General U.S. Grant up the Tennessee River, all Confederate positions except New Madrid
and Island No. 10 were abandoned. After the fall of New Madrid on March 14, 1862,
Union troops dug a canal through the swamps to allow their supply barges to bypass
the heavily fortified island. Union gunboats eventually succeeded in passing the island
and reduced its shore batteries. The large confederate garrison surrendered without a
battle on Apr. 7, after the Union troops seized the only escape route." Source: *Columbia
Encyclopedia*, 6th ed., Columbia University Press, 2005.

Mary went to Vienna this morning and tonight comes the great performance. I hope it will be interesting for it will be so muddy to go we must have some recompense. Whites [Benjamin and Lydia Coffin White—parents of Jo and Lyd] are very much out of humor about it and think it a disgrace to have anything to do with it. I think they are too rash about it, but everyone to their own opinion.

Thirdday, March 25th, 1862
The brightest day of the month excepting a few. Jane was here awhile this morning. Lyd and Steve are going to marry this week and are going to take dinner here on Seventhday. We went to the depot this evening. I asked the girls if everybody else came because we did or if we came because everyone else came. Jeff came up this evening and Will and him are working on the melodeon.[110] Two keys are out of tune, but I fear there will be many more out tune when they finish. We all went to the exhibition last night. It was very interesting. Had some good music. We did not retire till quite late and got up this morning accordingly. Jenny left for Richmond this evening and expects to remain. I do wonder if Lyd and Steve will be happy. Will and Jeff are trying the melodeon and Jeff says I do believe they are right, the notes. I do hope they are. They had an echo last night—"We will all meet again in the morning."

Fourthday, March 26th, 1862
Cloudy again this morning. I feel almost as bad as ever. I do wish I felt better. Lide Hiatt and Frank Randal[111] are to be married this evening so rumor says. I am afraid Lide is not going to do very well, but time will prove all things. Island "Number Ten" is not taken yet or was not yesterday. I am afraid we will not be the victors.

Melodeon

110. "A melodeon was a keyboard instrument sounded by the vibration of free reeds by wind. It is an American development of the harmonium, from which it differs in two principal respects. Its foot-operated bellows draw the air in past the reeds by suction, rather than forcing it out by pressure; and the characteristic size and form of the reeds and resonators result in a more even dynamic." Source: http://www.britannica.com/eb/article?tocId=9051907.

111. Benjamin Franklin Randall and Louisa J. Hiatt were married on March 26, 1862, by George G. Harris, J.P.

Fifthday, March 27th, 1862
It is such a beautiful morning. The birds singing gaily and all things seem invigorated by the fresh spring air and bright sunshine. "Lide Randal" It sounds so odd, but I suppose it is so for they were to be married at 7 o'clock. I am going down home this morning. Just one more day till Lyd [White] and Steve [Janney] are married. I have been home today. I was at grandfathers.

Sixthday, March 28th, 1862 [Lydia White and Stephen Janney's wedding day]
All is over. Jane came this evening to help me and we worried through the time to go to see the bride. She had a veil and white wreath and looked very becoming. We had a very nice supper. They are coming to our house tomorrow for dinner. I wonder how we will get along. There were more there than I expected. I felt very serious and longed for some dear friend to discuss something pleasant. I will be glad when tomorrow night comes.

Seventhday, March 29th, 1862
Well, well. It is evening. We dined at 3 pm. Let me see there was the two Miss Newbys, but first, the bride and groom, Jo and Jim, May and Edna, Cal and Jake, Alma and Ema Betts, George and Rebecca and Jane. There were some I did not have that I would like to have had, but I could not have so many. They spoke very highly of the cake. But they are all gone, but Lyd and Steve. It seems quite still now.

Sabbath, March 30th, 1862
I went to bed last night with a sad heart and my pillow was wet with tears, I wonder why I always have to cry? Oh, there is a beautiful Sabbath morning. Our bedroom window is open and the breeze comes in genial as summer wind. How I do love our little home. Just a little while ago I finished my morning work. We all got up so very late. We are invited to go to Matts for dinner, but I feel more like going to sleep.

Secondday, March 31st, 1862
A bright day. Alma came up this afternoon. Mother thought sure I was sick because I had not been down home. Jo was here awhile this evening. Our yard is getting so green and pretty. How nice it will look when we get the fence done.

April 1862

Thirdday, April 1st, 1862
April again. It seems but a short year and yet it has been long enough to bring more sorrow over this land than has been for many long years. It has been short to me, but how long it has seemed to those whose husbands or friends are upon the battlefield. No one save those can tell how thankful we should be. Will came

down and we stayed till dark almost and brought up something to plant. It looks so sweet among the trees at home. If father only would make a new fence. Wendell Phillips[112] speech was in the paper this morning. The one "the Cincinnati mob" . . . prevented there, I suppose.

Fourthday, April 2nd, 1862

This morning we spent some hours working in the yard. I wonder if I ever will forget how like a fright I fix up when I work in the yard. This morning I wore an old skirt pinned around my shoulders and old bonnet and veil and an old pair of gloves. I must have looked like a fright, but then there is no need to getting so black and having our hands so rough when we can help it. The wind is blowing very hard. A perfect hurricane almost. I cannot step out but my dress blows half over my head. Island Number Ten is not taken yet and report says there is a great battle yet to come off at that point. I think the war will last longer than may persons think of. The paper today has the "Exposition of the Knights of the Golden Circle," a band of traitors scattered all over the north and south for the overthrow of the government. There is no hope of quelling the rebellion when we have so many traitors anonymous. I hope the T.K.G.C. will be exposed and brought to punishment.[113]

---

112. "Wendell Phillips was born in Boston on 29th November, 1811. Educated at the Harvard Law School, he open a law office in Boston in 1834. Phillips was converted to the abolition of slavery cause when he heard William Lloyd Garrison speak at the Boston Female Anti-Slavery Society in 1835. Phillips was particularly impressed by the bravery of these people and during the meeting a white mob attempted to lynch Garrison. Phillips was so outraged by what he saw that he decided to give up law and devote himself to obtaining the freedom of all slaves. Phillips became a leading figure in the Anti-Slavery Society. A magnificent orator, Phillips was the society's most popular public speaker. Phillips also contributed to Garrison's *Liberator* and wrote numerous pamphlets on slavery. During the Civil War, Phillips criticized Abraham Lincoln for his lack of commitment to the abolition of slavery. In 1865 Phillips replaced Garrison as president of the Anti-Slavery Society. After the passing of the 15th Amendment, Phillips concentrated on other issues such as women's rights, universal suffrage and temperance. Wendell Phillips died in Boston on 2nd February, 1884." Source: http://www.spartacus.schoolnet.co.uk/USASphillips.htm.

113. "The Knights of the Golden Circle (T. K. G. C.) was a secret order of Southern sympathizers in the North. Its members were known as Copperheads. Organized in Cincinnati, Ohio it appealed to the South's friends in the North, particularly in areas where there was economic dislocation. It spread to other parts of Ohio, Indiana, Kentucky, Illinois, and Missouri. It became strongest among Peace Democrats, who felt that the Civil War was a mistake and that the increasing power of the federal government was leading toward tyranny. In late 1863 the Knights of the Golden Circle was reorganized as the order of American Knights and early in 1864, as the Order of the Sons of Liberty with Clement L. Vallandigham, most prominent of the Copperheads, as its supreme commander." Source: G. F. Milton, *Abraham Lincoln and the Fifth Column*, 1942, repr. 1962; R. O. Curry, *A House Divided*, 1964, www.factmonster.com.

Fifthday, April 3rd, 1862

Such a beautiful morning. We are going to Carmans to dinner. Will is working on our fence. I think it is going to be so pretty. I am anxious to see it done. I am so discouraged about the war I think the clouds grow darker all the time. I have not as much hope of peace as I had months ago, but I never believed we would have a short war. It is even asserted that McClellan is a T.K.G.C. I fear he is perhaps that is why he is so slow.

Sixthday, April 4th, 1862

I can hardly remain indoors this beautiful morning. I think I never loved spring and appreciated its beauties so much before. Alma and mother were here yesterday but I guess I will not go home today, not before evening anyhow. I am going to have so many flowers if I can, but I cannot arrange them nicely, I am afraid. Oh! the sweet little birds. How I do love to listen to their songs. If music is wrong, why do the birds sing so sweetly. I think if all things were harmless as music, this would be a good world. If we only could go to Pike's Opera [in Cincinnati] tonight to hear Parson Brobow speak. I wish I had enough books to keep me reading for a month.

Seventhday, April 5th, 1862

This morning I overslept myself—Will came in at last and I heard the astounding news that it was eight o'clock. Heston and Will were at Harrisses in the after part of the night. He is sick and I could hardly keep from getting afraid. There was a thunderstorm last night and this morning is cool. The rain freshened up the flower roots we planted. I do hope they will all live. Perhaps Lizzie Heston will board here. I wonder if we will like each other. I hope so it will be so nice to have someone to like real well. I feel like I am acquainted with her now. Will is going to begin the fence on Secondday—putting it up. I wrote to Matt the other morning I told her to come at quarterly meeting. It is always about six months between our meeting. The parting always comes soon enough.

Sabbath, April 6th, 1862

Went to church this morning. No preaching. It is such beautiful day, but cool. We took a nap this evening and a walk. We went to get some wild flower roots to plant out. We only found some violets. Jeff and Alma were here this evening. Alma stayed all night. Oh! if we only had our buggy done. I am so anxious to take a ride in it. I wore my new bonnet to church this morning. I did not feel ashamed of it.

Secondday, April 7th, 1862

The [third] anniversary of our wedding day. It is a wet gloomy morning. It was a lovely evening then. The sun came out from the vapor of clouds and I remember how bright and green the meadows looked. Strange if I could not remember three years. Alma and Cal are here. There was quite a little "episode" in our lives this evening. The girls were "tickled." They laughed and kept on laughing. Heston was here. I could see nothing to laugh at. They thought they would have the exquisite pleasure to seeing me cry. I was bound I would not. I asked Heston to sing a piece. He answered—it would be no use for him to sing. They would laugh all the music away. I said if they have no more manners than to laugh they can leave the room, all of which proved to be very insulting to the laughing beauties who came very near "laughing on the other side of their mouths." We went in where the melodeon is and Jeff played a tune. When we came back the seats around the fire were vacant. Where are the girls? I opened the kitchen door, but did not behold them. I opened the bedroom door and some little noise came to my ears. There piled on the bed, crinolines[114] and all . . . the girls almost drowned in tears. Their eyes red with much weeping. Afterward we read the Psalm [30:5] in which occurs the passage, "Weeping may endure for a night, but joy cometh in the morning."

Thirdday, April 8th, 1862
Dark again and the rain pouring in torrents every now and then. Alma is here but she is so interested in "White Lies." It is a hard matter to get her to bridge. What a "phrase" word. There is a terrible battle impending at Number Ten the paper says. I am afraid to hear the result for fear the victory will be against us, but the slaughter will be great before either the federals or confederates will surrender. In what suspense must the friends of those who are there be in daily expecting to hear bad news. How thankful we who are spared this sorrow should be. [See footnote for March 22, 1862, entry.]

Fourthday, April 9th, 1862
Such an awful day. Almost as stormy as in winter. The rain pouring in torrents and this evening the snow came down in great flakes. Alma is here yet. We have had such great times laughing. There has been no one in today. Will went to Holfords tonight. Holford is very bad. He locked the door and took the key with him. We were sitting by the fire talking when [we] were startled by a "rap." We started for the door, but we got to laughing and laughed all the time and for a long time could not tell them to go to the other door. It turned out to be Jeff. He is boarding here this week. He came from the city this evening, but it had been so long since the train came that we had no idea he would have come.

---

114. "The crinoline was introduced in the 1850s. It was considered very progressive, because it took the place of two or three petticoats and was named for its content, the French term 'crin,' which means horsehair, and 'lin' from linen. You may hear hoopskirts referred to as crinolines, but during the nineteenth century, they were referred to as cage crinolines to distinguish them from their earlier predecessor." Source: http:// demode.tweedlebop.com/crinoline.html.

Fifthday, April 10th, 1862
Some brighter today. Alma went home this evening. I played off on Alma this morning. I looked from the window and saw a "peddler" coming so when I heard a knock I was pretty sure who it was. I told Alma someone was there and then slipped in the bedroom. Jeff was here and we left him to entertain him and hid in the bedroom. In the midst of it Will came and called me, but I did not answer. But I cannot describe it or how we laughed so as I cannot do the subject justice I will leave it.

Sixthday, April 11th, 1862
Night again, but the stars did not mingle in the blue sky as beautiful as sometimes they do and the moon too looks like it had a cloud upon its brow. I gathered a tiny bouquet this morning of cedar and grass. One little sweet myrtle flower. It looks so nice on the table I think. We went to Moors this morning. Their baby is dead. Poor little thing. It seemed a mere shadow and its little coffin was but a miniature one. How happy it is now though. I wonder if it will grow in Heaven? Will moved our old fence this evening.

Seventhday, April 12th, 1862
Raining again. I will be glad when the warm days come. Lib and I went this morning to the meadow and got a little basket of flower roots to plant. I have been reading in the *Atlantic.* I think we must take that sometimes. The wind sounds lonely tonight and it is chilly and cold. I pity the poor soldiers.

Sabbath, April 13th, 1862
Company for dinner. Clarkson and Emma Hunt, Clay, Alma and Heston. We went over to hear Stillwell.[115] The sun came out beautiful this evening as a compensation for the dark morning. Every person looks inquiringly at our fence. Our old one turned wrong side out, but never mind. They will understand it when we get our new one. I am in hopes of seeing Matt at quarterly meeting.

---

115. Rev. J. R. Stillwell became a chaplain and served with the 70th Ohio Volunteer Infantry, 3rd Division, 20th Corps. A news article in the *Clinton Republican,* on August, 26, 1864, gives an account of Chaplain Stillwell while he served on the front lines in the Atlanta Campaign: "Our Regiment is very fortunate in possessing so good and energetic a man for its Chaplain. He not only devotes himself to the spiritual, but to the temporal welfare of the men. Rain or shine, he is actively engaged assisting the men in forwarding their letters, often carrying the mail ten or fifteen miles. He is a Christian gentleman, and is highly respected and admired by the entire Regiment. On the day of the battle, (the 20th ult.) Billy Baner, a brave and fearless lad, was stricken down by a minnie ball, whilst riding at the head of the Regiment. A few of the non-combatants of the Regiment lifted him up and conveyed him to a small grove. In a short time a grave was dug and poor Will was lowered to his last resting place. Chaplain Stillwell and the few friends stood around the grave with uncovered heads. The Chaplain commenced

Secondday, April 14th, 1862
I have the blues this morning. Everything comes crowding over my heart at once. How ungrateful [I] am to fret about little trivial things when there is so much real suffering over the land. The poor wounded soldiers. How they do suffer. I wish I was where I could do something for them. In what terrible suspense would I be in had I a brother or husband there. Aaron Ward's wife [Aaron Ward was a free black man raised by Evan and Priscilla Stevens.] was buried this evening. Alma, Cal and I went. I really felt real bad.

Thirdday, April 15th, 1862
Heston, Will and I went at fathers for tea this evening. Jeff is going to start home in the morning and perhaps he will bring Lizzie with him. Our fence is going to be so nice when finished. I am so anxious to see it alone. It has been such a warm day. There are so many wounded soldiers. How I do pity them.

Fourthday, April 16th, 1862
A beautiful day. Our fence progressing. No letter from Matt. I wonder if she is coming down. I hope so. Alma has been here this evening. Willie came up this morning and spent the day. I do hope he will be a good boy. We went in the meadow to gather flowers, but only found a few daisies. We went down to Holfords a little while this evening. He is not long for this world. It looks very cheerless there.

Fifthday, April 17th, 1862
Went to meeting. Came home very tired. Alma and mother came here. I wish Matt would write to me. It is always so good to get a letter from her. It has been raining today and this evening. Lyd and I started for a walk and were caught in a shower, but found refuge in Frank Moore's store. I do wish there was more energy and industry displayed here. Everywhere I go I see signs of neglect. The grave yard, the spot we should keep most sacred is open to every stray cow as it were, and every thing that comes along. All the trees and things planted on the graves are thereby destroyed. The schoolhouse too is greatly abused. No signs of care or pride in keeping it in any order can one see.

---

a chapter in the Bible, and had read but a few sentences, when the rebels made their charge. The bullets came whistling through the trees thick and fast, flying above and around the sorrowing few, screaming wild songs of slaughter. Without stopping or faltering an instant, the Chaplain finished the chapter, and then offered a prayer to 'Him that giveth and taketh away,' in behalf of the fallen brave. In a few moments the form of Billy Baner, passed forever from earthly view, and the clay lately so animate lay buried in the clay inanimate. The Chaplain's personal bravery is above questioning, and the men admire him the more for it. The 79th boys think they have about the best Chaplain in the army." Myra McMillan submitted the article to the *Clinton Republican*.

Sixthday, April 18th, 1862
Raining again, but now the clouds have scattered and this evening has been one of the most beautiful I remember to have seen. I can get 1,200 for our property "no indeed." This evening I looked from the window at the bright green grass, the budding trees and flowers and wondered can it be possible that spring is here again. Just a little time ago and cold winds of winter were sweeping over the earth all brown and bare. Now the spring breezes are at play and the violets and daisies are coming out again. Surely there is nothing too great to accomplish by our "Father who art in heaven."

Seventhday, April 19th, 1862
Chilly. I was so in hopes it would be a pretty day. This afternoon the raindrops are beginning to fall. I am afraid it will pour down so we will be disappointed about going home this evening. We are going to stay all night. It will have to rain very hard if it prevents me from going. Next Seventhday is quarterly meeting. Nearly six months since I saw Matt coming up the street with her blue veil flying. I was certain it was her then. I do hope they will come down. Capt J [John] E Bond is seriously wounded. He is at the hospital at Cincinnati. His wife went down. I hope he will get well. The rebels to claim a glorious victory at Pittsburgh. I think they had better wait till they are certain.

Sabbath, April 20th, 1862
At fathers. It has been raining all day nearly. Clay came down this evening. I wonder which Alma does like the best—Heston or Clay. Just pouring down rain. No going home tonight, I am certain.

Secondday, April 21st, 1862
Came home this evening. Will brought Julie down for me. She does go so easy and nice. I wish I could take a ride often. Such a poor fire. I must go and make it turn brighter before Will comes. John Bond is dead. I feel sorry for his wife. He died last evening at eight o clock.

Thirdday, April 22nd, 1862
The rain was pattering against the window frame this morning when I awoke and all prospect of a bright day vanished for the wind was chilly and sometimes a few little flakes of snow came down, but remembering it was April passed and the rain came, but after a time the rain ceased and the sun shone out bright and glorious. The raindrops glistening on the grass and the flowers drooping their tender forms looked bright and we can almost see them growing now. No letter. Mother gave me a new dress. I am glad of it for I need one and one +2.

Fourthday, April 23rd, 1862
Beautiful morning. All nature seems refreshed from the April showers. How sinful we are to murmur against anything that we cannot give the reason of.

How many times have we wished it would quit raining and felt worried because it was not bright and warmer. All the same it was all for our good and to make the flowers and trees grow. Jane is cleaning the kitchen. I do hope I can keep it clean. I think I must be very slovenly. I know I am.

Fifthday, April 24th, 1862
April—Winter again this morning. The trees and grass are dressed in white and the snow still coming down very fast. Snow in April. Whoever thought of such a thing when the flowers are budding and blooming and May sooner at hand. It is all just right though or it would not have been so. It is terrible to think of the sufferings of our brave wounded soldiers. I wish I could do something to help them. When the impending battle at Corinth is ended whether our troops meet with victory or defeat there is [written] upon record one of the most bloody battles that had yet been fought. At least the papers predict such a one and it is doubtless in time the rebels will try hard to retrieve their reverses and then brave federal soldiers will exert themselves to add yet another victory to become part of history.

Sixthday, April 25th, 1862
A beautiful morning again. How pleasant it seems to see the bright sunlight and hear the birds sing as they ever do on bright mornings. There is quite a contrast between this and yesterday morning. We had company to dinner and David and Deborah[116] [James] paid us their first visit. I am not going to expect Matt and then I will not be disappointed if she does not come. Alma received a letter from Heston. He and Lizzie anticipate coming on the Fourthday evening. I wonder if we will like Lizzie. We are getting anxious to see her.

Seventhday, April 26th, 1862
This morning when the train came I tried not to look for Matt, but would find myself peeping from the blinds to see if I could see her coming. She did not come, but her mother did and she brought me a letter. Matt said if I was looking for her she was sorry to disappoint me and if I was not she was sorry I did not miss her. Oh! well if she had come I would have been very glad but as she did not I am glad, for it would all be over so soon and now I can look forward to meeting her when the June roses are blooming and that will be a pleasure for she is the dearest girl. I went to meeting this morning. Alma and I came away before it concluded. We found Will had preceded us. There is a prophecy in today's paper. A confederate soldier slept and as he slumbered he dreamed and

---

116. David James was first married to Mary Hunt, Paulena's first cousin twice removed. It was their son's, Lindley James's, death that was recorded in the very first entry of Paulena's journal on April 17, 1859. Mary died in 1853 and David remarried Deborah Stevens, Paulena's aunt, the sister of her father, Evan Stevens. They were married on December 16, 1855.

it was revealed to him by his dream that he would die on the following day at 4 o'clock pm. There would be a battle fought. The most terrible of modem times in the last week of April early in May. Peace would come over the land more unexpected than had the war. The former has been fulfilled for he died at the exact hour mentioned. We must wait and see if the other be true. It was vouched for so says the *Richmond Whig* by a reliable officer. It seems very little like quarterly meeting to me. Will and I went fishing this evening. Had the fortune to catch enough for breakfast.

Sabbath, April 27th, 1862
Went to meeting this morning. Alma came here. She has gone out walking. Clay too. It seems like old times again I do think Alma likes Clay better than Heston. I do not believe she knows her own mind about [it]. This is a lovely Sabbath like spring indeed. We are up stairs in our pleasant little room. Will is lounging and reading. I think I could sleep. I feel so lazy. I hope we will get our fence finished this week.

Secondday, April 28th, 1862
Alma stayed last night and I went home with her this morning. We went to grandfathers this afternoon and Willie and Elva, Alma and I went to the creek[117] to get flowers. Jennie Hadley and her brother came to Uncle Williams this evening. It is reported that New Orleans is taken by the federals. I do not believe it though.[118] [New Orleans was captured on April 25.]

Thirdday, April 29th, 1862
Such a beautiful morning. I am going to Uncle Williams for dinner. I wish I had a new dress to wear. Jennie, John and Cal came by this morning and we went to the depot. I went to Uncle Williams for dinner. Alma came this evening. They went to the train to meet James and Jimmy.

Fourthday, April 30th, 1862
The last day in April has dawned bright and lovely. Our fence is done. It looks real nice. Oh, it is not painted yet. I am anxious to see the paper this morning. Perhaps there will be some more startling news. If so I hope it will not be unfavorable to us. I feel like I would like to go down home this morning, but I guess

---

117. The creek was the East Fork of Todd's Fork, which ran along Evan Stevens's and Aaron Betts's farm land. Today, a covered bridge crosses the creek near that land.

118. April 25, 1862, New Orleans: "The largest city in the Confederacy fell virtually without resistance to a Union naval squadron. Commanded by Flag Officer David G. Farragut, the 44-ship fleet battled its way past two forts, bristling with heavy artillery pieces, that guarded the mouth of the Mississippi River." Source: *Battles of the Civil War,* Supplement to the *National Geographic,* April 2005.

I had better defer it to some future time as I have been away two days this week already. Jeff and Lizzie came this evening. Will and I called there this evening. Lizzie did not talk much, neither did I. We seem very distant, but I think I will like her.

May 1862

Fifthday, May 1st, 1862

First of May. Just one year ago Matt was married.[119] It has come quickly again with its bright sunshine and beauty. I will ever love thee May. Hadleys, Jennie and Cal, Jeff and Lizzie took tea at fathers. We had such a pleasant time. At least they all seemed to enjoy themselves. I do like James and John so much and Jennie. She is such a sweet girl. Oh! if I only had two as nice good brothers. How I would love them. Lizzie and Jeff sang.

Sixthday, May 2nd, 1862

A pleasant time this evening for myself at least. They have all been here this evening. I think I will like Lizzie. James, Jennie and John went to Leesburg this evening. We went to the train with them. Lizzie is not going to remain all night tonight.

Seventhday, May 3rd, 1862

Have had a pleasant time this evening. Alma and Lizzie here for tea. After they were gone Cal and I went to Matts. A little whirl. Holford is very bad. I do not feel like writing and therefore cannot write. Alma and Lizzie are going to "Centre" in the morning, nothing prevents. I do wish we had our buggy done.

Sabbath, May 4th, 1862

A bright Sabbath morning. I went over to Sabbath School this morning. Ours begins next Sabbath. I expect to attend. We went to church and to Uncle Christopher's for dinner. Had a real pleasant time. Oh! it is such a beautiful evening. Holford is dead. He died last night.

Secondday, May 5th, 1862

Just forty-one years ago, Napoleon died at St. Helena. I wonder if it was as beautiful as is today. Yorktown is said to be evacuated. Why McClellen allows

---

119. Martha Ann "Matt" Ladd, daughter of Asa and Mary Chalfant Ladd, was married to "Adna" Pushee contrary to the discipline of the Quaker church and was condemned by the Fairfield Friends Meeting on December 16, 1861. They were married on May 1, 1861, probably near Leesburg, Highland County, Ohio.

the evacuation of so many places after spending months in preparation I cannot understand, but perhaps his policy will prove to be better than we think.[120]

Thirdday, May 6th, 1862
Such a lovely day. I think May is the dearest month. They all went Maying this afternoon and tonight. Hadley's are going to leave. I am real sorry for I have enjoyed their company so much. Jimmy left this morning for Richmond [Indiana]. Will says he would not be surprised if we lived there before long. I wonder if we will.

Fourthday, May 7th, 1862
Lovely again and very bright is the morning. It seems almost too sweet for such a wicked world as this. A good ride or a good laugh would do me good. I do wish we had our buggy. We have several places in view this summer. I hope we'll get to go. In May three years ago I was up to see Matt and Oh! what joyous times we had. I wonder if I will see her this May. I hope so.

Fifthday, May 8th, 1862
Just as beautiful as ever. I think I never saw lovelier weather. I took a walk this evening all alone. Jeff, Alma and Lizzie went riding this evening.

Sixthday, May 9th, 1862
I feel dull this morning and almost sick. What a lovely morning to go riding. We have Cola T at home again. I am sorry she ever left for she looks so much worse than when she went. Now if we only had a buggy. Williamsburg is in possession of McClellan. I suppose he will wait another year before he does anything of importance. I think if his name is very brilliant in history he will achieve something more than he has yet accomplished. I wonder if the war ever will be over. There is so much suffering everywhere that it is sad to think of it lasting another twelfth month—though it may be years before it is ended for it never seemed to me that the war would be short.

Seventhday, May 10th, 1862
Such beautiful days each succeeding morning and evening seems more lovely than the one before. Quarterly meeting. They have a nice time for it. I must surely write to Matt soon—dear girl how much I do love her. May is passing

---

120. May 5, 1862, "That night, successful in delaying the Union advance, the Confederates abandoned their redoubts and continued their withdrawal toward Richmond. Major General George McClellan telegraphed to Washington, 'The victory is complete.' Confederate General Johnston would later rebut, 'Had the enemy beaten us on the fifth, as he claims to have done, our army would have lost most of its baggage and artillery.'" Source: "Battle of Williamsburg," peninsular.org, http://www.peninsulacampaign.org/williamsburg.shtml.

quickly away and I fear I will not see the cliffs while the May sunshine falls from them. How pleasant it would be this evening to go riding. Sabbath school begins in the morning.

Sabbath, May 11th, 1862
Went to Sabbath School. Will and I went to George's. Matt, Cal and Jennie were there. Will and I took a ride with Cola. I did not feel a bit afraid of her.

Secondday, May 12th, 1862
May, Lizzie and I were up early this morning and had a walk down [the] street before breakfast. So here I sit by the window this delightful morning. All my work done while many others have the trouble of washing dishes. The birds are ever singing and ever happy in the bright summer days. The trees are getting green. It will soon be shady in the forest and a beautiful retreat from the dusty street. Lizzie and I are going down to the train at 10 pm.

Thirdday, May 13th, 1862
Sick today. Mother up here. I have nothing to write about now for I do not feel in the mood. Alma stayed tonight.

Fourthday, May 14th, 1862
Another bright day. Surely May is the dearest of months. I think I will not see Matt this May for it will soon be gone. Jeff and Lizzie did sing so sweetly tonight. I wish I could sing as well.

Fifthday, May 15th, 1862
Mother came up and Willie. It seems so good to have Mother a working around everything better. We have heard from Mrs. Adams at last, but it is sad to hear that they have parted. It seems so impossible to think about it and how kind he used to appear. Truth is stranger than fiction."[121] She has three children. How I would love to see her. She thinks of teaching school in Richmond. I hope she will.

Sixthday, May 16th, 1862
I have been so very hoarse that I had to whisper all the time. Mother came up this evening and brought some hot liniment.[122] I suppose I must take some of it

---

121. Quote from Mark Twain: "Truth is stranger than fiction, but it is because Fiction is obliged to stick to possibilities; Truth isn't." Source: www.brainyquote.com/quotes/quotes/m/marktwain122865.html.

122. "Watkins Red Liniment: The very first product sold by J. R. Watkins in 1868 is still a classic. The active ingredient in our legendary Red Liniment is camphor, from

tonight. Alma is going to stay all night. I was reading of Francis L. Osgood this afternoon. I think she was so lovely. There is a touching account of her death. She had two little girls Mary and Ellen. She prayed that they too might die. Her prayer was answered for they were all buried the same year and are now sleeping sweetly in that beautiful home of the dead—Mount Auburn.

Seventhday, May 17th, 1862
Up early this morning. Alma and I hurried with our work and had a long time to read before dinner. The paper this morning contained items from the rebel fighters. I hope they will be discouraged enough to become loyal again for oh! there has been so much blood already shed. They pretend to be boastful in some measure and think if they succeed in holding Richmond—foreign nations will interfere soon. Alma has gone home. Will gone fishing. Lizzie gone to Millers, so I am all alone, but not at all lonesome for I have the *Ladies Repository*[123] to read which I like very much. Yesterday as a convalescent soldier was waiting for the train at Camp with his father who came to take him home, he fell dead. How sadly disappointed will his friends be. I cannot keep it from my mind.

Sabbath, May 18th, 1862
Went to Sabbath School this morning. Came home sick. I was sick all evening. Alma here. I hope I will be better soon for I have felt so bad and everything for so long and I think it is so wicked to be grieving about little things when there is so much suffering. I expect we will hear of another battle soon and how much sorrow that will come. Try as I may I cannot become accustomed to strip war of all that is horrible. It seems worse and worse to me.

Secondday, May 19th, 1862
Again the bright May sun is shining and the birds joyous with their music. I feel better this morning than I did last evening, but I am not well yet. Alma is going to school or meeting. Mother has gone to meeting. Willie came from school this morning at recess. I fear for Willie. He has what will make a noble man if properly governed, but he is so quick to learn badness that I fear his evil propensities will overbalance his good. If he only had better society to go with, but I do not think his playmates are such as will improve him in any way rather the reverse. I received a letter this morning.

---

an Asian evergreen related to cinnamon. Together with red pepper extract, it works by stimulating nerve receptors that feel heat, masking the feeling of pain and relieving the discomfort of minor muscle pain, soreness and stiffness." Source: http://www.mommiescloset.com/saleitem.asp?si=1169.

123. *The Ladies' Repository* was a monthly periodical devoted to literature, art, and religion published in the nineteenth century. It began publication with the January 1841 issue and ceased publication with the December 1876 issue.

Thirdday, May 20th, 1862
How swiftly May is passing away. In just a little time the June roses will be blooming and the fall again where the flowers bloom. But alas! how many homes where it was joyfully greeted one year ago will it come bringing memories of happy Junes gone—brings memory of the bright little faces that have drooped and faded and were buried since last June or of the manly form that fell upon the battlefield or died far away from home in some dreary hospital among strangers. It seems almost impossible to look a few years back and see what a sad change has come. Nothing would give me more joy than to know that the war would be over, but it can not bring back again the dead ones nor fill with joy the hearts of bereaved ones and when the bells are tolling and the cry of peace is heard over the land there will be oh! how many thousands mourning for those who can return no more.

Oh! I do like the *"Repository"* so much. There are many times the tears come while I read, but I have often said I never weep over a story unless it touches some tender chord in my own heart, so I suppose there are a good many tender chords. It is real chilly this morning and I have a pleasant fire. It seems like old times all alone just now except Frank [Paulena's dog] who is up in the corner sleeping very sweetly.

Fourthday, May 21st, 1862
A wild stormy morning. The rain fell in torrents and the wind blew last night. For a time this morning the sun glimmered through the clouds and then after a great hush the thunder rolled like the distant rumbling of chariot wheels coming nearer, till at last there was a great black cloud in the west. I was so interested with a book that I scarcely noticed how dark it was getting, but soon the rain came down in torrents again and the wind blew bending the little trees till I was fearful they would break, but they did not. How like some hearts that the storms passed over. I have been reading of Harriett G. Hosmer[124] this morning and Cowper.[125] What a difference in the two persons. The former found

---

124. "Harriet Goodhue Hosmer born October 9, 1830, Watertown, Massachusetts, died February 21, 1908, Watertown, MA. She was an American sculptor, one of the leading female sculptors working in Rome in the 19th century and perhaps the only one to win complete financial independence through her artistic work." Source: *Encyclopedia Britannica Online,* http://www.britannica.com/eb/article?tocId=9041155. *Zenobia, Queen of Palmyra,* a marble sculpture by Harriett Hosmer, executed about 1857, was presented to the Art Institute of Chicago as a gift of the Antiquarian Society in 1993.

125. "[William] Cowper's name will always be associated with that of John Newton, his friend and pastor. Together they wrote many hymns familiar to us today [*Walking With God, Light Shining Out of Darkness* and most familiarly, *Amazing Grace* which was titled *Faith's Review and Expectation.* Cowper suffered from bouts of acute depression. Newton saved him from suicide several times. In fact, because his nervous system was so delicate, he was unable to hold a job. Therefore he spent his time in literary

enjoyment in everything, the water, the mountains and all that was grand. Found a true admirer in Harriet Hosmer all things were turned with the bright side out to her. On being asked by a friend whom she went to bid adieu before going to Vienna if she would not be homesick. She replied I can be happy any place with good health and a bit of marble. Cowper on the other hand, was always melancholy, in fact, he was insane for a time. The cloud with silver lining always had the clouded side to him. Here comes Lizzie down. What can we do just now, but tell our fortunes in coffee cups. We found a little bird. Will found it in the yard. We think it has it's wing broken. Poor little thing.

Fifthday, May 22nd, 1862
I went home this morning, but just as sure as I go any place I find something wrong when I return as often this evening I feel out of humor or something. Jennie Vance pulled two of my peonies and several little things have occurred to annoy me but I guess I will never mind. Alma has gone home tonight and Lizzie is not here yet. I wish she would come. I am not well yet and I feel like I am going to be worse.

> Old letters let's keep them in memory of the dear old time
> Though the dear dear hand
> Which penned them be in some far off clime
> Or in the Silent-Spirit-Land.

There is no one save those who have never had the enjoyment of receiving letters from dear friends that will feel a sad feeling steal over them as they sit down alone perhaps by a winter-fireside for it is then we feel most the need of that companionship that will draw forth the closest affections of our hearts and with whom we can converse with a freedom and a confidence that will leave no void when we have left them—but when there are no friends to join with us in conversation, what will come nearest filling their place than old letters.

We draw our easy chair to the fireside, we close the blinds—for we would have no one see the tears that perhaps may fall. We take one little delicate scented note and glance over it and we look at it half sorrowful and yet with almost a smile but we put it away—and think, oh that was long ago, it is nothing to me now—we open another perhaps the dear, dear hand that has traced this is not dead to any save us and we linger over the pages half tearful for in our memory came the dreams we used to dream together—also dreams that have been so sadly broken. We read farther and at last almost fancy we are friends

---

pursuits, including writing poetry. His poetry was quite influential. Many people who scorned evangelicals as 'Methodists' would read Cowper's poems. He addressed many social issues, such as African slavery, as well as spreading the Gospel." Source: "William Cowper, 1731–1800," www.puritansermons.com/poetry/cowpindx.htm.

again and long to clasp the writer to our breast and murmur our forgiveness when, the cold words and haughty look of that friend comes up before us as when last we met and we remember that no atonements nor words of reconciliation can ever make us friends such as we were years ago before we became estranged. What a barrier from happiness is pride.

Sixthday, May 23rd, 1862

Not so bright this morning. I would like so well to take a ride this evening, but I suppose I must wait till we get a buggy and I fear that will be a long time. Our little bird has left us. It did not appreciate our kindness at all. I wonder if I am to go anyplace this summer. If I am it seems a good piece off. I thought surely I would get to see Matt soon, but May is almost gone and I can not hope to see her soon. It has been more than a year since we were there. It will be good to be at the cliffs again and old bridge. What great times we used to have there.[126] The roses will soon be blooming again. How beautiful the flowers are. Now if I only could get a letter this morning.

I have been reading this morning of Mary Fletcher, Dinah Evans, Ann Cartler, Methodist women of whom nothing but good works can be told. Dinah Evans is the heroine of *Adam Bede*.[127] How much better I would feel if I knew I was leaving behind me such a record of those pure women. The sun has come forth bright again.

---

126. The Marietta and Cincinnati Rail Road bridge crossed over Lees Creek at a deep ravine near or on the Ladd family farm land near Leesburg, Highland County, Ohio.

127. "John and Mary Bosanquet Fletcher were the most famous example of preaching partners in eighteenth-century England. They were an important inspiration to many American Methodists. Another prominent partnership was that of Seth and Dinah Evans who served as models for leading characters in George Eliot's novel, *Adam Bede,* a tragic love story." Source: "You and I Are Partners, A Heritage for Clergy Couples in Nineteenth Century American Methodism" by William T. Noll, in *Methodist History* 26, 1, October 26, 1987.

"A review of *Adam Bede* by George Eliot (1819–1880) was given in the *Atlantic Monthly,* October 1859. Marian Ann Evans was a Victorian writer, a humane freethinker, whose insightful psychological novels paved the way for modern character portrayals. She used the nom de plume or "pen name" of George Eliot because in those days writing was considered a male profession. *Silas Marner,* her next novel, was published in April 1861. She was a contemporary of Dostoevsky (1821–1881), who at the same time in Russia developed similar narrative techniques. Among his novels were *Crime and Punishment* and *The Brothers Karamazov.*

Seventhday, May 24th, 1862
Jeff took Lizzie and I for a ride this evening. We had a very pleasant time. Went to Vienna to _____. I think I have not had as pleasant a time for a long time.

Sabbath, May 25th, 1862
Went to Sabbath School this morning. Had a very large school. Our class more interesting than usual. I did not remain for church but came home. How nice it is for a ride this evening. I wish we could take a ride. Dave Saunders and several gentleman called here this evening.

Secondday, May 26th, 1862
Lizzie and I got up early this morning. Went to see the train come in—went for a walk. It has been such a long day. Mother came up this evening. There is Matt's letter. I think I must answer it. I am never in the mood lately. I wonder where I will be this time next May and I wonder if the war will be ended. If not, how much more sorrow will be over the land than is already. Let us hope that peace will come long ere the May flowers bloom again. The battle at Corinth is still expected. I think we will have nothing very definite before as Halleck has concluded all correspondents from the lines. It will be terrible when it does come. How anxious many hearts are awaiting. How can anyone be brave enough to rush forward to meet death with such unconcern as many do?

Thirdday, May 27th, 1862
Bright again. How beautiful this May has been. Just a few clouds to make us appreciate the sunshine more. Everything seems so beautiful were it not for the cloud resting over our country which casts so many shadows on our hearts. The roses are blooming, all but ours. They must be June roses. Well I like June roses. May it seems adapted to violets, daisies. June perfectly smiled on roses. I am going home this morning. Lizzie is going to Millers to "keep house" a short time. I must go and see her. Will took Lizzie and I out riding this evening. Had a pleasant time.

Fourthday, May 28th, 1862
Lizzie is at Millers yet. I took a long sleep this afternoon, but Alma came in and made me go home with her as Mr and Mrs Brown were going down, so I got acquainted some with them. Lizzie wrote me a letter this evening and gave it to me. I must answer it some time. She is coming up in the morning.

Fifthday, May 29th, 1862
Bright and warm. The sun has come out his morning as though there was nothing but perfect happiness over all the land. Maybe mother will come up. I wish she would. I hardly know what to do with myself this morning, but I must begin something soon or I will never accomplish much. I wish we could take a ride this evening. It would be so pleasant. Now if I only had a pony to ride. I could

go when I pleased. I never saw how fast the weeks pass away. Lizzie, Jeff, Ella and B. Hunt sang tonight. It seemed to be a very attractive place for a time.

Sixthday, May 30th, 1862
Went to the train this morning. There were some dead soldiers taken up. How very sad their friends must feel. It is such a warm day. It is supposed the battle at Corinth is in progress or soon will be. I hope our side will be victorious, that of course is natural. Our strawberries are ripe. We have just as many as we please. I wish we had our buggy done and could take a ride this evening, but I suppose I must be patient and wait a little longer.

Seventhday, May 31st, 1862
Will and I were going to have a nice ride this evening, but the clouds grew thick and dark and the wind blew quite like a storm for a little time and then the rain came down like water for certain. So we did not enjoy a ride, but perhaps the rain will do more good than the ride so we are very well satisfied. Lizzie has gone to Millers again. I expect she would rather board there than here. I took a fine nap this evening. This morning Mrs. Brown came down to get some strawberries and found me looking very shabby indeed, but of course she could not expect me to look well so early in the morning. I think I will like her very much.

June 1862

Sabbath, June 1st, 1862
June again and such a lovely morning just suited to June. The rain last night has left a pleasant cooling in the air and everything seems refreshed by the genial showers. How perfectly in order is everything that God commands. The snow, the hail and the rain all came just in the right season. We were at fathers. Birdsall's were there. We took Cola T and went riding but dear me, I am afraid she is going to die. She looks so poor, but perhaps she will soon be better.

Secondday, June 2nd, 1862
I do think I have been real busy today. There has been so many here for strawberries this evening. Mother came up a little while this evening and brought something good. I surely must settle my self down to work for I had rather be out doors working with flowers or standing at the gate looking up the street seeing no person very often and sometimes some person.

Thirdday, June 3rd, 1862
McClellan has had a battle near Richmond and was successful. I am glad although it is dreadful to think of the many lives lost. Banks retreat from Winchester [May 25, 1862, the first battle of Winchester, Virginia, 2,419 casualties] last week was quite serious.

Fourthday, June 4th, 1862
A gloomy morning, raining, chilly and dismal. Just the kind of weather to make us appreciate beautiful days. I think I am getting to be very careless about writing. I thought I would keep such a neat journal, but I guess I am just as [much] a "bloky" as ever.

Fifthday, June 5th, 1862
Raining again. How glad I will be to see the sun shining again. I was at Gibson's a few moments this evening. He is going to war next week. Oh, if the war only was over. I hope we will have nice flowers this summer, but I am such a poor hand to arrange flowers. Anyhow I don't see why I cannot have more taste about such things.

Sixthday, June 6th, 1862
A beautiful evening. I am sitting in the door and it is so very pleasant. Lib Vance and I took a ride this evening, but good fortune did not follow us all the time. After enjoying ourselves at the creek for a time, we started home, had the misfortune to run against a fence rail and broke the buggy. Berry was mad. We were sorry—could not help it. He need not have scolded us. We would do better next time. "Guess you will when you get it again, you won't get it anymore." But for that we would have had a pleasant ride indeed.

Seventhday, June 7th, 1862
I wonder if I will get to go any place this summer. I want to go to Richmond to Jamestown and let me see if that is all, no to see Matt and so many other places, but it is doubtful about going any place.

Sabbath, June 8th, 1862
Went to Sabbath School. Had a very interesting class. I am very glad I did not change classes for I like ours just as well as any. Gibsons called here a while this evening. I think Sallie is so sweet. Will Robison preached this evening. I think he will make such a splendid preacher.

Secondday, June 9th, 1862
The fife and drum this morning reminded me of old times when the fife and drum were new sounds in our rural village one year ago, but alas our hearts have become accustomed to war and we hear of thousands being killed and rejoice over our great victory and such a victory. Surely, human lives are too precious to be given for the mere satisfaction of the generals who are eager to make their report and often there is nothing gained except they occupy the field of battle. A very little victory I call it. Jeff, Lizzie and I took a ride this evening as far as fathers. They sang and played so well.

Thirdday, June 10th, 1862
Lizzie and I took a ride this evening on Cola T. down in the pasture. Jeff and Will watched us so if any accident occurred they might assist us. Callers to-night. Mrs. Langstaff, Lide and Wilmer, Martha and Psace. The first time they ever were here. I do think we had so much fun riding.

Fourthday, June 11th, 1862
Very busy making jelly. I expect it will be real nice when it is done. Clay is going to leave in the morning. I feel real sorry for him.

Fifthday, June 12th, 1862
Mother and Willie came up today. I have made some preserves. I think I am getting used to such things for I worked very faithful at it for a day or two. If we only had our buggy done. It is such pleasant weather for riding. I am getting tired of waiting so long for it, aren't thee Will?

Sixthday, June 13th, 1862
Mother, Alma and I took a ride this afternoon and went to Uncle Thomases [Stevens]. I do not see how they can stand it away so far from every person. We went to "Literary" tonight. It was interesting.

Seventhday, June 14th, 1862
Lizzie, Jeff and Alma went riding this evening. It is so dreadful warm. The warmest day of the season. Lizzie and I have real good times. It will be lonely without her.

Sabbath, June 15th, 1862
Sabbath and Sabbath School again. A good class. Jim Hunt and Jeff more properly, Mr. Hunt and Mr. Heston dined here today. Willot called here this evening. I think he is a very interesting man to converse with. No ride this evening and it would have been so pleasant.

Secondday, June 16th, 1862
I wonder if Lizzie and Jeff will go away visiting when school is out—Lizzie anyhow. Mary West is very sick. Cal and I were going to see her this evening, but as usual got disappointed. Perhaps we will go in the morning. She is in Wilmington.

Thirdday, June 17th, 1862
Cal and I did go to Wilmington. Mary is very bad, but some better than she had been. We had a very pleasant time only as we came home it rained all the time, but we did not get very wet.

Fourthday, June 18th, 1862
A wet gloomy morning. Just like autumn almost. I feel very unwell this morning. Perhaps riding nine miles when the air was real chilly and the rain coming down all the time had something to do with the matter. Soon have potatoes and peas—goody.

Fifthday, June 19th, 1862
The sun is still darkened. The week almost gone and next week the last of school. No letter or anything. No news either. I wish I could hear something good.

Sixthday, June 20th, 1862
I hope we will go to "Literary" this evening. Oh, Pshaw, I think my journal is getting to be an old thing. Willie came up home with me this morning and mother is coming soon.

Seventhday, June 21st, 1862
Somehow or rather I like it the afternoon anyhow after all the rooms are swept and dusted, the flowers in the vases, the baking done. It seems so good to think for a little while, at least. Everything is in order. This evening we went to the train. There were several soldiers got off the train. Tomorrow is Sabbath. I wonder if I will know my lesson. I fear I do not as I ought for I have not read it over even. A great thing to put in my journal to be read perhaps, who knows, by my grandchildren. They would think their grandmother had not been very studious to delay it this long. Lizzie and I took exercise this evening by walking on the railroad iron.

Sabbath, June 22nd, 1862
Rained some this morning. We went down home for dinner. Had a good one. Clark, Milton, Sarah, Lydia, Jeff and Lizzie and others were there. We took a ride this evening. Will and I took Eva and Willie with us. It was such a pleasant evening for riding. Will and I went over to church tonight. Had some very sensible preaching. One week more and school will be over for a while.

Secondday, June 23rd, 1862
It has just poured down. Rain part of the time today. I hope it will not rain four days this week. Alma has been here this afternoon. She received a letter from Mary. She is coming over soon. I am glad of it. I wrote to her this morning and to Matt the other day. Oh! dear such a mean pen and ink in this journal will be a pretty thing indeed for anyone ever to read. I do wish Will had time to keep a journal so I could read it sometimes. It rained so hard this evening and is thundering again. Well, well, I must quit and get tea ready. What must I get. Let me see—Cheese, bread and butter and what else?

Thirdday, June 24th, 1862
I have got the dishes washed. I am glad of it for I always dread it. It certainly is going to rain again, but we will have potatoes all the sooner for it. I wish I could get a good letter from some kind of friend this morning. My letters are getting to be like Angel visits of late. I do want to go to Richmond so badly, but I fear we will get disappointed about it. When we have nothing to say we should say nothing and as the same rule will apply to writing. I had better quit for this morning. We took a ride this evening. Lizzie and I just a short one though. Alma and Lizzie and Cal had been riding and when they came home I suppose they took pity on me and let me go.

Fourthday, June 25th, 1862
Not raining this morning. Frank Smith washed here today and I fear I will be responsible for one story she told. I was in the parlor and heard someone talking and telling that I was at home and for him to go round to the front door. I just knew it was a peddler, so I slipped upstairs and told Frank I did not want to see him. She opened the door for him and said as innocently as could "She is not at home." So I feel responsible for that. I went home this evening and helped mother. Alma got tea up here. I brought up the buggy and we all took a ride. All of us three. Oh, Cal has a baby. It seems so funny.

Fifthday, June 26th, 1862
I was to see Cal's baby last evening. It is a sweet little girl.[128] I wish I had it or one like it—or a little girl anyhow. It is such a warm morning and I am so lazy.

Sixthday, June 27th, 1862
Up early this morning. I think I am always so sleepy in the morning, but after I am up I am glad of it. I do hope I will get Will in the notion of visiting some this fall. Going to try. Now let me see, there is Richmond, Ridgeville, Jamestown, Leesburg and so many places we might just as well go as not. Our Bible lesson—I wonder if we will have any more about it than we did last Sabbath. I really do hope so, for if our examination comes

"Lizzie" Russell Betts

---

128. Carolyn "Cal" Janney Betts, gave birth to a daughter on June 25, 1862, naming her Elizabeth Russell Betts. Carolyn Janney was the daughter of Joseph and Elizabeth Russell Janney and was an older sister of Will Janney. She was married to Madison Betts, the son of Christopher C. and Lydia Huff Betts, and was a first cousin to Paulena. Elizabeth R. Betts was later called "Lizzie," and her photograph later appeared in Paulena's album.

we will be in rather a tight place as they said. If I only had something good to read. I do want some new books so badly, but I suppose I must wait. I do wish I had a sweet little girl to play with and be with. How dearly I would love it.

Seventhday, June 28th, 1862
School closed this afternoon. The Lyceum was pretty good, only there was so much noise, it was not so interesting as it would be—would have been.

Sabbath, June 29th, 1862
Went to Sabbath School this morning. Had some visitors who asked our class questions. I did get so tired in meeting I could scarcely hold my head up. We went to Millers for dinner today. The first time we were ever there to eat. We had a real pleasant time. Lizzie is sitting by the window reading. Jeff and Will are out looking at the bees. They seem to have great affection for them. Oh, I do wish we had our buggy.

Secondday, June 30th, 1862
The last June of 1862 will pass away when the daylight fades away this evening. July will soon be here. Tomorrow is my birthday. Time has passed very gently with me since my eyes first saw the light 22 years tomorrow. 22 years, hence, if I live, I cannot say this, for trouble comes to us all and who can tell what will be my destiny ere then. It is very warm this morning, warm as July itself. Lizzie, Alma and I are going to enjoy ourselves, for a time, if we have no ill luck. For vacation will not last always. I do want to see Matt so badly. Bless her life. I wonder if she will ever change like some others have done.

[Letter found in back pages of journal written to her friend Matt]

> Matt Darling,
> Do not start—turn pale or faint—for I assure thee this is nothing more or less than a leaf from my journal. People who live in glass houses must not throw stones and the injunction "Do unto others as you would others would do unto you" is not so often observed as " do unto others as others do unto you"—no insinuations or, at least, no bad ones intended. For indeed, I do love thee more than I can tell and this morning as I am sitting up in Lizzie's room with my journal on my knee, my heart is longing for thy presence and this fine morning. Sunshine and balmy wind comes streaking in through the open window reminding me of those mornings we sat in our little room just as Lizzie and I are now—here comes Jeff upstairs with the paper and I simply say good morning without looking up and Lizzie laughs. I go on with my letter. I hoped to have seen thee before May was quite gone, but it has gone and June will soon be gone. Will we never meet again? The time seems very long indeed.

I imagine I can see thee this morning with thy sewing or a book—serving of course, for thee is an old woman thee knows. Well Lizzie and Jeff are talking about the objective elements, so I guess I will go downstairs and finish this after dinner. I am so dreadful tired of cooking—am I not simple. I sometimes think I am 'Anonconpros mentis' [*non compos mentis* is Latin for not of sound mind].

Home June 20th 1862

Thirdday, July 1st, 1862 [Paulena's twenty-second birthday]
My birthday. I wonder if I will be as happy one year from now as I now am. Lizzie, me and Cal were at father's for tea this evening. Had a very pleasant time. I took a ride on "Julia" this evening.

Fourthday, July 2nd, 1862
I am anxious to hear news from the battle at Richmond. If I only had faith in McClellan I would have so much more hope, but what has he ever done to gain our confidence? Tomorrow we want to go to Uncle David's. Alma came up this evening and we all tried to take a nap, but it was so very warm and the children made so much noise—not ours—that I did not enjoy my nap much.

Fifthday, July 3rd, 1862
We went to Uncle Davids. Had a very pleasant time. A good supper—all felt stupid. Bad news. The worst, almost, that could have come. McClellan is defeated. Oh, if he is a traitor what punishment is severe enough for him. Everything seems gloomy, for what could have been more unfortunate than the great army should be defeated and at a point where France and England have been watching with "Argusges." Surely something must be very wrong. Who is it? McClellan—or is it someone of the cabinet or else Stanton himself. There must be someone to blame for it and the blood of murdered soldiers call for vengeance. It is terrible to think of the wounded and dying upon the bloody field of carnage with the warm sun pouring down and no one to give them even a cup of cold water.

July 4th, 1862
Five minutes after ten this warm fourth of July. How little of independence can be celebrated today, but every heart will feel more deeply the blessing of a free and happy country years ago when the 4th of July came as a matter of course and was celebrated accordingly. More fully appreciated the great and noble work our forefathers had done in restoring liberty and independence on the American people, but today when our country is tottering upon the verge of destruction, all are awakened to our terrible danger and remembering other 4th of July's long past are determined to celebrate it even it be the last and would

it not be a coincidence if today our army should retrieve their misfortune at Richmond and achieve a great victory. There would it could be so, but how faint are the hopes of any good news today.[129] News a little better, but not very reliable.

Seventhday, July 5th, 1862
Such a warm day. Three hundred thousand more men called for by the president. Ohio's quota 40,000. I fear they will have to draft to get that many. Oh dear, what will I do if Will has to go. I do hope he won't. My Scripture, not looked at yet. How careless I am, but then I can get it yet. The girls had a very good time yesterday, but then I am sure I do not envy them. Bad news this evening. 40,000 men wanted within 40 days. I am so afraid they will draft and then what will become of us. I have had one cry already about it.

Sabbath, July 6th, 1862
Went to Sabbath school this morning, but few in our class. I have just been crying and crying. I am so afraid Will will have to go to war and what would I do. My life would not be happy any longer. Will and Jeff have been under the canopy of the heaven, lying on the green grass before the east window. At last we are all out here. There seems to be no better shrine. I pity the poor soldiers who are wounded or on duty this hot day. Oh, who can conceive this terrible suffering. If I only knew Will did not have to go to war how much happier would I be, but I am so fearful.

Secondday, July 7th, 1862
Just the same as other Seconddays. Lizzie and I went to the bridge this evening and saw the train pass. The old bridge. How like old times it seemed to be there again. I could not keep a feeling of sadness away when I remember the long warm noons when Elma and several of us school girls used to pass there, but alas! the old bridge would have been silent long ago. It had waited for our footsteps to break the silence for we are all scattered now and Elma is sleeping that last long sleep. Oh! many hours of happiness we used to spend together. [See May 23, 1860, entry for memorial poem written by Paulena for Elma.]

Thirdday, July 8th, 1862
Such a warm day. I wish I did not have to work any for I know I do not feel like it. The news is very discouraging. McClellan is receiving the censure of so many, I think there will be something done soon, for people will not stand such terrible defeats and butcheries as is carried on by McClellan. I almost think he is a traitor. I have not had any faith in him for a long time. If he ever does anything

---

129. It was the eighty-sixth anniversary of the signing of the Declaration of Independence and it was seventy-nine years after the signing of the Treaty of Paris, which ended the Revolutionary War.

worthy of praise l am willing to give him praise, but if he is as slow in the future as he has been in the past, I think his removal will be all that will conciliate the people. I almost hate him sometimes.

Fourthday, July 9th, 1862
We are so afraid they are going to draft and what will we all do if that does happen. I am afraid to build any air castles or plan any visits or anything for it will be so much worse to be disappointed about. It seems to me I can never be happy again if Will has to go to war. How could I pass our home.

Fifthday, July 10th, 1862
McClellan is recovering reinforcements all the time. We are all hoping he will have a victory at Richmond, but if he fails there how despairing will our prospects be—foreign intervention will be sure to ensue and war with France or England would certainly be a great misfortune to America. But if Will has to go to war it is no use to think of anything like pleasure for the future.

Sixthday, July 11th, 1862
I went down home this evening and Alma and I took a ride and Willie too who felt very important when he was driving. I am glad Willie is little now for he cannot go to war. I know I am not very patriotic, but it seems so bad to let our friends go and be murdered as it were by them. So often incompetent officers under whose control they are, are doomed to go on after to their death.

Seventhday, July 12th, 1862
A warm day after the fine rain, Lizzie and I alone again are going down home this evening. Mother is going to have fried chicken for me, Eva says. Tomorrow is Sabbath School again. I am afraid we will not have our lessons good. It seems like we are so careless about it. I must do better in the future.

Sabbath, July 13th, 1862
Went to Sabbath School. Did not know our lessons very well. Jeff and Lizzie were here for dinner. Alma also. Lizzie went away this evening. If we only had our buggy to go riding in. Will they never get it done. Alma is going to stay up here tonight. I certainly must write to Jennie.

Secondday, July 14th, 1862
Sick today. I am glad evening is coming for I have passed a very unpleasant day. I have been in so much pain. I could not stay in bed a minute and so I have been walking around and no one would have thought me sick. We are going down home this evening. Perhaps I will stay two or three days.

Fifthday, July 17th, 1862
Will and I went to grandfathers. Had a good dinner and supper. It just poured

down rain. Did not get home. Will stayed at fathers. Have been there ever since Secondday evening. There is not much news. Only Kentucky is in danger again. A great many troops pouring in to guard Lexington. Mrs. Frank Martin died last evening. Her death was very sudden.

Sixthday, July 18th, 1862
The moss roses are blooming and look very pretty. I love home so well. I am sure of never getting tired of it. Sometimes I get tired of staying here and long for a change, but it always seems good to get home again. I am so in hopes Will will not have to go to war, but someone has to go or the rebellion will never be crushed. If England and France will only let us alone. I hope the war will not last as long as I expect it will, but I never had an idea it would be a short war.

Seventhday, July 19th, 1962
It seems real good to be alone. No boarders or any thing to bother me. I am so worried about Will going to war. I am so in hopes he will not go.

Sabbath, July 20th, 1862
The same old routine. Sabbath School and church. I was teacher of our class. I think I should like to be a teacher real well. Emma and Sallie Miller and Alma were here for dinner. Will and I have been sitting in our grapevine retreat. It is such a cool and pleasant place.

Secondday, July 21st, 1862
No better news today. Everything looks so dark and I fear there is another chance that for Will to go to war. What will I do if he does. It will be such along time and perhaps he will never come home. I hope we will soon have better news though.

Thirdday, July 22nd, 1862
Nothing to encourage us yet. I will be glad when we hear to a certainty what we are going to do but oh, so sad if Will has to go. I feel so strange about writing a few days. I have always been so uneasy whenever anything was said about drafting and so afraid Will would go, but now I feel so much more in heart some way. Will either is not going or else it is right for him to go—which is it. A few days will decide it for the best, I hope.

Fourthday, July 23rd, 1862
Will and I canned up some blackberries[129] this morning. How much better

---

130. "John Mason, whose name canning jars are still known by, patented the screw neck bottle or the 'Mason Jar' on November 30, 1858. [The jars were threaded to accept a zinc screw-top lid.] By the time of the American Civil War (1861–1865) air tight lids had been made possible with the use of disposable rubber rings—or gaskets—that

would I feel if I knew he would stay at home for little good all the fruit would do me if Will went away. There was a war meeting held tonight addressed to several persons all of whom seemed anxious. Everybody else would go but they could not leave home quite so willingly. The principle speaker was Meane who made a very good speech and the young and handsome recruiting officer also made some remarks.

Fifthday, July 24th, 1862

Such a pleasant morning. Nothing to mar the beauty except this fearful war raging so fearfully over our land. How many hearts tonight feel the weight as of years that a little time ago beat with happiness. Alas this cruel war. How dreadful will be the sin of those who brought it on.

Sixthday, July 25th, 1862

We surely shall hear stirring news when action does begin and then for the long list of killed, wounded and again. If no person was killed it would not seem so bad, but someone must be killed and there is no telling who that someone is to be. Just as apt to be the poor imbecile without home or friends who will be spared as those who have friends waiting in painful anxiety for their return. Alma and mother were up this evening. Alma stayed to go to literary. She is going to declaim,[131] "Go my boy where duty calls you."

Seventhday, July 26th, 1862

I was up early this morning. Rumor says that the cabinet made some treaty with France concerning Mexico to prevent intervention. How much truth is contained in it waits to be told in future. Wilot was called home again this morning. His children are worse again. How I do hope they will get well. Our yard looks so pretty. I think I never saw it look so pretty before. If our flowers only would bloom like every one else.

Sabbath, July 27th, 1862

Took no interest in school this morning. Mary came up this morning, but did not stay long. She is going to board at fathers and attend the "Pustilate" [postulate]. I am not going to take any boarder, but Lizzie.

Secondday, July 28th, 1862

More news about drafting. I guess they surely intend to draft and what will

---

were set between the glass lid and jar." Source: http://digital.lib.msu.edu/projects/cookbooks/html/museum/object_054.html.

131. Declaim means: "To deliver a formal recitation, especially as an exercise in rhetoric or elocution." Source: *The American Heritage Dictionary of the English Language,* 4th ed., 2000.

become of us all if they do? I am so afraid Will will have to go. How good it would seem to hear some good news for everything has been so dark so long. Perhaps morning is not far distant for the darkest cloud is just before morning.

Thirdday, July 29th, 1862
I have not enough ambition to write anything worth reading. I am afraid my old journal will be no more interesting this time than my others, but I just can't write anything worth looking at. There is nothing at all to encourage the people in regard to them or unless the appointment of [Henry] Halleck as commander in chief of the army and I think that has not caused general satisfaction for although he is an improvement of McClellan. I fear he is too much a [illegible] to ever accomplish anything but we must give him time, and his defeat, would almost ruin us now. I hope there will be no more.

Fourthday, July 30th, 1862
We went down home this evening. There are two ladies besides Mary boarding there—Miss Stevens and Miss Ireland.

Fifthday, July 31st, 1862
The last day of July. Will another July find us in a worse or better condition. There seems to me no hope for us for a time for I think we will be purged to the utmost before the war is ended, but oh, why do the innocent suffer so much. Why not visit upon the hearts of those who brought the rebellion on, the punishment due. I think while we have as many mean generals as we have there will not be much change. It is going to be another hot day. I pity the poor soldiers. If I only knew [for] certain that Will would not have to go to war I would feel so much better and if we only had our buggy done, I am afraid we will never get the ride in it. There was a very sudden death this evening. Matilda McKay went to fathers this forenoon and after eating her dinner began spitting blood and in about three minutes was dead. It seems so bad for Alice and her father.

August 1862

Sixthday, August 1st, 1862
Everything as discouraging as ever. When will we hear any more good news. We went to the funeral this afternoon. She was buried in the cemetery at Wilmington near Prit and Lide. I thought as I stood by their graves what a mighty change has come over them. Just a few years ago they were full of life and their proud spirits scarcely dreamed of death and Alice petted and indulged by them all. It seems a great change for her now. Left almost alone with no mother or sister to care for her.

Seventhday, August 2nd, 1862[132]
We went to George's in the evening. The first time I had been there in a long time.

Sabbath, August 3rd, 1862
Went to Sabbath School. Did not recite—so few in our class. Came home. I have felt so bad all day. I take little interest in anything lately for everything looks so dark.

Secondday, August 4th, 1862
A dark morning. We are so in hopes it will rain for it is so dusty. No better news and everything to discourage us. I do wonder what will become of us.

Thirdday, August 5th, 1862
There was meeting at Morrisville this afternoon. We went over. There were only two volunteers, Captains, Spencer Allen and Hicks were there. They are to be here this evening. Oh, what a sad time it is. There is worse news than ever this morning. 300,000 men to be drafted again the tenth of next month. It seems like every hope is almost gone. If Will could only go for nine months without being drafted I could give up so much more willingly.

Fourthday, August 6th, 1862
Oh, what would I not give to feel once again as freehearted as in months gone by. Everything seems so dark now. I feel just like I had been to a funeral. Everything was so sad last night. Steve has volunteered. [See August 21 entry.] I feel sorry for Lyd, but I fear my turn will come next and there are only a few days to decide between being drafted and volunteering. If I only knew Will could come back again, but it is so dangerous. I have just been sick all day.

Fifthday, August 7th, 1862
Nothing to encourage us yet and I feel more like being in bed than anywhere else. If there only would be something to encourage us a little but all is so dark and I fear it is not yet the crisis.

Sabbath, August 17th, 1862
A week or more since I have written in my journal. I just did not have the heart to do anything for I thought Will would surely have to go to war or be drafted, but after days of suspense the good news came that the time for receiving

---

132. Stephen Janney's official Civil War records from the National Archives state that he was enrolled as a first sergeant, Company G, Seventy-ninth Regiment, Ohio Infantry, August 2, 1862, in Martinsville, Ohio, for three years. He was thirty years old, 5' 10", with a fair complexion, blue eyes, and dark hair. He was mustered in at Camp Dennison on August 20, 1862.

volunteers was extended, but oh! I do not know what we will do. Yet Will may be gone this time next week. Cary Cluxton[133] fell from a horse a few evenings since last Sixthday evening and has been insensible ever since. There is not much hope of his recovery. I hope he will get well. It was so sudden. Where will I be in four weeks from this evening.

The Voices in the Fire
[By Paulena Stevens Janney]

How they mingle with our fancies. Sometimes they are very merry and harmonize and are in perfect unison with our thoughts. We are happy and the voices we hear are Angelic ones and the forms we people are clothed in bright shining garments and dwell in temples rare and gorgeous. The voices call to us and beckon with their fairy fingers for us to come and revel amid the splendor and beauty we see shining through the portals of our fancy land. We long to go, but hands that we do not see, seem to bear us farther and farther away from our goal and the voices die away into a low murmur that reminds us we are yet afar off. Then the voices are sad and where a little time ago lifted high the castles and dreams and flitted the bright forms and where we heard the voices that awakened such hopefulness in our hearts in all one blackened mass and form the ruins come the voices we hear when we are unhappy and they sound like a dirge for our faded dreams. And the voices tell us that our lives are made up of happy and unhappy moments and that the nearer we attain to that city, which is no fancied one, but a city wherein there is no need of the sun neither of the moon to shine upon it, for the glory of God brightens it. The lamb is the light thereof the nearer will we attain to happiness.

Secondday, August 18th, 1862
I am getting rather careless about writing in my journal, but perhaps I will feel more like it after awhile. Our buggy is about done. How glad I am for we have waited so long for it. Steve [Stephen Janney] left for camp Denison.[134] I do hope Will will not have to go.

---

133. Cary Cluxton was married to Evelyn Hiatt, daughter of Clarkson Hiatt and Jane Hollingsworth. Evelyn was a second cousin to Paulena.

134. In 1861 General Rosecrans selected an area seventeen miles from downtown Cincinnati as a recruitment and training area for Union soldiers. Its proximity to the Little Miami Railroad and to Cincinnati made it a desirable location. It was thought that Cincinnati needed to be protected from Confederate attack. The camp was named Camp Dennison, after Ohio William Dennison, who was governor of Ohio at the outset of the Civil War. Today the Camp Dennison Civil War Museum is open to the public. It

Thirdday, August 19th, 1862
We have got our buggy home. It seems so good to think about it. We cannot take a ride until it rains for it is so dusty. It would ruin it almost. This is the last week of School. I have not been up at all. I have been so busy sewing this week that I have not taken time for much else. I have been hoping for it to rain, but as yet it has not come.

Fourthday, August 20th, 1862
Well I have had my wish for it has rained. But as "it never rains but it pours."[135] Of course it is muddy and we cannot go riding. Perhaps tomorrow. I am so afraid we will hear bad news for McClellan is such a poor excuse. I wish they would remove him and put Burnside in his place. It is so rumored. No letter from Matt or Jennie. Why don't they write. Because I was so slow writing to them, I expect.

Fifthday, August 21st, 1862
One first ride in our buggy at last. It is very nice to ride in. There were several that left this morning for Camp Chase. There was quite a crowd to see them off. Tomorrow is the last day for receiving recruits for new regiments. I am so afraid there will be drafting.

Sixthday, August 22nd, 1862
If I would write in my journal every day I would not make so many mistakes. We took a ride on Sixthday. Instead of Fifthday. I think I will be more careful in future.

Seventhday, August 23rd, 1862
Will went away this evening to help build those bridges that were burned by the rebels or their sympathizers on this railroad [Marietta and Cincinnati RR]. School closed tonight. It was not so very interesting to me. Lizzie and I are going to remain here tonight.

Sabbath, August 24th, 1862
Lizzie and I got up very late this morning and had breakfast accordingly. I did

---

is located on Ohio State Road 126, southwest of I-275. State Road 28 comes down directly from Martinsville and connects with SR 126. It was about thirty-seven miles from Martinsville.

135. "When it rains, it pours" is a cliche that means, "If something happens at all, it is likely to show up in excess." The phrase is old enough to have served as part of a title of a work by John Arbuthnot in 1726: *It Cannot Rain but It Pours.* Source: *The Dictionary of Cliches*, James Rogers, 1985.

not attend Sabbath School or church. Alma and Mary were here for dinner. I wish Will was here. There was a disgraceful scene transpired this evening. Alma, Mary and I were sitting in the door and had the misfortune to witness a fight.

Secondday, August 25th, 1862
I am anxious and yet almost afraid to hear this morning's news. Last Seventhday the news was rather discouraging. The letter from Washington began, "Oceans of water but not a drop to drink." Hundreds of brigades but not one in the right place and everything seemed to indicate a battle soon and the most terrible of the war. Surely if God is with us he will help us to conquer our enemies.

Thirdday, August 26th, 1862
Alma, Mary and I went to Amos Hunts today. Had a very pleasant time, rather late getting home. Seemed like the nearer we got home the longer the road was, but at last we saw the lights glimmering in town. All save our home which looked dark and alone. Will had not come home. Lizzie away. I am so in hopes there will be no drafting here.

Fourthday, August 27th, 1862
Will came home last night. He came to the window and called me. It did not frighten me at all though it was 2 o'clock and I had not heard the train come. Sarah A. West is very sick. Will went for some of her friends. We went home this morning. It seems so much better than when there were so many there. Cary is not improving very fast and I fear he will never be well again. There is no important news and nothing to encourage us unless it is that the foreign intervention is not so likely to occur as we thought for a time. The main object of England and France seems to be toward putting an end to this bloody war and they have too good sense not to see that any interference on their part would only prolong and make the war more bloody.

Fifthday, August 28th, 1862
We went to the funeral this morning. There were so many there. It is so much like autumn. Everything so lovely. Will cleaned the walks today and it improves the looks very much. We took a ride this evening and went to Will's old home. Alma, Mary and Cal went out to see Clay this afternoon. I wonder if they will ever make it all right again.

Sixthday, August 29th, 1862
Such a bright day. I guess we will not get to take any more rides soon, not for a day or two. The news is no more encouraging. I think something surely will be done soon, but oh! to accomplish anything how many lives must be sacrificed for the rebels are so determined. They will fight desperately. Jeff and Lizzie are going to Harveysburg.

Seventhday, August 30th, 1862
No news to encourage us rather the reverse. So much like September for certain. The leaves rustling in the breeze, the pleasant breeze of autumn. It seems sweet and sad for we know not but where this time next year our country will be much worse than it is now and so we should love this autumn for I think it is the turning point in our revolution. I read in a paper just now that bleeding may be stopped by the application of flour and salt in equal parts. I hope I will remember it, if I ever need to.

Sabbath, August 31st, 1862
Jeff and Lizzie came home this morning. They brought us a fine melon which we had for dinner. Alma, Will and I went to Birdsall's this evening. Had such a pleasant time. I do like to go there so well. I do not suppose Lizzie will board here much longer than this week.

September 1862

Secondday, September 1st, 1862
We had such bad news this morning. Our army which we have depended so much upon, has been given back to Washington. McClellan failed to reinforce Pope. Oh! the scoundrel, I detest him. What will become of us if he is kept and McDowell is a traitor. Surely, they are all demented at Washington—corruption: corruption thy name is Washington. We had such a pleasant ride to Wilmington this evening. So cool and the roads so nice.

Thirdday, September 2nd, 1862[136]
The news does not improve. So many of our men killed, murdered by McClel-

---

136. "There was a distinct threat once when twelve thousand Confederate troops led by Edmund Kirby Smith marched toward Cincinnati in an attempted invasion of the North. September 2, 1862, saw Cincinnati under martial law imposed by Union General Lew Wallace (who later wrote *Ben Hur*). A hasty pontoon bridge was thrown across the river. Within five days, seventy thousand men had crossed the river and were in place on the hills behind Covington. The Southern army turned back, and the Siege of Cincinnati was over. Nearly a year later, on July 13, 1863, John Morgan's Confederate raiders passed north and east of the city, and martial law was again declared. The fast-striking, hard-riding Morgan men vanished as quickly and as innocently as they had appeared.

"Nearly seventy thousand men marched across the pontoon bridge to head off an anticipated Confederate attack in 1862. The pontoons were in place near the site of the present Suspension Bridge, Cincinnati and its Kentucky neighbors were under martial law during the threat." Source: "War and Peace: 1860 to 1870," Luke Peck, *Yesterday's Cincinnati*, Cincinnati Public Library.

Stephen Janney's official Civil War record from the National Archives places Stephen and the Seventy-ninth Regiment, Ohio Infantry, crossing that pontoon bridge:

lan and McDowell. They both ought to be hung high as Ha-man.[137] I have so much to do this week. So much sewing. Oh! if I only had the power Lincoln has for a little while. How I would improve it. It just makes me almost despise everyone of them to see how unconcerned they are. I have lost all faith in all of them, but have the poor consolation of know[ing] that it will effect nothing. The fair begins next week, but I don't think we will go.

Pontoon Bridge over the Ohio at Cincinnati.
Library of Congress

Fourthday, September 3rd, 1862

I am so in hopes there will be no drafting here. Sometimes we hear there will be none and again we hear the reverse. So I suppose we will just have to wait and see. Lyd in much trouble for the 79th Reg left camp today I believe. She went to camp Denison to see him [Steven Janney].

Fifthday, September 4th, 1862

The startling news has come that Cincinnati is in danger. Thousands are hurrying to the rescue and the rebels will find that they cannot invade our free state without fighting desperately for never were people more determined—having lost all confidence in our cabinet, the cabinet of the Republic. There is nothing to rely upon, save the strong arms of the western boys. Shame on the wicked city and people of Washington. They should henceforth be deemed a blot upon our nation unless . . . in future, redeem themselves.

"From the camp at Dennison, Ohio, they were ordered south to repel General Kirby Smith's raid into Kentucky, and were opposed to General Bragg's forces for some time."

137. "Haman is known to Bible History from the book of Esther where, because Esther's cousin Mordecai (who was in fact very loyal to the king himself) would not bow down to him, Haman spitefully tried, and failed, to destroy all Jews within the kingdom. . . . Then said Harbona, one of the eunuchs in attendance on the king, 'Moreover, the gallows which Haman has prepared for Mordecai, whose word saved the king, is standing in Haman's house, fifty cubits high.' And the king said, 'Hang him on that.' So they hanged Haman on the gallows which he had prepared for Mordecai." "Esther 7:9–10 RSV". Source: "Daily Bible Study," http://www.keyway.ca/htm2001/20010107.htm.

Sixthday, September 5th, 1862
A great many went to protect Cincinnati and some went to Leesburg to the great Sabbath School examination—I did not care to go. Martial law has been proclaimed so we will all submit. What a dreadful state of affairs our country is in. Is there no hope but for us to be overpowered. Surely with our "Three hundred thousand more" we can free ourselves.

Waiting and Watching
[By Paulena Stevens Janney]

I am very, very lonely
As the shadows quickly fly
For I'm waiting and watching
For a darling one to die.

Her little hands are folded
And her breath comes short and low
And it will be but a moment
Till my darling one will go.

I have watched her all the evening
How her eyes grew large and bright
And she whispered to me fondly
Mother, I will die tonight.

Oh how sadly I am watching
By her little snowy bed
Putting back the golden ringlets
From her sunny baby head.

Now the twilight's growing deeper
And the sky first tinged with red
Cast a shadow upon the sleeper
For my darling one is dead.

Seventhday, September 6th, 1862
The news worse than ever. Many exciting rumors. The rebels said to be marching on Cincinnati.

   We took a ride this evening. Such a pleasant one. I am glad Will happened to be away yesterday or he would have been gone with the rest of them.

Sabbath, September 7th, 1862
So hot and dusty. Alma here. She is sick. We have been at home lazy enough. Lizzie went away this morning to her new boarding place. Her school begins tomorrow.

Secondday, September 8th, 1862
We took a ride again this evening. Went to Jo Hunts. They gave us such nice apples to bring home. The news is a little more favorable concerning Cincinnati, but still there is danger of an attack. I hope the rebels will get the worse whipping they get in their lives if they do come.

Thirdday, September 9th, 1862
Went home this morning early. Will brought the buggy down this evening and we had a nice ride. We went toward Charlie Orens. It was not very dusty and was much more pleasant. I am making my new calico dress this week. I think I have had it long enough to make it.

Fourthday, September 10th, 1862
Warm again. I do wonder if it ever will rain. Perhaps Alma, Will and I will go over to Wilmington this week and see Mary, but there is danger of us getting out of the notion as we often do. This evening Cal, Alma and I went down to the train. I had the good fortune or bad fortune to meet a lady alone in trouble. So what could I do but bring her home with me. She wished to go to Wilmington to see her husband. Sometimes I did not believe a word she said and then I thought, perhaps she tells the truth.

Fifthday, September 11th, 1862
Last night news came that Cincinnati was in danger again. Will, with several others went this evening. I hoped there will be no battle. We took that woman part of the way to Wilmington this morning. I wonder if she has seen all she says she has—the battle of Bullrun.[138] I wish Will was at home. We had a fine rain this evening.

Sixthday, September 12th, 1862
Alma, mother and I came up home this morning. I guess Alma and I will stay at

---

138. The Second Battle of Bull Run [Bull Run was the name of a water course], or Battle of Manassas, as the Confederates called it, was fought from August 28 to August 30, 1862, in Prince William County, Virginia. Maj. Gen. John Pope led the Union forces; Gen. Robert E. Lee and Maj. Gen. Thomas J. Jackson led the Confederate forces. This was the decisive battle of the Northern Virginia Campaign and a Confederate victory. There were 22,180 casualties (Union 13,830; Confederate 8,350). Source: Heritage Preservation Service, CWSAC Battle Summaries, Second Manassas, American Battlefield Protection Program, http://www.cr.nps.gov/hps/abpp/battles/va026.htm.

home tonight and perhaps Will will be at home tomorrow night as they have not attacked the city yet. Jim Hunt, Jr and Miss Cluxton [James E. Hunt and Sarah Cluxton] were married this evening.[139] I wonder if they will be happy. It seems to me there will have to be a great change in them both.

Seventhday, September 13th, 1862
I went home with Alma this morning. The news is better. The rebels have run. I am glad. I look for Will this evening. Will came for certain. I was so glad. I suppose Fannie Brown is for she was uneasy about "William." I like her real well.

Sabbath, September 14th, 1862
Such a lovely morning. So cool and pleasant. I am a bad girl. I am not going to school or meeting. I have no bonnet to wear. I have been reading *Rose Clark* by Fannie Fern. It is real good. Alley is very sick this evening. Will and I went to Blanchester to send a dispatch to Aaron and we went to Wilots. It seems so funny. I like his wife so well or think I will. I do wish they would come up. I would be so glad to have them come.

Secondday, September 15th, 1862
Alley is very bad, yet not much hope of his getting well. We have been putting up peaches today. Alma was here and helped us. We did not get done. We went to George's this evening. I am so afraid the crisis has not come yet in national troubles. We have not suffered enough yet, I fear, to purge us as we should be. I do hope that the war will be over sometime though. We have had some victories. One in Kentucky and we had a defeat someplace.

Thirdday, September 16th, 1862
Another day of fruit canning. I am so glad it is over. We have 24 cans put up of peaches. Will is tired and gone to bed. I must go soon. How thankful we should be that we can lie down at night in our own dear home, sleep sweetly and awake in the bright morning all refreshed while so many poor people are homeless, fearful or in some great trouble. How contented we should be. I received a good letter from Jennie the other morning—"Flora is dead," Jennie says, "consumption had so preyed upon her young life thee could scarcely have recognized her." [Flora was four years old, the younger sister of Jennie, John, and James Hadley, children of Jeremiah and Esther Smith Hadley.] There has been a terrible battle at Middletown, Maryland.[140] Lee commanding the rebels,

---

139. Jim Hunt was the son of Jonathan Hunt and Margaret Hadley. Sarah R. Cluxton was the daughter of William and Margaret Cluxton.

140. In September 1862, Lee began his invasion of Maryland and crossed the Potomac near Point of Rocks. The president asked McClellan to resume command of the Army of the Potomac.

McClellan the federals. It is said we have a great victory, but it is so uncertain about anything in that department. Lincoln seems to be in bad grace among some people. I think myself he has had too little energy.

Fourthday, September 17th, 1862
So warm again, Oh! I have been so sick today, but am better this evening and I guess we will go down home. I begin to feel like I would something good to eat. Our troops surrendered to the rebels at Harpers Ferry.[141] Col Miles was killed.

Middletown, Maryland, Frederick County, is located on the National Road (Route 40) near I-70 west of Frederick. Several Civil War Battles were fought around Middletown, devastating the community. Nearby at Sharpsburg, on September 16 and 17, 1862, the Battle of Antietam, in which 23,110 men died or were wounded, was fought.

141. "On September 15, 1862, Harpers Ferry with 12,000 men was surrendered to General Thomas J. Jackson. Harpers Ferry National Historical Park is located at the confluence of the Potomac and Shenandoah rivers in the states of West Virginia, Virginia, and Maryland. George Washington, Thomas Jefferson, Meriwether Lewis, John Brown, "Stonewall" Jackson, and Frederick Douglass are just a few of the prominent individuals who left their mark on this place.

"The story of Harpers Ferry is more than one event, one date, or one individual. It involves a diverse number of people and events that influenced the course of our nation's history. Harpers Ferry witnessed the first successful application of interchangeable manufacture, the arrival of the first successful American railroad, John Brown's attack on slavery, the largest surrender of Federal troops during the Civil War, and the education of former slaves in one of the earliest integrated schools in the United States." Source: http://www.nps.gov/hafe/.

"[I]t was the Leesburg [Virgina] home of John Janney where General Lee stopped en route to the fateful Battle of Antietam in September 1862. They were good friends; and their friendship went back many years." Source: *Loudoun Discovered*, vol. 1, p. 47.

The Janney and Lee families go back to the fourteenth century in England. The Janneys in the United States are descendants of the Janney Family of Cheshire, England. The Janney surname appears in official records of Cheshire, England, as early as 1324, and the Legh family is also among those records. In *The Cheshire Sheaf,* a publication of Cheshire Local Gleanings, Historical and Antiquarian, Chester, England, vol. II, 1883, p. 40, is an article based on the Calendar of Public Records of a list of the men of the county whose names were found as having served in Gascony and at Poitiers, France. The list also mentions the rewards granted these men by the Black Prince (the Prince of Wales in the reighn of King Edward III) for their services: "William Janney, Junr. Pardoned for his assault on William son of Thomas de Sale and Robert Fayrchild of Somerford, on account of his services at Poitiers, etc.

"In preparation for this battle, three hundred of the 'best and most skillful archers were to be raised and among them was recruited the 'hundred best and most skillful archers that can be found in the county [Cheshire.]' The leaders for the archers chosen by the Prince from Macclesfield hundred were Sir John Hyde and Robert Legh [reported to have been the ancestor of General Robert E. Lee] and Hamo de Mascy of Nantwich Hundred. These men were clothed in green and white uniforms and paid 3

Alley Betts [Albert Betts, son of Uncle William and Anna Hadley Betts—he was seven years old] is better. I am almost afraid to hear the news tomorrow for we have had so much bad luck lately. I feel it will not turn so soon. It is so very dry and no prospects of it raining.

Fifthday, September 18th, 1862
We went to Vienna this afternoon and came by Moons this evening. I am anxious to hear the news I hope our army will be victorious. It is time the tide was changing in our favor if we are ever going to be victorious and I think we will when our turn comes. I am so afraid there will be another call for men and then drafting will be sure to come.

Sixthday, September 19th, 1862
The news is not very good tonight, but we can hear nothing definite. "Rumors" fill the pages and creates all kinds of improbable things.

Seventhday, September 20th, 1862
A beautiful day. September indeed. The warm sunshine, the gentle breeze that rustles the leaves on the trees and sometimes sends the ones that have faded too soon to the ground. I love September so dearly. There is such a sweet sadness in everything. Lizzie came last evening, but I have not seen her yet. Jeff came this morning to get a dress for her. Just one week since Will came home. I am glad he does not have to go again or at least I hope he will not. How many many homes are tonight desolate indeed. Whenever I hear of a battle I think now how would I feel if Will was there and I did not know whether he was dead or wounded or taken prisoner. How terrible must be the suspense. How I hope I may never be called to suffer it myself.

---

weeks wages in advance. They went to Plymouth and were to leave 15 July 1355. Some were sick and unfit. The Prince of Wales landed his army at Bordeaux in December 1355.

"The Battle of Poitiers, September 19, 1356, was the second of Edward the Black Prince's great victories over the French. In 1355 the truce which had been concluded for eight years came to an end. . . . The following year he marched toward the Loire; but near Poitiers he found his way barred by 60,000 men under King John of France. The prince's army is said not to have exceeded 8,000, but it was very strongly posted behind lanes, hedges, and vineyards, which were lined with archers. His offers to treat were rejected, and the French horse pressed on up the lane. But they fell back in confusion before the arrows of the English. At the same time they were charged in flank by the English cavalry, while the main body of the English foot advanced on their front. The French fought desperately, but were completely routed. 8,000 of them were killed, and among the crowd of prisoners was King John himself." Source: *The Dictionary of English History,* Cassell and Co., London, 1897, p. 824.

Sabbath, September 21st, 1862
So many here this evening. Only Lizzie and Alma for dinner. We had some good singing—Lizzie, Jeff and Mr. Parker Osborn. We all went out walking this evening or part of us. Jim Hunt seemed to be attracted here this evening. It has been so dusty today, so many passing. I hope we will see Matt soon and we will have a good chat like we used to in the olden time and we will go to the bridge and cliffs. I wonder if it will seem like it used to?

Secondday, September 22nd, 1862[142]
I feel like I had not slept very well and I did not. Jim and Lizzie seemed to have a great deal to say which kept them very late. Another dusty day before us with no prospect of rain. I certainly must finish my dress this week if I ever expect to wear it for I put it off from one week to another so often.

Thirdday, September 23rd, 1862
Oh, it is so dusty. I do wish it would rain. We are going up to Ladds next Seventhday if it is not so dusty. The battles in Maryland must have been bad indeed. So many poor fellows murdered. How dreadful must be their sufferings and the suspense of their friends at home. Matt's baby is so pretty. So sweet. I wish we had a sweet little girl baby.

Fourthday, September 24th, 1862
It rained last night and so much more agreeable but it has been very gloomy all day. I went down home this evening. I wonder if Matt and I will enjoy ourselves as well as we used to. It has been so long. I hope there is no estrangement grown between us.

Fifthday, September 25th, 1862
We got up so early this morning and had a nice ride. Will went to Clarksville and I went as far as Lizzie's school. I enjoyed myself very well. She has a real good school. There were all color of eyes and hair and there were some intelligent looking faces so much brighter than the rest and one sweet little boy that I wanted to keep. I really do have so much to do. I think I will quit putting everything off so long.

Sixthday, September 26th, 1862
Night again and all the solemn things that come with night. There is no better

---

142. "Whereas on the 22nd day of September, A.D. 1862, a proclamation was issued by the President of the United States, containing, among other things, the following, to wit: 'That on the 1st day of January, A.D. 1863, all persons held as slaves within any State or designated part of a State the people whereof shall then be in rebellion against the United States shall be then, thenceforward, and forever free." This was the announcement that the Emancipation Proclamation would take effect in January.

time for reflection than when night has settled over all the earth. To me there is no sadder time. Well we expect to go in the morning if nothing preventing. Alma came up this evening. I hope we will have a good time. We expect to start very early if we do not sleep too late.

Sabbath, September 28th, 1862 [Leesburg, Highland County, Ohio]
Started early yesterday. Arrived safely. Glad to get there. Everything seemed so natural. Only Matt was not there to meet us. She came home in the evening train. We met them at the depot. Matt and I rode in the buggy and drove Cola. What heroines. Though we did go too far by the gate and have some trouble in getting Cola back. Today we went to Coxes for dinner and such a nice dinner. I like the girls so well. I was so tired last night. I could not sleep very well for we went to the cliffs and I am not so used to them as I used to be. We got home safe and we were very well pleased with our visit. Harris was buried this evening. We had not even heard of his being worse.

Secondday, September 29th, 1862
Morning. Sitting by the bedroom window. It is such a pleasant morning. We have been putting up some plumbs. They look so nice. I hope they will be as nice. Matt is coming soon. I will be so glad for it has been so long. I read some in [Ik] Marvel's *Dream Life*.[143] It is so good. Very much like his *Reveries.* I am going home this morning. Mrs. Alexander is going to be there.

Thirdday, September 30th, 1862
September almost gone. How quickly all the beautiful days have passed away. Will went away this morning. It seems very natural to be alone. We are really suffering for water and no place to go. I wish it would rain. General Nelson is killed. Col Jeff C. Davis shot him. No one seems to blame him much for Nelson was so mean.

October 1862

Fourthday, October 1st, 1862
Another week soon be gone. I wonder if our country will look as gloomy next year as it now does. I hope not, but oh! our mean generals. They seem determined to have all our men killed off and prolong the war as long as they can. I should think something would happen to them for being so wicked—but perhaps they are instruments in the hands of God to punish us for our sin and their time not yet come.

---

143. Ik Marvel was the pen name of Donald Grant Mitchell, who was the author of *Dream Life,* published in 1851, and *Reveries of a Bachelor,* which Paulena and Will had read earlier.

Fifthday, October 2nd, 1862
Elizabeth Alexander was here last night and we are going to Uncle Williams for dinner. We heard last night that the 73rd was going sometime in the night, but it happened not to be so. It looks odd to see a little girl here. I really think I must take one of my own sometime or someone else's. It would be such pleasure to play with them. I am going down home this evening.

Sixthday, October 3rd, 1862
Why don't it rain. Perhaps we will suffer for water and that would be dreadful indeed and the windows of heaven would soon be opened and the rain descended the water to the earth. How strange it seems that one little drop of water forms the rivers and oceans when ten thousand would not be enough.

Seventhday, October 4th, 1862
 A pleasant shower this morning. How refreshing it is this evening. It is cool and pleasant. The sun shown brightly though. There had been no clouds. Lyd received a letter this morning stating Steve was sick and that he had been very dangerous.[144] Lyd and Matt were going to start for Louisville, but the train did not arrive in time to take them to make connection with the other train. Lyd will be in great impatience until she hears.

Sabbath, October 5th, 1862
We were at Moons last night. Had a pleasant time. Had a nice ride home this morning. Went to church and then grandfathers. Cal, Jo, Jake and Jim were there. Had dinner. I could have a real good chat with them this evening. Yesterday's paper contained a sweet piece written [by] F. D. Prentice on the death of his rebel son who was killed at Augusta, Kentucky. "William Courtland Prentice was no common young man. He was remarkable in powers and in his powers and in his temperament a model of extraordinary intellectual energy, a strong thirst for strange and curious knowledge and a deep passion for all that is sublime and beautiful in poetry and nature. . . . O, if he had fallen in his country's service, fallen with his burning eyes fixed in love and devotion upon the flag that [more] than three fourths of a century has been the star of worship of his ancestors, his early death though still terrible, might be borne by his father's head."

---

144. According to Stephen Janney's official military record from the National Archives, on October 5, 1862, near Louisville, Kentucky, Stephen suffered a paralytic stroke, causing a paralysis of his entire left side, hip and leg, "induced and brought on from hard marching, over-extension and severe hardships and exposures he was compelled to undergo during the expected attack on Cincinnati, Ohio, by the enemy under Gen. Kirby Smith." His captain was called to his tent immediately when he was stricken. He was treated by the regimental surgeon and sent to a Louisville Hospital while his regiment moved on to Frankfort. He rejoined his regiment reaching them by train. He was not fully recovered but was able to write and make out reports while they were at Frankfort. He remained with his company through the remainder of the war.

Secondday, October 6th, 1862
A bright morning. The yellow leaves rustling upon the trees and perhaps autumn winds beginning to blow. The drying leaves and fading flowers remind us of one's own destiny. Another October passing swiftly away and our country deluged with blood and tears. How long will it last inquires each anxious heart and yet no answer comes. We have not suffered enough yet to purge us and I fear reformation is making slow progress among our officers, on whom after God, depends the fate of our nation and while their hearts are stirred with no higher longing than ambition, I have little hope.

Thirdday, October 7th, 1862
I think I would like to go away while it seems like my life is passing away to very little purpose, thus far, and I become very much discouraged sometimes when I think what a little amount of good I do accomplish. Lyd did not receive a letter from Steve and is very uneasy. I feel so sorry for her. I am in hopes he will be discharged. I hope Lincoln's determination of freedom to the slaves will hasten the end of the war and then what a joyful time it would be. Alma and I went to Vienna this afternoon.

Fourthday, October 8th, 1862
We took a moonlight ride this evening. It was so peaceful. It seems such a short week. I wonder if the weeks pass away as quickly for everyone.

Sixthday, October 10th, 1862
I am sitting in the kitchen. It seems good. Such a dark morning as it is and cold, but I do hope it stays this way for a while. Mother is coming up today. It has been a long time since she was here. I think I will make some potatoe soup for dinner. I think it is so good. I think my journal will be very interesting to look at in the years to come.

Seventhday, October 11th, 1862
A bright fire is burning in the grate. The clock upon the mantel ticking off the hours. The wind blowing and the leaves rustling. Just the same as last autumn. I wonder if when the next chill winds of October come there will be any change for me. I wish I had something real good, something new and interesting. I wish Lot would come and bring some books. He has *Les Miserables*.[145] I would like it, I expect. I want to go to Uncle Aarons soon and I can get something to read. Oh dear, I pity the poor soldiers with winter. They will suffer more than they did last winter. We took a ride this evening. I drove.

----

145. "Victor Hugo, novelist, poet, and dramatist is considered the most important of the French Romantic writers. He wrote that romanticism was the liberalism of literature. Hugo developed his own version of the historical novel, combining concrete,

Secondday, October 13th, 1862
Cloudy and cool. We had a shower last night. I went to Georges this morning and saw them at work at the sugarcane[146] and then we came back, went to fathers and grandfathers. I had a good time down there. Grandmother combed my hair and we had corncakes for supper and we brought home some chicken for tomorrow and some cider. We always come back home loaded. There has been a battle in Kentucky at Perrysville.[147] It is said we were victorious, but oh! the lives that were lost. It is so dreadful to think. I wish there was some progress of the war closing but everything looks very dark just now and if our cause grows bright it must be soon. I have almost finished a letter to Jennie.

Thirdday, October 14th, 1862
At home. Alma and mother were here. Perhaps Alma and I will visit Sarah Ellen's school sometime this week. We have a great family for visiting schools. I just love to go and study the different countenances. So many different comparisons. I really think it is a very good place to study human nature. We are thinking of going down to the colored school, but fancy we will not have so many

---

historical details with vivid, melodramatic imagination. His best-known works are *The Hunchback of Notre Dame* and *Les Miserables,* The latter story, published in 1862, has been filmed several times and made into a musical by the composer Claude-Michel Schönberg and the librettist Alain Boublil, which opened in 1980 in Paris, France. The English version was released in 1985 and the U.S. Broadway version in 1987." Source: http:// www.online literature.com/victor_hugo/.

146. George Janney grew and harvested sugar cane as had his father, Joseph Janney. Among the items in Joseph Janney's estate inventory were three molasses kegs and four sugar kettles.

147. "The Battle of Perryville, Kentucky, fought October 8, 1862, finalized Confederate General Braxton Bragg's famous 'Kentucky Invasion' with a tactical victory for the Confederacy, but an eventual retreat that set the stage for the end-of-year Battle of Stones River outside Murfreesboro, Tennessee. Perryville is near Danville, Boyle County, Kentucky." Source: http://www.battleofperryville.com/.
"Perryville Battlefield State Historic Site is the site of one of the bloodiest battles of the Civil War. A Confederate campaign to 'free' Kentucky was launched in 1862 under the direction of General Braxton Bragg, Army of Tennessee, CSA. Twelve thousand soldiers under General E. Kirby Smith fought northward and by the end of August controlled the central part of Kentucky. Bragg then moved his army with the intention of linking forces with Smith's, thereby gaining control of the entire state. Union forces in Kentucky under Major General Don Carlos Buell raced toward Louisville to save the major Union supply base from capture. Bragg let Buell beat him to Louisville, giving Buell a tactical advantage." Source: http://www.danville ky.com/BoyleCounty/perryenh.htm.

different eyes or different shades of complexion as some places. I am afraid I would laugh, but that would not do anyone good in the world for they would think we were "making fun" of them.

Seventhday, October 18th, 1862

I have been very busy this morning and I wish I had some new books to read. This is a bright October afternoon, the kind for one to go someplace or chat with a dear friend who will take all the beauty of this afternoons dreamy sunlight and appreciate it. The beauty of the autumn leaves gilded with the autumn gold. The fading flowers, the dead leaves, the sweet calmness of all things reminds us that summer will soon be gone and a little time ago that the grass was getting green and the flowers were opening all the beautiful things of spring coming. How true it is that "upon everything passing away is indelibly written 'Sic transit gloria mundi.' [*Sic transit gloria mundi* is Latin for "Thus passes the glory of the world."]"

Sabbath, October 19th, 1862

Afternoon of Sabbath again and such an afternoon is almost as beautiful as yesterday only the mind is higher. I went to church this morning. Will's eye was too sore for him to go. I came in with a bad headache. I think I will have to quit going to meeting for it makes me sick. We had no sermon. I wish we could have some good preaching sometimes. Perhaps next Sabbath. I will retire for a short time and dream either with my eyes open or shut. We had a nice ride this evening. It was so cool and pleasant.

Secondday, October 20th, 1862

A pleasant morning. I wish someone would come. Alma and I anticipated having such a good time today, but are disappointed. We were going to go to the old brown house where the weeping willows used to bend their long branches so near the ground and where so many things used to happen. When we used to go to see our old grandfather and grandmother [Gideon Stevens and Mary Coffin, who died in 1854 and 1855, respectively] when we were little girls. It has been years since we were there and I know there are many changes. The old willows are cut down. I am so sorry. I hope we will get to go sometime. Matt is coming down this week. I will be glad to see her.[148]

---

148. That house and property were conveyed in Gideon Stevens's will to his wife, Mary, and after her decease, it was to go to their daughter, Deborah, who married David James in 1855. The property was on the south side of the road leading to Martinsville, but in Union Township, Highland County, Ohio. Gideon's son, Thomas Stevens, received the farm on the north side of the road in Highland County, a short distance from the county line. Today these two properties are located on State Road 124, Union

Thirdday, October 21st, 1862
Not half so beautiful as yesterday. Alma and I are going to Wilmington-Jeffs school and we are going to call at Em Stevens school near Burtinville. I hope nothing will happen to us. I am always so foolish. I wish I had asked Will for some money, if I go.

Stirring moments on the Potomac are predicted soon. I almost dread to hear of what's being done there for, as yet, they have accomplished so little. Better a thousand times never have moved than to do as they have done. Had so many poor soldiers murdered and all to no purpose save to gratify the selfish commanders. I think it is time there is an end to this wholesale murder that has been going on so long. The battle in Kentucky was a bad affair, I think. Buell should be lining up someplace if anyone ought to.

Alma is determined to go. I think we should make out a report of a self appointed school committee. Tonight after our return I sit me down to record our days jaunt. This morning Alma and I started for a jaunt although the clouds were dark and lowering and the wind was loud and cold. We first went to Wilmington. Called at Miss Stevens school as we had intended. There were some bright little faces we noticed in particular. We arrived safely driving. We did a little shopping.

We started home on a new road. Had a fine time laughing. Said a great many very foolish things. It proved to be rather a long one and before I knew it we came to a creek. Alma said she would walk up the hill so I drove on. It proved to be a rather long one and before I knew it I was at Jeffs schoolhouse and Alma some distance down the hill. We opened the door of the schoolroom. Jeff did not faint, but blushed crimson or rather a "solfonia." He also had some very interesting little scholars. May Ireland and Jeff accompanied us to buggy.

We had much beautiful scenery on our road home. Splendid woods. The leaves crimson gilded by the autumn mantle and then the wind sounded so like music among the trees. The regimen for the dying leaves. At last the dilapidated little miserable town of Cuba. From our view nothing beautiful or anything else was seen there and the old buildings had a wo-be-gone look. There may be some good forefathers for all I know. "Judge not lest thou be judged" At present I am sitting alone by a bright fire and there is a kind of longing at my heart for I wish, Oh, I do wish something. Does anyone like me?

Fourthday, October 22nd, 1862
I had rather take a jaunt today than stay at home, but I think I will be as well off where I am and I am listening to the music of the washtub as I write instead of the wind music among the trees. I am so afraid Matt will not come. It is just a

---

Township, Highland County, Ohio, which leads to Martinsville and joins State Road 134 in Clark Township, Clinton County, at the county line. Source: Research notes of Christie Russell, 2002.

year this week, since she came the last time. It will be so good for her to be here again. I hope she will not be sick this time. There is an address of Garibaldi to the people of England. He is a great friend of America.[149] There is also an interesting piece of Ralph Waldo Emerson's. It was written for the *Atlantic Monthly.* It is an essay.

Fifthday, October 23rd, 1862
This morning Lib came over in a hurry and gave me a going over about Smiths. I know she meant me as much as anyone. Smith's wife is sick—got a baby boy and suffered for want of attention. I was quite innocent for I never thought of her suffering. I volunteered to tell Lib in the midst of it that they had many relations and why don't they do something for them. Nothing would convince Lib, but that it was because of their poverty that no one helped them. She says if they were rich people everybody would go. If Lib Haynes were sick, everyone would go to see her. She also said that "Phoebe" is going to meeting and complain of her neglect. I said I didn't care. I thought I had better go down after. I dislike the idea of anyone suffering. I took down her breakfast. She was sitting by the fire with a quilt wrapped around and everything looked so desolate and miserable. I cleaned up the room as well as I could. A little fresh air in the house. What a pity that there are so many miserable people and they have so many children to make them miserable. I feel sorry for anyone that is so poor that it provokes me to always hear them fling something about those who are worth a little more. In a great measure it is their own fault especially in this country. I think they must lack energy.

---

149. "1807 July 4, Garibaldi was born at Nice or Nizza (at that time part of France), the son of Domenico Garibaldi, a fisherman and coastal trader. The Great Liberator of the old world was born on the 31st birthday of the United States and just 2 years before the Great Liberator of the New World, Abraham Lincoln, in 1809. His birthplace Nice was always part of Italy until it was ceded to the French in 1796. 1862, (July) he began agitating in Sicily for another march on Rome, evidently with some encouragement from the King and Rattazzi, the Prime Minister. (August) Seriously wounded in a clash with Italian troops at Aspromonte, in Calabria. (October) After being imprisoned, he is granted an amnesty by the King." Source: http://www.reformation.org/garibaldi.html.

Giuseppe Verdi, Italian composer, "was excited by Garibaldi's stunning conquest, in 1860, of Sicily and Naples,—'By God, there truly is a man to kneel to! '—and by the concerted advance of the Piedmontese and Garibaldian troops on Rome later that year: 'Those are composers,' he wrote of Garibaldi and Cialdini, the Piedmontese genera. 'And what operas! What finales! To the sound of guns!'" "Verdi: the Liberal Patriot," *Viva la Liberta! Politics in Opera,* Anthony Arblaster, 1992, Veruso, U.K.

Sixthday, October 24th, 1862
Not raining yet. It is never going to rain. I do wonder if Matt is coming. I have received no letter from her and know what to depend on this time tomorrow. I have not had good success today with my cooking—my rising has not come yet. [She was waiting for the yeast to make her dough rise before baking.]

Seventhday, October 25th, 1862
Cloudy, drizzling and cold. Went to meeting. Did not remain till it was over. Mary was there, but she is not going to stay long—going home tomorrow. Matt did not come just as I expected. I feel disappointed. I hope she will come soon. We had no good preaching at least not eloquent sermons. Perhaps the preacher meant well. Lizzie came over this morning. I do wish Matt had come.

Sabbath, October 26th, 1862
Very cold. Snow. Snow, strange to see since when there has been so much dust. It is bitter cold. Jeff and Lizzie were here all night last night. A fire in the parlor. I pity the poor soldiers these days. How they must suffer. This afternoon had quite a good sermon.

Secondday, October 27th, 1862
Warmer than yesterday, but very different than this time last week. Will and I took a ride this evening. Were at fathers a little while. Will has gone up to the council. I wish he would hurry and come. I hope they will pass some good resolutions or whatever they are, and one of them, to take up all the hogs in the street.[150] It is true about Buell's removal. I think it time for he has been a disgrace to himself and the army.

---

150. "Hogs don't run off and it was more economical [to have them run loose] than having to pen them in. When slaughtering time came folks rounded them up." Source: Lynne Olver (IACP), editor, *The Food Timeline,* http://www.foodtimeline.org.

"Pork is the most widely eaten meat in the world, and from the time the first settlers came to the New World, it was a predominant meat in the American diet. Pigs have been domesticated since the Stone Age. . . . English, French, and all other Colonies found pigs easy to raise, for they foraged on their own and lived off scraps. . . . By the 1830s the streets of major cities were criss-crossed with hog tracks, for they were allowed to feed on the garbage . . . During this same era Cincinnati became the major pork-packing center, earning its nickname 'Porkopolis.' Pork itself was sometimes called in slang 'Cincinnati olive.'

"The demand for pork increased during the Civil War, when hog production doubled to provide meat for the Union troops while soldiers of the Confederacy starved for lack of it. After the war a new industry arose in meat-packing, led by Gustavus Franklin Swift and Philip Danforth Armour, who independently set up companies in Chicago in 1875." Source: *The Encyclopedia of American Food & Drink,* John F. Mariani, New York, Lebhar-Friedman Books, 1999, p. 250.

"This, That and the Other"

Paintings

"The Kidnappers"—painted to the order of Mr. Saunders. It represents two boys trading skates for three young pups. Great pleasure is expressed upon the countenances of the boys at the exchange but the mother of the pups is not so well pleased and tries to get them back again. I wish I could see some of the paintings—an artist's studio would be a delightful place for me provided there were nice pictures in it.

"The Falls of Minnehaha" painted by R. L. Dinncanson the fourth, "The falling waters appear to actually be endowed with wife and emotion and . . . it is difficult to divest oneself of the idea that it is nature itself we are amazed at.

"The Rag Pickers" by J. P Branmon.

"The Harp of a Thousand Strings."[151] *"The Soldier's Return.* ". . . *of the Mountain"* by Mr. Porter.

"Life is like wine; he who would drink it pure must not draw it to the dregs." Sir William Temple.

President Jefferson bought Louisiana for $15,000,000

Romanism was founded by a Spaniard named Ignatius Loyola. He appeared a short time before Christopher Columbus.

There has been nineteen Presidential elections. Thirteen times the southern people and democrats of the north have been successful in electing their President—6 times have the northern people elected men of the north—but some of them have proved to be traitors.

---

151. *The Harp of a Thousand Strings; or, Laughter for a Lifetime,* ed. Samuel Putnam Avery, New York: Dick and Fitzgerald, 1858. "An anthology of humor which includes. . . the first book appearance by 'Lewis Carroll,' a story entitled 'Novelty and Romancement: A Broken Spell,' pirated from English periodical *The Train. The Harp of a Thousand Strings* enjoyed great popularity and went through numerous reprintings from the same plates in the 19th century, but the first printing is scarce." Contributed by George Washington Harris. Source: *Bibliopoly,* The Brick Row Book Shop, http://www.polybiblio.com/brickrow/10153.html.

Thirdday, October 28th, 1862
Sitting alone by a pleasant fire, if I only had some one with whom I could have a chat. I wonder if Matt has entirely forgotten me, why does she not write? Really do think that she is too careless, for she promised to write me when she was coming and if she wasn't going to come. But never a line has she written to me. I feel like I could give her a good scolding when I do see her. We might have such pleasant times if she only had a little energy about going any place. Between my journal and myself, I think she might be a little more punctual.

How I wish some person would send me some nice presents. It would be such a treat to open the front door this morning and find a box of books and other things that I would like. Wish some unknown friend would be so kind to do all of the above. I really should make some calls but I had much rather stay at home unless I can go where it is preferably congenial.

Today's paper says "Mrs. Eliza Gurney had an interview with the President, she expressed the sympathy of the friends in England with him and appealed to him to trust in divine Providence." I think "Merry Old England" and the many eloquent expressions of admiration for England will not be quoted much if there should chance to be any trouble with "the Old Lady over the sea." There has always been a kind of bitter feeling at least existing between the two nations. Yet, in the heart of the Americans there has been a romantic interest for England and the English, for with the former so much of antiquity was connected—ruined castles and shrines and tombs of kings etc. Seems so grand to our imagination that we thought it all superior to anything we might even dream of.

Fourthday, October 29th, 1862
Just as quiet in Martinsville as ever. I think it is a very dreary place, but then there is no place like home. I went down home today and rode Cola up this evening. There is a special in the paper of Parson Brownlow.[152] It is very good.

---

152. "This article appeared as an editorial in the July 1862 *The Ladies' Repository. The Ladies' Repository* was published by the Methodist Episcopal Church North in Cincinnatti, Ohio. William G. 'Parson' Brownlow was a member of the Methodist Episcopal Church—North.

"Among the few who stood firm when many faltered the name of W. G. Brownlow stands conspicuous. Almost alone he breasted the storm of rebellion that swept over the South." Source: Parson Brownlow, "A Patriot Among the Rebels," July 1862, from *The Ladies' Repository,* http://www.ls.net/~newriver/tn/brownlow.htm.

"Born in Wythe County, Virginia, in 1805, Brownlow was an itinerant preacher and publisher of the Knoxville *Whig.* He fell out of popularity with the Confederate government in Tennessee by condemning the secession and had his paper shut down and himself arrested from 1861–62. In 1865 he became governor of Tennessee and led an oppressive Reconstructionist regime. He was governor of the state until 1869, when he was elected to the US Senate, where he served until 1873." Source: *Columbia Encyclopedia,* http://oneweb.utc.edu/~tnwriter/authors/brownlow.william.html.

He makes some very rash exclamations which seem hardly consistent for a minister. Yet I guess he doesn't feel any consternation for it. He is a very sensible man in some respects anyhow—just real sharp. He said he sent a message to "Victoria"—Queen Victoria's messenger was to give her compliments and to say to her he has known individuals in America and in whole neighborhoods that made a comfortable living by minding their own business. I suppose it will all be delivered.

Fifthday, October 30th, 1862
Alma and I had a pleasant afternoon. We went to Clay's school. There were so many things for us to look at as it was a strange road. Clay has a real nice schoolhouse and an interesting school. There were some nice little girls there— one in particular—Emma Barnes. She was quite young and was quick about everything and a good singer. As we came through Morrisville this evening there was such a sweet girl that came along by the buggy. We were talking to a lady. We thought she was so sweet and we took her in the buggy with us as we came by where she lived. We just kissed her and kissed her. Her name is Witly. Clay seemed well pleased that we had made him our visit. We had a real nice time and I am real glad we went.

Sixthday, October 31st, 1862
Gibson's sweet little baby. It looked indeed like a little angel. It's fat dimpled hands unfolded. Its eyes closed as if in infant slumber. I think I never saw a more beautiful picture. Baa is coming to preach the funeral sermon. I feel so sorry for Lib. They will miss it very much. It is better to have loved and lost than never at all. Someone has said.[153] Yet those who have no children have none to lose.

November 1862

Seventhday, November 1st, 1862
Dart preached so good. Why can not our preacher be more like him, I feel so sorry for Lib. Lottie did look so sweet. Little innocent girl. She knew nothing about her parents sorrow. I would be so glad if I could hear Dart every Sabbath. It does me some good. We left home about four o'clock. Got to Wests for supper. We were not long going. Jake and Ball started first and so they arrived there before us some little time.

Sabbath, November 2nd, 1862
Went to meeting. Not any very good preaching. A great many people there. Will

---

153. Alfred Lord Tennyson: "It is better to have loved and lost, than never to have loved at all," "In Memoriam," xxvii/4.

met one of his old schoolmates—Henry Hadley.[154] It just poured down rain as we started from Centre [Quaker Meeting]. We went to Jonathan Hadley's[155] for dinner. Had a pleasant time. We reached home about eight o'clock I expect. Was glad to be by the cheerful grate of our own home.

Secondday, November 3rd, 1862
I just cannot write anything fit to be seen. I was down home this evening. Elva is sick.

Thirdday, November 4th, 1862
This is a bright lovely morning, very different from Sabbath afternoon. I have been at grandfathers today. We had such a good time. Fried chicken and cornbread.

Fourthday, November 5th, 1862
I hope when we do have any news it will be something cheering for I have not much faith in the battles we have had lately although the federals are said to have been victorious. I believe we have lost a great deal more than we have gained. I have been reading a *Tale—Yale College.* It is not very good though and not at all improving. I went to school this evening. It seems so natural. I was down stairs awhile, so many little frisky children. They keep William busy. I was in to see Lide Miller. She had a little girl. I guess I was made for some other purpose. It has turned cool all at once and is going to rain, but in our comfortable rooms why should we dread the rain or sleet except in our pity for the soldiers—many of whom suffer not only for pleasant fires, but for all the comforts of life.

Fifthday, November 6th, 1862
All the clouds of last night are gone and the bright sunshine is out again. I was sitting in my easy chair by the cheerful fire wishing some person would come that I would be glad to see. I wished this morning that I would go to the front door and find a bunch of books. I have not been there yet, but will certainly look when I do go. Of course, I will find what I wish for. Now if we lived in a larger town I could go and get some books. I wonder if we ever will. The paper yesterday predicted a battle soon. Perhaps they are fighting now. I just dread to hear of so many fellows being killed. I do not see how they can be so anxious to fight as they appear to be. It would be the last thing I would want.

---

154. Henry Hadley was thought to be the son of John Hadley and Ann Wildman. He was born on March 5, 1838, in Clarksville, Clinton County, Ohio.

155. Jonathan Hadley, son of William Hadley and Sarah Lindley. He married Mary Lindon at Centre MM, near Wilmington, Clinton County, Ohio, August 22, 1838.

Sixthday, November 7th, 1862
The wind blows so cold. I have been reading some good pieces and wish I had some more to read. I fear I am getting very lazy indeed for I have no inclination to sew or do anything but to read and write. Anderson's have adopted a little baby. I was over to see it last evening. It is a sweet little innocent thing. I am sure I would love it. Oh, how the wind blows. Such days it is lonely indeed for those who have men on the battlefield or have lost them there. Now if I only had a sweet little girl to play with this afternoon. It would pass away much more pleasant, but then perhaps she would squall and be real mean so I could do nothing with her "perhaps" but I don't think she would for I would try so hard to make her good and sweet and pretty and smart and everything that I certainly wouldn't fail in every respect.

Seventhday, November 8th, 1862
Went down home this morning. Company there. One of Alma's school mates and her cousin. Will is coming—I hear his step—and goody he has got some butter—for that was the object of his search. Now the daily "Afternoon Dispatche." Affairs in Sigel's command—Jackson probably near Chester Gap UCUC.

Sabbath, November 9th, 1862
A beautiful autumn day. Will and I went riding. We had such a long ride—almost to Clay's schoolhouse. The roads are so beautiful for riding. Jim Hunt called this evening. If reports are true I think Lizzie is very anxious to have beaus. We hear that Mr. Parker Osborn is paying a great deal of attention to her. I wonder if it is so. I can hardly believe it, poor Jeff. I just know he would not like it.

Secondday, November 10th, 1862
The most important news of any for many weeks. McClellan is removed. I am glad for at best he did poor work. Burnside is appointed his successor and Hooker has the first command. I think we may almost say the destiny of the nation is changed. Perhaps I am wrong, but I think if McClellan had remained in command this war would have been prolonged to an indefinite period. The hope is that the war will be ended sometime.[156]

---

156. "Lincoln finally had had enough of George McClellan, relieving him of command on November 9, 1862. He was ordered to return to his home in Trenton, New Jersey and await new orders that never arrived." Source: http://www.swcivilwar.com/mcclellan.html.

"Steadily through the night and early morning, the Confederate columns crossed over into Virginia. McClellan did not actively pursue. As the days passed and Lee's army withdrew into the Shenandoah Valley, President Lincoln became impatient. The time was at hand, he thought, for the decisive blow. Calling upon McClellan on the field of Antietam October 1, Lincoln urged a vigorous pursuit of the Confederate army. McClellan insisted that his army required reorganization and new equipment.

Thirdday, November 11th, 1862
Mother was up today. The days are so short when she is here. I wish I could get a letter from someone. I hope Will will bring some "gossip" of some kind when he comes. He must find something very entertaining down the street.

Fourthday, November 12th, 1862
This is a very gloomy morning. The clouds are all mingled with clouds. I hope it will rain. It seems as though it will never rain. How dismal the town looks, now so dreary. Winter after winter the trees look brown and bare and the world rolls round and many changes and finds us at Martinsville and Martinsville itself almost as we were. I will be all alone today for I do not suppose anyone will come, I wish someone would come. I forgot Franky [probably pet dog] is here, so I am not quite alone.

Fifthday, November 13th, 1862
The birds sing as gaily as they sometimes do in the spring mornings. Alma and I had a pleasant walk this morning. It does me good to get a breath of fresh air these bright mornings. Now if I had a sweet little girl to play with. How pleasant it would be. I guess I will adopt one. I know I would like it so well. I wonder if I will ever see Jennie Wilot again. I think I should like her.

Sixthday, November 14th, 1862
Chilly. Has been such a beautiful day. Warm and summery. I never knew such lovely days could be in November—went down home this morning. Alma went to the Lycium tonight and is coming back, oh! pashaw I do not like my writing tonight. Oh, I so hope the war will be ended soon now that McClellan is away from it. But after that comes the king. I would not be surprised if McClellan was to be our king sometime, for I believe that in the next presidential election the generals will be victorious and before we know it we will be living under a monarch and a despotic one that for the hateful democrats will be so reinforced they will make good use of their power. [157]

Seventhday, November 15th, 1862
No news yet. I hope Burnside will not be so slow and do so little and be so measured as I think McClellan has been. I finished the book I had been reading *Lord Byron and Countess of Blessing.* I cannot help of having opinions of Byron not withstanding all his faults. Matt surely is never going to write to me. I am going to let her alone for I will never force anyone's friendship if there is not a

---

The President, having lost all confidence in McClellan, removed him from command on November 7." Source: http://www.cr.nps.gov/history/online_books/hh.

157. On August 22, 1863, General George McClellan was nominated as a presidential candidate by the Democratic Party at the convention in Chicago.

unison of feeling and a willingness to obligate and a respect of promises. There cannot be that kind of friendship. Oh, for some kind girlfriend whose every impulse would be congenial. I once almost thought I possessed such a friend, but all friends are liable to change. "I pres tutissimi caelis."

Sabbath, November 16th, 1862

Father, mother and all of us started this morning for a ride. We went to the old lonely looking house where grandfather [Gideon Stevens] used to live. It is very different from what it used to be. The willow trees are cut down and the appearance of things look so dreary and there was no old grandmother [Mary Coffin][158] there in the doorway with her kind welcome, I could not help thinking of those old times when we used to go up there and I looked in vain for the old tree in the corner of the yard where the leaves used to be under it. But those days do not remain.

Secondday, November 17th, 1862

A rainy morning—here all alone and am sick. A drove of mules went by and I was reminded of "Washington as a—Stubborn as a Mule" and in ever so many things and was really sorry when this last vestige of them was disappearing. I could almost have wished for a drove of mules long enough to take the whole day for them to pass through, for it was such a change from seeing nothing, that even a mule being a passable object, poor thing. I really felt sorry for them. Just think what dreadful times they will see this winter. Oh? I am so tired. I do not mean bodily, but I am tired for someone to engage my mind. I am sick and it is more tiresome to be alone.

Fourthday, November 19th, 1862

Oh! this rainy morning. It looks so dreary. Alma and Willie can not go to school if it rains this way. What a contrast between this week and last. It was so beautiful last week. Almost like summer and now just as dreary as it can be. The streets almost impassable already. I wish I had a good story to read today as "Regina" or "Beatrice Boyill." They are just suited for such days as this.

Fifthday, November 20th, 1862

Another dark rainy morning. Now that the clouds are opened. They know not when to cease sending the rain upon us. I am glad it has rained, we will not be so afraid of seeing a little water. John Hadley is dead. [John Smith Hadley died November 16, 1862, in Wayne County, Indiana. Hadley, twenty-three, was the son of Jeremiah and Esther Smith Hadley. He was a twin of James Hadley and brother of Jennie and Flora Hadley. See entries for September 16, 1862, November

---

158. It is through Mary (Coffin) Stevens that Paulena descends from the New England progenitors Tristram Coffin, Thomas Macy, Edward Starbuck, Richard Gardner, George Bunker, Robert Paddock, and Richard Sears.

28, 1862, and December 10th, 1862.]. I am so sorry just to think I will never see him again in this world. I pity them so much, poor Jennie—how dreary life seems to her now. So good a brother and another lost to her forever, within so short a time. There will be more to meet in heaven though. Well at last the "contraband" have been proved and bravely have they acquainted themselves the First Company of the First South Carolina Regiment. Have been brought into action and they "fought like veterans." I think Francis L. Gage must have written a piece in yesterday's paper. It is about the contrabands written from Beauford, S. C. I will quote a few lines.

> Among the slaves brought from the coast is a grandmother and members of one family. The elder woman is tall and stately. The blood of some proud race flashes across her almost white face. Her daughters are both white and darker than herself. Her grandchildren are whiter still and some of them are very beautiful. One babe is perfectly white. It's skin is very fair. Its eyes large, lustrous and warm.

Sixthday, November 21st, 1862
Clara and Cal took dinner with me today and this afternoon we visited the school. I always have a void in heart when I part from a person I know cares, but little about me or I for them, but how different when with those I love and whom I can have a perfect sympathy but always feel so much more hopeful and the world looks so much brighter after a chat with a true friend. I would be glad if I could often sit down and commune with someone whose aspirations were higher than mere gossip.

Seventhday, November 22nd, 1862
A bright morning. Went down home with Alma. Jeff called a little while tonight. I was in the middle of an interesting "episode" of a man in "Indian Days." I am a very child yet for I like to read about Indians. Sallie Gibson is such a sweet little girl. I never met with a child I loved better. If we only had such a sweet little angel as her. I would fully agree with the poet who says "A babe in the house is a well spring of pleasure."[159] I think I surely must steal one from someone, but then I could not enjoy it. I guess I will "wait and see" if some good angel will not bring one to the door or someplace. What a delightful sound it would be to be awakened some morning by a musical cry and in going to the door find a basket—a baby—a pretty one maybe. A dear little treasure to drive away care. With eyes of the darkest and hair of the brownest and cheeks that are dimpled, round and fair. A sweet little daughter we would love it, it should be with a

---

159. "A babe in the house is a well spring of pleasure, a messenger of peace & love; a resting place for innocence on earth; a link between angels and men.—Tupper." Source: http://www.scrapbooking poems.com/scrapbooking-poems babies.

pride and tenderness rivaled by none. A bright little boy we would love for it could be with a love just the same for a daughter or son.

Sabbath, November 23rd, 1862
We took a ride this evening. Stopped at grandfathers a little while. Jeff had long enough to make me mad, but then that is not very hard to do, so I will not dwell on it. Now, if Will was only going to stay at home tomorrow. I wish he did not have to be away so much.

Secondday, November 24th, 1862
Cal and I went down home this morning. Had quite a pleasant time. It has been a beautiful evening. We are looking to hear of a battle before long for Burnside is more energetic than McClellan. If not he had better be removed right away and not be left to kill a hundred thousand more men. I think we might make a parody.

How big was General McClellan?
What people call him great?
Was he like old Goliath, tall?
His spear a hundred weight?

Thirdday, November 25th, 1862
At home working on my hearth rug which I began yesterday. I hope I will get it done sometime. Burnside's army had reached Fredericksburg and demanded its surrender. I expect there will be a battle fought there. It seems so dreadful to think of so many being killed. How terrible a rebellion is. I wish Mrs. Wilot and I could write to each other. How glad I would be to see her sometime, but I suppose it will be a long time.

Fourthday, November 26th, 1862
The snowflakes came down softly this morning and it looked very much like stern old winter had come again for certain, but after a time the clouds cleared away a little and the sun almost shone, but it is very cold and how our poor soldiers suffer. I am so glad Will is not away in some dismal camp to suffer for everything at most. I am so afraid there will be another call or another draft for volunteering is about over. Tomorrow is Thanksgiving Day.[160] I wish we could have a good sermon.

---

160. The first Thanksgiving Day observance appeared in the *Massachusetts Centinel*, October 14, 1789. "This historic proclamation was issued by George Washington during his first year as President. It set aside Thursday, November 26 as 'A Day of Pub-

Fifthday, November 27th, 1862
Another cold day. Coming so close. Mother had been informed Alma will stay tonight. I expect this time last winter she was here. Oh! I feel so sorry for Hadleys. I do not see how they can bear so much trouble, but when a person has to do anything, there is help for it. I hope I will never have trouble, but I do not know what may be in store for me in the future. It is all a mysterious page that we have not turned.[161] My hearth rug is progressing finely, yet, I don't know how long I will be in the mood for working on it. I hope though it will be done. [A hearth rug was laid on the floor in front of the fireplace, the hearth, to protect the floor and carpet from sparks.] I dreamed last night of water in grandfathers garden and there were tulips and myrtle both in full bloom. The myrtle flowers being red and as I walked along the smooth walk admiring the flowers, I came to some of the most delicious raspberries I ever saw so ripe and delicious, as though it was reality. On one bed there were tomatoes growing up like beans, large ripe ones, I thought. Jennie and her father [Jeremiah Hadley] were there and that I was walking with Jeramiah in the yard. It seems we were all very solemn that grandfather was talking to us or something.

Sixthday, November 28th, 1862
Another sixthday evening drawing to a close. How quiet our life passes away, almost before we learned to live as we should live. I feel so sad when I remember that never more on earth will I see "John" [John Smith Hadley]. Just a little more than six months ago he was here the gayest of all and now his life is ended

----

lick Thanksgiving and Prayer.' Signed by Washington on October 3, 1789, and entitled 'General Thanksgiving,' the decree appointed the day 'to be observed by acknowledging with grateful hearts the many and signal favors of Almighty God." Source: http://early-america.com/earlyamerica/firsts/thanksgiving/s.

"While there were Thanksgiving observances in America both before and after Washington's proclamation, this represented the first designated by the new national government.

"The holiday we know today as Thanksgiving was recommended to Lincoln by Sarah Josepha Hale, a prominent magazine editor. Her letters to Lincoln urged him to have the 'day of our annual Thanksgiving made a National and fixed Union Festival.' The document . . . sets apart the last Thursday of November 'as a day of Thanksgiving and Praise.' According to an April 1, 1864, letter from John Nicolay, one of Lincoln's secretaries, this document was written by Secretary of State William Seward, and the original was in his handwriting." Source: *Collected Works of Abraham Lincoln,* ed. Roy P. Basler. Lincoln's Proclamation was issued on October 3, 1863. In 1941 President Franklin Roosevelt changed the holiday to the fourth Thursday in November where it remains today. Paulena notes the observation, which was Thursday, November 27, 1862. It would be the following year, 1863, that Lincoln designated the last Thursday.

161. Esther Smith Hadley, mother of James, John, and Jennie Hadley, was buried on November 29, 1861, at the Whitewater Friends Cemetery, Richmond, Wayne County, Indiana.

and his body tonight is resting in the cold grave but he has a brighter home for his last hours were calm and peaceful and his last words were, "Come Lord Jesus quickly."

Seventhday, November 29th, 1862
I went down home his morning although it was snowing a perfect hurricane. Em Hunt [daughter of Jonathan and Margaret Hadley Hunt] came down for them to go to Clarksville—perhaps they will go tomorrow as Alma was not well enough to go this afternoon. The girls brought me home in the buggy and I am sitting here by a cheerful fire. Will has gone for the paper and he paused at the door to receive my parting words which are always, "Now don't stay very long, Will" and he always obeys me pretty well, too. I wonder if there is any news today for I hate to hear of anyone being killed or wounded for they are somebody's friends.

Sabbath, November 30th, 1862
A gloomy morning, but not raining so I suppose the girls are glad to go their intended visit. If we only had the music of the church bells. How sweet it would be and seem so much more like Sabbath. I hope we will go travel some after this war is over. There are so many places I would love to go and if our lives are spared till that sometime comes, I think I would like to see some of the world. Clay asked me to write for the paper. He is going to have an examination in four weeks and the scholars are going to have a paper. I hope I can write something and that [I] can get to go. I think he has such a good school. Emma Barnes and a few more of the scholars are so intelligent, so different in their manners from any of the children here. I wish I had something to write about. I fear my journal will be filled with very uninteresting "items." The paper says a battle is imminent. I do hope our army will be successful. A defeat now would be a great injury to us.

December 1862

Secondday, December 1st, 1862
It seems not a twelfth month yet since it was here before, but how many days of thirty would all its transactions fill. At home all day. Miss Hayes returned my call this afternoon and it was a very short one as I have had the pleasure of building air castles which one is certain to do when alone and I am that very often.

Thirdday, December 2nd, 1862
Cold, cloudy and gloomy. Alma and Emma arrived at home all safe and seemed very much pleased with the visit for Alma. I have not seen Emma. Warners are such fine people I just like.

Fourthday, December 3rd, 1862
Mother has been up today. Our cousin has come from Virginia. His name is William Paxson. I have not had the pleasure of his acquaintance. I hope he will be similarly interesting and agreeable. Burnside's army has not done much yet, but I hope Richmond will soon be ours and then we may hope for the war to end sometime when the slaves are free. I am getting along finely with my hearth rug. I hope it will look pretty nice. Jo asked me to write for her paper, but I am not in a writing mood and it would be impossible.

Fifthday, December 4th, 1862
A bright morning going home. Been almost sick this afternoon. Had company till bedtime. Miltons and Matt and Cal—Lizzie is real sweet. I would not care if we had a baby if it would be sweet. I have not met our cousin yet. Tomorrow closes the first term of school. I don't think we will go until evening to the library. Will's aunt is dead and has been dead almost two months and we had never heard it, although they had written and sent word to us. They are lonely and would like for us to go over.[162] Nellie Weaver Lipton is at her fathers and has a son. It seems so funny. I am so anxious to see her for I like her real well. Will thinks we can go over before long.

Sixthday, December 5th, 1862
We went to the Lycum and I never came much nearer freezing. It seemed like the wind would just blow through us. Clay came in to get warm. It seemed like old times again. Alma, Clay and Mary all here at the same time.

Seventhday, December 6th, 1862
The coldest morning. Enough to freeze a person. Mary is going to her mothers. What a cold ride she will have.

Sabbath, December 7th, 1862
Cold as Greenland almost. We went to grandfathers this evening notwithstanding this cold. We got to meet our cousin at last. I did not get much acquainted with him but he is easy to get acquainted with. I wonder if Alma has got home yet. I know she will have a cold ride, but it is no matter for her. Will and I had a debate this evening, resolved that war is wrong. I took the affirmative and Will said I almost convinced, him. In fact, I am almost sentimental on the side I took.

---

162. Will's aunt could be Nancy Ann Russell Rhodes, wife of John Rhodes. She was an elder sister of Elizabeth Russell Janney, Will's mother. She died on July 12, 1861, in Clinton County, Ohio. Will's aunt also could have been the wife of John Russell, Jemima, who was living in Muskingum County, Ohio, but the date of her death is not known.

Secondday, December 8th, 1862

I have not had the energy to do much on my hearth rug. I am afraid it will be long time before I get it done. I am reading *Evening Entertainment*. It is such a curious book. I have the *Chambers Papers*[163] to read. Oh dear, I do not feel in the mood for writing and this will all be mixed up like . . . and not be worth reading if I ever live to be old and want to read it to my grandchildren.

Thirdday, December 9th, 1862

Went home and saw grandfather. Father's gone and we stayed with mother. There is no news of any importance whatsoever—all question the Rappahannock will become as familiar to our ears as was, "all quiet on the Potomac,"[164] last winter, but we have more faith in Burnside[165] than we had in McClellan and we are hoping that when he does move it will be to accomplish some purpose premeditated. They are looking for our cousin William James everyday now. He is coming from "My Maryland." I hope he will be intelligent.

---

163. This may refer to David Chambers: "David Chambers, a Representative from Ohio; born in Allentown, Pa., November 25, 1780; . . . was a confidential express rider for President Washington during the Whisky Insurrection in 1794; learned the art of printing; moved to Zanesville, Ohio, in 1810, where he established a newspaper and was elected State printer; volunteer aide-de-camp to General Cass in the War of 1812; served as recorder and mayor of Zanesville; member of the State house of representatives in 1814, 1828, 1836–1838, 1841, and 1842; clerk of the Ohio State senate in 1817; clerk of the court of common pleas of Muskingum County 1817-1821; . . . elected to the Seventeenth Congress to fill the vacancy caused by the resignation of Representative-elect John C. Wright and served from October 9, 1821, to March 3, 1823; member of the State senate in 1843 and 1844; president of the senate in 1844; delegate to the State constitutional convention of 1850; engaged in agricultural pursuits until 1856; died in Zanesville, Muskingum County, Ohio, August 8, 1864; interment in Greenwood Cemetery." David Chamber's Papers, American Antiquarian Society. Source: http://bioguide.congress.gov/scripts/biodisplay.pl?index=C000281.

164. Ethel Lynn Beers, "All Quiet Along The Potomac."

165. "Burnside was a tall burly sixfooter from Indiana. He was an 1847 graduate of West Point and accepted a commission in the artillery. He saw no action during the Mexican War and resigned his commission in 1853. Afterward, he started a firearms manufacturing company in Rhode Island. From 1855 to 1857 Burnside was a major general in the Rhode Island militia and became a colonel of the 1st Rhode Island Volunteers. He received a promotion to brigadier general after the Battle of First Bull Run. He successfully commanded forces sent to raid Confederate installations in North Carolina. Burnside declined two previous offers of command of the Union Army, but the third time was a charm and Burnside accepted after the Battle of Antietam.The Fredericksburg campaign was a disaster. Lincoln commented that it was like 'snatching defeat from the jaws of victory' and relieved him of his command. Burnside did see action at the Wilderness and Petersburg, but he was removed from his command for badly botch-

Fourthday, December 10th, 1862
We came to Uncle Williams this afternoon. Grandmother came too and walked. It seemed so funny for her to walk so far. [Anne Hunt Betts was seventy-seven years old at that time.] I could not get home for Will had forgotten and had taken the key with him. I read or heard a letter from James Hadley written since Johns death. I have never seen a more beautiful or affectionate one. It began, "The work is accomplished, the long and anxious agony is over, the earth angel has again visited the old east room."

Fifthday, December 11th, 1862
A beautiful morning, but cold. Mrs. Caleb B. Smith says the *Gazette* is going to make a Christmas dinner for 25 thousand sick soldiers. I think that will be very nice and it will do them a great deal of good. I am reading *Early Engagements*.[166] Very good.

Sixthday, December 12th, 1862
A beautiful morning. Almost like spring. It seems too bad for us to let all this lovely weather pass away and not use the splendid roads before they become a mire without us being benefitted by it in the way of buggy riding. Cal and I being of one mind on the subject anticipate taking a ride this afternoon. Why can we not meet in everyday life such characters as Florence than we do more often, but I mean Carrie, Theodore, Cliffton, and Florence although self willed and proud had yet many noble qualities which were brought into action by

---

ing the Federal assault there [Battle of Petersburg, seen in the movie *Cold Mountain*, following detonation of a mine under the Confederate line.] After the war, Burnside was the governor of Rhode Island, became a Rhode Island state Senator, and was the first president of the National Rifle Association." Source: http://www.collectorsnet.com/cwtimes/frederic.htm.

166. "Sarah M. Hayden was recognized at the 1893 World's Fair in Chicago as Illinois' first woman authoress. Her first novel, *Early Engagements,* was written when she was sixteen years old, but not published until 1854. Sarah was born in Shawneetown in southern Illinois in 1825, the year that Marquis de Lafayette visited her hometown. Sarah's father was John Marshall, who served in the Illinois Territorial Legislature held in Kaskaskia in 1818. John Marshall also operated a store and made frequent trips to Pittsburgh and Philadelphia for supplies. Sarah accompanied her father on one of the trips and stayed to attend the Sewickley School, a female 'seminary.' The school was to play an important role in her first novel. In 1843, Sarah married John James Hayden. Her first novel and its sequel *Florence* were not published until 1854. The Haydens moved to Cincinnati. Sarah continued writing both poetry and prose and the works were published in magazines and newspapers. Some of her works appear under the pen name Mary Frazer." Source: http://www.alliancelibrarysystem.com/IllinoisWomen/files/lg/html1/lg000001.cfm, from the John A. Logan College Library, Carbondale, Ill., *Early Engagements,* Mary Frazer, Cincinnati, Moore, Anderson, Wilstach & Keys, 1854.

her much suffering. I dearly love to read, would I could remember more that I read.

Seventhday, December 13th, 1862
Lizzy came late evening. We were entertained for we were not thinking of seeing her. We had a pleasant time, but she went home this morning. We had a shower this morning almost like a summer shower.

Sabbath, December 14th, 1862
Such a warm morning, but the wind is blowing. Mary came this morning. I was glad to see her. She has her bonnet retrimmed and it becomes her so well. Will and I are going to go riding, we spent the evening at Samuel's last evening. They brought in apples and wine and we were very clever. We also had some good music on the violin. George More was the performer.

Secondday, December 15th, 1862
Just pouring down rain. Such a lovely day. Jo and Cal were here a while this evening. It seemed very natural. Lydia Ann came home with Alma this evening. Oh dear, the armies that we have been expecting to meet in combat have at last begun their deadly work. The news is very bad tonight. If so, it said Burnside has retreated. Bragg defeated Rosecrans.[167] I do hope it is not so. Surely, if we are ever going to be victorious our "Luck" will soon turn.

---

167. "After McClellan's failure at the Battle of Second Bull Run Lincoln desperately wanted to replace him with someone possessed of a stronger fighting spirit. The Union Commander-in-Chief chose Ambrose Everett Burnside to shoulder the load and swing the momentum around to the side of the Federals . . . it was Burnside's reputation as a fighter that won him the position. Burnside reluctantly accepted and continued McClellan's march to Richmond.

"Lee had positioned Jackson in Winchester, Virginia, in the Shenandoah Valley to head off a potential Union attack to take the fertile lands which were a source of supplies for the Confederates. Longstreet followed Lee's orders and had taken up the area around Culpeper, Virginia, in case the Union army headed for Richmond. Once Lee realized that was indeed what the new Union general intended, he directed Longstreet to Fredericksburg to at least slow down the Union march to Richmond until Jackson could arrive from Winchester with reinforcements. Burnside's slow actions in directing his troops across the Rappahannock River gave Lee and his generals time to take up excellent defensive positions in and around Fredericksburg. The Union assaults were turned back time and again by the well entrenched Confederate forces. Union losses were heavy while the Confederate casualties were relatively light. Burnside lost Lincoln's confidence and was replaced in early 1863 by Major General 'Fighting Joe' Hooker." Number of Losses: Union 460 killed, Confederate 387 killed; Union wounded 1,124, Confederate wounded 1,582; Union Captured/Missing 1,312 Confederate 13. Source: http://www.collectorsnet.com/cwtimes/frederic.htm.

Thirdday, December 16th, 1862
The ground covered with snow and very cold and gloomy. Grandfather is very sick. I thought of my dream as soon as I heard it, for in my dream we were all in the room there and he was talking to us and we were very sad. I am so anxious to hear the news this morning.

Fourthday, December 17th, 1862
Will at home today. It seems so much better than to be here alone. It is cold, and disagreeable and we have had news in the bargain and all combined is enough to give us the blues. Burnside is across the river. What an immense loss of life and to no purpose. Our guess is surely our generals are not competent to be leaders of armies. Oh, what good will come of this bloody war sufficient to compensate for the desolated homes, the murdered sons and fathers, the destroyed cities, the demoralizing effect upon the people and the evil war is scattering abroad over our once beautiful and happy country.[168] Clay and Mary were here last evening. We had a pleasant time.

Fifthday, December 18th, 1862
Late this cold morning. I wish someone would give me a nice Christmas present, but of course that will not be so.

Sixthday, December 19th, 1862
"Sick" today. Have spent the day in reading and watching [out the window]. Alma is "editress" for this evening and has a piece for the "Sons of Arcanum" to read. We are going to form a society of five or six of us to meet once a week for the purpose of improving ourselves. I hope it will not fall in the talk as a great many things do. Ella and Lisa Wright and Jo, Mary, Alma and I and maybe Cal will form the society. Georgie ran off to Camp Denison.[169] I look for him home this evening. I presume he has had enough of soldier life already.

Seventhday, December 20th, 1862
Swiftly the old year is passing away. His looks are whitened and his steps are becoming feeble for much has been his suffering in all the months of his life and many will hail the dawn of his "New Year" with hope for a happier future. It is a very cold morning and I am not well, so Will is going to take me home in the buggy.

---

168. News from the Battle of Fredericksburg, Virginia, was delayed in reaching Martinsville by four days.

169. Georgie is George Janney, an older brother of Will. Camp Dennison is just outside Cincinnati to the northeast. George was to later volunteer in September 1863, at age thirty-three.

Sabbath, December 21st, 1862

Not ushered in by the sweet melody of the church bell and the glad sunshine, but by the thick dark clouds and the chilly wind of a December morning and the sleet too coming down with its form of frozen rain and it is going to make all things look gloomy enough. I feel awful. I guess I am sick though. We will not go home this evening or I will not. Will went to church. Benjamin was there. They had quite an eloquent sermon. The wind sounds very lonely this morning.

Secondday, December 22nd, 1862

The sun is shining brightly and melting all the sleet away. I am home again and have been reading *Poets and Poetry of the West*.[170] I wish I could remember all I have read. I think Sarah T. Bolton[171] is a good writer. She is or should be a lecturer and Amelia B. Wells is a sweet writer. One piece written on Laura W. Thurston,[172] a poetess begins:

---

170. William Turner Coggeshall, *The Poets and Poetry of the West: With Biographical and Critical Notices*, Columbus, Ohio, Follett, Foster and Company, 1860, http://www.wvu.edu/~lawfac/jelkins/lp 2001/kinney.html. Coats Kinney, Poet Laureate of Ohio: In the spring of 1840 he came to Springboro, Warren County, Ohio, where he spent most of his later boyhood. He was married on the seventeenth of July, 1851, to Hanna Kelley of Waynesville.

171. *Historical Sketches of Kentucky* by Lewis Collins and J. A. & U. P. James, Cincinnati, 1847, vol. 1, repr. 1968, Campbell County. *The Poets and Poetry of Kentucky*, page 577: "Mrs. Sarah T. Bolton, née Barritt, was born in Newport, Kentucky, in 1820, but removed with her parents before she was four years old, to Indiana—her home henceforth being at Madison and afterwards at Indianapolis, except while absent in Europe with her husband, when he was U.S. consul to Geneva, Switzerland, 1855–58. Between 1845 and 1858, Mrs. Bolton wrote numerous poems, some of them 'among the most beautiful of the day'; and while in Switzerland was a correspondent of the *Cincinnati Commercial*." [Poems shown: "If I Were The Light of the Brightest Star" and "Dirge for the Old Year," http://www.rootsweb.com/~kygenweb/kybiog/campbell/bolton.st.txt. Sarah T. Bolton Park is in Beech Grove, Indiana, just south of downtown Indianapolis. Bolton's home was Beech Bank, Bolton House, Sherman Drive, in Beech Grove, Indiana. She wrote "Paddle Your Own Canoe" and died in 1893.

172. "Laura M [Hawley] Thurston, poet, born in Norfolk, Litchfield County, Connecticut, in December, 1812; died in New Albany, Indiana, 21 July, 1842. . . . She was educated for the profession of teaching at the Hartford female seminary, and taught in Philadelphia, Pennsylvania, and New Milford and Hartford, Connecticut, removed to New Albany in order to take charge of an academy, and in September, 1839, married Franklin Thurston, a merchant of that place. She contributed to newspapers and magazines over the signature of 'Viola.' Her poems, some of which were descriptive of nature and some didactic, were highly esteemed, and many of them are preserved in Rufus W. Griswold's and other collections of American poetry." Source: *Edited Appleton's Encyclopedia*, 2001, Virtualology, http://www.famousamericans.net/lauramthurston/.

She has gasped like a bird from the minstrel throng.
She has gone to the land where the lovely belong.
Her place is hushed by her lovers side.
Yet his heart is full of his fair young bride.
The hope of his spirit are crushed and bowed,
And he thinks of his love in the long white shroud
For the fragrant sighs of her perfumed breath
Were kissed from her lips by his rival Death.

Thirdday, December 23rd, 1862

Beautiful, beautiful is this morning. The sun is shining, the birds singing and we almost forget that it is not April, instead of December. I wish I was an artist. How l could enjoy myself and I would make such beautiful pictures. There has been a division in the cabinet. Seward and Chase have resigned. I think our country is in a pretty state and will be in a worse condition if affairs are carried on by the same embacil leaders. I have not much confidence in any of them and think if about two dozen of the best leaders were kept in Fort Warren about six months things could progress. They ought to be hung for the murder of one soldier. I think they are guilty in the sight of God as is the midnight assassin, but then this is legal murder. I just believe it is the aim of those men to get all the men killed they can and then they think the North will be willing to compromise.

Fourthday, December 24th, 1862

This is Christmas eve again. It seems strange to think of it, but with what a chilling breath does it come to many a household that was joyous enough one year ago. Many a fireside will be cheerless and dark. A thought will recall the happy moments that are gone forever, perhaps, it is a husband who has fallen in the battlefield or been stricken by disease or a brother and the friend at home in anguish will remember they are coming never more. Oh, how my heart goes forth in sympathy to those who are mourning for those who will come no more and who may never come. How dreadful it is. It is almost strange how the sun can shine or the snow fall or the gentle rain can come when there is so much wickedness, misery and desolation. I hope in another twelve months, the future will be bright and the soldiers are at home. But I know it cannot be so if there is not a great change.

Fifthday, Christmas 1862

I wonder where we will be this time next year. We went down home today. It is so wet. This is vacation. I feel sad tonight. How can we help having the blues. It is just as natural what a reprocher night is. No difference in what form it comes whether the blue sky above is full of glitter of stars and the earth flooded with moonlight or the night dark and the winds abroad. All that we have ever said or done comes back to us and the past is spread before us as an open book with all our errors printed with business letters and we turn away "sick of what we are and what we ever hope to be."

Sixthday, December 26th, 1862
The rain comes pattering against the window pane and the wind sweeps by with its mournful music. The streets are dreary, muddy and deserted and in spite of myself, my heart feels lonely pain. Sometimes I think if God can spare our home circle I can stand anything else. I care naught for myself, but that bitter void in heart. God knows what that is and that is just as natural for any life to long for something. Oh! how I pity the poor soldiers out in this pitiless rain.

Seventhday, December 27th, 1862
A beautiful day almost like spring. We had a visitor for dinner. Thomas Wills—a minister—he used to be acquainted with mother and all of them. He can tell a great many interesting things. He is or expects to go to England in the spring. It is his land. I sometimes get in a great way about going to Europe, but my fear of crossing the "briny" waters puts me out of the notion, but oh, I do want to see something.

Sabbath, December 28th, 1862
The last Sabbath of the old year has come in with its bright sunshine streaming over the land as if all was peace and harmony and gone with the quiet hush never, never to return again. Who of us can really tell what mighty events will occur before the close of another year and we might say another week for only a few more days and as a nation we are free from the cross of slavery. We went to church this morning. Had a very good sermon from Wills. No one has been here this afternoon, as I told Will, "We live in a little world to ourselves." Poor Will, he is just now very much put out with the poor light and indeed it is rather bad.

Secondday, December 29th, 1862
It seems so good to greet the bright sunshine when we go out in the early morning so bright with sunshine. How much more beautiful things look when the sky is clear. We went down home this morning. Will took our poor hogs down to be executed with several more poor things. I was really affected to tears by their cries. It seems too bad to take the life of any living thing, but if I could be affected by the hogs, how much more deeply would I feel for the poor murdered soldiers could I be at their execution though their cries would be drowned by music and the roar of cannon. Yet it would not render the pain less acute. Morgan [John Hunt Morgan] is in Kentucky again. It is strange why our men cannot do as much as the rebels.

Thirdday, December 30th, 1862
I am all alone and the patter patter of the rain keeps time to my thoughts which come and go like the wind—sometimes far over the Atlantic again resting where the peaks of "Sierra Nevada" and then for a little time I am at home with my thought and so with my dreaming and my little domestic affairs. The rainy day is drawing to a close as is the old year. Alma will come here tonight.

Fourthday, December 31st, 1862
The last day of 1862 and the last time I will ever write it. Lizzie and Jeff came this morning. Alma, Lizzy and I sat up late tonight reading and talking. We read Prentice's *Flight of Years* which is very beautiful and appropriate for indeed the year has—"Gone, gone forever like a rushing wave and another year has burst upon the shore of earthly being and it is lost. Of earthly being —and its last low tones, wandering in broken accents in the air are dying to an echo."[173] Where will we be in one year or two or three. What a helping it is we cannot know.

1863
January 1863

> **[January 1st, 1863—Emancipation Proclamation]***
> President Lincoln issued the Emancipation Proclamation "declaring slaves in the rebellious states, 'thenceforward, and forever free.' Slavery continued, however, in the Border States of Missouri and Kentucky and elsewhere until outlawed in 1865."[174]

> *N.B.: Bracketed entries have been inserted by the editor.

---

173. George Denison Prentice, American newspaperman, editor, humorist and poet (1802–1870).

> Gone! gone forever!—like a rushing wave
> Another year has burst upon the shore
> Of earthly being—and its last low tones,
> Wandering in broken accents in the air,
> Are dying to an echo.

Source: *Flight of Years,* http://www.giga usa.com/gigaweb1/quotes2/quautprenticegeorgedx001.htm.

174. National Geographic Society, "The Making of America—Ohio Valley," Washington, D.C., December 1985.

Fifthday, January 1st, 1863
Since last I wrote January first how many changes have come. How many hopes have been broken and how many homes and hearths have been chilled with death. It is terrible to look back over the months and remember how many of them are gone and remember how many of them have been celebrated with the carnage of the battlefield. It is terrible to think of the homes that are wasted. The home circles that are broken, the many who have been stricken down in the pride of manhood and all just by this wicked, unholy war, but it is the scourge of the Egyptians and God will continue to punish us as a nation until we are willing to become purified and cast our idols from us and the idol of slavery.

Lizzy and I were at school this afternoon. There were some very interesting essays. We went to hear a lecture delivered by a colored man, Solomon Day, on the subject of Slavery. He looks very intelligent and spoke well. He was followed by Mr. Oren and Gibson. All seemed to rejoice that "Time will ere long reveal a new era to the nations." Eli [Newlin][175] visited us this evening. He seemed to dwell upon our love of ease and seemed to think we had not much good in us and because we love things neat and showed it—it was all vanity. Our love for the beautiful, false ideas of religion, just as if after God has made everything so lovely and perfection in nature that we could better display our love for him by letting everything around us be stark and void of beauty. Why did God make such beautiful flowers, such lovely trees and grand mountains and rivers and oceans unless it was for us to admire and look from nature up to God? Where do we find the most vice? Is it where everything is neat and beautiful or where it is the reverse? I think some of our friends have much to unlearn that they have learned before they can see as God sees and judge us as he judges.

Sixthday, January 2nd, 1863
Already the leaves are turning rapidly each day revealing something to our hearts. Some hope or joy or pain may each succeeding "leaf" bear the impress

---

175. "Eli Newlin, the oldest child of John and Esther Stubbs Newlin, was widely known among American Friends, as an itinerant minister. Over a period of twenty years his ministry took him to most of the Quaker meetings in America. In addition he made religious visits to thousands of homes and to numerous prisons, reformatories and houses of correction. His concern for the spiritual salvation of people was accompanied by a deep conviction that ways must be found to better the social and physical welfare of the unfortunate people scattered over the land who were often forgotten by society." Source: *The Newlin Family*, Algie I. Newlin, 1965. Eli and Lydia Newlin first settled in a Quaker community about twenty miles northwest of Richmond, Indiana. After the death of Eli's father they moved back to Clinton County, Ohio, to assist in the settlement of his father's estate. When this was done they all moved to the Sugar Grove community near Plainfield, Indiana. That appears to have occurred in about 1863, according to the Newberry MM records, Clinton County, Ohio W. W. Hinshaw, vol. V. Researched by Christie Russell.

of some noble light or action and not be worse than blank. William took dinner with us today for the first time. I think he is good hearted. He is nervous today. His proclamation [Lincoln's Emancipation Proclamation] did not come out today, but will soon. It will be a memorable year. The one just opening to us.

Seventhday, January 3, 1863

A stormy day yet not more gloomy than many hearts for there have been more battles in Tennessee. Morgan and Bragg defeated but at what severe cost it is hard to say. We have no definite account as yet but our loss must be heavy. Lizzie and Jeff are going to Hocketts this evening—would like to go along and hear some music. We sent for a copy of the *Louisville Journal* but there is too much democrat about it to suit us—the Editor cannot say enough in regard to the proclamation. He is so apposed to it. I wonder if Matt will come. I am not going to look for her.

Sabbath, January 4th, 1863

This morning the rain darted against the window pane and the wind blew a perfect hurricane, but after a time the clouds disappeared and the sun shone out bright and beautiful. Jeff and Lizzie were here for dinner, but now they are gone. It will seem real lonely I expect after having so much company so I am sitting here alone beside the window while the evening is deepening into twilight—occasionally some person or a carriage passes, but that affords me very little amusement. Not half so much as it did a while ago when Mary, Lizzie and I stood peeping through the blinds at everyone who passed. Will has come in now and I am going to get him to talk some.

Secondday, January 5th, 1863

A bright morning—mother is sick and I went down home. I hope she will be better by morning. This is a lovely day as we often have in spring. Oh, it is sad to read of the terrible slaying of our men, so many killed in the late battle, Stone River,[176] and the federals have reached Vicksburg and engaged the enemy. I hope we will conquer them.

---

176. "Maj. Gen. William S. Rosecrans's Union Army of the Cumberland followed Bragg from Kentucky to Nashville. Rosecrans left Nashville on December 26, with about 45,000 men, to defeat Bragg's army. He found Bragg's army on December 29 and went into camp that night, within hearing distance of the Rebels. At dawn on the 31st, Bragg's men attacked the Union right flank. The Confederates had driven the Union line back to the Nashville Pike by 10:00 am but there it held. Union reinforcements arrived from Rosecrans's left in the late forenoon to bolster the stand and before fighting stopped that day, the Federals had established a new, strong line. On New Year's Day, both armies marked time. Bragg surmised that Rosecrans would now withdraw, but the next morning he was still in position. In late afternoon, Bragg hurled a division at a Union division that, on January 1, had crossed Stones River and had taken up a strong position

Thirdday, January 6th, 1863
Raining and gloomy enough this morning. I cannot stand it here alone. I must go down home if I have to walk. I have not heard from mother this morning. I am going to stay down home a day or two.

Sixthday, January 9th, 1863
Have been down home this week. Mother has been right sick. Alma and I have had great times being kitchen girls. Mother is better and I came home this evening. It is sad to read the long list of names of the killed, wounded and injured. Everyone has someone to mourn for them, Lib Haynes brother, George West, is dead. They are going to send him home. I feel sorry for his friends. It will be so bad for them to have to meet him and he so still and unconscious. Oh, how could I ever bear it, but the many hearts that tonight are bowed over sorrow were once as light as mine. We have had so many men killed at Vicksburg[177] and have not achieved a victory, but have been repulsed. I hope they will yet be victorious. We received two letters this week from Jimmy and one from Cousin Mary H. Janney. We must answer them soon.

Essay
[By Paulena Stevens Janney]

The last goodbys were taken. The last one of the loved friends were over and I found myself gliding further with each succeeding moment from my inactive. Oh, how vain are all our ambitious longing, how fulfilled our brilliant dreams when our hearts feel the longing for home and friends. All that I had longed to see my imaginative . . . dreaming of the glorious things I should see in the old world sank into insignificance when I found myself floating along as gently watching until every vestige of the homeland should fade away. One lovely girl I noticed and my

---

on the bluff east of the river. The Confederates drove most of the Federals back across McFadden's Ford, but with the assistance of artillery, the Federals repulsed the attack, compelling the Rebels to retire to their original position. Bragg left the field on January 4–5, retreating to Shelbyville and Tullahoma, Tennessee. Rosecrans did not pursue, but as the Confederates retired, he claimed the victory. Stones River boosted Union morale. The Confederates had been thrown back in the east, west, and in the Trans-Mississippi." Source: http://www.civilwar home.com/stones.htm.

177. "Vicksburg is the key. The war can never be brought to a close until the key is in our pocket," President Lincoln said. Southerners agreed. "Vicksburg is the nail head that holds the South's two halves together," said Confederate President Jefferson Davis. Source: http://americancivilwar.com/vicks.html.

tears almost came in sympathy with her. She was very delicate. The bloom had left her cheek and her eye had a fatal luster. And she was accompanied by her father who seemed fearful for a breath of fresh air to fan his precious charge. I will not give you a definite history of everything that occurred on our journey suffice to say I made acquaintance the fair lady whose name [is]Fannie Lisle Archer. I found her very agreeable, educated and refined—do not fear for my heart—but remember I am a stranger in a strange land and who would not pass up at any chance of forming a friendship with so fair a friend. Many . . . are passed pleasantly as we read or talk of what we have read of the sea and the clouds. I do not feel fearful of storms like I supposed I would. So far the water has been so unruffled and looks so beautiful sparkling in the sunlight and the faces were all such a contented look now that the sickness if over. That was a matter of conscientiousness. Be cheerful and not mar anyone's happiness by my anticipation of evil to come.

Seventhday, January 10th, 1863
Dark, gloomy and raining in perfect unison with the mourning abroad over our land. The bright sunshine, the singing birds and the balmy air of spring would almost seem to be a mockery to the hearts laden with sorrow. But the wild wind, the storms seem in sympathy with the first strong passionate outbursts of grief—I want to see someone. I am all alone this dreary day and no one to speak a word to. Will is going to finish his work today. I am so glad.

Sabbath, January 11th, 1863
Went to church, but it was dreadfully muddy. Were at Carmans last night. Mr. and Mrs. Brown were there. I like Fannie so well. Carmans have such nice curtains and carpet. George West was not brought on the train last night as was expected. He will not come before tomorrow. Will is writing to cousin Mary. I am going to also. I am also writing to Jennie.

Secondday, January 12th, 1863
Bright this morning. Going home. January is passing very rapidly away and spring will soon be here again. I hope before it comes some great and important change for the better will have taken place, but if a certain prophet was a true one, it will be a change which will bring more sorrow than ever. The prophecy was "A dry fall, open winter, an early spring and then a king." I just feel almost sure from my own observations that we are to have a king. I think the democrats will be successful in electing their president next time and that president will be McClellan, perhaps, and our king. Maybe the democrats will be satisfied then.

Thirdday, January 13th, 1863
Went up home this afternoon. We rode old "Bell." Poor old thing. We felt sorry for her. We had a mind to walk. I spent part of the afternoon in the woodhouse and spent the remainder at the Vances for I did not get the door unlocked and after Will came we tried some little time before we could. I think we will leave the door unlocked. William James came this morning. He is very "polite." We did not get well enough acquainted to pass an opinion. There is no news of importance. France is more favorable. Napoleon in speaking to Slidell says as his government helped to form this one "I will also help to maintain it."

Fourthday, January 14th, 1863
Raining, raining. How dreary all things look. Nothing but mud and rain to be seen. How rejoiced I will be to see the bright days of spring returning to us laden with the breath of flowers and the sweet song of birds. Would that it's coming would restore the happiness to every heart that is now racked with anguish, but alas it cannot bring back the dead or bind up the broken heart. George West was buried yesterday. What a lonely day this must be to his friends. I was not at the depot when his remains were brought there. There were many persons there. He was in a metallic coffin. Dart preached his funeral at West Chapel. I would love the pleasure of hearing him every Sabbath, but it cannot be. Oh, the wind. How mournful it sounds. Its strains are of saddest music bringing sad feelings to our hearts that are impossible to resist. Will is at home. It seems much better than to be here alone. Near me are two letters. One from Matt and one from Josy. I received them long months ago. Josy's heart was breaking with sorrow and she could not confide in me as the truest and best friend. Have I changed? Have I ever been false? No, never and Matt, why is it that all the old love seems half forgotten. Surely my heart is just as true and loving as it was years ago. Why will others change? Oh, I could weep today with the old letters and the sad wail of the old memories spring up at other times that are half forgotten.

Fifthday, January 15th, 1863
Snow. Everything is snow and still coming. I wonder if it will ever quit. There is an old woman here a while ago and she said I think it will stop snowing at twelve o'clock or keep on coming. So we are sure it will. How I pity the poor soldiers out in this dreary snowstorm. Alma is here. She could not go to school. I never saw such a deep snow. Now if we could go out sleigh riding, but the snow is so deep it will not be very pleasant. The snow is covering many a newly made grave and the agony of hearts the friends feel to think of the snow covering those so short a time gone by were full of life and animation. Dreary, dreary indeed must the winter days pass away to those whose hearts are stricken with sorrow.

Sixthday, January 16th, 1863
This morning it was almost impossible for us to go out of the house without

being half buried in a snow drift. But Will took a shovel and cleaned paths around the house so it is not quite so difficult for us to go out—the snow has ceased almost, but the sky is full of . . . laden clouds again and there is no telling when the snow will be gone. Oh, what a miserable muddy time we will have, but if it was me I would risk it. Everything is getting so dirty and I think it would be a good plan to clean up but then it is so snowy.

Seventhday, January 17th, 1863
Just the same piercing cold air and the white glittering snow so deep we cannot venture far.

Sabbath, January 18th, 1863
Went to church this morning. Heard a good sermon from Benjamin. I think him a good preacher. We have had a few callers this evening. Jeff and Tim Moon came tonight and brought Jim Hunt. We attended church had a good sermon. William James is gentlemanly looking. I have a good opinion of him. I wish we could get acquainted with him. He is a member of the Methodist church. Will . . . is going to be a free man soon—out of debt. I think he will be much happier. Oh, it seems so funny. Jeff took Liz Wright home last night—tonight I mean, Alma and I sat up in the "Amen Corner." We carried over some warm bricks to put our feet on.

Secondday, January 19th, 1863
A gloomy day. The snow melting away and a drizzly rain began falling at dark. We went to church tonight. Benjamin was not there, but Nasy or whatever his name is preached. I do not like to hear him half as well as Benjamin though he may be a good man. He is very dignified in his appearance and I think a peculiar looking man. David Batter escorted Alma to church.

Thirdday, January 20th, 1863
Gloomy enough without. We received a letter from Lot this morning. Wonders will never cease. We are so surprised he is *going to marry*. Whoever heard of such a thing. [Lot Janney was thirty-seven years old and marrying for the first time.] He has invited us to go with him to Marietta [Ohio] where Fannie lives. We think of going. I hope we can go and have a pleasant time. Is it right for us to go? It seems like it must be for if the invitation had been given a month ago it would have been impossible for us to go. I will have to be in the inclination if we do go, for it will be long.

Fourthday, January 21st, 1863
l am becoming more and more contented the older I grow [twenty-two years old]. We are going to send a letter to Lot and tell him we think we can go. Fannie I think it is a pretty name. I do hope I will like her. It would be so nice to find a friend that would be just the one I need and she is older and will be like

my older sister. I hope but I am not going to pass any opinion before I see her. I think her mother is a tall dignified woman, a little cold perhaps. I wonder if we will go. I am just going to be calm about it and if it is right for us to go, we will go. After I went to Sanderson's this morning, I began to wonder and say within myself—invited or not invited, that is the question. It seemed so funny I could hardly realize it. I came to the conclusion I had been invited. We had a splendid dinner and a very pleasant time. True there was no congenial friend with whom I could chat but I got on very well with an elderly lady. Alma went home this evening. Mother is not well.

Fifthday, January 22nd, 1863
I am going home. Mother is like she was before. I am so sorry. I do wish she was not sick. I am going to stay till she gets better. If none of them would get sick but me I could stand it, but I am always so uneasy about the rest of them.

Fifthday, January 29th, 1863
Up home again. Mother better. William James took dinner here today. Burnside is removed and Hooker is in his place. I hope something will be accomplished now soon, but the men that must be killed first. It is horrible to think. There is a kind of new disease. Two children near us have it—they are deaf and I know not what else. The doctor can do nothing for them.

Sixthday, January 30th, 1863
We wrote again to Lot this evening for fear he had not received ours. We are beginning to be anxious to know what to do. Oh, it makes me feel so sad to think of the suffering and sorrow all over our land. We can not be thankful enough for the comforts we enjoy. It is not right to murmur again any of the little trivial things that is often beset us, but we are apt to be hasty in our judgment.

Seventhday, January 31st, 1863
I went down home this morning. Mother is not well yet. I hope she will be soon. Ella Bashimer was here. Something so terrible happened this morning. An Irish woman left her little children at home and her little girl got afire someway and when the mother got home she was burned so badly it did not survive long. Poor little thing. How it must have suffered and what must be the agony of the mother. I pity her very much for her husband is away—a soldier—and no doubt her fear of his anger will make her suffer all the more.

February 1863

Sabbath, February 1st, 1863
The day past away rainy and gloomy. I could not but remember the poor Irish girl who was burned. The hearse went by and but a few persons. The poor

mother looked sad enough. Oh, I pity her so much. I hope I will never experience such agony as must now be hers. We went to hear a sermon delivered tonight by a colored preacher. He is quite youthful in appearance. It was very good. I hope we will get the paper for our room tomorrow.

Secondday, February 2nd, 1863
Our paper came, but no letter. We did not do much with the papering in our room. We find it not such easy work to do. I wonder if we are going to Marietta. I think it is time we did know.

Thirdday, February 3rd, 1863
Nothing new. Cold and dreary, but we are quite busy and so time passes away quickly. We find it rather tedious work, this papering, and will be glad when it is done. Now if we could only see Wilots, I think we might enjoy our ourselves finely with them. I hope we will meet them sometimes. Oh, it just worries us so to be bothered with the old woman who lives near here, Not that I am unwilling to help her, but when she comes after "slop" she comes in and stays and tells so many things that does not interest us in the least, but I suppose we must put up with it for a little time, but I am going to tell her soon. Pshaw! What an interesting journal I am going to leave for my grandchildren and great grandchildren. I know they cannot fail to be deeply interested in reading, providing such, should be the case in time to come.

Fourthday, February 4th, 1863
There was a meeting last night for the contrabands. I was appointed on a committee to see that clothes will be made, but I am doing so little about it that I will not say much. I have a pair of pants to make—my first pair—no letter—why don't Lot write? is the query with us. . . . Our room is finished—almost all I can do. It will be so good to have things rectified once more.

Fifthday, February 5th, 1863
Well, well can it be so. It seems like a dream. A letter came this morning for me. George [Janney] took it out of the [post] office thinking it was for Jane—a terrible mistake. They read it. I am so provoked, but Will is more so. What will we do? Lot desired us to keep the knowledge of his marriage from the "folks." How could they be so dumb. They even read it all after reading our names which occurred before the close. Oh well, It cannot be mended now and we must make the best of it. Lot wants us to leave home on the 7th of March. He is to be at the Marietta's depot. The ceremony will take place the next evening. Oh, how much better we would feel if no one had seen the letter.

Sixthday, February 6th, 1863
William James is coming here tonight from literary. We are much pleased with our room. It looks so much better. I am reading a story in the *Ledger* entitled

"Warps and Weft."[178] I think it will prove to be very good. I hope I will begin in time so my work will be nearer done when the time comes for us to go, if we do go, as I am always so hurried when going anyplace. Such deep snow.

Seventhday, February 7th, 1863

The jingle, jingle of the sleigh bells float quite frequently on the winter air. Martinsville has not presented so stirring an appearance for some time as at present. Some changes from the monotony. We took our first sleigh ride of the season this evening. We went to Hayne's a little bit. Had a pleasant time and had the best apples and cider. Aunty Carman has been right sick and was sitting in the corner wrapped in a shawl and she says she never had looked [at] her hands so long in seven years. Well, I am sleepy.

Sabbath, February 8th, 1863

Well, the merry jingle of the sleigh bells will cease soon unless there is more snow. We went to grandfathers. Had such a good dinner. I almost hurt myself eating. Perhaps mother will come in the morning. I do hope she will. It will seem so good. "The joys and sorrows of life are more evenly balanced than is generally supposed" is the beginning of a short piece and I think it is very true. Then it goes on to say that though sorrow may find its way into the cottage, it also finds its way to those whose heads are crowned. Peter the Great suffered much sorrow from the misconduct of his son Alex, who kept on in wickedness not heeding the admonition and entreaties of his father, but at length he was arrested and sentenced to death for treason against his father. Alex died though in convulsions.[179]

Secondday, February 9th, 1863

This month is passing away so swiftly and now our hearts are beginning to be full of dread for what the coming spring may bring in regard to the war. Another draft is almost sure to come. I hope we will be fortunate enough to escape but someone will have to go. Mother was up all day. I hope she will get well soon again. A home would not be a home without a mother. How much I pity Jennie Hadley. How full of sorrow her heart must be the loss of a kind mother

---

178. The weft consists of the horizontal threads interlaced through the warp [vertical threads] in a woven fabric. The weft is also known as the woof. This article, however, most likely uses the term metaphorically.

179. "In 1724, Peter had his second wife, Catherine, crowned as Empress, although he continued to remain Russia's actual ruler. All of Peter's male children had died, and the eldest son, Aleksey, had been tortured and killed on Peter's orders in 1718 because he had disobeyed his father and opposed official policies. Aleksey's mother Eudoxia had also been punished; she was dragged from her home and tried on false charges of adultery. Aleksey's friends had also been tortured." Source: http://en.wikipedia. org/wiki/Peter_I_of_Russia.

and brother is very hard indeed to bear. The *Ledger* came today. I am anxious to get it, but Alma took it home tonight. The snow is all vanishing. I would not be surprised to wake in the morning to see every vestige removed.

Thirdday, February 10th, 1863
This is the brightest day we have had for sometime, but this evening the clouds begin to gather and before we know it I expect we will see the rain come pattering against the window. It will soon be time for us to go. I am getting anxious. The Contraband Society[180] meets tonight, but I do not feel well enough to attend. I hope I will not be appointed on another committee for I would rather assist myself than try to get others. The grass will soon be getting green again. How beautiful it will make all nature appear and then the flowers—the violet and the daisies will be springing up in the meadow. I hope I can wander glad and happy as I did last spring and gather them. Oh, if Will can only be spared from going to war. The best is beginning to come again and we must not get discontented yet. Oh, suppose it all comes out in the end.

Sabbath, February 11th, 1863
Went to church this morning. We went across the way to hear Benjamin. I still like him. His text was, "The Lord is my Shepherd and I Shall Not Want" [Twenty-third Psalm]. Clay and Cal were here a moment. Clay is on his way to see Alma. I suppose. If nothing prevents in the three weeks from this evening, we will be far from here. I hope it will be as pleasant a day as today has been. How very quickly a change will come this morning. It seemed like a spring morning, but soon the rain drops came pattering down and before long we had a real rainy day upon us again. Wind and rain and water seemed plenty to spare this season. But not standing winter is passing very rapidly and the spring buds and the spring sunshine will be making our hearts bright again. But I have been happy by the winter inside, but there is something so refreshing about spring that our hearts feel a new life and a new ambition to accomplish something more.

Secondday, February 12th, 1863
The day has passed away very pleasantly. Alma did not go to school so Cal and we had a nice time sitting by the fire talking of when we were children and how very happy the days were to us before our hearts learned to be in dread of sorrow and learn to meet it halfway.

Sixthday, February 13th, 1863
The fire is burning cheerfully in the grate. Alma and Cal are purchasing some

---

180. The Contraband Society was a group of members of the Newberry Meeting appointed to collect and make items for the Contraband, who were escaped slaves who fled to or were taken behind Union lines.

Valentines[181] for some of the boys. I remember I used to receive some such. I have been in a great notion this evening of Wilots moving up here, but of course it will not be so. Mother feels better than she has for some time. I am so glad. I hope she will get well now.

Seventhday, February 14th, 1863
The most beautiful morning we have had for a long time. It makes me feel so happy to see the bright sunshine and hear the music of the birds. How I do love the spring time, sad indeed that there is so much to mar the beauty. If we could all live in love and harmony how much misery might on temperance this evening at the school house. Jeff took dinner with us today. I think I must be avoided. This time last February Cal and I were looking forward with many anticipation to our going to Richmond and now Will and I are just as eager for our journey, but we do not talk so much about it as then we did. Charlie Oren delivers an address. I must be getting very romantic for l am becoming so fond of fried onions. We have had them for dinner three days this week. I even went so far as to borrow some today. I must not forget to return them. Three onions might do a great deal of good. I am afraid my journal will not be interesting for my grandchildren to review.

Secondday, February 16th, 1863
A bright day till evening. I went down home this morning. It seemed so good to see mother better. I do hope she will stay well. The time is fast coming around when we anticipate going our journey. I hope nothing will happen to us. Will Paxton came down this morning. He had been away such a long time—several weeks. There is a temperance meeting tonight. The "Rum Seller" of the town is going to pledge himself to discontinue the sale of intoxicating "liquors." I hope his heart is changed from principle as well as he is by fear, but it has been too sudden, I fear, to be lasting. I think he ought to be encouraged to be better now. Oh? the miserable Democrats. They are bound to ruin our government yet. I hope they will be checked before they go much further.

---

181. "Some experts state that it originated from St. Valentine, a Roman who was martyred for refusing to give up Christianity. He died on February 14, 269 A.D. . . . Legend also says that St. Valentine left a farewell note for the jailer's daughter, who had become his friend, and signed it 'From Your Valentine.' . . . Gradually, February 14 became the date for exchanging love messages and St. Valentine became the patron saint of lovers. The date was marked by sending poems and simple gifts such as flowers. . . . In the United States, Miss Esther [Allen] Howland is given credit for sending the first valentine cards." Source: http://www.pictureframes.co.uk/pages/saint_valentine.htm.

Esther Howland received her first English Valentine after she graduated from Mount Holyoke in 1847. She imported paper lace and floral decorations and began making her own Valentines. By 1850 her orders were so large that she recruited friends to help her. Eventually her business grossed $100,000 a year. In 1881 she retired and sold her business. Source: "Valentine's Day Card History," http://www.emotionscards.com/museum/estherhowland.htm.

Fourthday, February 18th, 1863
The ground was covered with snow this morning, but now it has almost all disappeared and the clouds are hanging dark and heavy as if ready to pour down something upon us. We will have great times after while. I am afraid for I guess the *conscription act*[182] will pass and almost everyone will have to go. I had rather give up our property than for Will to have to go. If the war only was over how bright everything would look.

Fifthday, February 19th, 1863
Oh, this beautiful evening, beautiful because this morning was dark and the afternoon ended with a hard shower. We, the committee of three—purchased goods for the contraband. I am making a wrapper and apron. I am going to save the pattern, for who knows, but I might need some little clothes of my own sometime. Alma has gone to Gibsons to tell Lib Canterfeld. Will received a letter from Lot. He was fearful we had not received his last letter. He sent us the photograph of the sweetest little girl. Mr. Utter presented Alma with a written delineation of her character. It is exact in almost every particular. I wish he would give me as good one. I have been reading the life of Murry, the father of Universalism. He was a good man anyhow and did what he believed to be his duty. If we all had the same faith in God we would be much happier.

---

182. "There was no general military draft in America until the Civil War. The Confederacy passed its first of three conscription acts 16 April 1862, and scarcely a year later the Union began conscripting men. Government officials plagued with manpower shortages regarded drafting as the only means of sustaining an effective army and hoped it would spur voluntary enlistments. But compulsory service embittered the public, who considered it an infringement on individual free will and personal liberty and feared it would concentrate arbitrary power in the military. Believing with some justification that unwilling soldiers made poor fighting men, volunteer soldiers despised conscripts. Conscription also undercut morale, as soldiers complained that it compromised voluntary enlistments and appeared as an act of desperation in the face of repeated military defeats.

"Conscription nurtured substitutes, bounty-jumping, and desertion. Charges of class discrimination were leveled against both Confederate and Union draft laws since exemption and commutation clauses allowed propertied men to avoid service, thus laying the burden on immigrants and men with few resources. Occupational, only-son, and medical exemptions created many loopholes in the laws. Doctors certified healthy men unfit for duty, while some physically or mentally deficient conscripts went to the front after sham examinations. Enforcement presented obstacles of its own; many conscripts simply failed to report for duty. Several states challenged the draft's legality, trying to block it and arguing over the quota system. Unpopular, unwieldy, and unfair, conscription raised more discontent than soldiers.

"Under the Union draft act men faced the possibility of conscription in July 1863 and in March, July, and December 1864. Draft riots ensued, notably in New York in 1863. Of the 249,259 18-to-35-year-old men whose names were drawn, only about 6% served, the rest paying commutation or hiring a substitute." Source: http://www.civilwarhome.com/conscription.htm.

Sixthday, February 20th, 1863
We spent the evening at Gibsons. Had a pleasant time. Sallie is so sweet. I just love her. Lib had a very nice supper. I do not see how she can think of so many good things to get. Alma was at Gibsons with us.

Seventhday, February 21st, 1863
Went home with Alma this morning. Mother is always glad to see us when we go. I almost have the blues today about something. I don't know what. I pity anyone who has no home or no place to sleep. My work for the contrabands is finished for the week. I must try and do my work next week for it will soon be time for us to go.

Sabbath, February 22nd, 1863
Snow again and everything is dreary as can be. We can not go sleighing though for it is muddy. I guess there is a sweet little bird singing. It sounds very happy, just as though we had no snow or cold chilling wind I am not in the mood for writing this morning. I fear my journal will be a sad failure and not be interesting, but I suppose it will do me some good to look over it in years to come if I am spared so long. I think we are going to have a revolution over here sometime before the war ends and I begin to be afraid.

Secondday, February 23rd, 1863
Cal sent me a note this morning to go and stay with her, so I took my silk dress and went. We got along with it very well. I wish it was all done. The *Ledger* came today. The stories are so good. I left "Earnest LeFevere" in rather a tight place. I am anxious to see how he will be extricated. I suppose he could not be killed and that he will come out all right yet and marry Pauline.

Thirdday, February 24th, 1863
Cal and I went to Millers, but Martha was not at home, so we called on Fannie Brown. It is a pleasant place to go. We are going to the contrabands meeting tonight. I have never been. Clarkson Hunt will address the meeting. The snow is almost gone and it is so muddy. Can hardly get anywhere.

Fourthday, February 25th, 1863
Chilly and disagreeable. Alma stayed at home today. William James is here tonight. I am going to try and get my dress done sometime, for the time is fast approaching for us to attend this great wedding.

Fifthday, February 26th, 1863
I have been in bed all day nearly sick, must get myself a little better for Mr. ____ is coming up tonight and he will be sure to tell us what he thinks of us—our character. There has been a great union meeting at Cincinnati. So many good

speeches. The Copperheads[183] get, but little encouragement, except about being hung. It would have been so pleasant to have heard all the proceedings, but the ladies were excluded so had I been there I would have been disappointed, but Will would have heard and that would do almost as much good as to have heard it myself.

Sixthday, February 27th, 1863
The brightest day we have had for many weeks. The sun is bright and everything looks like spring was almost here. The grass is getting green in the yard and the roses will soon be budding. If it was not for the draft, but it is surely coming. The conscription bill has passed both house and senate. The Indiana "Copperheads" are trying to take the military power from Governor Morton and put it in the hands of a Justice of the Peace. They are getting more bold everyday and meaner. I hope this will put a stop to them. They say there are so

---

183. "The Copperheads, according to Mark Boatner in his *Civil War Dictionary*, were 'Northern Democrats who opposed the Union's war policy and favored a negotiated peace' with the Confederacy. '[President Abraham] Lincoln assumed strong executive powers in suppressing them, including arrests, suspension of the press, suspension of habeas corpus, and censorship. Their organizations included the Knights of the Golden Circle, Order of American Knights and Sons of Liberty, and their strength lay mainly in Ohio, Illinois, and Indiana.'" Source: http://users.erols.com/kfraser/union/homefront/copper exp.html.

"Republican Abraham Lincoln was able to win the 1860 presidential election largely because the Democratic party had torn itself into several factions and could offer no united opposition. In the North the Democrats divided into two factions—the War Democrats and the Peace Democrats. Neither group agreed with the way the Republican administration conducted the war, but the War Democrats at least supported the fight for the Union.

"The Peace Democrats were opposed to the war and would have accepted a negotiated peace resulting in an independent Confederacy. Most Peace Democrats were from the midwestern states of Ohio, Illinois, and Indiana, but political dissent was widespread throughout the North. Midwesterners had close economic and sentimental ties with the South, and many of them bitterly opposed the Union's war against what one of them called 'the injured, incensed, downtrodden people of the South.'

"In 1861, Republicans started calling antiwar Democrats 'copperheads,' likening them to the poisonous snake. By 1863, the Peace Democrats had accepted the label, but for them the copper 'head' was the likeness of Liberty on the copper penny, and they proudly wore pennies as badges.

"The Copperheads mounted a forceful and sustained protest against the Lincoln administration's policies and conduct. The most popular of the Copperheads was Democratic Congressman Clement L. Vallandigham, who in 1862 introduced a bill in Congress to imprison the President." Source: http://civilwar.bluegrass.net/Home-Front/copperheads.html.

many K.G.C. [Knights of the Golden Circle][184] 80,000 in Ohio, 70,000 in Indiana and 100,000 in Illinois. I think there are worse times before us yet. I am going to try to write a letter in answer to one Jo wrote for the literary last week. If I only could write all I think it would do better but when I begin I cannot find language to express all I think and can never feel perfectly satisfied. I guess I am always in too much of a hurry.

Seventhday, February 28th, 1863
The morning came very beautiful, but now the clouds are gathering and I should not wonder if nature was accordingly. I wonder where the last day of next February will find us—none save God can know of all the changes to come before then. We can only wonder for many we know must come. Just one week and if we go, we will go. Alma went home last night. She was very anxious to go. I think Will and I will go pretty soon. Mary came this morning before I was dressed. As I said Dave Utter did tell our characters. Mary, Cal, Alma and Sallie Smithson were here. We had so much fun. He said, Alma and I were very much alike in everything, but I was more spunky and more suspicious and more un-approachable. He said if everyone was like he was they would not like me much at first. He said I was naturally affected, but it was all natural. He said so many things I can not tell all. Oh, dear we have heard such bad news. Aunt Eliza [Elizabeth Harris, wife of Thomas Stevens, brother of Paulena's father, Evan] is dead. How I regret it that we did not know she was sick. We might have done her some good. I wonder what will become of the poor little children.

March 1863

Sabbath, March 1st, 1863
A dark and gloomy afternoon. Aunt Eliza was buried this morning just after meeting. It is such a gloomy day to them—poor children. I hope they will all get good homes. Mr. Cable came on the train last night and he called here this morning. Jeff and Jim Hunt have come, so I must put off my journal. Our callers are gone. Jeff told Will he would like to talk to us real well, but he is going to defer it for a time. I would like to know what it is. Perhaps I can guess 1st of March 1863 and 1864 will be different and I wonder how. I hope the war will be

---

184. "Knights of the Golden Circle was a secret order of Southern sympathizers in the North during the Civil War. Its members were known as Copperheads. . . . Southern newspapers wishfully reported stories of widespread disaffection, and John Hunt Morgan's raid (1863) into Kentucky, Indiana, and Ohio was undertaken in the expectation that the disaffected element would rally to his standard. Gov. Oliver P. Morton of Indiana and Gen. Henry B. Carrington effectively curbed the Sons of Liberty in that state in the fall of 1864. With mounting Union victories late in 1864, the order's agitation for a negotiated peace lost appeal, and it soon dissolved." Source: http://www.bartleby.com/65/kn/KnightsG.html.

over but I don't think it will and then our king is yet to come. One week hence if a preventing occurrence, I suppose we will be at Woods.

Secondday, March 2nd, 1863
Sick today. Trying to get ready to go, but do not feel like trying. If my dress was only done it would be a relief to if mother could only come up, but all those children, I expect, will be there. Oh, I am so afraid mother will get sick. I wish someone would take them. . . . It is too much for mother to do it all [Thomas Stevens had five children].

Fifthday, March 5th, 1863
Have been real sick all week. Have been very much afraid we could not get to go, but I feel better today. I feel more like going and Will is better. Mother came up this morning. I have just cried all day pretty near for everyone of the five children coming to fathers to stay awhile. I pity them and it seems like there is no way to help it, yet for they cannot find homes for them, but just to think what a change for so long there has been such a small family and such a difference in the ages and now so many coming and younger than Willie and Eva, three of them, two anyhow. It seems too bad. It will be so different, so many children and everything. When Alma came home I told her and we both just cried and cried. We are so afraid mother will get sick too. Just think, eight children when Alma goes home. It is wicked trying for us to think so much about it for they cant help it, but then how can we?

Sixthday, March 6th, 1863
If nothing happens we expect to go tomorrow. We received a letter from Lot. He wants us to be sure to come. It is dark and gloomy this morning. My eyes feel very bad this morning. Alma and I are trying to be reconciled about the addition to the family, but it makes me almost cry, but Will has almost forbidden me from crying anymore before we go.

Seventhday, March 7th, 1863 [Traveling to Rainbow, just above Marietta, Ohio]
Left home looking wintery enough with the ground covered with snow and the trees bending beneath their light burden. We reached Marietta in safety after a pleasant journey. There was not much snow beyond Greenfield [Ohio] and it looked so good. Lot met us at the depot and took me to Fanny's aunt who is a maiden lady living alone. It seems so funny. She lived in a great big house. I should think she would be afraid, but I was not, so I went to sleep listening to the swishing of the waters which sounded like a sweet murmur of a waterfall. [The Muskingum River ran near the house.] I did not open my eyes until called to breakfast. It was a little breakfast in a little round table, but all good. I think it must be a pleasant place in summer. General Buells mother lives next house, I guess.

Sabbath, March 8th, 1863 [Muskingum River from Marietta to Rainbow, Washington County, Ohio]
We were almost ready to start to church when Lot came and said there was a boat going up the Muskingum in a short time, so we took passage and after a pleasant ride came to Woods. I think it is a very pleasant place and like them very well. It seems so funny to think of being away up here. I would like to live so near the river.

Secondday, March 9th, 1863 [Rainbow, Washington County, Ohio]
This evening the great wedding comes off perfect. The hearts are beating high. All is over. There was no fainting and everything passed away nicely. Had some sweet music and afterward some dancing. I had the pleasure of looking on. We had a nice supper. Tomorrow we start away. I wonder how it looks at home? We have a room which looks out over the river and hills and it must look very lovely in summer for it looks pleasant now.

Thirdday, March 10th, 1863 [Rainbow to Marietta, Ohio]
Took dinner at Mr. Oyeres. Had a pleasant time. After a weary waiting on the river bank the "Powell" came steaming up and we and our baggage were soon safe on deck. Cornelia [Nellie Wood, sister to Fannie Wood Janney] went to Marietta with us. I like her so well. When we arrived at Marietta the "Sultana"[185] was by our side and we just stepped over amid the noise and confusion—the clamor of porters and haste of passengers and we were soon safe in our stateroom and on our awakening we discovered we were at "Parkersburg" where we remained all day. Some of the Virginia [now West Virginia] ladies and gentlemen came on the boat and they drank an abundance of wine and were very merry—too merry

The *Sultana* at Helena, Arkansas, overloaded with former Union POWs. Library of Congress.

for ladies. We thought they made some good music for us though. One lady could whistle too admirably and she played the mockingbird and imitating it.

---

185. The *Sultana,* launched on January 3, 1863, was built in Cincinnati for Captain Pres Lodwick, well known on the Upper Mississippi for his *Northern Belle* and *Northern Light.* It was designed for the New Orleans cotton trade but ran from Cincinnati to Wheeling, West Virginia, at this time. See April 27, 1865, entry for the sinking of the *Sultana.*

It sounded pretty. Miss Ridgeway, a woman from Cincinnati, was designed on going to Vevay, Indiana. There was an Avis Bently and a Mrs. Northrup and an elderly looking lady who lived at Covington. We had pleasant company on the boat. The captain is a nice looking man very . . .

Fourthday, March 11th, 1863 [Cincinnati]
We arrived at Cincinnati about 1 1/2 o'clock remained on board till morning. Went to the Gibson House for breakfast. Saw finery. We went to the Hopkins store and saw that painting "North and South." It is very fine. Saw Mr. Lives— was at his store. Will got me a new veil, a brown one. There were a good many at the Gibson house more than could be accommodated with rooms. We came home on the evening train. Will having business in town, went to the depot and I stayed for the "buss." I just got there about two minutes too soon—found all safe at home—was tired and slept.

Seventhday, March 14th, 1863
Went home [her parents' home] this morning. I was glad to see them. It seems so strange to have so many little young ones running around. I am in hopes there will be some way provided for the children soon for it is too hard for mother to have them all there so long. The baby is so sweet. It will not let us do anything with it. I met Clay going down as I came home.

Sugar Grove Farm

Sabbath, March 15th, 1863
Went to church this morning—no sermon. Went to hear Benjamin in the afternoon and heard him deliver a temperance lecture in the evening. I just like him so well to hear him. Susy Betts [five-year-old daughter of Uncle Christopher Betts][186] is sick. Alma and I went to see her. It is very uncertain about her recovery. Clay and Alma took tea with us. I broached the subject and he took me in up in an instant and said he would build a fire so what could I do but get supper, but I guess it did not hurt me any.

---

186. Susan survived, married Benton Morrow, had two children, and died in 1919.

Secondday, March 16th, 1863
March is passing away very quickly and we are having some pretty days as it is going—the mud is drying up and the streets will soon be passable. Lizzie came this morning. Lib Vance is sick. I do not think she has very much to encourage her and she will look on the dark side, like I often do.

Thirdday, March 17th, 1863
Mother came up today. We went to see Susy. She is not much better. Lucy [Lucinda] Vance is sick. I do not think she will live long as she is in a . . . I have been cleaning the yard off some. It is satisfying and it seems so good to have some nice days. I guess we are going to lose our friend the Dr., but of course we will be resigned. He thinks of leaving our little Martinsville and going to the far west.

Fourthday, March 18th, 1863
I went down home this morning and made the baby an apron. Will came down this afternoon and we went to grandfathers. Had a real good supper. I like to go to grandmothers. I think they have too much work to do for such old people [Aaron Betts was eighty-one and Anne Hunt Betts was seventy-eight; they both died three years later]. It is much colder this evening and half as much like spring as it has been. The baby is not quite so afraid of us today. I hope it will get acquainted after awhile.

Fifthday, March 19th, 1863
Just like winter this morning. The sleet pattering against the windows and looking as cheerless as could be imagined. Quite a contrast from those pretty days we thought were so much like spring, but it is well enough to have the shadows sometimes for too much brightness would not do. I think we are having a sweet time here today. Will is experimenting with the sorghum and I have been making some wax.[187] Will let his molasses boil over and what a time it made. The wind sounds cold, but somehow or other I cannot complain. I think spring is not far off and when I am not looking I almost forget that the sun is not shining.

Sixthday, March 20th, 1863
Cheerless and gloomy enough for any winter day. The trees bending beneath

---

187. "Analysis indicates that sorghum wax, made from the coating on sorghum berries, has characteristics similar to carnauba wax, made mostly from Brazilian palms. . . . Sorghum wax's melting point is about 180 degrees, similar to carnauba and the wax makes a tough coating, like the imported wax. An IAPC [Industrial Agricultural Products Center, University of Nebraska] research team is studying the best ways to extract wax from sorghum hulls to provide a cost effective alternative to carnauba. . . . They also are comparing yields from sorghum grown under differing conditions to see if growing conditions affect yields." Source: http://agproducts.unl.edu/wax.htm.

their icy covering and the wind sounding dreary enough. Perhaps Alma will go away this summer and how I will miss her. If only I had someone to talk with how much more quickly the day would pass away. I must call Will in if I can get him to come in. When we were in the city we saw the picture called "The Volunteer's Return." It is so pretty. The hero is sitting with his soldiers clothes on and holding a little boy in his arms who is eagerly looking in his fathers face. Everything seems suspended to hear and see him. His sister is holding something in her hand just ready to put on the table which is standing, but she pauses to listen—behind her the cupboard door is not closed and the contents are visible and on one side the bookcase door is open and the books all show plainly. The mother and father are sitting near their son and listening to catch every word. I wish we were able to have such pictures in our house. Perhaps we will sometime. It seems like we will not always live here just as we do now and never see anything though our dear little home we love so well that I expect I would cry for a week if Will should take a notion to go away and leave it sometime but then there are many reasons why I should prefer some other place of residence or I think I would. Perhaps I would get homesick, would I?

Seventhday, March 21st, 1863
The clouds have been clearing away all day and this evening the sun came out right and beautiful. The birds were merry and everything looked like spring again. I felt like I wanted to be out instead of being indoors, but everything is so damp. The Confederates are getting very bold and things look very dark. The paper says it will be impossible to make a draft before June or July. I hope there will be none at all.

Sabbath, March 22nd, 1863
A balmy day. We went down home. So many there. Grandmother and grandfather, and aunt Lizzie—poor old woman.[188] It was quite a treat for them to get so good a rest. I wish they might have as good a time always. Rachel Hadley [daughter of Jonathan and Mary Linton Hadley] was there. They are going to live here perhaps somewhere. Little Lenna [Paulena Stevens, the young daughter of Uncle Tom Betts] was more social today and we are so glad. She would be real sweet if she would only be free with us. Alma perhaps will go away soon. I will be lonesome without her.

Secondday, March 23rd, 1863
Patter came the rain this morning, but after the clouds dispersed and the sun

---

188. Lizzie Betts appears on the 1860 census in the household of Aaron Betts and was two years older than Aaron. It is not known exactly who she was, but since Aaron had no sisters named Elizabeth or Lizzie, she might be the widowed wife of Aaron's older half-brother Hezekiah. It is not known whether Hezekiah ever married or had a wife named Elizabeth.

came out bright warm, so I bundled up and worked among the plants until meeting time and then Cal came by and we went to meeting. I also cleaned the closet. It showed how many things will accumulate in a short time. I am going to try and keep everything in order if I can. I was up to see Sallie Gibson in the afternoon a little while. I enjoy myself real well with her. We are going to have new neighbors. The new minister. Mary Sanderson's sons are going out west.

Thirdday, March 24th, 1863
The rain came down in torrents this morning and now the wind is getting loud and high blowing. A perfect gale. Spring sweet spring do hasten and come. The presence of those few bright days so generously sent us make us impatient for more, but the storms must come. It cannot be all sunshine. Everything is growing so and our yard is becoming so beautifully green. I think what a sweet little home we have got. Here comes Will with the "daily." So I must pause and see if there be any news. "Not" very much. Will says General Burnside has been appointed to the command of the Ohio. Good news predicted from Vicksburg. Better wait and see. I like Lizzie so much better than I did a while. I think I must tell her so.

Fourthday, March 25th, 1863
Another day of storms and darkness. The ground was whitened by the snow-flakes last night and this morning the rain is coming down in good earnest. Well I think I will appreciate fine weather when it does come. How delightful and how invigorating it will be to awaken in the bright morning to the music of birds and see the clear blue sky once more and then soon the flowers will be budding and then before we know it some bright morning we will find a full bloom flower greeting us like the day of sunshine to make our hearts pure and thoughts better. While I keep my mind engaged, I do not feel at all lonely, but if I pause awhile and look upon the gloomy prospect without I almost get tired. Yesterday looking over some of my old letters.

Fifthday, March 26th, 1863
Went down home this morning. Little Lenna is so sweet. We are becoming at-tached to her. We had a very affecting time this afternoon. We hear that Dr. Woodbury of Vienna and Williams will take two of the children. Alex and Lenna Woodbury will take Lenna. We just could not keep from crying. Alma began first and the rest of us followed suit till even mother was affected to tears either in sympathy with us or that Lenna has to go. They all have our pity but poor little helpless Lenna who is so innocent and has found such a warm place in our hearts that we hesitate to part her from us into strangers hands where she will forget all the love her little baby heart ever felt for us, but we think it is better for her and perhaps she will yet live to be a nice and true woman—a woman, not a lady, unless she can have the beauty and accomplishments of a lady and the true dignity of a woman combined, but a lady in the mere sense it is daily

used does not always embrace all that should belong to the true woman. We have taught or are teaching the baby to say please for everything and her please sounds very sweet to us.

Sixthday, March 27th, 1863
Alice brought Lenna up this morning and she has been in a good humor till this evening. She became fretful and her little eyelids grew weary and closed over her blue eyes. Oh, I do love children so dearly if ever such a fortunate event was to occur as "I even I" should have a baby just to love as much as I pleased. I cannot imagine what would happen to the sweet little thing in my efforts to have it so good and so pretty and so sweet and so everything would be in danger of being caressed to death almost and then if it should prove after all my training to be too smart or too pretty I should be afraid all the time it would not live. It would leave us and go up among the other angels, but time will prove all things and I had better not anticipate too many things, but work till the baby comes before I get the little fancy crib with the velvet cushions and the many other fine things I think I should have, but of all things I would try to make its heart pure and the most beautiful of all, for I have lived long enough to see and know the affects and sometimes have experienced them—the envy, deceitfulness and jealousy that impure hearts are filled with and striving to make the hearts of others pure we also would see the beauty there is in holiness.

Seventhday, March 28th, 1863
The sun came out for a little while and seemed like it would be spring, but this afternoon the clouds are full and heavy and the wind chilly. The snow is on the grass again. The wind blows so chill this evening. I wish it would be spring, but it will come in good time I suppose.

Sabbath, March 29th, 1863
Stayed down home all day. Lenna is so sweet. I think we will be sorry to give her up. We have had a pleasant time singing and playing this evening. The baby is so fond of music. Alma is going away. I will miss her so much. I wonder what I will do if we go to Richmond. That will cause the time to pass a little faster. I am anxious to see Coffins. It is so cold. Just like winter and we are glad to be by the warm fires and sometimes shiver a little at that. I wonder if Aunt Eliza would not have given Lenna to me had I seen her before she died. Sometimes I think we ought to keep her.

Secondday, March 30th, 1863
Cold yet not spring for awhile. The balmy days do not begin with March. Down home again today. Helping get Alma off. She is not so much up set with the idea she was when it was something farther in the future. I hope she will go and get home safe again.

Thirdday, March 31st, 1863
The last day of March. It is passing away not with bright sunshine and blue cloudless skies, but cold chilling wind and changing clouds. Sometimes a ray of sunshine and then the clouds grow dark again. Lenna so sweet today. I love her so well. Ella came down to see Alma this evening and we sang "Lorina." It is beautiful. We came to the conclusion that, so the truth of course, there are many Lorina's and now there is something in the words that will be a tender chord in our hearts. Oh, I have to send the books away and I feel sorry for they are like old friends and I have had many a beguiled happy hour as I recall the good things contained in many of them. I would like to keep them, yet a little longer, but no, tomorrow they must go.

April 1863

Fourthday, April 1st, 1863
April again and not a flower to be seen and so cold as much fire is essential. The winter days were here, but when the warm days come they will be so gladly welcomed. Only one more day till Alma starts. I am sorry. She is coming up this evening and Mrs. Sanderson ask to see if we would go in and hear some music. Maggie Vance is sick and I must go there as I promised as it is so near. I have really got my ironing done and I did dread it. It took me longer than usual—whether it was owing to the number of clothes or the *Candle's Lecture* which came very handy while waiting for the iron to heat. I will not say. Good bye old books. I am sorry to give you up, but may your contents be as much benefit to me as the pleasure felt by pursuing your many pages. I am beginning to wish I had been more studious. Oh, I am so anxious to see OUR sweet little Lenna. How can we give her up?

Fifthday, April 2nd, 1863
Went down home this morning with Alma. Lenna sweeter than ever. We love her better than we ever thought we should. Instead of a genial spring day it is cold and windy and more like winter—like February. It is no pleasure to work out among the plants for it is so cold and I have to bundle up so, but surely the bright days are coming soon anyhow. We will have a dry road if it does not rain soon again. Elizabeth Alexander had her sister N. Thornburg all down. I know she will feel so badly for when she was here before little Carrie was with her and now she is in the unknown land. I really dread to leave Lenna and come home. When I am down there I think I must bring her up here. I wonder if she would cry?

Sixthday, April 3rd, 1863
I really enjoy this morning for I thought it was a pretty nice day after all and with my gloves and shawl and veil I was getting along finely with my flower

bed with a few hints from Will occasionally. I came in a little bit and on looking I saw the snowflakes coming down in torrents, just like mid winter so my days work was ended. Perhaps we will have company tomorrow evening for tea. Mr. and Mrs. Sanderson. It seems so funny after hearing they have been our neighbors for three years and a half and now just as they are going away to make us their first visit. I hope they will enjoy it for we had a pleasant time when we made them our first visit. The wind sounds so lonely and I am sitting here just like I did in winter.

Seventhday, April 4th, 1863
Grandfather had a dinner today. Lizzie Alexander and her 3 sisters and several of the rest of us were here. We came home to receive our company, but I felt very tired after my long walk. Tomorrow Sarah M. Hiatt will be at meeting and strange to say Lizzie's mother has come. I am reading *Kenilworth*.[189] It is about Leicester and several others who we read of in history. I think it will be interesting. Oh, Lenna is so sweet.

Sabbath, April 5th, 1863
Have heard two sermons. Sarah M. Hiatt [Sarah M. Elliott married Asher Hiatt].[190] She is such a nice looking woman and a good preacher. This evening Jeff 's mother held a meeting. I feel so sorry for them for I know they feel bad yet, if they knew all they would feel worse. We took a buggy ride this evening for the first time, but it is not so pleasant as when the warm days were here.

Thirdday, April 7th, 1863 [Paulena and Will's fourth wedding anniversary]
Went home yesterday morning. Sarah M. took dinner there. Also Alma, Lizzie and grandmother and father. I like her so well. She has a meeting at the schoolhouse tonight concerning the suffering consigned upon the Indian depravations in Minnesota. Alma is gone. We received a letter from Call last evening and had to hurry to get Alma fixed off. Cal, Will and I went to the train. I hope she will get there safely.

Fourthday, April 8th, 1863
Company today. Lydia James and Mary Bailey.[191]

---

189. "Sir Walter Scott 1771–1832, a Scottish novelist and poet, was born in Edinburgh. He is considered the father of both the regional and the historical novel. His poem *Kenilworth* was published in 1821." Source: http://www.bartleby.com/65/ sc/Scott SirW.html.

190. Sarah M. (Elliott) Hiatt was a noted Quaker minister who lived much of her life in Minneapolis, Minnesota. Her husband, Asher Hiatt, was a first cousin to Paulena Stevens Janney.

191. Lydia James was the daughter of David James and Mary Hunt. She was

Fifthday, April 9th, 1863
Oh, I have been working so hard cleaning the yard. It is such a beautiful day that I cannot content myself within. I think we have such a dear little home. How truly thankful we should be for it, though there many thousands of homes, much more beautiful and grand. Yet there are many others not half so lovely. Lizzie and Jeff called tonight.

Sixthday, April 10th, 1863
Was nearly sick this morning, but got well enough to go on a promised visit to see Lide. Had a very pleasant time. Will came for us and we had a pleasant ride home. Lyd did not go till after tea as they had company. We have not heard from Alma. I am getting anxious. I want to see her. I have the pleasure of peeping from the window now to see the number of trunks and pairs of bedstands. One baby too. Everybody has a baby. It is just so natural as can be, but I guess they don't come down in whirlwinds—else why don't one come here?

Seventhday, April 11th, 1863
No letter from Alma yet. We do not know what to think of it for she should have written before this time. I have been home helping mother today. I am seamstress. Lenna is sweet. We could not give her up very well. I wish we could hear from Alma. It is not quite a week since she went away. Yet it seems like two. The thunder sounded tonight like it used to. It seems like summer is more welcome this time than ever before for there has been such a long blank. Last fall the flowers and grass were parched up by the hot sun and we could not enjoy them much. How glad I would be could we have the least trouble or expectations of peace soon, but to me it looks very gloomy ahead.

Sabbath, April 12th, 1863
Went to church this morning and heard Benjamin preach. Had a good sermon and this afternoon took a ride out and went to grandfathers.

Secondday, April 13th, 1863
Cal and I went to Walkers. Now with cousin Cal it is quite a different thing than from sister Cal.[192] Such a good dinner we did have and they gave us a variety of flower roots which we divided freely. It seems good to get home for I am almost run down. It is so cold and chilly.

---

a second cousin once removed to Paulena. David James married as his second wife Deborah Stevens, sister of Evan Stevens. Mary Bailey could be Mary Janney Bailey, a cousin of Will's living in Springboro, Warren County, Ohio.

192. Cousin Cal is Carolyn Betts, daughter of Uncle William S. Betts, and sister Cal is Will Janney's sister, Carolyn Janney Betts, who was married to cousin Madison Betts.

Thirdday, April 14th, 1863
Mag and Doc [Margaret and Dr. John Carmen, neighbors], Will and I had an invitation to dinner at Millers. Had a nice dinner. Lizzie, Jeff and their mother were here for tea and then we went to her meeting. She spoke very well but I felt so badly. After I came home and I took a good cry for Lenna is going away, I guess, and it is so hard to give her up. Woodbury's seem anxious to take her and we think it would be better for her to go. No letter from Alma yet. We cannot imagine what could be the matter unless she has written and her letter has gone somewhere else. Clay has not received one or anyone else, so it seems hardly likely that all would miss coming.

Fourthday, April 15th, 1863
Been cleaning up, but do not feel at all in the mood. No letter from Alma yet. What does it mean? Clay was up here. Guess he is getting anxious also. I am going to write to her tonight and see if I can find out what the matter is.

Fifthday, April 16th, 1863
Went down home this morning. Grandmother there. Had a good dinner, roast chicken. Lenna so sweet. When I came home I had received a letter from Alma. She is getting along very well—"A little homesick," has been to one "tea party" and "one grand party where everyone was there," has learned "Kingdom Coming" and heard so much music. Has taken some music lessons, but after hearing some girls sing and play it discouraged her of ever learning. Mother will be so glad to hear from her.

Sixthday, April 17th, 1863
Mother and Lenna and Eva up today. I hope I can keep Lenna up here part of the time this summer if Woodburys do not take her and I do not think they will for I have a premonition that we will keep her. It is such a sweet day so much more like spring than it has been. Americus Hiatt[193] was brought here and burned today. He has been dead sometime and they did not open the coffin. Cal and I went calling this evening to Mr. Maxey's to see Mrs. Hindman and Aunty Carman—we had a very pleasant time and came away favorably impressed with our new acquaintances. I wonder if Alma is homesick now and would be glad to see her.

Seventhday, April 18th, 1863
Such a lovely day. Genial and calm. I got my work all done early and went over in the meadow and got some wildflower roots to plant out along near the grapevines. I do hope Will will not dig them up. I received a letter from Jennie. She is anxious for me to go there. I wish I could. It would be so delightful, but I will not anticipate for the clouds of our national storm seem more threatening

---

193. Americus Hiatt was the son of Samuel L. and Mary J. Terrill.

and there is more talk of war with England. [England was making munitions for the Confederacy and there was great effort to recognize the Confederate States as a country. If that had happened, the Union would have been at war with England.] I hope it will not prove true. So what would become of us then, for it is just almost impossible for our government, so exhausted now with this bloody civil war and to have another war would be insanity.

Sabbath, April 19th, 1863
Went to church. Got caught in the rain or rather the flood for the rain came while we were in church. Went to Sabbath school this afternoon after taking a two hour nap. I wonder if Alma would like to be home. The week will pass away sometime I suppose and if nothing happens we will be glad we sent her. Fannie Brown is the first teacher of the class at Sabbath school.

Secondday, April 20th, 1863
Down home this morning. Mother has so much to do it just distresses me. I just wish there was some [assistance] provided for the children for it is hard for mother to have the care of them.

Thirdday, April 21st, 1863
A letter from Alma. It came when least looked for. She appears to be well satisfied and she is learning fast in music. She can play one tune and is going to learn painting and drawing. I hope I will get to learn it all sometime. They say they are going to make her so healthy and blackened we will not know her when she comes home. I hope she will get healthy but am not so particular about the blacken.

Fourthday, April 28th, 1863
My journal is becoming so near full that I will have to be rather prudent in the entries and skip part of the everyday affairs. Quarterly meeting is over. How unlike others it seemed there was more effect . It seemed more faces were away. I received a letter from Matt—how very different from some of her old ones—written on a half sheet of writing paper after having waited for so many months and also one from Fannie. She writes real good letters I think—must answer soon. We had no company to eat here and I was not sorry for I did not feel in the mood for company. Oh, everything is getting so beautiful and the flowers are coming out once more and the little birds make everything musical. Yesterday, mother, Lenna and I took a ride. Went to Langdons and Reuben Hunts for a little while.

Sixthday, April 30th, 1863
The last day of April. It past away very beautifully and the twilight shadows closed around just the same as though it had been yesterday instead of the last day. Mother and Lenna were up today and we received a letter from Alma, but

we cannot give up for her to stay that long. Maxy preached this morning in observance of thanksgiving.

May 1863

Sixthday, May 1st, 1863
This is bright beautiful May again. The day could be no more lovely. The birds are jubilant and the bees make music with their buzzy hum and all nature seems to be reinforcing it in the sunlight and the balmy air of May. I wrote Alma a long letter last night and hope she will not be disappointed as she was before and hope we are not going to let her remain twenty weeks. Can hardly wait for her to come now. There is going to be a Maying party this afternoon. This time last May Jennie, James and John were here all so full of life and now what a sad change has come upon them. Poor John. How unfortunately better off than any of us yet. He will be so sadly missed. I think I must go down sometime this afternoon. I wish Will was not so busy and it would be so pleasant to go riding somewhere this afternoon.

Seventhday, May 2nd, 1863
A bright day, but . . . there a few drops of rain. I hope my flower seeds will not be washed up. I went home this afternoon. I must quit going so often. Mrs. Hindman called while I was gone and left her card so I must return her call soon. Anyhow, if I do go home often it is the only place I go.

Sixthday, May 8th, 1863
Well, we have the cradle fixed at last, I put the finishing strokes of paint on this evening. We took a ride and went to Miltons and were surprised to find Emily [Janney, Will's sister] and Jesse Coffin there. We had not heard of their arrival. We received a letter from Steve and one from cousin Mary Ham.

July 1863

[July 1st, 1863, Paulena's twenty-third birthday]

[The Battle of Gettysburg, July 1–3, 1863, Gettysburg, Pennsylvania[194]]

> "In July of 1863, General Robert E. Lee's Army of Northern Virginia of 75,000 men and the 97,000 man Union Army of the Potomac under General George G. Meade met, by chance, when a Confederate brigade sent forward for supplies observed a forward column of Meade's cavalry.
>
> "Of the more than 2,000 land engagements of the Civil War, Gettysburg ranks supreme. Although the Battle of Gettysburg did not

194. Observing and reporting this historic battle was Charles "Carlton" Coffin,

end the war, nor did it attain any major war aim for the North or the South, it remains the great battle of the war. Here at Gettysburg on July 1, 2, and 3, 1863, more men actually fought and more men died than in any other battle before or since on North American soil." Source: http://americancivilwar.com/getty.html.

July 6th, 1863

My twenty-third birthday has passed away and left me almost without a shadow on my brow. How thankful I should be that the troubles of life have been spared me when so many others far more worthy have been afflicted. But while I can look back on the happy years that are gone and see where I so often erred, I cannot look with any certainty to those yet to come.

Secondday, July 13th, 1863

Militia all called out. Morgan making his way eastward. Great times generally.

Thirdday, July 14th, 1863

We all went to the depot this afternoon to see the boys off and the news came that Camp Dennison was in the possession of the rebels. The railroad torn up part way. The train on the Miami R.R. burned and the men taken prisoner, but paroled. Most of news was true, but not all. Camp Dennison not taken as the rebs were in such a hurry.[195] Great excitement. The train did not come. Lizzie,

---

a fifth cousin of Paulena. He was the official war correspondent for the Boston *Journal.* Coffin was the only reporter who covered the entire Civil War from beginning to end. He became noted as a stickler for accuracy who would venture onto the battlefield in order to obtain the facts. "His eyewitness accounts of events such as the battles at Manassas, the capture of Fort Donelson, and the fall of Richmond were the first real reports received by those waiting at home. Coffin's moving reports in the *Journal* about George E. Pickett's charge at Gettysburg, Grant's Wilderness campaign, and the retaking of Fort Sumter were the first to inform President Abraham Lincoln and his cabinet of the outcome of these events. When the president traveled to Richmond, Coffin was there to meet him and was part of Lincoln's official escort through the former capital of the Confederacy. His description of the president inspired Thomas Nast's portrait of Lincoln in Richmond." Source: *American National Biography,* vol. 5, Oxford University Press, 1999.

Thomas Nast—"As soon as *Harper's Weekly* was launched in 1857, Nast became determined to join the magazine. He had some drawings in the magazine but he did not obtain a full-time post until 1862. "Nast was a staunch opponent of slavery and throughout the Civil War, Nast produced patriotic drawings urging people to help crush the rebels. Abraham Lincoln is reported to have said: 'Thomas Nast has been our best recruiting sergeant. His emblematic cartoons have never failed to arouse enthusiasm and patriotism.'" Source: *Education on the Internet & Teaching Online,* http://www.spartacus.schoolnet.co.uk/USAnast.htm.

195. "In July of 1863, Rosecrans was menacing the southern forces at Tullahoma, General Burnside, in Cincinnati was gathering forces to penetrate into Tennessee. Bragg dispatched his officer, John Hunt Morgan, into Kentucky to sever communications

Miss Good, Alma and Elva all here all night did not say much so many rumors and Will gone to Vienna and away so late.

Fourthday, July 15th, 1863
The boys gone. The train heavily loaded, said to be 15 thousand. Morgan still at large doing great damage and taking many horses. I have not felt alarmed as yet as I do not think he will pay us a visit, but he might and then I would be frightened. Port Hudson has surrendered with 7000 prisoners, 60 from artillery, 10,000 stand of arms. A fearful riot in New York.[196]

---

between these two parties, thus delaying the possibility of attacks from them. Morgan conceived the idea of entering Northern territory to create panic and draw after him troops that might otherwise be sent to reinforce Rosecrans and Burnside. He crossed the river near Rising Sun, Indiana, on the 8th of July arriving at Camp Dennison the morning of the 14th. The speed and audacity with which he acted had enabled him to pass at night through the very outskirts of Cincinnati with hardly a skirmish. False rumors and the smugness of the citizenry nearly defeated the force of 50,000 Ohio Militia against a desperate 2,000. The Militia had been summoned as late as the 13th:

"All forces residing in Montgomery, Clinton, Warren, Fayette, Ross, Highland and Brown Counties, report forthwith to Colonel Neff, the military commander at Camp Dennison.

"A picket skirmish ensued at Camp Dennison and the rebel forces burned a park of government wagons, but one of their lieutenants and several privates fell prisoner to the Ohio forces . . . it was reported the wrecking and burning of a Little Miami Railroad locomotive and three coaches near Camp Dennison by Morgan and his raiders. . . . On July 26, Morgan was finally captured at Salineville and was imprisoned in the Ohio Penitentiary . . . Rosecrans with 57,000 men was pursuing Bragg who received reinforcement, and turned to meet his foe with 70,000 troops at Chicamauga [sic] Creek, Tennessee, September 1–20, 1863. Bragg broke through the line and Rosecrans was forced to retreat to Chattanooga, where Thomas took command. After weeks of bloody battle, Bragg's army was routed and driven back into Georgia. Burnside then finally accomplished the advance into Eastern Tennessee to relieve the Unionists there, but not until after the disaster at Chicamauga [sic]." Source: *Camp Dennison Civil War Museum, Stories and Articles*, www.incom.net/~tomt/dennison/stor.html.

Stephen Janney was in the Battle of Chickamauga.

196. "The nation is at this time in a state of Revolution, North, South, East, and West," wrote the *Washington Times* during the often violent protests that occurred after Abraham Lincoln issued the March 3, 1863, Enrollment Act of Conscription. Although demonstrations took place in many Northern cities, the riots that broke out in New York City were both the most violent and the most publicized. With a large and powerful Democratic party operating in the city, a dramatic show of dissent had been long in the making. The state's popular governor, Democrat Horatio Seymour, openly despised Lincoln and his policies. In addition, the Enrollment Act shocked a population already tired of the two-year-old war. By the time the names of the first draftees were drawn in New York City on July 11, reports about the carnage of Gettysburg had been published in city papers. Lincoln's call for 300,000 more young men to fight a seemingly endless

Fifthday, July 17th, 1863
Charleston surrendered. Hope it is true. Morgan on his way up the river doing much damage. The boys coming home this evening. Glad of it. A riot in Boston but not so bad as New York.[197]

My journal is ended—and I must say goodby—for never again will its pages be opened for my thoughts to be written upon—yet I will hope that if I am so fortunate as to possess one in the future to write something more interesting—more beneficial.

---

war frightened even those who supported the Union cause. Moreover, the Enrollment Act contained several exemptions, including the payment of a 'commutation fee' that allowed wealthier and more influential citizens to buy their way out of service.

"Perhaps no group was more resentful of these inequities than the Irish immigrants populating the slums of northeastern cities. Poor and more than a little prejudiced against blacks—with whom they were both unfamiliar and forced to compete for the lowest-paying jobs—the Irish in New York objected to fighting on their behalf.

"On Sunday, June 12, the names of the draftees drawn the day before by the Provost Marshall were published in newspapers. Within hours, groups of irate citizens, many of them Irish immigrants, banded together across the city. Eventually numbering some 50,000 people, the mob terrorized neighborhoods on the East Side of New York for three days looting scores of stores. Blacks were the targets of most attacks on citizens; several lynchings and beatings occurred. In addition, a black church and orphanage were burned to the ground. All in all, the mob caused more than $1.5 million of damage. The number killed or wounded during the riot is unknown, but estimates range from two dozen to nearly 100. Eventually, Lincoln deployed combat troops from the Federal Army of the Potomac to restore order; they remained encamped around the city for several weeks. In the end, the draft raised only about 150,000 troops throughout the North, about three-quarters of them substitutes, amounting to just one-fifth of the total Union force." Source: The Civil War Society's *Encyclopedia of the Civil War,* http://www.civilwarhome.com/draftriots.htm.

The Gangs of New York, written by Herbert Asbury, was used as the basis for a movie starring Leonardo DiCaprio and directed by Martin Scorsese. The movie was filmed in Rome and was released in Germany on February 20, 2003. The movie covers a period of New York City's history, from the 1840s through to the bloody *draft riots* of 1863, when graft and corruption permeated every level of government including the police department.

197. "History Lesson: The Gangs of Boston," Seth Gitell: "The climax of Martin Scorsese's latest film, *Gangs of New York,* takes place during the July 1863 New York draft riots. This was the time of the Civil War, when the rich could buy their way out of the draft for $300. While you wouldn't know it from the movie, which underplays the draft riots' racial aspect, almost 100 people were killed in the violence, most of them free blacks, who were lynched or beaten to death. And there's another thing you wouldn't know from the movie. On July 14, 1863, Boston had its own draft riot, markedly different from what happened in New York. The violence began when a crowd of

How can anyone live on year after year without the pleasant companionship of a journal. As I look over the pages of mine I can recall so many different emotions that have been the object of my mind at the time—and just how I felt when I wrote certain things—but one thing I am sorry for—that I did not take more pains to write correctly and write something better. I am always in such a hurry—Just now for example anyone could guess in a moment that I was in a terrible hurry when I wrote this or else that never could do well which is true. But after all it will be a consolation for me in years to come should I live to read this over and after I am done with it let someone else have it. I wonder who will be it's owner in 20 years—or perhaps before that time it will have been cast into the flames but who could do so mean a thing?

[Paulena's journal was filled. No pages were empty. There was a six-month gap with no entries made, and there was no indication whether the cradle was for an expected child that did not survive. Journal Three continues.]

[Newberry Monthly Meeting of Friends Held at Westfork, October 10–19, 1863]
"Moses Moon, James G. Hockett, Evan Stephens, Jonathan Andrew & Jab Simcox are appointed to attend the ensuing quarterly meeting as representatives and report to next meeting. The condition and wants of the Freedmen being brought to view by a circular from the Executive Committee appointed by our late Yearly Meeting, we now appoint the following friends to receive contributions of money and clothing to forward the same immediately the money to Isaac P. Evans Treasurer, Richmond, Ind. Clothing Books &c to Thomas Lambdin N.E. Cor. 34d and Elm. Sts. Cin. O. and report to this meeting in 12th mo. next." . . . Evan Stephens and 24 others . . .

Irish immigrants living in the North End—then the city's Irish immigrant enclave—attacked a federal marshal trying to distribute draft notices. The mob then turned on the local police, and the clash took on a definite ethnic flavor: 'Kill the damned Yankee son of a bitch,' rioters yelled, according to Jack Tager's *Boston Riots: Three Centuries of Social Violence* (Northeastern University Press, 2000). (See 'Boston's Days of Rage,' News and Features, March 2, 2001, for an interview with Tager about his book.) The mob tried to storm an armory on Cooper Street to get weapons. Soldiers fired cannons. Then the crowd stormed Faneuil Market, looting hardware stores and gun shops. Finally, the aptly named mayor, Ferdinand Lincoln, called in federal and militia troops to put down the insurrection. Nobody really knows how many people died, although the official tally counted eight killed. Notably, none of the dead were African-Americans." Source: http://www.bostonphoenix.com/boston/.htm.

[November 19, 1863—Lincoln's Gettysburg Address, Gettysburg, Pennsylvania]

"Four score and seven years ago our fathers brought forth on this continent, a new nation, conceived in Liberty, and dedicated to the proposition that all men are created equal. Now we are engaged in a great civil war, testing whether that nation, or any nation so conceived and so dedicated, can long endure. We are met on a great battle-field of that war. We have come to dedicate a portion of that field, as a final resting place for those who here gave their lives that that nation might live. It is altogether fitting and proper that we should do this. But, in a larger sense, we can not dedicate—we can not consecrate—we can not hallow—this ground. The brave men, living and dead, who struggled here, have consecrated it, far above our poor power to add or detract. The world will little note, nor long remember what we say here, but it can never forget what they did here. It is for us the living, rather, to be dedicated here to the unfinished work which they who fought here have thus far so nobly advanced. It is rather for us to be here dedicated to the great task remaining before us—that from these honored dead we take increased devotion to that cause for which they gave the last full measure of devotion— that we here highly resolve that these dead shall not have died in vain—that this nation, under God, shall have a new birth of freedom—and that government of the people, by the people, for the people, shall not perish from the earth."

[Book List and Names of Authors]
"Scrip Scraps"

All About it; or Mysterys of Common Things
Aids to Faith by William Tomson
Carlyle Hero Worship
Great Expectations by Charles Dickens

> [First published in America in 1861 by Harper & Bros., New York, in *Harper's Weekly.*] Charles Dickens traveled to America in 1842 to lecture against slavery. He was not at all impressed with what he saw in America. He wrote *David Copperfield* in 1849–50) and *Tale of Two Cities* in 1859. It was at this time that he wrote *Great Expectations*, 1860–61. It was the last of his widely known books and easily the darkest in tone.]

Great Truth by Great Authors
Home Dramas for the Drawing Room
Language of Flowers

Life and Letters of Washington Irving

> [Pierre M. Irving, *Life and Letters of Washington Irving,* Sunnyside Edit., 4 vols. New York, G. P. Putnam, 1864.]

Life of Havelock by L.T. Headby
Lovell, the Widower by Wm. M. Thackeray

> [William M. Thackeray 1811–1863
> "In 1860 the *Cornhill Magazine* was started with Thackeray for its ed., and to it he contributed *Lovell the Widower* (1860), *The Adventures of Philip* (1861–62), *The Roundabout Papers,* a series of charming essays, and Denis Duval, left a mere fragment by his sudden death, but which gave promise of a return to his highest level of performance. In addition to the works mentioned, Source: http://www.bibliomania.com/0/0/51/frameset.html.]

Reason Why
Saunterings in and about London

> [Max Schlesinger, English ed. by Otto Wenckstern, London, Nathaniel Cooke, 1853.]

Strange Story by E. Bulwer Lytton
Last Poems of Mrs. Browning

> [Elizabeth Barrett Browning died in 1861. *Works of Mrs. Browning,* ed. James Miller, New York, 1864, 5 vols. Very early collection issued in America.]

The Young Stepmother, by Miss Younge [*The Young Stepmother or A Chronicle of Mistakes,* 1861, London].

> ["Charlotte Mary Younge,1823–1901, English novelist. Her writing as well as her life was restricted by the rigid High Church tenets of her upbringing. In spite of their religiosity her books were long popular because of the excellence of their characterization and dialogue. *The Heir of Redclyffe* (1853), a novel, and *The Daisy Chain* (1856), a book for girls, are best known. She edited the *Monthly Packet* from 1851, and many of her stories first appeared there." Source: *The Columbia Electronic Encyclopedia,* 6th ed., Columbia University Press, 2003. Sources: http://www.answers.com/topic/1861 in literature and http://www.adam matthew publications.co.uk/collections_az/Women +VV 5/contents of reels.aspx.]

John Brent by Theodore Winthrope

["Theodore Winthrop, (1828–1861) a descendant of Massachusetts governor John Winthrop, was born in Connecticut. After graduating from Yale, he traveled to Panama and other locations throughout the Americas. At the outbreak of the Civil War, Winthrop enlisted in the Federal army. He was killed at the battle of Great Bethel, Virginia, in June, 1861. He wrote *John Brent; Cecil Dreeme; Edwin Brothertoft; The Canoe and the Saddle; Love and Skates; Life in the Open Air.* See *Atlantic Monthly,* August, 1861, and August, 1863; *Life and Poems* of, edited by his sister; *Nichol's American Literature."* Source: Electronic Text Center University of Virginia Library, Charlottesville, Virginia 22904-4148.]

Undercurrents of Wall Street

["Richard Burleigh Kimball, author, born in Plainfield, New Hampshire, 11 October 1816. He was graduated at Dartmouth in 1834, studied law, and in 1836 went to Paris, continuing "His studies in the university there. On his return he practiced his profession in Waterford, New York, and afterward in New York City. He founded the town of Kimball, in Texas, and built the first railroad that was constructed in that state, running from Galveston to Houston and beyond, of which he was president from 1854 till 1860. In 1873 he received from Dartmouth the degree of LB.D. He has published in magazines of travel, and essays on biographical, historical, and financial subjects . . . among them "Undercurrents of Wall Street" (1861)." Source: *Edited Appleton's Encyclopedia,* 2001, Virtualology, http:// www.famousamericans.net/richardburleigh kimball.]

Sarah Clarke—Grace Greenwood—

["Grace Greenwood (1823–1904). Grace Greenwood's real name was Sarah Jane Clarke Lippincott. She was one of the United States' first female newspaper correspondents. In 1844 Greenwood began writing for some of the best newspapers and magazines of the time, including 'Godey's Lady's Book' and the 'Saturday Evening Post.' She contributed poetry, fiction, and political commentary. In 1849, having been fired from a position at 'Godey's Lady's Book' for writing an antislavery essay, Greenwood accepted a position at the 'National Era' and moved to Washington, District of Columbia. She also became the Washington correspondent for the 'Saturday Evening Post.' In 1850, Greenwood began publishing her pieces in books. She married Leander K. Lippincott in 1853 and they began a children's magazine, 'Little Pilgrim.' [John Greenleaf Whittier's poem, 'The Barefoot Boy,' was first published in this children's magazine] . . . Greenwood joined the lecture circuit and spoke for abolition and against capital punishment. She continued to produce many books. Beginning in 1870 Greenwood was correspondent for the New York 'Tribune' and the New York 'Times.'" Sources: http://www.picturehistory.com/find/p/15865/mcms. html and http://www.bchistory.org/beavercounty/booklengthdocuments/AMilobook/4Clark.html.]

Marian Harlan author of *Nemesis* [Derby & Jackson, 1860]

[Mary Virginia Hawes Terhune (1830–1922) Courtesy, Passaic County (New Jersey) Historical Society.
"Known by her pen name Marion Harland, Terhune began publishing household advice and cookbooks in 1872, after she had struggled as a young wife, ignorant of housekeeping skills. Some of her later books were written in collaboration with her daughter Christine Terhune Herrick. Born and raised in Virginia, she married a New Jersey clergyman and after three years in Richmond, Virginia, moved to Newark in 1859. The family's summer home, Sunnybank, in Pompton was the setting of numerous books about collies by Terhune's son, Albert Payson Terhune."
Source: *Mary Virginia Hawes Terhune ("Marion Harland"): Her Life and Works,* by Mary Hudson Wright, George Peabody College for Teachers, 1934. The information below is taken, in part, from lists compiled by Kathleen Rais. The list of publications by Mary Virginia Hawes Terhune is taken, in part, from the Ph.D. dissertation Mary Virginia Hawes Terhune ("Marion Harland"): Her Life and Works by Mary Hudson Wright, George Peabody College for Teachers, 1934.
Alone (Morris, 1854)
The Hidden Path (Derby, 1855)
Moss—Side (Derby & Jackson, 1857)
Nemesis (Derby & Jackson, 1860)

Miriam (Sheldon, 1863)
Husks (Sheldon, 1865)
Husbands and Homes (Sheldon, 1865)
Colonel Floyd's Wards (Sheldon, 1866)
Sunnybank (Sheldon, 1866)
The Christmas Holly (Sheldon, 1867)]

Beulah, Miss Mary Anne Evans [George Eliot]

["George Eliot was the pen name used by Mary Anne Evans, born in Warwickshire, England, in 1819. From an early age she was attended various Boarding Schools. She was a very plain woman. It was her intellect and her soft voice, which were to be her saving graces. She first used the pseudonym George Eliot in a serial for *Blackwood's Magazine* in 1857 titled *The Scenes of Clerical Life*. She next produced the great novel *Adam Bede* (1859), then *The Mill on the Floss* (1860) and *Silas Marner* (1861). Later novels *Romola* (1862–3), *Felix Holt* (1866) and *Middlemarch* (1871–2) well display her breadth of knowledge. In 1880 she married John Cross, a long standing friend and financial adviser, nearly twenty years her junior. She however died within 8 months at the age of 61." Source: http://www.abacci.com/books/authorDetails2.asp?authorID=48&misspellID=166.]

Fredericka Bremer [1801–1865], the celebrated Swedish novelist

["*Hemmen i den nya verlden* (1853–4) is novelist Fredrika Bremer's 3-volume travel diary in letter form, a literary account of her two years' travel in the United States and Cuba. Bremer wove, into the America she 'wrote,' a number of American authors and their works." Source; Lund University, http://www.lub.lu.se/cgi bin/show_diss.pl?db=global&fname=hum_83.html.]

Fosdick, the poet "laureate" of the West

["William Whitman Fosdick (1825–1862) Ohio & Kentucky. William Turner Coggeshall, *The Poets and Poetry of the West: With Biographical and Critical Notices* 471–72 (Columbus, Ohio: Follett, Foster and Company, 1860): "William Whiteman Fosdick was born in the city of Cincinnati, on the twenty-eighth day of January, 1825. His father, Thomas

R. Fosdick, was long known as a merchant and banker of that city, and his mother, Julia Drake, as an actress of much merit. The boy Fosdick was first sent to school to Samuel Johnson of Cincinnati, afterward to the Cincinnati College. He was at this time more remarkable for brightness than application; and, though frequently proving a puzzling case to the pedagogic mind, was known amongst his fellows as a generous and whole-some youth, who scorned all meanness, and possessed a keen wit. Mr. Fosdick was graduated at Transylvania University, Lexington, Kentucky, and immediately went to Louisville.'" Source: http://www.wvu.edu/~lawfac/jelkins/lp 2001/ fosdick3.html.]

[Miscellaneous Items of Note Written by Paulena]

Napoleon born 1769 died 1821, Duke of Wellington died 1852, Baron Alexander Humbolt died 1859.

"Life is but a hurrying toward death"—Dante—written by Humbolt beneath portrait.

Line odis. Without hatred.

"Germany produced the first female sculptor of whom anything is known—Sabina von Steinbach"

"Harriet E. Hosmer was born in Watertown—Massachusetts, October 9, 1801"

"London covers one hundred and twenty-one square miles"

Hail Columbia was written by Joseph Hopkinson in 1798

> [Hail, Columbia! happy land! / Hail, ye heroes! heaven-born band! / Who fought and bled in Freedom's cause, / Who fought and bled in Freedom's cause, / And when the storm of war was gone, / Enjoyed the peace your valor won. / Let independence be our boast, / Ever mindful what it cost; / Ever grateful for the prize, / Let its altar reach the skies!

Hail, Columbia!
(Chorus)
Firm, united, let us be,
Rallying round our liberty.
As a band of brothers joined,
Peace and safety we shall find.

Immortal Patriots rise once more,
Defend your rights—defend your shore
Let no rude foe with impious hand
Let no rude foe with impious hand
Invade the shrine where sacred lies
Of toil and blood the well earnd prize
While offering peace sincere and just
In heaven we place a manly trust
That truth and justice will prevail
And every scheme of bondage fail
(Chorus)

Sound sound the trump of fame
Let Washington's great name
Ring thro the world with loud applause
Ring thro the world with loud applause
Let every clime to Freedom dear
Listen with a joyful ear
With equal skill the godlike pow'r
He governs in the fearful hour
Of horrid war or guides with ease
The happier times of honest peace
(Chorus)

Behold the chief who now commands
Once more to serve his Country stands
The rock on which the storm will beat
The rock on which the storm will beat
But arm'd in virtue firm and true
His hopes are fixed on heaven and you
When hope was sinking in dismay
When glooms obscured Columbia's day
His steady mind from changes free
Resolved on Death or Liberty
(Chorus)"

Source: http://pasleybrothers.com/jefferson/Hail_Columbia.htm.]

Rose Clark, a book written by Fannie Fern . . . very good showing that nothing is made by himself and mean Rose Clark the heroine was put in the Almshouse when very young by her aunt—and when She was of some age her aunt—a mean principled woman took her home to work for her—it shows how all her pure thoughts and noble aspirations were crushed by her hard hearted aunt NC. [New York, Mason Brothers, 1856, available electronically from Wright American Fiction, 1851–875, The Trustees of Indiana University, 2001. Source: http://www.letrs.indiana.edu/cgi/t/text/text idx?c=wright2; idno=wright2 1848.]

"Women that are the least bashful are not infrequently the most modest"

All that is beautiful is not innocent

Love's Philosophy

    The fountains mingle with the river,
    And the rivers with the ocean,
    The Winds of heaven mix forever,
    With a Sweet emotion:
    Nothing in the world is single
    All things by a law divine
    In one another's mingle
    Why not I with thine?"
                    Shelley

    [Verse continued from outside source]
    See the mountains kiss high heaven
    And the waves clasp one another;
    No sister-flower would be forgiven
    If it disdain'd its brother:
    And the sunlight clasps the earth,
    And the moonbeams kiss the sea—
    What are all these kissings worth,
    If thou kiss not me?
            Percy Bysshe Shelley[198]

---

198. "Mary (Wollstonecraft) Shelley, wife of poet Percy Shelley, was the author of *Frankenstein,* written in Geneva, Switzerland, in the summer of 1816, the Year Without a Summer. They were vacationing with the poet George Gordon, Lord Byron. Persistent heavy rain and gloom kept them in the house and Byron suggested they each write a story." Source: http://home 1.worldonline.nl/~hamberg/.
    What caused the Year Without a Summer? "The most likely cause was volcanic influences. Proponents note that a number of major volcanic eruptions preceded 1816:

["Leagues of blue ocean are between us ahead
And I cannot behold thee save in dreams.
I may not hear thy voice nor lyst thy tread
Nor see the light that ever remind thee gleams"

Sargent]

["—Tell me no more, no more/Of my soul's lofty gifts! Are they not vain/To quench its fainting thirst for happiness?/Have I not lov'd, and striven, and fail'd to bind/One true heart unto me, whereon my own/Might find a resting-place, a home for all/Its burden of affections? I depart,/Unknown, tho' Fame goes with me; I must leave/The earth unknown. Yet it may be that death/Shall give my name a power to win such tears/As would have made life precious."—"Properzia Rossi, a celebrated female sculptor of Bologna, possessed also of talents for poetry and music." *A Celebration of Women Writers*, Properzia Rossi by Felicia Hermans. Source: http://digital.library.upenn.edu/women/hemans/records/rossi.html.]

O sometimes grow weary of myself—that I do so little good.

To clean Canary birds of lice, place a clean white cloth over their cage at night—in the morning it will be covered. HC

Soufrière and St. Vincent in 1812: Mayon and Luzon in the Phillippines during 1814; Tambora in Indonesia during 1815. The volcanic theory of climatic influence relates increased volcanic activity with decreased temperatures due to the increased reflection of solar radiation from volcanic dust blown and trapped high in the atmosphere. The Tambora eruption has been estimated to be the most violent in historical times. The explosion is believed to have lifted 150 to 180 cubic kilometres of material into the atmosphere. For a comparison, the infamous 1883 eruption of Krakatau ejected only 20 cubic kilometres of material into the air, and yet it affected sunsets for several years after." Source: "Weather Events—The Famous Year Without a Summer," http://www.islandnet.com/~see/weather/history/1816.htm.

Book List of New Publications

The Stars and Stripes of Rebeldom

History of Frederick the Second—Frederick the Great Frederick the Great [*History of Friedrich the Second, Called Frederick the Great,* by Thomas Carlyle, New York, Harper 1858. Source: Making of America, Cornell University Online Library, http://cdl.library.cornell.edu/moa/browse.author/t.71.html.]

The Patience of Hope [This title is based on Thessalonians 1:3 "Remembering without ceasing your work of faith, and labour of love, and patience of hope in our Lord Jesus Christ, in the sight of God and our Father." There are possible sources from which Paulena may have read this material:

> "The Patience of Hope," *Atlantic Monthly* 10, 62 (December 1862); "The Patience of Hope, *The North American Review* 96, 198 (January 1863); "The Patience of Hope," by the author of *A Present Heaven. The Continental Monthly* 2, 5 (November 1862).]

After Dark, [Wilkie Collins (1824–1829)
> English novelist. *After Dark*—Six stories published in 1856.]

Ball Room . . .
Miriam, Marion Harland—dedicated to George T. Prentice [published by Sheldon, 1863]

"Les Miserables" Les Miserables appeared in five parts 1st Fantime, 2nd Cosett's, 3rd Maroons, 4th St. Dennis, and 5th ValJean

["Victor Hugo (1802–1885), born on February 26, 1802 in Besançon, France. He was a poet, novelist, and dramatist and the most important French Romantic writer of the 19th Century. Hugo is best known for his novels *Notre-Dame de Paris* (a.k.a *Hunchback of Notre-Dame*) (1831) and *Les Miserables* (1862)."]

The Slave Power, an English Work

["*'The Slave Power,* John E. Cairnes's seminal work on slavery, was widely acclaimed upon publication in 1862 as a brilliant attempt both to explain the essential cause of the American Civil War and to shape European policy concerning the struggle. It remains among the most important works on the political economy of Southern slavery. When Cairnes—one of the nineteenth century's preeminent classical liberal economists—characterized Southern slavery as inefficient and backward, his opinions carried enormous weight, earning him applause in the North and castigation in the slave-holding South. Casting the Civil War as a contest between an economically defunct and politically aggressive Southern slave power and a liberal, capitalist, free-wage-labor North, Cairnes offered an interpretation of the origins of the Civil War that has remained as compelling and controversial as it was when first published.'"

"Mark M. Smith's new introduction to the work places The Slave Power in historical context by explaining the intellectual milieu in which the book was written (including a treatment of classical liberal economic thought in Great Britain), the book's friendly reception in Union circles, and its rejection by war-torn Confederates. Smith also traces the book's reception by successive generations of historians of the slave South."

"John E. Cairnes (1829–1875) earned B.A. and M.A. degrees from Trinity College in Dublin. He held the Whately professorship of political economy at the University of Dublin before being named professor of political economy and jurisprudence at Queen's College in Galway in 1859. In 1866, Cairnes became professor of political economy at University College. London."

"Mark M. Smith received his Ph.D. from the University of South Carolina in Columbia, where he is now professor of history. The author of *Mastered by the Clock: Time, Slavery, and Free-*

dom in the American South; Debating Slavery: Economy and Society in the Antebellum American South: and *Listening to Nineteenth-Century America,* Smith is also editor of *The Old South.* He has published articles in a number of journals including the *American Historical Review,* the *Past and Present,* the *Journal of Southern History,* the *William and Mary Quarterly,* and the *Journal of the Historical Society.* Smith lives in Columbia." Source: December 4, 2003, parkerll@sc.edu, http://www.sc.edu/uscpress/2003/3522.html.]

"Bitter Sweet"—Horbilands "Bitter is always mingled with the sweet"

Jennie Henley Cousin Mary
When we meet round the fireside circle
There are in the world—333,000,000 of Christians; 5,000,000 of Jews; 600,000,000 professing Asiatic relations—160,000,000 Mohammedians and 200,000,000 of Pagans. The Christians 170,000,000 profess the Catholic, 76,000,000 the Greek and 80,000,000 the Protestant creeds

Number of Washings done by Mrs. Huelson an account from March 6th to October 12th. Each washing 25–50 cents. A full-page chart recorded the washings.

Childhood home passes away
just as it grows dearest.

The other feet tread the olden walks of the garden
where we have watched the flowers bloom,

And the sun sink in the west and dear, dear old playhouse,
it is hard to give thee up.

For my happiest days were spent
bringing violets from the brook
and acorns from the forest,

Decking thee with every toy
and broken dish
my hands could find.

Paulena Stevens Janney,
December 31, 1859

Journal Three

February 6, 1864—October 6, 1866

Paulena Stevens Janney
Twenty-six years old

Photograph by Lot Janney

[No entries for January 1864]

February 1864

*S*eventhday, Night February 6th, 1864

How glad I am that I can speak of my journal as something in my possession and not something that I would like to have here for ever so long. I have been wanting my journal feeling so sorry that so many days and weeks were passing away leaving no record for me only in my memory, but today Will came in very much pleased and in one hand holding my journal. A pleasant surprise for me indeed. Alma and Mary were here tonight and we have been sitting here talking of things not much benefit perhaps but just to be talking so expect we might have conversed about something of more importance and of more interest but as usual when starting upon a certain subject it is kept up. We were sitting close around the fire when something came against the window pane causing us to start. I looked around expecting to see a cat peering in, but instead was something we could not tell was fluttering at the window looking some like a bird or an owl. We could not tell what it was and were almost frightened, but after all our speculation Mary said, "Girls, I like to be scared this way," so I guess there was not harm done.

Sabbath, February 7th, 1864

Got up late this morning—such a bad habit—however pleasant a nine o'clock breakfast in New York may be, it is altogether a different affair in Martinsville when all the after work has to be done by our own hands instead of Bridgets. I wish there was someone who was going to deliver a sermon this evening. I think surely I am not all together adapted to country life. There is too much reality about it. I think sometimes we know too much about each other—for instance a stranger arrives, in just a little time someone knows the history of the whole family and the mother or father or some of them were not so good as they might have been. And so it goes. Every little thing raked up and told over and over again until it becomes a fact. Now to meet a person and like them for their friends sake and "vice versa." If a new minister comes somebody thinks he is affected. Another he is a kind of "fojo" I think and a great deal more. Really before we are aware, we lose interest in hearing those sermons we thought so "eloquent." Now if we did not think so ourselves and did not hear anyone else say so, no difference if there was a little truth in it would not trouble us in any way, but this everlasting criticism of one's friends is not very pleasant. I never had a friend that seemed some faulty and on every suitable occasion I am reminded of it and then I conclude if I try to defend them I will keep myself in a continual broil with all my other friends. I know I sometimes say things I ought not say but as a general thing I never speak to a person about their intimate and I just wish if my friends don't suit them they please not remind me of all their errors just as I—though I cannot like a person who is not worthy—as if any person is.

Secondday, Night February 8th, 1864
Alma up here yet. We have been having a great time this evening. I am looking for a cry next as that is the next thing in the "program" after I have a good laugh. We hunted up some of the old "Magazines of Art." They are so interesting telling so much of the artist and author and everything. I wish I could remember all I read as I get older. I think my taste for reading of a general character becomes stronger and books that I once cast aside as of not much interest I can devour now with great avidity. The more I read the more I want to know. I feel so discouraged sometimes when I think of how little I know and how unfit I am to pass in polished society should I be so fortunate as ever to have the opportunity of mingling in such. I do not know why, but I think sometimes perhaps my associates in some respects will be different—some of them at least—for I enjoy myself with some few of my friends now, but not as a general thing and I hope that sometime I will have it in my power to have a freer intercourse with books, works of art. How well I would enjoy it. It is strange to me that so many persons who are wealthy pass their life in some obscure place never caring for books or pictures or anything beautiful. I wish some such persons would leave me a few thousands and I would put it to better use.

Thirdday, February 8th, 1864
Another day gone. How quickly time passes away. We have so many things "laid off" today for next week but before we fairly begin the week is almost gone. The afternoon passed away and left me sitting in my little rocking chair sewing and thinking very hard and indeed with my fingers busy with my needle and my mind busy with the future I managed to get along very well until my lazy time which is between the hours of five and six, just as daylight is fading and twilight gathering. I sit and look into the fire or look out the window till my head and eyes become weary—dreading to budge to do anything and wishing Will would not get so hungry for it is such a change to come down from the sublime heights where my imagination takes me and do the more substantial mystery of cooking. That is making a little tea and perhaps some toast for as little cooking as possible does me for supper anyhow if not on all occasions. Tom Nooks was buried this evening. Poor fellow. He has few good actions to be recorded. He was buried in some secluded spot for dying of the disease he did. All were afraid to go near them. There have been so many colored persons died here this winter. I feel bad we did not pay more attention to Aaron,[199] but

---

199. Aaron Ward was enumerated in the 1850 census in the household of Evan Stephens, Paulena's father. Aaron was listed as a tanner, black, born in Virginia,

it was so bad and so unhandy to go—colored though he was. I would not have hesitated to have done all I could for his comfort had he been nearer. Living so long in the family and even when little calling our mother his mother—like we children—it would be strange indeed if we did not feel any emotion of sadness now that he is dead.

Fourthday, February 9th, 1864
Was surprised this morning. While finishing breakfast Will brought Jesse Coffin round to the kitchen door. The front one being fastened. He took dinner with us then went to Miltons. We are going there tonight. Kays are moving today.

Fifthday, February 11th, 1864
Got home this morning after a rough ride. A letter from Lot with five photographs—Daniel Coffins I suppose. I can remember that without writing it down. Lyd and Rebecca Ann were here for tea and Jake and Cal came up tonight.

Sixthday, February 12th, 1864
We went over and examined Cal's house. I do not think that any person wanted to move much worse and I am as anxious as Cal. Lot wanted us to come about the first of May when the hills are green and spring is in all her young beauty. I hope we can go, but I doubt it very much. [Lot and Fannie were living in Portsmouth, on the Ohio River, where he had a portrait photography studio.]

Sixthday, February 13th, 1864
I am so lazy and I have so much sewing to do that I wonder if I will get it done soon. Mother here today. I wish she would stay all night sometime. We are going down home tonight. It has been almost two weeks since I saw Lenna—little darling. We love her so much. Clay called last night. My dear journal, did I ever tell you of an accident that befell me the other morning? I did not, I was late getting up as usual—half awake and half asleep. But do believe I was wide awake that morning, but the door was shut and how could I know anything. I heard Will coming, I almost flew out of bed and reached the door as he opened the other one. But what a sight. The room was filled with smoke and on one side I beheld my clothes burning. My last "calico" dress, my blue skirt and my little chair. I rushed to the bucket of water and threw it on, Who says women have no presence of mind and then I quietly seated myself to see Will finish it. The thought struck me perhaps I can save some of my dresses and I am glad to record the saving part of the sleeves and "here and there a rag"—but my skirt,

---

nineteen years old. He would have been nine years old when Paulena was born. He was thirty-three when he died. It is believed that he was a free black child who was raised by the Stevenses as the Stevenses did not own slaves and, in fact, were very much opposed to slavery.

the blue one, was a total loss. Not even a button left to tell the story. I shivered around in my night dress for some time and at Wills suggestion that I had better put something on. I pretended I had nothing to wear and I got breakfast with a shawl on and told Will if he would only go away and not scold I would work and get another dress—but after the doors and windows had the appearance of a volcano for sometime and the traces of the fire removed I hunted among the things and found some clothes. I am sorry to say my skirt is too narrow for any hoops. I promised Will I would get up sooner hereafter and tried to convince him it might have been a great deal worse and so the matter ended. He, like a good fellow agreeing to what I had said and not scolding.

Sabbath, February 14th, 1864
At fathers all day. Had egg gravy for dinner. Alma went to Langdon's tonight with Alice. The smallpox is spreading in Morrisville. I fear it will come here, but I am not so much alarmed as to think of leaving if we get it. I believe I could be as good as any in town taking Wring for a standard. I think our doctors here have not had enough practice in it to be successful in it—"practice makes perfect." I would do just like "Wring" and some of Mr. Fred M.O.'s . . . for it is so treated.[200] If I could tear this leaf out I would for it is so dreadful in writing, composing and I promise in the future to try and do better and try and not be in such a hurry. But then dear journal the fire is almost out. Will is asleep and I am getting cold so you see just how it is and then I am so foolish anyhow.

Secondday, February 15th, 1864
We were at Jim's [James Hunt, a cousin, brother to Danny and Lydia] last evening awhile. I like Maggie someways. If I was only rich like she is I would have more style about it, but not be any prouder than I am now for I am already very proud. Maggie is a very good wife for Jim. I would think he would appreciate a home of his own after so long a time. If I was Maggie I would buy a nice home and have everything in style and be so kind to the poor and everything. She is perhaps—that is if she is as rich as "they say"—she is rather intelligent. When anyone is intelligent in my view they are naturally quick and learn anything and everything almost by intention and observe a thousand little things. After

---

200. "The preventive measures of vaccination and isolation drastically reduced the occurrence of smallpox in the early to mid-19th century. By the 1840's, vaccination was beginning to be neglected and there was a generation of Americans who had never been exposed to the disease. As a result, the incidence of smallpox began to rise in the decades before the Civil War. . . . Quarantine, vaccination and the destruction of infected clothes and bedding were the primary tools used to control the spread of smallpox in the armies. . . . The pressing demands of war often led authorities to institute programs that obtained the scabs from vaccinated humans . . . taken from vaccinated infants, each with a certificate listing the dispensary and the child's name." Source: *The Civil War News,* "The Medical Bag . . . Smallpox & Vaccination In the Civil War," October 2004.

all my idea of intelligence is being something above the ordinary, has good common sense and then she is more familiar with books than some others here.

Thirdday, February 16th, 1864
Bitter cold this morning. An addition to the family—a cat. It was so hungry and I gave it meat, but it refused it. The ungrateful cat. I was determined it should eat and it was stubborn as a mule as determined the other way. At last I turned it out, but still it lingered near and waited patiently till it cried. It compromised by eating hominy and is now quietly seated on a chair before the fire. I am resolved to bring it up right and as the beginning is the great starting point, I think it my duty to begin early which I did by making it obey me after speaking to it several times and as the last remedy I seized the "poker" when it submitted to "moral persuasion" and has not opened its mouth since to cry. I intend to bear in mind the maxim "Train up a child—or a cat as the case may be—in the way it should go and when it is old it will not depart from it." Will says it is an intelligent looking cat.

Fourthday, February 17th, 1864
Cold as ever. I just sit by the fire dreading to move. Surely a life in the country is a dull kind of life when one's whole life is passed away in its absurdity. Miss Dickinson speaks tonight at Mozart Hall [Cincinnati].[201]   Little good it would do me though. I really feel provoked sometimes to be stuck way off in the country where I never see or learn anything. All my tastes are congenial to town life and . . . here . . . well no matter perhaps it is better this and I should be thankful my life has been so pleasant instead of mesmerizing, but then is it mesmerizing?

---

201. "Anna Elizabeth Dickinson was born in Philadelphia to an orthodox Quaker family. Anna Dickinson began to write and speak about abolition while still in her teens. She contributed an essay to William Lloyd Garrison's *Liberator* in 1856, and addressed the Pennsylvania Anti-Slavery Society in 1860. Her intensity, youth, and dedication to emancipation attracted curious, sympathetic audiences and earned the notice of such well-known abolitionists as Hannah Longshore and Lucretia Mott. But Dickinson's greatest success came in 1863, when the Republican Party asked her to tour on behalf of its candidates. When Dickinson reached New York, an audience of 5,000 greeted her as the Joan of Arc of the abolition cause. Throughout the 1860s, Dickinson continued to lecture on the rights of women and African Americans. When popular taste shifted to light entertainment, she began a largely unsuccessful career as a playwright and actress, eventually dying in obscurity in New York. This carte-de-visite portrait of Dickinson was made on her triumphant Republican Party tour of 1863 and 1864." The albumen silver print was made by Mathew Brady Studio, National Gallery, Smithsonian Institution. Source: "Carte-de-visite," http://www.npg.si.edu/exh/brady/gallery/84gal. html; http://www.historyswomen.com/AnnaElizabethDickinson.html.

Fifthday, February 18th, 1864
Saunderson's case to be looked after. What will they do to him is the question. I would not be in his place for all his whiskey is worth. Poor man. I cannot but judge him for all his badness. I had a treat—some wax—but half its sweetness was having to burn myself over the fire watching it and after it was done I only had half of it, so that was too bad wasn't it.

Sixthday, February 19th, 1864
Washed today and my poor fingers, poor back, I had to raise up by degrees and the skin was off my fingers in more places than I can tell. Will had dinner to get which consisted of corn bread and onions—very good. I am going to learn Will to cook. It will be such an advantage to him. School closes today but I am too busy to attend.

Seventhday, February 20th, 1864
This evening we took a ride down home and to grandfathers. Polly Ladd is there with her little girl. Lenna is so sweet. We would take her if we thought she would ever like us and be satisfied to stay here. Meeting commenced today "across the way." I wonder if any person will be converted. There is need of something being done to check the dissatisfaction becoming so very prevalent here. Clay, as a matter of course was down home this evening. From his constant attention one would suppose that at some future period something serious would result. From accounts Ella and Ed are about "played out." I suppose it will be all right in the morning.

Sabbath, February 21st, 1864
Went to church this morning. Mary preached quite a good sermon. Had to nap this evening. Got up took a walk down the street. Did not go to church tonight. Was sitting quietly by the fire reading when the cry of "fire, fire" was heard in the street. I found great excitement when I went to the door, but I could not see any fire, but there really was a fire. It broke out in the house next to Jim Hunt's. In five minutes more it would have been in strong headway.

Secondday, February 22nd, 1864
A bright day almost like spring. I have been alone all day and am getting a little hungry. I wish Will would come for I am going to have some bean soup and cornbread.

Thirdday, February 23rd, 1864
Went a visiting today to Haynes. Mother and grandmother were there. We had such a pleasant time and a real good dinner. I am sorry I have not been there more for they are going away before long to Iowa. Shepard is going to preach tonight and Heston tomorrow night. The wind blew very hard this evening and for a little time the rain came down pretty fast, but when meeting was over the

moon was shining as brightly and it was a beautiful night. I am glad spring is so near at hand though there will be many dark days before the bright spring days come with all their attendant beauties.

Fourthday, February 24th, 1864
A beautiful morning. Mary Fisher [Mary Jane (Janney) Bailey Fisher, sister of Will] is here but is trying to sleep some now. Alma sent a note and wants me to go home, but I suppose I cannot go till Mary goes away. I am anxious to hear Mr. Nixon tonight. I think he is intelligent. I wish some person would join tonight. I will be sorry when it closes. I am going to have bean soup for dinner. It has got to be quite a favorite dish with me.

Fifthday, February 25th, 1864
Such a beautiful day. Only the wind blows so hard. I have been over at Vances all morning chatting with Lib. There is meeting again tonight. I wish some person would join. It is so discouraging to them. I feel so sorry for Mrs. Hinnman. Some person wrote a letter to Wilmington concerning her character. I think she is much better than the writer of the letter. It is too bad for her to be mined if she is innocent which I believe no reason to it.

Sixthday, February 26th, 1864
Such a lovely day. I have been out cleaning the yard and as usual I am with an accident. The fire poped out [on] the lounge and burned several things. I am getting so afraid of fire and am afraid our home will be burned sometime. The hyacinths and daffodils are peeping up and it will be just a little while when there will be buds on them and will be so glad when spring comes, Alma and Elva came up to go to church, I cannot go as James Fisher and Mary [Mary Jane Janney, Will's sister] are here. I do wish Cal and Jake would move.

Seventhday, February 27th, 1864
Will James, Mary and Alma were here for dinner. Us girls did laugh so much. I expect Will James thought we were very foolish which no doubt we were. I went down home with the girls this evening and we had some wax, I am so anxious for Harpers to come. I hope we will get four at once such a treat as it will be for me. I do not think in this case that anticipation will be better than possession.

Sabbath, February 28th, 1864
A gloomy day and I feel so dull and I feel so badly and I did not go to church. Will and Alma went. Meeting is over for this time. Alma and Elva are going to prayer meeting. It is raining and very disagreeable. Spring has been usurped by winter again. And it seems impossible that shorter time when the air was balmy and everything looked like spring. My yard cleaning did not agree with me and I feel I will feel worse yet. "Nobody to blame" is the leading story.

Secondday, February 29th, 1864 [Leap Year]
Chilly this morning. Alma and Elva gone and I can hardly bear to sit down and
I feel very bad. Cal must be very busy as she has not been up today. Today is the
last day of Feb and it has been a short month. Time passes away more quickly
than it used to. A year once seemed an eternity, but now slips away mingled
with tears and laughter, clouds and sunshine that its dying is almost unheeded.
Now, if I only had a little girl to be company for me today. The house would not
be so lonely. I think we must take a little girl sometime. How much we would
love it.

March 1864

Thirdday, March 1st, 1864
March indeed. The ground is white with snow and everything has the appearance of December only the birds are trying to be joyous but their poor little feet
must be suffering with cold as they are chirping in the cold. I have been reading "A Graceful and Touching Tribute" to the memory of "Thackeray."[202] It is
very good. He was found peacefully lying composed undisturbed and to all
appearances asleep on the 24th of December 1863. He was in the fifty-third year.
So young a man that the mother who blessed him in his first sleep blessed him
in his last. It is all so good I wish I could keep it all. I see in the *Commercial* the
name of Sarah Bolton[203] but with a new name "Reese." I suppose she is married

---

202. William Makepeace Thackeray wrote *Vanity Fair*, published in 1848. He
died suddenly on Christmas Eve 1863. He was buried in Westminster Abbey.

203. Sarah Tittle Barrett Bolton (December 18, 1814–August 4, 1893), poet, born
in Newport, Ky., was the daughter of Jonathan Belcher and Esther (Pendleton) Barrett,
pioneer settlers of Indiana. . . . Her early days were spent in the wilderness, about six
miles from Vernon, Indiana, where her father had staked a farm. Of this period her
poems entitled "Our Pioneers" and "A Pioneer Grandmother" are reminiscent. When
she was nine, her father sold his farm and moved to Madison [Indiana]. Here she got
some knowledge in the schools, and as much outside. Before she was fourteen, verses
from her pen had been published in the *Madison Banner,* and she soon became a regular
contributor to the newspapers of her home town and Cincinnati. In her seventeenth
year, October 1831, she married Nathaniel Bolton, a young newspaper man, and went to
live in Indianapolis. Thereafter her life was shaped by her husband's fortunes until his
death in 1858. He was first editor of the *Indiana Democrat;* then proprietor of a farm outside the city, his house there a tavern which became a stopping place for distinguished
men and something of a social center, Mrs. Bolton acting as housekeeper and cook,
besides running a large dairy. Later he was state librarian, then clerk of a United States
Senate committee, and finally consul at Geneva, which appointment gave Mrs. Bolton
opportunity for extensive travel. Two children were born to her. About five years after
his death, she married, Sept. 15, 1863, at Keokuk, Iowa, Judge Addison Reese, and for
the next two years lived with him at his home in Canton, Missouri. The climate there was

again. She wrote such a beautiful piece of poetry on the death of a lady—Mrs. Frank Smith of Indianapolis. One verse is:

> "She went in the dreamy night
> And she seemed to go alone
> For we could not see with our human sight
> The angels that guided her step all right
> Are the feet of the Holy One"

Fourthday, March 2nd, 1864
Such a sloppy time. The dreadest of all weather to me for it looks pleasant and yet we cannot step out without our feet getting so damp and cold. I washed today. A little washing. Matt's father is dead.[204] I feel sorry for her. Will said I might go but I did not think of such a thing for the train is

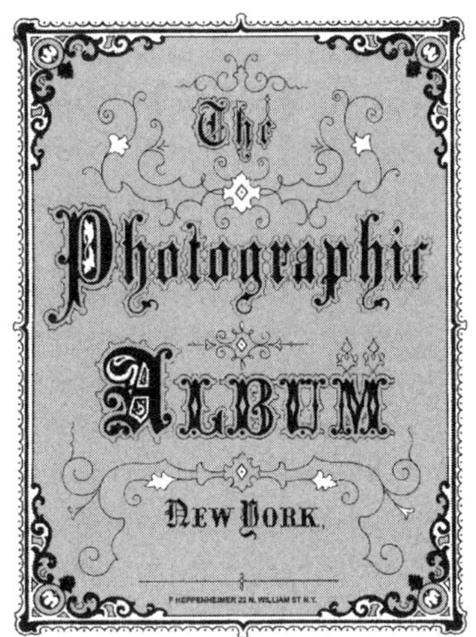

Title page of Paulena's
photo album

---

not favorable to her health, and she returned to Indianapolis, where she made her home until her death, though she spent two or three years abroad. She was always known as Sarah T. Bolton, and used the name "Reese" only for business purposes.

Her writings and participation in public affairs made her a prominent figure in Indiana. She was interested in various reforms, and was an active aid to Robert Dale Owen in his effort to secure property rights for women in the constitutional convention of 1850. She was a true child of the rising West, an ardent democrat and champion of freedom, full of fiery patriotism and faith in the country's future. These characteristics are reflected in many of her poems. As a whole these are of no great literary merit, but have the melody, sentimentality, and moral and religious flavor relished by the fireside magazine readers of their day. "Paddle Your Own Canoe" and a few others had wide popularity. Poems appeared in 1865, and a collection of her writings with a sketch of her career was published in 1880 under the title *The Life and Poems of Sarah T. Bolton*. A volume of selections, *Songs of a Life Time*, edited by John Clark Ridpath, was published in 1892. It contains an introduction by Lew Wallace and a poem by James Whitcomb Riley. Sources: *Dictionary of American Biography* by McMillan; and *Ladies' Repository*, Feb. 1852, pp. 69–73; Wm. W. Woollen, *Biography and Historical Sketches of Early Indiana*, 1883; J. P. Dunn, Greater Indianapolis, 1910; obituary in *Indianapolis Sentinel*, Aug. 5, 1893; and information furnished by Mrs. Adah Bolton Mann, H.E.S., http://www.bgpl.lib.in.us/Community/SarahBoltonPage.htm.

204. Asa Ladd died near Leesburg, Highland County, Ohio, on March 1, 1864. He was married to Mary Chalfant, a cousin of Paulena. Asa's will was recorded in Highland County, Ohio, on February 10, 1864. It named his wife, "Mary: Children, Elizabeth, Jonathan, Ruth, George, [Martha, "Matt,"] Ann Pushey [Pushee], Rebecca Alderman. Nieces: Marianna and Caroline Alderman. Executor: Franklin Ladd. Witnesses: J. L. Cox, John Hodson, John S. Roberts. Proven March 9, 1864. Sureties: John L. Cox, John Hodson. Appraisers: Evan Reese, John L. Cox, and Eli Milner."

so late getting there tonight and I am not able to walk so far when it does get there. My album came today and I have been fixing my pictures. I want to see Lenna so badly. Alma said the old "yellow cat" died and Lenna cried and cried about it. Cal thinks they will move next week or week after. I do wish they would hurry for Lib is going to move this week and I will have no place to go if I want to talk about anything.

Fifthday, March 3rd, 1864
Alma, mother and Lenna came up today. The day always seems so short when they come. Sallie Gibson is sick. It will be bad if she is taken from them. No letter yet from Miss Willett. Perhaps she never received my letter. We had chicken for dinner. It was a treat. Oh if Cal and Jake would only move it will be so nice. I do wish I had good taste in arranging flowers. I am so fond of them, but I must confess I cannot arrange them well. Carmans were here last night. The news came that Charley Oren was killed, but it is not believed. [Charley Oren was a captain in the Union Army. His home was next door to Madison and Caroline (Janney) Betts in Martinsville. He was not killed at that time.]

Sixthday, March 4th, 1864
Cal spent the afternoon here. We can always find something to talk about no matter how many times in a day we see each other. Vances have moved across the way and our "new neighbors" have come. It will seem so odd not to see Lib running around over there as usual. Cal says grandfather is going to give us our land, but has changed the program a little—Iowa instead of Indiana. [The land proved to be in Indiana after all, in Shelby County. The Flat Rock Farm, as it was designated because it was near the village of Flat Rock, was devised to the heirs in Aaron Betts's will in 1867. His will is in the Epilogue.] Well, I do not care much where it is, so it is worth something. Cal says we are to draw lots so there will be no hardness. I will almost be sure to get a poor piece for I am unlucky about such things. We are expecting to hear "startling news" from the Potomac soon. Let us hope it will be a kind not usually heard from there. Will is making great changes out doors. Cutting off peach trees.

Seventhday, March 5th, 1864
A cold dreary March morning. The ground covered with a light sprinkling of snow and no sunshine visible through the dark wintry clouds. Cola T is gone at last. I did not even get to bid her good-by, but took my last look at her through the window as she was being led away. I hope she will prove to be all she was to us. Report came to me this morning that our new neighbors were visited last night—sometime between dark and twilight by a little stranger. I was not told whether the baby was found in a basket on the doorstep or not. I presume not or I would have been told, I ought to go see it, but am ashamed to go and it would be funny if after all she has not got a baby at all. I am anxious to see the paper this morning. I wish it would contain an account of the capture of Richmond.

Sabbath, March 6th, 1864
Got up quite early this morning, but it was because I was sick and had to. It is such a beautiful morning. I would like to have the *Atlantic* for March. Will got breakfast and seemed to enjoy it. Finally he thought the coffee was splendid. I was much better to have a husband willing to do little turns when we are sick. I really do not think I could live with a "bear," but Will has become so accustomed to my whims he never thinks of objecting to anything he ought to of me when I ask him. The doves sound so sweet cooing. I read an extract from *The Beecher Family at Home*—an autobiography and corresponding of Lyman Beecher.[205] I see some critic remark that he hoped that Lyman Beecher learned more from his children than they from him. It seemed he was something of a Calvinist.[206]

Fourthday, March 9th, 1864
Will went to the city this morning and I am going down home to remain till he returns which will be nothing preventing till tomorrow. No *Harpers* yet. I am getting out of patience waiting for it. Lenna is so sweet and we like her better all the time. I wish she would come and stay with us but there is no such thing as getting her in the notion because mother is more to her than all else.

Fifthday, March 10th, 1864
Will came home this morning and I am happy to say brought me some new dresses too.

---

205. Lyman Beecher (1775–1863), "Congregational minister, educator, and vocal leader of American Protestants, Lyman Beecher embodied the shift from the harsh, demanding Puritan faith of the Second Great Awakening to a religion that found its expression in larger society. Beecher first received wide public recognition in 1806, with a sermon he gave against dueling after the death of Alexander Hamilton in a duel with Aaron Burr. From 1810 to 1826, as a minister in Litchfield, Connecticut, Beecher and his wife also ran a school for girls, with an unusually practical and serious curriculum. In 1833, Beecher and his family moved to Cincinnati, where he became president of the Lane Theological Seminary, a training ground for the religious leaders of the abolition movement. Beecher's ability to carry religious principles into daily life deeply influenced his children, especially Catharine Beecher, who became a national voice for practical domestic management, and Harriet Beecher Stowe, the best selling author of *Uncle Tom's Cabin*. The widespread fame of this virtuous family led a contemporary to joke, 'This country is inhabited by saints, sinners, and Beechers.'" Source: http://www.npg.si.edu/exh/brady/gallery/07gal.html.

206. "Calvinism, also known as Reformed theology, is a system of Biblical interpretation that focuses on the supreme sovereignty of God, His majesty, His holiness, etc. It relates this to man's fallen, sinful nature. Because of the great chasm between God and man and because of man's fallen nature, God must predestine people into salvation . . . or none would be saved. Therefore, salvation is the work of God and we are the mere recipients of His gracious election."

Seventhday, March 12th, 1864
Did not come home till this morning. Alma came up this afternoon and we went calling. The first place we went to was our new neighbors. We got a peep at the new baby and I got enough courage to say, "It is a little girl, is it?" I would be glad of that, but found she preferred little boys. After I was home and was telling Will about my calls and what I said—he just sat glancing over the paper and hardly made any reply. Why can't men be more appreciative!—Something I thought—Now why could he not have said, "I am glad thee went." Putting in some little word to prove he had some sympathy. And when I was telling him of our being at Saunderson's to see the little dead baby and was telling him of how sweet it looked with its little blue sack and white dress and how lonely Mrs. Saunderson looked all alone with no person but her and the sweet little babe. Will did manage to glance up long enough to say, "Why did you go?" and I almost cried in my effort to make him understand that we thought it would not be right to go right by there. Just because they are not as they should be to refrain from calling in a moment when they are so neglected—and such a little place. Will should have said, "You did right by going for they never injured you any and in such a case and in that case it is perfectly right to do so."

Sabbath, March 13th, 1864
So cold and gloomy looking and the wind blowing so hard. Every Sabbath passes away almost the same, very seldom we have a sermon and everything is so still. Will is going to make some molasses when the sugar water runs.[207] I can

---

"Basically, Calvinism is known by an acronym: T.U.L.I.P.

> **T**otal Depravity (also known as Total Inability and Original Sin)
> **U**nconditional Election
> **L**imited Atonement (also known as Particular Atonement)
> **I**rresistible Grace
> **P**erseverance of the Saints (also known as Once Saved Always Saved)

These five categories do not comprise Calvinism in totality. They simply represent some of its main points." Source: http://www.mslick.com/tulip.htm.

207. Paulena's "molasses" is surely what we would call maple syrup, particularly considering the time of year she mentions it. "Maple syrup is made from the sap of the maple tree. The sap rises from the roots and settles into the tree. In late February and early March, the thawing and freezing as the weather changes creates pressure. When a tap hole is made, approximately 1/2' deep through the bark of the tree, the sap can then flow into a bucket. (Placing a metal spout on the tree and striking it with a hammer creates a tap hole.) The sap is boiled until the water dissipates leaving maple syrup or sugar. Maple trees must be at least 30 years old before they can be tapped. One gallon of pure maple syrup requires 40 gallons of sap. Frigid weather makes it difficult to obtain a good sap flow. Warm days and cold evenings are needed to allow the sap to rise from the tree roots. The sap is primarily water. If the weather is particularly cold, the sap doesn't flow." Source: *Maple Sugaring Days*, Naperville, Illinois, http://www.romanceeverafter.com/maple_sugaring.htm.

have wax whenever I please. Will did get Hosmer's *Color Guard*[208] but we have not read it yet.

Secondday, March 14th, 1864
Sitting in my accustomed seat by the window, this morning I was busy upstairs cleaning things up a bit and burning old letters and papers. This time next week Cal will be living just over the way. If nothing prevents her she can come up this morning and put one carpet down. I wish Ella Janney and Nannie [daughters of Jonas and Ruth (Davis) Janney of Warren Co., Ohio] would come. I think we would enjoy ourselves finely and Will thinks so much of them. I would rather anyone would come that we both enjoy ourselves with. The snowflakes are coming down like December instead of March which is like almost like December itself. I must note it down here that Will was so fortunate this morning to procure five pounds of butter which will be quite a rarity.

Thirdday, March 15th, 1864
Snow, snow, just snow been coming down all evening and the ground is getting white. Will finished the frame for the honeysuckle. I think it will be so nice—when it is full of blooms. Will is busy cutting the leaves of *Harpers*[209] which came yesterday. I am waiting till I can enjoy a good read when I get the shirts done and the washing. It seems so funny that I am so much the "Bridget." I do it on my own accord and can quit any time I please. If Will made me and just wouldn't hire it done there would not be so much fun about it and I would not be so willing. I think I should try and help Will along and saving money is the way I can make it. One caller this afternoon—Abby. Tomorrow is the day Cal and Jake are going to move. I guess I hope, so anyhow, as I am getting tired waiting. I finished a book this evening entitled, *Married Not Mated* by Alice Carey.[210] It is good.

---

208. *"The Color Guard* is an account of the war experiences of Reverend James K. Hosmer who served as a corporal in the Civil War. Many scholars believe the book to be a classic in the genre of Civil War memoirs. His regiment, the 52nd Regiment of Massachusetts Volunteers, came from Franklin and Hampshire counties in the western part of the state." Source: Louisiana State University Library Special Collection, http://www.lib.lsu.edu/special/hosmer/index.html.

209. *"Harper's Magazine,* an American journal of literature, politics, culture, and the arts published continuously from 1850." Source: http://www.harpers.org/.

210. *Married, Not Mated* was published in 1856. "Alice Carey was born in the Miami Valley, eight miles north of Cincinnati, Ohio, April 26, 1820, and she died in New York, February 12, 1871. Her sister, Phoebe, was born near Cincinnati, September 4, 1824, and she died at Newport, R. I., July 31, 1871. Their parents were people of considerable culture. The education of Alice and Phoebe was limited to the meager opportunities of a newly settled country. Alice began writing verses at the age of eighteen years. For

Fourthday, 16th March 1864
Washed this morning—such a mess. Been assisting Jake and Cal put down the parlor carpet this evening. It looks real nice. In time, years from today, I wonder where we will all be, how many, many are the changes awaiting us in the coming years. We know that many of them are set and yet we are ever looking eagerly to some distant sometime in which we have promised ourselves so much pleasure and we never pause to remember that every long day is leading us nearer eternity. Our little room looks pleasant enough tonight—only the carpet. The fire burning briefly, the clock ticking away. Will after having had one nap on the lounge is actually nodding over *Harpers*. What can be more pleasant than to sit down by a cheerful fire with a table full of books and papers and be surrounded with congenial friends whose company make the hours to fly quickly away.

Fifthday, March 17th, 1864
Alma and I went to meeting this morning or started and I found my feet were rather damp so we returned home. Cal is getting pretty well fixed up, but their furniture has not come yet or did come but was taken up the road.

Sixthday, March 18th, 1864
Nothing to break the monotony. Mrs. Adam came up this afternoon to see about some potatoes. I suppose about her bakery. I was just fixing my yeast bread when she came and looked rather shabby. *Harper's* is real good. I glanced over it and the reading all looked tempting, but I have read only a little as yet. I noticed poetry of Jean Ingelows.[211] I never have read much of any of her poetry.

Seventhday, March 19th, 1864
Such a cold day. March a spring month—forsooth? It should be changed for if it is not winter now, when is it? Maria went away this morning but is coming back tomorrow. I wonder if she will talk about me when she goes home.

---

ten years she contributed prose and verse to newspapers. Her sketches of rural life, first published in the "National Era," under the signature of "Patty Lee," attracted considerable attention. In 1849 the *Poems of Alice and Phoebe Cary* appeared in book form in Philadelphia." Source: *Perspectives in American Literature—A Research and Reference Guide,* Paul R. Reuben, May 8, 2003, http://www.csustan.edu/english/reuben/pal/chap3/cary.html.

211. "Jean Ingelow, the English poetess and novelist, was born at Boston, Lincolnshire, England, in 1820. . . . Three poems were especially noteworthy: 'Divided,' 'High Tide on the Coast of Lincolnshire,' and 'Songs of Seven,' which consisted of seven poems portraying seven epochs in the life of a woman. This volume, published in 1863, quickly ran through several editions and verses were set to music and sung in every drawing room in England and America." Source: www.historyswomen.com.

Sabbath, March 20th, 1864
Went to church this morning. Heard a good sermon from Sarah M. Hiatt. Everyone likes her so well here, but she has enemies some places. This afternoon she preached at this meeting. Oh, it is so cold and the wind blows so hard. How glad I will be when spring comes. We are going to send flower seeds to James Vick.

Secondday, March 21st, 1864 [She has this as Seventhday]
Down home. Mother and I were at grandmothers this evening. Had a pleasant time and I came away loaded as usual. Alma and I have been very busy making our calico dresses. I do hate to make a dress so badly. It is so much trouble. I had rather be excused. Cody has come and is time for *Harpers.*

Sabbath, March 22nd, 1864 [Date confusion—March 20th also Sabbath]
Went to meeting. Sarah M preached. Alma and Clay and myself took dinner with Cal. Will was not here to participate. She had a real good dinner. Sara Hill had meeting at Reuben Hunt's tonight. We are going. Elva is going to help me wash tomorrow. It seems so funny that Cal lives so near. It is almost as if we were playing in a playhouse like we did when we were little girls. Such as running back and forth as we have. Will is going to fix a gate for us. It is so much trouble to climb and so inconvenient to go on the street every time.

Secondday, March 23rd, 1864
Such a big washing as we have done. I am getting to be almost a Bridget. My hands are as coarse and black. Instead of sending all my clothes away not caring how many—have to think more about it and wash them myself but Will says whenever I get tired he will have it done again. Lydia Ann brought some work for Cal and I to do for Sarah.

Thirdday, March 24th, 1864
Such a chilly gloomy day. The sun came out bright for a little while but soon disappeared. I was over at Cals this afternoon. It will be a hard matter for me to stay away one day from there.

Sixthday, March 25th, 1864
Nothing new has transpired this week. At night Sarah M. had meeting across the way and last night she attended prayer meeting. I am glad she did it. Alma is up today and it is such a gloomy morning. She will have to remain in a while yet. It is just pouring down snow. Will came up for us, so we are going down home to wait till Will gets through making molasses. Will received a letter from Lot. He insists on my coming to see them soon, but I fear it will be impossible as Cola is acting so badly. Will expects we will have to take her back.

April 1864

Sabbath, April 3rd, 1864

I will skip a few days in which I can think of nothing unusual as having occurred. No letter, nothing to make me real glad only our shutters have come, I wish someone would write something that would surprise me and please me both. It is so good to get a letter written in a strange hand and we wonder who it can be from and open it in a hurry and find something to please us very much. Elva has been living here this week. I did not suppose she would stay so long. Alma and Will are gone to church. I am not going this morning. It is a beautiful morning like spring but yet the air is a little too cold to be entirely pleasant. I have been reading my *Harpers*. It is so good. Specks, "Journey to the Nile" is very interesting but the account of the wicked superstition of the poor blighted sons of Africa is truly heart rendering.

Secondday, April 4th, 1864

A wet gloomy morning. Very much unlike spring. Cal had me to go over and take dinner with her after her company were all through. My dress is yet on hand and likely to before sometime to come. Clay called awhile this afternoon. He is going away in the morning to Virginia. I have been trying to move a few things in the yard, but it is so damp I can not feel interested. I am writing a letter to Lizzie. I think it is time but then I have not been in the mood lately. I am so busy. Oh, I will be so glad when fine weather comes. This dark gloomy weather is so disagreeable, but it will be all the brighter when the sun does shine.

Thirdday, April 5th, 1864

I am very busy making my dress. I will be so glad when it is made. It is so tiresome. Our seeds have come. I hope they will be as beautiful as we think they will. I have almost a mind to write to Matt. I wonder if she would answer it and yet why should she do otherwise? I am so sorry this kind of estrangement has come. We who have so many times said over and over how we will love each other, but I feel innocent of my offense and I know Matt is not angry. I fear it is that kind of apathy which often follows such burning friendship, but why should it, in our case, are we not congenial and do we not love each other. I hope it will all be right when we meet and the little secret of our coldness be out. I should not wonder if it was Ad's fault after all. He is so cold hearted. I think that he does not approve of my impulsive nature and often causes her to act more indifferent than she feels. [Matt Ladd was married to Addison "Ad" Pushee.]

Fifthday, April 7th, 1864 [Paulena and Will's fifth wedding anniversary]

Jeff has vacation this week. Lizzie is expected to reach Hillsboro tonight. Jeff was going to meet her at Blanchester. I am so glad.

Sixthday, April 8th, 1864
We dined at White's today. Cal and Jake also and Lide West. We had such a pleasant time talking of old times and about our housekeeping affairs. Lide prides herself on being a good cook which she is. We are both going to try our luck at baking cakes with sorghum in the morning. I like good dinners exceedingly when I do not have the trouble of getting them myself.

Seventhday, April 9th, 1864
A very bad day. Raining hard. I am so tired of having been working so hard—baking cakes and everything. Cal's cake will look whiter than mine. What is the matter with it. I think I will write to Ella Janney and write them to come soon and make us a visit. I like them so well.

Sabbath, April 10th, 1864
Did not go to meeting today.

Secondday, April 11th, 1864
Sarah M. spent the day at Cals and in a matter of course I was over. She is pleasant company and I think she is a good woman whatever some may say to the contrary. I begun braiding my apron this afternoon. I am not fond of such work. It is too much trouble. Lyd is embroidering a sheet. How she can ever find patience for such work is more than I can see. Mr. Bacon delivered a temperance lecture here on Seventhday night. It was very good. Aunt Lizzie is sick again and I really wish to go down and see her. It has been so long since I was there to stay any time.

Fifthday, April 14th, 1864
Nothing new to chronicle. Mrs Adams has an oyster supper tonight. Thomas Hunt [Thomas Elwood Hunt, son of Jesse Hunt and Anna Moon] is going to take Alma. Sarah E and May have been teasing her so much it almost got her crying.

Sixthday, April 15th, 1864
Down home and to grandmothers. Aunt Lizzie is sick again. Poor old woman suffers so much. Dear old grandmother hurried around to get me something good to eat and she always has such good victuals. Today she had saved a few pieces of chicken to make soup and it was very good. I came home loaded as usual. It is so good to have a home to go to and then such a good home. The draft postponed. Probably till June. It is very good news in one respect, but how is the army to be filled. I fear this far in the spring campaign our victories are few and do not promise much in the future, but perhaps it will all be alright. A

dreadful massacre at Ft Pillow.[212] The colored soldiers and most of the officers were butchered by the friends of rebels. After they had surrendered some were even burned alive—It is too dreadful to think of. How long will such fiends go unpunished. [Fort Pillow was on the Mississippi River on the Tennessee side about forty miles above Memphis.]

Seventhday, April 16th, 1864
Gone through the usual preliminaries of Seventhday—nothing new for me to put down. I tried my luck with some cakes and succeeded better than I expected. Cal had mean bread again today. I know she is provoked. My bread was good. It would fill all the slop buckets in Martinsville though I presume if all my mean bread could be gathered together.

Sabbath, April 17th, 1864
One early meeting across the way. Will was over but I went down home before. Mother had cooked a chicken and on purpose for me. She said so, we of course must go down home and after we had partaken of a hardy dinner. Clay is home from Virginia, but is going to return soon. He likes it very well for his business and says he enjoys being with the poor white trash for they seem so eager to learn all about Ohio and how we live here in the north. Just as though it were a thousand miles away. I would enjoy a trip there very much in the summer time. Just to think about it seems like such an easy task to go, but then the money— that is the question.

---

212. "Members of the Congressional Committee on the Conduct of the War investigated the 1864 massacre of Union soldiers at Fort Pillow, Tennessee. Reports of the massacre claimed Southern troops slaughtered many of the black troops who had already surrendered. The committee also investigated the condition of released Union prisoners of war in the spring of 1864. In both cases the committee found Confederate treatment of Union soldiers reprehensible. While some committee members, some in Lincoln's cabinet, and the general public urged retaliation, Lincoln demurred, perhaps realizing the futility of retaliation or fearing a series of reprisals. In early 1865 prisoner of war exchanges resumed and the pressure for retaliation disappeared." Source: Bruce Tap, "These Devils Are Not Fit to Live on God's Earth: War Crimes and the Committee on the Conduct of the War, 1864–1865," *Civil War History* 42, 2 (1996), pp. 116–132.

"On April 12, 1864, two Confederate cavalry brigades commanded by General Nathan Bedford Forrest overwhelmed a Union garrison of white Tennessee Unionists and former slaves at an outpost in western Tennessee. The Confederates then slaughtered the Federal troops in the Civil War's most notorious act of racial hatred. In his epic novel *The Falling Hills*, Perry Lentz uses the largely forgotten Fort Pillow Massacre to explore the erosion—or confirmation—of human character under the strain of war." See: *The Falling Hills*, Perry Lentz, 1994.

Secondday, April 18th, 1864
They are having great times in Congress. Long of Ohio and Harris of Maryland have both made speech worthy [of] the worst of traitors.

Thirdday, April 19th, 1864
Been very busy. Got up this morning late. Just hurried my best to get breakfast. Had eggs, coffee and bread and butter—our staple articles for breakfast, *Harpers* came this morning but as yet I have only had time to look through and anticipate what a good time I will have reading after awhile. Will put up part of the shutters and I had a time running to see how they looked. Everything is "at sixes and sevens"[213] all over the house.

Fourthday, April 20th, 1864
A beautiful morning. I am in the midst of house cleaning. Anything but a tidy housekeeper. One could not imagine a more slovenly looking affair than I am at this present moment—hair all on end, old dress, old apron, wet dirty ACUC. I hope no person will come. I am doing now what I used to hire done. I bought some bread this evening for tea. It is nice and good.

Fifthday, April 21st, night 1864
Tired—been working so hard, scrubbing, washing the windows. There is a panorama of the war tonight in the schoolhouse. Several are going. We are not. I will be glad when my work is done.

Sixthday, April 22nd, 1864
I am so busy working still at my home cleaning which seems an endless task almost for there are so many places for dirt. I am making so many changes one would hardly know the place.

Sabbath, April 24th, 1864
Just poured down rain this morning but this afternoon there was a calm and the

---

213. "At Sixes and Sevens"—"It's one of the more ancient expressions in the language, being recorded in the fourteenth century. There are various theories about its origin, but the most probable is that it arose out of an old game of dice called hazard, one in which one's chances of winning were complicated by a set of rather arbitrary rules. It is thought that the expression was originally to set on cinque and sice (from the French numerals, 'five' and six). These were apparently the most risky numbers to shoot for (to set on) and anyone who tried for them was considered careless or confused. Later, the number words shifted to their modern values, perhaps because the link with the game (and the original French words) had by then been severed, or perhaps it was a joke, as seven is an impossible number to throw with one die. The change may also be linked to the sum of the new numbers being thirteen, always considered unlucky. Its modern sense is simply 'to be confused.'" Source: *World Wide Words*, Michael Quinion, 1996–2004, http://www.quinion.com/words/qa/qa six1.htm.

sun came out beautiful and warm. We went over to Mans this afternoon. They are living in part of uncle Will's house. I wish we had a little girl. I hope we will have sometime. It would seem so nice to have a sweet little baby to play with. I never cared for one till lately. I begin to think I would not care. Marie Artry came up last evening. She is going to board at Beck's and says Triby is boarding there.

Thirdday, April 26th, 1864
I will be glad when I can be relieved of some of my work. I wish I could go to Portsmouth some time this summer. It will be such a pleasant time to go when the hills are really green and the weather beautiful. I am going to write to Ella Janney this week and write them to come and make another visit they promised I will be so glad to see them.

Seventhday, April 30th, 1864
Maggie and John [Dr. and Mrs. Carmen] and their young were here for dinner. Cal and I went down to the train this evening. There was an old beggar woman there, I felt so sorry for the little girl she had with her—a little thing about three years old.

May 1864

Secondday, May 2nd, 1864
May again but not the bright joyous we write of for the rain has been pouring down in torrents all morning nearly but we should learn to be contented anyway. Jane and Richard took tea here yesterday. We are going over soon. I feel so dull today.

Thirdday, May 3rd, 1864
I am busy making my dress. I will be glad when it is made.

Fourthday, May 4th, 1864
Down home today. Lenna with her little pink bonnet which she admires so much and her shawl on, trudged on to grandmothers. She is so sweet. I almost wish we had our own little girl. It would be so pleasant to have her running along with me when I go home or any place asking questions. I would take great delight in learning them all they could.

Fifthday, May 8th, 1864
Such a beautiful day. The sun so warm and everything so lovely. Cal and I had a time with our yeast again today. I think it ought to be good. Helen is sick. She looks so bad so pale and I hope she will be better soon. The baby is so sweet.

Sixthday, May 9th, 1864
The blue sky, the bright sunshine. Carl Moon was here a little while this morning. He says his seeds are coming up fine.

Seventhday, May 10th, 1864
Another bright morning. The 88th Reg is expected to go along sometime this morning. Mary and I are going down, I guess if anyone else goes. I am not very busy this morning—perhaps I might be. Will and I are going home this evening.

Fifthday, May 19th, 1864
A week gone and my journal has been neglected but I have not been in the mood having someone else to talk with. Our army in the east have been doing great execution. I feel the gain is not equal to the sacrifice though it looks very favorable as we read it. Yet it is hard to form a conjecture as to where the great victory lies. It seems the troops are massed in better order than was usual in a McClellan's campaign, but we had a fright last night. The news was Sigel who is between W Petersburg and someplace had been cut to pieces. Grant was retreating—400,000 men were called for which proved to be almost entirely a rumor but I fear we will have bad news. The west seems all right. The draft went off yesterday all right as far as Will was concerned. John D and George Cline were drafted. Lizzie, Cal and I had a good deal of fun about the honor of being a drafted man's wife, sister or as the case might be. Jake and Lizzie and Will and I were at Emas for tea on Thirdday evening. Lizzie went to Orens tonight.

Sixthday, May 20th, 1864
A beautiful day though warm. Oh! our poor wounded bleeding soldiers how they are suffering on the battlefield with this summer sun shining upon them or in the hospital while so many of us at home are enjoying ourselves just as though there were not thousands and thousands of poor fellows dying far off from home and friends. I think none of us can rightly appreciate or understand the full meaning of the word *soldier* unless we have a brother or husband or father suffering as only soldiers do. We can read of the terrible battles, read the long list of killed and wounded and feel sad but the next moment we turn away and are laughing or jesting. Perhaps until we feel the agony the terrible suspense of those who have loved ones. What we cannot realize is the full extent how terrible is war. The news last evening was Butler and "Beau" [General Pierre Gustave Toutant Beauregard] had had a battle in which if any difference Beauregard came off second best. It is so hard to know anything about the fighting. I am afraid to be very hopeful about it, so much is now depending on the success of Grant that should he have a defeat there, it would cast a gloom deeper than any ever caused by defeat on the whole country—saddening the heart of all save copperheads who of course will rejoice with unspeakable joy at our defeat and all the misery the terrible anguish of thousands of hearts will touch no tender feeling in their dark natures—I think the time will come when they will not be allowed to manifest their joy on such occasions unless it be some prison.

Seventhday, May 21st, 1864

Such a warm day. Oran was here for dinner today. Lizzie and I started to go to Nathan Hunts but we had not got very far when it began to thunder. We were undecided as to whether we had better go on or turn back again. At last we turned back and had got as far as town when we resolved to go to Reubins. We went. It rained and hailed. We had to be brought home in the buggy. Miss Trilby and Nana were here this evening.

Sabbath, May 22nd, 1864

Just hurried to get to Sabbath school, Had to even leave my dishes unwashed. Our class had finished reading our lesson. I suppose I had better go before breakfast time. We went out to Nathans after Meeting. Had a real pleasant time.

Secondday, May 23th, 1864

Been working real hard all day washing and been as lazy as need be in the bargain. It rained so hard this evening. I think it is such a strange summer. We have no news that is very encouraging as yet and it seems uncertain when this good news will come. We went last night across the way to listen to an appeal from a colored recruiting officer. There was several there of the sable line but he failed to make any impression on them and so they are all going to remain at home to be drafted.

An Unfortunate Man
[By Paulena Stevens Janney]

I am an unfortunate man, never saying or doing anything at the right moment. I cannot account for this dilemma of mine but my brothers are both accomplished gentlemen and make themselves agreeable to the ladies on all occasions with few exceptions. Thomas, who is quite a lady's man will when saying anything particularly witty, will finish it off with a possible squint—which by the way is a habit he got into when he was a boy by squinting at the schoolmaster when he was not looking. It still remains with him and amuses his friends sometimes when they are not too enamored to notice it. He has tried various ways to break himself of this habit but he has not succeeded. I almost envy him sometimes and I think I would take all his advantages with the slight disadvantage of having a squint for while he is conversing on some interesting theme, turning his mustache with his delicate fingers smiling and bowing and looking as if he really pitied everyone else but himself. Me, in particular, who is sitting in the corner now and replying to some question and coloring to the roots of my hair and I must add here on all occasions I am so unfortunate to have a red face in my calmest moments and when I blush you have at one look a helpless person. For I must tell you the form and substance of all my troubles is I am a bashful man in the fullest sense of the word.

Fifthday, May 26th, 1864
Such a hard rain today and the old affliction in Jakes yard blew down right in our gateway and so we have to go round or creep through. Mr and Mrs James Betts [James P. Betts, son of Uncle Wm. S. Betts and Anna Hadley, married Nannie Perry][214] —came yesterday. Lizzie and I did just get a peep at them as they went by. They returned this afternoon. Lizzie had another peep, but I was snoozing and missed it all. I hope I will get to see her sometime. We took supper over at Cals this evening. Lizzie is helping me about my dress which is almost done.

Sixthday, May 27th, 1864
Such a beautiful day. Mrs. Brown called this afternoon. Lizzie is at Frank Moore's tonight. Steve is wounded slightly. Lyd is anxious.[215] I feel sorry for her. Mrs. Moore was here a little while this evening. She looks so sad in her mourning. I feel sorry for her.

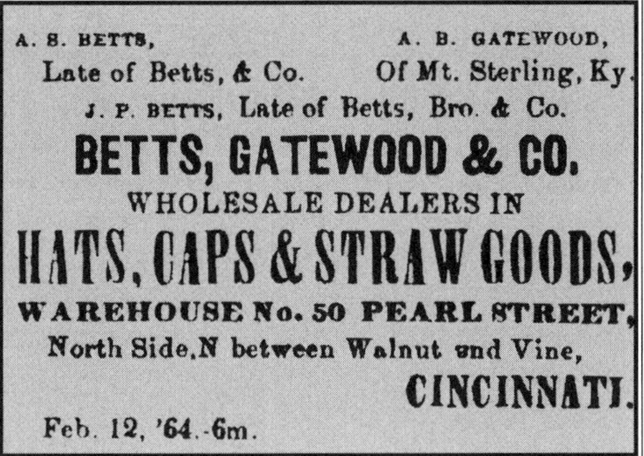

Betts, Gatewood & Co., and A. S. and J. P. Betts
Hats, Caps & Straw Goods, Cincinnati, Ohio

---

214. In the 1864 Cincinnati City Directory, James P. Betts was a partner with his brother, Aaron, in Betts, Gatewood & Co. (Aaron S. Betts, Asa B. Gatewood, and James P. Betts), Wholesale Dealers in Hats, Caps and Straw Goods, 50 W. Pearl, boarding at Burnet House with his brother, Aaron, until James married Nannie Perry. In the 1866 City Directory the partnership was listed as Betts Bro. & Co. (A. S. B., J. P. B., R. H. Perry & M. Betts), Wholesale Dealers in Hats, Caps & Straw Goods, 50 W. Pearl; living at 313 Longworth (Aaron S. Betts, James P. Betts, R. H. Perry, James' father in law, and cousin Madison Betts).

215. Stephen Janney was wounded slightly in the foot on May 15, in the Atlanta Campaign at the battle of Resaca, Georgia.
"All of William Tecumseh Sherman's troops were gathered on the morning of May 6, 1864 to begin the march to Atlanta. The Union Army of the Cumberland, under the command of George Thomas, was in the area of Ringgold; the Army of the Tennessee under James B. McPherson at Gordon's Mills, on the Chickamauga; and the Army of the Ohio under John M. Schofield near Red Clay, on the Georgia border north of Dalton. Facing Sherman were three corps of Confederate troops under the command of William J. Hardee, John Bell Hood, and Leonidas Polk, under command of Joseph E. 'Joe' Johnston, one of the South's best generals. Johnston's 45,000 to 50,000 troops and artillery stood in opposition to Sherman's combined total of 98,787 men. Based close to Dalton, the Rebels had a tactical advantage and had a superior cavalry of about 10,000 men under General Joseph Wheeler. . . . Johnston knew that he could not hold on to Resaca, but he could make the Union forces pay dearly, and not only with personnel. He

Seventhday, May 28th, 1864
Lizzie and I went down home this morning. Us and Alma had intended spending the evening at L_____ but they sent word for us to come tomorrow. So we remained at grandmothers.

Sabbath, May 29th, 1864
This morning, for a rare thing, I went to school in time and it seemed much better than going there after the chapter had been read. Alma was here for dinner—a splendid Sabbath dinner—corn bread and onions, but we seemed to relish it, after all. We took a walk to the graveyard. It was so pleasant there. Lizzie came back this evening, but is going to Moore's tomorrow.

Secondday, May 30th, 1864
Read *Our Mutual Friend.* The new story of Dickens in *Harpers* which will be continued for two years.[216]

June 1864

Fourthday, June 1st, 1864
Such a sweet morning. The first morning of the first day of the month of roses. The bright month of June and it is all too lovely to be stained with blood, for the sun does not rise in the beautiful morning without shining where hosts of armed men are preparing for battle or set without the last rays falling on bloody fields where for hours the poor soldiers has been falling and suffering and dying. Oh, dear, I must iron this morning and I am so lazy. It would be so much pleasanter to sit here in this cool place and read or write or something, but the sooner commenced the sooner ended.

Fifthday, June 2nd, 1864
How quickly the summer is passing away. Almost before we have enjoyed summer, the chilly wind of autumn will be with us. Went home this morning.

---

destroyed communication and railroad facilities, and burned the railroad bridge, interrupting Sherman's future supply line. After winning the battle on the 14th and 15th of May, Johnston retreated south across Oostenaula in the middle of the night, saving his men for future delaying actions and serious harassment to Sherman. On the morning of the 16th of May, Union troops entered Resaca. The first battle for this town was over." Source: http://ngeorgia.com/history/resaca.html.

216. "The publication of *Our Mutual Friend,* in the form of the earliest stories, extended from May 1864 to November 1865. Four years earlier Dickens had chosen this title as a good one, and he held to it through much objection." Source: http://lang.nagoya u.ac.jp/~matsuoka/CD Forster 9.html#V.

Grandmother up there. No news of importance, but some soon, as I expect I think it is dreadful so many of our poor soldiers suffering so. Lyd received a letter from Steve. He said he thought he would never come out of the battlefield alive, but he did escape with a slight wound. His reg or brigade or whatever it is, was detailed to bury the dead. They buried a thousand rebels. It must have been an awful sight to see a battlefield but I wish I could be where I could see just one. We surely have enough to see their suffering and try to comfort them all in our power—if they had all the pain to endure. I am reading a book, *The Old Farmhouse*—really good.[217]

Sixthday, June 3rd, 1864
We are just feasting on strawberries this week. Such large nice ones, too. Cornflowers do not grow fast enough to suit me. I am so afraid they will not be nice. It will be too bad. I never did want to go to the city so badly as I do now. It has been so long. I wish I could hear some good music. It would be such a treat to listen to some melody beside the squalling of children and the music of frogs. The inviting of Garibaldi to England[218] seems to have been something of a political scheme and they were glad to have him go for fear of some trouble.

Seventhday, June 4th, 1864
This is Saturday morning and pies to bake and so many little things to do. I don't like to cook. It is so much pleasanter to read or sleep or sew than to wash dishes or always keeping my hands like Bridgets. I finished *The Farmhouse*. It did not come out just like I wanted it to. "Beatrice" had to go and die away off in Italy before she found "Amy" and broke her husband's heart and died too and left Pauline in this strange land." Meyerbeer," the great music composer is dead. His death occurred on the 2nd of May. He was burned with great honor and magnificence at the railway station where the services took place—was elaborately draped in mourning at the expense of Baron Rothchild.[219] The ladies in the different cities are moving in a reform, as regards the use of imported goods, pledging themselves not to purchase during the war anything imported if not home manufactured. I wonder how long they will hold out. One good thing is, I have no occasion to bind myself to anything of this kind as my clothing does not consist of foreign goods to any great extent.

---

217. "The Old Farm House," *Putnam's Monthly,* November 1855. Source: "The Making of America," http://cdl.library.cornell.edu/moa/browse.author/o.18.html.

218. England's Queen Victoria supported Prussia, but her son Edward supported Denmark, his wife's country, and this view was shared by the prime minister. Edward angered the queen when he welcomed the Italian revolutionary Garibaldi to England in April 1864, when he came to encourage further support for Denmark. Source: *Biography of Edward VII.*

219. "Meyerbeer . . . was born in Vogelsdorf, near Berlin, on Sept. 5, 1791, as

Sabbath, June 5th, 1864
As an usual thing for me I was ready to attend Sabbath school this morning in plenty of time and we had a very interesting class. The question arose was Judas saved? For my part I think it not unlikely for though his sin was as scarlet why could he not be forgiven for we are told he repented of his sin. Alma and I came home and did not remain for church. I read a letter from George [Janney] this morning. He seems to think life is more uncertain where he is now than any place he has been so far as regards disease [yellow fever in the Florida Keys].

Secondday, June 6th, 1864
Alma and I went to Wilmington. As we went we made some poetry which I am going to pen down. Now one can see what little dunces we will be whenever we get old.

This morning Sister "Al" was bound
To take a jaunt today.
I didn't want to go one bit
But she wouldn't let me stay

And then we started from the door
O With heart full of alarm
For looking out into the west
We thought we saw a storm

And so we started down the street
As fast as we could go
For the sooner there we got
The sooner back you know

And now we'll tell you what we saw
As on our road we came
The first thing that we noticed
Was Julia getting lame

Yaakov Liebmann Beer. His father, Judah Herz Beer, was a wealthy sugar refiner in Germany and Italy. His mother, Malka Liebmann Meyer Wulff, also known as Amalia, was the daughter of a wealthy Berlin merchant and banker who made a fortune delivering supplies to Prussian troops, and also was the director of the Prussian lottery. Yaakov (or Jakob) was the eldest of three boys. His brother Michael became a well known German playwright, author of two successful plays, *Struensee* and *Der Pariah*. His other brother, Wilhelm, became a businessman and an amateur astronomer who achieved fame by publishing the first map of the moon in the 1820s. . . . Meyerbeer continued as an active composer until his death in Paris on May 2, 1864." Source: http://www.geocities.com/Vienna/8917/Meyerbio.html.

> We came upon a flock of geese
> And put them all to flight
> They never turned to look at us
> But ran with all their might
>
> We came into a little house
> Where copperheads did dwell
> And though we wished them nothing bad
> We wished them nothing well
>
> And then we got to Wilmington
> Where we had been before
> We hardly stayed five minutes
> And was out in a store.

Thirdday, June 7th, 1864

I did not wash and iron last night but I washed partly and this morning—I got it out early. It seems so funny that I washed this time yesterday. Last summer, I mean—I would not have thought of such a thing as my washing. I thought it an impossibility. It is a lovely day. Just cool enough to be pleasant and the trees look so stately in their rich green robes all ready for the summer banquet and I fear I am not appreciating all their beauty. I wish this afternoon I had some congenial friend to go with me out into the woods or sit in some dark place and share and enjoy a book or chat.

Fourthday, June 8th, 1864

Company this evening for tea. Ladd's and Browns. We had a very pleasant time as far as it concerned us. Fanny Brown spend the evening after tea. I think they are such nice people.

Fifthday, June 9th, 1864

No news from Grant. Morgan again in Kentucky. I hope he won't come over here again He might do more harm the next time. At any rate we would all be frightened worse next time. Mother was up today but she is always in such a hurry about going home. Mary and I are going to fool Al with a bouquet tonight. Lizzie is making a long stay at Moons. [John C.] Fremont has accepted the nomination,[220] and by so doing, has lost friends. He seems to have entirely given up to the Copperhead faction and is different from what we have ever looked upon Fremont as being—that is already producing quite a change inpublic opinion.

---

220. John C. Fremont was nominated for the presidency on May 31, 1864, by a small faction of the Republican party, but, finding but slender support, he withdrew his name in September. Source: http://www.civilwarstlouis.com/Bios/Fremont.htm.

Lincoln was nominated at the Baltimore convention.[221] We will have serious times this fall I fear. I think our worst days have not been yet.

Sixthday, June 10th, 1864
Been so lazy all day dreading to do anything. Alma and I called on Miss J Bells. We thought very well of her. I think she is not a person who will feel an elevated position as much as some people. She has had all her life a great many more advantages than I have. Mary and I are going to send Alma a bouquet to fool her and not signing a name.

Seventhday, June 11th, 1864
The long looked for letter came at last. A letter this morning from cousin Ella. They cannot at this present time come as a change has taken place in her family, but as soon as they can they are going to write.

Thirdday, June 14th, 1864
Nothing new and so I am going to skip a few days not knowing that I could write anything interesting of them. Lenna was here yesterday with me. She is so sweet. I love her so well. No news from Grant of any importance. Cal helped me about my dress today. I could not do without her for she is so much help to me about my clothing. She having a much better knack at fixing things than I have. We are so afraid our flowers are going to be burned up. Such a pity as it will be.

---

221. "Baltimore, Maryland, June 7 to 8, 1864, Nominated: Abraham Lincoln of Illinois for President. Nominated: Andrew Johnson of Tennessee for Vice President. The Republicans nominated Lincoln for a second term at the convention. They also changed the name of the party to the National Union party, with the hope of expanding its base. The most fateful decision taken at the convention was the decision to replace Vice President Hannibal Hamlin of Maine who was from a state that the Republicans were sure to carry with Andrew Johnson who was a pro Union governor of Tennessee." Source: http://www.multied.com/elections/Conventions/1864Rep.html.

"Although Andrew Johnson was a Democrat, the Republican Lincoln chose him as his vice president in the 1864 presidential campaign because Johnson was the only senator from a rebel state to remain loyal to the United States during the Civil War. When Lincoln was assassinated in 1865, Johnson succeeded him as President. In 1868, Johnson's battles with the Republican congressional leadership over plans for Reconstruction resulted in his being the first president impeached by the House of Representatives. He was acquitted by one vote following a trial in the Senate." Source: "North Carolina: Presidential History at James Polk, Andrew Johns Birthplaces," William Homes, *Beacon-News*, February 12, 2005, Paris, Illinois.

Seventhday, June 18th, 1864
We are going to Haworths this evening for our first visit.[222] I heard something so very strange today—cannot get it out of my mind. T______ L has gone off with another woman and left his poor suffering wife in sorrow. To any, not acquainted with it, will not seem so strange, but it is the last thing any of us ever would have thought of. It seems he was such a witch as to try to poison her too. It seems almost too strange to be. So surely truth is stranger than fiction. It seems he fell in love with that mean thing about a year ago. All that we have heard about it is shocking and to think of him trying to poison her.

Sabbath, June 19th, 1864
Had a pleasant time as could be expected. They were glad we went. We came home late. It seemed so good to get home again. Home is the best place after all. Vanlandingham has found his way back again to stir up contention among the traitors over here. The consequence we fear will not be favorable to our peace in the month and attempt though to roust him would cause trouble soon enough. We are afraid our flowers are not going to amount to much from the seeds we bought. Oh, it is so hot weather. We are anxious for it to rain.

Secondday, June 20th, 1864
Such a good shower. The rain drops pattering down through the leaves and against the window never made sweeter music. Everything looks so refreshed. I hope our flowers will grow fast now. Lyd Jackson was here this morning. She came to Cal's and Cal not being in, she just came in here. I like her right well. Been more fighting in the east. It is said Grant was victorious. Cal has a little son.[223] I have not seen the little stranger yet. We did hear we were going to have Clarks for neighbors on the left, but this morning we heard that Denniss are coming.

---

222. Richard M. Haworth married Jane Janney on December 1, 1963. Jane Janney was the sister of Will Janney. Richard M. Haworth inherited the homestead of 160 acres in Clark Township, Clinton County, Ohio, and took care of his parents until their death. In 1859 he traded with his brother George D. for a farm east of Wilmington. He increased his holdings, until, at one time, he had five farms of over five hundred acres in all. He invested very heavily in the pork packing business in Wilmington, Ohio, and reverses caused the loss of almost his entire property. In 1883 he moved to Hendricks County, Indiana, near Plainfield, and bought a small farm on the edge of Morgan County, where he did general farming. He and Jane are buried in Sugar Grove Friends Cemetery, Plainfield, Hendricks County, Indiana. Source: *History of Clinton County, Ohio*, Albert J. Brown, 1915, and research at the Plainfield Public Library by Christie Russell.

223. Thomas Wade Betts was born on June 17, 1864. He was the son of Madison Betts and Carolyn "Cal" Janney. Madison was a first cousin to Paulena, and Carolyn Janney was Will's sister.

Thirdday, June 21st, 1864
Nothing much to write about. I feel so void of energy that I do not feel like doing anything only sleeping. Uncle Tom [Stevens] is going to marry again. A Mrs. somebody out west. She having eight children—he five. 8 + 5 = 13. They will have a right respectable beginning. We would be so sorry for him to take Lenna. I do not think he will though. Eunice Winslow is going to have meeting here this morning, but I do not feel like going. The copperheads are going to nominate Alex Long for President.[224]

Dr. Dougan Clark, Earlham College
photo collection

Sixthday, June 24th, 1864
Asenath Clark[225] from Indiana. Her son Dr. Dougan Clark [a third cousin once removed] delivered a lecture at the school house last night—subject "Causes of the War" and also about the contrabands. He is a very intelligent man.[226] This afternoon he read an essay or lecture on education. School closed this evening. It is very different from what it used to be on such occasions.

---

224. "Alexander Long (1816–1886) was a Democratic congressman from Ohio from 1863 to 1865. Long was censured by the House of Representatives on April 9, 1864, for treasonable utterances. He was a delegate to the Democratic National Convention in 1864, 1868, 1872, and 1876." Source: http://www.picturehistory.com/find/p/5957/mcms.htm.

225. Asenath Hunt Clark was a member of the Greenwood–Eagle Creek Meeting, Hamilton County, Indiana, third month, 1860 original member. In the 1870 census she was enumerated under her father, Nathan Hunt, in Hamilton County, Indiana. Her husband had died in 1855. She died in 1873.

226. "Dougan Clark, A.M., M.D. His father and mother, Dougan and Asenath [Hunt] Clark; his grandfather, Nathan Hunt; and his great grandfather, William Hunt, were all ministers in the Society of Friends, At the age of eighteen he entered the Friends' Boarding School at Providence, Rhode Island, where he spent two years. In 1850, he entered Haverford College and was graduated there in 1852, and in the same year was married to Sarah J. Bates, of Hanover County, Virginia. Afterwards he attended a course of medical lectures at the University of Maryland, in Baltimore, and then removed to Indiana and practiced his profession, for eight years, at Carthage and Westfield, except that he spent the winter of 1860–61 at Philadelphia, where he received the degree of Doctor of Medicine from the University of Pennsylvania, with the class of 1861. Two years were then spent in Indianapolis as a practicing physician. In 1866 he was called to the chair of Greek and Latin in Earlham College, which position he held for three years,

Seventhday, June 25th, 1864

I went down home this morning. Almost starved for something to eat—that is something good, for I am so tired of all we have. It is dreadful warm this week Enough to nearly scorch us. Our neighbor children are none of the best and such squalling as we have from morning till night. I am awakened in the morning by a squall.

Sabbath, June 26th, 1864

Will has gone to see what can be the matter with Lizzie. I concluded I would stay at home. I went to Sabbath school this morning as usual. I tried to sleep this afternoon but I could not sleep very long on account of the flies, the heat, the chickens and the children. The wind blows and the sun shines down dreadful hot. I think Will and Lizzie will have an unpleasant ride. I am thankful I did not go. Our zinnias, we hope will be all right after all.

July 1864

[July 1st, 1864—Paulena's twenty-fourth birthday]

Sabbath July 17th, 1864

O My poor journal. Can you ever forgive me for neglecting you so long? I will not beg your pardon because of my many household duties, but simply— nothing but the same old everyday life has been with me and I have no ambition to write. Sometimes I get worn out with the same old wagon and get tired of hearing the same old bark and the same old children squall and so with it all I get so lonely and so long for a change for a little time or a long time.

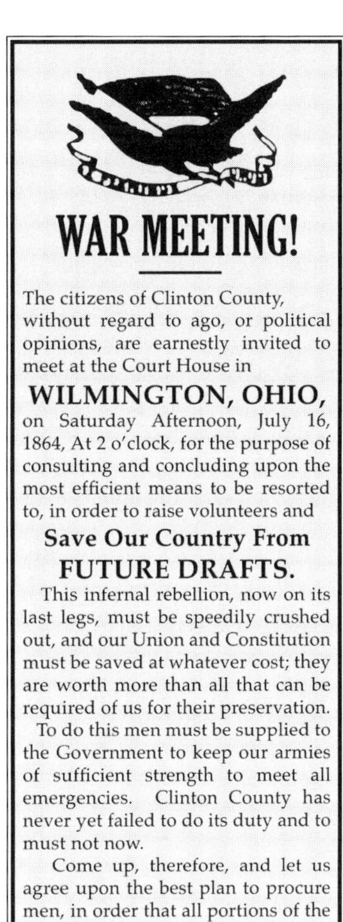

War meeting from *Clinton Republican,* July 15, 1864

---

when he resigned and moved to Richmond. He was recorded a minister of the Gospel, in 1869, and this was distinctively his life work. He was pastor of a Friends' church in Cleveland, Ohio, for thirteen months. From the beginning of 1882 till the end of 1883, he was the editor of the 'Gospel Expositor.' The following year he was again elected professor of Latin and Greek in Earlham College. With the establishment of the Biblical Institute, in 1888, Dr. Clark was promoted to the leadership of the new department, which position he held until 1894. He died at his home in Richmond [Indiana], October 10, 1896. Dr. Clark was the author of 'Offices of the Holy Spirit,' 'Instructions to Christian Converts,' 'Holy Ghost Dispensation,' and 'The Theology of Holiness.'" Source: *Memoirs of Wayne County and the City of Richmond, Indiana.*

Just a change to see different people. I have been reading *The Life of Theodosia Burr*[227] and in reading the life of the daughter we can not fail to have more respect for the father. There is something so touching in the affection with which she clung to her father through all his misfortunes and crimes and his love and tender thoughtfulness for her. When the mind is far above the ordinary. In fact Aaron Burr is in some respects my ideal of a man.[228] Moon's son was brought home yesterday—dead—it was all unexpected to the family excepting his father who had been with him.

Secondday, July 18th, 1864
Another warm day. I went to monthly meeting and remained until the business commenced.

---

227. "On December 31, 1812, the beautiful and vivacious Theodosia Burr, wife of wealthy Governor Joseph Alston of South Carolina, left her husband's plantation and sailed north on the Patriot to visit her beloved father, the famous Aaron Burr, in New York City. In early January the vessel was accosted off Cape Hatteras by ships of Great Britain, then at war with the United States, but was permitted to proceed on its journey. The *Patriot* was never seen again nor, with any certaintywas Theodosia.

"An angry storm that very night swept the coast of North Carolina. Some say that during the gale pirates boarded the *Patriot,* removed all valuables, forced passengers and crew to walk the plank, then sank the ship. But legend persists that Theodosia survived, that she was cast ashore in a small boat onto the Outer Banks, bereft of all possessions except a portrait of herself, and that, with her sanity completely gone, she was thereafter cared for by a Banker fisherman and his wife.

"The years went by. In 1869 [five years after Paulena had read the book] the strange woman became ill, and a doctor from Elizabeth City was called in to attend her. He did what he could, but it was clear that she had not long to live. As he was leaving the sick room, the poor fisherman's wife told the doctor that, as she had no money, he would have to choose something from the house for his pay. When he replied that he would like to have the handsome portrait hanging on the wall, the afflicted old woman sprang from her bed. 'It is mine! You shall not have it! I am on my way to visit my father in New York, and I am taking this picture of his darling Theodosia!' With that, she grabbed the canvas, rushed through the door, ran down the surf, and walked into the ocean. The next day, the portrait washed up on the beach. It is fact, not legend, that the doctor took the picture from Nags Head to his home in Elizabeth City, that a descendent sold it to an art dealer who in turn sold it to a member of the Burr family, and that it exists today." Source: *Classic American Ghost Stories*, ed. Deborah Downer, 1990, "The Portrait of Theodosia Burr," http://www.scaryhaunts.com/theodosia.htm. See also University of Missouri at St. Louis, Special Collections—http://www.umsl.edu/mercantile/special_collections/directory/slma 018.html.

228. Aaron Burr died in 1836, twenty-eight years before this journal entry. Aaron Burr and Alexander Hamilton dueled on July 11, 1804. Hamilton was mortally wounded. Dr. Benjamin Moore, a third cousin twice removed to Paulena, rector of Trinity Church, New York City, read the last rites to Alexander Hamilton. Dr. Moore's son, Clement Clark Moore, a noted biblical scholar, is best known as the author of the classical poem "A Visit from St. Nicholas," better known as "The Night Before Christmas."

Thirdday, July 19th, 1864
The news is 500,000 men called for. Cal came over to tell. Just as we [are] beginning to feel safe, here comes a call for so many more men. So what is to be done is still a continued question. No rain yet though the sky is full of white billowy clouds which look very fine and make one feel poetical, but at this time we would all much rather see some big black clouds looming up from the west, full of thunder and lightning and rain.

Fourthday, July 20th, 1864
Went to temperance meeting last night. Will read an article on tobacco. It did not set well with some of the old members. I had a nice little nap this afternoon on the floor. Our neighbors just over the fence do abuse their little children. It would be like bringing light out of the chaos when there is no light to bring order. It makes me feel bad indeed. This evening I could not refrain from going in the midst of a severe castigation. The screams of the poor child were more than I could bear. I did not know how I would be received, but at all events I resolved to try. I said a great many things and I hope some of them will have some effect. Poor Mrs. Dennis actually cried, telling me some of her troubles. I think she is not such a bad hearted woman after all, if she only had a chance. I talked pretty plain to her sometimes, but she did not seem angry. I am sure I meant it all for her good. She said "Sometimes I sit down and cry till every tear seems out of my heart and think I feel a little better." Poor woman. She is one of the many who has an unsympathetic husband and yet only last night I heard him say, "Everything that we do should be done to the glory of God"—wish as much as if he did all things in that way.

Oh, I hope I will be of some benefit in the world. Sometime when I do anything I think it is my duty to do, I feel so much better. What I said this evening I do think was my duty. At least I feel better for so doing it. I have heard so much about her. So many bad things and so many seem to hate her with such a perfect hatred that I really pity the woman and if I can do anything to make any change I will gladly do it. Of one thing I am sure. No person will hear anything from me concerning her bad qualities. I think we ought to have more sympathy for her than many of us do and for the poor and friendless. With her heart and hands both full, she has little chance of improving herself or from keeping her heart from becoming seared. I think of taking her a book to read.

Grapevine Cottage June [1864]
Dear Jennie,
I know it was not worth answering but I did not know it was quite so bad, but I have decided that you are the best judge and I will see about forgiving you. What do you think I had better do about it. How have you been prospering since last I heard from you? It has been such a long time. I hardly know how to write, but how do I know that you may be in some foreign land before this time as you have not entirely given up

the idea of some such freak even if you have such an append-
age or appendages. I should have said . . . of a husband and
three little responsibilities which however would only make it
the more pleasant. For with an artist who would enjoy all the
beautiful things you would see in your travels and the appreciative minds of your children you could enjoy their enjoyment
and also your own. I think it is such a pity to be with anyone
who cannot see anything lovely, don't you? Perhaps we will say,
"Oh, don't the sky look splendid?" Yes, it does look nice, but
then I believe it is going to rain. And how provoking it is to go
into ecstatics over a book and think it so good and someone else
says, "Oh pshaw, I cannot bear it" or paintings, for instance. We
have one of a little girl and boy. They are out on the hillside and
the goats are feeding around them. At their feet is a stream of
water, a river or something and in the distance almost hidden
by trees and hills looms up the old brown homestead. They are
there with their little barefeet and earnest looks soon to be in
some deep revere over something. Now sometimes I ask persons about that picture and they say it is about an old man and
woman. It almost provokes me.

Seventhday, July 30th, 1864
Such sad news. Charley Oren is dead. Sat [Sarah] is almost distracted, poor
woman. How much agony she feels. The body of Charley is to be brought home.
I don't know whether it will be brought here or Wilmington. Here, I suppose
though, and be taken there for internment.[229] I feel so sorry for Sat. Her agony
is almost more than she can bear. It was all they could do to keep life in her yesterday and when we think of how many thousands of such cases, it is enough to
keep us unhappy all the time. We have seen so little of it here. The Copperheads
are forming a conspiracy, but is in a way to be found out.

---

229. Charles Oren was killed on July 28, 1864, near Petersburg, Virginia, during
the siege of Petersburg. It was during that siege on July 30 that the Battle of the Crater
took place. A tunnel 511 feet long was dug by Union troops, former coal miners from
Pennsylvania. The tunnel was under Pegram's Salient, where gunpowder was placed.
When the explosion took place, it blew up a Confederate artillery battery and left a
crater about 170 feel long, 60 feet wide, and 30 feet deep. Union troops, instead of going
around the crater, plunged directly into it and were unable to go any farther. Confederate counterattacks retook the position, inflicting more than 4,000 Federal casualties. The
siege continued. The Battle of the Crater is portrayed in the movie *Cold Mountain,* produced in 2003. Source: Petersburg National Battlefield, Virginia Official Guide, National
Park Service, U.S. Department of the Interior.
Death Notice—*Clinton Republican,* August 5, 1864:
"It is our painful duty to record the death of our friend and late fellow citizen, Captain
Charles Oren, who was killed on last Thursday, the 28th ultimo, at the head of his Com-
pany near Petersburg [Virginia]. We have not yet learned the particulars of his death."

Sabbath, July 31st, 1864

Alma is sick. Poor Sat is very bad. I cannot get it out of my mind. Somehow everything looks dark. The effects of war are being felt nearer home now and makes us think more about it. No rain of any account yet. It seems like a famine would be no strange thing to come upon us now.

August 1864

Secondday, August 1st, 1864

A letter came from Charley to Sat, but they have not let her see it yet for fear she is very bad. They are looking for the body of Charley everyday. He will be buried here. Sat wants him given up to the scholars.

[August 3, 1864,] "In a Hole Near Petersburg, Virginia." For the *Clinton Republican,* reported by P.A. Stamats—published August 19, 1864.

Dear Republican:
"It is now more than a month since I wrote you before, and I had thought (after seeing what I had written in print.) that I would not attempt to write any more; but I now seize the pen for the purpose of giving to the citizens of the county some information of their late friend, Captain Charles Oren, who was mortally wounded on the morning of the 28th ultimo, and died the same evening. We were stationed in the second line of battle on Gen. Turner's front, acting as support, and at the same time doing fatigue duty at night, such as building forts, redans and parapets, behind which to set mortar batteries &c. It was in constructing one of these last named, that the Captain was killed. Unlike any other place that I ever heard of before the batteries in this siege are on the front lines, and the consequence is that it is very dangerous building them.

"On the night of the 27th of July he was sent out in command of a party and by some means did not get relieved till after daylight, and just as he was leaving the place he was struck. The ball entered his left hip and passing down came out on the top of his right thigh, severing the femoral artery of his right thigh, but not breaking the bone of either leg. A man came running up to my quarters and said that Captain Oren was shot. I ran down toward the place where I knew he had gone, and met the men carrying him on a stretcher. He had fainted and I thought at first that he was dead. As soon as they got out of range of the enemies' fire they set the cot down and then I saw that he was still living. I took off my coat and put it under his head and he seemed to revive. When we got him to the surgeon, he could talk and said that his hands were numb and asked if his wound was mortal. The Doctor did not think it was and immediately had him put into an ambulance and sent to the Division Hospital; and as it was not thought to be so serious a wound, I was not allowed to go with him. This was about 6 o'clock in the morning, and about 1 P.M., Lieut. Way came down and said that the Captain wanted to see me, and that he could not live twelve hours. I got permission to go, and when I got to the Hospital he was fast sinking and said that it hurt him to talk. I soon saw that he was dying, and to my questions, he only answered in short sentences. The Surgeons say that he lamented mostly because he could not live to see the end of this campaign.

"He was loved by all the officers who knew him; and commanded even more respect as a military man, (if it is possible,) than as a citizen. He was brave and cool on the battle field, kind and generous in camp, and his loss to the regiment is irreparable. He was in the charge on the 15th of June, when our Brigade charged and took the outer works of Petersburg. He was also in many other smaller encounters. He was on Gen. Stannard's line on the 19th of June, when the Regiment suffered more than it did on the 15th. But whether under a galling fire of grape and canister, or in camp, he was the same—cool and calculating. But he is gone—gone to rest, where wars are not known.

"I feel too deeply the loss that I have sustained, to be able to give utterances to the feelings of my heart on this most sad occasion; and therefore, I leave to others the task that I cannot perform. I am yours, P.A. Stamats"

Fifthday, August 4th, 1864

Charley came this evening. I think I never saw anything more solemn than it was when he was taken home at the request of Sat. The scholars went down. It was after night when he was taken. The box which contained his body was draped with the flag. The scholars all passed through Sat's room. She was very still, not even a tear came to her relief, but she just seemed immovable.[230] Dr. Sacan stood by the bed with his hand on her forehead, poor woman. Her sorrow

---

230. Sarah ("Sattie," "Sat") and her husband, Charley, were graduates of Antioch College, Yellow Springs, Ohio, at the time that Horace Mann was president of the college. She was a native of Clinton County, Ohio. She and Charley were both teachers in the Martinsville school.

Obituary: "Mrs. Sarah 'Sat' (Allen) Oren Haynes, the first woman to fill the position of State Librarian of Indiana, died last Sunday at the home of her daughter in Sault Ste. Marie, Michigan. In 1868 she came to this city [Indianapolis] from [Clinton County, Ohio] and became preceptress in what was then the City Academy, and in the next year she became a teacher in Shortridge High School, in which position she remained until 1873. In that year the Indiana Legislature selected her for State librarian. She held the office for two years, but the following Legislature, for political reasons, did not reappoint her. For four years, beginning in 1875, she was a teacher of botany and mathematics at Purdue University at West Lafayette. In 1879 she married Wesley Haynes, a farmer, near Peru, [Indiana] and they lived on a farm in Miami County until the death of Mr. Haynes, in 1897. Mrs. Haynes moved to Sault Ste. Marie and lived with her daughter until her death." Sources: *Indianapolis News*, April 25, 1907, p. 58; also *Indiana Biography Series, Volume 1*, p. 215, microfilm found at the Indiana State Library.

is very deep. I hope I may never have such suffering to undergo, but dark days
come to all and for all I know many such are awaiting me in the future.

Seventhday, August 6th, 1864
Such a large procession this afternoon. The largest funeral ever here. I presume
the estimated number was to be 1,000 quite a number for a small village like
this. Sat was very sick.[231] This afternoon the sun came down hot enough. It
almost scorched a person. Just burning everything up. Oh for some the rain we
used to grumble. Last spring it was hailed with gladness. I think we are very
hard to please, no doubt. Should a wet time come now we would soon think
it too wet and grumble about it. I will be pleased to see Lots baby. It seems so
funny—wonder if anyone will ever want to see our baby? I hope so any how.

Sabbath, August 14th, 1864[232]
A long blank in my journal. I fear l am sadly misleading my journal. Is it not that
I fear I will not be interesting in a few years for me or anyone else to read.

Secondday, August 15th, 1864
Cloudy this morning, but it is such an uncommon occurrence for it to rain. We
have almost ceased to expect it. Our zinnias neatly all proved to be single. Those
that are double are real pretty. D is trying for a ______ commission. I hope he will
succeed in getting one—if he wants to.

---

231. Captain Charles Oren was buried at the (I.O.O.F.) Independent Order of
Odd Fellows Cemetery, Martinsville, Clinton County, Ohio.

232. Lieutenant Colonel Wilder was made commander of the Light House Barracks
in Key West, Florida, on August 14, 1864. His journal accounts and family correspondence are preserved at Yale University. Portions are given here that were written the
time that George Janney was stationed there and living in the Light House Barracks
from which he wrote a letter dated October 18, 1864—see journal entry footnote. In describing Dress Parade at Fort Taylor, he [Lieutenant Wilder] wrote: "long lines of dusky
warriors with shining eyes and teeth, all covered with blue & glory & carrying Uncle
Sams muskets so polished & bright as to look like silver. Each man with shoes blacked,
brasses polished, white gloved & clean, going through the manual of arms with alacrity
& precision, not often seen in our armies."
On September 12, 1864, Lieutenant Wilder recorded, "at last had my attack of
yellow fever & I am just recovering therefrom . . . it was a light attack & only kept me
confined less than a week." He attributed his survival to being acclimated from a fever
he had previously. . . . "A man it is said, never has the yellow fever twice. . . . The Doctor
is trying to crowd me with calomel & sugar of lead & c, but I quietly throw the stuff out
the window." Sources: *Lt. Col. John Augustus Wilder*, Loomis-Wilder papers and letters
at Yale University; *The Civil War in Florida, Florida Keys and Fevers*, p. 887, Key West,
Florida, Public Library, collected by Christie Russell, May 18, 2000.

Grapevine Cottage

Dear Matt,
I wonder if thee ever thinks of me and if thee has forgotten how l look, for of course, my picture which thee has does not resemble me much now as it has been so long since I gave it to thee. Well Matt, how goes the world with thee? Is thee now as free from care as when in those happy days gone by. We had such merry times, such joyous rambles over the hills and such cozy little chats in some shady nook where the mummer of the waters and the singing birds made the sweetest music for us and whispered so much gladness for the future. Oh, give me the hills, the grand old hills that are wed to my native vale. They rock in their cradles the laughing rills and breathe an untainted gale. I presume we both have had much to sadden our hearts since the old times. Thee has felt the sorrow of a broken home circle, the sad changes which accompany such bereavement. I, as yet, have been spared that bitter anguish but it is but nature for us as we grow older to be more closely allied to influences which tend to make us shrink and feel more deeply.

Well Matt I intend only a short note this time. I will just ask why don't thee come down. Only 16 miles and yet it has been two years since we saw each other. It is too bad Ad is gone all the time. Thee might visit so much. I know we could have such pleasant times if thee would only come to pick up enough courage to get ready and come and spend a week or two anyhow. I will meet thee at the train. Just think how much like old times it will be and then I know thee can come if thee will only do so. If I was thee and thee me I would come I know. Aunt Lizzie is failing. I think all the time Lib Myres is living there now. The Institute is in session now and there are several students from a distance. Cal is my neighbor on the left and thee can imagine how many times in one day we see each other. It would not be possible for me to do without her. Now it seems that on the left there has been much changing. Some new neighbors came one morning and the next morning [didn't hear it squall] but there was one but the mother grew very weak and sick and they went away taking the little girl baby who was getting real sweet. Then pretty soon some more came with three little ones. One red and two white heads and then it was squall from morning till night for a time.

September 1864

Sabbath, September 4th, 1864
September is with us again and the leaves are already falling on their golden hue and are beginning to strew the ground. I love September so much. It is so beautiful and calm and its sunshine tinting the leaves and the wind rustling among the trees ever seems to be whispering to us of the bright summer passing away. My mind has been so occupied with thought of the draft that I

have entirely neglected my journal. Our debt is almost clear or that is, our understanding about it, but has cost great exertion on the part of some and money, too. Poor as Will is, he has had to put in $200 and our dear buggy is gone. I could not keep from crying but Lenna consoled me by saying, "Oh, we can get Uncle Evans buggy. He won't care." I am consoled with the hope that sometime when we come in possession of our carriage and those prancing black steeds I can see in my imagination it will all be right. For the last two weeks we have had Lenna up here. She is so much company.

Sabbath, September 11th, 1864
Went to church. Just a quiet sitting. I am not enough of a "Friend" to enjoy that kind of meeting very well. I like preaching to stir up better feelings and make us think. We went down home for dinner. Had a good one. Lenna did not come home with us this evening. She is tired of staying. Oh, dear I want to see some person, or go some place or something. I am so weary of this monotony. Everyday the same. Our flowers look prettier than ever. I am glad we sent for them nothwithstanding all the predictions of my friends. They proved to be all right and not a "burnbug." I think we are in a deplorable fix. No horse, no buggy, no money, no nothing, no baby. I mean we can just stay at home though, I suppose, and as to the latter named article we can borrow one.

Thirdday, September 13th, 1864
This morning I thought certain I would make some yeast vs dry yeast. So my hands were soon all daubed with corn meal and such a time I thought I never would get ready to go to Uncle David. Mother came along for me and I was in the midst of cornmeal. After a while it was all done and spread out to dry in the sun, but the sun changed and before evening instead of the hot September sun coming down, down came the rain and my poor yeast had to take it till I got home and I am afraid it is sour and will have to be put out in slop where all the sour raising goes. I was telling Cal last night, our slop bucket could tell a doleful tale considering our bread business, but it is not our fault.

Fourthday, September 14th, 1864
Such a sad morning. Lot's baby is dead.[233] I am sorry I did not get to see it. I feel sorry for them. McClellan does not entirely please the Copperheads. Vallandyham does not like him since he saw his letter of acceptance. I went down to see Beck. She has heard from George and feels much better.[234] I am

---

233. This son, whose name is unknown, was born on July 29, 1864, and died on September 4, 1864.

234. George Janney was a first Lieutenant, Company A, Second Regimental Infantry, U.S.C.T. [United States Colored Troops]. He was a white officer of African American Troops. He was appointed by President Lincoln from civil life. Mustered

glad. Lyd has heard from Steve also and is in good heart.[235]

Fifthday, September 15th, 1864
It seems so natural to sit down after my morning work is done and pick up my old journal which I fear has been sadly neglected of late. I am going to try and do better and so like autumn I feel like I wanted to go away in some beautiful lonely place and be with nature. If there was only a river where I could go and pick up shells or sit and watch the water hurrying along toward its ocean home. How sublime and how ennobling are all the works of God when we have the spirit to appreciate their beauty. Everything reminds us of his goodness and power and we feel a longing for something higher than the everyday life.

Sixthday, September 16th, 1864
Sick this morning. The house all dirty and I do not feel like cleaning it up. Mother and all the children went to Highland. Lenna excepted—who is here with me. Cal is gone too and I hardly know what to do with myself and then I feel uneasy about the draft which comes off on Secondday and this township is minus three men—unjustly though who those three men will be remains to be decided. I am so in hopes Will will escape this time. I wish I had the *Ledger* to read this evening. This is such a bright day. I feel like I ought to be enjoying it more than I am doing just now sitting here by the fire and cold at that.

Seventhday, September 17th, 1864
Alice came up to help me today. She is quite an assistance in my poor state of health. Good news about the draft. This township is free at last. Alma's melodeon has not come yet. I wonder why. I got a letter from Matt but it does not seem much like the good letters of the olden times that used to breath so much affection and fill my heart with gladness.

Sabbath, September 18th, 1864 [An outing in the woods]
Away out in the depths of the forest not in the Sylvan Shade where miniature lakes glisten like gems and birds of strange plumage hover and salute our ears with a melody unheard before, but here among the trees of our native woods

---

September 21, 1863, to take effect from same date, September 1863, mustered in Fort Monroe, Virginia for three years [Ft. Monroe is located at Hampton Roads, Virginia, where the Chesapeake Bay and James River converge.] joined Regiment with his Company A on January 15, 1864, at Ship Island, Mississippi. He was in action at Natural Bridge, near St. Marks, Florida, on March 6, 1865. He was on leave of absence for twenty days, beginning on September 4, 1865. Source: National Archives, Card Numbers 5533250, 5534162, 5534264, 5534364, 5534466, 5534565, 5534667, 5534767, 5534866, 5534964, 5535061, 5535151, 5535240, 5535334, 5535428, 9428412, O, 18, C.T. 1863.

235. Stephen Janney was with the Seventy-ninth Ohio Regiment in the occupation of Atlanta.

where they are rocked by the winds and the birds like those we heard in our childhood, sing their old songs—my heart is very full of something that I do not have the language to express as I sit here and muse—when we dwell upon the goodness and power of God in creating so much beauty, such lofty mountains, majestic rivers and a thousand other things that no man of earth could form or our minds imagine. In thinking of these things and fame often do a great many things so unholy that were God not very gracious he would long ago have cut us off, for we are but as grass so liable to wither and be cut off before we are ready. Will is getting in a hurry to go—so good-bye old woods. I wonder if when next your leaves are being tinged with the golden hue I will be as I am now. What untold sorrows, what agonizing tears are yet to be unfolded for many and why should I be spared, if not of my goodness I know. Don't forget me tree as I will think often of you.

Secondday, September 19th, 1864
Such a big washing for me and I had to be in such a big hurry for dinner. If it had not been for Elva I could hardly have got along. We were invited up to Carmans tonight to hear the musical performance of Messrs Ball and Gorman on the violin and guitar. The Misses Adams sang sweet songs. It was very nice. Now if I was in Matt's place after my arrival in New Hampshire [Matt's husband Addison Pushee was born in Lyme, New Hampshire—they might have visited relatives there] I would sit down and write a long letter to me.

Fifthday, September 22nd, 1864
The week passing away so quickly and I am not doing very much good. This is such a lovely afternoon. I am sitting over here in this shady doorway of the old church. The locust trees all shimmer, murmur and whisper as the wind sighs through them, but now the leaves are fading and every gust of wind sends a shower of them down until the ground is almost covered. How delightful it would be to have someone here to talk with. Mother is very sick with the diphtheria or croup.

> Ella Dear[236]
> This September morning sitting here all alone listening to the wind which sounds so sad, the rustling leaves and occasionally bringing down a faded leaf that budded and came forth glossy and green in the springtime. It is the saddest of all this year when the flowers are fading and dying and the foliage on the trees are deepening into the golden hue and should remind us forcibly of our own fading and dying.

---

236. These letter copies were addressed to Mary Ellen "Ella" Janney, the daughter of Jonas and Ruth Davis Janney, who lived in Waynesville, Warren County, Ohio, about forty miles west of Martinsville, Ohio.

Ella Dear

I have neglected the letter long, but not because I ceased to think of thee or wish for thy presence. We were sorry you could not visit us and sorry that such a sad occurrence prevented you. How many times do we learn the true meaning of the words, "We know not what a day may bring forth," and it seems the saddest of all things to me to stand beside a friend or relative when looking into the future, as far as mortal thought can reach. Again on earth everything seems so dark except as we can light our imaginations and picture a meeting in "That better land." I think if we would only pause and reflect in the sorrow shed abroad so abundantly over this land, it would be a sad world.

Sixthday, September 23rd, 1864

Poor little Walter dead. We were down to see him after the lecture but did not think of him dying so soon. Oh was someone coming to tell us bad news about him. No person but Dr. C [Carmen] was there with them excepting Billy and Jane. We hurried there as soon as possible. He looked just like he was sleeping. His face felt warm and looked flushed. Will and I came back to get clothes for him. It was a sad task, but there seemed to be no person to attend to things. Alma, May, Josey and I were all there to do anything We did not sleep any at all. It was our duty to dress him. It seemed so sad, but we did our best and kept our courage up enough to accomplish it. He looked so sweet. Fanny and Aaron came this evening but Willie is too far away for any word to reach him. I have been there most of the day and am almost worn out.

Seventhday, September 24th, 1864

The funeral is over. Dougless preached a good sermon. He was buried beside Arthur who was once such a pretty blue eyed baby and if it is true that infants grow in Heaven and that in Heaven they recognize their friends where they lie at this time Walter is in the midst of brothers and sisters. It seems such a mystery when we think about it and makes us long to know more. I was sick all night last night and do not feel near well yet. Lizzie and Jeff were here today. Lizzie is going to teach school in Leesburg this winter. I think I will go up and see her.

Sabbath, September 25th, 1864

Such a sad beautiful day. All day I have been lounging about feeling too near sick to do anything and not quite sick enough to go to bed for earnest. l am so restless. I get so tired of staying here all the time. I want to see something. We are having good news from every source, just now, if it only continues as good as it looks. More hopeful about the war being over sometime but there maybe much fighting to do yet. I hope Will will get to stay at home and I will be will-ing to defend with all the honors of his having been a soldier when this war is ended. Flowers and leaves and all things bear the impress of autumn. I am sorry to see them fading and yet I do not enjoy them as at first for their time for dying has come and our thoughts as winter approaches are counted on other things. The fair at Blanchester comes off this week. I think some of going, but Will is too busy. I will be glad if the time ever comes when we can live without him being so busy all the time. Clay got somewhat offended at Will the other night, but I guess it will not be serious. Aunt Lizzie is much worse.

Secondday, September 26th, 1864
I went to grandfather's today. Aunt L [Lizzie] is about the same. The Dr thinks it likely she may die at any time. The news is good if true. Sheridan has had more good luck. Captured 9000 prisoners. Breckenridge and Early. l am afraid it is not so. I wonder if I will go to the fair? I can hardly decide about going.

Thirdday, September 27th, 1864
It seems so lonesome for Cal to be away. She will not come up home this week.

Fifthday, September 29th, 1864
Got up early. Such a dark morning. In the notion and out of it several times before going to the fair. At last started, not hardly decided yet about going, but squeezed along with the crowd. I at last found myself in the cars and such a jam—no seats to be had. I found myself standing beside Dr. Noble. He is a surgeon in the army—was taken prisoner—exchanged—and is going soon to form his regiment. The rain fell in torrents part of the time but I took care of number one and kept myself dry although there were many completely drenched. We got home safe after being squeezed almost to pieces in the cars. I saw one lady I liked so well or thought I would and hope I will make her acquaintance sometimes. Her name, I think, is Mrs. Miller. I saw some sweet little dresses for children. I think I must make patterns sometime.

Sixthday, September 30th, 1864
A gloomy morning, but not raining. I am almost sorry we did not wait and go this morning, but it is no use in grieving over it now. Uncle P and his wife are coming this evening. I was introduced to Lake and Ella Lever. I liked them.

October 1864

Seventhday, October 1st, 1864
Uncle P and his wife arrived yesterday morning. Alice remarked, "I expect she will wish a good many times she had never seen father." Her daughter and cousin Cal Jackson[237] from Noblesville, Indiana, are coming this morning. I am

---

237. Cal Jackson is undoubtedly related to the family of Bowater and Jennie Mace Jackson, who were living in Hamilton County, Indiana, at that time. This family was related to Paulena through the Hunt and Mills family. Noblesville is the county seat.

anxious to see them. Rain, rain, it will come pattering against the window panes almost anytime now. It proved to be a wet evening and I did not get to go down home to see those ladies who came on the train. I just spoke with them a few minutes and did not have the chance to have a good look at Mrs. Watson.

Sabbath, October 2nd, 1864
All of us went over to church this morning. All signifies the company at fathers house. The new minister, Mr. Phillips, was there. He seems to be a very energetic man, but is not such a preacher in my opinion as D______ or B______ or even Stillwell who though he had opposite views about somethings from some here and had the independence to carry them through was always a favorite preacher of mine. We are going down home for dinner which is better than getting dinner at home. I think Mrs. Watson is right nice looking.

Sixthday, October 7th, 1864
Has been raining almost all week. Cal, Mother and Alma were up yesterday and we arranged for us to go to Vienna today—all three of us went. Took dinner at Thornburg's. Had a pleasant time there but on starting home the scene changed. A violent gust of wind and rain came dashing the rain in our faces until they were blue with cold. Judging from the feeling we reached home about dark having just passed through another little storm in which were almost drenched. I was really [worried] about Al [Alma] for I did not know but something might occur to her on her way home and several times when I would awaken for a minute and hear the wind and rain a picture of Al's poor little white face lying by the roadside chilled with the cold would come to mind and before morning I was almost fearful it would be so.

Sabbath, October 9th, 1864
Went to church and home with Matt. Baby getting sweet. Nothing to write about so will write nothing only I saw a little new baby at church with a blue hood.

Secondday October 10th, 1864
Went to meeting this morning. J Hoad from Iowa was there also R. Dougless. Clark child was buried and they had sent for D_____. He is such a good preacher. Tomorrow comes off the great election which is to decide so much for the good or bad for our country. Whoever votes for union men tomorrow will do the same in November. Clark and White had a discussion at Wilmington today.

Thirdday, October 11th, 1864
Up early this morning. Mrs. D went to camp Dennison this morning and she came near being left at home. I went down home to see Aunt Lizzie. She is very weak. Will says they have had interesting issues at the polls part of the time. Some discussion. There were several copperheads and I am all alone and I will be till midnight but I am not as big a coward as some people.

Sabbath, October 16th, 1864
Uncle Tom and Aunt Mary came up last night and spent the night. I would not like for Lenna to go to live there. This is a bright morning. Will being one of the trustees had to be absent all morning seeing about someone whom they are going to take to the poor house.

Secondday, October 17th, 1864
Another week passing away and bringing us nearer the end of autumn and soon the cold bleak winds of winter will be blowing chilling the poor soldiers to the bone or heart or anyhow almost freezing them. Jim West's oldest boy died this morning and his wife is very low. Death is ever busy and we know not what time its icy hand will be lain upon someone we love causing our hearts the most bitter anguish.

Thirdday, October 18th, 1864[238]
Cold and chilly this evening but the sun is shining and lighting with it beams this autumn afternoon but how many hearts there are that sunshine can not penetrate. I am going down to G___rs [Grandfather's] tonight to sit up with Aunt Lizzie. Beck is going too.

Fourthday, October 19th, 1864
It seemed almost impossible to get away this morning as there was no one to stay. B left me and came home to send someone down but nobody came down and at last I felt duty bound to come and get Will's dinner never thinking once that Alma would do it. It seemed so good to be out in the fresh air again and at home where I can burn as much wood as I please. If Will was like grandfather, not meaning to be irreverent, I would cry my eyes out or do something. I am sorry he is like he is. How much happier, more useful and how much better we might have been had our poor old grandfather had different ideas about some things.

---

238. Among the papers from George Janney's Civil War Service records from the National Archives is a handwritten letter by George Janney from Light House Barracks [Leight was his spelling], Key West, Florida, October 18, 1864, requesting a thirty-day leave of absence to return to his home in Ohio to settle some unfinished business and for a change of climate as his health was greatly impaired by recent sickness. Yellow fever had infected the company. The Light House Barracks was across the street from the Key West Light House on the southeast corner of present day Whitehead and Truman Ave. Also across the street from the Light House was the house that Ernest Hemingway lived in in the 1900s, which was in existence when George Janney was there. After the War, in 1868, a Canadian order restored the barracks building to create the city's first Catholic school and the Convent of Mary Immaculate.

Fifthday, October 20th, 1864
Got up early this morning. Expected to do so much. Going to wash. In the midst of my work—got so sick I could hardly stand on my feet, but it would never do to leave in such a plight. So work I must and when my clothes were ready to hang out I felt like I was ready to be put someplace too. Will being gone on a perilous journey to that poorhouse with some poor white trash I was all alone till almost dark. Hellena West died last night. Cal will keep Ida for a time anyhow.

Sixthday, October 21st, 1864
Just like old times, sitting here by the old east window looking at the same trees and the leaden sky. Aunt M___took dinner here today. Although I felt very badly, I was not able to attend the funeral. Will got back all right. They had a great time with them, but no one was hurt seriously. He said she was the worst of any of them—so wicked. Got *Harper's* today The last number—cannot afford to take it. The ensuing year so expensive or we are too poor.

Seventhday, October 22nd, 1864
Cloudy and cold. I am going to grandfathers tonight. Aunt Lizzie is very bad. I do not suppose she will last much longer. There are so many good pieces in *Harpers*—one is "My Refugees." I do not know what we had better take next year. I would like the old *Post* again. I believe it would seem so natural.

Sabbath, October 23rd, 1864
Had so much to do this morning. Sabbath, though it was, I could not help it and I told Will the "Good man" will know how it is. I feel so sorry for Aunt Lizzie. Last night she looked more deathly than I had seen her. I thought her time was almost _________out and the last "knot" will soon have been reached. I hope she will be more resigned than she has ever seem to be yet.

Secondday, October 24th, 1864
Been real busy part of the day and might be all day. Alma and C intend going with Tom H and his wife on their tour. It will be right pleasant, I expect. I hope I will get to go someplace sometime. I have been thinking of some plan to change our little old kitchen, but my plans are not so readily adopted by Will and I have concluded that fix it anyway we will—[it] will still be the same old kitchen—black and dirty. It seems an impossibility to have it clean for more than an hour or so at a time.

Thirdday, October 25th, 1864
This morning we had such awful news brought to us. Milton Moon killed himself. He was sick and being delirious got up in the night and taking his razors—two—he cut his throat from ear to ear. It was near the gate where he fell. It is dreadful and almost kills them. I feel so sorry for them, but all our sympathy avails but little. It seems like he was determined to kill himself for Rebecca

["Beck" Janney, sister to Will Janney] called him and he answered her and then finished his dreadful work.[239] It seemed like we have enough warning to make us more thoughtful than we are.

Fifthday, October 27th, 1864
A gloomy morning, but at noon the sun came out from among the clouds shining down upon us. Its glad light, chasing the raindrops from the leaves and grass and gladdening everything save the hearts of the afflicted. The funeral was a long one and a sad one. No one can help pitying the broken hearted wife and the poor old mother [Sarah Mills Moon was his mother and his deceased father was Henry Moon]. Upon all the relatives it was a dire calamity, but they seem more able to bear up than those two. Coffin's came yesterday. [Jesse and Emily Janney Coffin from Richmond, Indiana. Emily Janney was Rebecca Janney's sister.] They received the dispatch promptly.

Sixthday, October 28th, 1864
If I had been at home this morning I presume Coffins would have been here for dinner, but as I did not get home from grandfathers till late, they went to Haworths and called here this afternoon. We are going with them to Becks.

Seventhday, October 29th, 1864
Went to meeting. Good preaching, but the noisy children spoil half the solemnity of it. Bermidt is a good preacher, but has rather too much sing song about his sermons to send me, but the words are good. Richard and Jane [Haworth] came home with us from meeting and when the train came who should come but Lot. We were glad to see him, but I could not tell how Jane and he would meet. They met though better than I expected. Fannie has been to Rainbow for some time, but returned a few days ago. Her health is quite delicate.

November 1864

Fourthday, November 2nd, 1864
Last night Eliza, and Mph came. I do like them so well. Lide has not changed much in her appearance. Ellie is married. I am sorry to learn that Ella Janney is thought to be going down with consumption. I hope it is not so. I must write and see. They have bought property in Waynesville and it will not be so impossible for us to visit them now. Oh, how much I do love Ella. I would regret very much should I never see her any more.

---

239. "Died, on October 24, 1864, last Monday, Milton Moon, suicide by cutting his throat with razor. From Martinsville, Ohio, Age 48 years." Source: *Clinton Republican,* Wilmington, Ohio.

Fifthday, November 3rd, 1864
Went to grandfathers this afternoon and Lizzie still the same. It seems strange that she lingers so long. I think I must write to Ella Janney soon.

Sixthday, November 4th, 1864
Only a few days till the election. How anxious we will all feel to be to hear the results. I fear sometimes that we all expect too great a victory.

Seventhday, November 5th, 1864
Been down home this morning. Came up to put some letters in the office. Hurried down but was a few minutes too late. So much for five minutes. "The Diamond Seeker" is another story I am reading. I wish I could remember all I read, but I read history and other things and there being no person to converse with I forget or at least could not tell anything correctly anyhow.

Sabbath, November 6th, 1864
There is a funeral this morning. Pleasant Moon's son. Dougless is to be at meeting. I am sorry I could not go, but my cloak was not at home, so I could not go. I dreamed of Ann so much last night. I expect she is in great trouble now if living. Poor woman. Her pleasures have been few. I wish it was in my power to offer her some assistance for she must be suffering from poverty. George F. Train[240] has leaned to the right side again and is making speeches for the cause of the union. I am sorry we miss all the speeches when we would enjoy them so well. I hope sometime it will be so we can have more advantages than we have ever yet had. I think we would appraise them more than some. I think I must go and stay at grandfathers tonight. Someone has to go and it is quite a task. I intend writing to Ella Janney this afternoon if I can find a pen good enough. They are so bad—the most of them. I fear I am going to have a cold which I [page missing].

Thirdday, November 8th, 1864
Election day.[241] How much depending on today's results. There are several who will not vote. Uncle Christopher Hiatt [married to Paulena's mother's sister,

---

240. "George Francis Train was an American merchant, promoter, author and eccentric. He was born in Boston in 1829. He engaged in business there for several years and then went to Australia in 1853 where he founded the house of Caldwell, Train and Co. He traveled extensively, went to England, and made vigorous efforts to introduce street-railways into London in 1859, but met with violent opposition and was unsuccessful, returning to the United States in 1862. He announced himself a candidate for the presidency in 1869, traveled around the world in eighty days in 1870." Source: http:// www.collectimaniac.com/p81 14428 maj george eliot military sci autho.html.

241. Presidential Election, 1864. "Lincoln's chances for reelection appeared dim for much of 1864. No president had won a second term since Andrew Jackson more than 30 years ago. More importantly, Lincoln was weakened by widespread criticism of his

Jemima Hunt] for one and Elwood his son. The copperheads had their big program fixed out, but have been found out. They anticipated burning Chicago and St Louis. Hundreds of them have been arrested. Some of them ought to be hung if anyone ought.[242] Matt will not be down soon, I fear.

Fourthday, November 9th, 1864
Down home today. Uncle Tom's packing up to leave in the morning. I feel right

---

handling of the war. The Union had suffered a long string of disappointments and many faulted the president's strategy. Further, conservative forces in the North were outraged by the Emancipation Proclamation and feared its impact on the future of society. Much maneuvering occurred in the Republican Party prior to the convention because of Lincoln's apparent vulnerability. Various names were advanced as presidential possibilities: General Benjamin F. Butler was thought to be popular with the War Democrats. Vice President Hannibal Hamlin enjoyed strength among the growing ranks of Radical Republicans. General U.S. Grant received a newspaper endorsement Treasury. Secretary Salmon P. Chase had supporters among the extreme abolitionists and other Radical Republicans.

"All of these early possible candidates disavowed interest in advance of the convention. However, the strident anti-slavery forces coalesced around the candidacy of John C. Frémont, a bitter foe of Lincoln. The president had twice dismissed Frémont from military commands and had reversed his order to free the slaves in Missouri in 1861. These anti-slavery forces held an early convention in Cleveland and nominated Frémont. The regular Republican Party met in Baltimore and used the name National Unity Party in the hope of attracting War Democrats.

"Lincoln was selected on the first ballot and offered no preference for a running mate. The convention chose Andrew Johnson of Tennessee, a seemingly attractive candidate thanks to his Southerner and War Democrat background. The platform promised to prosecute the war effort until the Confederacy's unconditional surrender.

"The Democrats adopted a platform that called for a cease fire and a negotiated settlement with the South. They gave their nomination to George B. McClellan, who promptly repudiated the platform and simply pledged to conduct the war more skillfully than Lincoln.

"During the campaign, Frémont relinquished his bid, fearing that he would split the Republican vote and enable the Democrats to win. The turning point came in early September with Sherman's capture of Atlanta, a victory that lifted spirits throughout the North and revitalized the Lincoln campaign. The Republicans warned the voters, Don't change horses in the middle of the stream. Also, leaving little to chance, federal officials arranged liberal furloughs for Union soldiers—a source of significant support for Lincoln. McClellan managed to capture 45 percent of the popular vote, certainly a respectable showing, but the electoral tally was a landslide for Lincoln." Electoral votes 212 to 21. Source: http://www.u s history.com/pages/h201.html.

242. The more radical members of the "Peace Democrats were called 'Copperheads.' They obstructed the war, they resisted and attacked emancipation." They claimed the war had become a war to free the slaves, and these Northern Democrats would have none of that. Source: www.hobbsschools.net/HobbsHigh/AP%20History%20Lessons/AP%20US%20HISTORY/Review%20for%20AP%20Exam.doc.

sorry to see the children all go away for all it will be a great relief to mother for them to be away. Oh, dear I do not know what will happen next. M and I had almost a quarrel this afternoon. I think it awful there be so much contention. I felt so mad part of the time I could hardly see. Oh dear, if we only could go away. I do hope we will before long. I think it will be better a deal for us at least I think so. The rain has been pouring in torrents most of the day till this evening a beautiful rainbow . . . [page missing]

Sixthday, November 10th, 1864[243]

Cold this morning—no all day. I have been very busy all day—ironing and baking bread. I wonder if Matt will come down any time soon. I wonder how she will look. It has been so long since I saw her over two years ago. In 10 years—no thrice—I wonder where I will be. Not in this little sitting room sitting by the window, I presume, but living some other place. I hope if no worse no better. I do not know how the fuss will come between Clay and the rest of them. One thing certain, it is time some of the relations were so altering is we always have been too near each other to get along right. All our view and opinions of all kind always being at variance.

We think of taking the old *"Post"* again this winter. It will be like an old friend. Oh, I am getting so tired of this monotony. I want to see some one or go

---

243. Lincoln on the 1864 Presidential Election—Response to a Serenade—November 10, 1864. "It has long been a grave question whether any government, not too strong for the liberties of its people, can be strong enough to maintain its own existence in great emergencies. On this point the present rebellion brought our republic to a severe test; and a presidential election occurring in regular course during the rebellion added not a little to the strain. If the loyal people, united, were put to the utmost of their strength by the rebellion, must they not fail when divided, and partially paralized [sic], by a political war among themselves? But the election was a necessity. We can not have free government without elections; and if the rebellion could force us to forego, or postpone a national election it might fairly claim to have already conquered and ruined us.

"The strife of the election is but human-nature practically applied to the facts of the case. What has occurred in this case, must ever recur in similar cases. Human-nature will not change. In any future great national trial, compared with the men of this, we shall have as weak, and as strong; as silly and as wise; as bad and good. Let us, therefore, study the incidents of this, as philosophy to learn wisdom from, and none of them as wrongs to be revenged.

"But the election, along with its incidental, and undesirable strife, has done good too. It has demonstrated that a people's government can sustain a national election, in the midst of a great civil war. Until now it has not been known to the world that this was a possibility. It shows that, even among candidates of the same party, he who is most devoted to the Union, and most opposed to treason, can receive most of the people's votes. It shows also, to the extent yet known, that we have more men now, than we had when the war began. Gold is good in its place; but living, brave, patriotic men, are better than gold." Source: http://www.nps.gov/liho/writer/1864.htm.

someplace or something, but I know I must not murmur for my situation is so much better than many. All I want is change or excitement of some kind.

Seventhday, November 11th, 1864
Gloomy this morning. I wonder if any person will come I will be glad to see. Grandfather has been here giving me a lecturing about Clay. If all is as bad as they say Alma had better let him alone. I think some of those who encouraged the intimacy between Alma and him ought to be ashamed now. Oh, I am so tired. I don't know what to do with myself. If I could only go away.

Thirdday, November 22nd, 1864
My journal has been neglected for a long time. What excuse can I offer that will satisfy you journal. Must I say I have been so busy and had company and been out of the mood for writing for that is just the reason. Ada and Alf [Coffin] left here on last Fourthday morning. I like them so well. Will received a letter from Fanny [Lot's wife] inviting us to come and visit them. Perhaps we will soon. Aunt Lizzie is very bad—poor old thing. Her suffering is very great indeed. It seems strange to think of her as the same old woman who a year or so ago was always so ready and willing to wait on others. No difference how weary, she would do anything for our comfort and now, though it is a hard task, we surely ought to do all for her we can. Vances little William came very near dying the other night. Everyone there thought it almost gone when all at once a change came for the better. They would not give it up. Perhaps the time came when they will wish it had died, but I hope not. This is such a cold day—winter for certain. I am sick today and I am not going to get supper.

Fourthday, November 23rd, 1864
Such a cold night last night and still cold. I do not do much, but sit here by the stove and listen to the wind and hear the fire burn in winter. I always crave for something—books or someone to talk with or something. I have not been down the street for so long. I do not care about going soon. There is but little attraction there for me. It seems to me I would shed few tears on leaving here for good only on account of our little home and father and mother. I do hope we will get to go someplace soon if Will can go too. Jim Hunt's have a little daughter—so much for them. I think it is time for ours to be coming.

Fifthday, November 24th, 1864
At home, no letter. I think some person might write. I wonder if I have no friends at all. It seems they are few and far between. Perhaps though I will sometime meet my ideal. Oh it looks so dreary and is so cold. The clouds hang in an uncertain attitude. It seems just ready at any time to hail or snow or do something cold. I have a very pleasant fire though and the cold air without does not chill me like it does so many poor creatures. Mrs. D does not get any letters from D____ and every morning comes in for consolation. I have told her all that I can

think of, but still no letter greets her morning after morning. Sometimes she gets so bad she thinks she could just _____ him. I do not know what the result may be if he does not write soon. Oh, dear, I am so tired staying here. If we could only get a away for awhile. It may be wicked but I am so tired I do not know what to do. I am ready to leave anytime for an indefinite period. I do not mean to murmur though for I know I have many things to be thankful for, but I can't help being tired of Martinsville.

Sixthday, November 25th, 1864
At grandfathers all night and day and Lizzie about the same. This morning I heard a knock and going to the door I was met by three old women. All had quilted bonnets on just alike—all sisters. It looked so funny and reminded me of the three old maids in "Left Alone." They seemed like such a happy old women too. Like they had never done anything wrong in their lives. I wonder if we will go to Portsmouth. It seems like we ought to go somewhere for awhile. Just always stay here.

Seventhday, November 26th, 1864
Just like all seventhdays. Nothing to disturb the usual quiet. Only that Clay has come home. Al sent a dispatch to him telling him that charges injurious to his character were being circulated. I hope he will make some of them suffer if he is innocent. It is time that some of the tattle of "Tattle Town" should be traced home to its original source.

Thirdday, November 28th, 1864
Came up home this morning feeling badly having sat up with Aunt Lizzie last night. The poor old woman still suffers on. Her time not come yet. Oh dear, I do not know what all of us will do. There seems no other way than to have a fuss. Grandfather is so bitter against Clay and if we offer any defense of any kind he is just as bitter against us. I hope things will come out all right. Poor old man. I cannot help pitying him. A letter from Lib Janney. Poor Ella is sick.

November, 30th 1864
The last day of November and soon another year will be bursting upon us with its realities all untried. None of us know how many bitter tears it has in store for us. Poor little Ida is sick. How much better she will be off when she is taken away if she does die. Cal and I were talking this morning about her mother. How glad she would be to see her baby in Heaven. It is so mysterious. Will they know each other. Will has serious notions of selling, but I fear it will be impossible for us to get another home soon. We cannot decide where to go or what kind of a place. I want a nice one. Will says it will take more money than we have to buy just such a place as we would like to live. We have exalted ideas about farming. I expect we would have funny experiences to relate should [we] be so fortunate to get a farm. Dear Ella Janney is sick. Consumption they fear. I am so sorry. For

any person I like real well is sure to be situated some way so I never see them hardly and now if Ella dies it will be sadder still. I think sometime it is no use for me to ever try to have any friends. I guess there is no attraction to make any one care for me anyhow.

December 1864

Sixthday, December 17th, 1864
Poor old Aunt Lizzie is gone at last. Alma, Emma and I were there last night. I sat up until two o'clock. Alma then got up but we did not wake Em as Aunt Lizzie had not needed any attention. She was lying on one side with her hand to her face. She looked like one who had cried themselves to sleep. We kept noticing her every little bit. I had not been in bed long when Alma came to the bed saying I believe Aunt Lizzie is dead. I was up in a moment and by her side, but her hand was icy cold. Her suffering ended. We hope and trust for though she did not give us such manifestations of her peace with God, as we would have wished, yet she has ever tried to do good to others so many times and was ever willing to give the "cup of cold water."[244] For her sane moments she had said many things which made us think that as far as she knew she had no fear of death, but last week her mind has been in such a shattered condition that there was nothing to be said on the subject. It was hard for her to die thinking we all treated her so mean and not tell us farewell or say anything to show us she was all ready and willing to go. It would have been so much more comfort. When any dies with whom I have been intimately associated with every unkind word or action reoccures to me with a bitter pang and all the kind words bring pleasant and I wonder why I did not do a little more when it was so easy. I think we should learn by this bitter experience to be kind to everyone and then we will have no regrets, no trouble. But human nature is so frail.

Seventhday, December 18th, 1864
Evening. Sitting by the window. Douglas preached such a good sermon. It seems hard to think of putting anyone down in so dark and dreary so damp and loathsome a place as the grave. Douglas called here this evening. We had a pleasant time. One does not feel afraid of him. We went into Jakes with him. I feel so lonely. Not lonely, but sad. We are not going to Lots until the morning after Christmas.

---

244. Mark 9:41: "For truly I tell you, whoever gives you a cup of water to drink because you bear the name of Christ will by no means lose the reward." Matt. 10:42: "and whoever gives even a cup of cold water to one of these little ones in the name of a disciple—truly I tell you, none of these will lose their reward."

Fifthday, December 22nd, 1864
Will is away. I wish he would hurry. Ever since Aunt Lizzie died I feel so lonely when alone, Everything sounds too lonely and tonight I feel more sad than usual. Perhaps I have more on my mind. Anyhow my heart feels very heavy somehow. I wonder if something is going to happen or if it is the circumstances now existing that produces my feelings. There is another call for men 300,000 more—oh dear. Will must not go and how can he help it is the question now to be answered. Yesterday the paper contained the account of an awful accident on the railroad. I think near Detroit. It was by a collision. Several persons were burned to death and one man in particular was spoken of who was sensible of his terrible fate, but was so situated they could not get him out. It is horrible to think of it. I can not get it out of my mind. Oh, dear, the wind sounds so lonely like some solemn dirge to be in unison with thousands of breaking hearts. When I think of all the misery and despair now over our country it seems a sin almost for others who have nothing to trouble them to enjoy themselves. I think as I grow older I grow all the time sadder. Sometimes I think more for the grief and anguish of others than anything connected with my own life yet—I know time will prove.

Sabbath, December 25th, 1864
Christmas. Phillips preached a sermon lecture it should have been called "The Morals of Revolution." We anticipate starting to Portsmouth in the morning. Mother, Lenna, father, Alma were up today. Mother has not been up for so long. I hope nothing will happen to us tomorrow. My S [sewing] finger is sore and I have not been well for a day or so. I feel so lonesome at night. Oh pshaw! I do not feel like writing one bit so I will quit.

Secondday, December 26th, 1864 [Traveled to Portsmouth, Ohio]
Got up early, flurried to pieces and with the help of Cal and Alma got ready. Went to the depot. Waited a long time. The cars came at last. Several on, so of course I put all I had on and myself into the bargain, then sunk into insignificance in my own estimation anyhow. Got to Portsmouth all safe. Did not like the country between Camden and here. It looks too natural.

Fifthday, December 28th, 1864 [Portsmouth, Ohio]
Am reading *Hannah Thurston* by Taylor.[245] Good, had a long walk this evening just after the streets were lighted [oil or gas street lamps]. Enjoy city life very much so far. One lady called here this afternoon. I liked her appearance so much. Her name is Mary Soul.

---

245. "Bayard Taylor (1825–1878) was one of the most celebrated writers of his time. His travel-writings are still widely read. He was born in Chester County, Pennsylvania. Apprenticed to a printer, he wrote a book of poems, and then visited Europe, and then gained a post as a traveling correspondent for the 'New York Tribune.' This

Sixthday, December 30th, 1864 [Portsmouth, Ohio]
Finished that book, then began, "A Life for a Life Mrs Muloch." Quite a snowstorm if it keeps on snowing. I fear it will be too bad for my walk this evening. Think I will go a little way. Got my hat fixed—like it very well. Can go on the street with more comfort.

January 1865

[No entries for January 1865]

February 1865

Fourthday, February 1st, 1865
When the 1st of next February comes I wonder where we will be. I hope nothing bad will happen where we will be and yet how much lies enshrined in it. Mysteries of the coming summer—how many hearts that are beating now full of life and hope will be still in death or dumb with agony when another summer has passed away. The train was very much detained this morning and did not reach here till noon. I hope there will be a letter. Alma, Lenna and Mother were coming up but I suppose they are not coming. M___ will be decided soon whether Will will volunteer or not. I cannot want him to be drafted and can see no other chance for him to go but oh I hate it so bad. I have a little hope they will not accept him, but am afraid to think much about it. Jake is at present a full member in the Friends church that has been in a thriving condition of late. I hope they will hold out faithful and not prove their minorityness in some little mean trick which I know, without great change in their hearts, some of them are capable of. Oh, I do hope something will turn up to help Will at home.

Fifthday, February 2nd, 1865
Real sick last night. My head hurt me so badly and to tell the truth it never does feel any better after I cry and how could I help but cry when I thought Will would have to volunteer. There seemed to be no escape and in my extreme anxiety I said to Will—

American tale was probably composed while he was Secretary to the Legation at St. Petersburg. 'I do not rest the interest of the book on its slender plot, but on the fidelity with which it represents certain types of characters and phases of society. That in it which most resembles caricature is oftenest the transcript of actual fact . . . which may now and then be heard in almost any country community of the Northern and Western States.'"
Source: *Hannah Thurston: A Story of American Life,* P.G. Putnam, New York, 1863.

"Oh, I do wish thee was conscientious. Can't thee be?" and the answer was, "No, not to be a man." I don't know how about that, but I suppose if he thinks it wrong for him to try to get off by assuming conscientious motives, when not really so, it would be sinful.[246]

Mother, Grandmother, Lenna and Father and grandfather were here for dinner. Lenna is sweet and fat as a little pig. Grandmother, as she was going through the parlor on starting home, looked around the room and said, "Well, sis, I wouldn't leave this house for anything." She cannot think how easy to fix another room much nicer than our little rustic parlor, but indeed to me it has a pleasant look. Such a hard time to clear the T. P. [Trustees of the Poor]. The friends are not willing to assist any—only few—and so it comes pretty hard off of some others.

Sixthday, February 3rd, 1865
A gloomy day alone. I heard my character as given by this ______. A person whom of all others in town should have kept it to herself for how many times have I defended her from the accusations of others. Not that I could not see the defects in her nature, but because she was a neighbor and I knew she had many good traits as qualifying her to be a friend, neighbor at any rate. What I did not like, I held to myself but after having been so near for five years in that time we never had any difficulty but we both of not willing to oblige and I should think she had little case to think me so formal, too proud for anything on the earth. Just wanting to be a lady, never ever getting a potato and among the rest never having invited her to eat and Oh I don't know what all even referring to my borrowing her fine dishes which I confess I did sometimes borrow some when I had much company, but what of it. How many times did she borrow mine and say she never could have company unless it was for me letting her have things. Oh deceit how I do hate thee with thy kind smile and kind words. Thy outward forms of affection thy inward impulse of hate if there are many sins I am innocent of I am sure deceit must not be one. J is not going to help the poor men out of their difficulty this time. I would be ashamed if I was him, but perhaps the poor fellow has no money. Last fall he was interested, as much as any, but this time is going to claim protection from the "friends" and of course feel safe. I think in consideration of last fall, for his 50 dollars was but a drop in the bucket he might assist a little. I am in the notion, if Will is, of not moving to Springfield—what a mean thing. I can hardly write at all. I have subsisted on crackers since breakfast—that is a few and must go to work and prepare something for supper. I think so much would taste good and it is healthy and so little trouble—so I guess it shall be done.

---

246. "A conscientious objector is one who on the basis of religious or moral principles refuses to bear arms or participate in military service." Source: *The American Heritage Dictionary of the English Language,* 4th ed., Houghton Mifflin Company, 2000.

Seventhday, February 4th, 1865

Such awful news. A dispatch received states that Lees Creek bridge gave away—the one by Ladds. The train fell through—several were buried and mangled, but oh the burning. If pity could do any good they have it from a thousand hearts. Poor things. I cannot get them out of my mind. It seems almost a sin for us to enjoy ourselves when others feel so miserable. The poor friends of the dead and wounded. It is ascertained to a certainty that four men and four women were buried—16 killed altogether. How can we imagine the suffering. The cars tumbled down end ways. All in a heap mashing up all so no one could do anything. One man got on at Greenfleld with 10,000 going to Cincinnati for the purpose of urging the credits of volunteers to free that PT from draft. Poor fellow he is free from it forever. His hand was all that was left. I hope we may never experience such misery. Why must anyone suffer and endure such torture of such unfortunate beings and of body as they themselves. Why cannot we take warning and prepare ourselves for death so if it came unlooked for in whatever form it might, we would not need to think.[247]

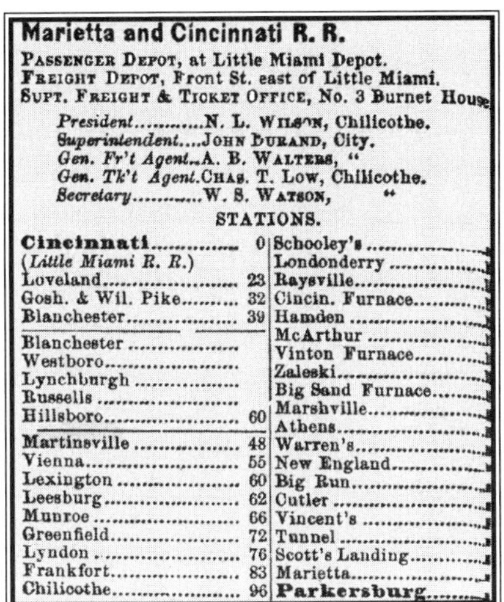

Marietta and Cincinnati R. R.
PASSENGER DEPOT, at Little Miami Depot.
FREIGHT DEPOT, Front St. east of Little Miami.
SUPT. FREIGHT & TICKET OFFICE, No. 3 Burnet House.

President............N. L. WILSON, Chillicothe.
Superintendent....JOHN DURAND, City.
Gen. Fr't Agent..A. B. WALTERS, "
Gen. Tk't Agent.CHAS. T. Low, Chillicothe.
Secretary............W. S. WATSON, "

STATIONS.

Cincinnati	0	Schooley's
(*Little Miami R. R.*)		Londonderry
Loveland	23	Raysville
Gosh. & Wil. Pike	32	Cincin. Furnace
Blanchester	39	Hamden
Blanchester		McArthur
Westboro		Vinton Furnace
Lynchburgh		Zaleski
Russells		Big Sand Furnace
Hillsboro	60	Marshville
		Athens
Martinsville	48	Warren's
Vienna	55	New England
Lexington	60	Big Run
Leesburg	62	Cutler
Munroe	66	Vincent's
Greenfield	72	Tunnel
Lyndon	76	Scott's Landing
Frankfort	83	Marietta
Chilicothe	96	**Parkersburg**

Marietta and Cincinnati
Railroad schedule

---

247. *The Clinton Republican,* Friday, February 10, 1865: "Frightful Railroad Accident on the Marietta and Cincinnati Road—11 Persons Killed and 5 Injured:
"We are indebted to Mr. Duran, President of the Cincinnati & Marietta Railroad for the following full and concise statement of the shocking accident that occured on that road Saturday morning last. Immediately after hearing of the catastrophe he proceeded to the locality where it occurred, and has given his personal attention to the care of the unfortunate victims.

"The Chillicothe Accomodation Train, consisting of a locomotive, tender, one baggage car and two passenger cars bound to Cincinnati, on Saturday morning, was precipitated into Lee's Creek—sixty-five miles from Cincinnati—by the falling of the bridge over that stream. The number of passengers on the train cannot be ascertained with certainty, as the Conductor is among the seriously injured; but from the best information that can be obtained there were eleven persons in the rear car, and five in the forward car.

"The Conductor, Express Messenger, Baggage Master, Telegraph Repairer and newsboy, were in the baggage-car. The cars immediately caught fire, and were rapidly consumed. Of the persons in the rear car but one, St. Burkeley, escaped. In the forward car Mr. McElroy was killed, and the others escaped death, but were all more or less injured. Eight bodies were recovered from the wreck up to last evening, but so much burned that but few of them can be identified. The following is as correct a list as could be made out yesterday, of the killed and wounded: Killed—Mr. And Mrs. C.G.

[The following portion of a poem describes the train wreck as report-
ed in this Journal and in the newspapers. It was written by A. Homer
Betts, a first cousin of Paulena, the son of Christopher Columbus Betts
and Lydia Huff, in a collection of his writing published in 1924 entitled
*"Some Idles" From A Busy Farmer's Life Written For Exercise, Recreation and
Enjoyment Not For Inspection, Criticism or Praise.*]

One minute of time as the train onward rolled,
And this sorrowful tale would have never been told,
That minute once past all efforts were vain
For the bridge giving way 'neath the ponderous train.
Down, downward it went in the valley below,
Where the ice had retarded the waves in their flow,
Yes, downward it went with a terrible fall
With a fate to the many, a warning to all.

Hill, of Rose Hill, Darke county, Ohio; Mrs. Louden, of Chillicothe; Elizabeth Merritt
and brother, of Indianapolis; Lawrence Lenox, Ross county [Ohio]; Thomas McElroy,
Fayette county; Joseph Furrey, East Monroe [Highland Co., Ohio]; Libins Tuttle, telegraph repairer, injured, and since dead.

"Injured—Lieut. A.A. Callahan, Logansport, Indiana, leg broken and head
bruised; Matthew Bonner, Clark county, O., not seriously; St Burkeley, Chillicothe,
slightly; P. Cronan, Clinton county, O., slightly; M. Conway, Clinton co., slightly;
S.E. Mozier, engineer, not seriously; D. Purdee, fireman, slightly; S. Gideon Severs,
conductor, seriously; Henry Bradbury, baggage master, thigh dislocated and other
injuries; E.A. Holyoke, express messenger both ankles broken;—McKibben, newsboy,
spine injured;—Nugent, brakeman, slightly.

"The catastrophe was occasioned by the channel of the stream having become
gorged with ice, the current changed into a new channel, which directed the swollen
stream against the stone pier of the bridge with such force as to undermine its foundation, and cause its fall before the train reached the bridge. The bridge was new,
and very substantial; both spans were framed together, with entire and continuous
chord, and it remained in position after the pier fell until the train reached the center
and caused it to give way. The persons injured are unable yet to be removed to their
homes, are in the families of citizens of Leesburg, and vicinity, and are receiving
every attention which surgical skill and kind nursing can afford. The bodies of Mrs.
Susannah Hill and Mr. McElroy have been identified.—The remaining bodies that
were burned are in the hands of the township officers, and will be kept for identifica-
tion by friends unless it should become necessary to inter them.

An inquest was held by a coroner's jury of citizens, but a verdict has not yet
been "rendered. It will, however undoubtedly accord with facts stated above. It was
impossible for the engineer to have observed the injury done the bridge, as the track
retained its proper position.

The report published on Saturday, that a man heard the pier fall, and failed to
warn "the train, has been ascertained to be false.—(*Cincinnati Gazette* 6th)." Source:
Monday, February 6, 1865, *Indianapolis Daily Gazette,* from microfilm at the Indianapolis State Library. gives a similar account: "Distressing Railroad Accident."

Sabbath, February 5th, 1865
The sun shone out bright this morning, but there were many hearts its rays could not penetrate. So think the wall of misery which had arisen since last it roared. No dispatches have been received today from Leesburg. Those who went up say it was the most awful sight they ever could see. Will came home from Wilmington last night, strong in the notion of buying property there if we can sell ours. It will be funny. I hope it will all come out right about it.

Fifthday, February 9th, 1865
Been indoors all week. Not seeing anyone only as someone called and callers have been few and far between times. When I become settled down to this way of living I like it very well. I wonder if we will move to Wilmington. I would like to be finding out about it. All that will make me give up to go would be on Will's account. He thinks if he can buy that property he can make a speculation by selling it if we want to sell. A letter came for Will from Jeff , Will has gone to W_____ on business for the T.P. [Trustee of the Poor]. It is no fun to be trustees. Willie is staying here for a night or two. He has been a good boy. I do hope he will be a good man. I think with much care he will be but his disposition is one that can be much inspired by bad influences. He is inclined to be a little selfish, but I hope the dear little fellow will come out all right. Elva got a letter form Alma. She is coming home on Seventhday next week.

Sixthday, February 10th, 1865
A bright morning—cold. A letter from Fanny. She says the house seemed so silent and lonesome when we came away and that we did not stay near long enough. Will did not come home till so late last night. I was so uneasy about him and thought perhaps some one had killed or robbed them for $14.00. It would not have been a small amount to some people. It was such a lonely road from Brittains. He came at last and right glad I was to hear his well known foot steps. Such a fire in Philadelphia. So many burned. It is awful many bad things happened daily almost.

Seventhday, February 11th, 1865
Went to Birdsalls. Had a real pleasant time as we always do there. Like to go so much. Stayed at fathers all night. It seems good to be at home to stay all night. Sometime Alma is coming home on the morning train on Sixthday provided nothing prevents.

Sabbath, February 12th, 1865
At grandfather's today. Had a good dinner. Could hardly keep G R [Grandmother] from killing a chicken, but at last prevailed on her not to. It seems strange to not see Aunt Lizzie there. I am in the meanest mood and am not in the mood for writing so I am going to quit and go to bed.

Thirdday, February 14th, 1865
Meeting this afternoon. David H. Bennet. I wonder if we are going to sell. It seems not soon if anyone intends buying. I wish they would hurry and not wait till everything looks so pretty here that we will hate to leave it. I wish we were able to buy a place in Xenia. I think we could like to live there. We do not like to go to Wilmington as well as we would someplace and if we go will not go with the intentions of staying there always.

Sixthday, February 17th, 1865
As I have not felt in the mood for writing and nothing having occurred to put me in the mood I have skipped a day or two. Alma came running in this morning just as natural as life. We were not looking for her much till tomorrow, but were the more glad to see her. Had several new styles. It seems they go on style a good deal there. Alma spent the day at Mollie Barners. She has five little children—boys. She wants me to visit her.

Seventhday, February 25th, 1865
In truth my journal has been a kind of a drag for some time and has been sadly neglected. Alma went back Secondday evening. She and grandmother were here for dinner. Poor little Hannah Hulford was burned to death last week. She caught fire when her mother was away. I dread to hear of any one suffering so. A letter from Lizzie last week. Not answered yet. Am not in the mood.

Success seems to elude our armies on every hand. Charleston the starting point of the rebellion evacuated, Wilmington captured and all points seem ready to give way, but I fear something will come to mar our good fortune. A letter from Jesse Coffin. School out this afternoon.

Thirdday, February 28th, 1865
Been out calling a little this evening. Was at Browns to see the baby. It is sweet. I almost envy them but in time perhaps we will be equally as fortunate. They have not named it yet. Mrs. D still continues to give me hail when away from me but is very kind when I see her. Mrs. D is making my dress. It is some consolation to think I have never considered her a friend and that it does not hurt me. She will miss me more than I will her.

March 1865

Fourthday, March 1st, 1865
Grandmother got her arm put out of place. Insisted the other morning she is helpless. I went down and stayed all day with her. We looked over poor old Aunt Lizzie's drawers. It makes one feel sad to see her dresses and things folded away. I can not make a selection of hers as we are all to have one, but must make up my mind. Poor old grandmother. It is a sad for us to go away. In her view she

cannot see the need of any change and thinks we might be unsatisfied to remain here. I will hate to leave the home, friends and our dear little home, but think we will go and that it is better for us. Feel the need, though it may be worse for us. We can only try.

Fifthday, March 2nd, 1865
Nothing new. No letter from anyone. Felt so badly this morning but recovered almost. Called at 6 to see how they did. It was accidental for I had not thought of it two minutes before, but she was friendly as usual. Just as if she was the same as always and I suppose I must go to keep up appearances and not get her mad. Not sold our house yet—no prospects.

Sixthday, March 3rd, 1865
Such a dark day. Been real sick. Suffered so much in the morning, but could sleep in the afternoon. Closed the shutters. Had a good fire and it was pleasant.

Fourthday, March 8th, 1865
Ella N called this morning. Cloudy day again. Will got a *Times* this evening. No news of importance. Have not sold yet. Think some of going west to live instead of Springfield. Do not know as we can be satisfied to stay there. The week almost gone already. Only a funny thing or a bad thing happened this evening. Mrs. D thinks Smiths have her chicken. She went down to see about it. Took Will along to identify it. They got into a fight. Will had to part them. I _______ him so much about it. I think it is the last time he will interfere in a woman's fight. Mary here today.

Fifthday, March 9th, 1865
March like winter morning. This evening and very chilly. My clothes are getting a good wetting but perhaps it will make them look whiter and was not in the mood for washing this morning. I have been very idle this afternoon. Not doing much good for myself or anyone else. Will thinks of going to Illinois after harvest providing nothing prevents him. I begin to fear the draft again, but hope there will not be any. I think I could not bear for Will to go to war. Steve's time will be out in August.

Sixthday March 10th, 1865
Very cold this morning and frozen. Going down home. I wonder if I will not miss the going down home when we are so far away and it will be impossible to go. I think we will go for Will is more determined than ever to sell and I have almost given up to go to Illinois though I once thought I never would go there. We will hate to leave our little home and the trees we have planted and even when they become so beautiful. The white pine tree is my favorite. It looks so stately and the wind has such a sighing among its branches sounding far off—the passing into a murmur.

Seventhday, March 11th, 1865
So windy can hardly step out with comfort and then so cold. Beck was at father's yesterday. Grandmother is not much better. It makes me feel bad to think how grandfather has always been about everything. His nature is so hard some way, not that he intends being cruel. A letter from Alma wants a new dress and some money. School out in two weeks. Our seeds came today.

Sabbath, March 12th, 1865
The wind is high and loud today sounding like a tempest shaking everything within its reach. I have been sitting in here all day not going to church. Will went. Carter preached. I feel so idle—not inclined to read and Will is always so interested in a paper. It is of no use to say anything to him. Have not finished all the books I brought home. Somehow have not been much inclined that way for a time.

Secondday, March 20th, 1865
A week not recorded yet. There has nothing unusual transpired during that time to any of us. I made Lizzie a visit at last. I received a letter from her and she insisted so strongly for me to visit her. I went up Sixthday night. Lizzie was not in waiting as I expected, but soon came. Had a pleasant time part of the time and the other part not so good. Liked Borems very much. Came home this morning on the train. Found Will in readiness to receive me with a band box—not baby—wish so. Have been feeling badly all day, but went to church. Monthly meeting a good meeting. Sarah M [Sarah M. Elliott Hiatt, wife of Asher Hiatt] returned from her town. Came on the morning train. Left this afternoon. Poor woman, her cup of sorrow seems full, the sad news has reached her of the death of her mother, sister and sister in law. A sad blow and hard to bear as her trials seem many. So many persons came here—in many ways unjustly I think. God only knows but she has many warm friends. All my sympathy is for her. It has been a lovely day. Spring indeed. I hear Will's well-known footsteps returning from up town.

Thirdday, March 21st, 1865
The clouds seem clearing away from me this morning and I wonder why I can ever do anything or feel in anyway indifferent to all the goodness of God, the manifestations of which I see more plainly the older I grow. However it may be or how it may look to some I do not forget even when my actions are otherwise that I have very much to be thankful for.

God knows the working of all our hearts so not even the most secret thing can be hidden from his watchful eye, therefore he can judge us wisely and in all truth and not as others. Sometimes my heart is full of something irrepressible,—a longing for something higher and nobler and I feel so insignificant, a mere nothing, doing no particular good for anyone or myself; it makes me very unhappy indeed and it seems no one knows me. How should they when I do not know myself. They attribute wrong motive when I mean well and although I do many things I ought not to do, I think I am not quite so bad as people sometimes think and they could tell nothing if questioned.

My living here has done me good, in others much harm. It has made me too sensitive, caused me to be more selfish and suspicious. On the other hand perhaps it has caused me to cherish a deep appreciation when I do meet with anyone I can trust and enjoy myself with and has made me long for higher things. I received a letter yesterday from cousin C and their photographs. Sweet little Jennie, I would be so glad to see her.

Fourthday, March 22nd, 1865
Went down home. The wind blowing a perfect hurricane. Mother is not well. Am so uneasy about her. Alma and her friend are coming home tomorrow—vacation is for two weeks. We had much rather Alma would come alone, but will do the best we can. I wish I could feel perfectly reconciled to going to Illinois. Will is so anxious to go and all that keeps me from being so in the parting from mother and the rest. Perhaps I might like it after awhile.

Fifthday, March 23rd, 1865
So windy I will be glad when there comes a calm. Tomorrow is the day Alma is coming. I am going to have them here for dinner. Nothing would do Will, but I must write a letter to Mary Bond in reference to buying our home, but I do not think they will buy it. I want Matt L to come and see me once more before we go away. We have had so much pleasure in the days gone by and it will be much like old times to be with her again if she has not changed. I am going to send her a letter. I would love to visit the cliffs before we are so far away and cannot go. Mother nature and mine are different in some respects. I could not be content to live nestled down among the hills, shut out from the world and all society, but perhaps she can be happier than I for discontent being unhappiness. At home—baked bread. Jo came down this evening—stayed a long time. She is going out to Illinois and Aunt Lizzy is coming tomorrow evening or I expect she will. The wind is blowing a perfect tempest and so cold. I wish spring would come. I wrote a letter to Matt this morning. I hope she will answer it.

Sixthday, March 24th, 1865
Alma and Dicy came this evening. Remained here for dinner. Had roast chicken—good. A letter from Fanny. In the afternoon all went away leaving me alone, but sitting in the parlor by a pleasant fire reading *Dora Dean*. The afternoon passed rapidly away. At last the train came. Lizzie too. The wind has been so cold. I think we will certainly appreciate spring when it does come.

Seventhday, March 25th, 1865
A letter from Lib Janney. Good news. She says contrary to all expectations Ella is some better. I am in hopes it will continue. Matt thinks perhaps she will come

and visit us before long. Steve is a prisoner—was captured in South Carolina. Bad news, but no one can feel as Lyd. I pity her. The particulars have not been heard.[248] Cold again and I am suffering with sore lips. A cold in my head. I wish I could feel right well for a while and see how it would seem. I have felt so much indisposed of late. I wonder if we are going to sell. I will hate leaving worse when everything is green and beautiful around our home.

Secondday, March 26th, 1865

Lizzie and I went down home this afternoon. Stayed at home all day yesterday not even going to church I not being well enough. I am so much in hope Ella Janney will get well. It will be such a joyful thing for them. Lenna is so sweet. I hope she will not learn any badness like other little W girls do. Lizzie is reading *Dora Dean.* She likes it so well. Sallie Hadley was buried today. I pity them so much. How hard it is to bear the life of a mother.

Singer Sewing Machine advertisement from 1862 Cincinnati City Directory

---

248. Memorandum from Prisoner of War Records, no. 299, National Archives. Stephen Janney was Captured at Wadesboro, N.C. March 5, 1865, confined at Salisbury, N.C., for 3 weeks and confined at Richmond, Virginia [Libby Prison], March 29, 1865. From Stephen Janney's biographical sketch from the *History of Crawford County, Kansas* published in 1905: "Mr. Janney was also in General Benjamin Harrison's brigade for a time when the latter had command of the First Brigade, Third Division, of the Twentieth Corps. Among the battles of this campaign in which he participated were Resaca, Kenesaw Mountain, New Hope Church, Burnt Hickory, Peach Tree Creek. From Atlanta they went on the famous march to the sea, thence up through the Carolinas, and toward the end of the campaign, while leading a foraging squad, Mr. Janney was captured by the Rebels, being first lieutenant at that time. He was taken prisoner on March 5, 1865, was held three weeks at Salisbury, North Carolina, then taken to Richmond and kept in Libby prison a week and a day before the fall of that city was sent down the James river to be paroled at Aiken's Landing, Virginia. He reported at Camp Parole, [Annapolis] Maryland on April 2, 1865. On April 8, 1865, he was given leave of absence for 30 days. [He went home to Martinsville and en route, he learned of Lee's surrender and of Lincoln's assassination soon after.] He returned to his company from leave, and was assigned to duty at Camp Parole, Maryland, May 15, 1865." Camp Parole was in Annapolis.

Thirdday, March 28th, 1865
Lizzie and I are going down home after while. If that man brings the sewing machine we are going to learn to sew. No letter from Matt yet. I wonder if she will ever write. Down home the machine came. Learned some—so many there for dinner. I have not much love for farm life taking all things in consideration.

Fourthday, March 29th, 1865
We went to see Sattie Oren. I pity her so much. Her heart is broken. Poor Charlie dead and Butler near the grave. Poor little fellow. It is hard to see him running and playing around and yet know that he must die soon.[249] I hope I may never know such anguish as hers, but we know not what in the future will come. Lizzie and I had so much fun coming home in the rain walking too, but we got along fine and made the best of it. I sounded very funny to Lizzie when in the midst of a little shower I proposed to her that we had better get from the umbrella and run. She said it would come harder. Some new shoes. Did not know which pair to take. Brought three pairs home and as a matter of course too, the most expensive.

Fifthday, March 30th, 1865
A stormy day. Glad we did not defer our visit until today. I had a nap this forenoon. Felt so badly after our long walk.

Sixthday March 31st, 1865
Lizzie and I have been singing nearly all day. I think it would help my voice to sing more. Lizzie went away this evening. Cal and I went to the train. Butter seems numbered with the things that have been. "No butter" is getting to be as common as "no letter." Dicy is such an innocent girl, We like her so well.

April 1865

Secondday, April 3rd, 1865
Glorious news—if are true. Richmond is ours. A battle has been raging for four days. Grant captured 12,000 prisoners and a number of cannon. Richmond was evacuated. Petersburg also.[250] I hope the worst is over now and that peace will soon come. Gold has fallen $165. Cal and I went down home this afternoon. J

---

249. Butler Oren had swallowed an eight-penny nail in January 1865. See August 15, 1865, entry.

250. *"'I think it is absolutely necessary that we should abandon our position tonight.'* [Telegram from Robert E. Lee, in Petersburg, to Jefferson Davis, in Richmond, April 2, 1865.] At approximately 7 A.M. on Sunday, April 2, 1865, Ulysses S. Grant's army attacked Confederate lines at Petersburg, Virginia. By mid-afternoon, Confederate troops had begun to evacuate the town. The Union victory ensured the fall of Richmond, the

came down and we rode up in the buggy. What great times people are having tonight over the news. But those whose friends have fallen will feel little joy. When hearts are too sad to enter into the manifestations of joy, however thankful they may feel that the victory is ours. I wish Will would hurry.

> Dear Jennie
> I only write to inform you of a remarkable dream I have had. I dreamed a letter came from you. It was full of photographs. The principle ones were "Shem and Ham" and a little brick church in Washington.
>
> Yours Truly
> Lena Janney

Thirdday, April 4th, 1865

Dark this morning and promising rain. Will went to Wilmington, expects to have a tooth drawn. I have my morning work done and am going to iron—tired of being Bridget. I have had Margaret to do my washing for a time. It seems much pleasanter than to do it myself—slopping around till my back is almost broken and my clothes wet from top to bottom. Perhaps Jeff and Lizzie will come on the train this morning. Oh dear, must go and iron but feel more like going to bed and taking a snooze.

Fourthday, April 5th, 1865

A letter from Lizzie this morning. She is coming tomorrow. Alma and Dicy are coming this evening as Dicy intends starting back in the morning. I am out of the notion of selling this summer, but prefer remaining till autumn. It maybe that I will prefer remaining longer the fact of it is that I have not been quite so anxious to leave since Will got in such a great notion of Illinois. It is so far from mother. We are having such splendid news now from our army of the Potomac. I should have been delighted to have been in some safe corner and watched the troops marching into Richmond. It must have been grand. I think it looks some more like peace, but am afraid something will turn up to prevent it.

Fifthday, April 6th, 1865

Lizzie came this morning Such a dark dreary time as it is and the wind blows so hard. Alma is looking so badly now with a cold.

---

capital of the Confederacy, located just 25 miles north of Petersburg. President Jefferson Davis received word of the events in Petersburg while attending services at St. Paul's Church in Richmond. He abandoned the capital late that night on a train bound for Danville, Virginia.

"Richmond, meanwhile, burned, as fires set by fleeing Confederates and looters raged out of control. Davis was eventually captured by Union soldiers, but not until May 10, 1865." Source: http://memory.loc.gov/ammem/today/apr02.html.

Sixthday, April 7th, 1865 [Paulena and Will's sixth wedding anniversary]
Lizzie and I went to school this afternoon. Spent most of the time upstairs in Mr. Nixons room. M[ilton] having gone to fill a place in the bank in Wilmington. We liked Mr _____ H so much. Think he will be a good teacher. Had a few calls.

The news came this afternoon that Lee and his army were captured, but we do not know as it is time, but not withstanding the doubt there are many manifestations of joy.

Went to see Fanny B[rown]. The room was shaded so we could hardly see. I suppose the light hurt baby's eyes so I cannot say how it does look—sweet though of course.

Seventhday, April 8th, 1865
Remained down home this morning. Alma has gone. Lee's army is captured. The particulars will come out soon. Such a dark day, but I should not think of such a thing for how much have I to be thankful for. Will safe at home. Steve, none of us know where, and Lyd in such suspense and thousands of others the same. I received a letter from M [Matt]. It was not much like the letters I used to get in the olden time, not so full of tender epithets and gentle reminding of other days—never breathing a wish that our friendship might prove much improved—not so good as those I used to get, but I know of no cause only her weakness and maybe she thinks I have changed. Perhaps when we meet again it will all be right. Poor girl. Her health is so poor. She cannot half appreciate life. Her aches and pains seem to be her entertainment. I would just give anything if we could have as pleasant times together as we used to, but it has been long since we met and the time seems far distant yet for us to meet.

> **[April 9, 1965]**
> "Appomattox Court House, Virginia was site of the surrender on April 9, 1865, of the Army of Northern Virginia commanded by Confederate Gen. Robert E. Lee to the Army of the Potomac led by Union Gen. Ulysses S. Grant, ending the Civil War. The surrender took place at the home of farmer Wilmer McLean, one week after the fall of Richmond and Petersburg. The terms were quite generous. The Confederate soldiers were to surrender their weapons; they were given a day's rations and told they could return to their homes and keep any horses or mules they owned. Officers were allowed to keep their side arms."

Thirdday, April 11th, 1865
Just pouring down rain. I am sitting in the little old kitchen by the stove too lazy to make a fire in the sitting room. It seems the news is too good to be true and it makes me feel real bad to think we can not be some place where we can have the privilege of witnessing the gladness it causes those loyal hearts. Sixthday is to be a great day in remembrance of Ft. Sumter. I wish we could be some place. It just seems like a prison here.

Fourthday, April 12th, 1865
Been real busy all morning sweeping. Such a cold windy morning. Oh dear, I want to be in Cincinnati on Sixthday. There is going to be such a great time. The beginning of the programme is to be the ringing of all the bells in the city and then there is to be speaking. I would be so glad to be there, but instead I presume I will be at home where all things will go along in the old trudging routine. I may have the pleasure of hearing a dinner bell, now although we would not do anything but look. I would listen if we were in the midst of a jubilee, yet we could say mentally "that is my mind" with quite as much truth as ever any of our old friends say it at quarter meeting. My journal I think is getting pretty near filled up with nonsense.

Fifthday, April 13th, 1865
Went down home this morning. Been real busy sewing. Think it fun to sew on the machine. Feel so sorry because we can not go to the city tomorrow—such a great time and we will miss it all. Am sitting here all alone waiting for Will who has gone up town to hear something. I hope he will hear some gossip if nothing more.

Sixthday, April 14th, 1865
The 14th of April such a bright joyous morning. All nature so beautiful. There is much more gladness over the land this morning than has been for so long and yet how much sadness—sorrow if when the war is ended all the boys could come marching home. How much more joy, but the absent ones who are sleeping on the many battlefields of the South can never come again. Oh, if we could only be in the city today. I felt like this is a prison almost sometimes and yet there are many pleasant things connected with a home in the country. My nature though is not adapted to country life, however delightful may be many features of it. I must become more settled in my reading. Great demonstrations. Cannon fired, bonfires lighted and the principle buildings illuminated. Speeches, songs—so much of Martinsville. One or two accidents. The one I know the most about is of a girl or woman wearing a blue dress falling down and hurting herself as she was coming from the depot. The boardwalk being out of repair.

Seventhday, April 15th, 1865
One extreme has followed another in quick succession. The nation is shrouded in gloom. Lincoln is dead or dying, killed by the hand of an assassin in Fords Theater in Washington last night. Seward hardly wounded, his son also. Booth, the actor, suspected of the murder of the president.[251] Great excitement and

---

251. *Clinton Republican*, Wilmington, Clinton County, Ohio, April 14, 1865: "The President and Mrs. Lincoln were listening to the performance of 'Our American Cousin,' occupying a box in the second tier. At the close of the third act, a person entered the box occupied by the President, and shot Mr. Lincoln in the head, the shot entering the

indignation. Copperheads will suffer now in killing the president. They have injured all traitors. No one will prove as lenient as Lincoln. We fear Johnson will not prove all true as he is in the habit of drinking and makes us fearful. Oh, if it had not happened. The nation now will feel as much sorrow as it had full of joy.

[The following portion of a poem describes the assassination of Abraham Lincoln as reported in this Journal and in the newspapers. It was written by A. Homer Betts, a first cousin of Paulena, the son of Christopher Columbus Betts and Lydia Huff, in a collection of his writing published in 1924 entitled *"Some Idles" From A Busy Farmer's Life Written for Exercise, Recreation and Enjoyment Not for Inspection, Criticism or Praise*]

But that moment the ruffian had entered the door,
Sent forth his dread missive, his labor was o'er.
Then leaped to the stage in his fiendish delight
And flourished his dagger, then vanished from sight.

We mourn as a nation that moment of time
That filled us with sorrow and stamped us with crime.
Then is there a man on the face of the earth
That ever can tell what a minute is worth?

[On April 15, 1865, Walt Whitman wrote his now famous tribute to Lincoln, "O Captain! My Captain!" Walt Whitman was another of Paulena's New England cousins.]

O Captain! my Captain! our fearful trip is done,
The ship has weather'd every race, the prize we sought is won,
The port is near, the bells I hear, the people all exulting,
While follow eyes the steady keel, the vessel grim and daring
But O heart! heart! heart!

---

back part of his head and coming out above the temple. The assassin then jumped from the box upon the stage and ran across to the other side, exhibiting a dagger in his hand, flourishing it in a tragical manner, and shouting the same words repeated by the desperado at Mr. Seward's house [the motto of the state of Virginia is *sic semper tyrannis*, Latin for "perish all tyrants"] adding to it, 'The South is avenged,' and then escaped from the back entrance to the stage, but in his passing dropped his spur and his hat. Mr. Lincoln fell forward in his seat, and Mrs. Lincoln fainted."

O the bleeding drops of red,
Where on the deck my Captain lies,
Fallen cold and dead.

O Captain! my Captain! rise up and hear the bells;
Rise up—for you the flag is flung—for you the bugle trills,
For you bouquets and ribbon'd wreaths—for you the shores
a-crowding,
For you they call, the swaying mass, their eager faces turning;
Here Captain! dear father!
This arm beneath your head!
It is some dream that on the deck,
You've fallen cold and dead.

My Captain does not answer, his lips are pale and still,
My father does not feel my arm, he has no pulse nor will,
The ship is anchor'd safe and sound, its voyage closed and done,
From fearful trip the victor ship comes in with object won;
Exult O shores, and ring O bells!
But I with mournful tread,
Walk the deck my Captain lies,
Fallen cold and dead.

Walt Whitman (1819–1892), from *Leaves of Grass,*
http://www.poets.org/poems/poems.cfm?prmID=1733.

Sabbath, April 16th, 1865[252]

Steve came home last night. Did not see him till this morning as I was down home. Will was at the train. Great excitement in Cincinnati yesterday. Persons who expressed joy at the news were shot down without argument—bad times coming. It seems all does not look so bright as few days ago. Phillips preached a sermon for the occasion. Thompson preaches in Blanchester two weeks. We would like to go but it is quarterly meeting.

Secondday, April 17th, 1865

Nothing much is thought of, but the murder of Lincoln. His murderer, Booth, not yet arrested. Seward not dead, but better. His son some better. Mrs. Lincoln's grief is said to be agonizing. Mobile has surrendered with many prisoners. If it were not for the gloom caused by the death of Lincoln everything would be much brighter, but I fear there are too many traitors in the north to let peace come.

---

252. "Sermon Upon the Assassination of Abraham Lincoln, Br. Rev. M.P. Gaddis, Pastor Sixth Street, M.P. Church, Delivered in Pike's Opera House, April 16, 1865." Source: *Cincinnati Daily Times,* Monday, April 18, http://www.mnu.edu/~fjohnson/313/gaddis/licsermon.html.

Thirdday, April 18th, 1865
A dark morning, but has cleared off bright and fair this afternoon. Mrs. Lincoln is said to be dangerously ill no doubt caused by her great grief. How great has been the change within a week. I can hardly sit down and work alone. It seems so still. Clay went to the city and got a carpet. Mother sent forty dollars. It cost $55. We have not seen it yet. Will's strawberry plants came today only four and he sent for six so they have cheated him out of a dollar. I want to go to Cincinnati so badly think I must go soon.

Fourthday, April 19th, 1865
A day of mourning over the whole nation in every village town and city where the loyal hearts reside. Businesses have been suspended. Meetings in honor of the President have been attended. P[hillips] preaches a good sermon. More were in attendance than I had expected would be. It was very solemn as if it had been a funeral in reality in our midst. Letters from Alma this morning. She likes Mrs. Thompson so well. I think we will go to Hillsboro sometime this summer. I wish we could have the privilege of attending church in Cincinnati now. I know if there is anyone who would enjoy living in a place where one could have the opportunity to going to hear lectures, sermons and all such things improving to the mind and affording present enjoyment it is I. I try to be thankful for being so pleasantly situated in many respects but there is ever a void in my heart, a lack of something felt which cannot be filled.

I do not like to feel so insignificant, of so little worth. Any soul longs for something higher than this plodding of everyday life. Not that I mean its many duties, for until we can appreciate them we are not capable of higher things, but then there are so many petty things—so many mean things each day causing us to forget our good resolutions—so many things contrary to right. I feel like saying sometimes, "Save me from my friends and I will take care of my enemies" for more reason than one ever since old enough to think of such things. I have been surrounded by those who view this poorly, causing a kind [of] bitter feeling. They perhaps not always intentionally attributing many motive to my actions and I perhaps thinking hard of them, but aside from all this the trouble has been we have not been congenial enough. I have thought often maybe I am to blame a great deal. I will try and conform more to the ways of those around me but using a slang, "It was no go!" Anything by force is hard. There was a longing I could not stifle and thus it is, "Oh dear what a simple little goose I am," but I can't help it. Perhaps sometime everything will be different. I will be ashamed of this maybe when I read it over.

Fifthday, April 20th, 1865
Been working real hard all day helping mother about the carpet. Got it done and down. A letter from Cornelia Wood.[253] She writes good letters. I took a little

253. Cornelia "Nellie" Wood was the younger sister of Fannie Wood, who had married Lot Janney. Nellie was born in 1841.

walk up the street alone. Just at dark. Everything seemed so lonesome. Willie Betts[254] came home this afternoon evening. He has been away for some time.

Seventhday, April 22nd, 1865

Lyd, Steve and Jo here all day. No news of importance. Booth not captured yet. The train having the remains of the President left W[ashington, D.C.] yesterday morning. Cincinnati will be missed in the journey. It will be quite a disappointment as he will be taken to the principle cities in the states.[255]

Sabbath, April 23rd, 1865

Cold almost freezing Went to church—heard two sermons and a prayer. Had a cold. Dinner—went to sleep on the floor before the fire. Will slept the most though. I think Jo and Mother came a little bit.

[April 27, 1865—Sinking of the Sultana]

On March 10, 1863, Paulena and Will were returning to their home in Martinsville from attending the wedding of Will's brother, Lot Janney and Fanny Wood at Rainbow, on the Muskingum River, just north of Marietta, Ohio. They boarded the *Sultana* at Marietta on the way to Cincinnati and soon were settled in their stateroom. The *Sultana* was 660 tons, 260 x 42 x 7 with four tubular boilers and twenty-four 5″ flues. Its paddlewheels were 34 feet in diameter working 11 foot buckets. It was launched January 3, 1863, built for Captain Pres Lodwick, well known on the Upper Mississippi for his *Northern Belle* and *Northern Light*. It was designed for the New Orleans cotton trade but due to the uncertainties of war, she was entered in the trade between Cincinnati and Wheeling

---

254. William "Willie" Clyde Betts was the son of Uncle William S. and Anna Hadley Betts. The 1876 Atlas of Jasper County, Missouri, gives the following biographical information: "In September, 1864, then yet under twenty years of age, he went to Memphis, Tennessee, and engaged in business. At the time of Forrest's raids through Tennessee, and his attacks on Memphis, in 1864, Mr. Betts entered the First Tennessee Regiment, State Troops, and served six or eight months as a private of Co. C. In August, 1865, he went to Cincinnati, and engaged with his brothers [Aaron and James P.] in the wholesale hat and cap business."

255. "The route Lincoln's train took him roughly mirrored his journey from Springfield to Washington, District of Columbia, with the addition of a stop in Chicago. It traveled through 8 states and took nearly two weeks. The body was placed on prominent display in city halls and other public arenas." It traveled from Washington District of Columbia, to Baltimore; Harrisburg; Philadelphia; New York City; Albany, New York; Syracuse, New York; Buffalo, New York; Erie, Pennsylvania; Cleveland, Ohio; Columbus, Ohio, on April 28–29, the nearest point to Martinsville; on to Richmond, Indiana, April 30; Indianapolis, Indiana; to Michigan City, Indiana; Chicago, Illinois, on May 1, 1965, Bloomington and Springfield, Illinois, on May 2–3, 1965. Source: Source: http://www.eliillinois.org/30108_87/funeraltrain/.

on February 12th which she continued until mid-March 1863.[256] Will and Paulena traveled on it just before it was under U.S. military auspices.

"The U.S.S. *Sultana* was built in Cincinnati, Ohio, in 1863. The steamer's run was from Saint Louis to New Orleans. In the year 1865 on April 27, the U.S.S. *Sultana* left Memphis on the Mississippi River headed for the United States' worse river disaster. Days earlier on April 23, Captain Mason had brought the *Sultana* into Vicksburg with a boiler leak for repairs. There, Union soldiers released from Andersonville prison in Georgia and Castle Morgan prison in Alabama had been released to return home as the war ended. General Dana, the Union Commander for the Department of the Mississippi, had ordered that the soon-to-be paroled prisoners at Camp Fisk be sent northward from Vicksburg on private steamers. The Captain, who was part owner of the *Sultana,* was paid $5 a head for enlisted men and $10 for Officers, so he did not complain when the steamer was overloaded with passengers returning home. The *Sultana* was certified to carry 376 passengers but was loaded with over 2000 [other reports say 2,400] sick, hungry, and war torn soldiers anxious to return home. The steamer left Vicksburg and reached Memphis on the evening of April 26, 1865. Soldiers, while in port, heard the news of President Lincoln being shot. From Memphis they stopped at a coaling station on the Arkansas side of the river and then headed for Cairo, Illinois. [They were seven miles above Memphis when they reached the crossing at Paddy's Hen and Chickens.] About 2 A.M. that evening one of the boilers exploded and the blast toppled the smokestack cutting the deck in two. Many were killed instantly by the fire and steam, the rest began going over the side. Many of the wounded were put over the side to avoid the fire, only to drown. Many died jumping overboard and landing on others in the water. The steamer was in midstream and the shore was about four miles away. Approximated 800 survivors were found, leaving the death count at 1547 according to the U.S. Customs count. No one is sure of the exact count of soldiers on board. The tragedy was made worse because most of the country was not aware of it due to the news of Lincoln's assassination." Source: "The U.S.S. *Sultana* Disaster," http://goodies.freeservers.com/sultana.html.

Of further interest in this narrative is the fact that John H. Janney[257] was one of the casualties of the *Sultana* disaster.

---

256. Way's Packet Directory, 1848–1994, comp. Frederick Way Jr., Ohio University Press, 1994.

257. John Hayden Janney was the third son of Joseph and Sarah Ellis Janney. He enlisted when he was twenty years old and was living in Delaware County, Indiana. Muncie is the county seat for Delaware County. It is reported by survivors that in the

The Memorandum from Prisoner of War Records 272, National Archives: "John H. Janney, Private, No. of Reg. 36, Indiana, Infantry, Company B. Confined at Andersonville, Georgia. Admitted to the Hospital at Andersonville, Georgia, Sept 3, 1864, treated for Vul. Sclof. [He had been wounded at the battle of Atlanta and was in Andersonville Prison for eight months]. He was paroled at Vicksburg, Mississippi on or about April 21, 1863. He perished on board the *Sultana*, April 27, 1865—killed by the explosion of Steamer, *Sultana*, in Mississippi River. This Information was Obtained from the Rolls furnished by Surgeon General." [The remains of the Sultana today lie several feet deep in a soybean field now lying on the Arkansas side of the river.

May 8th, 1865
The weeks have been wet, cold and chilly now and then a few bright days coming to remind us how pleasant is spring. Not answered Fanny's, Lizzie's nor Cornelia's letters—Alma came home at quarterly meeting and is still here. We think she ought not to go back till better. Booth gone to his account days ago. He was shot by a soldier, Corbert, as they were trying to capture him in Maryland. He was secreted in a barn.

Fourthday, May 10th, 1865
Rain. When it rains on Secondday it is sure to rain for days. It has been pouring down nearly all day. Lyd and Steve went to the city yesterday. I presume L [Lydia White Janney] will go on to Annapolis. There is to be a grand review of Sherman's army at Washington. It will be splendid. The remains of the President everywhere was received with great honor and by immense crowds. Am sorry we could not witness some of the demonstrations. The news of his assassination was the cause of deep feelings of regret and indignation in Europe. I must not forget to chronicle our visits last week. Two invitations in succession and two of the best dinner places.

Fifthday, May 11th, 1865
Rain rain pattering down all day just as if it had not rained for a month but all for the best I suppose. Over at Cals as a matter of course. It has been so long since I saw Matt. Seven years ago in May since we had such great times over at the cliffs and meadows, laughing talking, sleeping and reading—passing many hours away very foolishly no doubt, but we were very thoughtless then.

---

explosion, John was caught under heavy boards. He asked his friend John Maynard [Ninth Indiana Cavalry; he also perished] to get an axe and cut him loose but drowned before John returned with the axe. He died at the age of twenty-four years and seventeen days. John H. Janney was a first cousin once removed to Will Janney. It is presumed his body went down with the ship. Source: *The Janney Family* by Uva and Geneva Janney of Delaware County, Indiana.

Sixthday, May 12th, 1865
At grandmothers. Mother, Lenna, Alma and I had such a good dinner. Grandma hurried around and got a chicken and had good corn bread, and sweet potatoes. Believe her whole life she will just do anything for us. It seemed like we ought to see Aunt Lizzie in her old place at the table. I could not help thinking about it. Grandmother, in the midst of the dinner got uneasy about her little turkey's—went out stayed and stayed. We finished our dinner without her and afterward on going to the door we saw her driving the old hen and her little turkeys along. We laughed but grandmother was in real earnest thinking she had lots of trouble with them. I wonder if I will ever have chickens or turkeys to care for. Mother says Alma and I can attend to them after they are cooked which I think is the case. I sent a letter to Fanny this morning.

Sabbath, May 14th, 1865
Company. Rebecca M____, Cal and her children. Cal has such a pretty bonnet. Looks so much nicer than she used to before going to the city. Lizzie is a little sweet thing yet. Went over to see Berry's baby. Better. They do not seem to like Mrs. D___much. I think they had better not have talked so much about her until they were right sure they would not like her and that she would not tell.

Secondday, May 15th, 1865
A bright morning once more and it is pleasant to meet the sunshine and listen to the humming bees and singing birds. *Clarions* news.—Jeff [Jeff Davis] and his tribe captured in Georgia. Jeff was trying to get away by putting on his wife's dress but the boots were visible, so the ruse failed and he will be kept secured.[258] I reckon for disposal hereafter. It seems too good to be true. I want to see *Harpers Weekly* pretty soon. Alma is going to be here in the morning I expect. Tompson is coming here to preach next Sabbath.

[This was the final date of discharge for Lt. Stephen Janney.]

Fourthday, May 17th, 1865
Been so busy. Washed—Hoed the peas, and the flower beds, ironed some—scrubbed the floor and then let me see what else did I do—nothing of much importance. I was so lazy this morning and could hardly bear to wash. Was discouraged the first piece or two. I almost got in the notion of putting it off

---

258. "[Jefferson] Davis was captured by Union soldiers near Irwinville, Georgia, in early May 1865 and was indicted for treason against the United States government on 24 May. Whether by accident or design, Davis was wearing his wife's dark gray raglan (a short-sleeved cloak) and black shawl when he was captured. Although one of Davis's own aides was persuaded his chief had indeed disguised himself as a woman to abet his escape." Source: http://memory.loc.gov/cgi bin/query/r?ammem/mcc:@field(DO CID+@lit(mcc/005.

for Margaret thinking that she would not stop after having commenced. I persevered and am real glad of it. I think I will wash next week. I would not mind working if I was a man, but we have so many disadvantages to undergo. For example, afraid of getting sunburned, and getting our hands rough and black, and our clothes dirty and our hoops are forever catching on something when we get in a big hurry. Some kinds of work are pleasant. Alma stayed here last night. She almost missed the train this morning. I hope we will get to go to Hillsboro [seat of Highland County, Ohio] and see her.

Fifthday, May 18th, 1865
I just love summer. Everything is so bright and it is more pleasant to do anything. I am getting to be quite a gardener. This evening I thought I had found some of our lost cucumber seeds that we had planted some time ago. To be sure they were in a new place, but how easy it was for them to wash any place in the last flood. I was very careful to put the dirt around them good. Sprinkled ashes around them, but to come to the point "Halicamassions" coming along. Soon remembered that I had been setting out radishes. Radishes indeed. Just as if I could not tell them from cucumbers. Had a nap. While I slumbered somebody's old chickens came and scratched my flower seed all to flinders. I told Mrs. D_____ they had to be killed. I just would not stand for it. It was too bad etc. She consoled me by telling me I should have set the box up. I replied that was too bad to have to put everything up to keep other people's chickens from scratching them. She said she would tie her old hen, but I know she will not. What a foolish journal for children and grandchildren to read when their old grandma is gray headed and wearing caps and glasses—gold ones of course.

Sixthday, May 19th, 1865
Quite a shower this morning. I was so sleepy could hardly bear to get up, but at last determined to not put it off any longer for who would grind the coffee, make the bread if I did not do it. I had corn cakes, fried eggs and coffee—good. Wonder if Martinsville was not where Robinson Crusoe lived so many years. It must have been at a period when children were scarce of course. They were absent there. Now they are in abundance, screaming, squalling, fighting and scratching. I think two mean children never were born than Alma Dennis and Newt Moore. I told Mrs D this morning what I thought and do not know if I was responsible for a sound thrashing he got soon after. Unless I can raise our boys better I never want anyone to say. I think if a mother cannot train them who can.

Seventhday, May 20th, 1865
All my work done. Did not dread it today. A letter from Alma. She is as well as when she went back. Mrs. T _____ has had them to change their room for a larger one. She is so kind to them. Alma and Dicy changed their room. Not all of them did. The sun is shining bright enough this afternoon as it had not hidden among

the clouds for so long and the rain pouring in torrents. I would enjoy a ramble among the cliffs where Matt and I used to have such happy times. I want to see the dear girl so badly. I wonder how we will meet in the sometime we have been talking about so much. I think I have changed some in the six years. I hope a great deal for such a little flirt as I was. Everything is so still I can almost "hear the silence"—that is, indoors—nothing but the old clock ticking off the hours all so still, but when I stop from writing, the songs of little birds and the chirping of insects and the wind stirring among the leaves tell me that with out my darkened room there are plenty of joyous creatures, life and beauty.

Sabbath, May 21st, 1865
At church this morning. Mr. T preached a splendid sermon. He called this evening. I like him. He is very pleasant, polite and agreeable. Complimented Alma and Liz. Gave us a pressing invitation to go to Hillsboro. Mr. T___ is going to preach again tonight. I could listen to him everyday almost. I wish I could feel like I was hearing something all the time instead of feeling like I was of no benefit to anyone or to myself I think the trouble is I ought to have a baby or two to claim my attention and I could put my time in better.

Secondday, May 22nd, 1865
Monthly meeting. Went but did not remain all meeting. No person "gave in" at the meeting. Cal and I went out calling after tea. Seems Brown's baby is a great baby. Will and I are going up to Carmans tonight to play dominoes. Have not written to Lizzie yet.

Fourthday, May 24th, 1865[259]
Down home. Company there. Maggie Hunt, Cal, Beck M baby is so sweet. I almost envied her. Just as fat as butter and as white as a lily and so good. Brought Alma's *Repositorys* home to read.

Fifthday, May 25th, 1865
Rain, rain patting against the window pane and making music in the room. A day of

Stephen Janney, First Lieutenant, Co. G, Volunteer Infantry, Union Army. Photo taken in Washington, D.C.

---

259. The Grand Review, May 24, 1864, in Washington, District of Columbia. First Lieutenant Stephen Janney was in the review and had his photograph taken in his uniform while there.

darkness. The sun never once succeeding in showing its light. Have been reading the *Repository*.[260] It is so good.

Sixthday, May 26th, 1865
Storming this morning like everything and all night in the bargain. Slept with the window up most of the night. Felt sure would be sick as consequences of it. Who should come this evening but Alma. It was Clay's work as we were not looking for her. Going back Secondday. The thirteen wonders of the world: 1) The Tower of Babel. 2) The Pyramids of Egypt. 3) The Lighthouse of Alexandria. 4) The walls and hanging gardens of Babylon. 5) The Temple of Diana at Athens. 6) The Statue of Olympian Jupiter. 7) The Manslevian of Artensia. 8) The Colossus of Rhodes. 9) Solomon's Temple. 10) The Catacombs in Rome. 11) The Cretan Labyrinth. 12) The Great Wall of China. 13) The Leaning Tower at Pisa.

Seventhday, May 27th, 1865
Been down home all day. Intended making my chesterfield but "there is many a slip twixt the cup and the lip"[261] and when just beginning the important part of cutting it out found I lacked just a yard—so goodby to my sack for a while. Have been feeling most miserable bad all day. Hardly able to sit up, but walked up home. Alma came with me and as we came got frightened at a cow. Al did at first and it was hard work convincing her that the poor old cow did not move its horns back and forth at will. They were such a funny shape I got a little frightened too, but marched past her bravely while Al climbed over the fence. Had a few strawberries for tea. Such a few.

Sabbath, May 28th, 1865
Whenever I was awake long enough last night I could not keep moaning with pain for indeed I felt so badly my poor arms, my poor back and all the rest afflicted from my eyes to my feet. Will got breakfast after I had taken a bath and eaten a boiled egg. I recovered enough to go to church. Will told me of a discovery he had made in our meadow. The water forms a little branch. The surface of the water is covered with a scum not unlike oil. I walked down to see it. We took

---

260. In 1864, the paper's offices were burned during the Confederate siege of Chambersburg, but the Repository quickly began republishing from the lecture room of the Chambersburg Presbyterian Church. Source: *Repository Transcript,* http://www.iath.virginia.edu/vcdh/xml_docs/valley_news/html/about/repos.html.

261. *The New Dictionary of Cultural Literacy,* 3rd ed., Hazlett, 2002. The English proverb means, "Between the time we decide to do something and the time we do it, things often go wrong." Also found in 1588: "Though men determine, the gods do dispose; and oft times many things fall out between the cup and the lip." Sources: Greene, *Perimedes the Blacksmith* (1588), http://www.bartleby.com/100/pages/page190.html and http://www.bartleby.com/59/3/theresmanyas.html.

a spoon along and skimmed off some and put it in a bottle. It would be so good if it would prove oil, but we have no expectations on the subject.

Secondday, May 30th, 1865
Alma off again this morning for F. C. H. _____ F. C. Lenna and mother came up this afternoon. I am always glad to hear Lenna's little feet patting on the ground and see her fat little face at the door for I am always sure Mother is not far off. Willie's Julia has a little cold. He is always so certain to tell of every addition to the animal family that he was cautioned this time in particular not to say anything about Julia's cold. To Clay he kept from it as long as he could but this morning at breakfast T___ had to come. He said, "Well Alma, the colt is about gone up." They asked him if it was dead. No, he said. It was not dead, but it was so pretty near dead. Little fellow, I only hope he will be good. I can see very plainly that the association of his daily life will not bring out the best part of his nature. So many bad boys to go with. We went down to Hocketts this evening. Saw Gulielma's photograph and Elwood's, it makes me feel sad thinking of the old happy times we had at school. Their earnest faces looked so natural. I could hardly realize that they grew pale in death years ago and were buried from our sight. I think I can never forget the night when Elma kissed us for the last time when she was dying. If it is true that friends will know each other in heaven how many glorious meetings there will be.

Thirdday, May 31st, 1865
Dear old May passing away and has only given us a few of her smiles but many of her tears. What has become of the May. It used to be prized for its beauty, its balmy days, its flowers and singing birds. The birds we have now we cannot appreciate their songs so well. Other things are not in unison everyday. The clouds come and the air is cool. A fire would not be uncomfortable much of the time and this is May. I think it would be a good idea to strike spring out of the catalogue and class it all winter. I was up bright and early this morning but not withstanding the fire was nearly gone. I think the reason of that was it was made too soon. I am just as mad as I can be at the old rooster. Could almost stand by and see it hung or beheaded or something. There is no such thing as giving it a hint. Common people have sense to see when they are not wanted but this old rooster seems impregnable to any persuasive power no matter how much force is used, brickbats and other things involved.

June 1865

Fifthday, June 1st, 1865
Got up early this morning. Done a big washing. Scrubbed the floor. Went down home and was busy all the rest of the day sewing. Came up home, gathered strawberries for supper. Helped Will water the sweet potato plants. Almo Domiss and Newt Moore had been in the garden helping themselves to

strawberries. If either of those boys ever do much good in the world it will surprise me. Never saw a boy so totally depraved as Almo Domiss. I will be glad when they move. I think A will get the finishing touch in the city.

Sixthday, June 2nd, 1865
A beautiful morning. A letter from Alma yesterday. Has had her teeth extracted. Four hurt her so badly. I am glad they are out. Fanny Fern's real name is Mrs. Parton, wife of James Parton, the biographical writer.[262] James Gordon Bennett is nearly 70 years old.

Seventhday, June 5th, 1865 [Date confusion—it was actually June 3rd]
Up at six. Got my work all done long before noon. Made good cherrie fire for dinner from our trees. Had a nap since dinner. Evening Beck and Lyd called. Went to Browns and played dominoes. Fanny and I beat at last. They pretended it was all wrong and it was to their gallantry in letting us do so. The baby is sweet. The little dear got so hungry and cried and Fanny was ashamed to let it nurse before Will and so it was more awake when we left near 11 o'clock. Had strawberries for tea.

Sabbath, June 4th, 1865
June the loveliest month. So bright and warm and full of beauty. I could hardly bear to get up this morning. Felt so sleepy. I could have slept much longer. Oh, I wish somebody would come that we would be glad to see. It seems such a long time since we have had company that afforded us real pleasure. Just seems half the time like we are nearly out of the world although home is pleasant and I enjoy it, but there are times when my nature craves something beyond its boundaries—a little more insight into the great world around us. So much to learn and so little chance to learn. If I read there is no one to talk with about things and so I forget a great many things I want to remember.

Secondday, June 5th, 1865
Went to the lecture this afternoon. It was principally to the children but I think many older ones might learn something also if they would all follow his advice in regards to raising children they would have more pleasure with them. It came up to my ideas exactly but perhaps I might not be able to do just that way and

---

262. Sarah Willis Parton (1811–1872) wrote under the pseudonym of Fanny Fern. "As an exception to the 'damned mob of scribbling women,' Hawthorne praised Fanny Fern's Ruth Hall for breaking the mold of the 19th century women displaying 'female delicacy.' Fern satirizes men's domination of women and children and exposes their economic and social victimization. Fern was also criticized for praising Whitman's *Leaves of Grass*.

"Her Primary Works were *Fern Leaves from Fanny's Portfolio*, 1853; *Ruth Hall*, 1855; *Rose Clark*, 1856; *Folly As It Flies*, 1859."

not have the perseverance. He is going to lecture tonight again. Called at Becks and Jims. The baby May[263] is so sweet. Maybe ours will be as sweet. I wonder if it will? Night—the lecture would not suit the old foggies, I am sure, for he came down heavily on calomel the poisons that are administered in fevers and all diseases. Getting very biter sometimes in his denunciation of such.

My Portfolio

June 1865

Have been upstairs looking over some of my old papers. My portfolio came first. Its leaves are torn and it is getting old and worn, but yet it is not so old but what it can still hold some treasures of the olden times. One dear old letter of M [Matt Ladd Pushee] beginning her usual style.

"I am so tired of rain and storm clouds coming between me and the sun's hopeful light, but it was ever thus I never laid my deeply cherished plans but they were suddenly lashed to earth. As the letter continued in a way that reminded me vividly of the old happy times. One place she said, "And Thee don't know how sick I have been or thee would have thought of me often seriously too, but today I am propped up in the arm chair drawn beside the table to write to thee, but with a trembling hand. A cheek, a little paler than usual on which but now glistens a tear, a tribute to a fond memory."

Dear M. I expect a tear has often glistened there since and her cheek been many times paler. I wonder often if she is changed and if when we meet there will be anything to remind us of how dear we were to each other, or will we be just like other people never saying a word of the old times and part just as formal. Oh, no (think not for my own pain). I think I will always love her.

But there were many other things in my portfolio about this and that and the other. Some of our school whispering, for as we were not allowed to whisper, we used strategies all about this person and that one party and all such things that interested school girls. One might have the pleasure of a sleigh ride and did not go. I thought the next morning "it was so much pleasanter to be at home by a good fire than freezing." Jo did hope no one would take her anymore. Just as if she could not refuse and so many things as we had to talk about. What bad girls we were, but what happy times we had. It is very sad to reflect on the many changes that have taken place in the intervening years and although we might say that to many of us "The winters have drifted like flakes of snow and the summers like lands between, yet many things have transpired to throw shadows over our spirits. Some of these we mingle with are dead, others are changed. We meet, but where is that feeling of friendship, that intimacy of soul that bound us together when school

---

263. Abigail "May" Hunt was born on January 7, 1864. She is thought to be the daughter of James Hunt and Margaret "Maggie" C. Atkinson.

girls. The clasp of the hand is not the same, the kiss is not the same. It comes more from the lips, less from the heart. There is something between that is deepened by each succeeding year. Why is it natural that friends should grow cold and love grow old. Is [it] because the cases of troubles and frivolities become so mingled with our lives that we find no time to think of old friends. I believe our lives would be purer and happier if we would cherish our friendship more. Have fewer and truer.

My Garden

What a wonderful garden it is. I called it that because I have to worked in it as "Halicarnassis." [Halicarnassus][264] has proportioned the left hand side of the garden for special care and benefit. The onions are to be hoed first although almost it discouraged me—so many weeds. Some of them came up with some of the onions. I thought seriously of pulling them up and taking the weeds out and planting them back again. The peas needed attention. I began my operations just before a storm of rain. I must have looked a fright an old skirt on, hoops sticking out, dress pinned up, old slab bonnet without the slab—wrong side out and in such a hurry. They were all fixed now and I have planted peas in three different places. Since I had a handful what was to be done with them was the next question. I could not tell. At last the happy idea struck me that I could dig a little hole and put them all in a bunch which I did accordingly and they remain there to this day unless they have been exhumed by "him." That is Halicarnassis was quite disappointed at one time about some cucumbers that weren't cucumbers, but I guess it is not worthwhile to mention.

Secondday, June 12th, 1865
June passing away rapidly and have not written in my journal for nearly a week. Nothing has happened though more than usual. I was sick a day or so and did not feel like writing. No letter from Fanny—wonder why this is a beautiful morning, but I failed to see it's earliest beauty having slept quite late got breakfast at last, rang the bell twice. The last time pretty fast. Will says he can just tell a woman's temper by the way she rings the bell. I dreamed last night that I had really succeeded in killing the old rooster and just as I had him killed Liz Vance came along and told her they might have him to eat if they wanted him. She was rather inclined to be offended as she said the rooster belonged to them. But I defended myself very well. Who knows but it will all seem so.

---

264. In 377 B.C., the city of Halicarnassus was the capital of a small kingdom along the Mediterranean coast of Asia Minor.

I received a letter from Lizzie last Fifthday. I think I have acted real mean in not writing to her sooner as she had written three times to me. My linen sack came very near being spoiled by some unaccountable mishap of which I have so many. I got grease on it in several places, not because I am such a sloven, I know. I suppose it was off the machine. A lady called the other morning with some pictures for sale. I would have taken her for a perfect lady had I met her at home and as it was I did not feel like being suspicious of her for I do not think it dishonorable for a lady to earn her living. She was real intelligent. She had read and could talk about so many things. She remained some time. I am going to have onions for dinner. They're sweet fragrance is already filling the house from attic to all over the house.

Thirdday, June 13th, 1865
At home it is raining this morning but all the better for my rosebush which I moved yesterday I hope it will live for Will spoke rather doubtful about it since I moved it. The 79th[265] passed down this morning on their way to Camp Dennison. I don't know what to get for dinner. We live on such a light diet here that I never have much left for another meal. Went to writing school this evening. Am almost sorry I started for I fear I will not learn much.

Sixthday, June 16th, 1865
Rained hard. Went to writing school. Think I am improving some. A letter from Fanny. She has a new bonnet and shawl. I wish they would come and make us a visit. Before I write I want to get a new bonnet so I can have the pleasure of describing it to her. My rosebush is fading day by day. It's leaves are all withering and soon there will not be one to tell the story of its death. I know it had blossomed and faded and was budding again when a restless hand tore it from its home in the cozy little flower bed and transplanted it in a place not at all congenial. So much for not minding Will.

Seventhday, June 17th, 1865
A bright pleasant morning up early and have my work almost done. It is pleasant in our bedroom of a mornings. I hope I will get a letter from Lib today. I think it was time she was writing—we are so anxious to hear from Ella. I am afraid she is not living. We hear that James Hadley has the consumption—so sorry.

---

265. The Seventy-ninth Regiment Infantry was organized at Camp Dennison, Ohio, in August 1862. Stephen Janney served in Company C, enlisted by I. B. Allen, and was designated a first sergeant n the day of enlistment, later to be promoted to first lieutenant.

Been very lazy all day. Not doing very much but writing. It is very warm today. My rising did not come today[266] so I will have biscuits to bake. Had two lessons in writing. This evening and I got very tired writing. This is a specimen of my penmanship after taking lessons of L M McPherson that I did not know what to do. I do hope I will be in the first class but fear not. I have nothing new to write about. I will be glad when I can hear some good news of some kind.

Fifthday, June 22nd, 1865
A bright morning. Not any too warm and a pleasant breeze. Have been quite busy all morning. Attended to my flowers. Made a pair of sleeves. Been writing some and have some peas gathered for dinner. A very few though. Our neighbors on the west are preparing to move to Cincinnati. I have gathered raspberries for dinner. Wish we had some good cream for them.

July 1865

[July 1st, 1865—Paulena's twenty-fifth birthday]

Fourth of July 1865 [She traveled from Hillsboro, Ohio]
Am home and with the expectation of remaining here for one very good reason—no way to go any place. I had a good time at Hillsboro—heard good music and saw so many paintings and had a good time generally. Alma and I took tea at Mollie Barriers on Sixthday evening. Lib Haynes is dead.[267] She died on Fourthday night. It is a terrible shock to her family. We called there a little bit. We came home on Seventhday morning. Mother was up home and had a good dinner for us. I was so fortunate as to get in the first class as relates to the writing school, but anyone reading this would think I did not deserve it. But then I am not doing my best. Have a miserable pen. Ella cannot last long. I am so sorry we cannot go and see her, dear girl. If I could only see her once more. It is a warm, but pleasant day. There is a pleasant breeze stirring and in the woods it must be delightful.

---

266. She meant that the yeast in the bread mix did not rise and she had neither enough time nor enough yeast to make another batch; therefore, she would have to make biscuits, which would be quicker, because they do not require rising. The purpose of any leavener is to produce the gas that makes bread rise. Yeast does this by feeding on the sugars in flour and expelling carbon dioxide in the process.

267. Elizabeth West Haynes was the daughter of James West and Elizabeth Leggett. She was the sister of George Washington West, whose death is noted in these journals in the January 9, 1863, entry. Lib West was married to Asa Haynes in 1849.

Sixthday, July 7th, 1865
Very warm—ironed this morning. Part of my ironing. Still like summer—though
it makes the sweat pour. No not quit either. I prefer it to winter. The conspirators
in the assassination trail are to be hung—four of them. Sentenced among them
is Miss Suratt.[268] It seems hard to hang a woman but when they are guilty as
men why not meet the same fate. I would not care about seeing the executing of
the unfortunates. I hope no one that is anything to us will ever do anything to
merit such a punishment. It must be terrible for their friends. Went over to see
Aunt Lyd [Aunt Lydia Betts, wife of Christopher Betts, uncle to Paulena] and
Cal is better. The parrot would not talk much. I would like so well to have one
to play with. No letter from Lizzie or Matt.

Seventhday, July 8th, 1865
Sick this morning, but am not sorry. Baked such nice cake for tomorrow out of
sugar. Carmans have got home from Illinois. Liked their visit very much. Spent
the 4th in the city. Saw Dennses. They like living there very well.

Sabbath, July 9th, 1865
It is cloudy and warm. Wish it would rain. Going down home after the meeting.
Feel very much indisposed. I really think too bad but the truth is I have not been
to our Sabbath school this summer. The same old routine which has been com-
mon for years—if home and friends were not here it would be very dead to me.
I would not live here.

Thirdday, July 11th, 1865
Stayed down home till afternoon. Felt so badly and it rained. Mother is not well
at all. I feel so uneasy about her—if there is any person meets trouble farther
than I do they must be unhappy one indeed. I hear our neighbors pounding
away. Moons, but I cannot imagine what they can be pounding for I do not
think they have very much. Jim H and Beck have moved into Mrs. Carmans
house—am going to send for the *Phrenology Journal*[269] or think so.

---

268. Mary E. (Jenkins) Surratt (1817–1865) was "the accused No. 8: Mother of
John H. Surratt, Jr.; Arrested for Conspiring to Kill President LINCOLN; She was
alleged to have provided BOOTH and HEROLD Carbines, a Rope and Whiskey on Friday, April 14, 1865, at about 11:00 A.M. at her Surrattville Tavern." Source: "The Lincoln
Conspirators," Paul R. Surratt Jr., http://freepages.genealogy.rootsweb.com/~prsjr/
0mary/mary 00.htm.

269. "Phrenology had particular appeal to pre–Civil War Americans. Discovered by a physician from Vienna named Franz Gall and imported into the United States
in 1832, phrenology exerted an extraordinary impact on popular culture. One American
phrenology journal claimed a circulation of 50,000, and many employers required prospective employees to have their heads read. One of the earliest examples of a 'science
of human behavior,' phrenology held that distinct portions of the brain were devoted to

Fourthday, July 12th, 1865

Very pleasant. All alone as usual. Am sorry we did not get to bid them goodby. I sent the money for the *Phrenological Journal*. Hope it will come soon. Our neighbors seem very busy. I wonder if we will ever move. Well old journal, you are almost finished and what will I do with you. Put you away up stairs with the rest of your companions. l am sorry this one like all my journals is not written with something more interesting, but perhaps I will do better in the future.

Fifthday, July 13th, 1865

Went down home to make a sack for Lib Vance. A silk one. A letter from Mary Fisher [Mary Jane Janney Fisher was a sister to William]—Poor Josy[270] is dead—killed in battle near Selma, Alabama. It must be a hard trial for her—her only boy and not even the satisfaction of knowing where his grave is. How many such bereavements. The papers just overflow with accounts of accidents by various means. Oh dear, I must get dinner. Wish I did not have to. It is so much pleasanter sitting here by the window than cooking over the fire. When we get rich, I am not going to work only when I want to—maybe not—do hope hope something right would turn up to keep Will from going to Illinois. I do not want to go and think I never will. Any place in Ohio, but not Illinois.

---

distinct impulses such as combativeness, amativeness (sexual love), and adhesiveness (comradely affection)—and that people's mental attributes could be read through their facial features. Phrenology claimed to offer young men and women a way to evaluate potential spouses and employers a tool for judging potential employees." Source: "The Birth of American Culture," *Digital History,* http://www.digitalhistory.uh.edu/database/article_display.cfm?HHID=648.

270. Joseph "Josey" Bailey was the son of David and Mary Jane (Janney) Bailey, born in 1845. After David died in 1858, Mary Jane married James Fisher in 1860. Mary Jane Janney was an older sister of William Janney, husband of Paulena.

"Battle of Selma, 'Southern Heartland Falls,' April 2, 1865. By the spring of 1865, the territory of the Confederacy consisted only of isolated areas, and its commercial and industrial capabilities were in shambles. Only 100,000 ragged, poorly equipped men were left in the Southern armies. The North, more powerful than ever, had 1,000,000 men in the field, and were attacking on every front. Selma, Ala., was one of only a few manufacturing and munition centers remaining in the South, and on March 22, Union Gen. James H. Wilson started from his base in southern Tennessee to conquer it. He set out with two divisions of cavalry, 13,500 veteran troops armed with Spencer carbines, three batteries of horse artillery, and a supply train of 250 wagons. His only obstacle would be the son of a poverty-stricken backwoods blacksmith, Confederate Gen. Nathan Bedford Forrest.

"The Confederacy's shortage of men and supplies, however, had taken a frightening toll on Forrest's command. He had fewer than 8,000 men, many of whom were new recruits and impressed citizens—old men and young boys who had previously escaped the Confederate draft. While setting up a defensive position in his front, Forrest sent his veteran troops to attack the rear of Wilson's column. Wilson,

Sixthday, July 14th, 1865
At home sitting by the window it is pleasant this morning, but rather too cool to suit me for I like warm weather much better. Can not think of anything to get for dinner but peas and potatoes which we have been feasting on for two weeks. I do not know what will fill the place of the peas when they are gone. How dull it is here—perhaps if I were to go to the gate and stand half an hour I might probably see a man or two—and maybe an old wagon or so. I know I look awful this morning so slovenly—but am too lazy to dress—oh dear, I don't like such cold weather in such hot weather.

Seventhday, July 15th, 1865
Morning—dark cloudy and cool. Think we will go to Moons this evening. Our relations think we do not visit them much and I suppose we might as well strike out indeed. I have not been to Moons since last winter. I wish Gibsons had moved here instead of Moons.

Sabbath, July 16th, 1865
It is raining this morning. We had to be brought home. It is so much pleasanter riding than walking. I hope we will be able to own a buggy and horse sometime again. I am in trouble about going west. Do not want to go. Will thinks it best. Wish something would turn up to keep Will in Ohio. I feel so bad, stupid and sick this morning. Ed Coffin came last night and looks very natural. I wish we could sell if we are going to and get fixed up some place. Not Illinois though. Can't bear to think of going there. Believe I will go to bed and put a wet rag on my head. I never want to live in a little town if we move from here.

Fourthday, July 18th, 1865
Wet, wet this morning and the rain still pattering down. Sounding the melancholy music as the drops fall among the leaves. A dreary kind of moaning. The wind has also an accompaniment for the rain. I think anyone in trouble must feel more miserable such days as this when everything without seems in such harmony. If it were not for hope, how many hearts would sink, but how very true it is that we live in the future. Even the happiness of the present is mostly

---

however, intercepted a dispatch containing Forrest's plans and used the information to isolate and delay the raiding party. Then, on April 1, Wilson attacked and overran Forrest's inexperienced troops in the Battle of Ebenezer Church. Forrest fell back 18 miles to Selma, where he put all his available men—3,000 untried militiamen, spread very thinly in the 3.5 miles of earthworks surrounding the city.

"At 5:00 pm on April 2, Wilson attacked and quickly drove the Confederates out of the works. By the end of the day, Wilson had captured 2,700 Confederate prisoners and the city of Selma, with only 46 killed and 300 wounded among his own men. Forrest and a few of his companions escaped. Forrest, at last, had been beaten." Source: *Civil War, Bluegrass Battles and Campaigns,* http://civilwar.bluegrass.net/battles campaigns/1865/650402a.html.

made up with that delightful discontent which hopes better things for the future. I read a letter from Jennie Willett. She insists on me making her a visit soon and makes many promises what she will do. I want to go real bad. Ed Coffin was here all night and is here now.

Sabbath, July 23rd, 1865

Came up this morning from down home having been there ever since Fourthday night. Will was helping them harvest. Have had a pleasant time. Things are coming to a crisis yesterday—Letters were received from Clay. One for father and mother asking for Alma. I hope if they do marry it will all be right and prove contrary to the predictions of friends and relations. We dread the fuss there will be about it though. I must write to Jennie Willett soon and tell her if I am going. Alma is here. We are going to church.

Secondday, July 24th, 1865

Oh gracious, what a time I have had washing. I was so warm and tired. Several times I came very near giving out entirely I was so wet. Mother often says and used to, "now thee is wet to the hide I know"—it was never more true for it was really so this time—my dress, apron and all and besides that the perspiration just rolled off. Such a washing. Four sheets and after that the floor was scrubbed and all things done. My bread real nice. I put some more clothes on and Will's slippers and took it easy in the rocking chair in the parlor.

Sabbath, July 30th, 1865

Stayed at home from church on account of having no bonnet to wear. Mine being at the milliners. Alma and Aaron Hunt were here for dinner. After dinner I thought I had better sweep the parlor before dressing. Commenced accordingly and had not finished when a rap at the door startled me. I flung the broom in the bedroom—a nice place truly—and opened the door to half a dozen callers all strangers, except one—Jake Vance. The ladies were not introduced—were quite green—wanted boarding. I said I had thought if I took boarders I would prefer gentlemen. They were not so much trouble and put the finishing touches by saying one reason is they are not about the house so much as girls. One with a hat on turned in red and green ribbon with a plain linen gingham dress with a hem about three inches and a half inch wide hemmed on the machine defended herself by saying that is quite different from where I boarded. Everybody wanted to board her. One place stayed eight weeks. Only paid three dollars which quite astounded me as I had not meant to be personal in my remarks. They departed at last to my great relief and edification.

Secondday, July 31st, 1865

Went home. Mother not there. It never seems like home unless she is fixing my blue checked gingham dress. Do hope mother will keep it for Elva. There was quite an accident here the other morning. An engine exploded injuring several men. One they think will die. The engineer—they sent for his wife—he was taken home on the evening train. The A.P. [*American Phrenologist*] came all right. Have received two numbers. Like it very well.

August 1865

Thirdday, August 1st, 1865
A rain this evening. Uncle Jacob and Matt came this evening. We were not looking for them quite so soon My bonnet will be done this week. I hope I will like it, but I must expect to pay a big price for it, but it will be cheaper than a new one.

Fourthday, August 2nd, 1865
I made a mistake by neglecting to write daily for a time. Our company came on the 2nd instead of the 1st. Nothing to write about.

Fifthday, Night August 3rd, 1865
Went to Steves and with them tonight. Went up to hear a man lecture. A traveler. Has been all over Europe—Pretty near anyhow. Has been to China twice. Told a great many interesting things. Was at the city of Rome, in the Holy Land, at the garden of Gethsemaine, on the Mt. of Olives. Oh, I wish I had seen or could see all he has. I would not begrudge thousands of dollars. Tomorrow night he is going to give a more extensive description of his travels etc., etc.

Sixthday, August 4th, 1865
Been lazy all morning had to get breakfast—had the unfortunate to break a can full of black berries—buried can and all in the garden along with the rest of the articles. A letter from Jennie W____. Another photo of Luies, the baby. She is looking for me to visit her soon which I intend doing nothing preventing. Will went with them to Moons. We are going to Vienna this evening.

Seventhday, August 5th, 1865
Went to Vienna this evening for our bonnets.

Thirdday, August 15th, 1865
We are in trouble about Alma. Clay has come home. They are in the notion of marrying and then they will go to Alabama. We hate very much for her to go so far away fearing accidents and all manner of evil. And then we know it will be a bad affair with grandfather and dread it so much. Hope it will all come out right—that none of the predictions made will come true. Poor little Butler Oren[271] was buried this afternoon. Sat [Sarah "Sattie" (Allen) Oren] looked very

271. Charles Butler Oren died on August 14, 1865, He is buried in the I.O.O.F. Cemetery, Martinsville. The death notice in the *Clinton Republican* reads: "Died on

sad. Her trouble of last year is still fresh in her memory. I have not written to Jennie Willett yet, do not know what to tell her about going up there.

Fourthday, August 16th, 1865
The students from the Institute went to father's grove this afternoon to practice elocution and gymnastics. We went down as spectators. Feel very bad. I do wish I could get better and not be half sick so much. I know Sattie feels sad. I feel so sorry for her. We are taking the *Phrenological Journal,* and the *Agriculturist* and a city paper. If I were to start to borrow anything I might possibly find a *Clinton Republican,* but as I can read that down home I would not be benefited. I wish I could have the chance of reading more.

Fifthday, August 17th, 1865
Could not sleep hardly. Cyrus Hunt came this evening. I felt so bad. Could hardly go at all, but managed to get a little supper. Cyrus is a good boy. I feel sorry for him He is lonely, I know. His wife and child both dead. I wish we had a little boy or girl—one we would love it so well.

August 14, 1865, Charlie Butler Oren, youngest son of Capt. Charles & Sarah A. Oren died from swallowing 8 penny nail, last January. He was 20 months old."

Sattie had lost her husband, Charlie, when he was killed the year before on July 28, 1864, in the Battle of Petersburg, Virginia, and had now lost one of her three children. Her remaining son, Horace Mann Oren, and daughter Cata, survived to adulthood.

In 1868 Sattie went to Indianapolis, Indiana, and became preceptress in what was then the City Academy, and in the next year she became a teacher in Shortridge High School, in which position she remained until 1873.

In that year the Indiana Legislature selected her for state librarian. She held the office for two years, but the following Legislature, for political reasons, did not reappoint her. For four years, beginning in 1875, she taught mathematics and was chair of the Botany Department at Purdue University at West Lafayette. In 1879 she married Wesley Haynes, a farmer, near Peru, Indiana, and they lived on a farm in Miami County until the death of Mr. Haynes, in 1897. Then Sattie Oren Haynes moved to Sault Ste. Marie, Michigan, and lived with her daughter, Cata, until her death in 1907. Source: Obituary, *Indianapolis News,* April 25, 1907, p. 58; also *Indiana Biography Series,* vol. 1, p. 215. Microfilm found at the Indiana State Library.

"Horace Mann Oren was Attorney General of the state of Michigan, 1899–1901 and 1901–3. He was born in Oakland, Clinton County, Ohio, Feb. 3, 1859. His father, Captain Charles Oren, having been killed in the siege of Petersburg, himself and mother moved to Indianapolis in 1868. Mr. Oren graduated from the Indianapolis High School in 1877, and from the Michigan University (classical course) in 1881, and law in 1883; came to Sault Ste. Marie in 1882 [p.160]; was editor of the *Soo News* for three years; began the practice of law in 1883; held the office of Circuit Court Commissioner one term; served as Prosecuting Attorney two terms, and was Village Clerk and Attorney for several terms. He was elected on the Republican ticket for Attorney General." Source: Michigan Biographies, pp. 159–160.http://search.ancestry.com/db lhbum7004b/P134.aspx.

Thirdday, August 22nd, 1865
Cannot feel well. Feel so weak and void of energy. Things do not seem half so bright as they used to. It just rained. Poured this morning and everything seems just like autumn, so lonely. We are sitting in the kitchen by the fire. Fire in August. I wrote to Jennie Willett yesterday. Hope I will get an answer soon.

Items

Table Rock is on the Canada side at Niagara near the Horse Shoe Falls and the terminus of the carriage road in this direction, June 26th 1860 a part of the Rock fell making a tremendous crash it's size being nearly 200 feet long, 60 feet wide and 100 ft thick. Burning Spring two miles above the Falls on the Canada side. The Whirlpool on the American side, 3 miles below the Falls. Goat Island I mile 1/4 round.

Fourthday, August 23rd, 1865
Cyrus started home this morning. Did not think of him going so soon. Been home. Clay was there. I think it is time they were getting married for they cannot be apart. I hope they will always be so affectionate. Night we have been to hear Edwards recite some poems. He did well and we were much interested. His poems were "Eugene Aram"[272] and "The Golden Bee" which was beautiful and three or four others.

   [August 31, 1865]
   Josephine "Joe" White was married to Milton Morgan in Clinton County, Ohio.

   [Thirdday, September 19, 1865]
   Mary "Alma" Stevens married Henry "Clay" Cowgill. She was a Quaker, and he was from a Methodist family. The Newberry Records show that on December 17, 1866, Mary Alma Cowgill" (formerly Stevens) was condemned for marrying out of unity. After she acknowledged her failure to follow Quaker discipline, she was retained as a member in good standing.

---

272. "Eugene Aram 1704–1759, English philologist, b. Yorkshire. A self-taught linguist, Aram was the first to identify the Celtic languages as related to the other languages of Europe. In 1758, while at work on an Anglo-Celtic lexicon, he was arrested and later hanged for the murder 14 years earlier of his friend Daniel Clark. The story of his crime inspired Thomas Hood's poem *The Dream of Eugene Aram*, and Bulwer-Lytton's novel *Eugene Aram*." Source: *The Columbia Encyclopedia*, 6th ed., Columbia University Press.

September 1865

Seventhday, September 23rd, 1865

Have been so careless about my journal, but have had so much to do that I have not had time for writing. The great wedding came off on Thirdday night 19th. Alma looked sweet in her white tarleton dress vail and flowers. Rev E. McHugh said the ceremony. There were about twenty-four for supper. The old heathanish custom of "belling"[273] was observed on the occasion to our great annoyance. On the next day we went to Cowgill's. They had a nice dinner. Farrens girls were there. I have not been in the mood for writing lately. Have had so much to do. They intend starting on Thirdday for Alabama. We hate to see them start. I am not going to the depot.

October 1865

Thirdday, October 16th, 1865

Night—A long time has elapsed since I wrote in my journal partly neglect and then I have been so busy for a long time. Will and Matt Hunt are in Michigan selling territory—for Patent Churn [a butter churn]. I am at fathers. I want to see Will so badly. Have had two letter from him. The last one from Hillsdale, Michigan. Jim Winn ______ is not expected to live. He has the typhoid fever. Grandmother is here and Grandfather has gone to Indiana. I am so busy serving can hardly take time to read any of late but must make it up after while. Whites and Lyd and Steve have all gone to Illinois.[274] Only one letter from Alma. We are so anxious to hear from them since they have gone to Florence. I want to go to Willetts after quarterly meeting if nothing happens.

Sabbath, October 22nd, 1865

At home all day. Lenna and I. It has been a long day. If Will was only here it would not seem so long. I am so afraid Will will not do very well. I do hope he will.

---

273. *"Shivaree* is the most common American regional form of *charivari,* a French word meaning a noisy mock serenade for newlyweds and probably deriving in turn from a Late Latin word meaning headache. . . . Some regional equivalents are *belling,* used in Pennsylvania, West Virginia, Ohio, Indiana, and Michigan; *horning,* from upstate New York, northern Pennsylvania, and western New England; and *serenade,* a term used chiefly in the South Atlantic states." Source: *American Heritage Dictionary of the English Language,* 4th ed., 2000.

274. An Ash Grove Quarterly Meeting was established in 1865, and an Onarga Quarterly Meeting in 1867. Ash Grove and Onarga are both located in Iroquois County, Illinois. By 1868 Stephen and Lydia were members of the Ash Grove Monthly Meeting. Source: *Iroquois County History,* 1985.

November 1865

[No entries for November 1865]

December 1865

Seventhday, December 16th, 1865
After a long time my journal is resumed. It has been along time since I wrote any. My time has been so occupied. Mother was sick for sometime and I had so much to do. After she got better I went to Washington [Washington Court House, Ohio]. Had a pleasant time. Was gone nearly two weeks. Made several acquaintances. Mrs. W_____ gave me a large picture of herself. I returned on Sixthday and on Seventhday night Will surprised us all by coming home. Was so glad to see him. It will be something to get used to housekeeping again. Still in the notion of selling our house, but no buyer yet. I wish we could go to Springfield. I know I would like it if we only had the money to go there. I would be willing to try ever so hard. Fanny has a boy. I am anxious to see him. His name is Russell. I wonder if the time will come ever when anyone will say of me, "she has a girl or a boy." Cal and J got home all safe from Va.—found William P—southern people—rebels and bitter ones at that. I don't want them to come here. Alma and Clay are getting along finely. If we may take their word for it they have bought property. The last letter they wrote like they had some notion of coming home to stay. I wish they would come nearer. It would be so handy.

Fourthday, December 20th, 1865
Will gone to Wilmington. Such a dreary day. The snow coming down fast and the wind blowing a perfect hurricane. It is very still in doors. Carmans were here last night and we played dominoes. It is so much fun. I must settle myself and do some good at something some but I am alone so much. I dread sitting down to sew alone but rather read or write.

Fifthday, December 21st, 1865
Cold this morning. Cal and I have been playing chequers. I had the good luck to beat her all but twice. I don't see what makes Will stay so long there. It is almost three o'clock and no Will and what his business is I can't imagine. Our bed is moved in the sitting room. It is pleasant to sleep by the fire.

Sixthday, December 22nd, 1865
Will and I visited the school this afternoon. It does not seem much like old times so many strange faces. I feel like a stranger when I go there and it makes me sad thinking of old times and old faces that have passed away. Got a book this evening. *Lives of British Essayists* by McCauly. I think it will be interesting.

Seventhday, December 23rd, 1865
Had a nine o'clock breakfast this morning. Shall be lazy all day I expect. It is so easy to get lazy when there is a little to do. I wonder how Mrs. W____ is prospering. She is sick. A curious woman—one minute you think you don't like her one bit and wonder why you ever did, the next minute one forms a better opinion and at last think you like her real well after all. She told me of a little episode in her life when she ran off intending to be an actress but she changed he mind before it was late. She was quite young. I wonder what she would do if "Pris" should be late. A notion to be like her "ma" was. I must quit to go to work.

Secondday, Christmas 1865
Been at home all day. Not much Christmas but enjoyed myself well. Made a little skirt for Hannah James little girl. Sent a dress, a skirt, two little shirts and some more little fixings. Lenna up here today. She grows so fast. I am afraid she will not be so sweet when big. There is a festival at the schoolhouse tonight. We are not going up—I suppose they will have a splendid supper. I am going to send for a specimen number of the *Post* and see if it is good enough to take.

Fourthday, December 27th, 1865
The old year passing away rapidly soon, instead of 65 it will be 66. This time last year a cruel war was filling our land with mourners and now though many hearts are full of anguish we do not have to read daily long lists of killed and wounded for the war is ended. How thankful ought we to be. Elva is up here. I am in hopes she is going to be a better girl if she would only get her attention turned to reading more. It would do more for her than we can say. This is dreary day. Chilly and damp. I have not written to Jo yet. I have read the lives of Bacon, Frederic the Great, Madam Darblay an English lady who married a Frenchman. She is a writer. Lord Bacon born January 22nd 1561. Frederick the Great king of Prussia was born Jan 1712. I think the *Phrenological Journal* so good. It came today.

Fifthday, December 28th, 1865
A letter from Fanny and three different photographs of baby. A little bump of something wadded up in clothes and wrappings of a little nose and eyes reminds us it is a baby. Fanny seems very much pleased and says it is right pretty and a real nice baby. I wonder if we are going to sell and if we will be sorry for it. I hope not the latter. If we only can get settled once more and feel contented. Will feels so out of heart and thinks he can do nothing here. I think we will get to Carmans tonight and play dominoes if Will wants to go.

Seventhday, December 30th, 1865
A beautiful day. Not at all like winter was. No one was ever so unfortunate about being caught in the dirt as I was. I had my old calico dress on, my hair

combed strait back looking very much like Bridget when as usual there was a knock. Mrs. Carman came first then before I got the dishes washed and a clean dress on here came Jesse C and George. I was ashamed but could not help myself. We were at George's yesterday all day. I think G has the consumption but he does not think he has—I hope he is right. Linton is worse. [Linton Moon, son of John Milton, deceased, and Rebecca Janney Moon. Linton died on January 6, 1866.] It is not likely he will live long. Will has gone out there now.

Sabbath, December 31st, 1865

The last of the old year. Never again will the year 65 return. It is almost gone and has been full of events making it a year long to be remembered. I wonder where we will be this time next year. How many changes may occur in the coming year for us. I hope nothing sad though how unlikely it is that we can live as we do so full of enjoyment. If we only appreciate it. While so many others have such sorrow meted out to them. Will is at Moons' tonight. Linton is very low. Elva and I are alone. We think of hanging up our stockings but I expect "Santa Claus" will never think once of us and our stockings will be as empty in the morning as usual. The old fellow never has paid proper respect to me anyhow. Maybe he will think of me sometime.[275]

---

275. It is interesting and surprising that Elva and Paulena were even thinking of hanging up their stockings on New Year's Eve, a week after it was traditionally considered the time when Santa would visit. Quakers also did not follow such traditions in exchanging gifts or celebrating Christmas other than by attending meeting. Santa Claus or St. Nicholas had become a more familiar Christmas figure since the publishing of the poem "A Visit From St. Nicholas," or "T'was the Night Before Christmas," written by Clement Clarke Moore.

"Clement Clarke Moore, educator, born in New York City, 15 July, 1779, died in Newport, Rhode Island, 10 July, 1863, was graduated at Columbia in 1798. Although educated and prepared for the ministry, he never took orders, but devoted himself chiefly to oriental and classical literature. In 1818 he made a generous gift to the General theological seminary, just organized, on condition that its buildings be erected on the ground where they are now standing. He was appointed by the trustees professor of biblical learning in 1821, and afterward of oriental and Greek literature, and served the institution for nearly thirty years. In 1850 he was made professor emeritus. Dr. Moore published a 'Hebrew and Greek Lexicon,' the first of the kind in America (2 vols.. New York, 1809); 'Bishop B. Moore's Sermons' (2 vols., 182.4); 'Poems' (1844); 'George Castriot, surnamed Scanderbeg, King of Albania,' a condensation of the old English translation of Jacques Lavardin's 'Historie' of that hero (New York, 1850); and also at various times made contributions to journals and magazines, he was the author of the well known ballad " 'Twas the Night before Christmas,' and is considered the pioneer of Hebrew lexicography in this country." Source: *Edited Appleton's Encyclopedia,* Virtualology, 2001, http://www.famousamericans.net/benjaminmoore/.

Clement Moore was the only son of Dr. Benjamin Moore, president of Columbia College and bishop of the Protestant Episcopal Church in New York. Both Benjamin and his son, Clement, were fourth cousins of Paulena Stevens Janney through her Betts, Chamberlain, and Stoughton ancestors of Long Island, New York.

January 1866

2nd of January 1866

At home sitting by a cheerful fire. Yesterday we went out to Moons for dinner. Linton cannot live long. I feel so sorry for them. They are so unfortunate. Coffins would like for us to move to Richmond and I am very willing to go live there as Springfield and mother had rather we would go to Richmond than any other place I guess. I hope we will not regret it if we sell. The fact of it is, although in many respects it is much ahead of other little towns, yet it is like them in the advantages and taking all things into consideration I think it would be better for us to go to some more thriving place.

January 8th, 1866

This is Will's 31st birthday. It is true we are growing old as the years come and go leaving their impress on each. How a shadow on each heart bringing changes for joy and for sorrow while the past year brought joy to many hearts by the return of some loved ones who had been amid danger of many kinds—passing through battles, unhurt while others fell wounded and dead. How very many were saddened by the death of some dear one at home or abroad. Albert [brother of Clay Cowgill] started for Florence[276] [Alabama] this afternoon. Alma will be pleased I know so many things as she will get. Al got her

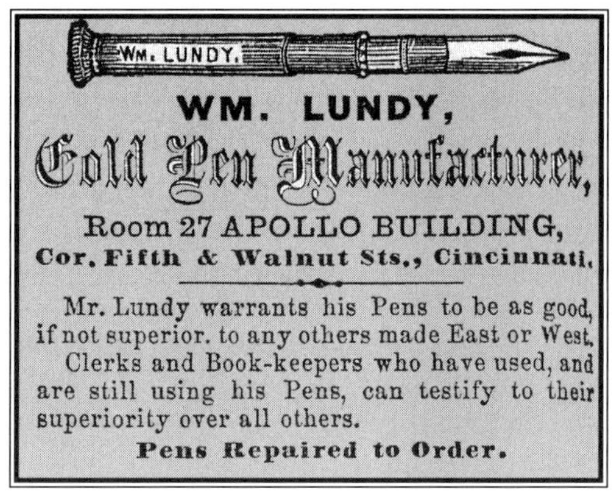

Wm. Lundy, gold pen manufacturer, from an advertisement in the Cincinnati City Directory

a present of a blue silk hood, so pretty. Father sent her a silver pen handle with gold pen and gave me one also. I am going to be very careful of it and keep it a long time. When I get my nice writing desk it will be a nice appointment. I am busy saving things for some future time and do not always enjoy the present as I should. My journal I feel will be very much out of order. I do not feel like writing very often. Things are so much alike. Nothing stirring. I just spent nearly everyday like I feel like I am living a very aimless life.

---

276. "There was an outstanding college for young ladies in Florence [Alabama] known as 'Florence Synodical College.' It was established in 1847 as the Florence Female Academy by Professor S. S. Stevens, native of Pennsylvania. In 1855 it came under the sponsorship of the Presbyterian Synod of Nashville, Tennessee. . . . This college, which survived the Civil War, closed its doors in 1893. The location of the college was at the site of the present Florence Post Office and Judge John McKinley Federal Building." Source: William L. McDonald, City Historian, sent to Christie Russell, July 13, 2005, from Martha Murphy.

Fourthday, January 10th, 1866
A lonesome looking day—cloudy and been hailing. Linton died yesterday morning and is to be buried tomorrow at 1 o'clock.[277] They have so much trouble. I
am here all alone. Will gone to Moons and perhaps will stay all night. I hardly
know how to put my time in. If I could only walk out and see something.

January 24th, 1866
This has been such a dreary day raining or sleeting and the ground covered with
snow. A letter came to mother yesterday from Alma. It is like Springtime there.
The grass green and the trees putting forth their leaves. It must be a delightful
climate. I would enjoy a winter in the south so much. I hope Alma and Clay will
get home all safe. They think of coming in 4 or six weeks. I wish we could meet
them in Cincinnati, but cannot think of such a thing. No money, no nothing. It is
very "inconvenient" to be poor. Decidedly so—maybe something will turn up
though. I am busy cutting carpet rags.[278] I wonder if I will ever get my carpet
done. Poor Will is so discouraged as everything is so dull. No building going on
and if he gets anything to do there is no money for so long, and yet we cannot
sell to go any other place.

February 1866

February 1st, 1866
Along time has elapsed since I opened my journal. How very careless I am getting, but indeed one day is so near like another that I feel no incentive to write.
Get up late of mornings, eat breakfast, clean the rooms and sit down to my
carpet rag cuttings or have I told you journal that I have commenced making
a carpet. Well I have and no wonder I find no time to write. We are looking for
Alma home soon. Are so glad. Can hardly wait till she comes. It will be so like
old times. I hope I will be more punctual in the future about my writing, but
before I quit I must not forget to Chronicle one important occurrence that will
cause at least the Newman tribe to wonder. Newman has fallen heir to 25,000
dollars. I should think they should move out of the swamps in quick order. They
will afford the rest of us some consolation to see how they dispose of it. They
will hardly know what to do with it. I do wonder if it will make any difference

---

277. Linton Moon was the son of John Milton Moon and Rebecca Janney. He was
eighteen years old. John Milton Moon had committed suicide on October 25, 1864, as
recorded in this journal. Ella Moon had died on July 1, 1861. Rebecca Janney Moon died
on April 29, 1868, and all of their children except Dora were deceased before her. Dora
Moon married Benjamin David Jay, removed to Whittier, California, in 1898, and was
listed in the 1930 census as living in Pasadena, California.

278. Carpet rags were strips of cotton sewed together and rolled into balls of
various single or mixed colors, ready to hook into carpets.

in them—if it will be Mr. and Mrs. Newman instead of old Newmans. Strange things will happen. Will is going to try for a patent on a fruit pan. I do hope he will succeed. Anyone as honest and who would use the money to so good advantage as I know Will would, ought to succeed in something and I think he will sometimes. Oh, how discouraged we will feel if he fails with the patent. I will hope for the best though.

Sabbath, February 4th, 1866
Very cold and windy this morning. Rolla preached a good sermon. How glad I would be if we could have the opportunity of going to hear a good sermon every Sabbath. The house is very cold like a barn and I think the energy of the people here is below par. Members of the Methodist church getting few and far between. The old house is getting more dilapidated each succeeding year and more unable to resist the wintry wind which blows through the crevices affording ample ventilation for the most rigid believers in fresh air. In the morning Will intends starting on his mission. I hope so much for it in 3 months. I wonder how we will think and feel about it. Now we are constantly alternating between hope and fear. I told Will this morning I thought the Good news ought to let us make something.

Sabbath, February 11th, 1866
Alma is at home all safe again. Came on Fifthday. Were glad to see her. She had no difficulty in getting along. Will and I helped paper the rooms down home. They look so much better. Will's mission to the city was not entirely fruitless. Whatever may be the result in the future Mr. Gibson thinks his fruit pan a good thing and does not see why there will not be a patent.

Fourthday, February 14th, 1866
I am sure careless this winter about writing in my journal letting days and weeks slip away without opening my journal. The fact is I have nothing to write about. I have taken my seat by the east window. My old favorite place of sittery in winter. It is the place I can look from into the street and of course I find a great deal to attract my attention. Will and I were at grandfathers on Seventhday night. It does them so much good to have any of us go there. I wonder if we will live as they do. If we live to be old and care as little about things outside the precinct of home. It is making butter, etc than for a book or poem or a trip? I don't think we need let our domestic affairs interfere with our higher aspirations, but our dear old grandmothers did not cultivate any love for such things as we now feel the need of and become absorbed entirely with other things. I think this is certainly the dullest place. I get so tired it almost makes me sick. I felt like I could almost vomit this morning when Will came from the office and said "no letters." Well I must be more industrious, I suppose, but even then when busy I feel the need of someone to talk to. It is so dreadful muddy. I cannot go home nor Alma can come here isolated from all congenial spirits by the rivers of mud.

February 23rd, 1866
Spent part of the afternoon with Lib. Willie rather cross. I think babies are so sweet if they would not squall. The one I have pictured in my mind is a dear little creature with brown eyes and curls of the same. A sweet little thing always playful and interesting, smiling even amid it's tears and always looking as clean as a lily, as pure as a rosebud and as cheering as a sunbeam. Will I not be discouraging, if after my vivid imagination, it should prove to be a rose with thorns, a lily with dew that is liable to squalls and to be annoying on all occasions especially before people. I am going to send for Mary to come and help me sew carpet rags tonight. Milton and Mary, Jim Hunt and Maggie were here tonight. Mary helped me sew carpet rags.

February 26th, 1866
This month nearly gone and the winds of March preparing to give us a salute serenading us with the winds in every crevice. I am glad. Birdsalls have bought a place in Richmond for I think we will go there to live come time and it will be a real nice to have some acquaintances there we like. I am going to be industrious this week for I must get my new dress done and clean up things real nice. I think everything looks out of order, so much now, as it is always so cold and I am so lazy. We are reading *Bayard Taylor's Travels.*[279] It is so good describing the people of Greece and Russia. I am not writing according to principle. It is too much trouble when writing with my journal on my knee, even if I could.

March 1866

March 4th, 1866
This morning we went over to hear Rolla preach. Had a good sermon. He is going to be at church tonight. I am glad of it. We have had beautiful weather for a few days past but today the wind blows very hard. Mother has been here today. The exhibition on Sixthday night was pretty good in some respects but a few things to mar the interest. I was nearly sick all last week, but did not quite make it out. Wonder if I will finish this week, but I feel so much better now. Cal told me something so funny, but we will have to wait till September to see if no one knows it yet, but us. I wish it were true to keep her company.[280] Oh, I am so tired. I wish Will would come in. I see Alma and Clay passing. They have been to Clay's mothers [Susan Ann (Doggett) Cowgill].

---

279. Bayard Taylor, *A Visit to India, China and Japan, in the Year 1853*, New York, G.P. Putnam & Sons.

280. Cal, Carolyn (Betts) Jackson, Paulena's first cousin, suspected that she was pregnant with her first child, William Betts Jackson, to whom she gave birth on September 27, 1866.

Secondday, March 5th, 1866
A beautiful day, but cool. I am so lonely I do not know what to do with myself this afternoon. There is a meeting tonight. Rolla preaches. I do not know whether to go, but of course I will though.

Thirdday, March 6th, 1866
Going down home this morning. The trial of the murderer of the Roosa family is in progress. I hope they have the right man this time. I would like to be in court during the trial. It must be interesting. Grandfather has been sick again. No prospect of selling yet. I do wonder if we will sell this spring. I can never feel in the mood for writing lately—have nothing to excite me to be industrious or anything.

Fourthday, March 7th, 1866
My thumb is so sore I can hardly hold my pen at all and must not write much. Will and I stayed all night at fathers, came up this morning and I have been home all day, although I tried to occupy my time by reading and cutting carpet rags. We made some enigmas last night.[281] Clay made one which solved was a big fat boy—said article being desirable in every family. I made one a big fat girl etc, etc. This is a perfect March day. The wind blowing so hard and cold. Jimmy's have a little girl.

Sabbath, March 11th, 1866
Just like all Sabbaths here. Went to church this morning. Heard a few words from Nathan, came home, and feel so dull and sleepy. Began reading Griffith Garnet on *Jealousy in the Atlantic*. Only have two numbers though. Birdsalls have had a sale and are going away this week. I wonder if we will ever sell. I wonder if I will ever be as tired being away from Martinsville as I am staying here. Perhaps I may. Alma, Clay, Will and I went to Uncle Hiatts on Fifthday. My thumb is so sore I can hardly write at all , so I must not write for at best my journal will be a botched up affair.

Fifthday, March 15th, 1866
Just poured down rain this morning, but is not raining this evening. I am sitting here all alone. The wind sounds quite lonely. I wish I did not have to be alone so much, It is so tiresome. It is well enough when I feel real well. Have plenty to read or do and am in a certain mood, but when feeling almost sick it is very tiresome to be penned up here in this little room no one to say a word to but to go to the window and not see anything, but mud. Who wouldn't get tired. I am almost wicked enough to wish sometimes Will had a sore finger or something

---

281. "Enigmas are related to mysteries, conundrums, puzzles, and riddles. Some have solutions, others are yet to be solved. Some so-called solutions remain unproven." Source: "Investigating Enigmas," http://projects.edtech.sandi.net/grant/enigmas/.

not bad the matter with him. Just enough to keep him in the house with me. I think I will write to Matt someday, but then I do not know if she would ever write to me. It is strange thinking of how very intimate in the truest sense we used to be and how cold and distant we are now. I had a feeling for her I used to think I could not feel for anyone else. There was such a bond of sympathy between us some way. She always seems to know me so well and then the fun we had. Did anyone ever have more? I wonder if she had forgotten all about it. I have a good lecture laid up for her if I ever get to see her. There is not one bit of sense when anyone is married of neglecting their old friends in such a manner even if they have got a baby. Just two months ago I was sick in bed. Well I am getting stout for I have not been so bad since.

March 16th, 1866
Such a cold day. The wind howls around the house so lonely. I think we should not anticipate spring until June for with the cold wind and snow and all the accompaniments of winter, March is anything but spring. I have been busy most of the day and now it is near night and Will will soon come for his supper. Let me see, I think I will have eggs, toast and tea. I am so hungry for chicken. I think as much as we are bothered with the chickens, Mrs. C____ might afford to give me part of one anyhow. I just wonder how I would feel if we raised chickens running over there to get the eggs if they bothered them as they do us. I wish Will would hurry and come home so I could have someone to talk with who would not get tired. I do wish I had a baby for company. The dear little thing.

March 19th, 1866
We spent Seventhday night and Sabbath down home. Mother had roast chicken for dinner which I have been longing for so long. Went to monthly meeting today. Sarah Smith and her husband from Milton, Indiana were there. She is such a good speaker. Oh, dear. I am so in hopes—something, perhaps will now be after awhile—could such a good thing for me be possible? If so how different will life be. So much brighter. I think it entirely too good to be true. I will not get my expectations up too high. [She suspected that she might at last be pregnant after almost seven childless years—and indeed she was.] Alma and mother were here for dinner. A letter from the man who was to look at our house in the fall. Perhaps he will buy it after awhile.

Fourthday, March 21st, 1866
Cold. A letter from Lizzie this evening. She is teaching at Bartlett.[282] I must be

---

282. Bartlett, Ohio, is twenty miles directly west of "Marietta, Washington County, Ohio, on State Road 550. From 1865 to 1892, Bartlett Academy, a school of higher learning, educated the best and brightest in the region. The school building and its bell can still be seen, just across the street from the Bartlett Restaurant and next to the old boarding house, which is now a private home." Source: http://www.mariettatimes. com/communities/bartlett.asp.

more industrious, but when I have not got much to do and feel so little energy, how can I do much and think it best for me to have my mind occupied. I feel better for it, now if I only had two or three babies.

Fifthday, March 22nd, 1866
A beautiful morning, but cool enough to make a fire quite desirable and indeed indispensable. I think it will be delightful when spring comes. Will is so discouraged about his affairs and wants to make money so badly. I hope some good thing will turn to his advantage soon.

Sixthday, March 23rd, 1866
Dark and raining. I was real sick yesterday evening, but am better today. Elva is doing my work. Does very well. It is so funny. A letter came from Marion, Indiana. It said "Pellina Janney. Dear Sir. It is about the land wanting to know the lowest cash price." Pikes Opera was burned last night.[283] I am sorry I never got to see it. It was so splendid. I want to go to Cincinnati so badly. It has been so long since I was there.

March 26th, 1866
A cold day. Just like winter. I never was so tired of winter in my life. I think I will appreciate spring when it comes. It will be so delightful to get up in the morning and dress without nearly freezing or scorching by the fire to raise the windows and open the shutters and not be chilled. I do not think I will say a word to get ever so warm. Sent a letter to Fannie after a long a time. Protracted meeting begins or has begun. Rolla preaches tonight. I think it doubtful if any one joins. They are all so cold. I am much better this week than last. If it will only continue. Oh dear I do wish for something that would make me real glad would occur before long. I would be delighted beyond measure.

Thirdday, March 27th, 1866
Have my mornings work nearly done. Am half sick of eating onions yesterday for dinner. Tired of gravy, soup and eggs. I just had to force my breakfast down this morning. It was a perfect burnbug. Went to church last night. Think generally a good man, but do not like to hear him so well as some others—though

---

283. An Article titled "The Great Fire in Cincinnati, March 22, 1866, Burning of Pike's Opera" appeared in *Harper's Weekly*, April 14, 1866. "We give on page 228 illustrations of the recent conflagration in Cincinnati, sketched on the spot by our artist, Mr. Waud. The fire broke out in Pike's Opera-house. This building—the most splendid structure of the kind in the West—was completely destroyed. Very fortunately the immense audience, congregated to hear 'Midsummer Night's Dream,' had dispersed before the accident occurred, otherwise we should have occasion to detail the horrible features of another human holocaust devoted to the Moloch of Flame." Source: http://www.rootsweb.com/~ohhamilt/pics004.html.

he is talented. So cold this morning winter still lingering in the lap of spring. I do not know what to get for dinner. Will is such a good man likes good dinners so well. I would like to get something good. If some good genius would appear I would astonish Will wonderfully. Oh those onions. It makes me sick to think of them. It was strange I did not dream of a mountain of onions last night. We are reading Taylors *Eldorado*.[284] It is good. I finished reading *Captivity of the Oatman Children*.[285] What suffering they endured. I would like to see some of the poor Indians strung up for their cruelty. I am not one who sympathies with them. I think the sooner they are extinct the better.

Fourthday, March 28th, 1866
Patter, patter goes the rain against the window pane as the wind sighs round the house with solemn moan. So the day began. Every day we wonder what tomorrow will bring mingled with some hope or fear, some dread undelivered or some secret joy. Thus our lives pass by. Willie came in the morning wet as a rat, but not minding it the least. Telling me he had a pen in one pocket, ink in the other, etc. I wonder what kind of a man he will be. He has so many qualities about him if rightly developed would make him much more a man than many other little boys I know. I am gong to write to Jennie H. this morning.

Fifthday, March 29th, 1866
Cold and cloudy. Just like winter. I am all alone and do get so tired of being so much alone. I am not in the mood for writing this evening. I wish I could get a letter from some person. seems as if no one cares enough about me to write of late. There is a meeting tonight again. Tom Hunts wife joined last night.

Sixthday, March 30th, 1866
The brightest day we have had for sometime, but when the weather is bright we have so much wind. Hattie Hart is sick this morning. She is very bad. I feel so sorry for her—anyone has to pay dearly for a little life. I hope she won't die. There is meeting again tonight. There were several at the mourners bench last night.

---

284. Bayard Taylor published *Eldorado* in 1850. "Taylor was an American traveler and man of letters. He wrote for newspapers and magazines and published poetry and novels. He was appointed secretary of legation under the U.S. minister to Russia at St. Petersburg in 1862. From 1870 to 1877 Taylor was a nonresident professor of German literature at Cornell University." Source: *Picture History*, http://www.picturehistory.com/find/p/4965/mcms.html.

285. "In 1851 nine members of the Oatman family set out for California. Seventy miles from California a group of "Apache" Indians came to their camp to beg, grew angry, massacred the family, and took two of the Oatman children captive. This 1857 book of their experiences is one of the few authentic, early accounts of life among the SW Indians currently in print. An amazing and interesting saga." Source: *Captivity of the Oatman Girls*, R. B. Stratton, 1857, http://www.scholia.net/captivity_oatman.htm.

April 1866

[April 7th, 1866—Paulena and Will's seventh wedding anniversary]

Seventhday, April 12th, 1866

A bright morning. We went a fishing last evening. Will, Willie and I, but as usual were unlucky. Caught no fish. I think it too bad for we are so fond of them. Have been almost sick for three months. I do not know why. I have not been sick in earnest. Will has started on a butter expedition. I am so in hopes he will be fortunate enough to get some. I do not see much chance to keep from starving if we have no butter. Poor Will is so discouraged, but I hope things will grow brighter soon. I think anyone so good and so industrious as Will ought to succeed. I hope I will live to see the day when Will can live easy and have plenty of money too. There has been protracted meetings here for over two weeks. Many have been converted among the number—Brown, Willie Betts, Bill Hunt and Sue. I hope they will all hold out faithful.[286]

Sabbath April 15th, 1866

We went to church this morning. Heston preached. The rain is pouring down this evening and it looks very gloomy indeed. I am sure I will be glad when spring comes in earnest. The weather is so unsettled I feel badly this evening. In two weeks it will be quarterly meeting. I wonder if we will have any company. Got plenty of butter now.

Secondday, April 16th, 1866

Cloudy and cool this morning. Lyd has a baby. I wonder if anyone will ever say Will has a baby. I think Will is getting in the notion of going to Iowa now. Mercy I hope some good fortune will turn up for us and we can choose a more desirable place than Iowa. I never could feel any desire of going to a new country to live. We have disadvantages enough here. I do wish we could sell. I think it will be much the best thing for us and am quite willing if we only had money to buy a farm.

---

286. "As Donald Scott states, the key to understanding Evangelicalism in the 19th century is the experience of conversion. Even more, that 'conversion was an experience.' Conversion was 'something that happens to you.' It was an intensely emotional experience, a 'catharsis,' and a 'heartfelt rebirth.' Those who led the Great Awakening of the 18th century were from the Reformed background. They placed the emphasis in conversion on the inner transformation affected by the Holy Spirit to awaken faith in the Gospel. However, they were not averse to visible changes and expressions accompanying conversion. But, for Revivalists in the 1800s, conversion was recognized by the 'power and character of emotions that accompanied' conversion. A second aspect of conversion was a 'profound psychological transformation.' It consisted of an 'altered sense of self' which led to an awareness of 'identity as a new kind of Christian.'" Source: *In Christ Alone!*, http://www.inchristalone.org/CharacRevivalism.htm.

Thirdday, April 17th, 1866
Went down home this morning. Am going again in the morning to help sew. I am wishing so much to know if something be true. I hope so—will know before many weeks, I think. Alma went to Vienna this morning to see about some of her things.

Fifthday, April 19th, 1866
Did anyone ever like babies better than I do. It seems like we ought to have one we are so fond of them. Maybe sometime we will, but I fear it will be a long time first. I wish I had something real good to get for dinner.

Sabbath, April 22nd, 1866
This lovely Sabbath morning how bright everything looks. It is strange how anyone can be moody or discontented when all things are so lovely and the grass is green. The sun so warm, the birds so merry and all things are saying in their language spring has come. Yet how often not withstanding the beauty we suffer ourselves to become blinded to its elevating influences and cannot understand the many voices of nature speaking to our hearts. I must go to church this morning as I have missed going to Sabbath school—for indeed I did not get up early enough. When I start to Sabbath school I will be more punctual—get up early. I am reading *Very Hard Cash*.[287] I wish I had some hard cash instead of reading of it.

Secondday, April 23rd, 1866
So stormy all day. It seems as if the day had been a week long almost, although I have been in bed most of the time. Got up at six, had breakfast went to bed again till eight, ate some more, did the dishes, went to bed till noon. How lazy I am, but I am all alone and feel so stupid. Oh I do get so tired of being alone.

---

287. Charles Reade, *Very Hard Cash,* 1st American ed. New York, Harper & Brothers, 1864. From Columbia Encyclopedia, 6th ed., 2004: "READE, CHARLES 1814–84, English novelist and dramatist. He is noted for his historical romance *The Cloister and the Hearth.* After being elected a fellow of Magdalen College, Oxford, he was called to the bar. His interests, however, soon turned to the theater. He achieved his first success with *Masks and Faces* (1852), written in collaboration with Tom Taylor. The play, concerned with life in the theater, was used as the basis for his first novel, *Peg Woffington* (1853). An ardent reformer, he began a long series of propagandist novels with *It's Never Too Late to Mend* (1856), describing the cruelties of prison discipline. Others in the series included *Hard Cash* (1863), and *Put Yourself in His Place* (1870). He also wrote the novels *Griffith Grant* (1866), *Foul Play* (1869), and *A Terrible Temptation* (1871). His masterpiece, *The Cloister and the Hearth* (1861), is a picaresque novel concerning the adventures of Gerard, the father of Erasmus. In 1879 Reade collaborated with Charles Warner in writing *Drink*, a dramatization of Zola's *L'Assommoir*. Bibliography: See biography by M. Elwin (1931); study by W. Burns (1961)."Source: http://www.highbeam.com/ref/doc3.asp?docid=1E1:Reade Ch.

Thirdday, April 24th, 1866
A bright morning, but the wind is beginning to blow and it is cloudy—so much for our expectations. If a pretty day, our hopes in life are not clouded. I hope we will get a letter today with something cheering in it, but if one comes I will expect something discouraging. I wonder if anyone will come here after Quarterly meeting. Anyone I will be glad to see. It has been a long time since I saw anyone I care much about seeing. Willie is staying here now. He is a very good boy. I hope he will be good when he is older. Will has made a new churn for Freeborn to take. It is the best one ever made. I hope it will be of some benefit to them.

Fourthday, April 25th, 1866
Bad again. I think we can appreciate nice weather. When it does come I am not very busy. Wish I was but cannot think of anything to do. I wish I had a baby to keep me occupied. Think the "Good Man" ought to give me one anyhow for I would be so much better off. Wish we had something good to get for dinner as my appetite is very good. I get so hungry. No letter yesterday. Hope there will be one today from Richmond. The sun is shining a little. Hope it will be bright soon and not so windy.

May 1866

Sabbath, May 13th, 1866 [At her parent's home]
Very unpleasant weather most of the time. Have been down home two weeks. Will is working there. They are having things fixed much better. Oh, I am so in hopes something is true. It seems too great a happiness. I cannot realize it and am afraid to think much about it yet. Oh, if it can only be so. How thankful I will be. Wait and see how it will be. That is all I know about it. Will thinks of going to Hillsboro to work. I will be so lonesome up home. Cannot stay here alone.

Seventhday, May 19th, 1866
A bright morning. So different from the cold chilly mornings of last week. I enjoy it so much more. Jeff is to be buried this morning. I feel so sorry for his mother and he was not willing to die which makes it much more sad. I am going to spend the afternoon at Tafts. I do so much hope for something. Am continually alternating between hope and fear. Why cannot it not be true. It would be something bright to look to in the future. I must write to Lizzie soon.

Fifthday, May 24th, 1866
Up home today. Nothing to get for my dinner. I do not live alone very well, so dreary and I dread to cook when no one is here but me. I am not certain yet about something. I am afraid it is all a hoax about it. It does not seem possible for it to be true. Will is going to Hillsboro next week. I will be so lonesome but I do not intend staying at home much of the time.

Secondday, May 28th, 1866
Cold and cloudy very unlike summer. How tired we are of such dreary weather. Will is going to go to Hillsboro in the morning. I will miss him so much. He will not be at home anyhow for two weeks. I hope we will be able to live together and not be separated. Received a letter from Jo. She was much more punctual than I was. I am so in hopes that something long hoped for will be true. Although I am afraid to get my expectations up too high for fear of being disappointed. Nineteen weeks next Fifth day since I was very sick, but have felt bad enough many times since.

Thirdday, May 29th, 1866
All alone sitting in the little kitchen by the fire for May as it is it is very unlike it. Will is gone I am sorry he had to go and he hated so much to have to go. I will miss him so much for he is so good and kind. I hope the time will soon come we can live together again if we could only sell and go where Will could do well. I think it would be so much better. If I only had a little sweet baby to keep me company now. I really think we need one worse than anyone else I know.

Fourthday, May 30th, 1866
A bright morning but cool. Wish it would go to warm. It was lonesome without Will. I do not know how to stand it so long. Willie and Lenna stayed all night with me. I thought there was going to be a heavy frost and covered up things but nothing was burnt. Living alone is so tiresome. I want something more to occupy my mind. If we only had a baby. Little sweet thing. We would love it so much. I want to see Will already. Can hardly wait till he comes home.

June 1866

Thirdday, June 5th, 1866
Up home tonight. It is quite lonesome without Will. I am so tired of living this way. Sarah M. Hiatt and Aunt Ester came last Fifth day. She is going to try to settle up the difficulty she is in. They have told so many mean contemptible things it will be hard to trace them up. I would be ashamed of myself. I think it looks so little in them to talk so much about a poor woman. If it ever comes out that she is in the wrong which I do not believe, I will not regret that I am her friend. I do hope it will all be right for her. I pity her so much. A letter from Will came last Seventhday. He will be so glad to get home. I know I am so anxious to see him. I am so in hopes of something. Can it be possible if it will only come out all right how thankful we will be.

Fifthday, June 7th, 1866
Stayed up home again last night. Another letter from Will. Was glad to get it. Am so glad he is coming home on Seventhday, but am sorry he has to go back.

I hope the time will soon come when we can live at home again. Will seems so happy and is so good. I wish I could feel the same way. Oh. I am so in hopes we will have a sweet little baby to love. How we would love it. I think we would try to raise it up to be of some use to all. I so hope we will have the chance. This is a beautiful June morning. The air so warm and everything looks so bright and pleasant. I am reading *Queechy.* It is very good. I think Sarah H. and Aunt are going to start home in the morning. I hope I will get to see them before they go. Five months today since I was VERY SICK. What a long time.

Fifthday, June 12th, 1866
Been down home all week. This afternoon Alma and I went to the depot to meet Fanny and were so fortunate as to find her. The baby[288] is so sweet and I like it already. It is just as fat as butter. I would give anything if we had a baby as sweet, I wonder if the time will ever come when we will speak of the baby as something really in our possession. I hope so, but fear to hope too much. Will must come home while Fannie is here, anyhow and see the baby. I expect Will is homesick tonight. I hope he will come home soon. Fanny and baby are both sleeping already. There is a blindman preaching tonight. I must go out to the gate and listen.

Sabbath, June 17th, 1866
Just poured down rain nearly all day—a rainy Sabbath for certain. Fanny and I at home alone. Did not even put on our other dresses. I wrote to Will to come home next Seventh day. I hope he will come. I do not know what to do about going to Richmond with Fanny. Sometimes I think it an impossibility. We have a fire in the sitting room as it is cool.

Sixthday, June 29th, 1866
Fanny and baby left this morning. I hated to see them start. She has gone to Richmond. I think she will have a nice time if she gets there all safe. I wish we could live there sometime. Maybe we will. I am all alone. It will be so lonesome now no baby. One little shoe is left to remind me there has been a baby's foot in it. I hope sometime we will possess a sweet baby of our own. It will be so nice. I do hope nothing will happen to disappoint us. We were just in time for the train this morning. No time to spare. I am thinking of making a visit next week. I would like to see her real well and her baby.

---

288. Russell Janney was born on November 15, 1865, in Portsmouth, Ohio. He was the son of Lot and Fanny (Wood) Janney.

July 1866

Sabbath, July 1st, 1866 [Paulena's twenty-sixth birthday]
A bright morning. Came up home this morning early. Am going to Sabbath school. My 26th birthday. It does not seem I am 26.

Fifthday, July 5th, 1866
Very warm. Been up home since yesterday. I did not go to Leesburg. I think it a fortunate thing. I wish Will would hurry and come home. It is lonesome without him. George is so much worse. I am so sorry about him. A letter from Fanny yesterday. Got to Richmond safe.

Sixthday, July 6th, 1866
At home. Yet had a lonely time this afternoon as it rained and was dark for a time. I waded around much more than I ought, but that is the way lone women have to do. I will be glad enough when Will comes home to stay. I was down to see George this evening. He looks very bad indeed. I am so sorry for them. Alma and I expect to go to Leesburg in the morning. It has been so long since I saw Matt. I wonder if she will be like she used to. I hope George will get better. How badly would I feel if Will looked as weak as George. Elva is with me tonight. I had much rather have some company than to be alone. When dark comes I begin to feel lonely.

Sixthday, July 13th, 1866 [Traveled to Leesburg, Highland County, Ohio]
Very warm today, but pleasant for me as I have not much to do. A letter from Lizzie this morning. Her school is out at Bartlett and she was to start home yesterday. Alma and I had a very pleasant time at Leesburg. Matt is very much like she used to be only she stays at home so much and lets herself get old and she is so weakly. I fear if her baby lives it will never have much health.[289] I am so in hopes we will have a sweet little baby and that I can do just right with it. I must go down to George's this afternoon. 25 weeks yesterday since I was VERY SICK.

Seventhday, July 14th, 1866
Very warm. Alone—am not looking much for Will, but received no letter. Would be glad to see him coming, but he would have a hot walk from Lynchburg this evening. I am still up home. Like to stay here pretty well, but get tired of being alone so much. I am so glad Will will soon be at home to stay. It will be so much better than living this way.

Sabbath, July 15th, 1866
So hot. Willie and I got up so late this morning, but managed to get breakfast in

---

289. Matt (Ladd) Pushee was expecting her second baby, who was born on December 3, 1866. She was named Nellie F. Pushee.

time to go to Sabbath school, but I remained at home almost from necessity. My dresses which I can wear at present are few and far between and I am ashamed to wear the same dress all the time. I dreamed last night I had a baby. A girl all perfect and well and that I was not bad at all. I wonder if so good a dream will ever be true. I hope so earnestly. After all I dread and long waiting of so many months. It must be too bad to not have a sweet baby. I will think anyone sweet if perfect and sensible if it is ugly.

Secondday, July 23th, 1866
Pouring down rain. Will and Emma Hiatt came Seventh day. Had to go home on the train this evening. Emma is a very nice little girl. Poor old grandmother is very sick. I fear she will I never get well, we will miss her so much for she has ever been kinder than we deserved denying herself to pleasure.

Sixthday, August 24th, 1866
Elva and I came up yesterday. Moved up rather, for we had a load. Clay brought the spring wagon. I think I will stay at home nearly all the time now for things get out of order so much when I am away. I expect it will be rather lonesome for us. I wish Will would hurry and come home to stay. I do not know when to look for him, but it will not do for him to stay away very much longer. Oh, our sweet little darling, that is to be will it be all right and live and will I live to take care of it. How glad we will be—It seems too good to be true.

The Sunbeam
Written long ago

A tiny sunbeam came one morning after there had been many days of gloom. It came to cheer the sick, the sorrowing and to shed beauty all over the land. It glided into the sickroom and the sufferer turned to catch it's radiance and a smile lighted up the pale features as the sunbeam lingered upon the white brow. Alas for the sick one. Soon the sunbeam will come again when the bed will be draped in white and the eye open no more to the beautiful light. It will come again when all in the room is still—when the death angel has come and gone. It lingered again beside a sleeper, a rosy cheeked babe and it seemed to grow brighter and brighter as it fell upon the sunny curls of the little cherub and the red lips half parted in a smile as though the angels were whispering to the beautiful boy as he slumbered. Oh will the sunlight always bring such gladdening influences in the future years when the crib is put away and the baby clothes laid by? When the tender limbs are strengthen and developed by the strong sinews of manhood. Sleep on innocent child for thy happiest moments are now when the sunbeams are playing around thee and the angel keeping watch by the downy pillow. For the time will come when there will seem to be no sunbeam in all life's way. They lingered in another home. There is an aged man and woman and a beautiful young woman one hand on the cradle, the other clasping a bright boy. They listen while the old man reads. "Come unto me all ye that are weary and heavy laden and I will give you rest." It is a beautiful picture. The sunbeam is gleaming upon them now and it sped gladly on its way. But there were other homes where discord reigned where the sunbeam could not fulfill its mission on the obdurate and hardened heart. It was all unappreciated. So it took its flight through the green woods tinting the leaves and warming the flowers into life and all nature seemed rejoicing and thankful for nature is so appreciative and just before the last beam died away it lighted up a beautiful chamber where a child was repeating as its mother taught it, "Our Father who art in Heaven hallowed be thy name" and then it sank in slumber as the beam faded away. Let us all be sunbeams and fulfill our mission by doing all in our power to make others happy, be as a sunbeam gliding into dark places where the spirit of dwellers are darkened and at last when our time has come we can, like the little child, lie down to our deep sleep with the murmured words, "Our Father who art in heaven hallowed be thy name."

August 1866

Some of my poetry

Oh why should we love to live
When the world is so full of pain?
When our friends are falling one by one
Like sheaves of ripened grain—

Oh why should we cling to life,
When death comes like a gentle sleep

Sealing the eyes of those we love
With a slumber soft and deep.

It is death that frees us from pain
It is death that a rest can give
It will take us to those we love
Then why should we love to live?

Grandmother [Anne (Hunt) Betts] was buried the 1st of August. I did not go to the funeral as mother was sick. Went down to see her for the last time. I could not realize that I should never see her more. She looked calm and peaceful like one in a quiet slumber, but her brow was cold as marble and she could not give us the kindly greeting she had so often given us before. Never again would we see her dear form and as [I] looked around the desolate room after they had taken her away, I could sympathize more than ever before with those who looking at the vacant chair or some familiar garment of an absent one, realize with anguish that the one they miss is gone, gone forever. Poor old grandfather [Aaron Betts] is brought very low by his trial. He seems very different from the "cold hearted" man we have so often thought him. He does not look like he would be long behind grandmother and he seems anxious to meet her in the better world when we have the assurance she is waiting to welcome those she loved on earth.

Seventhday, August 25th, 1866
A bright morning. Everything looks lovely. Elva and I still live here and are not tired yet. If the rest of the time will pass as quickly and pleasantly away I can get along very well. All that is lacking now is Will and I hope he will not be away much longer every week makes his stay that much shorter. I am trying to get things fixed up some. I dislike disorder very much. How glad it would be if I could only be in my present mood all the time. It is a much happier feeling than the way I often feel. Perhaps when a baby comes it will all be right. How I will love the little sweet thing. I am so afraid there will be something to mar the pleasure, I anticipate, but try not to think too much about it for fear of being disappointed. Two months more will tell the story. Good or bad. When I let my imagination picture a little crib with its baby features and fancy myself bending over it to see the baby all bright and sweet and perfect nestled among the pillows, it seems impossible for such a good fortune to be ours, and yet, why not. God gave others beautiful children who do not care for them like we would.

Sabbath, August 26th, 1866
Went to Sabbath school across the way [at the Methodist Episcopal Church]. Enjoyed it better than our own. There is more interest manifested. They sing real well and have learned new songs. It is so beautiful this morning, bright and cool and pleasant. I succeeded in getting the grass cut and the wood house cleaned out last evening. It looks much better. Alma and I spent the afternoon at Mackafees. Had a very pleasant time.

Secondday, August 27th, 1866
Another beautiful day. We are getting along finely. Have plenty to eat and have no notion of going down home to beg supplies as Alma predicted we would. I did not get any letter from Will this morning. I am nearly provoked at him. I will let him look for a letter this week, but I do not think I will write unless he gives

me a very good excuse—a pretty story indeed if a man can't find time to write to his wife once a week—as it is the first time, I suppose something besides business prevented. We are going to have chicken soup for dinner and baked potatoes. I expect to go visiting this week as I have had two or three invitations and I might as well go as not. If I keep on I will go till the late pinch I reckon. I think every week I cannot go out much longer.

Thirdday, August 28th, 1866
Cloudy this morning. A letter from Will. He is coming home in three weeks to stay. I am so glad of it. I hope the next time I hear it will not still be three. Oh, I wonder if our baby will be sweet and smart. How anxiously we will await its coming and how disappointed will be our hopes if it does not live, but I must not look on the dark side for why will it not be as sure to be right as anyone. I am going to write some letters soon. How very careless I am of late. I wonder if anyone will ever feel any interest in reading this journal and since it will not be very interesting.

Fourthday, August 29th, 1866
The day almost gone. Another beautiful evening. I enjoy such evenings so much. Only two more weeks after this till Will comes to stay. I hope it will soon pass away. 32 weeks tomorrow since I was very sick. I hope in 10 more we will have a sweet little baby all ours. Oh, I wonder how it will look. I hope it is all right and with good sense. How glad I will be and will not care for the pretty so much for it will be sweet enough anyhow. Little pig of a thing. I hope it will be fat and hearty. I cannot imagine such good fortune to be possible. I will wait and see. I bought some splendid apples this morning, but I could eat them all in two days. They are so good, but I must not be that extravagant.

September 1866

Secondday, September 3rd, 1866
A hard rain this morning. The thunder and lightning was terrific enough to frighten anyone timid, but I think I am not a very big coward. I went with Alma and Clay out to his mothers and sisters. Seventhday evening and yesterday we went to Holmes. They live in such a large nice home and everything is so convenient. I think it is a model farm and he a model farmer. I wish more of the farmers were like him and it would not be so tiresome living in the country. I am at home yet. I hope in two more weeks Will will be here. I am so tired of living this way. I just intend to keep Will at home when I get him here.

Thirdday, September 4th, 1866
Another beautiful morning. How anyone can prefer winter to summer I cannot see for there is so much to admire and enjoy in spring, summer and autumn

that is not thought of in winter. All our better and finer feelings are awakened if we only pause from our daily routine long enough to see and feel the beauty around us. It cannot but give us purer hearts to cultivate love for the higher and more beautiful objects of nature and art. The time is drawing nearer for Will to come home. I know he is glad. If I only knew "our baby" would be as we could wish how pleasant would it be to think about it. I get so discouraged sometimes and feel it impossible almost that it will be all right and then when I think of the thousands of babies that come every day and many of them so unwillingly received. I think nothing is impossible with God. A baby is not to me like many persons a dreadful nuisance, but something to cherish and love. How I could love a child of our own I think nothing would be more pleasant than the care of children provided they are anyway lovable and I think that depends a great deal on the training.

Fifthday, September 6th, 1866
Went with mother over to Uncle Christopher's to see grandfather. He is no better. I went to Sid Randal's for supper, I do hope Will will come home next week. I am getting so tired living this way and in fact I am getting very scarce in the provision line. We will travel to get a supply of nearly everything before long or else do something.

Sixthday, September 7th, 1866
Such a dreary day. The rain just pouring down and no prospect of quitting soon. Mrs. Fan has a boy. I am glad it is. If I only can get along so well and possess a little tiny girl or boy on some of these mornings how happy I will fee. Aunt Anna [Anna Hadley Betts, wife of William S. Betts] is real sick. I must go and see her when it quits raining.

Seventhday, September 8th, 1866
Clear this morning. Have been busy doing nothing much. I feel in a bad humor this morning. I wish I could feel in a better mood. Elva provokes me so. It keeps me out of humor half my time when with her. I do not know what she may be but I know she never was a more obstinate headstrong girl ever lived than she is now, so provoking. [Elva was fourteen years old.]

Sabbath, September 9th, 1866
Up home this morning. A very bright day but do not appreciate as I should. I feel disappointed. I got a letter from Will this morning. Came yesterday and he will not be at home for two weeks more. Every time I hear it is a little longer I am just so provoked I can hardly keep from crying. I just won't let him stay any longer than that for I need him at home now if ever I did. Night all alone and feel in an unhappy mood. It is so lonely all the time on Sabbath anyhow or in the evening I will be so glad when Will comes home. I am sure he will not go

away anymore and leave me. But I ought not to be so selfish as it is just as hard for him to be away as for me to have him away.

Thirdday, September 11th, 1866
Pouring down rain when we awoke this morning and we did not hurry ourselves getting up. Have been very busy all day and this evening. Our chickens caused a vast amount of trouble, but at last we got them all quiet. Cal came in just now and told me Jennie Henley was dead. Oh, can it be that I will never see her more. I am so sorry and I have been so careless about writing to her. The letter I received weeks ago is unanswered. I feel very sad indeed and the memory of those days we spent together at Earlham comes back with more sadness than ever before.

Fifthday, September 13th, 1866
A beautiful morning so bright it looks impossible for it to ever rain anymore. Was over to see grandfather last evening. He is failing rapidly. It is sad to see him brought so low, I dreamed last night he was dead, that he died sitting up. I think he cannot live long. The week is passing rapidly away. Only a few more days till Will will be at home to stay. How glad I will be. Anyway only a few more weeks till something else will happen. I am so in hopes it will be nothing bad when it does happen and that a sweet little baby will be in our possession. It seems too good to be true.

Seventhday, September 15th, 1866
A beautiful evening. A September evening indeed. I have been at Vances sewing for Lib on the machine. No letter from Will. I wonder why he did not write. I think it is too bad to disappoint me so for I felt sure I would get one this morning. Maybe he is coming home tonight. I am glad it is Seventhday again. Perhaps in another week Will will be at home. I am very sure he will if he is well for I do not think I will let him stay away any longer done or not done. It is time he was at home helping me fix up things a little before I am unable to see to anything. Oh, when the dread is all over and if it only happens that there is a sweet little babe to care for I cannot be thankful enough. I get discouraged sometimes and think it is of no use for me to indulge in any pleasant fancies about the future for it will be impossible for me to possess a sweet baby. I would be asking too much, but I am going to hope for the best and perhaps the "Good Man" will make it all right.

Sabbath, September 16th, 1866
Bright and pleasant this morning, seeming as ever Sabbath morning here all so quiet. No ringing of church bells filling the air with music, only passing along quietly to Sabbath school or church. Poor old grandfather is very low—will not live long. It appears a long, long time and yet but a little time since grandmother was busily engaged with the household duties and grandfather working with

so much energy in his garden. Now the old house is all vacant and lonely and the inmates have left it forever. How good it would be to go to grandfather's once more, but it cannot be. One week and Will will be at home I expect it will be so much better for him to have to go back again.

Secondday, September 17th, 1866
Gloomy today. Have been almost sick and have not done much. I wonder if I will get a letter from Will tomorrow saying he will not be at home for two weeks yet. I expect him home this week certain. Oh, I wonder if in 7 weeks we will have a little baby all sweet and bright or will something else sadder have occurred. I hope not. How delightful to think. Maybe we will be talking of the baby as something that really is in that time.

Thirdday, September 18th, 1866
Very gloomy. Just like fall. I wonder if we will have anymore pleasant weather before cool weather comes. I am looking for a letter from Will this morning. Will be much disappointed if I do not get one. I wish he would write that he would be home about sixth day. I wish the train would hurry and come. We got up so late this morning and yet it seems long. Night. A letter from Will. He wrote he was coming home before the week was out, but did not say what day. George and Grandfather are both so bad. I wrote him to come as soon as he could.

Fourthday, September 19th, 1866
Raining this morning like everything and looks dark enough to rain all day. I look for Will tomorrow. Almost regret having written to him to come for I am sure he will not know what to do. I do wish we could sell our house. I think I will not care to leave much of course will regret it on some accounts, but yet am anxious to try the experiment. Had rather go to Richmond than Hillsboro, but expect the latter place will be better on some accounts.

Fifthday, September 20th, 1866
Such a dark morning. Just pouring down rain. Lonely enough for anybody. After awhile when the baby comes how much more pleasant it will be. In the first place it will be such a curiosity to see a baby in the house and then it will be improving all the time. A constant source of enjoyment. I do hope I will not be disappointed about it. Grandfather is just alive. Cannot last much longer. I dreamed so much of grandmother last night. It always makes me feel so sad to dream of her as she used to be and wake up to find it all a dream. How good it would be to see her again. I was at Georges last evening. He is not able to sit up this week. The baby is real sweet if we only had one so sweet. [Joseph G. Janney was born on July 16, 1866, but died on May 16, 1867.] How glad I would be. Evening—Grandfather [Aaron Betts] is dead. A few minutes ago. How sad the evening. The rain pouring down. Every little while the yellow leaves falling

giving it more the appearance of a November than a September evening. I am so in hopes Will will get home in time.

Friend

According to promise I write to you most willingly—it is usual when any one becomes possessed of any treasure to be exceedingly glad we are at present the possessors of a jewel most rare—we esteem it of priceless worth—value it more highly than we would the brightest gem that glitters in the crown of Prince or Princess—in our admiring eyes it seems no polish or embellishment of any kind could enhance its beauty or value—but we hope by patient and unceasing efforts to keep it bright—and "at last" it will be fitted to be a Jewel in the upper world. I must now describe it—brown eyes with drooping lashes, cheeks soft as velvet and fat, dimpled arms—do not infer that is bald headed from my not having described hair—brown hair with which a little coaxing for a season will curl beautifully—and so summing it all up you will see it is a baby—brown eyed, sweet—and fat, a chubby little thing we think the world of and can say in very much truth "And though she is nothing to another she is all the world to us."

Sixthday, September 21st, 1866
So lonely today. Grandfather buried at 3 o'clock. Will did not get home in time for the funeral, but has come at last to stay. I am so glad. George is so bad. I expect he will not live long. I feel very sorry for Beck. This is her first great sorrow. How could I bear it if Will were to die.

Secondday, September 23rd, 1866
Dark and raining. If Will was away I would feel very lonely indeed. Poor George is very low.[290] May not live till morning. They have sent for Steve and the rest of them, but I fear they will not see him alive if they come. Will is there. I am afraid to be there very much as it might do some harm. I do not see how it can though.

---

290. George Janney's health had been greatly diminished when he contracted yellow fever while serving in Key West, Florida, during the Civil War. "Transported to the new World aboard slave ships, the mosquito-borne diseases of yellow fever and malaria 'proved a lasting threat to the eastern seaboard of North America.'" "Disease and Our Ancestors, Mortality in the Eighteenth and Nineteenth Centuries," *New England Ancestors*, Holiday 2002, vol. 3, nos. 5–6. "Consumption [tuberculosis] was widespread in the Old Northwest and serious enough to account for one-fourth of the deaths." Source: "Death and Disease in the Old Northwest," Thomas H. Shawker, National Genealogical Society, January/February 2002.

Thirdday, September 24th, 1866
Cloudy this morning and been raining. Cal is sick. I am so anxious to know the result. I can hardly wait till it is over. I hope she is not very bad, but I expect she will think she is for at best it is bad enough. If I can only get along without suffering so much I will be thankful. I am sure. George is very bad. Cannot live much longer. How dreary everything must look to Beck. Nothing bright for the future. What a lonely winter it will be for her.

Sixthday, September 28th, 1866
Been bright for a few days. Seems so much more pleasant. Cal and baby. A big boy are getting along finely. It seems so strange to think Cal has a baby. [William Betts Jackson was born on September 27, 1866]. Why will it be impossible for me to have one. I hope I will have no cause to envy Cal this winter to own a little pet of my own.

Sabbath, September 30th, 1866
Went to the meeting of the Alumni last night. It was very good. The new members are to be taken into full membership this morning. I thought I had better stay at home. Several are to be immersed. I never saw any one baptized in my life, but never felt so anxious about it as some persons. Such a beautiful day. Calm and bright. A September Sabbath. The last one of 1866. I wonder if I will ever see another September and if it will be as bright to me then as now. Our little girl, if nothing bad happens, will be nearly a year old then. I hope so.

October 1866

Secondday, October 1st, 1866
A beautiful October day. In one month I suppose my fate as to the coming event will be decided for good or bad. Good I hope, but time will prove. Will has gone to Georges tonight. We went over to church. The new minister Gregg preached. Like him very well. I wish our baby was here all safe and sound as Cal's. I know she must feel awful glad.

Seventhday, October 6th, 1866
Ann Stevens spent the afternoon here. We had a very pleasant time. Such beautiful weather as we have now. Oh, I feel nearly discouraged when I think of all I have to go through with before long. I am so in hopes I will get along all right. How thankful I will be. My old journal full at last to be laid away for what?

[At this point, the journal was completely full. No other journals are known to exist. Just over three weeks after this last entry, on October 30, 1866, Alma Fawceit Janney was born to Paulena and William. Both mother and child survived. While the journals were finished, the story continued. See Epilogue.]

Alma Fawceit Janney

Recipe

Washing Soap
Dissolve one pound of soda and a half a pound of hot lime[291] in one gallon of boiling water. Dissolve one pound of sliced hard soap in two quarts of boiling water. When cool mix them together soak the clothes and boil them half an hour in the suds of this soap. Then rinse.

Pudding
Boil one quart milk with the rind of a lemon, strain and boil again. Mix 1 tablespoonful of flour with two of cold milk. Stir it in the boiling milk. When cool add 3 well beaten eggs. Sweeten to taste and bake in crust in a quick oven.

Tapioca Pudding
Four tablespoonfuls of tapioca. Soaked in one quart of new milk overnight. Stir it over the fire in the morning till it comes to a boil, add grated lemon rind, one tumbler of sweet cream, half a tumbler of wine with sugar enough to fill the glass and four egg whites and yolks beaten separately to be added just before baking. Bake five minutes in a quick oven. Eat cold.

Dressing for Cole Slaw
To the well beaten yolk of one egg add a little milk, two or three table spoonfuls of vinegar and a small piece of butter. Stir it over the fire till it come to a boil.

Corn Starch Cake
Stir to a froth three quarters of pound of butter, one lb of sugar, half cup of sweet cream and whites of nine eggs beaten very light. Take a pound of cornstarch, two large spoonfuls, replace with flour add it as the above. Flavor with lemon.

---

291. A chemical with the formula CaO, commonly called quicklime or hot lime. When hydrated with one mole of water, quicklime forms slaked lime, $Ca(OH)_2$, which is used to make calcium-fatty-acid soaps.

Italian Cream

One pint of cream—half milk make it hot, sweetening to taste and flavoring with lemon peel. Beat the yolks of eight eggs, beat all together set over a slow fire till it thickens. Have an ounce of icing glaze melted and strained. Add to the cream. Whip it well and pour in the mold.

Sponge Cake

Four eggs, two cups sugar, three cups flour, butter the size of an egg, one teaspoonful cream of tartar, half teaspoonful soda, one cup of milk.

Fire Protection

To protect roof from fire, a wash composed of lime, salt and fine sand or wood ashes. Put on like white wash.

We meet, but where is that feeling of friendship,
that intimacy of soul that bound us together when school girls?

The clasp of the hand is not the same,
the kiss is not the same.
It comes more from the lips, less from the heart.

There is something between that is deepened by each succeeding year.
Why is it natural that friends should grow cold and love grow old?

Is [it] because the cares of troubles and frivolities
become so mingled with our lives
that we find no time to think of old friends?

I believe our lives would be purer
and happier if we would cherish our friendship more.

Paulena Stevens Janney

June 1865

Epilogue

Paulena's Story Continues . . .

Fifthday, July 17, 1863

**How can anyone live on year after year without
the pleasant companionship of a journal? . . .**

**It will be a consolation for me in years to come
should I live to read this over,
and after I am done with it
let someone else have it.**

I wonder who will be its owner in 20 years.

Paulena Stevens Janney

Epilogue

*T*he days following the last entry of Paulena's journal were filled with the expected arrival of the couple's first child, a daughter, Alma Fawceit Janney, named for Paulena's sister, Alma [Mary "Alma" Stevens Cowgill], born in Martinsville on October 30, 1866. She was a healthy baby and Paulena apparently had a safe delivery.

The Will of Paulena's grandfather, Aaron Betts, was proven on January 18, 1867, in Clinton County Probate Court. In the will the distribution of property was made to the heirs. The real estate was located in Clinton County, Ohio, and Shelby County, Indiana. By May 24, 1867, eighty acres of a 400-acre tract of land known as the Flat Rock Farm in Shelby County, Indiana, was sold by the heirs for $3,200. There still remained 320 acres to be sold, but no record has been located for the sale of that land.

The Will of Aaron Betts

"Be it remembered that heretofore to-wit on the 29th day of December A.D. 1866 at a Probate Court held in the Court House in Wilmington, Clinton County Ohio, before J. West—Judge, thereof. This day came William S. Betts and produced in open Court the last-Will and Testament of Aaron Betts late of Clinton County deceased which is in words and figures following to-witt:

"**1st** The State of Ohio, Clinton County; Will of Aaron Betts Deceased, I Aaron Betts of Clinton County, Ohio, in this my last will and Testament —Provides as follows That my Son Wm S. Betts Shall have the farm where he now resides said to contain one hundred acres (100) also that known as the Patterson Farm in Steuben's Survey No 2697 Said to contain Seventy-five (75) acres also one hundred (100) acres adjoining the first named piece, on the south in Bradfords Survey No 2371 also 62 1/2 Sixty-two and one half acres part of a tract of one hundred and fifteen acres purchased by me of James Taylor survey No 10.744. The said sixty-two and one half acres to be off of the East side of said tract and adjoining land now owned by him W.S. Betts: also 5 (five) acres lying on the west of and adjoining the Village of Martinsville and town lot No. 64 of said Village which land and lot have at my instance been deeded to said Wm S. Betts by Nathaniel Hunter. Also lot No 57 adjoining the last named lot. Also the proceeds of Fractional Lot No 2 in Johnsons and Daltons addition to the village of Martinsville previously deeded for his (Wm Betts) Benefit. The above named lands and lots all lying in the county of Clinton and State of Ohio. I also bequeth him one third of that known as the "Flat Rock Farm" situated in Shelby County, Indiana.

"**2nd** To my Son Christopher C. Betts I give the farm where he now resides adjoining Martinsville on the East Side said to contain (90) ninety acres. Also 30 Thirty acres in Bradfords Survey No 2390 purchased by me of Wm. Moon as known as the Calvin Watson land also that known as the Milton Hollingsworth land Situated on Glady Run in Clark Township and said to contain Two-hundred acres. Also the proceeds of (22 1/2) twenty two and one half acres deeded to John Davie for (his CC Betts) benefit—being part of the one hundred and fifteen acres tract named in W.S. Betts bequest. Also town lots Nos 1 and 4 in Johnsons and Daltons addition to the town of Martinsville the above lands and lots all situated in the county of Clinton and State of Ohio. I also bequeath him one third of the "Flat Rock Farm" situated in Shelby County Indiana before mentioned in the bequest of W.S. Betts.

"**3rd** To My Daughter Prescilla Stephens I give my home farm of one hundred and fifty-two acres also (160) one hundred and Sixty acres in Taylors Survey No 10744 and 10.570 being lands deeded to me by James Taylor & Son. Also (30 1/2) thirty and one half acres balance of the one hundred and fifteen acre tract before me mentioned in the bequest to W.S. and CC Betts. Also Lot No (2) two and fraction adjoining on the East in the town of Martinsville. Of the above lands all situtated in the county of Clinton State of Ohio. I also bequeath her one third of the "Flat Rock Farm" situated in Shelby county Indiana before mentioned in WS and CC Betts's bequeths.

"**4th** To my Grandchildren I bequeath Eight-Hundred dollars each. They having been provided for and to be provided for as follows Madison Betts, Rebecca A. Janney, Paulina A. Janney, Caroline A. Jackson, Edwin Betts, Homer Betts, Alma Cowgil, and Wm.C. Betts and Emma Betts and Rachel Betts have already been provided for by lands deeded to them by me in view of this revision. Aaron S. Betts and James P. Betts have been provided for by the payment of money to them by me for said purpose and for the further provision of the minor Grandchildren I have placed in the hands of W.S. Betts (1723 3/100) Seventeen hundred and twenty three & 33/100 Dollars and in hands of Christopher C. Betts Thirty-one hundred and thirty three Dollars and in the hands of Evan Stephens Thirteen hundred and thirty three Dollars which Sum each Wm S. Betts and CC Betts and Evan Stephens Shall pay to his own children Five Years from the time they arrive at age and for the payment of which the bequests herein made to my children shall be responsible as follow Wm S. Betts to his own children for 1723 33/100 Dollars.

"**5th** CC Betts his own children 3133 33/100 Dollars and Priscilla Stephens for 1333 33/100 Dollars the amount placed in the hands of Evan Stephens. Any deficiency to make Eight Hundred dollars to each and all of my Grandchildren shall be made from property not mentioned in this will. I do hereby nominate and appoint—Wm S. Betts and Christopher C. Betts and Evan Stephens executors of this my last will and testament–hereby authorizing them to compromise adjust-release and discharge in such manner as they deem proper the Debts and claims on me.

        "I have hereunto Set–my hand and Seal this 27th day of 11th month in the year of 1865.

Signed and acknowledged (Aaron Betts)
by Said Aaron Betts as his last will and testament in our presence
and signed by us in his presence Thomas F. Atkinson
James Hunt

6th Codical A
"That my will concerning the disposition of my property as above intended to be expressed may be more properly understood the following interlineations and additions being necessary. I have caused the same to be made is-Interlineation marked A. in the bequest to Precilla Stephens after the figure 2. as follows two and fraction on the East-Interlineations Marked B in the bequest to my Grandchildren inserting the name Pauline A. Janey invertantly [inadvertently] left out in the above writing and in further testimony of my will be it understood that—Evan Stephens shall have and hold a life estate for the term of his natural life in the bequest to his wife Precilla Stephens said interest—to be existant with the interest of Prescilla Stephens and to vest with the date of the above will Should the same not be revoked by me and further that Ann Betts wife of Wm S Betts and Lydia Betts wife of Christopher C. Betts Shall have and hold a dower interest—in the Estate of their husbands above granted which interest–shall vest with the date of the above mentioned of Wm S. Betts for 1723 33/100 Dollars CC Betts for 3135 33/100 dollars and Precilla Stephens for 1333 33/100 dollars be it understood that the same is for funds placed in their hands to be paid to their children in pursuance of the above bequest to my grandchildren and that they are responsible as follows Vis Wm S. Betts for 1723 33/111 dollars to his children George Betts, Eva Betts and Albert Betts. CC Betts for 3133 33/100 dollars to his children Mary Betts, Daniel Betts-Ella Betts and Susan Betts and Precilla Stephens for funds placed in her hands for 1333 33/100 dollars to her children Elva Stephens and Wm Stephens. If any of the above named Grandchildren should die before becoming entitled to payment as provided then the parent of such child should be released from all obligation for the payment of said childs portion. Interlineation of is made by reason of Emma Betts and Rachel Betts grandchildren having been provided for since writing the foregoing Will In Conformation of the above will and testament with the additions and explanations herein made I have here unto Set—my hand and Seal this 9th day of 8th Mo A.D. 1866."

Aaron Betts
Signed and Acknowledged by Aaron Betts as his last will
and testament in our presence and signed by us in his presence—
James Hunt
Aaron B. Betts

"Will proven January 18, 1867

"Original will filed in Clinton Co. Ohio Court House Will Book No. 2 page 152. Another copy of this will is found in the deed records of Shelby Co. Indiana when a portion of the Flat Rock farm property was sold following Aaron's death."

Shelby County Deed—William S. Ensley Deed from Betts & Stephens

"This Indenture witnesseth that William S. Betts and Anna Betts his wife, C.C. Betts and Lydia his wife and Evan Stephens and Priscilla his wife of Clinton County in the State of Ohio Convey and Warrant to William S. Ensley of Shelby County in the State of Indiana for the sum of Three thousand two hundred dollars the following Real Estate in the Shelby County in the State of Indiana to wit:

"The West half of the South West Quarter of Section twenty-four (24) in township Eleven (11) North of Range Six (6) East—containing Eighty-acres more or less.

"In Witness where of the said William S. Betts and Anna Betts his wife C.C. Betts and Lydia his wife and Evan Stephens and Priscilla his wife have hereunto set their hands and seals this twenty fourth day of May A.D. 1867.

"Signed sealed and acknowledged in presence of

"James H. West

Wm. H. Brown

A.J. Taft

State of Ohio

Clinton county

    Wm S. Betts

    Anna Betts

    CC Betts

    Lydia Betts

    Evan Stephens

    Priscilla Stephens

"Before me A.F. Taft a Notary Public in and for said County this twenty-fourth day of May AD 1867 Wm. S Betts and Anna his wife CC Betts and Lydia his wife and Evan Stephens and Priscilla his wife appeared and acknowledged the execution of the as said deed."

The 1867 Platt Map of Shelby County, Indiana, shows this property in Washington Township of Shelby County about eight miles southwest of Shelbyville and a mile north of the village of Flat Rock and about ten to twelve miles east of Interstate 65, I-65 that runs from Chicago to Florida through the state of Indiana. The above mentioned property is listed under Ensley; however, an adjoining one-half section of Section 23, which consisted of 320 acres was still listed under Aaron Betts. The property referred to in the will consisted of at least 400 acres. No deed of transfer, gift, or sale of the 320 acres was located on my initial search. Source: Notes of Christie Hill Russell.

Aaron Betts's son, Christopher Columbus Betts, was the only one of that generation who remained in Clinton County. He would die in 1870, not long after the other families moved out west.

"Christopher C. Betts, Clark Township, a son of Aaron and Anna (Hunt) Betts, the former a native of Bucks County, Pennsylvania, and the latter of North Carolina. Aaron Betts came to Clinton County by 1818 and settled one mile west of Martinsville where he purchased a large tract of land from the original survey. He was listed as a tanner in the early years and was found on the 1820 census in Clark township of Clinton County.[292] Subsequently he bought eighty acres of land, a part of which formed a portion of the homestead [Sugar Grove Farm] later occupied by his son C. C. Betts.

"In 1836, Aaron engaged in the mercantile business with his sons, William S. and Christopher Columbus Betts, under the firm name of A. Betts & Sons. In 1838, the firm changed to C. C. Betts and Lazenby, who did business together until 1849, when the latter withdrew and David Sanders entered as a partner. This company, C. C. Betts & Co., continued merchandising till 1860, when the firm dissolved, and C. C. Betts retired from mercantile pursuits and followed farming up to his death, which occurred October 14, 1870.

"Christopher C. Betts was for many years prominently connected with all the secular, religious and educational interest of Martinsville. He was largely instrumental in securing to Martinsville the schoolhouse as well as the school itself (built by William and George Janney in 1857).

"Christopher C. Betts was married September 30, 1845, to Miss Lydia Huff, the youngest child of a native of Highland County, Ohio, where she was born February 28, 1815. Mr. and Mrs. Betts had eleven children as follows: Madison, born February 13, 1837, Cashier of Clinton County National Bank; Rebecca A., born June 13, 1849 [should be 1839], wife of George Janney; James E., born March 14, 1842; Aaron 'Homer,' born February 6, 1845; Martha E. born January 25, 1847; Rachel A., b. June 13, 1849, wife of Jasper Axline; Mary O., b. Nov. 16, 1851, wife of Jefferson McKibben; Daniel W., b. January 7, 1854; Lydia L. b. March 23, 1856; Susan, b. April 8, 1858; Sarah E., b. March 26, 11840, and died July 27, 1840." Source: History of Clinton County Ohio, 1882, W. H. Beers & Co., pp. 951–52.

---

292. Aaron and Ann Hunt Betts are listed among "First Families of Clinton County, Ohio," since they were enumerated on the 1820 census.

Obituary of Christopher Betts's Son, Madison Betts
Clinton Democrat [Wilmington, Ohio], September 26, 1907

"Honorable Madison Betts Closes an Active Career

Honorable Madison Betts died at his beautiful country home near Martinsville last Thursday morning at 5 o'clock. He had been in ill health for several years with a nervous affliction and was very feeble during the last several months of his life, although he was able to get about until the day preceding his death and was in Wilmington about a week prior thereto.

"The death of Madison Betts marks the passing of a man who for many year was one of the most active factors in the affairs of this community.

"He was a son of the late C.C. Betts and was born February 13, 1837, on the farm on which he died. Mr. Betts was educated at Martinsville and the Friends' Boarding School, now Earlham college, Richmond, Indiana, he graduated from that institution as a civil engineer, and subsequently assisted in surveying the Cincinnati and Marietta railroad. He was deputy collector of internal revenue for a year and a half under the late David Sanders and was for the succeeding three years bookkeeper for a large wholesale firm in Cincinnati.

"He was admitted to the bar of Clinton county in 1867, he in the meantime having served as deputy auditor, and was a partner of Judge A.W. Doan in the practice of law for three years. He represented Clinton county in the legislature in 1868–9, and introduced a bill, which passed the house but failed of passage in the senate by a tie vote, prohibiting railroads from consolidation, extortion or charging exorbitant rates. He was also the father of the bill which authorized the erection of the West school building. He was a member of the Wilmington school board for many years. For fifteen years he was cashier of the Clinton County National Bank, and during the many years of his residence in Wilmington was actively identified with its best and most progressive interests. He resigned the cashiership of the Clinton County National Bank and was subsequently appointed U.S. bank examiner. He soon established his ability as an expert in this capacity and was sent by the government to all parts of the country to examine the large banks and untenable intricate complications produced by the chicanery of dishonest or derelict bank officials.

"After several years service he resigned this position to accept the vice presidency and management of the Third National Bank of Cincinnati. After filling this responsible position with marked success for a number of years he resigned on account of failing health and retired to his beautiful country home at Martinsville, where his declining years were peacefully and happily spent with his wife and daughter.

"Madison Betts was united in marriage June 30, 1859, with Miss Caroline Janney, a native of Clinton county, then residing in Richmond, Ind. Of the two children born to this union, the son, Wade, died some years ago. Miss Lizzie R., the daughter, remains to share the bereavement of the widow.

"Mr. Betts was a great friend of Wilmington College and a member of the board of managers for many years.

"The funeral service was held at the residence at 1 p.m. last Saturday, conducted by Mrs. Emma S. Townsend. Interment was made in Sugar Grove cemetery, Wilmington Commandery, Knights Templar, acting as escort from South street and observing the Knight Templar service at the grave." Source: Microfilm, Clinton Democrat, March 1, 1906–November 28, 1907, Wilmington Public Library, Wilmington, Ohio.

The Westward Migration

With the close of the Civil War came the opening of territories west of the Mississippi River and a vast influx of settlers eager for a fresh start in an expanding country. With the passing of Aaron and Anne Hunt Betts and the distribution of the Betts estate to the heirs, plans were made for several family members to move to southwest Missouri. It is not

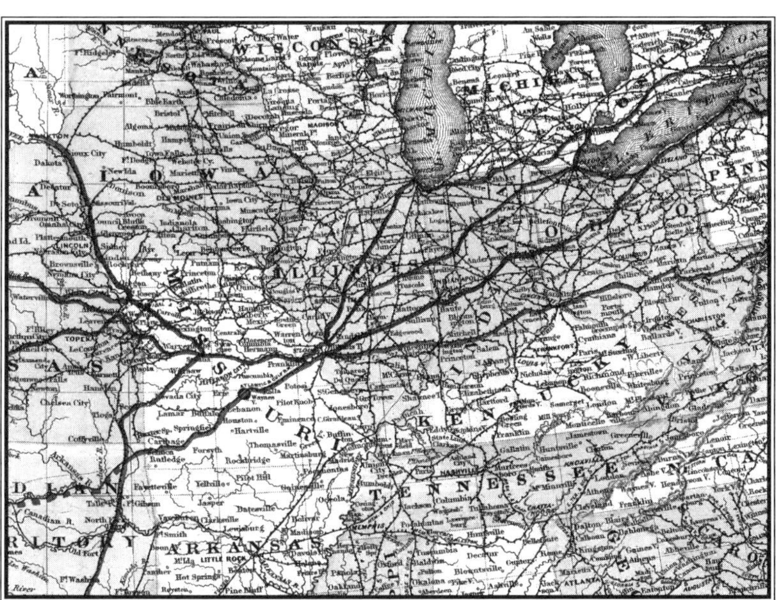

Martinsville, Ohio, to Carthage, Missouri, on the Atlantic and Pacific Railroad System (Map 1873)

known exactly why that particular location was chosen except that there was a Quaker meeting already established at Alba, Jasper County, Missouri, about twelve miles from Carthage, the county seat. Union Monthly Meeting, Jasper County, Missouri, was established by the Kansas Quarterly Meeting at the request of Union and Fairview Preparative Meetings on August 1, 1868. All Charter members were formerly members of Spring River Monthly Meeting Kansas. [Hinshaw Quaker Records, unpublished notebooks 46, 48, and 92a, Earlham Quaker Collection.] On November 6, 1869, Evan, his wife, Priscilla, and their children—Lydia Elva, William Land, and Lenna—were received on a certificate from Newberry Monthly Meeting, Ohio, dated August 23, 1869.

Family tradition has stated that the families migrated from Ohio to southwest Missouri in 1868. From a deed in Jasper County, Missouri, William Janney and Paulena bought lot 26 in Lamb's Addition to the town of Carthage on October 2, 1867, from Mary Searle for $150, Warranty Deed Book K, pp. 51 52. William and Paulena must have been among the first of the families to make the move to southwest Missouri. Lot 26 is the south half of the block on 11th Street between Main and Lyon streets. The records for Union Monthly Meeting, Jasper County, Missouri, show that William Janney, wife, Paulena, and child Alma F. were received on certificate from Newberry Monthly Meeting, Ohio, also dated August 23, 1869, the same date as for Evan and Priscilla Stevens.

Alma would have been about one year old in 1867. It was in Carthage that William and Paulena had their second child, Carl Russell Janney, on December 8, 1869. This birth date gives reason to believe that they moved in 1867 or 1868, as it was not likely that Paulena would have been able to make such a strenuous journey in a late pregnancy in 1869. A *Carthage Press* article stated that Carl Janney was born on South Main St. between Tenth and Eleventh Streets. That would appear to have been lot 26 of the Lamb's Addition. It is one block south of the Christian Church and across the street from the home of Judge Perkins, grandfather of zoologist Marlin Perkins.

Death of Paulena Stevens Janney

When Alma was six years old and Carl was only three, their mother, Paulena Stevens Janney—author of these journals—died on September 9, 1873. She was thirty-three years old. The cause of death was consumption, or tuberculosis. William Janney recorded his last conversation with her in his day book:

Diary of William Janney (1872–1909)
Lena died Sept. 9, 1872
Last words spoken by her to her dear husband were such as these:

"Will, Forgive me for all the hasty words
spoken unthoughtfully by me."

I forgave her truly and wished to be forgiven all . . . lived her forgiveness. She said if she had her life to live over again, she would be a very different wife to me. She told me her besetting trouble was her ambition. She told me to be good to the children. Said I would have to have a great deal of patience with them, said not to be to [too] hard on Carl. Wanted me to try to make them to be good Christians.

Another sweet expression, said she would have to ask God to forgive all her sins.

She said, "Oh, how I do hate to leave the children. Oh, how can [and again] I leave the children."

Remarked to me when I was so overwhelmed with grief. "Poor fellow, what a hard time I would have." She hoped we would meet again as a family in heaven—as for her father all was right—2 children happy. God be praised for his great goodness to her and may her devoted and pure life and happy death be the means of making her husband a better man—that he may . . . his two motherless children to profit by the example of their beloved mother!

William Janney

Paulena A.
Wife of Wm Janney died Sept. 9, 1872
Aged 33 years
A loving Wife
a kind and affectionate mother has gone
home to her Savior, where she awaits
for the happy reunion with those she loved
best while on Earth

Obituary, Carthage, Missouri, *Weekly Banner*

"DIED On Tuesday, Sept. 9, 1873, of consumption Paulina, wife of Mr. Wm. Janney, aged 33 years.

"The following verses, by [John Greenleaf] Whittier, so truthfully descriptive of her life, are published at the request of her friends:

"Her path shall brighten more and more
 Unto the perfect day:
She cannot fail of peace who bore
 Such peace with her away.

O sweet, calm face that seemed to wear
 The look of sins forgiven!
O voice of prayer that seemed to bear
 Our own needs up to heaven!

How reverent in our midst she stood,
 Or knelt in grateful praise!
What grace of Christian womanhood
 Was in her household ways!

For still her holy living meant
 No duty left undone;
The heavenly and the human blent
 Their kindred loves in one.

And if her life small leisure found
 For feasting ear and eye,
And pleasure, on her daily round,
 She passed unpausing by,

Yet with her went a secret sense
 Of all things sweet and fair,
And beauty's gracious providence
 Refreshed her unaware.

She kept her line of rectitude
 With love's unconscious ease;
Her kindly instincts understood
 All gentle courtesies.

An informed charm of graciousness
 Made sweet her smile and tone,
And glorified her farm wife dress
 With beauty not its own.

The dear Lord's best interpreters
 Are humble human souls;
The Gospel of a life like hers
 Is more than books or scrolls.

From scheme and creed the light goes out
 The saintly fact survives;
The blessed Master non can doubt
 Revealed in holy lives.

Source: Copied from microfilm by Christie Russell, November 2002, at the Missouri Historical Society newspaper collection Columbia, Missouri.

Paulena was first buried in the East/Cedar Cemetery, just outside Carthage, but in 1891 her remains were removed to the Stevens Plot in Park Cemetery, Carthage, Missouri.

John Greenleaf Whittier, who wrote the above poem, "The Friend's Burial," was Paulena's fifth cousin once removed.

William Janney

remarried, to Sarah Johnson in 1877, four years after Paulena's death. Alma was eleven and Carl was eight years old. The 1880 census listed the family—William Janney, Sallie, Alma, and Carl—living on the Chestnut Street farm in Madison Township, Jasper County. The family moved to Garden Plain, Sedgwick County, Kansas, in 1883 when Carl was fourteen, but family tradition states that Carl was so unhappy that he ran away from home and it is believed that he returned to Carthage where he probably lived with his Stevens grandparents, Evan and Priscilla, or his aunt Alma Stevens Cowgill. By the time he was about nineteen years old, he was listed in the 1888–89 Carthage City Directory as a miller, boarding at 302 N. Garrison. The Galesburg or Carthage City Mill, which was operated by Carl's Uncle, Clay Cowgill, and Frank Hill, was where he learned the milling business.

Alma Janney,

daughter of William and Paulena, moved with her father and stepmother, to Garden Plain, Kansas, in 1883 and died there a year later in 1884. She is buried in the Calvary Methodist Cemetery, Garden Plain, Kansas. William and Sarah adopted a daughter, Ethel, who was born on September 30, 1886. They remained in Kansas until 1902 when they removed to Neosho, Newton County, Missouri, where they lived on a forty-acre tract of land. William Janney died on April 9, 1909, and is buried in the Thrasher Cemetery, outside of Neosho, Newton County, Missouri. Ethel married Albert Sweeney and lived in Springfield, Missouri, until the early 1950s when Christie and her parents visited her. She gave the three journals that constitute this book to Georgia Janney Hill.

Carl Russell Janney,

the only surviving child of William and Paulena, married Fannie Elizabeth "Eliza" Kendrick in 1893 when he was a little over twenty-three years old and she was eighteen. Fannie's mother, Elva Britten Kendrick, had died in 1888 when Fannie was thirteen. How she and Carl Janney met is still not known, but it is possible that it was through the milling business. J. D. P. Kendrick, Fannie's father, probably used the Galesburg or City Mill. Whatever the circumstances of their meeting, Carl and Fannie were married at the Methodist parsonage by the Reverend Darby in Jasper, Jasper County, Missouri. Although Carl's mother, Paulena, author of these journals, showed interest in the Methodist denomination while they lived in Clinton County, Ohio, she still retained her Quaker affiliation.

Joshua Draper Palmer Kendrick

was a member of the Cumberland Presbyterian Church in Carthage, but his daughter, Fannie Kendrick, was a member of the First Methodist Church in Carthage. It is not known why Fannie and Carl were not married at the Kendrick House. Perhaps it was because J. D. P Kendrick had served in the Confederate militia in the Civil War and the family had owned slaves at one time. To have his [J. D. P. Kendrick's] daughter married to a young man with Quaker, anti-slavery, and Union sympathies might have been unthinkable at that time.

In the 1900 census, J. D. P. Kendrick was enumerated under his son, Thomas Kendrick, along with Tom's wife, Della Primm, and their adopted son, Frank. Next to them in the Kendrick house were Carl and Fannie with their one-year-old son, Walter. John Primm, father of Della and her brother, S. John Primm, were in the next house. J. D. P. Kendrick died on May 22, 1901. Of the seven children born to J. D. P. and Elva Kendrick, only four were living at the time their father died. With the settlement of the estate, Fannie Kendrick Janney received the Kendrick House and some acreage, Tom Kendrick and Della Primm went out to Portland, Oregon, where they lived and are buried. William D. Kendrick went to Phoenix, Arizona, where he is buried. Electa Kendrick Phillips was suffering from tuberculosis, and her doctor advised that she remove to a warmer, dryer climate. Therefore, in about 1902, Electa, her husband, William Phillips, and their children loaded their belongings on a wagon and headed for New Mexico. Her doctor thought fresh air would be better for her. Fortunately,

Electa's health returned in the New Mexico climate, and they moved on to California, where she lived in Long Beach until she died on May 12, 1950. William had died there on March 2, 1941. They are buried in Mt. View Cemetery at San Bernardino, California. Their children were Anna Bernice, Miriam Palmer, Fannie Fay, Della Arete, and Eugene Frank.

George and Rebecca Betts Janney

Two weeks after Paulena gave birth to Alma Janney, the son of George and Rebecca Betts Janney, Madison—"Maddie"—died at the age of six on November 15, 1866, and was buried in the Newberry Friends Cemetery. George Janney died on January 19, 1867. He was buried in the Newberry Friends Cemetery. He died of tuberculosis as a result of contracting yellow fever during the Civil War while he was stationed in Key West, Florida. His regiment lost three officers and twenty-four enlisted men killed in battle, but the greater toll was the loss of one-third of the company—eleven officers and 135 enlisted men—who died of disease. That number did not include George, as his death occurred almost two years after the war was over. Just four months after George's death, his son, Joseph Janney, aged eight months, died and was buried in the Newberry Friends Cemetery. Rebecca "Beck" Betts Janney had lost her husband and two of her three sons in less than six months.

Reynold Janney,

the only surviving child of George and Rebecca (Betts) Janney, was born near Martinsville, Clinton County, Ohio, on July 4, 1858. He was the nephew of Will Janney and a first cousin once removed to Paulena Stevens Janney. Reynold and his mother, Rebecca, were listed in the 1870 census in the household of Christopher C. Betts, Rebecca's father and uncle of Paulena Stevens Janney. On October 22, 1883, Reynold Janney and his mother, Rebecca, were granted a certificate of transfer from Newberry Monthly Meeting to the Wilmington, Ohio, Monthly Meeting, about seven miles away. While a student of Professor Levi T. Edwards at Wilmington College, Reynold, his fellow student Milton Farquhar, and Professor Edwards built a thirteen-inch telescope that was housed in the observatory on Wilmington College Campus, the second building erected on the campus.

For twelve years, Reynold Janney served as a teacher and high school principal in Wilmington and Chillicothe, Ohio. He married Ella Cerinthia Dixon on August 15, 1882, in Londonderry, Ohio. Although elected professor of mathematics and astronomy at Wilmington College, he moved east, where he was the manager of Densmore-Yost Company in Westboro, Massachusetts, and was four years in Worcester, Massachusetts at Prest Cycle Improvement Company.

In 1893 and 1894, Reynold Janney was corresponding with Professor Samuel L. Langley, who was an astrophysicist and pioneer student of aeronautics, and later became the third secretary of the Smithsonian Institution. Reynold suggested the use of two propellers and a small engine, which he believed would support the weight of a man as well as the equipment in Langley's experimental aerodrome. It is not known whether Langley used any of the suggestions offered by Janney. Langley's twelve-foot unmanned aerodrome was tested on August 8, 1903, with encouraging results. The model flew a distance of 600 yards and then sank in twenty-two feet of water. However, the successful manned flight of the Wright brothers' airplane took place four months later on December 17, 1903, eclipsing any further successes of Langley's aerodrome.

In 1894 Reynold moved his family to Keene, New Hampshire, where he was the superintendent of Trinity Manufacturing Company for four years. While there, he built an experimental auto. "The experimental machine, a light pleasure wagon, was given its trial run on June 26, 1900. The car had three cylinders attached to a revolving shaft. The shaft activated gears that powered the vehicle. Steam power was used to run the engine. The trial run was successful and in January of 1901 the Church Street factory began producing the new auto. During the next month the 'Keene Sentinel' announced that the Steamobile Company of America, a Delaware corporation with capital stock of $500,000, had acquired the factory, machinery, and patent rights of the Trinity Cycle Company and were to commence the manufacture of the new auto under the name 'Steamobile.'" Source: Historical Society of Cheshire County, New Hampshire, *Era 7: Emergence of Modern America—1890 to 1930*, Steamobile Company of America. 2002, Webworks3.com, http://www.hsccnh.org/mm/mm016.cfm.

By that time, Reynold Janney was at Bridgeport, Connecticut, as superintendent of the Locomobile Company of America and from there he went to Glen Ridge, New Jersey, with Thomas A. Edison as manager of his Storage Battery Company. Among Reynold's noteworthy inventions was the Edison storage battery (an alkaline, nickel-iron storage battery), the result of many thousands of experiments. The Edison storage battery was extremely rugged and had a high electrical capacity per unit of weight. By 1901 Reynold was in Jackson, Michigan, where he was superintendent of the Buick Company and at the same time vice president and chief engineer of the Waterbury Tool Company at New Britain, Connecticut. His work and experiments proved successful in developing a reversible turbine, but his principal achievement was the hydraulic speed gear. It was during World War I that his invention was most extensively applied on battleships for manipulating guns, turrets, and rudders. He was awarded the Howard N. Potts Gold Medal from the Franklin Institute of Philadelphia on April 3, 1918, for his invention of the Waterbury Hydraulic Speed Gear. Engraved over the entrance to the Franklin Institute are the words, "In Honor of Benjamin Franklin, Recognizing the world's leading men and women of science is one important way the Institute keeps its commitment to Franklin's legacy."

In his work, Reynold Janney crossed the ocean eighteen times and made one trip around the world. For several years, he and his wife maintained their residence in New York City, 21 Claremont Ave., now owned by Columbia University, but also lived in London and Paris. But, because he had to be in England, France, Italy, Germany, Austria, Russia and Japan so often, they often spent more time abroad than in New York. Reynold died on October 7, 1938, in Chillicothe, Ohio, where he is buried in the Grandview Cemetery with his wife, Ella. "Mrs. Reynold Janney, Chillicothe, Ohio, Ella Dixon Janney died last night eight days after seeing the movie made from best-selling novel written by her son, Russell Janney. Her age was 86. Mrs. Janney crippled for the last ten months, by a hip fracture saw the movie, 'The Miracle of the Bells' on May 20. She is the widow of Reynold Janney, Chillicothe High School Principal who died in 1938." Sources: *New York Times*, Sunday May 30, 1948, p. 34; Christie Russell, *The Clinton Chronicle* XIII, April 2, 2002, *History of Clinton County, Ohio*—1915, *Encyclopedia of American Quaker Genealogy*, W. W. Hinshaw, vol. V, Ohio, Genealogical Publishing Co., 1946.

Evan and Priscilla Betts Stevens

Union Monthly Meeting Quaker records dated May 1, 1869, show that Evan and Priscilla Stevens and their children—Lydia Elva, William Land, and Lenna [adopted child—daughter of Thomas Stevens, brother of Evan]—were received on certificate from Newberry Monthly Meeting on February 22, 1869. From land records in Jasper County, Missouri, for Evan Stevens, we learn that on November 18, 1867, "Wilkinson R. Ross and Elizabeth H. M. Ross of Champaign County, Illinois, conveyed to Evan Stephens of Jasper County, Missouri by a bond of $55 for Lot 1 & 2 of a tract of NW fractional quarter and the east half of the SW quarter and the NW quarter of the SW quarter of Section 2 and seven acres off the E side of NE quarter of the SE quarter of Section 8—Twp 28, Range 31 containing in all 297 acres." The final sale was for $4,455. That tract is on the east of Carthage and appears to be very near land that William Janney later owned, which was referred to as the East Chestnut Street farm, owned today (2006) by David Knost. On March 9, 1868, "Isaac Lamb and Sarah J. Lamb conveyed to Evan Stephens of Clinton County, Ohio, South half of W quarter of NE quarter of Sec. 10, Township, 28 Range 31 containing 20 acres except for 30 feet in width off the south side of said tract for a road. WD L/92 Jasper County, Missouri. February 3, 1869. Jacob Young and Caddie Young to Evan Stephens of Jasper County, Missouri, tract of land Lot #105 of the Town of Carthage in Missouri, being 100 feet front by 200 feet deep for $2,000. WD 0/138 139." The 1876 Jasper County Atlas shows a tract of land of 132.99 acres in Township 28, Range 31, Sections 6 and 7, designated to Evan Stephens. This land is adjacent to and west of the Morgan Heights section of Carthage.

Historic Route 66—the Mother Road, as John Steinbeck called it in *The Grapes of Wrath*—was to run through a portion of that tract of land long after the Stevenses' ownership of the land was over. Route 66 began in 1925 with an act of Congress. Many existing roads, from Chicago to Los Angeles, were joined to create the new highway, which ran for 2,400 miles. The last stretch of that road was decommissioned by the federal government in 1985 and was officially replaced by Interstate 40. Evan Stevens died on September 1, 1891, and Priscilla died on November 27, 1894. Both are buried in the Stevens plot in Park Cemetery, Carthage, Missouri.

Alma Stevens and Clay Cowgill

Alma and Clay Cowgill reportedly migrated to southwest Missouri in 1868 and settled in Carthage. According to the Union Monthly Meeting, Jasper County, Missouri, Quaker Records, May 1, 1869, Alma Cowgill and her daughter Lily D. were received on a certificate from Newberry Monthly Meeting dated February 22, 1869. Clay Cowgill opened a dry goods store on January 1, 1870. Two years later, he formed a partnership with Frank Hill and carried on the mercantile business until March 1876. He purchased an interest in the Center Creek Mills in 1872, and he and his brother were owners of the Galesburg Mill. In January 1876, the Carthage City Mill, operated by Cowgill and Hill, opened for business.

Lydia Elva Stevens and Curtis Brinton Wood

On April 22, 1871, Lydia Elva Stevens married Curtis Brinton Wood in Carthage, Missouri. In the census of Carthage, Jasper County, Missouri, taken on June 18, 1880, they were living in the household of Evan Stevens. Curtis was thirty-two, born in Massachusetts, and was employed with an engineering firm. Elva was twenty-eight, son Edward L. was eight, and Walter E. was two.

William "Willie" Land Stevens

Willie Stevens, the younger brother of Paulena, died on July 21, 1872, in Jasper County from the accidental discharge of his gun while he was out hunting. He was sixteen years old. He was first buried at East/Cedar Cemetery, and his remains were removed to the Stevens Plot in Park Cemetery in 1891, at the same time that Paulena's were moved.

Paulena "Lenna" Stevens

Paulena "Lenna" Stevens, the daughter of Thomas Stevens and Elizabeth Harris, was the youngest of their five children. When her mother died, she was adopted and raised by the family of Evan Stevens, her uncle. She migrated with the family and was listed in the 1870 and 1880 censuses of Jasper County in the household of Evan Stevens. She died in 1886 at the age of twenty-four and was buried at East/Cedar Cemetery. Her remains were removed to Park Cemetery in 1891. It is not known where her father and the rest of her family lived, but it is strongly believed that they were in Aurora, Lawrence County, Missouri, just a few miles from Carthage. This is based on 1880 census records. Her older brother Cyrus is believed to have remained in Clinton County, Ohio, with a family.

Stephen and Lydia White Janney

In 1867, 12th month, 13th day, Newberry Meeting condemned Stephen Janney's military service and his marriage as contrary to discipline, however, he was not disowned and remained a member in good standing with the Newberry Meeting. His Civil War pension file stated that he removed to Illinois on September 1, 1865. His membership from Newberry Meeting was not sent until March 23, 1868, to Ash Grove, Illinois,

in Iroquois County. In 1870 he moved on to New Sharon, Mahaska County, Iowa, where he owned fifty acres of land and served as school director and township trustee. He then removed to Crestline, Cherokee County, Kansas, in 1886. He moved to Cherokee, Crawford County, Kansas, in 1902. The next Quaker records for him appear on December 16, 1905, at the Timbered Hills Monthly Meeting, Cherokee, Crawford County, Kansas. He and his wife, Lydia, died there in 1912 and 1922, respectively, and are buried in the Cherokee Cemetery, Crawford County, Kansas.

Josephine "Jo" White

Josephine "Jo" White, sister of Lydia White, and her husband, Milton Morgan, moved to New Sharon, Mahaska County, Iowa, at the same time that Stephen and Lydia Janney moved. They remained there, and she died on May 12, 1882. It was after that time that Stephen and Lydia moved to Kansas.

William S. Betts and Anna Hadley

From Quaker Records, Missouri Monthly Meetings: Union Monthly Meeting, Missouri, Jasper County. "William S. Betts (brother to Priscilla Betts Stevens) 5 1 1869 (5th month, 1st day, 1869, which is July 1, 1869), wife Anna (Hadley), children George E., Evaline, and Albert, were received on certificate from Newberry Monthly Meeting, dated 2 22 1869." These records are found in the Friends Collection, Lilly Library, Earlham College, Richmond, Indiana, and at Swarthmore College, Philadelphia, Pennsylvania.

William S. Betts and Anna Hadley Betts were the parents of ten (fourteen children were born, but four died in infancy or early childhood). The twelfth child, Eva Betts, married Edwin Erastus Hussey and to this union four daughters were born: Nellie, Blanche H., Anna Margaret, and Mattie May. William Janney's record book shows several days that he worked on the Erastus Hussey house in 1874 in Carthage, Missouri. Stephen Hussey was married to Martha Bunker in 1676, on Nantucket Island, Massachusetts. The Husseys were the ancestors of Edwin Erastus Hussey, who married Eva Betts. Martha Bunker was the ancestor of Paulena Stevens Janney through the Coffin family.

Jacob Jackson and Carolyn Betts

According to Union Monthly Meeting Quaker Records dated May 1, 1869, Jacob Jackson and wife, Carolyn, and William H. and Armilla Jackson were received on a certificate from Newberry Monthly Meeting dated February 22, 1869.

William Clyde Betts and James P. Betts

(sons of William S. and Anna Hadley Betts). "William C. Betts, Clerk of the Court of Common Pleas of Jasper County, Missouri, was born in Clinton County, Ohio, on October 7, 1845. . . . He attended the common schools, and not two years a student at Earlham College in Indiana. In September 1864, he went to Memphis, Tennessee, and engaged in business. At the time of Forrest's raids through Tennessee, and his attacks on Memphis, in 1864, William C. Betts entered the First Tennessee Regiment, State Troops, and served six or eight months as a private of Co. C. In August 1865, he went to Cincinnati and engaged with his brothers (Aaron and James P.) in the wholesale hat and cap business. After four years' residence in Cincinnati, due to declining health, he went to Southwest Missouri, and located at Carthage. He accepted a position as clerk in the dry goods store of Ruffin & McDaniel until the end of 1870 when he was elected Clerk of the Court of Common Pleas and served four years in that office and was re-elected in 1874. On February 1875, he was married to Sarah McKerrick, of Carthage. They had four children, Albert Harland, William McMerrick, Curtis Aaron, and Katharine Olive Betts. William C. Betts died in Aurora, Missouri, in 1901, and his wife died in Carthage in 1944." Source: 1876 Jasper County, Missouri, Atlas.

Curtis Aaron Betts was a longtime reporter and correspondent for the St. Louis Post Dispatch. He died in 1972 at age ninety-one at a convalescent home in San Mateo, California.

James P. Betts was a partner with his brother, Aaron S. Betts, in Hats, Caps, and Straw Goods, a wholesale dealership in Cincinnati. He married Nannie Perry and had four children. By 1872 he was a justice of the peace in Carthage. James P. Betts was listed as an abstract maker living at the corner of Seventh and Lincoln in the 1876 Atlas of Jasper County. He died in 1927 and is buried in Park Cemetery, Carthage.

Eva Betts

Eva Betts, daughter of William S. Betts and Anna Hadley, married Erastus Hussey after her family arrived in Jasper County. She was included in her parents' Quaker certificate of removal and was enumerated in her parent's home in the1870 census. William Janney noted in his day book that he worked on the Isaac Newton Hussey house in 1871 and the Erastus Hussey house in 1874, which was about the time they were married, since their first child was born in June 1875. Joshua and Martha Ann Johnson Hussey were the parents of Erastus Hussey. They lived in Hillsboro, Highland County, Ohio, and joined their children in Jasper County later.

Lot and Fanny Wood Janney

Lot and Fanny Wood Janney left Portsmouth, Ohio, about the same time the other family members were moving west. They appeared in the 1870 census in Olathe, Johnson County, Kansas. Three years later Fanny died at the age of forty-two, and three years later, in 1876, Lot died at age fifty. That left Russell, age eleven, and Ralph, age six, orphans. William Janney, identified as Lot's brother in the Johnson County, Kansas, probate administration, estimated the value of Lot's estate at $4,500 [the final account showed the value at $8,346.98]. Gustavus Wood, brother to Fanny, was appointed guardian of the two minor sons. In the 1880 census, Russell and Ralph were enumerated in the household of Gustavus Wood, age forty; also listed were his mother, Sophia Hall Wood, age seventy-nine, and his sister, Cornelia "Nellie" M. Wood, age thirty-six, all living in Muskingum, Washington County, Ohio. Ralph Janney committed suicide in 1896 in the Samoan Islands, and Russell Janney married, had five children, and was living in Santa Barbara, California, in 1917.

John C. Lazenby and Mary Hiatt

John C. Lazenby and his wife, Mary Hiatt, who was a first cousin once removed to Paulena Stevens Janney, were neighbors of the Evan Stevens and Aaron Betts families in Clinton County, Ohio. They left their Cottage Grove Farm, near Martinsville, Ohio, and went to Carthage, Missouri, in 1868. Both died there and are buried in Hackney Cemetery, ten miles northeast of Carthage, Missouri.

Benjamin J. and Lavinia Coffin White,

parents of Lydia and Josephine, moved to Iroquois County, Illinois, at the same time as their daughter Lydia and Stephen Janney, and their daughter Elizabeth "Lizzie" and her husband, Elmer Hull. Lavinia, Lizzie, and Elmer are all buried in Ornarga, Iroquois County, Illinois.

Parker Moon and his wife, Mary Emily Green, emigrated from Martinsville, Clinton County, Ohio, to Jasper County in 1868. Parker founded the Fairview Friends Meeting, near Carthage.

Notable Kin

Notable Kin of
Paulena Stevens Janney

The Kendrick House
Painting by Jerry Ellis

The Kendrick House, one mile north of Carthage, Missouri, was to become the home of Paulena and William Janney's only surviving child, Carl Russell Janney, and his wife, Fannie Kendrick. Fannie Kendrick and all of her siblings were born in the house. She was born in 1874. Fannie inherited the house from her father's estate in 1901. That house would be the birthplace of all of the Janney children, Elva Pauline, Norman Guy, Walter Kendrick, Carl William, Georgia Clara, Russell Francis, and Andrew Palmer "Jack" Janney.

On February 14, 1925, Georgia Janney and Clayton G. Hill were married in the parlor of the house. Fruit punch and angel food cake were served to their guests. The children of Clayton G. and Georgia Janney Hill were Fannie Hill White, Clayton R. Hill, Betty Hill Kochan, and Christie Hill Russell. Jacqueline Janney Stroud, the daughter of Jack and Lucille Janney, was born in the house in 1932.

The Kendrick House and 540 acres were acquired by William and Elizabeth Palmer Kendrick in November 1860 from Sinnet Rankin. They were the grandparents of Fannie Kendrick. Their son, Joshua Draper Palmer Kendrick, inherited the house from his father's estate in 1868. The house remained in the family for 139 years and is now owned by Victorian Carthage, Inc. as a museum. For more information, see www.kendrickplace.com.

$\mathcal{P}$aulena's early New England ancestors who settled in the Massachusetts Bay Colony from England were the Coffins, Macys, Starbucks, Gardners, Paddocks, Austins, Searses, Bunkers, Stoughtons, Chamberlains, Bettses, and Fieldses. A number of notable persons, all of whom are related to Paulena Stevens Janney, are among their descendants. We will first introduce descendants of the Coffin, Starbuck, Macy, Gardner group, referred to as "Nantucket Soup" by Gary Boyd Roberts in his two-volume *Notable Kin.* These individuals were instrumental in making our country what it is today—a leader of the free world.

Part I

The genealogical key that was to unlock much of my New England ancestry came to me in a letter from my uncle, Jack Janney, just ten days before his death in December 1985. In that letter, he related the latest research information, which was that Paulena's grandmother was Mary Coffin, wife of Gideon Stevens and daughter of Samuel Coffin and Mary Duana Carr. The Coffin family was significantly linked to numerous early New England lines. The other major family line was the Betts family. My research for that link took me from Bucks County, Pennsylvania, to New Jersey and finally to Long Island, New York, and then back to England.

Paulena was undoubtedly well aware, if only by name, of her cousins who were active in the abolition, Underground Railroad, women's suffrage, and temperance movements. She may not have been entirely aware of the notable literary, political, artistic, and scientific figures of the nineteenth century to whom she was related. Virtually all of them greatly influenced the generations that followed in the twentieth and twenty-first centuries.

Nantucket Fathers

Thirty miles off the coast of Massachusetts and about twenty miles south of Cape Cod lies the island of Nantucket. It is fifteen miles long, approximately three and a half miles wide, and has an area of thirty thousand acres. Thomas Mayhew had purchased the island in 1641 from Lord Sterling, who held title through a land grant from the king. The First Purchasers of Nantucket were originally nine men (Mayhew retained a one-tenth share, thus making the tenth member, but he never settled there). Of the nine members of the company, five were direct ancestors of Paulena Stevens Janney. A purchase agreement with the Indians living on the island was also made. Eventually ten more members chosen by the original ten would join the company. These men had already demonstrated substantial ability in the communities in which they lived before settling in Nantucket. In this book, I will refer to those ancestors of Paulena Stevens Janney as the Nantucket Fathers.

Scrimshaw by Michael J. Vienneau of Nantucket

Thomas Macy[293]

is credited with being the first permanent English settler of Nantucket. Born in 1608, he came from Chilmark, County Wiltshire, England, to Newbury, Massachusetts Bay Colony, sometime before he was made a freeman on September 6, 1639. Later he helped found Salisbury and Amesbury and served as selectman. Obed Macy records that Thomas Macy was the owner of 1000 acres of land, "a good house and considerable stock." The house he built in Amesbury in 1654 is now preserved as a museum. He married Sarah Hopcott in about 1643, probably in Salisbury, because that was where all of their children were born.

Massachusetts had strict laws against the Quakers, and any settler could be fined up to five pounds for every hour he entertained one in his home. Macy was a Baptist, but during a heavy storm he had given refuge to four Quakers: Edward Wharton, William Robinson, a merchant from London, and Marmaduke

---

293. *Patronymica Britannica* spells the name Macey and traces it to Macie near Avranches in Normandy; the name is also an old Norman form of Matthew.

Stephenson of Yorkshire, England. William Robinson and Marmaduke Stephenson were hanged in Boston on October 27, 1659, for being Quakers. Macy was summoned to court and fined for providing them shelter. That may have hastened his departure from the mainland a little, but Nantucket had been purchased several months before, and his plans for moving to the Island had already been made.

The Macy family of five children and parents was settled on Nantucket in a crude dugout structure in the side of a hill in the fall of 1659, a few months after its purchase from Thomas Mayhew, the first of the new owners to settle on the island with their families. In a letter to the governor of New York in 1676, Macy refers to Mayhew as "my honored cousin."

In addition to his one share as a purchaser of the Island, Macy had another half share as a weaver. He took an active part in the affairs of Nantucket and at one time served as a magistrate. Josiah Coffin, an early historian, described him as "a merchant, and enlightened man . . . a man of fortitude, courage, good sense and education." Thomas Macy died in 1682 at the age of seventy-four. Sarah lived to be ninety-four. Paulena Stevens Janney was descended from Thomas and Sarah's daughter, Mary Macy, who married William Bunker.

Tristram Coffin

was the most prominent and influential of the First Purchasers of Nantucket. Born in 1605 in Brixton, Devonshire, England, Tristram Coffin belonged to the landed gentry. The Coffin family has been connected with the county of Devon from the time of William the Conqueror to this day. The Domesday Book, a survey of English lands, was compiled in 1086. In it, Coffins were listed as owners of several hides of land in Devon. A "hide of land" was a term applied in Anglo-Saxon times to the amount of land sufficient to support a family—usually sixty to 100 acres.

The great civil and religious unrest in England in early 1640 must have played a large part in Tristram's departure from England. He gave up a 500 year lease on land and sailed for America with his wife (Dionis Stevens, daughter of Robert Stevens), five small children, two unmarried sisters, and his widowed mother. He first settled in Salisbury in the Massachusetts Bay Colony but soon moved to Haverhill. It is said that he was the first person to plow land at Haverhill, having made his own plow. He moved to Newbury where records show that he was given a license in 1644 to keep an ordinary (tavern or inn), sell wine, and operate a ferry on the Newbury side to Carr's Island across the Merrimac River.

He purchased woodlands and with his sons built a sawmill. A house belonging to his son, Tristram Coffin Jr., in Newbury is now preserved as a memorial by the Society for the Preservation of New England Antiquities. The original part of this house was built about 1653. In 1654 Tristram Senior returned to Salisbury and lived there until the company that purchased Nantucket was organized. He and Dionis settled on Nantucket in the spring of 1660. Tristram served as the first chief magistrate on the island in 1671 and in 1677.

If any one man could be considered the patriarch of Nantucket, it would be Tristram Coffin. He and Dionis had nine children. They had seventy-five grandchildren, and by 1772, forty-one years after Tristram's death, he had more than 1,100 descendants. Tristram died in 1681.

Paulena Stevens Janney descends from Tristram and Dionis's son, John Coffin, and his wife, who went to Martha's Vineyard, where he worked as a blacksmith, and some of his descendants are still there.

Edward Starbuck

was born in 1604 in Draycot, Derbyshire, England. Edward Starbuck came to New England in 1635. His wife, Catherine Reynolds, was from Wales. They settled in Dover, New Hampshire, not far from Salisbury, Massachusetts, where Tristram Coffin and Thomas Macy settled a few years later. Edward first appears in the records of Dover, New Hampshire (at that time it was part of Massachusetts Bay Colony), in 1640, when he is found on a list of inhabitants of Dover. He was named as a proprietor in 1642. In 1643 and 1646 he was chosen as representative from Dover to the General Court of the Massachusetts Bay Colony. He was one of the men appointed by the town in 1644 to manage the fisheries in the river. He was a partner with Richard Waldron in lumbering on the Maine side in 1648. He was granted the right to erect sawmills in 1647, 1650, and 1652.

While in Dover, he came under the influence of the Anabaptists. On October 18, 1648, Edward was charged with refusing to join with the established church in the rite of baptism. There is some question if these religious differences played a part over the next few years in Edward's decision to move his family from Dover. Whatever the reason, Edward gave all his property in Dover to his son-in-law, Peter Coffin, on March 9, 1659, and moved himself and his family, except for Abigail (married Peter Coffin, son of Tristram) and Sarah (married Joseph Austin), to Nantucket. Although not one of the original ten, Edward Starbuck accompanied Tristram Coffin on his first voyage to the island and was also a companion of Thomas Macy when he left Salisbury to make a new home at Nantucket. When the original ten selected ten others as partners, Thomas Macy selected him. Macy and Starbuck did most of the negotiations with the Indians; Starbuck especially was a good linguist and diplomat and got along well with the natives. His name appears there on the earliest Indian deed in 1660 and on many other deeds and documents in the succeeding years. He served as a selectman in 1673. On March 18, 1685, Edward deeded all his property and goods to his son, Nathaniel. Edward died at Nantucket on March 4, 1690, at age eighty-six.

William Bunker,

the son of George and Jane (Godfrey) Bunker, was of Huguenot origin and was born in 1649. Originally, the name was Bon Coeur, meaning "good heart" or "great heart." William was the grandson of William Bunker, a French Huguenot who fled to England to avoid the religious persecution to which he was subjected in France. William came to Nantucket with his stepfather, Richard Swain, who had married his mother, Jane, after his father, George, died. The Bunker children brought to the island with Richard and Jane (Godfrey) Bunker Swain were Elizabeth, who married Thomas Look; William, who married Mary Macy, daughter of Thomas Macy Senior; Mary, who married Stephen Coffin, son of Tristram Senior; Ann, who married Joseph Coleman, son of Thomas, Senior; and Martha, who married Stephen Hussey, son of Christopher. William Bunker married Mary Macy and the next in our lineage was their daughter, Abigail Bunker, who married Nathaniel Paddock.

Richard Gardner Sr.

and his brother John were sons of Thomas Gardner who moved from Salem, Massachusetts Bay Colony to Nantucket. They had come from England with their father, Thomas Gardner, who had come in 1624 to oversee the plantations of the Dorchester Company at Cape Anne. Richard was the first of the two brothers to remove to Nantucket, where he was granted a half share on March 22, 1666, to exercise his trade as a seaman. Richard married Sarah Shattuck, daughter of Samuel. They had ten children, among whom was Sarah Gardner, who married Eleazer Folger, the uncle of Benjamin Franklin. Sarah Gardner's brother, Richard, was the next in the direct lineage to Paulena Stevens Janney. Abiah Folger, mother of Benjamin Franklin, was Paulena's fifth great-aunt by marriage.

Sources: *The History of Nantucket County, Island, and Town,* Alexander Starbuck, Charles E. Tuttle Company, 6th edition, 1986; *The Coffin Family,* Louis Coffin, Nantucket Historical Association, 1962; *Seventeenth Century Colonial Ancestors,* Mary L. Hutton, 1987; *Directory of the Ancestral Heads of New England Families,* 1620–1700, compiled by Frank R. Holmes, Baltimore, Maryland, Genealogical Publishing Co., 1980; Susan Rogers Clement, *Reynolds Family Association,* 1992; *The Beard Family, A Bundle of Relations, A Knot of Roots,* Ruth Beard McDowell, 1978.

Part II

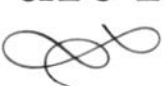

Charles A. Beard—Historian

"Charles Austin Beard (1874–1948), American historian, born near Knightstown, Indiana. A year at Oxford as a graduate student gave him an interest in English local government, and after further study at Cornell and Columbia universities he wrote, for his doctoral dissertation at Columbia, *The Office of Justice of the Peace in England* (1904, repr. 1962). While teaching (1904–17) history and politics at Columbia, he joined James Harvey Robinson in promoting the teaching of history that would encompass all aspects of civilization, including economics, politics, the intellectual life, and culture. Together they wrote *The Development of Modern Europe* (1907) and compiled an accompanying book of readings. Beard was especially concerned with the relationship of economic interests and politics. His study of the conservative economic interests of the men at the Federal Constitutional Convention, *An Economic Interpretation of the Constitution* (1913), caused much stir; he also wrote *Economic Origins of Jeffersonian Democracy* (1915, reprinted 1965) and *The Economic Basis of Politics* (1922). His interest in city government led to *American City Government* (1912) as well as the long-standard *American Government and Politics* (1910). After resigning from Columbia in World War I, he helped to found the New School for Social Research, was director (1917–22) of the Training School for Public Service in New York City, and was an adviser on administration in Tokyo after the disastrous Japanese earthquake of 1923. Beard wrote *A Charter for the Social Sciences in the Schools* (1932), which had an enormous influence on the teaching of history. Beard became widely known to the general reading public through *The Rise of American Civilization* (2 volumes, 1927, reprinted 1933) and its sequels (Volume III and Volume IV), *America in Midpassage* (1939), and *The American Spirit* (1943), all written in collaboration with his wife, Mary Ritter Beard (1876–1958). This panoramic work is an example of the broad historical view that Beard championed; the great store of fact is laid open with easy and graceful literary style. With his wife he also later wrote a brief survey, *The Beards' Basic History of the United States* (1944, revised edition 1960). Charles Beard, much criticized as a radical in his earlier years, was just as much criticized by the liberals in his later years for his violent opposition to Franklin D. Roosevelt's administration, especially in the struggle over the Supreme Court and in foreign policy. Beard's last work was *President Roosevelt and the Coming of the War, 1941* (1948, reprinted 1968). Mary R. Beard, a historian in her own right, was particularly interested in feminism and the labor movement and wrote a number of works on the subjects, notably *Women's Work in Municipalities* (1915), *A Short History of the American Labor Movement* (1920), *On Understanding Women* (1931), and *Woman as Force in History* (1946)." Source: *The Columbia Encyclopedia*, 6th ed., Columbia University Press, 2004.

Catherine Drinker Bowen—Author

"Bowen came from a prominent Quaker family and was a descendant of John Drinker, the first baby boy born in Philadelphia. She was an accomplished violinist, playing with string quartets in Philadelphia and New York. But it was as a writer that she gained her fame.

"Her first biography was *'Beloved Friend: The Story of Tchaikowsky and Nadejda Von Meck,'* followed by *'Free Artist: The story of Anton and Nicholas Rubenstein.'* . . . *'Yankee from Olympus: Justice Holmes and His Family'* (1944); *'John Adams and the American Revolutions'* (1950); *'The Lions and the Thorns: The Life and Times of Sir Edward Coke'* (1957).

"She also wrote *'Miracle at Philadelphia: The Story of the Constitutional Convention'* (1966), and *'Family Portrait,'* a history of her own family, in 1970. During her lifetime she was awarded numerous literary and civic honors, as well as honorary degrees. She was also the holder of two of the city's top prizes: the Philadelphia Award and the Gimbel Award.

"At the time of her death she was working on a study of Benjamin Franklin. The book was published posthumously in 1974 as: *'The Most Dangerous Man in America: Scenes from the Life of Benjamin Franklin.'* She was buried at West Laurel Hill Cemetery, Philadelphia, Pennsylvania." Source: http://www.forever care. com/gen_view.php?id=21or.

Phillips Brooks—Episcopal Bishop of Massachusetts

"Phillips Brooks (1835–1893) has been called 'the greatest American preacher of the 19th Century.' He attended the Boston Latin School, Harvard University (where Phillips Brooks House was named after him) and Episcopal Theological Seminary in Alexandria, Virginia. He became an Episcopal priest in 1860, and became Rector of the Church of the Advent, Philadelphia, Pennsylvania. He was known for his support of freeing the slaves and allowing former slaves to vote. In 1869, he became Rector of Trinity Church in Boston. In 1872, he helped design the Trinity Church building which today stands in Boston's Back Bay. In 1891, he became Episcopal bishop of Massachusetts." Among several hymns he wrote, the best known is "O Little Town of Bethlehem" written in 1868. Brooks wrote about his horseback journey from Jerusalem to Bethlehem, where he assisted with the midnight service on Christmas Eve, 1865: "I remember standing in the old church in Bethlehem, close to the spot where Jesus was born, when the whole church was ringing hour after hour with splendid hymns of praise to God, how again and again it seemed as if I could hear voices I knew well, telling each other of the Wonderful Night of the Savior's birth." After Abraham Lincoln's death, Brooks gave the sermon over his body at Independence Hall in Philadelphia. Source: http://www.cyberhymnal.org/bio/b/r/o/brooks_p.htm.

Dr. John Goodrich Clark

"John Goodrich Clark, physician and surgeon, was the son of Thomas E. and Nancy (Goodrich) Clark, of Quaker ancestry. He matriculated at Ohio Wesleyan University but at the completion of his sophomore year joined a surveying and engineering party of U.S. engineers in Idaho and Utah. Deciding to follow the medical profession he entered the medical school of the University of Pennsylvania from which he was graduated with honors in 1891. He was resident physician in the St. Agnes and Children's hospitals in Philadelphia and the surgical wards of Belleview Hospital, New York City, and then entered the gynecological department of Johns Hopkins University Medical School under Dr. Howard A. Kelly, serving successively as anaesthetist, assistant resident physician, and resident gynecolgist. He was also associate in gynecology in Johns Hopkins University medical school.

"In 1898 he went abroad for a special course of study in the anatomical laboratory of the University of Leipsic, and the pathological laboratory of the University of Prague. At the former he made a study of the life history of the corpus luteum under Profs. His and Spalteholz. Upon his return in 1899 he accepted the professorship of gynecology at the University of Pennsylvania, succeeding Dr. Charles B. Penrose, and held the chair until shortly before his death. He was also consultant gynecologist to the Woman's College, Bryn Mawr, Germantown and Chestnut Hill hospitals.

"Dr. Clark attained a foremost place among American authorities on gynecological diagnosis and at the university he developed one of the outstanding gynecological clinics in America. As a surgeon he had few equals in his delicacy of touch, knowledge of anatomy and dexterity and as a diagnostician his skill was almost uncanny. He was one of the first to advocate a radical operation for cancer of the cervix. He was one of the pioneers in the employment of radium for gynecological lesions and was an accepted authority on this subject. He was not only a great surgeon but a teacher of unsurpassed ability, with the happy faculty of imparting knowledge easily and in an unforgettable manner which commanded the devotion and respect of his student. . . ." [He was the author of numerous articles published in medical journals.]

"As a member of the Rockefeller Commission Dr. Clark accompanied John D. Rockefeller, Jr., to Pekin, China, in 1921 for the dedication of the Union Medical College there. He was president of the Clinical Congress of Surgeons of North America in 1917, was a member of the American Gynecological Society (president 1918); the American Medical Association (chairman of the obstetrical section and board of public instruction), and the Philadelphia Medical Club (president 1923). During the world war he was a member of the general medical board of the council of national defense." Source: Abstracted from National Cyclopedia of American Biography by Christie Russell. Dr. Clark is related to Paulena Stevens Janney through her Gardner line. He was a half first cousin once removed to Pierre Goodrich.

Alice Virginia Coffin—Co-founder of the P.E.O. Sisterhood

"One of the pioneer societies for women, P.E.O. was founded on January 21, 1869, by seven young college women on the campus of Iowa Wesleyan College in Mount Pleasant, Iowa. Originally a small campus society, P.E.O. soon chose to go entirely off campus. Today, P.E.O. has grown from that tiny membership of seven to over a quarter of a million members in chapters in the United States and Canada. From its inception, the P.E.O. Sisterhood has taken an active role in the promotion of educational opportunities for women. Today, education continues to be the only philanthropy of P.E.O., as evidenced by the promotion of five international projects designed to assist women. . . . Grant, loan, and award recipients, as well as Cottey College students, need not be members of P.E.O. To date, P.E.O. has awarded Educational Loan Fund dollars totaling nearly $92 million, International Peace Scholarships exceeding $16 million, Program for Continuing Education grants topping $22 million and Scholar Awards in excess of $6 million. In addition, more than 7,400 women have graduated from Cottey College." Source: P.E.O. *International*, http://www.peointernational.org.

Alice Virginia Coffin (1848–1888) was one of the seven founding members. Alice was a seventh-generation descendant of Tristram and Dionis through the line of John. Born on March 29, 1848, in Louisville, Kentucky, she was the fourth child of Martha (Thompson) and Matthew Starbuck Coffin. Matthew purchased a steamboat, the *Monroe*, plying the waters between St. Louis and New Orleans on the Mississippi River, to use in connection with commissions at New Orleans. Matthew returned to his farm near Salem, Washington County, Indiana, when his daughter, Alice, was two years old (1850). He remained there five years, but finding that farming did not prove sufficiently profitable, he sent his wife and children to live in Indianapolis with Martha's father, Judge John Hadley Thompson, while Matthew went to Newton, Iowa, where he and a partner planned to open a dry goods store. The next year, in May 1855, Alice and her mother and siblings moved to Newton, Iowa. Due to storms ruining his inventory the first year, the company went bankrupt. In 1857, when Alice was only nine years old, her mother died from complications following childbirth. Just two weeks after giving birth to a baby boy, she died, along with the baby.

During the Civil War, her father, who had become a successful businessman, was appointed Supervisor of Transportation of Troops and Supplies on the Mississippi and Ohio Rivers. He moved the family to Mount Pleasant, Iowa, so that his children could obtain a good education at the Iowa Wesleyan University.

At college, Alice made the decision to be a schoolteacher.

In 1869, during her senior year at school, Alice and six of her closest friends decided to form a sisterhood to perpetuate what had become a beautiful friendship. The young women formed their own group, a Philanthropic Educational Organization—P.E.O. Alice suggested their emblem—a star—and wore it proudly in her blonde hair or pinned to her dress. They had wanted to help women cultivate their physical, mental, moral, and social powers.

Alice received her Bachelor of Science degree in June of 1869. She taught briefly in Des Moines, Iowa, and soon thereafter started teaching in Chariton, Iowa, where she remained for several years. It was in Chariton that she left the Methodist Church of her mother; her father was a Quaker. Her reason for leaving the Methodist Church was that she was never allowed to dance. She became an Episcopalian. In her new church, she found the ritual and ceremony satisfying, and attended church faithfully for the rest of her life.

Alice poured her enthusiasm and love into teaching her students. Wanting to be with her father and sister again, Alice moved back to Newton and taught grammar school there. "Hitch your wagon to a star," she told her pupils. "Never mind if you never attain your star; the effort will be a development." She provided financial assistance to three young women in her lifetime. A woman of many talents herself, Alice encouraged her female students and family members to recognize their own creative powers and self worth. At age forty, Alice was stricken with Bright's disease and died in her sister Mary Skiff's home on July 28, 1888. She is buried next to her parents in Newton's Coffin family plot. Sources: "Alice Virginia Coffin," Kirsten Alexander, *Coffin Family Newsletter,* February 1993; *Alice Virginia Coffin, One of the Seven Founders of the P.E.O. Sisterhood,* written for the Washington County Indiana Historical Society by Lillie D. Trueblood, 1943.

Charles Albert Coffin—First President and Board Chairman of General Electric

"'A man born to command, yet who never issued orders.' This phrase sums up the leadership qualities of Charles A. Coffin , General Electric's first president. His executive skills helped establish GE's place in the front rank of American corporations.

"Electrical manufacturing was Coffin's second career. At 18, he moved from Fairfield, Maine, where he had been born in 1844, to enter his uncle's shoe business at Lynn, Massachusetts. He later found his own shoe manufacturing firm, and by 1883 had established himself as an outstanding success in this line.

"In that year, Silas E. Barton, a Lynn businessman, proposed bringing to the city the struggling young American Electric Co. of New Britain, Connecticut, whose major asset was the inventive genius of Elihu Thomson. A businessman was needed to supplement Thomson's technical skills. Coffin was prevailed upon to take the post.

"He led the new company, Thomson Houston, to parity with Thomas Edison's companies, the previous leaders of the field. When negotiations in 1892 led to the formation of General Electric, a key step in creating a viable enterprise was the installation of Coffin as its first chief executive officer.

"Coffin's associates (and he always made a point of calling them 'my associates,' not 'my subordinates') knew him as a gracious gentleman and delightful companion. He never ordered one of them to do anything, preferring to rely on his powers of suggestion. In his turn, he graciously sought and welcomed suggestions from those around him—and then decisively made up his own mind on key questions.

"Customers and competitors knew him as both the outstanding statesman and the outstanding salesman of the electrical manufacturing industry. He took a personal interest in major negotiations, often writing business proposals to important customers in his own hand. At tense meetings he knew how to relieve the pressure with an appropriate anecdote, and how to add the key words to bring matters to a successful conclusion.

"His greatest test came in the depression of 1893. A cash shortage threatened GE's existence. He coolly negotiated a deal with J.P. Morgan whereby New York banks advanced the needed money as payment for utility stocks which GE held. The tactic saved the company and made possible its rapid recovery and growth during the remainder of his tenure. The strength and wide ranging excellence of the company he passed to Owen D. Young and Gerard Swope when he retired from the board chairmanship in 1922 was—and remains—his greatest monument." Source: *Hall of History Biographies*, http://tardis.union.edu/community/project95/HOH/Biography/coffin.html and http://www.ge.com/en/company/companyinfo/at_a_glance/bio_coffin.htm.

Charles Carleton Coffin—Civil War Correspondent and Author

"Coffin, Charles Carleton, author, born in Boscawen, New Hampshire, 26 July 1823. He worked on his father's farm till he was of age. His means of education were limited, but he was so desirous to acquire knowledge that he studied at night. He worked as a civil engineer from 1845 till 1848, and then bought a farm, but abandoned it on account of failing health. He then gave his attention to telegraphy, constructed the time line between Harvard observatory and Boston, in 1849, and, when in charge of the Boston telegraphic fire alarm, sent out the first signal over the system, 29 April, 1852. After writing for some of the New Hampshire papers, he began contributing to the Boston press in 1851, spending much time upon his articles, some of which he rewrote ten times before sending them to the printer. From 1855 till 1860 he held various places on the Boston

Journal, the *Atlas,* and the *Traveller.* When the civil war began, Mr. Coffin became war correspondent for the *Journal,* writing under the pen name of 'Carleton.' He witnessed many important battles, and was in almost every engagement from the Wilderness to the taking of Richmond, often rendering important service to the military authorities by his knowledge of engineering. He was also the *Journal's* correspondent during the Prusso Austrian war of 1866, and at its completion made the circuit of the world, returning part of the way from San Francisco by stage, the Pacific railroad not being completed. During his travels, which lasted two and a half years, Mr. Coffin wrote a weekly letter to the Boston *Journal.* He has lectured before the Lowell institute, and was for years a popular lyceum lecturer. He has also appeared several times before congressional committees, to present arguments on the labor question. He has been for some time a resident of Boston, and was a member of the Massachusetts legislature in 1884 and 1885, serving on important committees. He has published 'The Great Commercial Prize,' advocating the construction of a railway over the Northern Pacific route (1858); *Days and Nights on the Battle Field* (Boston, 1864); *Following the Flag and Winning His Way, a story* (1865); *Four Years of Fighting* (1866); *Our New Way Round the World* (1869); *The Seat of Empire* (1870); *Caleb Krinkle. a Story of American Life* (1875); *History of Boscawen* (1877); *Boys of '76* (New York, 1879); *Story of Liberty* (1878); *Old Times in the Colonies* (1880); *Life of Garfield* (Boston, 1880); *Building the Nation* (New York, 1883); and *Drum Beat of the Nation,* the first volume of a series (1887)." Source: *Edited Appleton's Encyclopedia,* Virtualology, 2001.

Elizabeth Rebecca Coffin—Artist

"Elizabeth Rebecca Coffin [was] a groundbreaking artist, educator, and philanthropist. . . . Like many women artists of her generation, Coffin's work richly deserves wider recognition. Born and raised in Brooklyn, New York, Elizabeth Coffin had Quaker roots firmly embedded in the sandy soil of Nantucket Island. She was an eighth generation descendant of Tristram (1605–1681) and Dionis Stevens Coffin (1609–1676), who were among the first English settlers on the island in 1660. Her grandfather Gorham Coffin (1784–1850) and her father, Andrew Gardner Coffin (1816–1897), were born on the island and prospered in the whaling industry. Her mother, Elizabeth Sherwood (1818–1855), was a native of Brooklyn and a staunch Quaker.

"The young artist spent her early years in New York and California, where her father had established a wholesale drug company in the 1840s and 1850s. After acquiring a Quaker education at the Friends Seminary in Manhattan, in 1865 she enrolled in Vassar College in Poughkeepsie, New York, where she took classes in drawing and painting from the Dutch painter Henry Van Ingen (1833–1899). At Vassar, the fine arts were considered a central component of a student's moral life and education. Coffin was encouraged to attend the college by the Nantucket born Vassar astronomy professor Maria Mitchell (1818–1889), a pioneer in the women's rights movement and an influential and lifelong friend of Coffin.

"In the early 1870s, when the American woman's sphere was still primarily the home, Coffin boldly ventured to Europe for further art training. She enrolled in the Academie van Beeldende Kunsten (Academy of Fine Arts) in The Hague, the oldest art school in the Netherlands, which had only begun to accept women students in a special separate course in March 1872. Coffin joined this group in the fall of 1872, the first American woman to enroll. She took classes in drawing from plaster casts of Greek and Roman sculpture, which was the typical initial instruction offered at most European art academies. She also studied painting privately with the director of the academy, Johan Philip Koelman (1818–1893), and copied Dutch masterpieces in the extensive collection at the Mauritshuis.

"Something of a renegade, Coffin requested permission to take the classes reserved for men in the antique, anatomy perspective, and history of architecture, and the academy's director granted her request. She thrived in this competitive atmosphere, and by the time she left the academy in June 1875 she had won six awards, four of them, according to her, were in competition with male students. . . .

"Family obligations brought Coffin home to Brooklyn in late 1875, and by the following year she was back at Vassar College. In the spring of 1876, after passing an examination and completing a thesis entitled 'The Progress of Art in Ancient Times,' she became the first person ever to be awarded a master of arts degree in fine arts in the United States—a remarkable achievement for a young artist.

"After settling into the family home in Brooklyn Heights, Coffin was elected a member of the progressive Art Students League of New York in 1877. There, over the next decade, she took classes with the well known American painter William Merritt Chase (1849–1916).

"It was in Brooklyn that Coffin first met and studied with Thomas Eakins, who became a lifelong friend and whose style of painting had a lasting impact upon her. From 1881 to 1885 Eakins traveled from Philadelphia two days a week to give classroom critiques and lectures at the Brooklyn Art Association. After studying with Eakins there, Coffin enrolled in his life class for women at the Pennsylvania Academy of the Fine Arts in Philadelphia in February 1883." Source: http://www.findarticles.com/p/articles/mi_m1026/is_5_160/ai_80116459.

Howard Earle Coffin—Pioneer in Automobile Industry and Developer of Sea Island, Georgia

"A successful pioneer in the automobile industry, Howard Coffin rebuilt an abandoned antebellum mansion on Sapelo Island and revitalized the agricultural potential on it, developed St. Simons Island and Sea Island as Georgia's premier coastal tourist destinations, and provided seed money for the mighty pulpwood industry that continues to thrive in the state's Coastal Plain.

"Born in 1873, Howard Earle Coffin grew up on an Ohio farm and in Ann Arbor, Michigan, where he studied engineering at the University of Michigan. It was there that he constructed his first automobile. It was steam-powered, and he used it to deliver the mail around town. He also made use of the university's engineering shop in 1898–99 to build his first internal combustion engine. In 1902 the Oldsmobile Company hired him as chief experimental engineer. By 1905 Coffin was Oldsmobile's chief engineer. Later he worked for the E. R. Thomas Detroit Motor Car Company, the Chalmers–Detroit Motor Company, and the Hudson Motor Car Company, serving as vice president and chief engineer of each and designing many of their early models.

"Coffin is known in automotive circles as the Father of Standardization, a result of his initiative in standardizing material and design specifications and in arranging for automobile manufacturers to share their patents. These accomplishments enabled the American automobile industry to grow quickly.

"Before World War I, Coffin served on the Naval Consulting Board, which helped plan the possible involvement of the United States in that conflict.

"Coffin led the 1916 preparedness campaign, including an inventory of the nation's industrial capacity, something that had never been attempted before. When the United States entered the war, President Woodrow Wilson named Coffin to the Council of National Defense, which served as the country's unofficial war cabinet. Coffin's job was aircraft production. Through his leadership the U.S. Army Air Service ultimately became a significant arm of the military. He also led in building the revolutionary Liberty airplane engine.

"After the war Coffin helped launch the nation's commercial aviation program. He helped found and served as board chairman of the National Air Transport Company, a forerunner of United Airlines. In 1925 he served on the Morrow Board, which President Calvin Coolidge named to investigate and make recommendations regarding the federal government's role in air safety and in creating an air defense system. The board's recommendations established the principle of federal regulation of civilian flying, a vital step toward a federal air law.

"Automobile racing first drew Coffin to Georgia. He considered racing as a means to test and advertise early automobiles, several of which he had designed. At a 1911 contest in Savannah, he learned that Sapelo Island was for sale. Coffin and his wife, Teddie, who had visited the coastal area, jumped at the chance to buy 20,000 acres of the Sapelo Island land and marsh for $120,000. He constructed a palatial home on Sapelo Island, using the existing tabby walls and foundation that had constituted Thomas Spalding's antebellum mansion. What followed were numerous improvements to the island: he had drainage ditches blasted, fields cleared, an oyster-canning facility constructed, and roads cut. Soon Sapelo was host to a number of dignitaries, including aviator Charles Lindbergh, President and Mrs. Calvin Coolidge, and President and Mrs. Herbert Hoover. During this period Coffin bought vast tracts of land along coastal Georgia, and when paved roads began penetrating the area, he foresaw the potential for tourism. This prompted Coffin to purchase several plantations on St. Simons Island, where he began extensive development, including a golf course, a yacht club, paved roads, electricity, and a residential subdivision. Almost as an after-thought he purchased an adjacent island, which he named Sea Island. This is where he eventually built the Cloister, an exclusive resort.

"A causeway constructed during the 1920s between the mainland and St. Simons Island enabled tourists and day visitors to reach the beach area eas-ily. Coffin used his floating dredges to strengthen the existing causeway and also to build a causeway between St. Simons and Sea Island. This ensured the success of the Cloister, the only major resort between Miami, Florida, and the golfing community of Pinehurst, North Carolina.

"Coffin made another major contribution to coastal Georgia's economy by recognizing the area's potential for growing pine trees that could be used as pulpwood. In 1927 he invested $10,000 in an experiment to determine if pine chips from Georgia trees could be processed into paper pulp. The success of this led to the creation of the Brunswick Pulp and Paper Company, one of the many pulp mills that now dot the eastern seaboard.

"Coffin died in 1937. His Sea Island resort, still run by family members, is scheduled to be razed and rebuilt closer to the Black Banks River by 2006. His Sapelo Island mansion is owned and operated by the state of Georgia. Georgia's vibrant coastal area is his most visible and significant contribution, along with the pulpwood industry he foresaw and actively supported." The United States hosted the 2004 G8 Summit at Sea Island, Georgia. Sources: *The New Georgia Encyclopedia, Business and Industry*, Maxwell Taylor Courson, Valrico, Florida, 2003; read also Maxwell Taylor Courson, "Howard Earle Coffin, King of the Georgia Coast," *Georgia Historical Quarterly* 83, summer 1999, pp. 322–41.

John Huntington Crane Coffin—Mathematician

"John Huntington Crane Coffin, mathematician, born in Wiscasset, Maine, 14 September, 1815. He was graduated at Bowdoin in 1834. Two years later he was appointed professor of mathematics in the United States navy, and in that ca-pacity served on the 'Vandalia' and the 'Constellation,' in the West India squad-ron, at Norfolk navy yard, and on the Florida surveys, until 1843, when he was placed in charge of the mural circle in the United States naval observatory in Washington. After 1853 he was intrusted with the department of mathematics, and subsequently that of astronomy and navigation, at the United States naval academy. In 1865 he was appointed to the charge of the 'American Ephemeris and Nautical Almanac,' then published in Cambridge, Massachusetts, but since 1867 in Washington, District of Columbia. In this capacity he remained until 1877, when he was placed on the retired list, having been senior professor of mathematics since 1848. Prof. Coffin is a member of the American academy of sciences, Boston, the American philosophical society, Philadelphia, and was one of the original members of the National academy of sciences. In 1884 he received the honorary degree of LL.D. from Bowdoin. Besides many smaller articles, he has published 'Observations with the Mural Circle at the United States Naval Observatory, with Explanations, Formulas, Tables, and Discussions, 1845–9,' in the volumes of the observatory for those years; 'The Compass,' local deviations (1863); 'Navigation and Nautical Astronomy' (New York, 1868), the last two having been prepared for use in the United States naval academy; 'The American Ephemeris and Nautical Almanac,' edited (1868 till 1879); also 'Personal Errors in Observations of the Declination of Stars' in 'Gould's Astronomical Journal' (1850); and 'Observations of the Total Eclipse of the Sunday, August 1869'. (Washington, 1884). Sources: *Edited Appleton's Encyclopedia,* Virtualology, 2001, http://www.famousamericans.net/johnhuntingtoncranecoffin; *Appleton's Cyclopedia of American Biography,* ed. James Grant Wilson and John Fiske, 6 vols., New York: D. Appleton and Company, 1887 1889.

Levi Coffin—President of the Underground Railroad

"Levi Coffin was born in Greensboro, North Carolina, on 28th October, 1798. After a brief education he became a school teacher. A member of the Society of Friends, Coffin attempted in 1821 to start a school for slaves but their owners refused to allow them to attend. In 1826 Coffin moved to Newport, Indiana. This was on the route where fugitive slaves made their way from the South to Canada. During the twenty years they lived in Indiana, they helped in freeing 3,300 slaves. An average of 106 fugitives a year slept under their roof. Readers of "Uncle Tom's Cabin" will remember the elderly Quaker, Simeon Halliday, and his kindness to fleeing slaves. Mrs. Stowe had Levi Coffin and his wife in mind when she wrote of Simeon and Rachel Halliday. Eliza, who crossed the Ohio River on blocks of floating ice, was also a real person who was sheltered in the Coffin home on her way to Canada.

"Coffin moved to Cincinnati in 1847 where he opened a store selling goods made exclusively by freed slaves. He also visited England to raise funds for the cause and in 1867 he was a delegate to the International Anti-Slavery Conference in Paris.

"Levi Coffin, whose autobiography, *Reminiscences,* was published in 1876, died in Cincinnati, Ohio, on 16th September, 1877." He is buried at Spring Grove Cemetery, Cincinnati, Ohio. Sources: http://www.shockfamily.net/underground/levicoffin.html and http://www.spartacus.schoolnet.co.uk/USAScoffin.htm.

Vestal Coffin—Founder of the Underground Railroad

"The Underground Railroad was started in 1819 by Vestal Coffin at New Garden in Guilford County, North Carolina. Coffin had joined the Manumission Society begun by Benjamin Lundy in 1816. The Friends in North Carolina had mostly freed their slaves in 1772, but many of these freed slaves stayed with their owners rather than run the risk of capture by other southerners. Such was the case with Aaron and Samuel Henley of Randolph County, both of whom had freed slaves living on their property in 1840. These slaves had been inherited through their wives' families. The leader of the Underground Railroad in Indiana was Levi Coffin, an uncle of Vestal Coffin who had emigrated west to Newport, Indiana, near the border of Ohio and Indiana. For twenty years Levi and Catherine Coffin opened their home as a way-station for more than 2,000 escaped slaves. On the escape route were homes of relatives of the Coffins. The way-stations and routes were kept secret and never put in writing to protect the lives of the home-owners and the slaves. However, it is known that some of the stops or overnight refuges were at homes of relatives of the Coffins and their fellow Friends." Source: http://olympus.as.arizona.edu/~mccarthy/JILL/C7.html%25.

John Calvin Coolidge—President of the United States

"At 2:30 on the morning of August 3, 1923, while visiting in Vermont, Calvin Coolidge received word that he was President. (President Warren Harding had died.) By the light of a kerosene lamp, his father, who was a notary public, administered the oath of office as Coolidge placed his hand on the family Bible. Coolidge was 'distinguished for character more than for heroic achievement,' wrote a Democratic admirer, Alfred E. Smith. 'His great task was to restore the dignity and prestige of the Presidency when it had reached the lowest ebb in our history . . . in a time of extravagance and waste. . . .'

"Born in Plymouth, Vermont, on July 4, 1872, Coolidge was the son of a village storekeeper. He was graduated from Amherst College with honors, and entered law and politics in Northampton, Massachusetts. Slowly, methodically, he went up the political ladder from councilman in Northampton to Governor of Massachusetts, as a Republican. En route he became thoroughly conservative.

"As President, Coolidge demonstrated his determination to preserve the old moral and economic precepts amid the material prosperity which many Americans were enjoying. He refused to use Federal economic power to check the growing boom or to ameliorate the depressed condition of agriculture and certain industries. His first message to Congress in December 1923 called for isolation in foreign policy, and for tax cuts, economy, and limited aid to farmers.

"He rapidly became popular. In 1924, as the beneficiary of what was becoming known as 'Coolidge prosperity,' he polled more than 54 percent of the popular vote.

"In his Inaugural he asserted that the country had achieved 'a state of contentment seldom before seen,' and pledged himself to maintain the status quo. In subsequent years he twice vetoed farm relief bills, and killed a plan to produce cheap Federal electric power on the Tennessee River.

"The political genius of President Coolidge, Walter Lippmann pointed out in 1926, was his talent for effectively doing nothing: 'This active inactivity suits the mood and certain of the needs of the country admirably. It suits all the business interests which want to be let alone. . . . And it suits all those who have become convinced that government in this country has become dangerously complicated and top-heavy. . . .'

"Coolidge was both the most negative and remote of Presidents, and the most accessible. He once explained to Bernard Baruch why he often sat silently through interviews: 'Well, Baruch, many times I say only "yes" or "no" to people. Even that is too much. It winds them up for twenty minutes more.'

"But no President was kinder in permitting himself to be photographed in Indian war bonnets or cowboy dress, and in greeting a variety of delegations to the White House.

"Both his dry Yankee wit and his frugality with words became legendary. His wife, Grace Goodhue Coolidge, recounted that a young woman sitting next to Coolidge at a dinner party confided to him she had bet she could get at least three words of conversation from him. Without looking at her he quietly retorted, 'You lose.' And in 1928, while vacationing in the Black Hills of South Dakota, he issued the most famous of his laconic statements, 'I do not choose to run for President in 1928.'

"By the time the disaster of the Great Depression hit the country, Coolidge was in retirement. Before his death in January 1933, he confided to an old friend, 'I feel I no longer fit in with these times.' He descends from Tristram Coffin's sister, Mary Coffin, who married Alexander Adams." Source: *Past Presidents,* http://www.whitehouse.gov/history/presidents/cc30.html.

Henry S. Drinker, Philip Drinker, and Catherine Drinker Bowen

were the children of Henry S. Drinker Sr. and Aimee Beaux. They were descendants of Thomas Gardner of Salem, Massachusetts, and also of Mary Janney of Cheshire, England. Henry S. Drinker Senior was President of Lehigh University from 1905 until 1920.

Henry S. Drinker—
Drinker Biddle & Reath, LLP, Philadelphia

"August 1904 marked the arrival of Henry S. Drinker, Jr., who became a dominant presence in the firm for 50 years. Drinker was the executive voice of the firm from the time he emerged in the 1920s until the 1950s. Educated at Haverford College, Harvard, and the University of Pennsylvania, Henry Drinker worked for several months without a salary, until finally collecting $50 and $100 in January 1905. He was admitted to the partnership in 1918, and was named counsel to the University of Pennsylvania in 1927. His passion for the law was equaled by his love of music. Drinker was a recognized musicologist and translated texts of Bach and Mozart. In 1931, he was appointed an associate trustee and member of the University of Pennsylvania's Board of Fine Arts.

"When war once again engulfed Europe in the first half of the 20th century, Henry Drinker's love of choral music earned him a footnote in the well-known story of the Trapp family. In October 1939, family patriarch, Georg Von Trapp, asked Henry Drinker to intervene when the family was detained at Ellis Island with visa problems. Their Philadelphia lawyer and benefactor would repeatedly come to their rescue during the war years." Source: Drinker Biddle,http://www.drinkerbiddle.com/about/history/#Henry%20S.%20Drinker.

Philip Drinker—Co-inventor of the Iron Lung

"Nothing worked well in keeping people breathing until 1927, when Philip Drinker and Louis Agassiz Shaw at Harvard University devised a version of a tank respirator that could maintain respiration artificially until a person could breathe independently, usually after one or two weeks. The machine was powered by an electric motor with two vacuum cleaners. The pump changed the pressure inside a rectangular, airtight metal box, pulling air in and out of the lungs." Source: *The Iron Lung and Other Equipment,* http://americanhistory.si.edu/polio/howpolio/ironlung.htm.

Allen Welsh Dulles—OSS and CIA leader

"He was born Allen Welsh Dulles, the son of famous Presbyterian minister Reverend Allen Dulles in Watertown, New York. His father often stressed the merits of public service with his five children. He was educated in the local school system then went on to Princeton and with graduation entered the diplomatic service. He returned to George Washington University earning a law degree and with it in hand took a job at the New York firm owned along with a partner by his brother John Foster Dulles. During World War II, he was a station chief (spy) in Berne, Switzerland. Dulles supplied the U.S with much sensitive information about Nazi Germany, then played an important role in negotiations leading to the unconditional capitulation of German troops in Italy. Congress created the Central Intelligence Agency and Allen Dulles was closely involved with its development and named deputy director. Under President Eisenhower, he became its director. The CIA was instrumental in the overthrow of many governments through covert activities. The U-2 Plane was devised, gleaning important information with its flights over Russia. It discovered the hidden missiles in Cuba resulting in subsequent removal. However: They hit a snag when President John F. Kennedy held Dulles responsible for the failed Bay of Pigs invasion of Cuba because of faulty information and forced him to resign. In retirement, he wrote articles defending the CIA and rejected charges it was to blame for the Cuba failure. He closed out his amazing career by serving on the Warren Commission on the assassination of President Kennedy adding credibility to the final report. Eight years later, at the time of his death, he still carried the mythical tile of 'Spymaster' and was still respected in the country and throughout the world as the most talented, effectual American spy in history. He contracted influenza which developed into pneumonia taking his life at age seventy five. Prior to his resignation he toured the newly constructed Central Intelligence Headquarters, a project he spearheaded, situated in a college campus-like atmosphere creating an ideal atmosphere in which to pursue intelligence work. He never was able to occupy the office of director. After his death a bas-relief sculpted by Heinz Warneke depicting him was placed on the north wall of the main lobby honoring his long service and contributions to the CIA." Source: http://www.findagrave.com/cgi bin/fg.cgi?page=gr&GRid=305&pt=Allen%20Dulles.

John Foster Dulles—Secretary of State under President Dwight D. Eisenhower

"John Foster Dulles, a Senator from New York; born in Washington, D.C., February 25, 1888; attended the public schools of Watertown, N.Y.; was graduated from Princeton University in 1908; attended the Sorbonne, Paris, in 1908 and 1909; graduated from the law school of George Washington University, Washington, D.C., in 1911; was admitted to the bar and commenced the practice of law in New York, N.Y., in 1911; special agent for Department of State in Central America in 1917; during the First World War served as a captain and a major in the United States Army Intelligence Service 1917–1918; assistant to chairman, War Trade Board 1918; counsel to American Commission to Negotiate Peace 1918–1919; member of Reparations Commission and Supreme Economic Council 1919; legal adviser, Polish Plan of Financial Stabilization 1927; American representative, Berlin Debt Conferences 1933; member, United States delegation, San Francisco Conference on World Organization 1945; adviser to Secretary of State at Council of Foreign Ministers in London 1945, Moscow and London 1947, and Paris 1949; representative to the General Assembly of the United Nations 1946–1949 and chairman of the United States delegation in Paris 1948; trustee of Rockefeller Foundation; chairman of the board, Carnegie Endowment for International Peace; member of the New York State Banking Board 1946–1949; appointed as a Republican to the United States Senate to fill the vacancy caused by the resignation of Robert F. Wagner and served from July 7, 1949, to November 8, 1949, when a duly elected successor qualified; unsuccessful candidate for election to the vacancy; United States representative to the Fifth General Assembly of the United Nations 1950; consultant to the Secretary of State 1951–1952; appointed Secretary of State by President Dwight D. Eisenhower 1953–1959; died in Washington, D.C., May 24, 1959; interment in Arlington National Cemetery, Fort Myer, Va." Source: Arlington National Cemetery, http://www.arlingtoncemetery.net/jfdulles.htm.

James A. Folger—Founder of Folgers Coffee

"The Folgers Coffee Company began in 1850 in San Francisco as the Pioneer Steam Coffee and Spice Mills. James A. Folger, a Nantucket native, journeyed across Panama to San Francisco with two of his brothers to join the 1849 Gold Rush. While his brothers sought their fortunes in the hills, James Folger joined William Bovee and bought a mill to grind roasted coffee beans, tea, and spices. Folger traveled through the California gold camps selling his goods, and took over the entire business in 1859 when his partner left to mine for gold.

"The company grew, survived the 1906 earthquake, and eventually became the leading coffee brand west of the Ohio River. The spice business was sold to A. Schilling & Co. in 1929. The Folger Company was sold to P&G in 1963. Americans remember Mrs. Olson, who promoted Mountain Grown Folgers on American television in the 1960s and 70s." Source: P & G Global Operations, 2006, Procter & Gamble, http://www.pg.com/en_CA/product_card/bf_folgers.jhtml.

Henry Clay Folger—Chairman of Standard Oil and Founder of Folger Shakespeare Library

"Henry Clay Folger 1857–1930, American industrialist and collector of Shakespeareana. His connection with Standard Oil companies, beginning in 1879, continued until his retirement 49 years later as chairman of the board of the New York company. He was an enthusiastic student of Shakespeare during his college days and became a discerning collector. His wife, Emily Jordan Folger, (died 1936), was his associate in this work. Their collection, quietly acquired, became one of the largest and most valuable of its sort in the world. The Folger Shakespeare Library, east of the Library of Congress, Washington, D.C., was dedicated in 1932. Its major collections contain more than 250,000 volumes, primarily 16th- and 17th-century works of literature, drama, and history of the

English Renaissance. It is administered by Amherst College trustees." Source: *The Columbia Electronic Encyclopedia*, 6th ed., Columbia University Press, 2005.

Lydia Folger Fowler—Medical Doctor and Professor of Medicine

"Lydia Folger (1822–1879) was born in Nantucket, Massachusetts, on May 5, 1822. She attended the Wheaton Seminary in Norton, Massachusetts, from 1838 to 1839 and taught there from 1842 to 1844. In 1844 she married Lorenzo Niles Fowler, a well known phrenologist and one of a family of promoters in that field. Lydia Fowler soon took to the lecture circuit as a phrenologist herself, and she wrote "Familiar Lessons on Physiology (1847)," "Familiar Lessons on Phrenology" (1847), and "Familiar Lessons on Astronomy" (1848) for the family publishing firm of Fowlers & Wells. In 1849 she entered Central Medical College, an eclectic institution in Syracuse, New York. During her second term by which time the college had moved to Rochester, New York, she served also as principal of the female department. On graduating in June 1850 she became the second woman, after Elizabeth Blackwell, to receive a medical degree.

"In 1851 Fowler was appointed professor of midwifery and diseases of women and children at the college, becoming thereby the first woman professor in an American medical college. From the closing of the school in 1852 until 1860 she lived and practiced in New York City. She also lectured frequently to women on hygiene and physiology, championed the further opening of the medical profession to women and became active in the women's rights and temperance movements. During 1860–1860 she studied medicine in Paris and London, and in 1862 she became an instructor in clinical midwifery at the New York Hygeio Therapeutic College in New York City. In 1863 she and her husband moved to London permanently. In that year she published a temperance novel, 'Nora: The Lost and Redeemed.' 'The Pet of the Household and How to Save It' (1865) was a collection of lectures on child care, and 'Heart Melodies' (1870) was verse. Fowler died in London on January 26, 1879." Source: *Encyclopedia Britannica*, 1999

Margaret Getchell— Macy's Department Store Senior Executive

"Margaret Getchell was on her way to pioneering the entry into the ranks of management in major American Corporations. Getchell began her rise through the glass ceiling as a cashier in R.H. Macy's New York department store. Rising through the ranks to an executive position at Macy's, Getchell became one of the first women in America to hold a senior executive position purely on her own merits.

"As early as the 1860s, women held very high positions in the store's management. Macy's first three superintendents were women. R. H. Macy's cousin, Margaret (Getchell) La Forge, was his first store manager. She remained in the position until the birth of her first child in 1870." Source: R. H. Macy and Company Collection, Catalog Record, Mss 776 1858 1919 M177, Box 1, http://www.library.hbs.edu/hc/wes/indexes/alpha/content/1001954460/.

Nathaniel Gorham Jr.—Signer of the U.S. Constitution

"Nathaniel Gorman was born in Charlestown, Massachusetts, May 27, 1738. He received an excellent education, and possessing uncommon talents, he always appeared to be an advantage in company with literary men. He settled in business at the place of his nativity, but being a constant, fearless, and independent lover of freedom, seemed to be formed more for public life than to succeed in mercantile pursuits. Mr. Gorham was chosen representative for Charlestown, in 1771, and every year till the commencement of the Revolutionary war. He was a very assiduous attendant on the house of representatives, and was a leader in all their debates. In 1779 he was elected a delegate of the convention which formed the constitution of his native State. In 1784 he was chosen a member of the Congress of the United States, and soon after elected president of that honorable body.

"In 1787, Mr. Gorham was a member of the grand convention which formed the federal constitution. In this august body, he sustained a high reputation for his knowledge and integrity. He stood high with all parties for his wisdom and prudence, and eloquence in debate. He was on this account one of the most influential members of the State convention, which adopted the constitution. He died, June 11, 1796, at the age of fifty-eight years." Source: Marshall, James V., *The United States Manual of Biography and History,* Philadelphia, James B. Smith & Co., 1856, pp. 165–166.

"During the convention which drafted the new constitution, Georgia delegate William Pierce, and others for various reasons, left the convention before September and did not sign the new constitution. However, while in attendance Pierce made private notes on each representative as found above." Source: http://www.laughtergenealogy.com/bin/histprof/founders/const/gorham.html.

Nathaniel Hawthorne—Author

"Nathaniel Hawthorne (1804–1864), American novelist and short story writer, was most famous for his novel *The Scarlet Letter.* He was born at Salem, Massachusetts, on July 4th, 1804, son of a sea captain. He led there a shy and rather over protected life; yet not wholly uncongenial to his artistic development. Hawthorne turned to writing after his graduation from Bowdoin College. He wrote several successful short stories which were collected in *Twice-Told Tales* (1837). Insufficient earnings as a writer forced Hawthorne to take a job in the Salem Custom House. By 1842, he was able to earn enough to marry

Sophia Peabody[294] and move to Concord, which was then the center of the Transcendental movement. Hawthorne returned to Salem in 1845, and in 1850, his most famous novel, *The Scarlet Letter* was published. His next novel was The *House of the Seven Gables* (1851). He also wrote two classic works for children, *A Wonder Book* (1852) and *Tanglewood Tales* (1853). He wrote another novel, *The Marble Faun,* in 1860 and an account of a journey to England, *Our Old Home,* in 1863. Nathaniel Hawthorne died at Plymouth, New Hampshire, on May 18th, 1864." Source: http://www.online literature.com/hawthorne.

William Wade Hinshaw—Metropolitan Opera Baritone and Compiler of the *Encyclopedia of American Quaker Genealogy*

"William Wade Hinshaw was a highly educated man. He graduated from Friends Academy, New Providence, Iowa, in 1886; received degrees in Engineering (1888), Music (1890), and Law (1897) from Valparaiso (IN) University. He continued studying music at the Chicago Music College in 1890 and during following years studied singing and operatic art under various outstanding teachers. He taught music and was Dean of Music Dept. of Valparaiso University 1895–1899. During 1907–1909 he was president, owner and director of the Hinshaw Conservatory of Music and Dramatic Art, Chicago. He was leading baritone of the Castle Square Opera Co., of Boston for three seasons in concerts and operas 1890–1918. From 1910–1913 he was the leading American baritone with Metropolitan Opera Company. He continued in operas and musical festivals until June, 1926 when he retired from the music field.

"For twenty one years, 1926 until his death on 27 November 1947, he devoted his life to locating and making Quaker records more available to genealogists. He believed that Quaker records contain the most detailed genealogical data of perhaps any religious group. Because he knew that these records were often lost, destroyed or decayed, he conceived the idea of trying to locate as many as possible and extracting genealogy information. His goal was to compile and publish a set of Encyclopedia of Quaker Genealogy. . . .

"The responsibility of continuing the work of Wm. Wade Hinshaw after his death was assumed by his 2nd wife, Mrs. Mable Hinshaw . . . she made financial arrangements for more of his records to be published. She gave most of his unpublished data to the Friends Historical Library, Swarthmore College, Pennsylvania, and provided the college with funds to continue her husband's project. The unpublished collection at the time of his death included Quaker

---

294. Her sister, Mary Tyler Peabody, married Horace Mann, who is called "The Father of American Education." He was President of Antioch College, Yellow Springs, Ohio, when Charles and Sarah (Sattie) Oren were students there. Charles and Sattie were friends and neighbors of Paulena and William Janney. They were also distantly related to Paulena.

records of California, Kansas, Iowa, more Pennsylvania records, Colorado, Idaho, Minnesota, Missouri, Nebraska, more New Jersey, Oklahoma, and South Dakota.

"Mr. and Mrs. Hinshaw lived at the Mayflower, Washington, D.C. He was a Mason, Shriner, Republican, member of Society of Friends, Knights of Phythias, Elk, and various country clubs. He was an expert golfer." Source: *Biographical Sketch of Wm. Wade Hinshaw,* compiled in 1990 for Selby Publishing Printing Co., Kokomo, Indiana.

R. H. Macy—Founder of Macy's Department Store

"Rowland Hussey Macy's family had lived on Nantucket Island, Massachusetts, for eight generations by the time he was born in 1822. At age 15 he shipped out to sea on a whaler, where he was tattooed with a red star that was later adopted as the trademark for Macy's. On his return Macy opened the first of his doomed dry goods stores in Boston; two years later he wrote the final entry in his account book; 'I have worked two years for nothing. Damn, damn, damn.' Macy tried his luck as a Forty Niner in California, and in six other retail ventures that all failed. Why he made another attempt, and how he convinced someone to lend a man with his record $20,000, is a mystery. But the store he established in lower Manhattan, on 14th street near Union Square, in 1858 took off.

"Rowland Macy had an uncontrollable temper, an ulcer, and a severe case of stinginess; but he also had a flair for advertising and the ability to hire the right people. Much of the store's success after 1860 must be credited to Margaret Getchell, a cousin of Rowland Macy who became store superintendent the first woman executive of a large business. Getchell's motto was, 'Be everywhere, do everything, and never fail to astonish the customer.' She had a reputation for fixing anything with a hairpin.

"The store continued to thrive under Macy's four point plan: 1) sell at fixed market prices; 2) sell for less; 3) buy and sell for cash only (credit cards were added in 1939); 4) advertise heavily. By 1880 Rowland Macy and all original partners had all died. Eight years later the store passed into the hands of three people who had run the china department at Macy's: Lazarus Straus and his two sons, Isidor and Nathan. The Straus family still serves on the board of directors." Source: *The Business & Industry Hall of Fame,* Weekly Featured Exhibit: Rowland Macy.

Dr. Obed Macy—First Medical Doctor in
Los Angeles, California

Dr. Obed Macy, son of William Macy and Mary Barnard, was born in Guilford County, North Carolina, in 1801. The family removed to Union County, Indiana, where Quaker records state that on August 8, 1818, Obed Macy (along with his parents and siblings) was received on certificate from Center Monthly Meeting,

Guilford County, North Carolina, endorsed by Whitewater Monthly Meeting, Indiana, to Silver Creek–Salem Monthly Meeting, near Liberty, Union County, Indiana. In 1824 he married Lucinda Polk, daughter of Charles Polk and Margaret McQuade, at the Maria Creek Baptist Church in Knox County Indiana. The Quaker records state that on December 24, 1825, Obed was disowned by Salem Monthly Meeting for marrying out of unity; that is to say, he did not marry a Quaker.

Obed Macy was a medical doctor for the Bruceville community in Knox County, Indiana. It is reported that in 1850 the Macy family and a large party of other Knox County families left Indiana at the end of April, crossing the Wabash River at McCarter's Ferry, present-day Russellville, Illinois, and traveled overland to the Mississippi River, which they crossed on a ferry according to Dr. Macy's daughter, Lucinda, then up the Missouri River to Kansas City, where they bought nine wagons and oxen and other provisions to the westward move. Their son Charles, about nine years old, died along the trail in Nebraska, and they had no choice but to bury him alongside the trail. They proceeded west to get to Salt Lake City where their grandchild, Randolph Cheesman, was born, on September 15, 1850. They continued their journey, finally reaching the San Gabriel Mission on New Year's Day 1851 with only one wagon remaining. The family camped about two months at San Gabriel, then moved to El Monte, building a "stick and mud" house under a great oak tree. In 1852, the family moved to Los Angeles, where Dr. Macy bought the Bella Union Hotel, establishing his family in one of two small houses on the northwest corner of Los Angeles and Commercial Streets.

They lived here for some time, and the children attended school in the new two-story brick schoolhouse on the northeast corner of Second and Spring Streets. Then Dr. Macy acquired a site on the Zanja Madre at what is now the corner of North Main and Macy Streets, where he built a low spreading building, a portion of which was fitted up as a bathhouse, water for the baths being taken from the Zanja by means of a large waterwheel. The bathhouse was not of adobe brick, but of mud poured into forms in the manner of concrete construction today.

While this house was being built, the Macy family lived nearby in an adobe on the east side of Olvera Street. Dr Macy died on July 9, 1857, and was survived by his widow, Lucinda Polk Macy, who, with other members of the family, continued to live in the home until her death on August 3, 1872. Macy Street has recently been renamed Cesar Chavez Blvd. Sources: *History of Los Angeles City and County, California*, William A. Spalding, Los Angeles, Finnell & Sons Publishing Co., 1931; *Footsteps Through Time, A Macy Family Newsletter*, October 1, 1986; The Macy Roots Web List, Don Cordel, January 8, 2002.

John Macy—Judge

John Macy, son of John Winchester Macy and Sarah Edger of Winchester, Randolph County, Indiana, practiced law with Pierre Goodrich from 1920 to 1923. Pierre Goodrich was the son of John Baldwin Goodrich and Elizabeth Edger, sister of Sarah Edger. John Macy and Pierre Goodrich were first cousins once removed. John Macy was a seventh cousin twice removed to Christie (Hill) Russell. John Winchester "Chas" Macy was a third cousin twice removed to Dr. Obed Macy of Knox County, Indiana, and later Los Angeles, California. Sources: *History of Los Angeles City and County, California,* William A. Spalding, Los Angeles, Finnell & Sons Publishing Co., 1931; *Footsteps Through Time, A Macy Family Newsletter,* October 1, 1986; Macy Roots Web List, Don Cordel, January 8, 2002.

Herman Melville—Author and Poet

"Born in 1819 into a once-prominent New York family, Herman Melville was raised in an atmosphere of financial instability and genteel pretense. After his father's death, Melville attempted to support his family by working various jobs, from banking to teaching school. However, it was his adventures as a seaman in 1845 that inspired Melville to write.[295] On one voyage, he was captured and held for several months by the Typees; when he returned unscathed, friends encouraged Melville to write the escapade down. *Typee: A Peep at Polynesian Life* became his first literary success; the continuation of his adventures appeared in his second book, *Omoo.* After ending his seafaring career, Melville's concern over his sporadic education inspired him to read voraciously. In 1847, he married Elizabeth Shaw and moved first to New York and then the Berkshires. There he lived near the reclusive writer Nathaniel Hawthorne, who was to become a close friend and confidant. Intoxicated by metaphysics, Melville penned *Mardi and a Voyage Thither,* a philosophical allegory. The book failed, and though discouraged, Melville dashed off *Redburn,* a comedy. Although the book proved a financial success, Melville immediately returned to the symbolic in his next

---

295. The last whale ship that Melville served on was the *Charles and Henry.* "In the late fall of the year 1842, the (Charles and Henry) ship was lying at Tahiti, and Captain John B. Coleman, disheartened by the poor quality of his boatsteerers (harpooners), signed on a young American he found ashore looking for a berth. In signing on the young man he wrote, in a bold hand, the name 'Herman Melville.' Melville was to serve until July of the next year (1843), when he received his honorable discharge at Lahaina, the port on the island of Maui in the Hawaiian Islands. From his experience on the *Charles & Henry* the author incorporated a number of passages in his books. It is to be noted that Captain Coleman received better treatment than the master of the *Acushnet,* Melville's first whaler." *Nantucket Doorways: Thresholds to the Past,* Edouard A. Stackpole, 1974. Editorial note: Herman Melville was related to both Charles and Henry Coffin and to Captain Coleman as well as Paulena Stevens Janney through their mutual Coffin lineage.

novel, *White-Jacket; or, the World in a Man-of-War.* In 1851, he completed his masterpiece, *Moby-Dick, or the Whale.* Considered by modern scholars to be one of the great American novels, the book was dismissed by Melville's contemporaries and he made little money from the effort. . . .

"During the 1850s, Melville supported his family by farming and writing stories for magazines. He later traveled to Europe, where he saw his friend Hawthorne for the last time. During that visit in 1856, it was clear to Melville that his novel-writing career was finished. In 1857, after returning to New York still unnoticed by the literary public, he stopped writing fiction. He became a customs inspector, a job he held for twenty years. And he began to write poetry. [It will be remembered that Paulena Stevens Janney read Melville's short novel *Israel Potter: His Fifty Years of Exile.* It appeared serially in *Putnam's Monthly Magazine* in 1854 and 1855, and in book form in 1855.]

"The Civil War made a deep impression on Melville and became the principal subject of his verse. With so many family members participating in various aspects of the war, Melville found himself intimately connected to events, and also sought out conflict for himself. He observed the Senate debating secession during a visit to Washington, D.C., in 1861, and made a remarkable trip to the front with his brother in 1864. Melville's first published book of poems was *Battle-Pieces and Aspects of the War* (1866), a meditation. The volume is regarded by many critics as a work as ambitious and rich as any of his novels. Unfortunately, Melville remains relatively unrecognized as a poet.

"Herman Melville died of a heart attack on September 28, 1891, at the age of 72. At that time, he was almost completely forgotten by all but a few admirers. During the week of his death, *The New York Times* wrote: 'There has died and been buried in this city . . . a man who is so little known, even by name, to the generation now in the vigor of life that only one newspaper contained an obituary account of him, and this was but of three or four lines.'" It wasn't until the 1920s that the literary public began to recognize Melville as one of America's greatest writers. Source: *The Academy of American Poets,* http://www.poets.org/poets/poets.cfm?45442B7C000C040109.

Maria Mitchell—Astronomer

"Maria Mitchell, astronomer, was born in Massachusetts on the Island of Nantucket, the second daughter and third of ten children of William and Lydia (Coleman) Mitchell. Her ancestors were members of the Society of Friends who had migrated from England to America. Her mother she later remembered as stern and hardworking; her father was said to be 'mild and winning in his manners, firm and resolute in his purposes.' Originally a cooper, William Mitchell became in 1827 master of the first free school on Nantucket and in 1836 cashier, or principal officer, of the Pacific Bank. He had, however, a scientific bent, which was inherited not only by Maria but also by her brother Henry, who became a leading hydrographer. In the early nineteenth century, when Nantucket was the greatest whaling port in the world, knowledge of the skies was imperative for those who navigated distant oceans.

"William Mitchell became interested in astronomy and soon added to his other tasks the rating of chronometers for the Nantucket whaling fleet— checking them by stellar observations. When she was still a child, Maria began to help him as he worked on 'the widow's walk' on the roof of their house. In 1831, while they watched a solar eclipse, the twelve-year old girl recorded the time. Asked in later years what had led her to astronomy, she cited her love of mathematics and her father's example, but credited her environment as well: 'In Nantucket people quite generally are in the habit of observing the heavens, and a sextant will be found in almost every house. . . .'

"[S]he became librarian of the New Nantucket Atheneum, a position she held for twenty years. The library was open to the public in the afternoons and on occasional evenings; she had the rest of the day to explore its rich resources undisturbed. Soon she was studying Bowditch's *Practical Navigator,* reading the works of Lagrange, Laplace, and Legendre in French, puzzling over Latin passages in Gauss' Theoria Motus Corporeum Coelestium, and teaching herself German. The lyceum lectures of Emerson, William Ellery Channing, Theodore Parker, Lucy Stone, and Horace Greeley furthered her intellectual awakening.

"Most of her evenings were spent in the observatory her father erected on the roof of the Pacific Bank, assisting in stellar research of a breadth and accuracy that soon won the attention of such men as William C. Bond, director of the Harvard College Observatory, his son George Bond, and Alexander Dallas Bache, superintendent of the United States Coast Survey. The Nantucket lookout became a station of the Survey, and in 1848 William Mitchell was appointed to the visiting committee of the Harvard observatory. As Maria continued to help her father with his work for the Coast Survey, they made thousands of observations of meridian latitudes of stars for the determination of time and latitude, and of moon culminations and occulations for longitude. Later they turned to the observation of double and variable stars. Their instruments included an altitude and azimuth circle, a four inch equatorial telescope, and a two inch Dollond telescope.

"With this last, Maria Mitchell, on the night of October 1, 1847, discovered a new comet. When it was established that she was, indeed, the first discoverer, the comet was named for her, and she gained worldwide fame as the King of Denmark awarded her a gold medal. In 1918 she became the first (and until 1943, apparently the only) woman elected to the American Academy of Arts and Sciences in Boston. In the same year Elias Loomis devoted an entire chapter to 'Miss Mitchell's Comet' in his survey of *The Recent Progress of Astronomy; Especially in the United States.* In 1849 she was appointed one of the original computers for the new American Ephemeris and Nautical Almanac, a post which augmented her salary as Atheneum librarian. She was elected to the American Association for the Advancement of Sciences in 1850, on the nomination of Louis Agassiz. On a long desired trip abroad in 1857–58 she met many famous European scientists, including Mary Somerville, Sir John Herschel, and Alexander Von Rumbold. Upon her return a group of women, led by Elizabeth Peabody, gave her a five inch Alvan Clark telescope. Despite such recognition, she felt that her reputation was undeserved. . . . In 1861, after her mother's death, she moved with her father to Lynn, Mass., where a married sister lived. The shape of her future was soon changed unexpectedly by Matthew Vassar, a wealthy brewer of Poughkeepsie, N.Y., who had founded a woman's college to rival the best men's colleges in America. Eager to add a woman of Maria Mitchell's stature and reputation to his first faculty, he offered to build and place her in charge of an observatory with a twelve inch telescope (the third largest in the country). The prospect was enticing, yet she hesitated. Never having attended college, she questioned her own qualifications for teaching. She finally agreed to try, however, and moved with her father to Poughkeepsie in time for the opening of Vassar Female College in September 1865.

"Through her years at Vassar she continued her own research. She pioneered in the daily photography of sunspots and faculae, noting that the former were whirling vertical cavities, not clouds above the sun's surface as many astronomers still believed. Her publications also included reports on solar eclipses as well as on changes observed on the planetary surfaces, particularly of Jupiter and Saturn and their satellites. On a second trip abroad in 1873 she renewed her European contacts and visited the great Russian observatory at Pulkova. Always she inspired her students to share her research. Night after night they worked with her in the observatory. Nine even bought their own telescopes. On two occasions groups of them journeyed west with her to observe solar eclipses, the first at Burlington, Iowa, in 1869, the second in Denver in 1878. Many followed in her path after graduation, sometimes in science, often in other fields. Twenty five found a place in *Who's Who in America,* including such leading women scientists as Ellen Swallow Richards and Christine Ladd Franklin and Miss Mitchell's own successor, Mary W. Whitney.

"Maria Mitchell's influence was not, however, restricted to Vassar or to her work in astronomy. She was a founder in 1873 of the Association for the Advancement of Women, a group of moderate feminists in whose annual congresses women in the professions, social service, and other aspects of public life met together to discuss the work and problems of their sex. For two years (1875 and 1876) she served as its president and until her death was chairman of its science committee. Year after year, at scientific meetings and A.A.W. congresses and in lectures, she pleaded for recognition of women's scientific abilities. She wished, also, to see the scientific method applied to other fields, and repeatedly urged that the experimental approach, with its basis in 'the law of growth through failure,' be brought to bear on social problems. In recognition of the breadth of outlook she was in 1869 elected to the American Philosophical Society—again the first woman so honored—and in 1873 was made a vice president of the American Social Science Association.

"Her health failing, Maria Mitchell retired from Vassar early in 1888 to return to Lynn, hoping to continue work in the small observatory she had built there. She died the next year in Lynn, however, of 'brain disease,' at the age of seventy. She was buried in Nantucket. . . . In 1922 a bust of Maria Mitchell was placed in the hall of Fame of New York University." *Notable American Women, 1607–1950,* vol. II.

Lucretia Coffin Mott—Political and Social Reformer
"Political and social reformer Lucretia Coffin Mott was born on January 3, 1793 in Nantucket, Massachusetts. Inspired by a father who encouraged his daughters to be useful and by a mother who was active in business affairs, Lucretia Mott agitated for the oppressed while raising six children. She devoted her life to the abolition of slavery, women's rights, school and prison reforms, temperance, peace, and religious tolerance. . . . With the placement of the Stanton-Mott-Anthony sculpture in the Capitol Rotunda in June 1997, and the sesquicentennial of the historic Seneca Falls Women's Rights Convention of 1848, Mott's life is receiving renewed attention." Sources: http://www.mott.pomona.edu/; http://courses.temple.edu/IH/IH52/Enlightenment/Mott/MottBio.htm.

O. Henry—Author
"Born William Sidney Porter, this master of short stories is much better known under his pen name 'O. Henry.' He was born September 11, 1862, in North Carolina, where he spent his childhood. His only formal education was received at the school of his Aunt Lina, where he developed a lifelong love of books. In his uncle's pharmacy, he became a licensed pharmacist and was also known for his sketches and cartoons of the townspeople of Greensboro.

"At the age of twenty, Porter came to Texas primarily for health reasons, and worked on a sheep ranch and lived with the family of Richard M. Hall, whose family had close ties with the Porter family back in North Carolina. It was here that Porter gained a knowledge of ranch life that he later described in many of his short stories.

"In 1884, Porter moved to Austin. For the next three years, he roomed in the home of the Joseph Harrell family and held several jobs. It was during this time that Porter first used his pen name, O. Henry, said to be derived from his frequent calling of 'Oh, Henry' the family cat.

"By 1887, Porter began working as a draftsman in the General Land Office, then headed by his old family friend, Richard Hall. In 1891 at the end of Hall's term at the Land Office, Porter resigned and became a teller with the First National Bank in Austin. After a few years, however, he left the bank and founded the *Rolling Stone,* an unsuccessful humor weekly. Starting in 1895 he wrote a column for the Houston *Daily Post.*

"Meanwhile, Porter was accused of embezzling funds dating back to his employment at the First National Bank. Leaving his wife and young daughter in Austin, Porter fled to New Orleans, then to Honduras, but soon returned due to his wife's deteriorating health. She died soon afterward, and in early 1898 Porter was found guilty of the banking charges and sentenced to five years in an Ohio prison.

"From this low point in Porter's life, he began a remarkable comeback. Three years and about a dozen short stories later, he emerged from prison as 'O. Henry' to help shield his true identity. He moved to New York City, where over the next ten years before his death in 1910, he published over 300 stories and gained worldwide acclaim as America's favorite short story writer.

"O. Henry wrote with realistic detail based on his first hand experiences both in Texas and in New York City. In 1907, he published many of his Texas stories in *The Heart of the West,* a volume that includes 'The Reformation of Calliope,' 'The Caballero's Way,' and 'The Hiding of Black Bill'. Another highly acclaimed Texas writer, J. Frank Dobie, later referred to O. Henry's 'Last of the Troubadours' as 'the best range story in American fiction.' Porter died on June 5, 1910 in New York City at the age of forty-seven. An alcoholic, he died virtually penniless.' 'The Gift of the Magi' is one of his best known and loved short stories." Source: *Lone Star Junction,* 1995–96, http://www.lsjunction.com/people/porter.htm.

Francis Parkman—Historian

"Francis Parkman (1823–1893), American historian, was born in Boston. In 1846, Parkman started a journey along the Oregon Trail to improve his health and study the Native Americans. On his return to Boston he collapsed physically and moved to Brattleboro, Vermont. There Parkman dictated to his cousin *The Oregon Trail,* published in book form as *The California and Oregon Trail* (1849); the shorter title was resumed in later editions. Despite ill health, he labored on his *History of the Conspiracy of Pontiac* (1851) and wrote an unsuccessful novel, *Vassall Morton* (1856). Following a trip to Paris in 1858 to seek medical aid, he was for several years unable to continue his historical researches. He took up the study of horticulture and became an expert in the field. In 1866, *The Book of Roses* was published, and from 1871 to 1872 he was professor of horticulture at Harvard. He eventually resumed his studies of the history of Canada and the early Northwest, publishing *Pioneers of France in the New World* (1865), *The Discovery of the Great West* (1869; 11th and later editions pub. as *La Salle and the Discovery of the Great West), The Old Régime in Canada* (1874), *Count Frontenac and New France under Louis XIV* (1877), *Montcalm and Wolfe* (1884), and *A Half-Century of Conflict* (1892). Parkman served for a time as overseer of Harvard and later as a fellow of the Harvard Corporation (1875–88). He was a founder of the Archaeological Institute of America (1879) and was president of the

Massachusetts Horticultural Society (1875–78). Parkman's superior literary gifts, combined with his careful historical research, gained him wide contemporary prominence. His work showed both anti-Catholic and anti-democratic prejudices, but it usually managed to combine accuracy and vigor of expression." Source: *The Columbia Encyclopedia,* 6th ed., Columbia University Press, 2004.

William Henry Seward—Lincoln's Secretary of State

"William Henry Seward was a Senator from New York. He was born in Florida, Orange County, N.Y., on May 16, 1801; after preparatory studies, graduated from Union College in 1820; studied law; admitted to the bar and commenced practice in Auburn, N.Y., 1823; member, State senate 1830–1834; unsuccessful Whig candidate for governor in 1834; Governor of New York 1838–1842; elected as a Whig to the United States Senate in 1849; reelected as a Republican in 1855 and served from March 4, 1849, to March 3, 1861; unsuccessful candidate for the Republican nomination for president in 1860; Secretary of State in the Cabinets of Presidents Abraham Lincoln and Andrew Johnson 1861–1869; while Secretary of State concluded the convention with Great Britain for the settlement of the Alabama claims and the treaty with Russia for the purchase of Alaska; died in Auburn, Cayuga County, N.Y., October 10, 1872; interment in Fort Hill Cemetery." Sources: "Seward, William Henry," *American National Biography; Dictionary of American Biography; William Henry Seward,* ed. Frederick Seward, 3 vols, New York, Derby and Miller, 1891; John M. Taylor, *William Henry Seward: Lincoln's Right Hand,* New York, Harper Collins, 1991.

Edward McMasters Stanton—Lincoln's Secretary of War

"In 1860, Edwin M. Stanton (1814–1869) was appointed the Attorney General for the last remaining months of James Buchanan's administration. He left office upon the inaugural of Abraham Lincoln but later accepted the post of Secretary of War for the sixteenth president. He performed well in the job, and was kept on when Andrew Johnson assumed the Presidency after Lincoln's assassination. Stanton and Johnson did not get along, and in 1868, Johnson removed Stanton as head of the War Department on grounds of disloyalty. Congress claimed Johnson violated the Tenure in Office Act by removing Stanton, and tried to impeach Johnson. After Johnson survived the impeachment trial, Stanton resigned his office and returned to private legal practice. President Ulysses S. Grant appointed Stanton to the Supreme Court in 1869, but he died before he could take this oath of office. He is buried in the Oak Hill Cemetery in Washington, D.C." Source: *World History,* http://www.ehistory.com/world/PeopleView.Cfm?PID=68.

Stanton's grandmother was Abigail Macy whose eighth great-grandparents (that is, eight "greats") included one Macy, one Coffin, one Bunker and three Gardners.

Mercy Otis Warren—Poet, Dramatist, and Historian

"Mercy Otis Warren (1728–1814) was born in Barnstable, Massachusetts, on September 25, 1728. Mercy Otis was the sister of the political activist James Otis, who was early active in events leading to the American Revolution. She received no formal schooling but managed to absorb something of an education from her brothers' tutors. In 1754 she married James Warren, a Massachusetts political leader. Knowing most of the leaders of the Revolution personally, Warren was continually at or near the center of events from 1765 to 1789. Her vantage point combined with a talent for writing was to make her both a poet and historian of the Revolutionary era. She wrote several plays, including the satirical *Adulateur* (1772). Directed against Governor Thomas Hutchinson of Massachusetts, the play foretold the War of Revolution. *The Defeat*, also featuring the character based on Hutchinson, followed, and in 1775 Warren published *The Group*, a satire conjecturing what would happen if the British king abrogated the Massachusetts charter of rights. The anonymously published *The Blockheads* (1776) and *The Motley Assembly* (1779) are also attributed to her. In 1788 she published *Observations on the New Constitution*, whose ratification she opposed. ['She unsuccessfully urged that equal rights for women be included in the U.S. Constitution. She outlined her objections to that document as originally drafted in *Observations on the New Constitutio . . . by a Columbian Patriot* (1788). Many of her criticisms were met by the Bill of Rights and later amendments.' Source: *The Columbia Electronic Encyclopedia*, 6th ed. Columbia University Press, 2005.]

"Warren corresponded with her friend Abigail Adams on her belief that the relegation of women to minor concerns reflected not their inferior intellect but the inferior opportunities offered them to develop their capacities. In 1790 she published *Poems, Dramatic and Miscellaneous*, a collection of her works. In 1805 she completed a three-volume history entitled *A History of the Rise, Progress, and Termination of the American Revolution*, which remains especially useful for its knowledgeable comments on the important personages of the day. The book's sharp comments on John Adams led to a heated correspondence and a breach in her friendship with the Adamses that lasted until 1812. Warren died on October 19, 1814, in Plymouth, Massachusetts." Source: *Encyclopædia Britannica*, 1999.

John Greenleaf Whittier—Author and Poet

"John Greenleaf Whittier (1807–1892), American Quaker poet and reformer, was born near Haverhill, Massachusetts. Whittier was a pioneer in regional literature as well as a crusader for many humanitarian causes. Whittier received a scanty education but read widely. An introduction at the age of 14 to Robert Burns' poetry inspired him to write verse; his first poems were published (1826) in the Newburyport *Free Press*, edited by William Lloyd Garrison, the abolitionist, who became his lifelong friend. In the years from 1828 to 1832, Whittier edited and contributed stories, sketches, and poems to various newspapers. His first two published books, *Legends of New England* (1831) and the poem *Moll Pitcher* (1832), warmly portrayed everyday life in his rural region. . . . In 1834–35 he sat in the Massachusetts legislature; he ran for Congress on the Liberty ticket in 1842 and was a founder of the Republican party. He also worked staunchly behind the political scene to further the abolitionist cause and was an active antislavery editor until 1840, when frail health forced him to retire to his Amesbury home. . . . He wrote over 100 hymns of which he is best known for 'Dear Lord and Father of Mankind.' As the voice of the New England villager and farmer prior to industrialization, his work portrays an important period in American history." Source: *The Columbia Encyclopedia*, 6th ed., Columbia University Press, 2001.

Thomas Lanier "Tennessee" Williams—Playwright

"Thomas Lanier Williams was born in Columbus, Mississippi, on March 26, 1911, the first son and second child of Cornelius Coffin and Edwina Dakin Williams. His mother, the daughter of a minister, was of genteel upbringing, while his father, a shoe salesman, came from a prestigious Tennessee family which included the state's first governor and first senator. The family lived for several years in Clarksdale, Mississippi, before moving to St. Louis in 1918. At the age of 16, he encountered his first brush with the publishing world when he won third prize and received $5 for an essay, 'Can a Good Wife Be a Good Sport?,' in *Smart Set*. A year later, he published 'The Vengeance of Nitocris' in *Weird Tales*. In 1929, he entered the University of Missouri. His success there was dubious, and in 1931 he began work for a St. Louis shoe company. It was six years later when his first play, *Cairo, Shanghai, Bombay*, was produced in Memphis, in many respects the true beginning of his literary and stage career.

"Building upon the experience he gained with his first production, Williams had two of his plays, *Candles to the Sun* and *The Fugitive Kind*, produced by Mummers of St. Louis in 1937. After a brief encounter with enrollment at Washington University, St. Louis, he entered the University of Iowa and graduated in 1938. As the second World War loomed over the horizon, Williams found a bit of fame when he won the Group Theater prize of $100 for *American Blues* and received a $1,000 grant from the Authors' League of America in 1939. *Battle of Angels* was produced in Boston a year later. Near the close of the war in 1944, what many consider to be his finest play, *The Glass Menagerie*, had a very successful run in Chicago and a year later burst its way onto Broadway. Containing autobiographical elements from both his days in St. Louis as well as from his family's past in Mississippi, the play won the New York Drama Critics' Circle award as the best play of the season. Williams, at the age of 34, had etched an indelible mark among the public and among his peers. Following the critical acclaim over *The Glass Menagerie*, over the next eight years he found homes for *A Streetcar Named Desire, Summer and Smoke, A Rose Tattoo,* and *Camino Real* on Broadway. Although his reputation on Broadway continued to zenith, particularly upon receiving his first Pulitzer Prize in 1948 for *Streetcar*, Williams reached a larger world-wide public in 1950 when *The Glass Menagerie* and again in 1951 when *A Streetcar Named Desire* were made into motion pictures. Williams had now achieved a fame few playwrights of his day could equal.

"Over the next thirty years, dividing his time between homes in Key West, New Orleans, and New York, his reputation continued to grow and he saw many more of his works produced on Broadway and made into films, including such works as *Cat on a Hot Tin Roof* (for which he earned a second Pulitzer Prize in 1955), *Orpheus Descending,* and *Night of the Iguana.* There is little doubt that as a playwright, fiction writer, poet, and essayist, Williams helped transform the contemporary idea of the Southern literature. However, as a Southerner he not only helped to pave the way for other writers, but also helped the South find a strong voice in those auspices where before it had only been heard as a whisper. Williams died on February 24, 1983, at the Hotel Elysée in New York City." Source: Eric W. Cash, *The Mississippi Writers Page,* University of Mississippi English Department, 2004.

John Woolman—Abolitionist

"Man's ideas of liberty and life have always harbored a conflict of civil law and civil rights. Disobedience of civil law takes place when an individual's conscience interferes with society's rules. Socrates, Plato, Jesus, the Sadducees and the Pharisees of Biblical times, all displayed civil disobedience by going against government, current philosophy, tax collectors and the worship of idols. People are continuing to increase their stand on issues of conscience. Individuals great and small have influenced and inspired enthusiasts for every cause. One such man, perhaps the most prominent man of his day, was 'the earnest Quaker,' a man who not only preached brotherhood, but also practiced it. John Woolman, (1720–1772) early Quaker abolitionist, devoted much of his life to freeing black slaves through civil disobedience.

"The Woolmans came to the new world in 1678. They settled in West New Jersey and were prominent businessmen and substantial landholders by Quaker standards. Woolman, as was his father, was active in politics, business and religion. He achieved the knowledge of reading, surveying, accounting, medicine and the drawing of legal documents without the benefit of conventional schooling. Woolman's life was based on morals of love and conscience. At an early age, he learned the writings of God's word and amplified his interpretation of the Bible into his life. This strong belief in the scripture systematically led him into a life of trying to correct the evils of society. He used his belief in God to justify his defiance of the keeping of slaves. Woolman claimed it a sin to keep slaves; and insisted, '[t]he black men and women in bondage in America must be freed.' Woolman believed all life precious and deserving of freedom. As a young boy, he took the freedom of life from another creature [a bird] and was haunted by it." He was a first cousin four times removed to Paulena Stevens Janney. Source: http://tntn.essortment.com/johnwoolmanbio_rwfy.htm.

Part III

The Chamberlain line originated with the Stoughtons, a minor Kentish gentry family whose descendants include more than a hundred major figures in American or British history. Only a few are listed below. The Field line married into the Betts line on Long Island and New Jersey. The Field family originated in Sowerby, Yorkshire, England, and Richard Betts came from Hertfordshire, England.

Richard Betts arrived about 1648 in Ipswich, Massachusetts, and removed to Newton, Long Island, New York, by 1656.

It was from Joanna Chamberlain Betts, Elizabeth Scudder Lathrop/ Lothrop, Thomas and Israel Stoughton, and John Scudder that many notable kin descended. The major sources I have consulted for these relationships are the compiled work by Jane Fletcher Fiske, F.A.S.G., reported in *The American Genealogist* 72, 1997, pp. 285–300, entitled "A New England Immigrant Kinship Network," and Senior Genealogical Researcher at the New England Historic Genealogical Society Gary Boyd Roberts's *Notable Kin*, vols. 1 and 2.

Hiram Bingham—Missionary

Hiram Bingham (1789–1869), an American Congregationalist missionary, was born in Bennington, Vermont. In 1819 he founded the first Protestant mission in the Hawaiian Islands. He adapted the Hawaiian language to writing and translated the Bible into Hawaiian. His son, Hiram Bingham Jr. (1831–1908), born in Honolulu, was also a missionary. In 1857 he founded a mission in the Gilbert Islands and later adapted the island language to writing.

Hiram Bingham III—Professor, Explorer, Archaeologist, Statesman

"Hiram Bingham (1875–1956) was born in Honolulu, Hawaii, November 19, 1875; educated at Punahou School and Oahu College, Hawaii, 1882–1892, Phillips Academy, Andover, Mass., 1892–1894, Yale University 1894–1898, University of California at Berkeley 1899-1900, and Harvard University 1900–1905; professor of history and politics at Harvard and then Princeton Universities; South American explorer, credited with the discovery of the Incan ruins at Machu Picchu; delegate to the First Pan American Scientific Congress at Santiago, Chile, in 1908; captain, Connecticut National Guard 1916; became an aviator in the spring of 1917; organized the United States Schools of Military Aeronautics in May 1917; served in the Aviation Section, Signal Corps, and attained the rank of lieutenant colonel; commanded the flying school at Issoudun, France, from August to December 1918; lieutenant governor of Connecticut 1922–1924; elected as a Republican to the United States Senate on December 16, 1924, to fill the vacancy caused by the death of Frank B. Brandegee in the term ending March 3, 1927; reelected in 1926 and served from December 17, 1924, to March 3, 1933; Committee on Territories and Insular Possessions (Seventieth through Seventy-second Congresses); censured by the Senate in 1929 on charges of placing of a lobbyist on his payroll; appointed a member of the President's Aircraft Board by President Calvin Coolidge 1925; engaged in banking and literary work in Washington, D.C.; during the Second World War, lectured at naval training schools 1942–1943; chairman of the Civil Service Commission's Loyalty Review Board 1951–1953; died in Washington, D.C., June 6, 1956; interment in Arlington National Cemetery, Arlington, Va." Bingham is most noted for heading archaeological expeditions sent from Yale in 1911, 1912, and 1914–15 to South America and investigating the Inca ruins of Vitcos and Machu Picchu in 1911 and 1912, bringing them to the attention of the outside world for the first time. Sources: *Biographical Directory of the United States Congress, Dictionary of American Biography;* Frank L. Miller, *Fathers and Sons: The Bingham Family and the American Mission,* Philadelphia, Temple University Press, 1982; Woodbridge Bingham, *Hiram Bingham: A Personal History.* Boulder, Bin Lan Zhen Publishers, 1989.

Thomas Dewey—Governor of New York and Presidential Candidate

"Thomas Dewey (1902–1972) was born in Owosso, Michigan, on March 24, 1902. He graduated from the University of Michigan and went on to receive a law degree from Columbia University in 1925. Dewey's reputation grew with his appointment as special prosecutor of New York. He became known for breaking up organized crime. His success gave rise to a political career and he was elected the district attorney of Manhattan in 1937. Dewey continued to pursue his political career by running in the 1938 gubernatorial race. He promised to end corruption in New York politics; however, Dewey lost the election. Although he thought the New Deal excessive, Dewey believed the federal government had a responsibility to promote the public interest.

"In 1940, he tried to gain the Republican presidential nomination, but lost. His success came in 1941, when he was elected governor of New York State. Dewey kept his promise by setting in place reforms, including the first statewide civil rights legislation in the nation, and an increase in aid to the New York State Education Department. In 1944, he won the Republican presidential nomination and campaigned vigorously against FDR. Although he lost the election, he won 46 percent of the popular vote, the highest Republican total since Herbert Hoover's 1928 victory. Reelected Governor of New York in 1946, a fiscally conservative Dewey introduced progressive education, health, civil rights, and transportation policies while insisting upon a balanced budget. Dewey received the Republican nomination again in 1948 to run against Harry

Truman after he defeated Harold Stassen in the Oregon presidential primary by attacking Stassen's proposal to outlaw the Communist party. Unexpectedly, Truman won with 49 percent to Dewey's 45 percent in a four-party race. Dewey ended his third term as governor in 1955 and returned to private law. He died in March of 1971, still an active member of the GOP." Source: *The Concise Dictionary of American Biography*, 5th ed., New York, Charles Scribner's Sons, 1997, p. 304.

Marshall Field—Founder of
Marshall Fields Department Store

"Marshall Field (1834–1906), American merchant, born in Conway, Massachuetts. In 1856, after five years' apprenticeship in a general store in Pittsfield, Massachusetts, he went to Chicago and became a clerk for Cooley, Wadsworth & Co., a leading dry-goods house there, of which he became a junior partner in 1862. In 1865 he became a partner in the firm of Field, Palmer, and Leiter, the company that became Marshall Field and Co. in 1881. He amassed one of the largest private fortunes in the United States and pioneered in establishing many modern retailing practices.

"He made the first of his major philanthropies when he was a charter member of the corporation formed (1878) to found the institution which became the Art Institute of Chicago. In 1890 he gave the original tract of land for the University of Chicago, ultimately becoming one of the largest donors to the school. In 1893 he gave $1,000,000 to the fund for the museum at the World's Columbian Exposition. Its collections were the nucleus of the Field Museum of Natural History, now housed in a magnificent building on the Chicago lake front that was provided by a bequest of $8,000,000 from Field." http://www.1911encyclopedia.org/Marshall_Field.

Marshall Field III—Founded the Chicago *Sun* and
Bought the Chicago *Times*

"1893–1956, son of Marshall Field 2nd, was educated at Eton and at Cambridge University then served in World War I. He engaged in numerous business activities until 1936, when he gave up all of them to devote himself to his various social projects. In June, 1940, Field helped found the New York City liberal newspaper PM. He was the publication's largest stockholder and, from October, 1940, its owner. He took no part in its editorial direction, but offered it financial support until Apr., 1948, when the paper was sold; soon afterward it went out of business.

"In 1941, Field started the Chicago *Sun*, and in January, 1948, he bought the Chicago *Times* and merged the two papers. Field took a more active part in that journalistic enterprise, ultimately becoming the paper's dominant personality. Through Field Enterprises, Inc. (est. 1944) he also published the *World Book Encyclopedia*. His charities included many child welfare organizations. Field's political and social beliefs are expressed in his book *Freedom Is More than a Word* (1945). See also L. Wendt and H. Kogan, *Give the Lady What She Wants: The Story of Marshall Field and Co.* (1952); biography of Marshall Field III by S. D. Becker (1964); J. Tebbel, *The Marshall Fields: A Study in Wealth* (1947)." Source: *The Columbia Electronic Encyclopedia*, 6th ed., Columbia University Press, 2005.

Hamilton Fish—Governor of New York, U.S. Senator, and Secretary of State under Grant

"Hamilton Fish (1808–1893), American statesman, born in New York City, graduated from Columbia, 1827 He was the son of Nicholas Fish (1758–1833). He studied law and was admitted to the bar in 1830.

"Named for his father's friend, Alexander Hamilton, and heir to the Federalist tradition, Fish naturally gravitated to politics as a Whig. He served as U.S. Representative (1843–45) and was elected lieutenant governor of New York in 1847 and governor, for a two-year term, in 1848. From 1851 to 1857, Fish was a U.S. Senator, serving on the foreign relations committee in 1855–57. A moderate anti-slavery man, he opposed both abolitionist and pro-slavery excesses and deplored the breakup of the Whigs as a national party. Slow to join the new Republican party, he lost his national political standing but became prominent in civic activities in New York.

"Fish was one of many to lionize the victorious Civil War general Ulysses S. Grant, but his appointment (Mar., 1869) as Grant's Secretary of State, to succeed the grossly miscast Elihu B. Washburne, came as a surprise. He accepted reluctantly and expected to hold the office for only a few months, but actually remained in the cabinet longer than any other member, serving through both of Grant's administrations.

"Fish was one of the ablest of U.S. Secretaries of State. Grant was much impressed with Fish's character and ability, and he called upon Fish's aid in the administration of domestic affairs as well. Fish's greatest achievement as Secretary was bringing about the treaty (Treaty of Washington) that paved the way for settlement of the Alabama claims and other long-standing disputes with Great Britain. This was accomplished amid great difficulties, especially those offered by the vigorously anti-British chairman of the Senate foreign relations committee, Charles Sumner. The period was one of constant trouble with Spain, arising out of the Ten Years War, and Fish was hard pressed to persuade Grant not to recognize the belligerency of Cuba. Under Fish's vigilant eye filibustering expeditions from the United States to Cuba were kept to a minimum, but the Virginius affair in 1873 nearly brought the nation, long sympathetic to the Cuban cause, to war with Spain. To secure Grant's support of other policies Fish supported without enthusiasm the President's unsuccessful project to annex the Dominican Republic." Source: *Columbia Electronic Encyclopedia*, 6th ed., Columbia University Press, 2005.

Stuyvesant Fish—Railroad Executive

"Stuyvesant Fish (1851–1923), American railroad executive, born in New York City; son of Hamilton Fish (1808–93). He became (1877) a director of the Illinois Central RR, and as its president (1887–1907) he built the railroad into a large system. Fish was ousted from the presidency by E. H. Harriman after Fish's participation in the state committee that investigated (1906) the Mutual Life Insurance Company of New York." Source: *The Columbia Electronic Encyclopedia*, 6th ed., Columbia University Press, 2005.

President Ulysses Simpson Grant— President of the United States

"At the outbreak of the Civil War, Grant was working in his father's leather store in Galena, Illinois. He was appointed by the Governor to command an unruly volunteer regiment. Grant whipped it into shape and by September 1861 he had risen to the rank of brigadier general of volunteers. He sought to win control of the Mississippi Valley. In February 1862 he took Fort Henry and attacked Fort Donelson. When the Confederate commander asked for terms, Grant replied, "No terms except an unconditional and immediate surrender can be accepted." The Confederates surrendered, and President Lincoln promoted Grant to major general of volunteers. At Shiloh in April, Grant fought one of the bloodiest battles in the West and came out less well. President Lincoln fended off demands for his removal by saying, "I can't spare this man—he fights." For his next major objective, Grant maneuvered and fought skillfully to win Vicksburg, the key city on the Mississippi, and thus cut the Confederacy in two. Then he broke the Confederate hold on Chattanooga. Lincoln appointed him General-in-Chief in March 1864. Grant directed Sherman to drive through the South while he himself, with the Army of the Potomac, pinned down Gen. Robert E. Lee's Army of Northern Virginia.

"Finally, on April 9, 1865, at Appomattox Court House, Lee surrendered. Grant wrote out magnanimous terms of surrender that would prevent treason trials . . .

"[A]s the symbol of Union victory during the Civil War, he was their logical candidate for President in 1868. As President, Grant presided over the Government much as he had run the Army. Indeed he brought part of his Army staff to the White House. Although a man of scrupulous honesty, Grant as President accepted handsome presents from admirers. Worse, he allowed himself to be seen with two speculators, Jay Gould and James Fisk. When Grant realized their scheme to corner the market in gold, he authorized the Secretary of the Treasury to sell enough gold to wreck their plans, but the speculation had already wrought havoc with business." Source: "Past Presidents," http://www.whitehouse.gov/history/presidents/ug18.html.

Mrs. John Hart—Wife of Signer of the Declaration of Independence

"Sarah Scudder was married to John Hart (1711–1779), New Jersey signer of the Declaration of Independence. 'John Hart was a New Jersey farmer. His father had moved from Connecticut to a farm near Hopewell, New Jersey. He helped to build, and later inherited, that very successful farm and was a leading member of his community. His first public service was a justice of the peace. In 1761 he was elected to the New Jersey Assembly, there annually reelected until the assembly was dissolved in 1771. In 1775 he was appointed to the local Committee of Safety, the Committee of Correspondence, and a judge to the Court of Common Pleas. He was elected to the newly formed Provincial Congress of New Jersey in 1776, and sent as a delegate for New Jersey to the Continental Congress that year. Hart's property was looted in the course of the war. His wife died on October 8th, 1776. When the area was overrun by the British in November of that year, he was forced to hide for a time. He was engaged in public service throughout the war, twice reelected to the Congress and also serving the Commitee of Safety and as Speaker of the New Jersey assembly. On June 22nd, 1778, he invited the American army to encamp on his farm. Washington had lunch with him, then had his famous Council of War at the nearby Hunt House. Twelve thousand men camped on his fields during the growing season. After resting and preparing for battle the troops left on the 24th. On Tuesday, May 11th, 1779, he died at the age of 66.'" Source: *Signers of the Declaration of Independence,* 1999–2005, the Independence Hall Association, a nonprofit organization in Philadelphia, Pennsylvania, founded in 1942. See ushistory.org, on the Internet since July 4, 1995.

Oliver Wendell Holmes Sr.—Author and Physician

Oliver Wendell Holmes Sr. "was born in Cambridge, Mass., graduated from Harvard (B.A., 1829; M.D., 1836) and was the father of Oliver Wendell Holmes, Jr. He began his medical career as a general practitioner but shifted into the academic field, becoming professor of anatomy and physiology at Dartmouth (1838–40), dean of the Harvard medical school (1847–53), and Parkman professor of anatomy and physiology at Harvard (1847–82). A stimulating and popular speaker, he published two important medical lectures, one in opposition to the practice of homeopathy and the other on the nature of fevers. His first important poem, 'Old Ironsides' (1830), was a protest against the scrapping of the fighting ship *Constitution.* A collection of his witty occasional poems was published in 1836. In 1857 he began to contribute to the *Atlantic Monthly* (which he named) the famous series of 'Breakfast-table' sketches, which were collected in *The Autocrat of the Breakfast-Table* (1858) and several subsequent volumes. These urbane pieces present imaginary conversations at a Boston boardinghouse, reflecting Holmes's opinions, charm, and wit. The first volume includes several poems, of which the most famous are the ironic 'Deacons Masterpiece' and 'The Chambered Nautilus.' Among his other notable works are three novels presenting a scientific approach to psychological traits, most notably *Elsie Venner* (1861); and biographies of his friends John Lothrop Motley (1879) and Ralph Waldo Emerson (1855)." Source: *Columbia Encyclopedia,* http://www.bartleby.com/65/ho/HolmesOdad.html.

Oliver Wendell Holmes Jr.—Jurist

"Oliver Wendell Holmes Jr. was born on March 8, 1841 in Boston, Massachusetts, and was named for his famous father, the writer and physician. His keen intellect, humor, and ability to express himself helped Holmes direct American thought as a member of the United States Supreme Court for over 30 years. At the end of his service in the American Civil War Holmes entered Harvard Law School. Early in his career he became co-editor of the 'American Law Review,' a commercial legal periodical, and wrote his great work 'The Common-Law' in 1881. In 1882 Holmes became professor of law at Harvard, and was appointed to the Massachusetts Supreme Court in 1899. President Theodore Roosevelt appointed Holmes to the United States Supreme Court in 1902. A cornerstone of Holmes's judicial philosophy was his opinion that, 'The life of the law has not been logic, but experience.' He insisted that the court look at the facts in a changing society, instead of clinging to worn-out slogans and formulas. Holmes convinced people that the law should develop along with the society it serves. He exercised a deep influence on the law through his support of the doctrine of 'judicial restraint' which urged judges to avoid letting their personal opinions affect their decisions." Source: http://www.lucidcafe.com/lucidcafe/library/96mar/holmes.html.

Nedenia Marjorie Hutton (Dina Merrill)—Actress

Dina Merrill was the stage name of Nedenia Hutton, the daughter of Marjorie Merriweather Post and E. F. Hutton. She was married for the second time to actor Cliff Robertson, who won an Academy Award in 1968 for his title role in *Charly*.

Russell Dixon Janney—Author, Writer, Press Agent, and Theatrical Producer

"Russell Dixon Janney . . . was the son of Reynold Janney, a builder of bicycles and [inventor], and Ella Dixon. Soon after his birth his family moved to Chillicothe, Ohio, where his father served as principal of the high school. In 1894 Janney's father gave up his career in education and moved his family again, this time to Keene, New Hampshire, where he set up in business as a mechanic.

Keene was at this time often a stopover town for theater companies traveling between Boston and Montreal, and Janney developed an interest in working in the theater. He enrolled at Yale University, where he wrote and produced several plays for his fraternity, Beta Theta Pi. After he graduated in 1906 he settled briefly in New York, but the following year he departed for London to pursue a career as a press agent and freelance writer. . . .

"Returning to the United States in 1910, Janney co-managed stock companies in Indianapolis and Milwaukee. . . . He contributed to such popular magazines as "Smart Set," created sketches for the "Ziegfeld Follies," and represented Stuart Walker's Portmanteau Theatre in New York and on tour. . . . His first successful production in New York was a stage adaptation of Booth Tarkington's 'Seventeen' (1918), but Janney did not really begin to make his mark as a producer until 1925, when he coauthored and produced (with Professor Brian Hooker of Yale) 'The Vagabond King,' based on the life of the colorful French poet Francois Villon. The popular composer Rudolf Friml provided the music for this major success, which had 511 performances on Broadway and was later performed across the country by seven road companies simultaneously. Other well known productions by Janney include . . . 'Sancho Panza' (1923), based on the island Barataria sequence in 'Don Quixote,' by Melchior Lengyel, with music by Felix; . . . and a historical operetta, 'The O'Flynn' (1934), based on Justin McCarthy's novel and play, with book by Janney and Hooker and music by Franklin Hauser. He also served as manager for Otis Skinner and as play doctor for many New York productions.

"Although Janney remained a familiar figure in the New York theater scene, reviving the popular 'Vagabond King' in 1943, he essentially suspended his stage activities to write his first novel, 'The Miracle of the Bells' (1946). The novel is a highly romanticized and somewhat autobiographical story of a cynical, big city press agent and the religious events he witnesses in a small, Polish American Catholic town, where he is involved in the funeral of a beautiful young actress. The work was . . . a great popular success and the basis for a much loved film of the same name [starring Fred MacMurray in the lead role and a young Frank Sinatra as the priest].

"The popularity of 'The Miracle of the Bells,' along with its sentimental advocacy of such themes as religious tolerance, the redemptive power of faith, and the pleasure of smoking, earned Janney the attention and support of the National Conference of Christians and Jews, who organized and sponsored a nationwide lecture tour, and of major tobacco companies, who provided extensive advertising. Janney's pleas for religious tolerance often included condemnations of communism, seen by him as a serious threat to tolerance and a source of civic divisiveness. When he was selected in 1949 as a juror in the New York trial of Communist leaders accused of threatening the United States, his public statements against communism were recalled, and a bitter controversy, led by the leftist newspaper 'The Worker,' surrounded his appointment. The judge nevertheless refused to remove Janney from the jury or to declare a mistrial. When at last a verdict was returned, finding Gus Hall and others guilty of conspiracy to bring about the violent overthrow of the U.S. Government, Janney was seen by many as the manifestation of a compromised judicial process.

"The highly publicized trial cast a shadow over Janney's final years, and, clearly suffering from the attacks on his character and motives, he largely withdrew from the public eye. . . . Despite his active career in theatrical production and his close association with many important figures of his time, it is for his one highly successful novel, 'The Miracle of the Bells,' that Janney is most remembered." Source: *American National Biography,* Marvin Carlson, vol. II, Oxford University Press, 1999.

Mrs. Richard King—Texas Rancher

"Henrietta Maria Morse Chamberlain King (1832–1925), rancher and philanthropist, the only child of Maria (Morse) and Hiram Chamberlain, was born on July 21, 1832, in Boonville, Missouri. Her mother's death in 1835 and her father's Presbyterian missionary work in Missouri and Tennessee often made her childhood lonely; as a result she became strongly self-reliant and introspective, and she maintained close attachments to her family. She attended Female Institute of Holly Springs, Mississippi, for two years, beginning when she was fourteen. She moved to Brownsville, Texas, probably in 1849, for she was living there when her father organized the first Presbyterian mission in South Texas at Brownsville, on February 23, 1850.

"In 1854 she taught briefly at the Rio Grande Female Institute before her marriage to Richard King on December 10, 1854; they had five children. In 1854 Henrietta and Richard King established their home on the Santa Gertrudis ranch. Their original dwelling was a mud and stick jacal, but this was eventually replaced with a house overlooking Santa Gertrudis Creek. Not only was Henrietta King wife and mother, but she also was supervisor of housing and education for the families of Mexican-American ranchhands. During the Civil War the ranch was an official receiving station for cotton that was ferried first to Mexican ports and then on to England. When King left the ranch to escape capture by Union forces in 1863, a pregnant Henrietta remained. After the house was plundered she moved the family to San Antonio until they could safely return home. Upon her husband's death in 1885 Mrs. King assumed full ownership of his estate, consisting chiefly of 500,000 acres of ranch land between Corpus Christi and Brownsville and $500,000 in debts.

"Under Henrietta King's skillful and personal supervision, and with the assistance of her son-in-law, Robert Justus Kleberg, the King Ranch was freed of debt and increased in size. By 1895 the 650,000-acre ranch was engaged in experiments in cattle and horse breeding, in range grasses, and in dry and irrigated farming. That year King gave Kleberg her power of attorney and increased his ranch responsibilities. The ranch continued to grow, reaching a size of 1,173,000 acres by 1925. One of the horses bred at the ranch won the Triple Crown in 1946. The Santa Gertrudis cattle developed there were a boon to the Texas cattle industry because of their resistance to disease and heat. King was also interested in the settlement of the region between Corpus Christi and Brownsville. About 1903 she offered 75,000 acres of right-of-way to Uriah Lott and Benjamin Franklin Yoakum, who planned to construct the St. Louis, Brownsville and Mexico Railway. In 1904 she furnished townsites for Kingsville and Raymondville, located on the railway. She founded the Kleberg Town and Improvement Company and the Kingsville Lumber Company to sell land and materials to settlers in Kingsville. As the town grew she invested in the Kingsville Ice and Milling Company, Kingsville Publishing Company, Kingsville Power Company, Gulf Coast Gin Company, and Kingsville Cotton Oil Mill Company. She constructed the First Presbyterian Church building there and also donated land for Baptist, Methodist, Episcopal, and Catholic churches; she constructed a public high school and presented it to the town. Among her many charities were donations of land for the Texas-Mexican Industrial Institute and for the Spohn Sanitarium. In her last years she provided land and encouragement for the establishment of South Texas State Teachers College (now Texas A&I University). Henrietta King died on March 31, 1925, on the King Ranch and was buried in Kingsville. At her funeral an honor guard of 200 vaqueros, riding quarter horses branded with the ranch's Running W, flanked the hearse. Each rider cantered once around the open grave." Sources: *The Handbook of Texas Online,* Edgar P. Sneed, Ann Fears Crawford, and Crystal Sasse Ragsdale; *Women in Texas,* Burnet, Texas, Eakin Press, 1982; *The King Ranch,* Tom Lea, 2 vols., Boston, Little, Brown, 1957; Texas Mothers Committee, *Worthy Mothers of Texas,* Belton, Texas, Stillhouse Hollow, 1976.

≈ ⚐ ≈

Mrs. Rufus King—Wife of Signer of the U.S. Constitution

"Mary Alsop was married to Rufus King, 1755–1827, signer of the U.S. constitution, Federalist statesman and presidential candidate, U.S. senator, diplomat.

"King, Rufus, 1755–1827, American political leader. He was born in Scarboro, Maine (then a district of Massachusetts). He served briefly in the American Revolution and practiced law in Massachusetts before serving (1783–85) as a member of the Massachusetts General Court. He was (1784–87) a delegate to the Continental Congress, where he helped draft the Ordinance of 1787 and was chiefly responsible for the exclusion of slavery from the Northwest Territory. At the Federal Constitutional Convention (1787), he was an effective supporter of a strong central government and helped to secure Massachusetts's ratification of the Constitution. Moving to New York City, King was elected to the state assembly and was chosen (1789) as one of New York's first two U.S. Senators. He strongly supported Alexander Hamilton's financial measures and later defended *Jay's Treaty.* As minister to Great Britain (1796–1803) he reconciled many differences between the two countries and proved himself an able diplomat.

He was the unsuccessful Federalist party candidate for Vice President in 1804 and 1808 and for President in 1816. From 1813 to 1825 he again served as U.S. Senator. Although at first an opponent of the War of 1812, he later came to support the administration's war measures. King opposed the *Missouri Compromise* and advocated solving the slavery problem by emancipating and colonizing blacks outside the country on the proceeds of the sale of public lands. In 1824 he declined reelection but was again minister to Great Britain (1825–26). Charles King (1789–1867) was his son." Sources: C. King, ed., *The Life and Correspondence of Rufus King,* 6 vols., 1894–1900, repr. 1971; biography by E. H. Brush, 1926; study by R. Ernst, 1968; *The Columbia Electronic Encyclopedia,* 6th ed. Columbia University Press, 2005.

Henry Wadsworth Longfellow—Poet

"Probably the best loved of American poets the world over is Henry Wadsworth Longfellow. Many of his lines are as familiar to us as rhymes from Mother Goose or the words of nursery songs learned in early childhood. Like these rhymes and melodies, they remain in the memory and accompany us through life.

"There are two reasons for the popularity and significance of Longfellow's poetry. First, he had the gift of easy rhyme. He wrote poetry as a bird sings, with natural grace and melody. Read or heard once or twice, his rhyme and meters cling to the mind long after the sense may be forgotten. Second, Longfellow wrote on obvious themes which appeal to all kinds of people. His poems are easily understood; they sing their way into the consciousness of those who read them. Above all, there is a joyousness in them, a spirit of optimism and faith in the goodness of life which evokes immediate response in the emotions of his readers.

"Americans owe a great debt to Longfellow because he was among the first of American writers to use native themes. He wrote about the American scene and landscape, the American Indian ('Song of Hiawatha'), and American history and tradition ('The Courtship of Miles Standish', 'Evangeline'). At the beginning of the 19th century, America was a stumbling babe as far as a culture of its own was concerned. The people of America had spent their years and their energies in carving a habitation out of the wilderness and in fighting for independence. Literature, art, and music came mainly from Europe and especially from England. Nothing was considered worthy of attention unless it came from Europe. But 'the flowering of New England,' as Van Wyck Brooks terms the period from 1815 to 1865, took place in Longfellow's day, and he made a great contribution to it. He lived when giants walked the New England earth, giants of intellect and feeling who established the New Land as a source of greatness. Nathaniel Hawthorne, Ralph Waldo Emerson, Henry David Thoreau, Oliver Wendell Holmes, and William Prescott were a few of the great minds and spirits among whom Longfellow took his place as a singer and as a representative of America.

"The first Longfellow came to America in 1676 from Yorkshire, England. Among the ancestors of the poet on his mother's side were John and Priscilla Alden, of whom he wrote in 'The Courtship of Miles Standish.' His mother's father, Peleg Wadsworth, had been a general in the Revolutionary War. His own father was a lawyer. The Longfellow home represented the graceful living which was beginning to characterize the age. Henry was the son of Stephen Longfellow and Zilpah Wadsworth Longfellow. He was born February 27, 1807, in Portland, Maine. Portland was a seaport, and this gave its citizens a breadth of view lacking in the more insular New England towns. . . . From the beginning, it was evident that this boy was to be drawn to writing and the sound of words. His mother read aloud to him and his brothers and sisters the high romance of Ossian, the legendary Gaelic hero. Cervantes' *Don Quixote* was a favorite among the books he read. But the book which influenced him most was Washington Irving's *Sketch Book.* Irving was another American author for whom the native legend and landscape were sources of inspiration. . . .

"Longfellow's father was eager to have his son become a lawyer. But when Henry was a senior at Bowdoin College at 19, the college established a chair of modern languages. The recent graduate was asked to become the first professor, with the understanding that he should be given a period of time in which to travel and study in Europe.

"Much tribute is due him as a teacher. Just as he served America in making the world conscious of its legend and tradition, so he opened to his students and to the American people the literary heritage of Europe. He created in them the new consciousness of the literature of Spain, France, Italy, and especially writings from the German, Nordic, and Icelandic cultures.

"In 1831, he married Mary Storer Potter, whom he had known as a schoolmate. When he saw her at church upon his return to Portland, he was so struck by her beauty that he followed her home without courage enough to speak to her. With his wife, he settled down in a house surrounded by elm trees. He expended his energies on translations from Old World literature and contributed travel sketches to the *New England Magazine,* in addition to serving as a professor and a librarian at Bowdoin.

"In 1834, he was appointed to a professorship at Harvard and once more set out for Europe by way of preparation. This time his young wife accompanied him. The journey ended in tragedy. In Rotterdam, his wife died, and Longfellow came alone to Cambridge and the new professorship. The lonely [Longfellow] took a room at historic Craigie House, an old house overlooking the Charles River. It was owned by Mrs. Craigie, an eccentric woman who kept much to herself and was somewhat scornful of the young men to whom she let rooms. But she read widely and well, and her library contained complete sets of Voltaire and other French masters. Longfellow entered the beautiful old elm-encircled house as a lodger, not knowing that this was to be his home for the rest of his life. In time, it passed into the possession of Nathan Appleton. Seven years after he came to Cambridge, Longfellow married Frances Appleton, daughter of Nathan Appleton, and Craigie House was given to the Longfellows as a wedding gift.

"The marriage was a happy one, and the Longfellow house became the center of life in the University town. The old Craigie House was a shrine of hospitality and gracious living. The young people of Cambridge flocked there to play with the five Longfellow children—two boys and the three girls whom the poet describes in 'The Children's Hour' as 'grave Alice and laughing Allegra and Edith with golden hair.' From his friend Nathaniel Hawthorne, Longfellow got a brief outline of a story from which he composed one of his most favorite poems, 'Evangeline.' The original story had Evangeline wandering about New England in search of her bridegroom. Longfellow extended her journey through Louisiana and the western wilderness. She finds Gabriel, at last, dying in Philadelphia. 'Evangeline' was published in 1847 and was widely acclaimed. Longfellow began to feel that his work as a teacher was a hindrance to his own writing. In 1854, he resigned from Harvard and with a great sense of freedom gave himself entirely to the joyous task of his own poetic writing. In June of that year, he began 'The Song of Hiawatha.' Henry Schoolcraft's book on Indians and several meetings with an Ojibway chief provided the background for 'Hiawatha'. . . . The publication of 'Hiawatha' caused the greatest excitement. For the first time in American literature, Indian themes gained recognition as sources of imagination, power, and originality. The appeal of 'Hiawatha' for generations of children and young people gives it an enduring place in world literature.

"The gracious tale of John Alden and Priscilla came next to the poet's mind, and 'The Courtship of Miles Standish' was published in 1858. It is a work which reflects the ease with which he wrote and the pleasure and enjoyment he derived from his skill. Twenty-five thousand copies were sold during the first week of its publication, and 10,000 were ordered in London on the first day of publication.

"In 1861, the happy life of the family came to an end. Longfellow's wife died of burns she received when packages of her children's curls, which she was sealing with matches and wax, burst into flame. Longfellow faced the bitterest tragedy of his life. He found some solace in the task of translating Dante into English and went to Europe for a change of scene.

"The years following were filled with honors. He was given honorary degrees at the great universities of Oxford and Cambridge, invited to Windsor by Queen Victoria, and called by request upon the Prince of Wales. He was chosen a member of the Russian Academy of Sciences and of the Spanish Academy. When it became necessary to remove 'the spreading chestnut tree' of Brattle Street, which Longfellow had written about in his 'Village Blacksmith,' the children of Cambridge gave their pennies to build a chair out of the tree and gave it to Longfellow. He died on March 24, 1882. 'Of all the suns of the New England morning,' says Van Wyck Brooks, 'he was the largest in his golden sweetness.'"
Source: Roberto Rabe, eclecticesoterica.com / longfellow_bio.html.

Ellin Mackay—Wife of American Composer and Lyricist Irving Berlin

"Ellin Mackay was a journalist and a contributor to the *New Yorker*. Her millionaire father Clarence Mackay was a devout Catholic and a society figure in New York. He was the head of the Postal Telegraph Cable Company. Clarence Mackay bitterly objected to an engagement refusing to allow his daughter to marry an immigrant Jew. However, Berlin and Mackay married in a civil ceremony in 1926 and lived happily together for the rest of their lives. Ironically, when the stock market crashed in 1929, it was Berlin who financially rescued his father-in-law.

"Irving Berlin, born May 11, 1888, was an American composer and lyricist. Born Israel Isidore Baline, in Tyumen (or Mahilyow [Mogilev]), Belarus, he emigrated to the United States in 1893 with the rest of his family. Following the death of his father in 1896, Irving found himself having to work to survive. He did various street jobs including selling newspapers and busking [the practice of performing in public places to receive donations of money]. The harsh economic reality of having to work or starve was to have a lasting effect on the way Berlin treated money. In 1911 the song "Alexander's Ragtime Band" launched a musical career that would span over a thousand songs including many hit Broadway musicals.

"Irving Berlin's first credited song lyrics were for "Marie from Sunny Italy" in 1907. He was paid 37 cents for this song. Due to a misprint on the record Balin became Berlin.

"In 1917 during World War I, he staged a musical revue, *Yip Yip Yaphank*, while at Camp Upton in Yaphank, New York. The revue was a patriotic tribute to the United States Army. Berlin composed the song "God Bless America" for the revue but decided against using it. It was also considered for the National Anthem, but was rejected by the press for coming from a Jewish composer. The revue was later included in the 1943 movie *This Is the Army*, featuring other Berlin songs, including the famous title piece, as well as a full length rendition of "God Bless America" by Kate Smith.

"He was responsible for many Hollywood film scores including *Top Hat* (1935) as well as songs such as *White Christmas* from the film *Holiday Inn* (1942). Berlin was equally as prolific on Broadway, where he is perhaps best known for *Annie Get Your Gun* (1946), although he stopped writing after the failure of *Mr. President* in 1962. Other well known hits include: "Always"; "Blue Skies"; "Change Partners"; "Cheek to Cheek"; "Easter Parade"; "Heat Wave"; "Hostess With the Mostest"; "How Deep Is the Ocean?"; "I"; "Let Yourself Go"; "Let's Face the Music and Dance"; "Marie"; "Oh, How I Hate to Get up in the Morning"; "A Pretty Girl Is Like a Melody"; "Puttin' on the Ritz"; "Say It Isn't So"; "Steppin' Out With My Baby"; "There's No Business Like Show Business"; "Top Hat, White Tie and Tails"; and "What'll I Do?" His friend and fellow songwriter Jule Styne said of him: 'It's easy to be clever. But the really clever thing is to be simple.' In spite of his musical career, Berlin never learned how to play a piano or read music beyond a rudimentary level. He owned a special piano that mechanically transposed keys and an assistant wrote out the music scores. . . .

"He was married twice. His first wife, singer Dorothy Goetz, sister of songwriter E. Ray Goetz, died of pneumonia and typhoid fever, contracted on their honeymoon to Cuba and five months after their wedding in 1912. . . . His second wife was Ellin Mackay, a Catholic heiress to the Comstock Lode mining fortune as well as a writer who was published in *The New Yorker*. They were married in 1926 and had three daughters—Mary Ellin, Linda, and Elizabeth, all of whom were raised Protestant—and a son, Irving Berlin, Jr., who died before his first birthday, on Christmas Day. Irving Berlin died of a heart attack in New York City at the age of 101 [September 22, 1989] and was interred in the Woodlawn Cemetery in The Bronx, New York." Source: *Wikipedia*.

Dr. Benjamin Moore—Episcopal Bishop of New York and President of Columbia College

"Benjamin P. Moore, Episcopal bishop, born in Newtown, Long Island, New York, 5 October, 1748; died in Greenwich Village (now part of the city of New York), 27 February, 1816. He entered King's (now Columbia) college, and was graduated in 1768. He then engaged in teaching Greek and Latin, and prepared for entering the ministry. He went to England in May, 1774, and was ordained deacon in the chapel of Fulham palace, 24 June, 1774, by the bishop of London, and priest in the same place the following day by the same bishop. Soon after his return he was appointed an assistant minister of Trinity church, and he was made rector of Trinity parish, 22 December, 1800. He received the degree of S. T. D. from Columbia in 1789. Bishop Provost resigned his jurisdiction in 1801, and Dr. Moore was unanimously elected his successor, he was consecrated bishop co-adjutor (during Bishop Provost's life, which lasted till 1815) in St. Michael's church, Trenton, New Jersey, 11 September, 1801 [200 years to the day before the Attack on the World Trade Center]. He was also president of Columbia college from 1801 till 1811. Early in 1811 he was attacked by paralysis and disabled from further active service. Bishop Moore published a few single sermons and a controversial pamphlet in defense of his church. His son, Clement C. Moore, published selected sermons of his father's." Trinity Church (Wall Street at Broadway), which is literally in the shadow of the Twin Towers, miraculously escaped damage during the attacks of September 11, 2001. Source: *Edited Appleton's Encyclopedia*, Virtualology, 2001, http://www.famousamericans.net/benjaminmoore/.

Clement Clarke Moore—Educator and Poet

"Clement Clarke Moore, 1779–1863, American educator and poet, born New York City, graduated Columbia, 1798. He was a biblical scholar, and was professor of Asian and Greek literature at the Episcopal General Theological Seminary, erected in New York City on land that he had donated. He is remembered for the well-known poem 'A Visit from St. Nicholas,' which begins, ' 'Twas the night before Christmas'; it was first published anonymously in the *Troy Sentinel* in 1823." Source: *The Columbia Electronic Encyclopedia,* 6th ed., Columbia University Press, 2005.

William Moore—Physician

"Benjamin Moore's brother, William, a physician, was born on Long Island, New York, in 1754; died in New York, 1824, was educated by his brother. He went to London in 1778, and thence to Edinburgh, where he was graduated in medicine in 1780. He then returned to New York, where he practiced for forty years, making a specialty of obstetrics. He was president of the New York county medical society and a trustee of the College of physicians and surgeons. He contributed to the 'American Medical and Philosophical Register,' to the " New York Medical Repository," and to the 'New York Medical and Physical Journal.'" Source: *Edited Appleton's Encyclopedia,* Virtualology, 2001, http://www.famousamericans.net/benjaminmoore/.

Anne Spencer Morrow—Pilot, Author, Mrs. Charles Lindbergh

Anne Morrow Lindbergh was born on June 22, 1906, in Englewood, New Jersey. "Known in her own right as a writer, she was also co-pilot and navigator for her husband, Charles Lindbergh. The couple met when Anne's father was ambassador to Mexico when Lindbergh came to visit and took the family on sight seeing flights.

"Under her husband's tutelage, Anne earned her pilot's license in 1931. In the wake of the media feeding frenzy that accompanied the kidnapping and murder of the couple's twenty-month-old son in 1932, they took on a five-month project of flying around the world to survey the proper airlines for transatlantic flights. She wrote and published books about their journeys. One of her most notable books, *A Gift from the Sea* (1955), reflects on the meaning of a woman's life. She continued to write and to add to her growing list of publications until her death in 2001." Source: *Information Please Database,* Pearson Education, 2005, http://www.infoplease.com/ipea/A0763073.html.

Walter Loomis Newberry—Newberry Library

"Walter Loomis Newberry, (1804–68), American merchant and banker, born East Windsor (in the section now South Windsor), Connecticut. In 1822 he entered the shipping business with his brother Oliver in Buffalo, and in 1826 they went to Detroit, where they established a prosperous dry goods business. In 1833 he moved to the newly established town of Chicago, where he had previously made extensive investments in real estate. He engaged in the commission business, prospered, and later entered banking and also became president of the Galena and Chicago Union RR. He was active in civic affairs, founded the Young Men's Library Association, and made numerous philanthropic gifts. His will provided for the founding and endowment of the Newberry Library in Chicago, a free reference library that specializes in the fields of history, literature, music, and philology and has gained an international reputation. It has a fine collection of Americana." Source: *The Columbia Encyclopedia*, 6th ed., Columbia University Press, 2002, http://www.bartleby.com/65/ne/NewberryW.html.

Frederick Law Olmsted—Founder of Landscape Architecture

"Frederick Law Olmsted (1822–1903) was a landscape architect before the profession was founded. He was a visionary who foresaw the need for national parks, devised one of America's first regional plans, and designed America's first large suburban community.

"Olmsted is perhaps best known for his designs for the United States Capitol grounds. Collaborating with Calvert Vaux, Olmsted also designed Central Park in New York City, Prospect Park in Brooklyn, New York, and the Riverside Community in Illinois. He created the Buffalo, New York Park System and a Boston, Massachusetts system of parks and parkways known as the Emerald Necklace. After Olmsted's death, his son, stepson, and their successors continued the landscape architecture firm he founded. Records show that the firm participated in 5,500 projects between 1857 and 1950.

"Although Olmsted is famous today for his landscape architecture, he did not discover this career until he was 35. During his youth, he pursued several professions, and became a respected journalist and social commentator. Traveling through the southern United States, he wrote treatises against slavery. His book *A Journey in the Seaboard States* was not a great commercial success, but was highly regarded by readers in the Northern United States and England." Source: http://architecture.about.com/library/blolmsted.htm.

C. W. Post—Cereal Manufacturer

"Charles William Post (1854–1914), cereal manufacturer and developer, was born on October 26, 1854, in Springfield, Illinois, to Charles Rollin and Caroline (Lathrop) Post. After graduating from the Springfield public schools he entered Illinois Industrial University (now the University of Illinois) at Urbana; he remained for only two years before abandoning school 'for hard physical work.'

"At seventeen he went to Independence, Kansas, where he worked as a salesman, clerk, and store owner. He returned to Springfield in 1872 and worked for the next fourteen years as a salesman and manufacturer of agricultural machines. During this period he invented and secured patents on such farm equipment as cultivators, a sulky plow, a harrow, and a haystacker.

"On November 4, 1874, Post married Ella Letitia Merriweather. They had one daughter. After living apart for several years they were divorced in 1904, and on November 7 of that year Post married Leila Young of Battle Creek, Michigan. After a nervous breakdown in November 1885 caused by strain and overwork, he went to Texas in 1886 and in Fort Worth became associated with a group of real estate men who were developing a 300 acre tract in the eastern part of the city, an area now known as Riverside. Other members of the family, including Post's brother Rollin, followed C. W. (as he signed his name) to Fort Worth. In 1888 the Posts acquired a 200 acre ranch on the outskirts of the city and began the development of a subdivision on their property; they laid out streets and lots for homes and constructed a woolen mill and a paper mill.

"In 1891 Post suffered a second breakdown and moved with his wife to Battle Creek, Michigan, where he entered a sanitarium. With rest and the ministrations of a Christian Science practitioner came recuperation, and soon he was experimenting with a cereal drink he called Postum. He subsequently developed Grape Nuts and Post Toasties, breakfast foods that by the end of the century made him millions of dollars. He served as president of the American Manufacturers Association and of the Citizen's Industrial Association. Post was a bitter opponent of labor unions and an advocate of the open shop.

"His health failed again in 1914, and he died, probably by suicide, on May 9, 1914, at his home in Santa Barbara, California. He is buried in Battle Creek, Michigan." Sources: C. W. *Post's Colonizing Activities in West Texas,* Austin, Texas State Historical Association, 1952; Nettie Letich Major, C. W. Post, Washington, Judd and Detweiler, 1963.

Marjorie Merriweather Post—
Heir to Post Cereal Fortune and Founder of General Foods

"The Hillwood Museum and Gardens [Washington, D.C.] are a constant reminder of Marjorie Merriweather Post, the forceful woman who lived in this former home and who was a unique member of American upper-crust society. She was an heiress, American-style, and a legend in her own time. Post was the epitome of style and grace, a woman of wealth who married often, whose parties and movements were duly charted and reported by the press, whose fashion set trends, and who presided over countless foundations, institutions and charities." Source: "Fashion Plate Hillwood Exhibit Celebrates 100th Anniversary of Post's Debut," Gary Tischle, *The Washington Diplomat,* September 2003.

Anna Eleanor Roosevelt—Wife of President Franklin D. Roosevelt

"Eleanor Roosevelt . . . was born in New York City on October 11, 1884, daughter of lovely Anna Hall and Elliott Roosevelt, younger brother of Theodore. When her mother died in 1892, the children went to live with Grandmother Hall; her adored father died only two years later. Attending a distinguished school in England gave her, at 15, her first chance to develop self confidence among other girls.

"In her circle of friends was a distant cousin, handsome young Franklin Delano Roosevelt. They became engaged in 1903 and were married in 1905, with her uncle the President giving the bride away. Within eleven years Eleanor bore six children; one son died in infancy. 'I suppose I was fitting pretty well into the pattern of a fairly conventional, quiet, young society matron,' she wrote later in her autobiography. . . .

"When Mrs. Roosevelt came to the White House in 1933, she understood social conditions better than any of her predecessors and she transformed the role of First Lady accordingly. She never shirked official entertaining; she greeted thousands with charming friendliness. She also broke precedent to hold press conferences, travel to all parts of the country, give lectures and radio broadcasts, and express her opinions candidly in a daily syndicated newspaper column, 'My Day.'

"This made her a tempting target for political enemies but her integrity, her graciousness, and her sincerity of purpose endeared her personally to many—from heads of state to servicemen she visited abroad during World War II. As she had written wistfully at 14: 'no matter how plain a woman may be if truth & loyalty are stamped upon her face all will be attracted to her. . . .'

"After the President's death in 1945 she returned to a cottage at his Hyde Park estate; she told reporters: 'the story is over.' Within a year, however, she began her service as American spokesman in the United Nations. She continued a vigorous career until her strength began to wane in 1962. She died in New York City that November, and was buried at Hyde Park beside her husband." Source: "The White House, Biographies of The Presidents and First Ladies," http://www.whitehouse.gov/history/firstladies/ar32.html.

Franklin Delano Roosevelt—President of the United States

"Franklin D. Roosevelt was born in Hyde Park, New York, on January 30, 1882, the son of James Roosevelt and Sara Delano Roosevelt. His parents and private tutors provided him with almost all his formative education. He attended Groton (1896–1900), a prestigious preparatory school in Massachusetts, and received a BA degree in history from Harvard in only three years (1900–03). Roosevelt next studied law at New York's Columbia University. When he passed the bar examination in 1907, he left school without taking a degree. For the next three years he practiced law with a prominent New York City law firm. He entered politics in

1910 and was elected to the New York State Senate as a Democrat from his traditionally Republican home district. In the meantime, in 1905, he had married a distant cousin, Anna Eleanor Roosevelt, who was the niece of President Theodore Roosevelt. The couple had six children, five of whom survived infancy: Anna (1906), James (1907), Elliott (1910), Franklin, Jr. (1914) and John (1916).

"In Chicago in 1932, Roosevelt won the nomination as the Democratic Party candidate for president. He broke with tradition and flew to Chicago to accept the nomination in person. He then campaigned energetically calling for government intervention in the economy to provide relief, recovery, and reform. His activist approach and personal charm helped to defeat Hoover in November 1932 by seven million votes.

"The unending stress and strain of the World War II literally wore Roosevelt out. By early 1944 a full medical examination disclosed serious heart and circulatory problems; and although his physicians placed him on a strict regime of diet and medication, the pressures of war and domestic politics weighed heavily on him. During a vacation at Warm Springs, Georgia, on April 12, 1945, he suffered a massive stroke and died two and one-half hours later without regaining consciousness. He was 63 years old. His death came on the eve of complete military victory in Europe and within months of victory over Japan in the Pacific. President Roosevelt was buried in the Rose Garden of his estate at Hyde Park, New York." Source: Franklin D. Roosevelt Presidential Library and Museum, http://www.fdrlibrary.marist.edu/fdrbio.html.

Edith Carow—Wife of President Teddy Roosevelt

"Edith Carow Roosevelt (1861–1948) was the second wife of Theodore Roosevelt, who served as president of the United States from 1901 to 1909. While first lady, she had to manage both her White House social duties and a large family of six children. She skillfully handled both jobs.

"Mrs. Roosevelt, whose maiden name was Edith Kermit Carow, was born in Norwich, Connecticut, on Aug. 6, 1861. She grew up in New York City. She was born into a family that had become wealthy from a shipping business. While growing up in New York City, Edith Carow was a friend of Theodore Roosevelt and his sister Corinne. Theodore married Alice Hathaway Lee in 1880, but she died in 1884. After Alice's death, Edith and Theodore renewed their acquaintanceship. They married on Dec. 2, 1886. The couple had five children between 1887 and 1897. The children were, in order of birth, Theodore, Jr.; Kermit; Ethel Carow; Archibald Bulloch; and Quentin. In addition, Theodore had another child, Alice, with his first wife in 1884. Edith Roosevelt raised Alice along with her own children. (Alice Roosevelt married Nicholas Longworth, the grandson of Nicholas Longworth, whose garden Paulena Stevens Janney visited in 1859.)

"When Theodore Roosevelt became president in 1901, the family's six children ranged in age from 3 to 17. The presence of so many children made the

White House a lively place. In addition, President Roosevelt enjoyed playing with his children at home. Edith Roosevelt was generally in charge of disciplining the children.

"Edith Roosevelt also made organizational changes in the operations of the White House. She arranged to have the family's living quarters moved so the family would have more privacy. She was the first president's wife to hire a personal secretary to help with social functions. She also greatly expanded the White House china collection.

"Mrs. Roosevelt lived almost 30 years after her husband's death in 1919. She traveled widely after his death and spent her later years at the family home in Oyster Bay, New York. She died on Sept. 30, 1948." Source: *World Book,* 2004, http://www2.worldbook.com/wc/popup?path=features/presidents&page=html/roosevelt_edith.htm&direct=yes.

Charles Scribner III and IV

"The following brief history is extracted from a lecture delivered at the Rowfant Club of Cleveland, 11 October 1978, by Charles Scribner III. . . .

"In 1913 Charles Scribner's only son, another Charles (III), graduated from Princeton and began his own career in publishing. He was a contemporary of Perkins and Wheelock, and his age gave him a ready grasp of the importance of the new writers who were beginning to appear on the scene. Another era in American literature was dawning and the firm's enthusiasm for the new authors was to yield it a rich harvest. There was Alan Seeger, whose *Poems* came out in 1916, best remembered for his "rendezvous with death." Four years later, F. Scott Fitzgerald heralded the Jazz Age with his first novel, *This Side of Paradise.* Stark Young's *The Flower in Drama* appeared in 1923 and, in the following years, Ring Lardner's *How to Write Short Stories* (1924), James Boyd's *Drums* (1925, a year best remembered for *The Great Gatsby*), and John W. Thomason, Jr.'s *Fix Bayonets* (also in 1925). In 1926 Ernest Hemingway's *The Torrents of Spring* and *The Sun Also Rises* were both published. In view of Hemingway's later achievements and his equally enduring loyalty to the firm, we shall always think of that as a year set apart. Thomas Wolfe, at the end of this glorious decade, made his debut with *Look Homeward, Angel* in 1929.

"Around this time, the long career of Charles Scribner II was drawing to a close. In 1928, he turned over the presidency to his younger brother Arthur and continued on only as chairman of the board. Happily, he lived to see the first published volumes of the *Dictionary of American Biography,* a project which extended from 1928 to 1936 and a work to which he had given his utmost support: it was probably the most important project the firm had ever undertaken and was developed with the American Council of Learned Societies, which has subsequently collaborated with Scribners on other reference projects. In 1930 Charles II died, as did the loyal and patient Arthur in 1932, leaving Charles III to preside alone. He was only forty-one at the time.

"It would be hard to think of a more difficult time in which to take over the management of a large publishing house. The Great Depression was in its worst stage, and the future must have appeared most uncertain for books. Yet the firm continued to look for fresh talent and take chances on new authors in a way that marks this as one of the most enterprising periods in all our history, an achievement that testifies to the aims and courage of C. S. III and to the devoted support that his associates, Max Perkins in particular, gave him. In the following years many important new works appeared, not only by already established authors such as Fitzgerald, Hemingway, and Wolfe, but also by unknown writers who were later to become famous. Among these firsts by new authors were Marcia Davenport's great biography of Mozart, published in 1932 and still in print; Nancy Hale's *The Young Die Good*; Marjorie Kinnan Rawlings's *South Moon Under* in 1933, followed by her most famous novel, *The Yearling,* five years later; Hamilton Basso's *Beauregard* in 1933; Taylor Caldwell's *Dynasty of Death* in 1938, and Christine Weston's *Be Thou the Bride* in 1940. An extraordinary decade of debuts.

"In 1952 Charles III died very suddenly; he had just finished reading the manuscript of Hemingway's short classic, *The Old Man and the Sea,* which was dedicated to him and Perkins. After his father's death, Charles Scribner, Jr. moved back from Washington, where he'd been sent as cryptoanalyst during the Korean War, and took the helm at the age of thirty-one.

"Now in a different spirit Scribner set out to recapture some of the past, the 'back list'– you might say the literary 'capital'– most of which had by this time been licensed to paperback and cheap hard-cover reprints. He wanted to bring these books back under the Scribner imprint. This move was soon to prove invaluable. He did not believe in paperbacks. But he soon changed his mind and invented the Scribner Library, a line of quality paperbacks, at which point he now had at his disposal an incredible list of classics to convert into paperback, *The Great Gatsby, Tender Is the Night, The Sun Also Rises, Ethan Frome,* and so on. His industry colleagues credited him with uncanny foresight and patience in reverting all those licenses in preparation for Scribners' new paperback line.

"He completed the *Album of American History* and began the *Dictionary of Scientific Biography,* a fifteen-year project sponsored by the American Council of Learned Societies with a grant from the National Science Foundation. It has since become the model for multi-volume reference works of original scholarship. There followed the *Dictionary of the History of Ideas,* then the *Dictionary of Foreign Policy* and, with the American Council of Learned Societies, the *Dictionary of the Middle Ages.*" Source: Board of Trustees of the University of South Carolina, http://www.sc.edu/fitzgerald/scribner.html.

Jane Lathrop Stanford—Co-founder of Stanford University

Jane Lathrop Stanford (1824–1893): "One of the 'Big Four' who built California's Central Pacific railroad, Leland Stanford brought a sweeping political influence to the partnership that insured this privately financed project all the advantages of public funding.

"Stanford was born into a well off farming family in Watervliet, New York. After a superb secondary education and several years of higher education, Stanford entered an elite law office to prepare for a career as an attorney, passing his bar exam in 1848. He soon moved to Wisconsin, where he began to practice his profession.

"After three years in Wisconsin, Stanford and his new wife [Jane Lathrop] decided to move to California, where several of his brothers had already found success as merchants. Stanford joined them in 1852 and soon began making enormous sums of money by selling equipment to miners in northern California. He also became involved in politics, first as a justice of the peace, then as the unsuccessful 1857 Republican candidate for state treasurer, and in 1859 as the unsuccessful Republican gubernatorial candidate. Stanford was finally elected governor in 1861, when the Civil War split the Democratic vote, and he played a part in keeping California loyal to the Union.

"During his tenure, Stanford made no attempt to separate his political office from his private business interests. With Mark Hopkins, Collis Huntington and Charles Crocker, Stanford was one of the 'Big Four' planning to build the eastbound section of the transcontinental railroad, and his contribution to the partnership was to come in the form of political influence. As governor, Stanford kept this pledge, despite his responsibilities to the public, by helping to secure massive state investment and land grants for the railroad project.

"When his term ended in 1863, Stanford declined to run for governor again, choosing instead to become president of the Central Pacific, a post he held until his death. He was also a major stakeholder in and longtime president of the Southern Pacific, as well as owner of many of the construction companies that did most of the actual railroad building. Later in the century, as public pressure mounted for government regulation of such monopolies, Stanford's political connections in California continued to keep his railroad business interests on track.

"The immense wealth Stanford acquired from railroad building enabled him to live a lavish life. He maintained enormous vineyards and owned a large horse raising ranch near Palo Alto. In 1884, the death of their fifteen year old son [Leland Stanford, Jr.] prompted the Stanfords to found and endow Stanford University in his memory. In 1885, Stanford arranged for the California legislature to appoint him to the United States Senate, where he served without distinction but with pleasure until his death in 1893." Source: http://www.pbs.org/weta/thewest/people/s_z/stanford.htm.

Rev. Thomas Stoughton—Puritan Minister

"The Reverend Thomas Stoughton (1550–1622) matriculated at Trinity College, Cambridge, in 1573 but received his A.B. degree from Queens College, Cambridge, in 1577. He was a fellow at Queens in 1579 and received his M.A. from there in 1580. He was ordained a deacon and priest [in the Church of England] at Lincoln in 1582. He was rector of Naughton in Suffolk until deprived of his living. He was named vicar of Great Coggeshall in Essex, but his zealous Puritanism forced his removal. He was a member of the Dedham Classis, an organization of Puritan ministers in East Anglia, that met frequently to discuss ecclesiastical affairs and was a major force within it. After losing his pulpit, he wrote pamphlets, including 'To the Christian Readers,' 'The Dignitie of God's Children,' 'To the Nobility and Gentry of Great Britain,' 'Two Profitable treatises,' and 'The Christian's Sacrifice' as set forth in Romans XII, 1 2. Thomas Stoughton and his wife, Katherine Montpesson, were the parents of our next ancestor, Elizabeth, who married first John Scudder. Following the death of John Scudder, Elizabeth married Robert Chamberlain who died in 1639 in Strood, County Kent, England. She was left to raise Joanna and Samuel Chamberlain as well as her children from her first marriage, John and Elizabeth Scudder. Thomas and Israel Stoughton, brothers of Elizabeth, as well as her son John Scudder immigrated to New England between 1630–1635. Elizabeth joined her brothers and son in New England around 1640. Joanna Chamberlain (See *The American Genealogist* 72: 285–300) immigrated to America with her mother, Elizabeth (Stoughton) Chamberlain, brother Samuel Chamberlain, and half sibling Elizabeth (Scudder) Lathrop/Lothrop. She was born October 1630 in Strood, Kent, England. Joanna Chamberlain[296] married Richard Betts about 1648 in Ipswitch, Massachusetts, and they removed to Newton, Long Island, New York, by 1656."
Source: A New England Immigrant Kinship Network, Jane Fletcher Fiske.

Mrs. Charles Lewis Tiffany—Tiffany Jewelers

Harriett Olivia Avery Young was the wife of Charles Lewis Tiffany and the mother of Louis Comfort Tiffany.

"The year was 1837, Charles Lewis Tiffany and his schoolmate John Young traveled from New England to New York City with an idea and a dream that were to become Tiffany & Co. While the first day of business brought in a mere four dollars and ninety eight cents, the world of jewelry and luxury goods would never again be the same.

---

296. "The origins of Joanna Chamberlain are well laid out in a presentation in *The American Genealogist* 72, 1997, pp. 285–300, by Jane Fletcher Fiske, in a very interesting network of the Scudder family. This kinship network ties together Betts, King, Lathrop, Very and Scudder immigrant families." Source: *Genealogical Thoughts* by Gary Boyd Roberts, no. 22.

"Charles Tiffany's tireless search for one of a kind objects charmed and fascinated the wealthy of New York. But when the store obtained some of the French crown jewels in 1848, Tiffany's fame spread far and wide.

"Charles Tiffany went on to introduce the nation's first retail catalogue. And, his obsession with the simple elegance of classic silver design earned Tiffany & Co. the highly coveted Award of Merit at the Paris Exposition Universelle in 1867. This was the first time an American company had been recognized by a European jury.

"Of the many individual achievements made under the leadership of Charles Lewis Tiffany, the introduction of the celebrated engagement ring in the 6 prong Tiffany Setting is one of the most noteworthy. But, of course, Charles Tiffany's grandest accomplishment was to establish America's preeminent house of design and the world's premier jeweler." Source: *Who's Who in America.*

Louis Comfort Tiffany—Glass and Jewelry Designer

"Louis Comfort Tiffany (1848–1933), the celebrated jewelry and glass designer, was born the son of Charles Lewis Tiffany, founder of Tiffany & Co. His remarkable career designing jewelry, windows and decorative glass spanned 57 years including his tenure with L.C. Tiffany & Associated Artists, the Tiffany Glass Company, Tiffany Studios, Tiffany Furnaces, and L.C. Tiffany Furnaces. In 1902 he became Tiffany & Co.'s first Design Director, creating fantastic jewelry designs inspired both by nature and the art of other cultures. His patent for opalescent window glass in 1881 and his commissions for Mark Twain, Cornelius Vanderbilt and many others earned him an international reputation. His work has been honored by museums and treasured by collectors around the world." Source: http://www.infomat.com/whoswho/charleslewistiffany.html.

Mrs. George Washington Vanderbilt—
Wife of G. W. Vanderbilt, Builder of Biltmore

Edith Stuyvesant Dresser married George Washington Vanderbilt (1862–1914), brother of Cornelius Vanderbilt II and William Kissam Vanderbilt. "He was born on Nov. 14, 1862, on Staten Island, was the least involved of William Henry's three sons with the family businesses and investments. He built a huge estate, named Biltmore, near Asheville, N.C. There he carried out experiments in scientific farming, forestry, and stock breeding. He died in Washington, D.C., on March 6, 1914, after an operation for appendicitis." Source: *Encyclopedia Britannica Online,* http://www.britannica.com/ebi/article?tocId=209750&ct=.

Walt Whitman Jr.— Poet

"Walter 'Walt' Whitman (1819–1892) was born on May 31, 1819, the second son of Walter Whitman, a housebuilder, and Louisa Van Velsor. The family, which consisted of nine children, lived in Brooklyn and Long Island in the 1820s and 1830s. At the age of twelve Whitman began to learn the printer's trade, and he fell in love with the written word. Largely self-taught, he read voraciously, becoming acquainted with the works of Homer, Dante, Shakespeare, as well as the Bible. Whitman worked as a printer in New York City until a devastating fire in the printing district demolished the industry. In 1836, at the age of seventeen, he began his career as teacher in the one-room school houses of Long Island. He continued to teach until 1841, when he turned to journalism as a full-time career. He founded a weekly newspaper, *Long-Islander,* and later edited a number of Brooklyn and New York papers. In 1848 Whitman left the Brooklyn *Daily Eagle* to become editor of the New Orleans Crescent. It was in New Orleans that he experienced at first hand the viciousness of slavery in the slave markets of that city.

"On his return to Brooklyn in the fall of 1848, he founded a 'free soil' newspaper, the *Brooklyn Freeman,* and continued to develop the unique style of poetry that later so astonished Ralph Waldo Emerson. In 1855, Whitman took out a copyright on the first edition of *Leaves of Grass,* which consisted of twelve untitled poems and a preface. He published the volume himself, and sent a copy to Emerson in July of 1855. Whitman released a second edition of the book in 1856, containing thirty-three poems, a letter from Emerson praising the first edition, and a long open letter by Whitman in response. During his subsequent career, Whitman continued to refine the volume, publishing several more editions of the book.

"At the outbreak of the Civil War, Whitman vowed to live a 'purged' and 'cleansed' life. He wrote freelance journalism and visited the wounded at New York–area hospitals. He then traveled to Washington, D.C., in December 1862 to care for his brother who had been wounded in the war. Overcome by the suffering of the many wounded in Washington, Whitman decided to stay and work in the hospitals. Whitman stayed in the city for eleven years. He took a job as a clerk for the Department of the Interior, which ended when the Secretary of the Interior, James Harlan, discovered that Whitman was the author of *Leaves of Grass,* which Harlan found offensive. Harlan fired the poet.

"Whitman struggled to support himself through most of his life. In Washington he lived on a clerk's salary and modest royalties, and spent any excess money, including gifts from friends, to buy supplies for the patients he nursed. He had also been sending money to his widowed mother and an invalid brother. From time to time writers both in the states and in England sent him 'purses' of money so that he could get by.

"In the early 1870s, Whitman settled in Camden, where he had come to visit his dying mother at his brother's house. However, after suffering a stroke,

Whitman found it impossible to return to Washington. He stayed with his brother until the 1882 publication of *Leaves of Grass* gave Whitman enough money to buy a home in Camden. In the simple two-story clapboard house, Whitman spent his declining years working on additions and revisions to a new edition of the book and preparing his final volume of poems and prose, *Good-Bye, My Fancy* (1891). After his death on March 26, 1892, Whitman was buried in a tomb he designed and had built on a lot in Harleigh Cemetery." Source: http://www.poets.org/poet.php/prmPID/126.

Theodore Dwight Woolsey—President of Yale University

Theodore Dwight Woolsey, 1812–1889, educator and anti-slavery leader, President of Yale University, 1846–1871. Source: *Grove Street Cemetery,* www.grovestreetcemetery.org/Grove_Street_Cemetery_Chronicle_of_Eminent_People.

William Wrigley III

"Throughout William Wrigley III's early years at the family firm, Wrigley's gum enjoyed a substantial lead in its industry. However, by the time he assumed the presidency in 1961, sugarless gum, and later bubble gum, were chipping away at that lead. Wrigley began to invest heavily in research and eventually produced several new lines, including Freedent for denture wearers, the sugarfree *Orbit,* the bubble gum *Hubba Bubba,* and the cinnamon flavored *Big Red.* Under William III's leadership, Wrigley's was able to maintain its position as the world's largest manufacturer of chewing gum." Source: *20th Century Great American Business Leaders,* President and Fellows of Harvard, 2004, http://www.hbs.edu/leadership/database/leaders/988.

Entertainment Industry Icons

These entertainment industry icons are from the Stoughton-Chamberlin-Betts-Hussey family lines.

James Dean—Actor

"The actor James Byron Dean (1931–1955) starred in only three movies—*East of Eden, Rebel Without a Cause,* and *Giant.* In the first two, and to some extent the third, he played adolescent rebels at a time in American life when "teenagers" were defining themselves as neither children nor adults, but something special, and specially tortured. Dean's roles, and his early death in an automobile accident, seemed to many of his generation to embody and extend their own life situation and existential trauma. . . .

To many young people seeking to break away from their parents or construct an individualized but viable identity, Dean became almost a cult figure, and a myth was created somewhat tainted by the suggestion of danger or evil. But his co-workers often found him charming, and gossip columnist Hedda Hopper is said to have enjoyed "mothering" him. Despite the rebel aura, Dean was born and raised in the quiet environment of largely Quaker Fairmount, Indiana, an area redolent of the Hoosier life." Source: *New England in Hollywood, Part Four: The Ancestry of James Byron Dean* (1931–1955), by Richard E. Brenneman.

Clint Eastwood—Actor, Director, Producer

"Clint Eastwood was born May 31, 1930 in San Francisco, California. He won attention in the television series *Rawhide* (1959–66) before his roles in three of Sergio Leone's "spaghetti westerns" (1964–66) made him an international star. He returned to the U.S. for the successful *Dirty Harry* (1971), the first of a series of action films in which he played laconic and dangerous heroes. He combined directing with acting in films such as *Play Misty for Me* (1971), *Pale Rider* (1985), *Unforgiven* (1992, Academy Award), *A Perfect World* (1993), *The Bridges of Madison County* (1995), and *Million Dollar Baby* (2004, Academy Award). His interest in jazz led him to direct and produce *Bird* (1988). . . . His minimalist style of acting and direction garnered critical acclaim to accompany his long-established box-office success." His most recent films, *Flags of Our Fathers* and *Letters from Iwo Jima*, opened in October and November, 2006. Source: *Britannica Concise Encyclopedia*.

Lillian Gish—Actress

Lillian Gish was born in 1896 in Springfield, Ohio, the elder sister of actress Dorothy Gish. In 1912, their friend, Mary Pickford, introduced the sisters to D. W. Griffith, and helped get them contracts with Biograph Studios. Lillian would soon become one of America's best-loved actresses.

Having appeared in over twenty-five short films and features in her first two years as a movie actress, Lillian became a major star, becoming known as "The First Lady of the Silent Screen" and appearing in lavish productions, frequently of literary works such as *The Scarlet Letter* (1926). MGM released her from her contract in 1928 after the failure of *The Wind*, now recognized by many as among her finest performances and one of the most distinguished works of the late silent period.

With her debut in talkies only moderately successful, she acted on the stage for the most part in the 1930s and early 1940s, appearing with distinction in roles as varied as Ophelia in Guthrie McClintic's landmark 1936 production of *Hamlet* (with John Gielgud and Judith Anderson) and Marguerite in a limited run of *La Dame aux Camélias*.

Returning to movies, Gish was nominated for the Academy Award for Best Supporting Actress in 1946 for *Duel in the Sun.* She appeared in films from time to time for the rest of her life. Lillian Gish made numerous television appearances from the early 1950's into the late 1980's. Her most acclaimed television work was starring in the original production of *The Trip to Bountiful* in 1953. Gish received a special Academy Award in 1971 "for superlative artistry and for distinguished contribution to the progress of motion pictures." In 1984 she received an American Film Institute Lifetime Achievement Award, only the second female recipient (Bette Davis was first in 1977) and the only recipient who was a major figure in the silent era. She has a star on the Hollywood Walk of Fame at 1720 Vine Street." She died at the age of 99 on February 27, 1993. Source: *Wikipedia.*

Ruth Hussey—Actress

"Ruth Hussey was born in Providence, Rhode Island, in 1911. Her father died when she was seven years old from the 1918 flu. He was just thirty-four years old. She graduated from Pembroke College, which was then the women's college at Brown University, in 1933. She never landed a role at Pembroke in any of the school plays she tried out for. She then studied drama in post graduate school at the University of Michigan School of Drama, and worked as an actress with a summer stock company in Michigan for two seasons.

"After working as an actress in summer stock, she returned to Providence and worked as a radio fashion commentator on a local station. One day she was encouraged by a friend to try out for acting roles at the Providence Playhouse. At the Biltmore Hotel in Los Angeles she was spotted on opening night by MGM talent scout Billy Grady. MGM signed her to a players contract and she made her film debut in 1937. For a 1940 'A' picture role she was nominated for an Academy Award for her turn as Liz Embrie, the cynical magazine photographer and girlfriend of Jimmy Stewart's character Macaulay Connor in *The Philadelphia Story.*

Hussey also worked with Robert Taylor in *Flight Command* (1940), Robert Young in *H.M. Pulham, Esq.* (1941), Van Heflin in *Tennessee Johnson* (1942), Ray Milland in *The Uninvited* (1944) and Alan Ladd in *The Great Gatsby* (1949). In 1946 she starred on Broadway in *State of the Union,* the Pulitzer Prize play. In 1960 she co-starred in *The Facts of Life* with Bob Hope. Hussey then was active in early television drama, focused much of her attention on family activities and in 1964 designed a family cabin in the mountain community of Lake Arrowhead, California." She died April 21, 2005. Source: *Wikipedia.*

Bruce Springsteen—Singer, Songwriter, Guitarist

"Bruce Springsteen (born September 23, 1949) is an American rock singer-songwriter and guitarist. Springsteen has frequently recorded and toured with the

E Street Band, in addition to recording and performing as a solo artist and with other musicians. Springsteen is most widely known for his brand of heartland rock infused with pop hooks, poetic lyrics, and Americana sentiments centered around his native New Jersey.

His eloquence in expressing ordinary, everyday problems has earned him numerous awards, including several Grammy Awards, an Academy Award, and induction into the Rock and Roll Hall of Fame, along with a very large, devoted, and long-lasting fan base. His most famous albums, *Born to Run* and *Born in the U.S.A.,* epitomize his penchant for finding grandeur in the struggles of daily life." Source: *Wikipedia.*

Patrick Swayze—Actor, Dancer, Songwriter

"Patrick Swayze was born in Houston, Texas, the son of Jesse Wayne Swayze and choreographer and ballet school owner Patricia Yvonne Helen "Patsy" Karnes Swayze. Patrick's brother, Don Swayze, is also an actor. Swayze formally trained at the Harkness and Joffrey Ballet Schools in New York City.

His first professional appearance was as a dancer for *Disney on Parade,* then in the Broadway production of *Grease,* before his debut film role as *Ace in Skatetown, U.S.A.* (1979). He also appeared in the *M*A*S*H* episode "Blood Brothers" (Episode 9.18, 6 April 1981).

He is probably most memorable for his roles in the popular films *Dirty Dancing* (1987), *Ghost* (1990), and *Point Break* (1991). He also appeared in *Red Dawn* (1984), *Road House* (1989), *Black Dog* (1998), and *Donnie Darko* (2001). He is also famous for the *North* and *South* miniseries. Swayze received Golden Globe Award nominations for his roles in *Dirty Dancing, Ghost* and *To Wong Foo, Thanks for Everything! Julie Newmar* (1995). Additionally he wrote and composed the hit song "She's Like the Wind" for *Dirty Dancing.* He has been starring as Nathan Detroit in the London production of Guys and Dolls." Source: *Wikipedia.*

Thoughts from . . .
Paulena Stevens Janney's
Great-Granddaughter

What began as a simple effort to transcribe my great-grandmother's journals to a more stable and readable manuscript resulted, ten years later, in sharing this treasured family heirloom in book form.

It has been an enriching experience for me to read, in Paulena's own words, a personal account of her life, her words of wisdom and strong faith in a life hereafter where we will be united as a family once again. I have watched her grow from a young, romantic bride of ten days through seven difficult, war-torn years into a mature wife and soon-to-be mother.

Her rhythm of life was marked by Sabbath worship and study in her Quaker Meeting. Like her mother and grandmother, she assumed the responsibilities of providing food and shelter for Quakers attending Quarterly Meetings and for family and friends. She made garments for use in the Underground Railroad and watched trains carrying dead soldiers to be buried by their loved ones. She planted little gardens, cooked and baked, visited friends and relatives, and wrote letters and essays. Her poems and prose reflect a sorrowful reality of life and death which constantly surrounded her.

I learned valuable lessons in history and in nineteenth-century life and literature. I saw myself reflected in her philosophy of friendships, her joy of making a home for her family, her love of gathering flowers, and her childhood pleasure of little playhouses.

I hope that Paulena's descendants and other interested readers will also be enriched by her presence in the writing.

Christie Russell

Index

Coffin, Charles Carleton, 379–380
Coffin, Daniel, xxx
Coffin, Elizabeth Rebecca, 380–381
Coffin, Howard Earle, 382–383
Coffin, Jesse, xxx
Coffin, John Huntington
    Crane, 383–384
Coffin, Levi, xix, 384
Coffin, Tristram, 371–372
Coffin, Vestal, xix, 385
Coggeshall, William Turner, 172n170
conscientious objector, 278, 278n246
contraband society, xxi, 185, 185n180
Coolidge, John Calvin, 385–386
Cook, John E., 47, 47n68, 50n72
conscription, 187, 187n182
conversion, 326n286
Copeland, John Anthony, Jr., 51n72
Copperheads, 189, 189n183, 271n242
Coppoc, Edwin, 51n72
Cowgill, Henry "Clay," 84n84, 362
Cowper, William, 120, 120n125
Crassus, Publius Lucinius, 85n87
crinoline, 110n114

D

Davis, Jefferson, 297, 297n258
Dean, James, 431–432
Dennison, Camp, skirmish at, 204n195
Dewey, Thomas, 406–407
Dickens, Charles, 21n41, 246, 246n216
Dickinson, Anna
    Elizabeth, 227, 227n201
Donelson, Fort, 93, 93n95
Douglass, Frederick, 24n44
Drinker, Henry S., Jr., 387
Drinker, Henry S., Sr., 386
Drinker, Philip, 386, 387
Dulles, Allen Welsh, 387–388
Dulles, John Foster, 388–389

E

Eastwood, Clint, 432
Eliot, George (pen name of Mary Ann

Evans), 122n127, 212
enigmas, 322n281

F

Field, Marshall, 407
Field, Marshall, III, 407–408
Fish, Hamilton, 408
Fish, Stuyvesant, 409
Fletcher, John, 122n127
Fletcher, Mary, 122n127
Folger, Henry Clay, 389–390
Folger, James A., 389
Fosdick, William Whitman, 212–213
Fowler, Lydia Folger, 390
Fox, George, xiii–xiv, xiiin5
Fremont, John C., 249, 249n220
Earlham College, xv, 41, 100
Friends' Boarding School, xv, 41

G

G. W. Coffin Buckeye Bell
    Foundry, 4, 4n2
Gardner, Richard, 373
Garibaldi, Giuseppe, 154, 154n149
Gaskell, Elizabeth, 14n36
Getchell, Margaret, 390–391
Gettysburg Address, 208
Gettysburg, Battle of, 203
Gish, Lillian, 432–433
Gorham, Nathaniel, Jr., 391
Grant, Ulyssess Simpson, 409
Green, Mary Emily, 366
Green, Shields, 51n72
Greenwood, Grace, 210

H

Hadley, Anna, 364
Hadley, Esther Smith, 165, 165n161
Hadley, Henry, 159n154
Hadley, Jonathan, 159n155
Haman, 141n137
Harland, Marion. *See* Terhune,
    Mary Virginia Hawes
Harp of a Thousand Strings; or,

Notes

Notes

Notes

Notes

by McClelland — — I almost think he is a traitor I have not had any faith in him for a long time - if he ever does any thing worthy of praise I am willing to give him praise but if he is as slow in future as he has been in the past I think his removal will be all that will coincide to the people — — I almost hate him sometimes....

Fourth day 8th 1862

We are so afraid they are going to draft and what will we do if that does happen? I am afraid to build any air castles or plan any visits or any thing for it will be so much worse to be disappointed about...........

It seems to me I can never be happy again if Will has to go to war — how could I part with him

Fifth day 10th July

McClellan is receiving reinforcements all the time but we are all hoping he will have a victory at Richmond but if he fails there how dispairing will our prospe - foreign intervention will be sure to ensue and war with France or England would certainly be a great misfortune to America — — — — how I do want to see Matt it has been such a long time since she was here.... But if Will has go to war it is worse to think of anything with pleasure for the future.. Lizzie is going away visiting in a few days...

Sixth day 11th 1862

I went down home this evening and Slim and I took a ride and Willie too who felt very important when he was driving.. I am glad Willie is little now for he cannot go to war. I know I am not very patriotic but it seems so bad to let our friends go and be murdered it were by these so often incompetent officers in